Frau Engeli

Thanks for your help!

Gerhard [illegible]

CAADfutures '91

CAAD futures '91

Computer Aided Architectural Design Futures

Education, Research, Applications

Edited by Gerhard N. Schmitt

vieweg

Prof. Dr. Gerhard N. Schmitt
Chair for Architecture and CAAD
Department of Architecture
Swiss Federal Institute of Technology
ETH Zürich, 8092 Zürich, Switzerland

Vieweg is a subsidiary company of the Bertelsmann Publishing Group International.

Cover design by Philippe Mouthon.
Image: Axonometric of the Lineamenta-CAAD exhibition by Leandro Madrazo.
Rendering Eric van der Mark
Printing and bound by W. Langelüddecke, Braunschweig
Printed on acid-free paper
Printed in Germany

ISBN 3-528-08821-4

Preface

Computer Aided Architectural Design (CAAD) is the art of design and computation. Since the establishment of the CAAD futures organization in 1985, experts meet every two years to explore the state-of-the-art and postulate on future development in Computer Aided Architectural Design. The fourth international CAAD futures conference took place in July 1991 in Zürich at the Swiss Federal Institute of Technology (ETH Zürich), organized by the Chair for CAAD. More than 220 participants from 25 countries attended the conference. Presentation topics were education, research, and application. The mission of CAAD futures '91 was to provide an international forum for the dissemination and discussion of future oriented developments and new experiences in the field of Computer Aided Architectural Design. This book is one result of the conference and is divided into three sections:

Education. The first section describes new approaches to teaching design and to teaching CAAD in a cross section of methods and experiments in design education. Educators see the computer in the design studio as a maturing instrument to support tasks from presentation to developing new design strategies. They focus on presentation techniques, evaluation of design interfaces, and application of generative approaches to the exploration of form.

Research. The second section focuses on new research topics and on new findings in already established research areas. Researchers present implementations of prototype systems and explore promising and innovative directions. They concentrate on creativity, case-based reasoning, semantics inherent in shapes, and abstractions supporting evaluation.

Application. The third section describes projects in which the new technology had an impact on presentation, system integration, and previously manual activities. Developers make use of earlier research findings to implement practical applications in all design related fields. Authors describe new computer-based tools that support knowledge-based energy-conscious design, retrofit, property reuse, virtual reality, stereolithography, and multimedia.

This international overview of the 1991 state-of-the-art in Computer Aided Architectural Design will serve as a reference for design teachers, researchers, and application developers interested in CAAD. Acknowledgements and thanks are directed towards the following groups:

The authors of papers and their contributions to this book. After a two-stage selection process they submitted all material in electronic form and standard format to facilitate the production of this document.

The poster presenters who had the difficult task of describing complex topics in a limited space. Contributors were Kamal Fuleihan, N. K. Garg, Maurice Herman, Ludger Hovestadt, Peter Jordan, Christian Kühn, Alan Lee, Raymond McCall, J. L. Fleury de Oliveira, Ivan Petrovic, G. G. Schierle, Marc Schiler, André Streilein, Mark Tapia, Francisco Garcia Vallejo, Stefan Wiesmann, Jerzy Wojtowicz, Ruth Zohar. Special thanks to Geert Smeltzer and Marlyn Aretz for the virtual reality installation.

The session Chairs for their written summaries of the sessions which helped to structure the presentations. They were Peter Jordan, Tom Maver, William Mitchell, Antonino Saggio, Rik Schijf, and Edna Shaviv.

The international review committee for reviewing and selecting the papers. It consisted of Ömer Akin, Aart Bijl, Harold Borkin, Gianfranco Carrara, Chen-Cheng Chen, Per Christiansson, John Danahy, Bharat Dave, Boi Faltings, Ulrich Flemming, John Gero, Armin Grün, Robert Johnson, Yehuda Kalay, Herbert Kramel, Ramesh Krishnamurti, Robin Liggett, Leandro Madrazo, Earl Mark, Tom Maver, John McIntosh, Patricia McIntosh, William Mitchell, Werner Oechslin, Irving Oppenheim, Rivka Oxman, Robert Oxman, Gernot Pittioni, Sharon Refvem, Daniel Rehak, Rik Schijf, Shen-Guan Shih, Geert Smeltzer, James Turner, Harry Wagter, Stefan Wiesmann, and Robert Woodbury.

The editing team consisting of Chen-Cheng Chen, Bharat Dave, Leandro Madrazo, Christopher Mason, Hans Uli Matter, Sharon Refvem, Werner Riniker, Shen-Guan Shih, Sibylla Spycher, Claude Vezin, and Annelies Zeidler. Special thanks to Eric van der Mark for producing the final version of this book.

Palo Alto, October 1991

Gerhard Schmitt

Contents

Computer Aided Architectural Design Futures 9
Gerhard Schmitt, Werner Oechslin

Section 1: Education

1 Integrating Shape Grammars and Design Analysis 17
William J. Mitchell, Robin S. Liggett, Spiro N. Pollalis, and Milton Tan

2 Designing with Grammars 33
Terry W. Knight

3 Experiments in Architectural Design Development Using CAD 49
Charles M. Eastman and Jurg Lang

4 DAC or Design and Computers 65
Alan H. Bridges

5 Design Education with Computers 77
Leandro Madrazo

6 Imagining Light: A Visualization of Daylighting Data 97
Brian Sumption, Bruce Haglund, and Alexander Zabrodsky

7 A Stratified Approach to the Integration of Low Cost Modeling with Advanced Technology Rendering 105
Robin Liggett, William Jepson, and Stephen Teodosiadis

8 The Computer-Aided Studio Critic: Gaining Control of What We Look At 121
John Danahy

9 An Evaluation Module for "An Interface for Designing" (AID): A Procedure based on Trichotomic Segmentation 139
Elena Mortola and Alessandro Giangrande

Section 2: Research

10 On Knowing - Feeling and Expression 157
Aart Bijl

11 An Intelligent Simulation Approach in Simulating Dynamic Processes in Architectural Environments 177
Filiz Ozel

12 Intelligent Systems for Supporting Architectural Design 191
Gianfranco Carrara, Yehuda E. Kalay, and Gabriele Novembri

13 Solid Modeling of Architectural Design with PLASM Language 203
Alberto Paoluzzi, Claudio Sansoni

14 Use of Data Modeling in the Conceptual Structuring of Design Problems 225
Charles M. Eastman

15 A Framework for Modeling and Communicating Abstractions of Constructed Facilities 245
M. Kiumarse Zamanian and Steven J. Fenves

16 Mutation and Analogy to Support Creativity in Computer-Aided Design 261
John S. Gero and Mary Lou Maher

17 Computational Modalities of Evaluation and Prediction in Design 271
Yehuda E. Kalay

18 What's in a Case: The Use of Case Bases, Knowledge Bases, and Databases in Design 285
M. A. Rosenman, J. S. Gero, and R. E. Oxman

19 Case-based Representation and Adaptation in Design 301
Shen-Guan Shih

20 Refinement and Adaptation:Two Paradigms of Form Generation in CAAD 313
Rivka E. Oxman and Robert M. Oxman

21 BAU: A Knowledge-Based System for the Investigation of a Basic Architectural Unit 329
Herbert Kramel and Chen-Cheng Chen

22 Reading Architectural Plans: A Computable Model 347
Sally McLaughlin

23 Intra-Medium and Inter-Media Constraints 365
Stephen M. Ervin

24 Recognizing Structures: Some Problems in Reasoning with Drawings 381
Richard White

25 What Could Artificial Intelligence Know about the Knowledge Involved in the Design Process? 395
Khaldoun Zreik

Section 3: Application

26 The Impact of Computer Use on Design Practice 413
Richard Coyne

27 ESP — An Expert System for Property Revitalization 425
Robert E. Johnson

28 XNET2 - Methodical Design of Local Area Networks in Buildings: An Application of the A4 Intelligent Design Tool 443
Hartmut Ayrle

29 Architecture of a Knowledge-Based-System for the Detailing of Reinforced Concrete Columns 451
Christoph Meinecke and Raimar J. Scherer

30 An Integrated KB-CAAD System for the Design of Solar and Low Energy Buildings 465
Edna Shaviv and Uriel J. Peleg

31 Design Tools: Future Design Environments for Visualizing Building Performance 485
Murray Milne

32 The First CAAD Package (sketch based cad) 497
Mark de Vries and Harry Wagter

33 Interactive Scene Walkthrough Using a Physically-Based Virtual Camera 511
Russell Turner, Francis Balaguer, Enrico Gobbetti, and Daniel Thalmann

34 Leaving the Planar Universe 521
Peter Durisch, Edoardo Anderheggen

35 Creating Architecture Models by Computer-Aided Prototyping 535
Bernd Streich

36 The Reconstruction of the Past: the Application of New Techniques for Visualization and Research in Architectural History 549
Patricia Alkhoven

37 Free Hand Plotting - Is It Live or Is It Digital? 567
W. Davis van Bakergem and Gen Obata

38 Data Generation for CAAD with Digital Photogrammetry 583
Horst A. Beyer and André Streilein

Computer Aided Architectural Design Futures

Gerhard N. Schmitt

Chair for Architecture and CAAD
Swiss Federal Institute of Technology

Werner Oechslin

gta Institute
Swiss Federal Institute of Technology

Computing has become a recognized art in the discipline of architecture, moving from the periphery towards the core of the design process. Research, education, and application are the critical areas that provide the development platforms for the future of design and computing. Seen in perspective, the term lineamenta *describes related activities in historical architectural research.* Research *also shaped the origins and early directions of CAAD. The first* applications *emerged after computers and software were powerful enough to implement high level ideas. Meaningful* education *of a wider audience of designers only became possible after the results of research proved promising.*

Figure 1. LINEAMENTA - CAAD. Instruments of a science of architecture. Poster for the Exhibition at ETH Zürich by Werner Oechslin and Gerhard Schmitt. Design Philippe Carrard.

Lineamenta - an Historical Perspective

CAAD can build on a history and scientific theory of architecture which reveal an astonishing richness of ideas few of which have been fully explored. Many of the apparently new CAAD research paths have been tested before with different intentions. The findings of Werner Oechslin's research on the subject of architectural drawing serve as a good example (Oechslin 91). Since the era of humanism, when the modern theory of architecture was established based on Vitruvius, there have been repeated attempts to define and develop the architectural drawing as an instrument of scientific research. According to Alberti (1452) architectural drawing and design process are virtually identical: *lineamenta*. Literally translated, lineamenta stands for line, lines, or collections of lines. In Latin, a distinction is made between the abstract "lineamentum" and the literal "linea". Since Cicero, "lineamenta" has taken on a more precise meaning. Together with other attributes - form, interval, size - "lineamenta" becomes a part of geometry, a distinction that indicates the architectural significance of this label. Later two directions emerge. There is the desire to achieve coherence and compatibility between projections (plan, facade, section), stretching the meaning of Vitruvius' text more than is appropriate, re-interpreting *scenographia* as *sciographia*. Parallel to this is the search for new and boundary crossing architectural possibilities per se, exemplified by (as an extreme case) Caramuel's *arquitectura obliqua*. The interrelationship between architectural drawing and the design process has always served to explore and redefine the creative possibilities of architecture.

The situation after the institutional crisis of the French revolution is characterized by the attempt to simplify complex drawing processes and by the reduction of means to a minimum. Economy governs Durand's arguments in his "Précis des Leçons d'Architecture données à l'Ecole Polytechnique" of 1802. He summarizes all relevant previous literature in his book "Recueil et Parallèle des Edifices de tout genre, anciens et modernes". His contribution is the achievement of the ultimate degree of abstraction - "dernier degré de brièveté" - by reducing the drawing to its fundamental linear quality. The compressed drawing and composition methods of Durand demonstrate once again the relation between geometry and architecture. He also develops a new design method on a radically different basis, a different design method which he later calls "Marche à suivre" and from where he moves from the simplest drawing definitions - according to Albertian tradition - to higher degrees of detail. We have to keep this in mind when we use Durand's famous diagrams as a point of departure or justification for computer implementations.

Durand's most significant scheme in this context is "Ensembles d'Edifices, résultants des divisions du quarré, du parallélogramme, et de leurs combinaisons avec le cercle". Here he implies that even the most complex building typologies can be generated from geometric primitives and that therefore architectural richness can be achieved by deduction and generation. This is in accordance with the originally humanistic assessment of the relationship between "more geometrico", syllogism, science, and drawing. Durand's generative grammar proves a new quality of relation between lineamenta and the disciplines of geometric drawing and systematic design process and has therefore been a most influential book for decades.

Even more interesting for future CAAD systems are the attempts at systematic formalization of the aesthetic. Alberti's term "concinnitas", often too directly translated as aesthetic in the modern sense, still maintains in its definition the relationship with geometry and mathematics. Following the discussions of style and taste in the 18th century, the triumph of the sensual view, and even after the definition of the modern term aesthetics, there were still attempts to define the aesthetic dimension of an artifact by quantification or other scientific means. In the tradition of a geometry-based architectural theory, the richest form could become the most desirable. Hogarth in "The Analysis of Beauty" (1753) uses the double serpentine line as a symbol of variety and understands the combination of triangle and serpentine as "order of form". John Ruskin defines a "line of beauty" for the integration of a "British Villa" into its surroundings in his article "The Poetry of Architecture", published in 1839 in Loudon's Architectural Magazine. He maintains that nature and architecture should be composed and orchestrated in their interaction as firm geometric lines.

Towards the end of the 19th century, notions on the causal relationships between form and aesthetic value and form and significance appeared in increasing numbers in text books on ornaments. Even the classical work of George D. Birkhoff, "Aesthetic Measure" (1933) points in this direction. The concept of "numerical aesthetics", which sought to capture the aesthetic value of Velasquez' famous "Hilanderas" by quantifying the elements and configurations appearing on the surface of the canvas (G. Cavallius 1972), came to yet more extreme conclusions. Such attempts were as futile as those made to capture the aesthetic value of modern or historic buildings through arbitrary grids for geometric primitives alone. They do, however, point to a fundamental challenge to the digital world: Now that the new instruments have proven their potential usefulness, they are expected to become intelligent and knowledgeable, after which they may be expected to show taste and style and eventually truly support architectural design. This brings us to the present and the efforts to improve the worldwide state-of-the-art in CAAD. For the first time in history, progress is being monitored in real time.

CAAD futures '91

The triad of CAAD research, education, and application is very dynamic in character and has undergone radical changes in its short history. Universities and sizable design firms were the original institutions of *research*. Today, large CAD software firms and some hardware producers have their own CAD research centers or directly subcontract universities. Not surprisingly, this has influenced the direction of inquiry, placing greater emphasis on applications rather than fundamental research. Although *education* has traditionally been the domain of universities, the high demand for CAD literate personnel in architecture and design offices has lead to the establishment of independent training centers in design firms and CAD software houses. Universities have also become more dependent on commercial software to keep up with the rapid advances in capabilities and the new principles of thinking. *Applications* were and are developed for practice. This field has undergone the most dramatic change in the past decade: from a few thousand installations and users in the early 1980's the base has grown to more than one million CAD users worldwide. In the same period, architectural CAD installations have increased from a few hundred to almost 200,000 worldwide. The sheer number of users indicates the growing importance of applications in shaping the future of CAAD. Developing CAD programs has become an industry as well; whereas individuals developed and sometimes even marketed earlier programs, this has now become the exception. Teams consisting of several dozen members (IEZ in Bensheim with Speedikon) and up to several hundred members (Dassault in Paris with CATIA or AutoDesk in Sausalito with AutoCAD) are now involved in the development, updating, and marketing of CAD programs.

Figure 2. Lineamenta - CAAD. Generation of form with parameterized elements, using ArchiCAD. Models Doenz, Fries, Osman, Graser and Steiner in a CAAD course at ETH Zürich by Gerhard Schmitt. Rendering Eric van der Mark with Wavefront Advanced Visualizer.

CAAD Research Futures

It appears that a research environment is ideal for defining and shaping the future of CAAD: Relatively free of economic, time and special interest group pressure, researchers can search for the truth. They would work according to Ulrich Flemming in two areas: (i) gaining insights into the design process and the human cognitive apparatus, and (ii) finding methods to improve the design process or its results (Schmitt 90). Supported by a large and steady stream of funding, they would finally solve the problem of knowledge representation, break the complexity barrier, define the relation between geometric and symbolic representations and find the ideal graphics and information exchange standards. All knowledge gained could be recorded and made available for future generations as fundamental truth.

Reality is different. Research in CAAD is both benefitting and suffering from the fragmentation of the design and building industry. In most industrial and post-industrial countries, the AEC industry contributes a major share of the GNP, yet there exists no category for architectural design research in national research programs. Thus, architectural researchers must creatively collect their support from various sources under different funding schemes. Within the design research community, discussions about fundamental versus applied research are common. In addition, the design of new computer programs is also referred to as research which poses a similar problem to that of labeling architectural design as research. Understanding and formalizing the design process are at the core of many projects, because it seems a prerequisite for the development of intelligent design support systems. The developers of such systems must acknowledge the fact that there is no single design process, and that for any given design process properties of the results of traditional scientific research such as repeatability and quantifiability may not be found. Built architecture provides architectural historians with some of the opportunities which researchers in the fields of physics or chemistry take for granted. In such cases, one can expect to discover elemental principles and fundamental laws. Yet exploring the dynamic and under-constrained process of design is research on a moving target which calls for new methods and instruments.

Not surprisingly, research and development in CAAD had split into several branches by the beginning of the 1990's. In this book, exponents of some of these fundamental streams report on their progress and findings. The discussion about the advantages of *design automation* versus *design support* is ongoing. The consensus seems to be that there will not be, and should not be an autonomous architecture machine, but rather that research should focus on the invention of intelligent design support systems. Investigation of *generative systems* and *grammars* in particular has already resulted in a number of elegant implementations (Mitchell 90). So far, grammars have mainly proven useful for the partial analysis and reconstruction of past architecture rather than in the complete synthesis of new architecture. *Knowledge-based systems* (KBS), a much used AI term in recent years and long believed to offer a solution to some of the problems of architectural design, are being fundamentally challenged from several sides. There are claims that knowledge not connected to the human being is useless or worse, and that without common sense knowledge KBSs cannot perform even the simplest tasks. *Case-based reasoning* may be a superior method for representing complete cases and their inherent knowledge without searching for causal relationships between function and form. Case adaptation and case combination appear to be promising techniques for handling the complexity of architectural design. *User interfaces*, besides representing the largest part of the source code in any CAD program, are finally recognized as a key research area.

As exciting as findings in these areas are, a few words of caution are necessary: The field has grown so rapidly that no single human being can be an expert in all areas, which has effectively placed the goals that Sutherland and Negroponte placed on the agenda more than two decades ago out of reach. The historic perspective seems to be dangerously missing in most of the projects, the absence of which poses the question of relevance. Knowledge is being gained vertically much more rapidly than horizontally, thus creating the impression of islands of knowledge that are unable to communicate with each other. It has become necessary to specialize in order to survive the competition for resources. This reaffirms the importance of fundamental discoveries that are of value for the entire field. Most of all, it appears critical to keep in mind the overall goal and vision of architectural research: To improve the quality of the built environment we live in.

CAAD Education Futures

In the 1990's software tools and hardware have reached a quality that requires a major re-evaluation of previous assumptions. A new generation of architects, educators and students has evolved which approaches CAAD with less bias and prejudice than was the case just ten years ago. Surprising and unexpected directions in architectural form and presentations are the result. A new agenda for CAAD education is essential.

The needs of practice and the availability of new tools, taught at increasingly competent training centers, define the agenda for CAD *training*. The future agenda for CAAD *education* is more difficult to define as human and financial factors within academic environments will influence its development.

The human factor. The easy days of teaching CAAD are over. Competition from other courses is strong and the field has grown to such an extent that educators must make decisions about which topics are most important. The quality and nature of commercial products reduces the chances for individual educators to have an impact on future CAD products. CAAD educators face the dilemma of becoming obsolete - once new software becomes powerful and user-friendly enough - or of invading the domain of design teachers. The latter is inevitable if the advantages of computing in design are to be taught professionally and convincingly. The number of software users is increasing at a much greater rate than the number of software developers, which might explain the lack of fundamentally new ideas over the past 15 years. It also indicates the need to educate more concept and program developers.

The financial factor. Taken seriously, CAAD education will turn architecture into one of the most capital intensive teaching subjects. Extremely high demands with regard to graphics speed and quality, unusual output media and sizes, differentiate architecture from other disciplines. Hardware donations may subside, in which case all hardware and software would have to be purchased and maintained within restrictive academic budgets. This would give financially strong universities a significant advantage.

Education in CAAD has moved from the fringe to the mainstream. There are few architectural schools in North America that do not include one or more CAAD courses as essential components of their curriculum. Europe is following quickly. The relatively late introduction of CAAD in Europe has had an interesting and possibly revolutionary side effect. Educators are of a younger generation. They view the instruments that they teach with differently than the pioneers of CAAD who are still familiar with the awkward earlier tools. The even younger students begin with highly superior instruments compared to their colleagues of a decade ago and have access to a fairly large body of work on the reconstruction of past architecture. What they still lack are examples of good architecture that has been produced with the new tools. So they set out and explore - a most exciting example is the recent "Soft Targets - Visions in Space" exhibition completed by students from the Technical University of Munich in October 1991. By using all of the modeling, projection and visualization technologies that have been developed in recent years, they were able to create an excitement that changed people's view of CAAD (Schallhammer 91). The "Lineamenta - CAAD" exhibition at the ETH Zürich presented in conjunction with the CAAD futures '91 conference in July 1991, also used student work to show new possibilities for generating, modeling, and visualizing virtual architecture.

Given the availability of data bases, knowledge bases and the new possibilities in visualization and presentation we must not forget to educate students to ask fundamental question about the purpose of design and technology. As the space for exploration opens up with the introduction of new instruments, an historic perspective and a convincing theory and discipline for applying computers in design become even more important.

CAAD Application Futures

The area of applications is expanding most rapidly. With few exceptions, applications concentrate on what could be termed design support at various levels. Yet there is still no conclusively integrated design package. Insular solutions to selected problems characterize the market. There are few programs which integrate more than two aspects of design such as graphics and structures or energy and cost evaluation (Haldemann 91). Some reasons for this are, the limitations of design data bases and representations, and the lack of semantic filters in modeling and presentation. With the number of users still growing rapidly and in the absence of a broad CAAD educational strategy which focuses on the new possibilities for designing with computers, traditional paper-based metaphors and paradigms are still understood best, they are the easiest to learn and therefore dominate the application market. Several authors in this book will point to the fact that a paradigm change in design will have a serious impact on the practice of architecture and the AEC industry in general. Here again, a convincing application, successfully marketed to architects, might change the perception of what can and cannot be done. It appears that new developments in application programs do not necessarily take hold due to their merits, but rather due to successful implementation. As an example, several viable standards for exchanging design information such as IGES and STEP have been proposed. Yet the market has made DXF the de-facto industry standard, although it is in some aspects inferior to the two others. A second example is the sudden widespread proliferation of graphics libraries such as GL, although theoretically the system independent GKS or PHIGS graphics packages offer greater advantages.

Natural user interfaces are of crucial importance for CAD application programs, particularly for novice users. New interface paradigms still do evolve and the range of physical input devices is growing even faster: keyboards, screens, mouse, pen, dials, space ball, data glove, just to name a few. It is interesting to note that pen-based computers are now marketed as the latest in technical development while they rely on a traditional input mechanism perfected over centuries.

The majority of new programs fall into the category of CAD productivity tools. As in research, progress has occurred vertically within design activity areas but not horizontally. A typical example is the DOE-2 energy simulation program: After more than 15 years of development, there is still no graphical or at least user-friendly interface, although it has been proven that DOE-2 can be used as an effective design tool. Specialists in energy simulation do not need graphical input, and designers do not use the program because of its awkward non-graphical input mechanism and overwhelming set of options.

Similarities between natural language and design language do exist and have been the subject of extensive research. Yet differences become clear very rapidly when one searches for the design counterpart of word processors, outliners, spelling and grammar checkers. In the restricted and - compared with architecture - highly constrained space of natural language vocabulary, there are enough conventions and sufficient known semantic content to allow the processing of data from different points of view or through different filters. Even so, countless unexpected and undesirable confusions can occur, thus effectively preventing automation. In parallel, design productivity could definitely improve if a shape processor, a design element checker, a design grammar checker, and design outliners would exist in an integrated program. Then even designers might use computers.

Conclusions

It has become clear that CAAD will have not one but many futures, shaped by academia, practice, and business. Scientific methods in architectural research have helped to create a foundation of knowledge on which new CAAD research can build. Consequently, CAD programs first concentrated on the most formalized product, the architectural drawing. The art of abstraction, essential for the communication of architectural ideas, will not lose its significance even in the age of virtual reality. Lineamenta can serve as the link from the past to demonstrate possible future developments.

Future CAAD systems should be useful, intelligent and eventually support properties in the class of taste without limiting creativity. For this, we must understand the link between architect, drawing, and completed building. At the same time, we must understand the pragmatism and precision of leading architects such as Botta or Campi which point to the research directions of case-based reasoning and adaptation. We also must realize what we may surrender by replacing the traditional process of design with new modeling and interaction techniques. Aesthetics is one of the challenges for the next generation of CAAD systems because there is no reason to exclude any of the properties of architecture from the processes of understanding, formalizing, and explicating. Whether or not we shall succeed is not the question, but rather how we will proceed to investigate such seemingly unquantifiable properties of architecture. Nothing would be more devastating for the young science of computer aided design and for architecture than the creation of new taboos.

References

Haldemann, Samuel. 1991. "CAAD - Eine Herausforderung an den Architekten." *Hochparterre,* vol. 4, no. 11: 70-74.

Mitchell, William J. 1990. "Introduction: A New Agenda for Computer-Aided Design." In Malcolm McCullough, W. J. Mitchell, and P. Purcell (eds.). *The Electronic Design Studio*. MA: MIT Press.

Oechslin, Werner. 1991. *Lineamenta - CAAD*. Exhibition and opening remarks at CAAD futures '91. ETH Zürich, Switzerland: gta Institute.

Schallhammer, Johannes, and F. Wenz. 1991. "Neugier Einsamkeit Wirklichkeit." *Leonardo*. October. Kissing: WEKA Fachverlag.

Schmitt, Gerhard, U. Flemming, L. Madrazo. 1990. "Design Support Systems." *archithese* 3-90, 28-37.

Education

1 Integrating Shape Grammars and Design Analysis

William J. Mitchell, Robin S. Liggett, Spiro N. Pollalis, and Milton Tan

Graduate School of Design
Harvard University
48 Quincy St.
Cambridge, MA 02138, USA

This paper demonstrates how design problems can be solved by combining a shape grammar to generate alternatives with standard engineering analysis procedures to test them. It provides a detailed worked example, and discusses practical applications of the idea in design teaching.

Introduction: Generating and Testing Design Alternatives

If we take it that design is a generate-and-test process, then it follows that design knowledge may be embodied in the generator, in the tester, or in both (Mitchell 1990). In other words, effective design processes (whether manual or automated) may combine blind generation of alternatives with highly effective selection (evolution's strategy), or employ such foolproof generation techniques that there is no need for further testing to weed out mistakes (God's strategy), or divide the labor between generator and tester in some appropriate way (the demigod's strategy).

It has been shown that the shape grammar formalism (Stiny 1980) provides an effective way to encode knowledge of how to put various types of artifacts together so that they function as required, and that generation of designs in the languages specified by such grammars can be supported by appropriate computer software. It has also been shown, in many contexts, that standard engineering analysis procedures can be applied to computer models of design alternatives in order to determine whether these alternatives are satisfactory. These two observations suggest that a powerful knowledge-based computer-aided design system might result from combining a shape grammar as the generator with analysis procedures for testing. This approach has the additional technical advantage that the shape grammar rigorously and precisely specifies the range of inputs with which the analysis procedures must deal. In this paper we consider such a combination.

The Primitive Hut Problem

The problem chosen as a vehicle for the study was design of a fairly simple three-dimensional framed structure—a modern equivalent of Laugier's archetypal "primitive hut". The structure is rectangular in plan, with a column at each corner (figure 1). Primary structural members span between the columns and support secondary members, which in turn support a roof of planks. Length, width, and height of the enclosed volume can vary arbitrarily.

Normal roof loads for a small garden pavilion are assumed. The designer's problem is to choose, arrange, and connect primary and secondary roof members so as to transfer loads to the columns, to provide adequate lateral stability, and to size all members appropriately.

Figure 1. The primitive hut as depicted in Laugier's *Essai sur l'Architecture*.

This is, of course, quite an elementary problem—but a moment's reflection reveals that the knowledge needed to solve it is by no means trivial. For a start, you have to know that beams and trusses are appropriate types of spanning members for use in this context. Next, you have to know something about the various types of flat and pitched trusses, the arrangements of their constituent members, and the reasons for choosing one type rather than another in a particular context. Once you have an idea of what the spanning members might be, you need some basis for choosing the direction in which the primary members will span, and for choosing the number and spacing of the secondary members. Given a basic topology, you need to know how to resolve connection details—particularly at the corners. You need to know the various ways that lateral stability can be provided. And finally, you need to know the rules for sizing beams, columns, and truss chords correctly.

Experienced designers have all this knowledge at their fingertips, and so can produce solutions very quickly and confidently. But inexperienced designers often lack some of the necessary knowledge, and it seems clear that even a small knowledge deficiency can produce considerable uncertainty and can greatly hinder the production of a sound solution. (Beginning students can often be observed struggling with this sort of problem.) The consequences of gaps in knowledge show up in several ways: a designer may fail to produce a solution at all, or may produce a solution without being confident that it is satisfactory, or (worst of all) may believe that a proposed solution is satisfactory when, in fact, it would fail.

The function of a knowledge-based computer-aided design system (in general, and for this problem in particular) is to supply knowledge that might be missing, and so to enable inexperienced designers to perform at the level of experts. An effective system should allow inexperienced designers to produce solutions quickly, and it should guarantee that these solutions are adequate.

Vocabularies and Rules of Usage

The knowledge needed to solve problems can often be encoded in the form of conditional rules, and knowledge-based computer-aided design systems usually incorporate such rules. Each such rule specifies a condition, and associates with that condition an action which may appropriately be taken in response. To apply knowledge that is expressed in this form, you first try to find a match between the conditions at hand and the condition part of a rule. Then, when you find a match, you follow the instructions in the action part of the rule. Consider, for example, the problem of crossing the road safely. A traffic light has three possible conditions: red, yellow, and green. The rules that you need to know are: if red then stop; if yellow then continue if started else stop; if green then go. To apply these rules you need to look at the light, find a match between the condition of the light and the condition part of a rule, then act as instructed by the action part of that rule. Notice that it does not help to know the rules when you are unable to recognize conditions—if, for example, you are color-blind. Nor does it help to recognize the conditions if you cannot associate actions correctly—if you can see that a light is red, but do not know what this means.

In architectural contexts, it is particularly convenient to express conditional rules graphically. In other words, you draw a context (the condition that is to be recognized), and you also draw an appropriate design response to that context. Some simple examples of such rules are shown in figure 2. These are rules of usage for the architectural elements that show up on the right (action) sides of rules. In other words, rules of usage specify the contexts in which elements such as pedestals, columns, and entablatures can be used, and show the possible relationships of these elements to other elements.

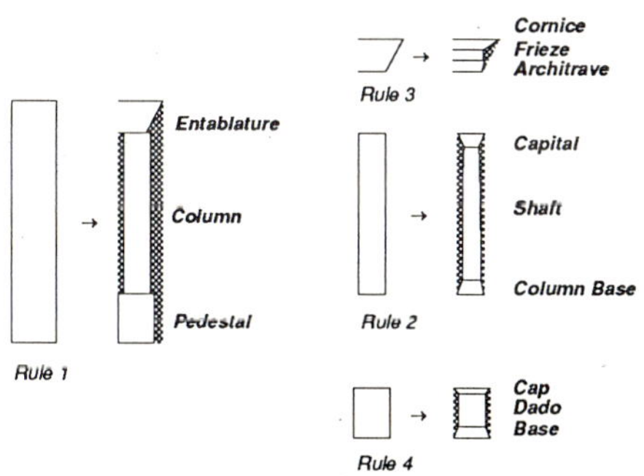

Figure 2. Rules of usage for some architectural elements.

The elements that appear in rules of usage may be actual construction elements and spaces, or they may be abstract shapes and volumes that serve as construction lines, grids, axes, place-holders for later substitution of something else, and other devices that guide the development of a design. These marker elements are removed when they no longer serve a useful purpose, they do not explicitly form part of the final design, and they do not show up in bills of materials or space inventories. We distinguish them from terminal elements, which do show up in final designs, and do appear in bills of materials. In figure 2, rule 1, for example, a simple rectangle initially serves as a marker for the whole design. The rule specifies replacement of this marker by an assembly of lower-level markers showing the outlines of pedestal, column, and entablature. Then rules 2, 3, and 4 show how these lower-level markers can, in turn, be replaced by terminal vocabulary elements: cornice, frieze, architrave, capital, shaft, column base, cap, dado, and pedestal base.

Exhaustive specification of the ways to use some architectural element (whether a terminal or a marker) requires identification of all the contexts in which that element can appear, and specification of one or more rules for each of those contexts. By establishing a vocabulary or marker and terminal elements, and writing complete rules of usage for these elements, we can define a shape grammar that specifies a language of architectural form. Formally, such a grammar consists of a marker vocabulary Vm, a terminal vocabulary Vt, a set R of rules of usage, and a starting shape S. Designs in the language specified by the grammar are derived by recursive application of the rules R to the starting shape S. A rule applies when its left side matches a subshape of the current design in progress. The result of application is replacement of that subshape by the shape shown on the right side of the rule. A derivation terminates when no further rule applications are possible. If the resulting design contains no markers, then it is a complete design in the language specified by the grammar. (If it does contain markers it is a design dead-end—a configuration which cannot be developed into a complete design under the given rules of usage.) The language specified by the grammar consists of all the complete designs derivable in this way.

To describe how to put together a primitive hut, then, we need to specify an appropriate terminal vocabulary, a marker vocabulary, and rules of usage. A reasonable terminal vocabulary consists of the following: timber columns, masonry columns, timber beams, parallel-chord timber trusses, pitched timber trusses, bow timber trusses, knee braces, cross braces, one-way braces, and masonry shear walls (figure 3).

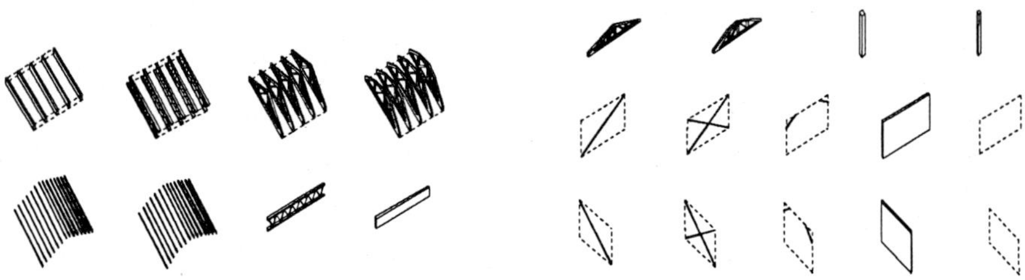

Figure 3. Terminal vocabulary for the primitive hut.

These terminal vocabulary elements can be put together to form subsystems that provide necessary functions (figure 4). For example, we can put together four columns to produce a supporting substructure that holds up the roof. We can put together beams, parallel-chord trusses, and pitched trusses in various combinations to become roof structures that hold up a plank roof and so provide shelter. And we can put together a support structure, a roof structure, and braces or walls to produce a system that has lateral stability.

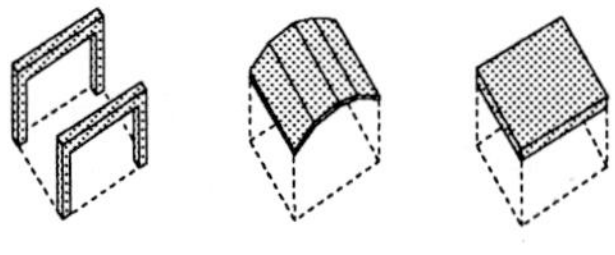

Figure 4. Some subsystems of the primitive hut.

When we want to represent a subsystem without committing ourselves to details of its internal organization, we can show it as an abstract volume. Figure 5 illustrates the various subsystems of the primitive hut, depicted in this abstract way. These abstract volumes constitute the marker vocabulary of the primitive hut grammar. Markers serve as the intermediate abstractions that we use in thinking about how to put terminal vocabulary elements together in subsystems so that they function as required. By combining markers in different ways, and substituting different arrangements of terminals for the same marker, we can generate different hut designs.

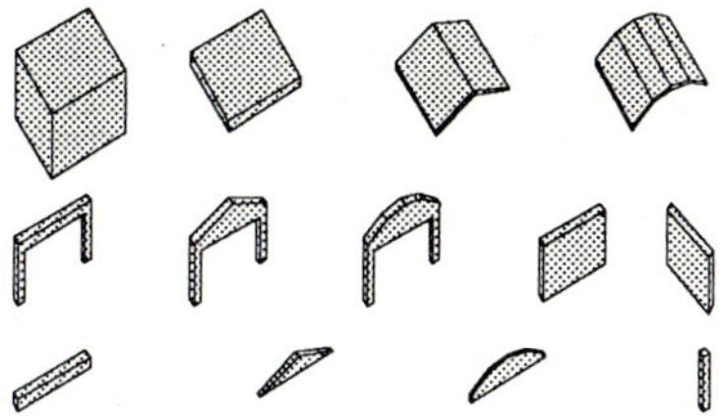

Figure 5. Marker vocabulary for the primitive hut.

Notice that the markers correspond to architectural roles. The rules of usage, then, must specify ways to use terminals and combinations of terminals *in* these roles. They must show how to use timber and masonry columns *as* structural supports, beams and trusses *as* primary structural members, beams and trusses *as* secondary structural members, and knee braces, cross braces, and shear walls *as* lateral stability systems. Figure 6 shows our rules of usage for putting together terminal vocabulary elements to produce subsystems, and for putting together lower-level subsystems to produce higher-level subsystems. (The design variables introduced at each step are listed in italics on the right.)

REFINEMENT OF THE PRIMARY STRUCTURE:

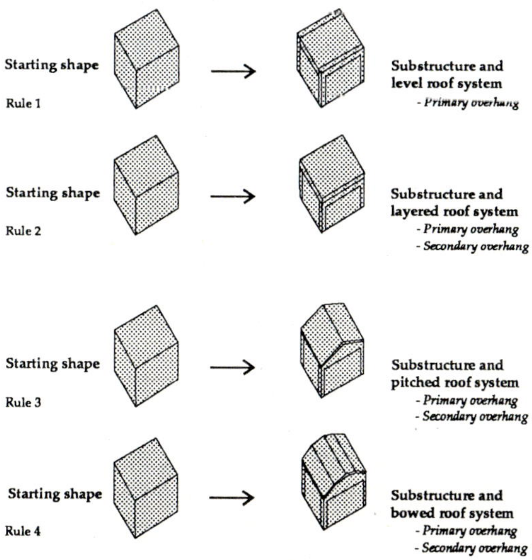

REFINEMENT OF THE PRIMARY STRUCTURE:

Flat primary structure
Rule 5
(applicable without primary overhang)

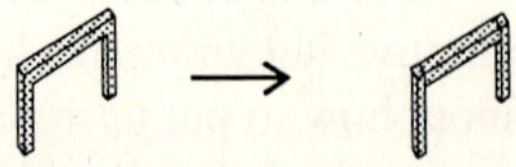

Primary roof support abuts columns

Flat primary structure
Rule 6

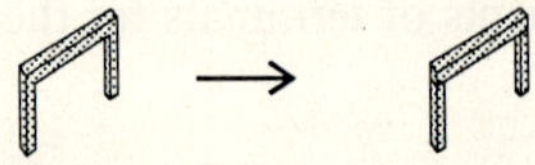

Primary roof support above columns

Pitched primary structure
Rule 7

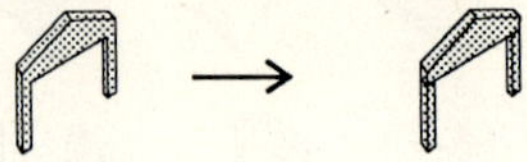

Pitched roof support above columns
- *Primary truss height*

Bowed primary structure
Rule 8

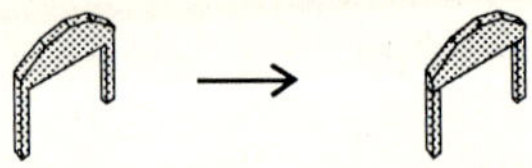

Bowed roof support above columns
- *Primary truss height*

SUBSTITUTION OF SECONDARY STRUCTURE TERMINALS:

Flat-bottomed secondary roof structure
Rule 9

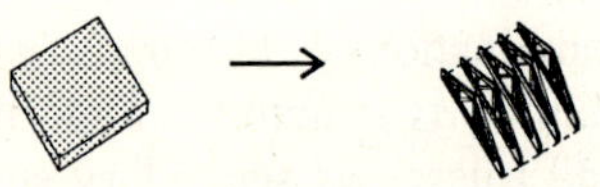

Pitched trusses
- *Spacing*
- *Top depth*
- *Bottom depth*
- *Width (calculated)*
- *# divisions*
- *Secondary truss height*

Flat-bottomed secondary roof structure
Rule 10

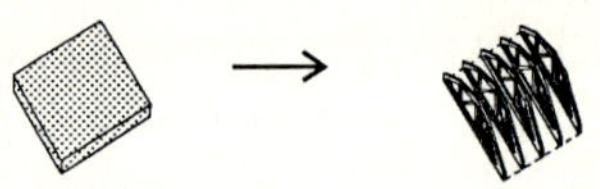

Bowed trusses
- *Spacing*
- *Top depth*
- *Bottom depth*
- *Width (calculated)*
- *# divisions*
- *Secondary truss height*

Flat-bottomed secondary roof structure
Rule 11

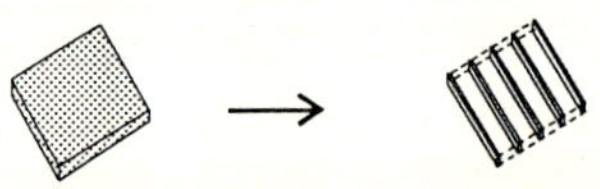

Beams
- *Spacing*
- *Joist depth*
- *Joist width (calculated)*

Flat-bottomed secondary roof structure
Rule 12

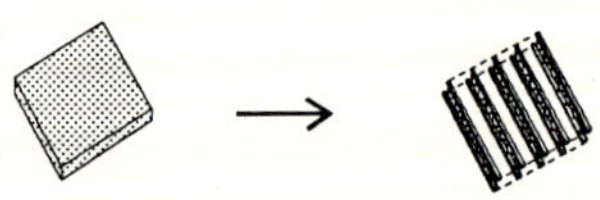

Flat trusses
- *Spacing*
- *Top depth*
- *Bottom depth*
- *Width (calculated)*
- *# divisions*

Pitched secondary roof structure
Rule 13

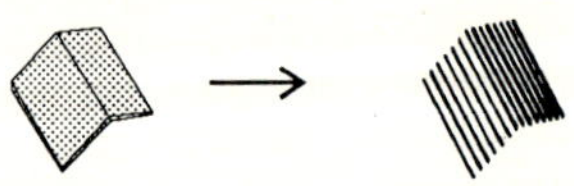

Joists
- *# divisions*
- *Depth*
- *Width (calculated)*

Bowed secondary roof structure
Rule 14

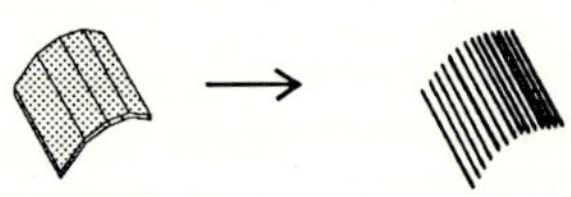

Joists
- *# divisions*
- *# joists / divisions*
- *Joist depth*
- *Joist width (calculated)*

SUBSTITUTION OF LATERAL STABILITY TERMINALS:

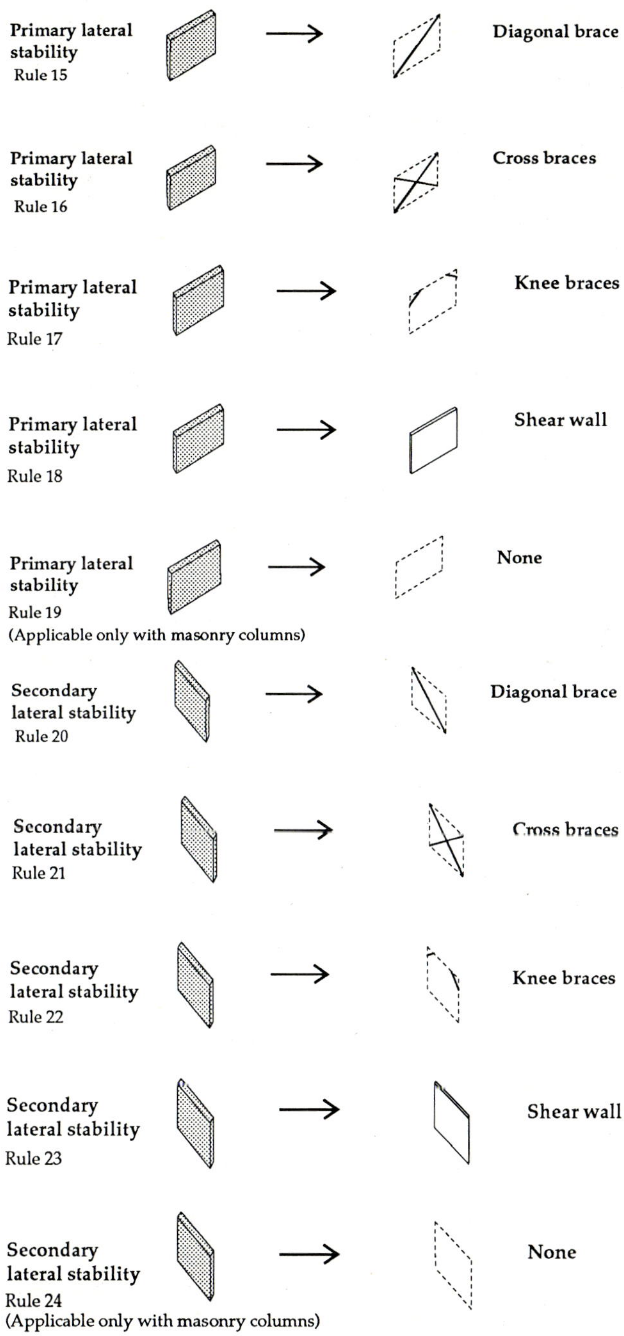

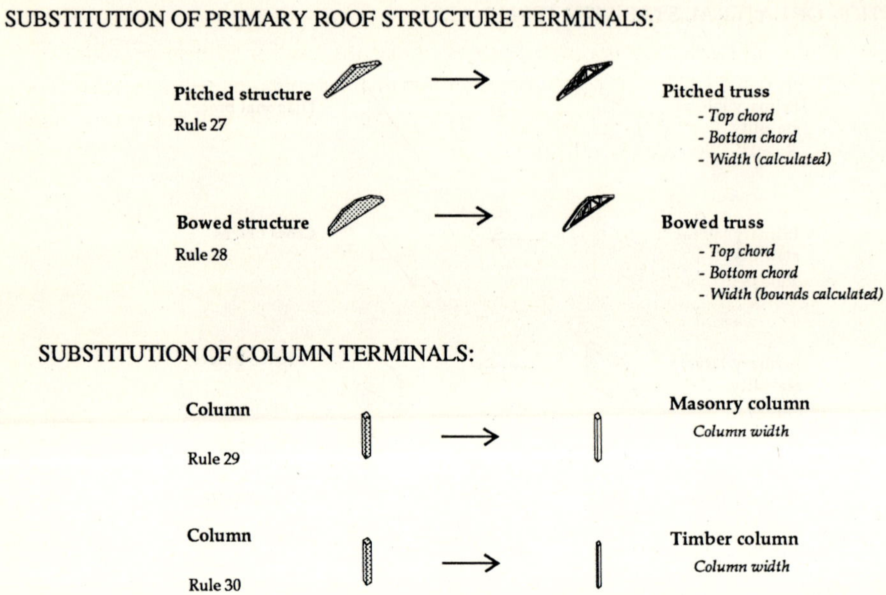

Figure 6. Rules of the primitive hut grammar (variables are in italics).

Thus by drawing terminal vocabulary elements we specify their forms, and by defining rules of usage we specify their functions. (Similarly, a dictionary specifies the forms of words, while grammatical rules describe their functions in sentences—how to use them as nouns, verbs, adjectives and so on.) Of course you can argue with our rules: there may be ways of using these elements to make primitive huts in ways that we have not considered, and you may not like some of the usages that we allow. The rules simply represent some empirical knowledge of how things work, and like all empirical knowledge it may be incomplete and imperfect. If you know better, then you can change the rules.

The starting shape S to which these rules are applied is a simple rectangular box, as illustrated in figure 7. The length, width, and height of this box can be varied to specify huts of different sizes.

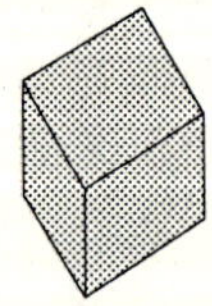

Figure 7. The starting shape of the primitive hut grammar.

Under the rules of the primitive hut grammar, certain elements can be used in different roles. A beam, for example, can be used as either a primary structural element or as a secondary structural element. On the other hand, some contexts allow use of alternative elements in a role: roof support can be provided either by masonry columns or by timber columns, and so on. Thus the rules of usage allow different combinations to emerge: they specify not just one primitive hut design, but a language of primitive huts. Figure 8 illustrates the derivation of one design in this language by recursive application of the rule system to the starting shape. Different sequences of rule applications are possible, and yield different designs. If we have written our rules correctly, all of these designs should prove functionally satisfactory in the sense that they shelter a rectangular volume, carry roof loads down to the ground, and provide lateral stability.

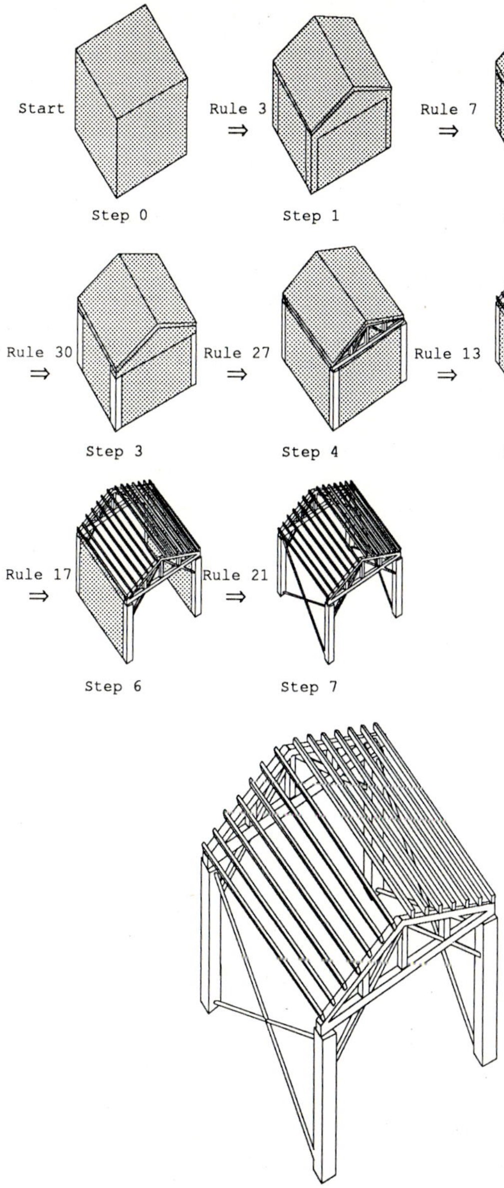

Figure 8. Derivation of a design in the language.

The rules of the grammar assign a hierarchical structure of elements and subsystems to any design in the language. Figure 9 illustrates this structure (the syntax tree) for the design that was derived in figure 8.

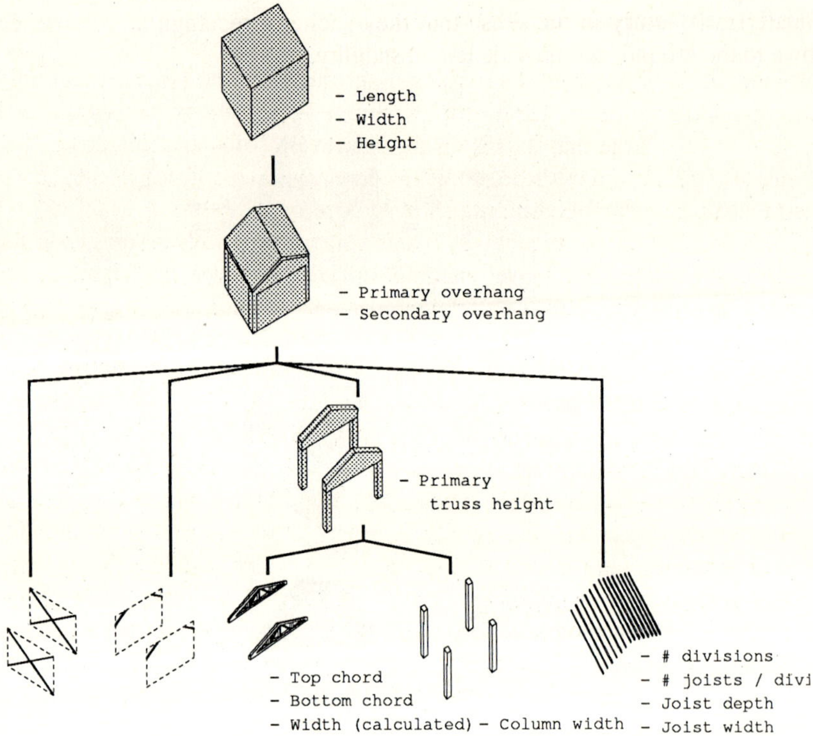

Figure 9. Syntax tree for the derived design.

Parametric Variation

All of the terminal and marker vocabulary elements in this language are defined as parametric objects. In other words, their dimensions are variable, and different instances can be specified by assigning different values to the variables. This is necessary if we want to be able to adapt hut designs to different functions and contexts, but it creates some complexities.

The basic problem is that the dimensions of some elements must depend on the dimensions of others if functionality is to be maintained as dimensions are varied. A beam, for example, must span between columns if it is to be able to hold up the roof. If we take the length of the beam as an independent variable, then column spacing must depend on it. Alternatively, we can take the column spacing as an independent variable and make the length of the beam depend on this. In any case, we establish chains of dimensional dependencies when we fit elements and subsystems together to produce hut designs.

The problem of tracing dependencies can be simplified considerably by assuming that dimensional dependencies are always propagated top-down through the syntax tree, so that lower-level subsystems fit within the envelopes established by higher-level subsystems. (Figure 9 illustrates how variables may appropriately be introduced at various levels in the syntax tree that was shown earlier.)

Structural Analysis of Alternatives

In general, the dimensional variables of terminal vocabulary elements are subject to constraints. A timber beam, for example, must be large enough to support the load that it carries, but not so large that it exceeds the dimensions of available timber. Thus, when we attempt to trace a chain of dimensional dependencies and adjust a design accordingly, we may find that a constraint violation results in some terminal.

This problem can be handled by making some reasonable assumptions about loads on the system as a whole, then using standard formulae to check the adequacy of terminal members. Whenever an inadequate terminal member is found, the designer can attempt to adjust its dimensions to achieve adequacy. If this proves impossible within the space available, then the designer can back up the abstraction hierarchy, and attempt to adjust the higher-level subsystem so that the problem in the terminal becomes solvable. If this also fails, then the designer can back up again, and so on to the top of the tree.

Notice how formulae and grammar interact. First, the grammar establishes the structural roles of elements and hence the types of analyses that are relevant—whether, for example, a particular rectangular element should be analyzed as a column or a beam. Second, the grammar often can be (and in this case is) written to assure that no unanalyzable conditions develop: every design in the language is a well-formed object of analysis with the available formulae. (This is analogous to the property of a computer programming language that every syntactically correct command is processable, or the property of a spoken language that every grammatical declarative sentence is meaningful—either true or false.)

The Topdown Primitive Hut System

To explore the possibilities of combining a shape grammar and structural analysis of alternatives, the Topdown system (Liggett, Mitchell, and Tan 1990) was used to implement the primitive hut grammar (as described above) for putting together timber and masonry columns, timber beams and trusses, and various kinds of lateral stiffeners in configurations such that shelter is provided to a rectangular area, vertical loads are transferred to the ground, and there is stability under lateral loading. (In other words, the generator encodes knowledge of how to satisfy these requirements, together with considerable knowledge of how to resolve the detailing problems that arise when elements are put together in different combinations.) Structural analysis calculations were integrated so that member sizes could automatically be tested for adequacy. (That is, knowledge of how to size structural members was built into the tester.)

The user of Topdown sees three windows on the screen (figure 10). The peek window always displays the current state of the design. The poke window depicts the design in terms of intermediate abstractions at any chosen level in the abstraction hierarchy—from a rectangular box (the starting shape) to the current configuration of terminal elements. The poke window also shows dimension line. Finally, the message window displays textual suggestions, reminders, critical comments, results of analyses, and so on.

All interaction takes place via the poke window. Clicking on an intermediate abstraction in the poke window brings up a dialogue box displaying possible substitutions—elements that can play the role defined by the intermediate abstraction (figure 11). Selecting one of these substitutions then results in performance of the substitution and depiction of the result in the peek window. Clicking on a dimension line brings up up a slidebar which can be manipulated to vary the corresponding dimension (figure 12).

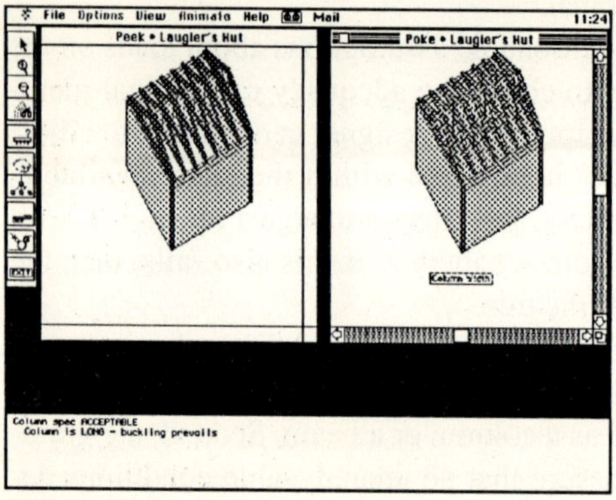

Figure 10. The Topdown interface.

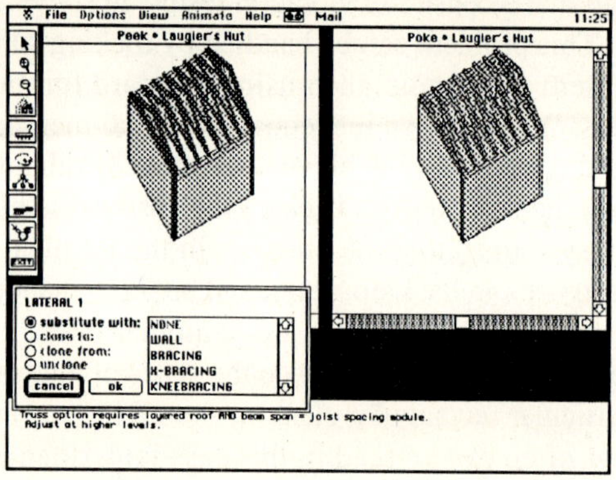

Figure 11. Topdown substitution dialog.

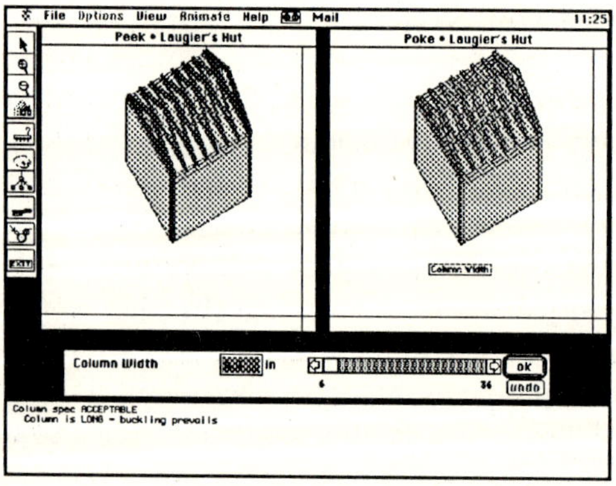

Figure 12. Topdown parametric variation dialog.

The user of this system is able to select from among alternative elements and subsystems to use in various contexts, and to vary dimensions at any level within a hierarchy—from individual member sizes up to overall dimensions of the entire system. All operations are in realtime or close to it in versions implemented on Macintosh II and IBM PS/2 machines.

Realtime Visual Feedback

Load and strength calculations are carried out on the fly, in realtime, as dimensions are chosen and varied. (Reasonable simplifying assumptions, and use of elementary beam, truss, and column formulae, make this feasible even on a Macintosh or PS/2 (Pollalis 1990). Implementation on a more powerful workstation would make more sophisticated analysis feasible, but there would probably not be a lot of advantage in this.) Feedback of evaluation results is simple, direct, and graphic: adequately sized members are shown in green, inadequately or prohibitively sized members are shown in red, and members on the threshold of inadequacy or prohibitiveness are shown in yellow.

Red conditions can usually be eliminated by appropriately resizing elements or subsystems. For example, a red primary beam might be made green either by increasing its depth or by reducing the overall dimension of the hut and hence its span. Sometimes a green condition can be achieved by choosing and substituting a more appropriate element or subsystem for a particular role—a truss instead of a beam for a long span, for example.

Thus the designer's objective is to find a configuration that responds to whatever nonstructural objectives are relevant, while keeping all the members green. (The system is, then, a demonstration of the *Logic of Architecture* thesis that design can be seen as search within a language to discover alternatives that satisfy specified predicates. The alternatives that satisfy the predicates have no red members.) Users typically find that the system allows them to explore a very wide range of alternatives in just a few minutes, and to converge quickly on one that is both technically adequate and aesthetically interesting (so refuting Kermit the Frog's well-known assertion that "It isn't easy being green.").

Renderings and Animations

The result of a successful Topdown session is a fully detailed three-dimensional model. This is represented internally, in extremely compact fashion, as a set of parameter values. Simple procedures can then expand these values into DXF, IGES, or other types of files for export to geometric modelers, renderers, or animators, so establishing a particular close linkage between exploration of construction possibilities and consideration of corresponding visual and spatial qualities.

Applications in Teaching

This system has been used by more than one hundred students in large introductory structures and computer-aided design classes at the Harvard Graduate School of Design. Most students grasped the idea of the system instantly, were able to begin working with it right away, and could produce satisfactory designs after just a few minutes of work. Thereafter, they were able to explore alternatives and variations freely—so developing an understanding of the interrelationships between element, arrangement, material, and dimension choices, and gaining a sense of the domain of possibilities structured by the grammar.

Our experience suggests that the approach may have wide have wide applicability in teaching construction, structures, and environmental systems. It has the advantage of allowing students to learn in a self-directed, exploratory way, by considering a wide variety of interesting and diverse examples. It combines some of the best features of the design studio (rich and complex problems and encouragement of formal exploration, but little analysis) with those of technical classes (careful analysis, but often simplified examples, and little opportunity for wide-ranging exploration of alternatives), while mitigating the disadvantages of both.

Reflecting on Rules

It is sometimes objected that this type of knowledge-based system reduces design to rule-following. But this objection only has force if the grammar is closed and rigid, and if it is used unreflectively. A more interesting view is that a grammar expresses a set of working assumptions about how to put together a design with the properties that you want. These assumptions are provisional, and subject to change as you discover that certain choices and arrangements cause difficulties, that elements can usefully be arranged in ways that you had not anticipated, that the given rules do not provide sufficient adaptability to satisfy particular requirements of context and function, and so on. A grammar should be used reflectively, with constant attention to whether it is helping to solve the problem at hand, and it should be amended continually. In this way, a grammar becomes an evolving repository of explicit, machine-processable design knowledge.

One of the main problems in developing rules is that you must identify all the conditions requiring attention that can emerge in the derivation of a design, and specify rules for dealing with these conditions. Otherwise, if unexpected conditions emerge, derivations may not terminate. Thus, for example, you must solve the corner detailing problem in a general way—for all the different combinations of timber and masonry columns, beams and trusses as primary structure, beams and trusses as secondary structure, and different choices of lateral stability systems, that alternative derivations may produce. Consequently, rule systems must often be modified to respond to conditions that were not initially anticipated.

A second problem is that you must choose an appropriate hierarchy of intermediate abstractions, and the best way to do this may be far from obvious. Instead of parsing the hut as we have done, for example, you might parse it into two frames with a roof structure slung in between, as illustrated in figure 13. This structures a designer's thinking in quite a different way. Whenever you choose one particular way of parsing a design, you illuminate some issues and open up certain possibilities at the expense of others. In development of the primitive hut grammar, many alternative ways of parsing were considered. All had both advantages and disadvantages.

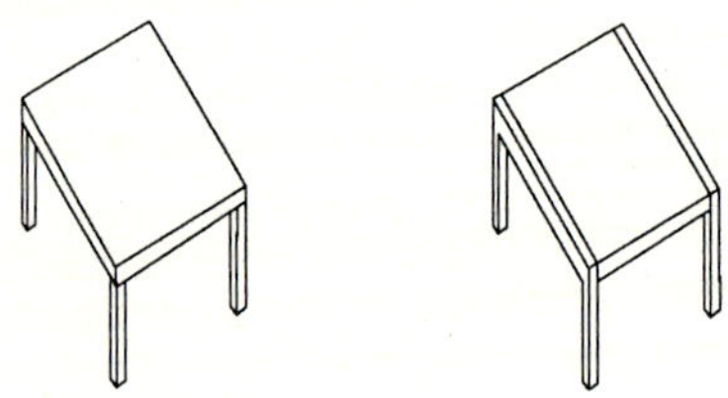

Figure 13. Alternative support structures.

And a third problem is that you must try to specify a language that is sufficiently extensive to allow response to different contexts and functional requirements, and provides a designer with adequate expressive power, but does not include a lot of irrelevant possibilities and architecturally meaningless variations. Our primitive hut grammar certainly errs on the side of restrictiveness. Everything that it produces is functionally sound, but it does not produce enough to establish an extraordinarily interesting domain for design exploration.

All of these issues provoked extensive and interesting discussions among the authors as the primitive hut grammar was under development. We explored the advantages and disadvantages of several different parsing schemes, and devoted a great deal of effort to finding general solutions to arrangement and detailing problems. A particular point of contention was the priority of spatial versus tectonic decisions. Should you first choose a general spatial arrangement then explore feasible tectonic realizations, or should you first choose a tectonic vocabulary then explore the spatial possibilities that it establishes? Such questions probably have no general answers: it seems that different designers take characteristically different attitudes toward them, and so produce characteristically different responses to similar problems.

Limitations of the Approach

The Topdown system has certain significant limitations. Most importantly, it imposes a predefined, fixed, hierarchical decomposition on designs. Thus it lacks the capacity to recognize and transform emergent shapes, as a fully general shape grammar system would have. However, there is considerable practical justification for treating terminal vocabulary elements as indivisible atoms, since they are both real physical components and natural units of structural analysis.

Conclusion

Implementation of the primitive hut grammar in Topdown has demonstrated the feasibility of capturing sufficient practical knowledge in a grammar to support very efficient solution of a fairly elementary, but certainly non-trivial, three-dimensional architectural design problem. In the implementation and testing process, this grammar evolved through many versions: in its current state it expresses a much more complete and refined theory of how to design a "primitive hut" than it did in earlier versions. Others might take it even further—so enacting a cycle of theory-building, criticism, and modification that produces an accumulation of practical design knowledge in accessible, computer-processable form.

References

Liggett, Robin S., William J. Mitchell, and Milton Tan. 1990. "Multi-Level Analysis and Optimization of Designs." In Yehuda E. Kalay (ed.). *Evaluating and Predicting Design Performance: Proceedings of the SUNY Buffalo 3rd International Symposium on CAD*. (To appear in Yehuda E. Kalay (ed.). *Evaluating and Predicting Design Performance*. New York: John Wiley.)

Mitchell, William J. 1990. *The Logic of Architecture*. Cambridge MA: MIT Press.

Mitchell, William J., Robin S. Liggett, and Milton Tan. 1990. "Top-Down Knowledge-Based Design." In Malcolm McCullough, William J. Mitchell and Patrick Purcell (eds.). *The Electronic Design Studio*. Cambridge, MA: MIT Press.

Pollalis, Spiro N. 1990. "Topdown: The Structural Engineering Assumptions for the Design of the Primitive Hut." Unpublished report, Harvard University Graduate School of Design.

Stiny, George. 1980. "Introduction to Shape and Shape Grammars." *Environment and Planning B* 7: 343-51.

2 Designing with Grammars

Terry W. Knight

Graduate School of Architecture and Urban Planning
University of California
Los Angeles, CA 90024-1467
U.S.A.

Shape grammars that generate languages of designs have been used widely over the past several years to describe and understand a diversity of architectural and other styles of designs. These grammars have been developed to address two fundamental concerns in design: 1) the analysis of contemporary or historic styles of designs, and 2) the synthesis or creation of completely new and original styles of designs. Most applications of shape grammars so far have been concerned with analysis. The creative use of shape grammars - the use of grammars to invent new architectural or other designs - has not been exploited nearly as well. A new series of exercises for designing with shape grammars, and also with color grammars, *is sketched informally here. These exercises are currently being used in classes in the Architecture and Urban Design Program at U.C.L.A.*

Introduction

Shape grammars (Stiny 1975, Knight forthcoming) that generate *languages of designs* have been used widely over the past several years to describe and understand a diversity of architectural and other styles of designs. These grammars have been developed to address two fundamental concerns in design: 1) the analysis or description of contemporary or historic styles of designs, and 2) the synthesis or creation of completely new and original styles of designs. Most applications of shape grammars so far have been concerned with analysis. For example, shape grammars have been defined to understand languages of Chinese ice-ray lattice designs (Stiny 1977), Palladian villas (Stiny and Mitchell 1978), Hepplewhite chairs (Knight 1980), Japanese tearooms (Knight 1981), Frank Lloyd Wright prairie houses (Koning and Eizenberg 1981), and Queen Anne houses (Flemming 1986), among other kinds of designs. However, the creative use of shape grammars - the use of grammars to invent new architectural or other designs - has not been exploited nearly as well as the use of grammars to do analysis. Designers and design students are often intimidated by the formal aspects of grammars and incorrectly assume that the use of grammars requires a technical competency beyond their means or interests. To bring the use of shape grammars into the design studio and into architectural practice where the potential of shape grammars can be fully realized, an appropriate programme for developing new and original grammars is needed. The groundwork for such a programme has been laid by Stiny (1980). Stiny's programme is illustrated using the building blocks of the 19th century educator Frederick Froebel. Froebel, the inventor of the kindergarten method of education, is well known among architects through Frank Lloyd Wright's numerous testimonials to his Froebel training as a child, and the impact this training had on his design philosophy and work. Stiny has shown how Froebel's kindergarten method of education for children, which closely resembles the studio method of architectural education, can be exploited in a sophisticated programme for developing grammars for original languages of designs.

Stiny's programme has recently been reworked and expanded into a series of coordinated design exercises using the Froebel blocks or other 3-dimensional forms. This new programme of exercises is being used in elective classes in the Design Theory and Methods area of the Architecture and Urban Design Program at U.C.L.A. Students in these classes come from the four degree programs in the school (M.Arch. I, M.Arch. II, M.A., and Ph.D.) and have a variety of backgrounds and levels of experience in architectural design and formal methods. Students from the Department of Design frequently participate in these classes as well. The programme of design exercises with grammars is in two parts. One part is comprised of exercises for developing shape grammars; the other part is comprised of exercises for developing color grammars. Color grammars (Knight 1989), an extension of shape grammars, describe qualitative aspects of designs such as color, texture, materials, function, and so on, in addition to spatial aspects of designs. Both series of exercises deal initially with simple, abstract forms. However, the goal of the exercises is to develop these simple forms into more detailed architectural or other designs. An informal and partial overview of both series of exercises is given here. The formal and complete details of these exercises are described elsewhere (Knight forthcoming).

Designing with Shape Grammars

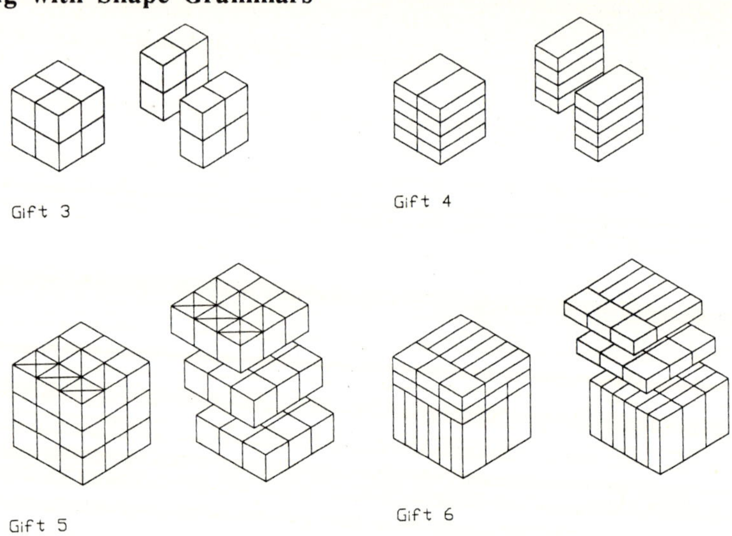

Figure 1. Froebel's building gifts.

In the first part of the programme, exercises begin with the definition of simple shape grammars that lead to the definition of more complex ones. The development of shape grammars begins by specifying a *vocabulary* of 3-dimensional forms or *shapes*. The shapes in a vocabulary are the building blocks for designs. In class demonstrations, vocabularies are made up of various blocks from the four building gifts of Froebel - cubes, half-cubes, quarter-cubes, oblongs, squares, and pillars (figure 1). In class projects, students are free to use any 3-dimensional shapes in defining their own vocabularies.

A vocabulary of shapes by itself does not determine designs; it merely determines the pieces from which designs may be made. To actually construct designs, the ways that shapes in a vocabulary can be combined with one another must also be specified. These particular ways of combining shapes are given with *spatial relations*. Figure 2, for example, shows a spatial relation between two oblongs from the Froebel gifts.

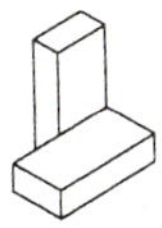

Figure 2. A spatial relation between two oblongs.

Spatial relations, such as the one shown in figure 2, are compositional ideas for making designs. They provide different contexts for either adding shapes in a vocabulary to one another or subtracting these shapes from one another, to create designs. In more traditional terms, they fix the ways that shapes may be either drawn or erased as a design is made. These two basic actions of adding and subtracting shapes are specified more precisely with *shape rules*.

Given two shapes A and B that are arranged to form a spatial relation, denoted by A + B, four different shape rules can be determined. Two of these rules correspond to adding a shape to a design, two correspond to subtracting a shape from a design:

addition rules:	(1) $A \rightarrow A + B$
	(2) $B \rightarrow A + B$
subtraction rules:	(3) $A + B \rightarrow A$
	(4) $A + B \rightarrow B$

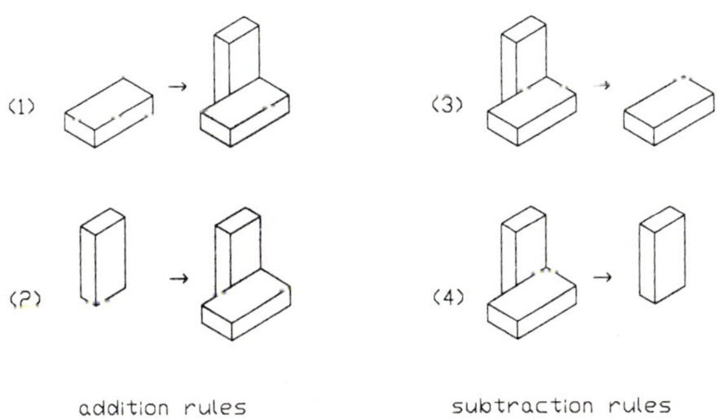

Figure 3. The four shape rules that can be defined from the spatial relation in figure 2.

Once a compositional idea or spatial relation is chosen, a set of simple grammars, called *basic grammars*, is defined. Basic grammars are defined using one or both of the two addition rules defined from the chosen spatial relation. If the shapes in a spatial relation are the same - for example, two oblongs - then only one addition rule is necessary to define each basic grammar. (Basic grammars defined from either of the two addition rules determined from a particular spatial relation generate the same designs but in different orientations.) If the shapes in a spatial relation are different - for example, an oblong and a pillar - then both addition rules are necessary to define each basic grammar. A starting or *initial shape* to begin the construction of designs is also included in each grammar. The initial shape is one of the two shapes in the chosen spatial relation.

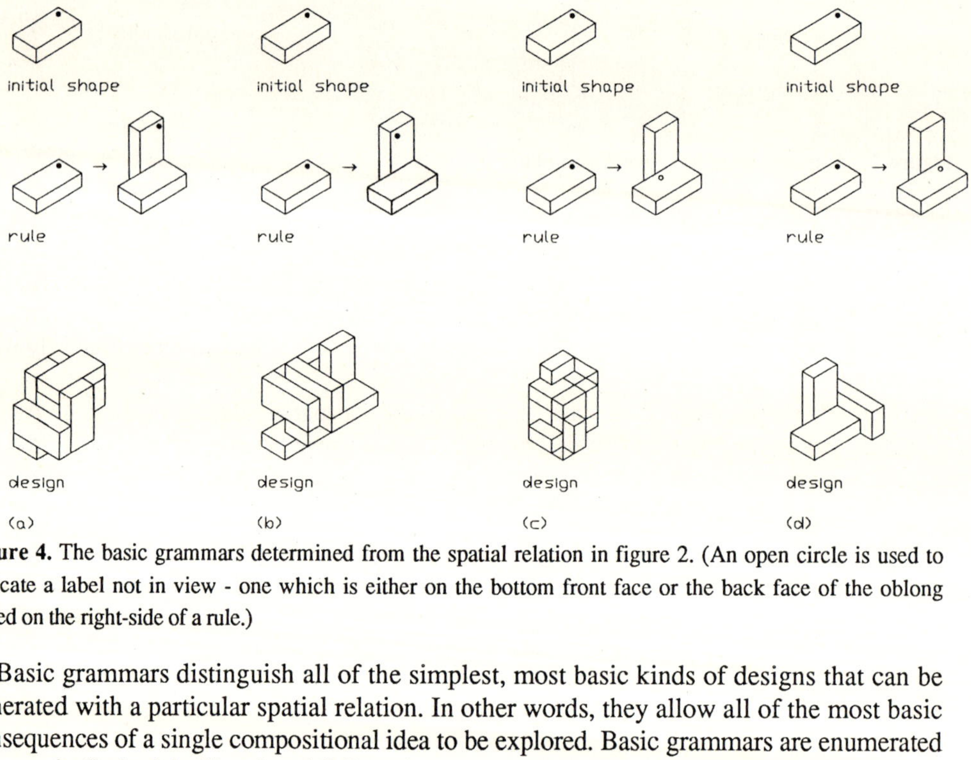

Figure 4. The basic grammars determined from the spatial relation in figure 2. (An open circle is used to indicate a label not in view - one which is either on the bottom front face or the back face of the oblong added on the right-side of a rule.)

Basic grammars distinguish all of the simplest, most basic kinds of designs that can be generated with a particular spatial relation. In other words, they allow all of the most basic consequences of a single compositional idea to be explored. Basic grammars are enumerated systematically by *labelling* the addition rule (or rules) defined from a spatial relation, according to the symmetry properties of the shapes in the rule. Briefly, the symmetry of a shape is determined by the different isometric transformations that keep the position and orientation of the shape invariant. The transformations that determine the symmetry of the shape on the left-side of a rule can be used to identify the different ways (the different transformations under which) the rule can be applied. The application of a rule can then be restricted to each one of these different ways by adding labels to the shapes in the rule. Each different labelling of a rule, according to the symmetries of the shapes in it, determines a different basic grammar. Each different basic grammar generates designs with distinct spatial properties.
Figure 4, for example, shows all of the basic grammars that can be determined from the spatial relation in figure 2. Eight basic grammars are defined, corresponding to the eight possible symmetry transformations of the oblong. The eight basic grammars are identical except for the labelling of the addition rule (rule (1) in figure 3) in each grammar. The posi-

tion of the label (a dot) on the oblong on the left-side of each rule is the same; however, the position of the label on the oblong added on the right-side of each rule is different. These different positions of labels correspond to the eight different symmetry transformations of the oblong. Although each basic grammar is based on the same vocabulary, the same spatial relation, and the same rule, each different labelling of the rule produces unique designs. A design generated by each grammar is shown figure 4. (Technically, each basic grammar must also include a rule to erase labels. For simplicity of presentation, these rules are not shown here and in the grammars that follow.)

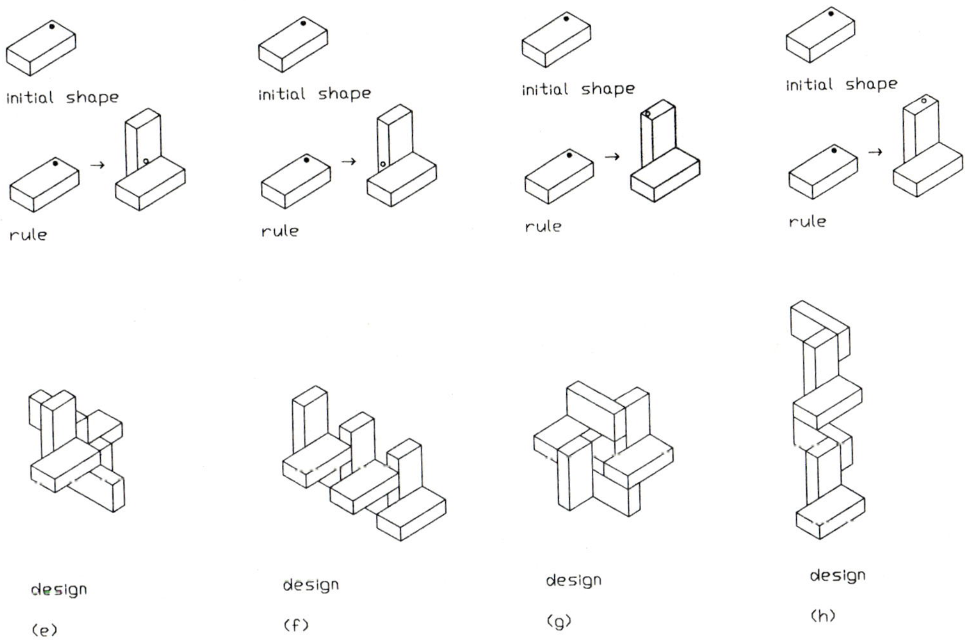

Figure 4. (continued).

Figures 5 and 6 show some student work produced with basic grammars. The designs in figure 5 are generated by basic grammars determined from a spatial relation between two elongated pillars set apart from one another. Sixteen basic grammars can be defined with this spatial relation (the symmetry of the pillar is 16); six designs generated by six of the basic grammars are shown here.

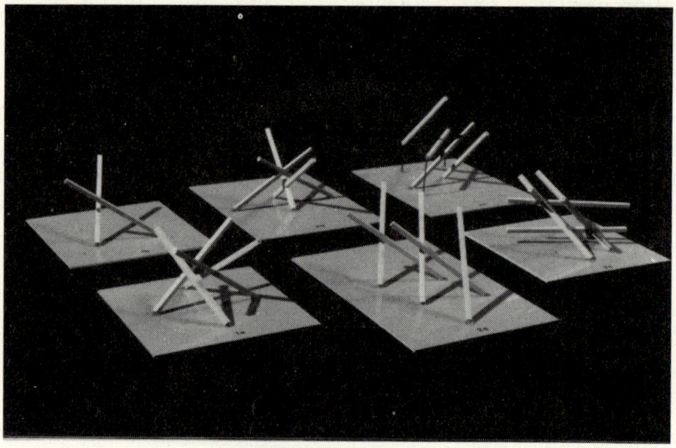

Figure 5. Designs generated by basic grammars determined from a spatial relation between two separated pillars (Djordje Krstic).

The designs in figure 6 are generated by basic grammars determined from a spatial relation between an oblong and a cube. Three-hundred and eighty-four basic grammars can be defined with this spatial relation (the symmetry of the oblong (8) multiplied by the symmetry of the cube (48)); four designs generated by four of the basic grammars are shown.

Figure 6. Designs generated by basic grammars determined from a spatial relation between an oblong and a cube (Jeng Tay-Sheng).

Once some or all of the most basic designs implied by a particular spatial relation are identified with basic grammars, more elaborate shape grammars are developed. These more elaborate grammars, called *complex grammars*, generate more elaborate designs that combine spatial properties of the designs produced by basic grammars. Complex grammars are defined by elaborating the rules and/or elaborating the initial shapes of basic grammars.

Rules are elaborated by combining the rules of basic grammars in various ways. For example, one of the simplest ways of elaborating rules is to combine the rules of two or more basic grammars, determined from the same spatial relation, into a single grammar. The complex grammar so defined will generate designs that are spatial combinations of the designs generated by each of the basic grammars alone. No matter how complex these designs become, however, they are all still based on a single spatial relation. Figure 7, for instance, shows a complex grammar with two rules from two basic grammars - one from basic grammar (a) in figure 4, the other from basic grammar (h).

Still more complex grammars can be developed by combining rules of basic grammars determined from different spatial relations. These grammars allow designs to be created using more than just one or two shapes and more than one compositional idea. For example, figure 8a shows a basic grammar determined from a spatial relation between two oblongs (the same grammar as basic grammar (b) in figure 4); figure 8b shows a basic grammar determined from a spatial relation between an oblong and a pillar. The rules of these two basic grammars are combined to define the complex grammar shown in figure 8c. This new grammar generates designs that combine in various ways the properties of designs generated by each of the two basic grammars from which it was formed.

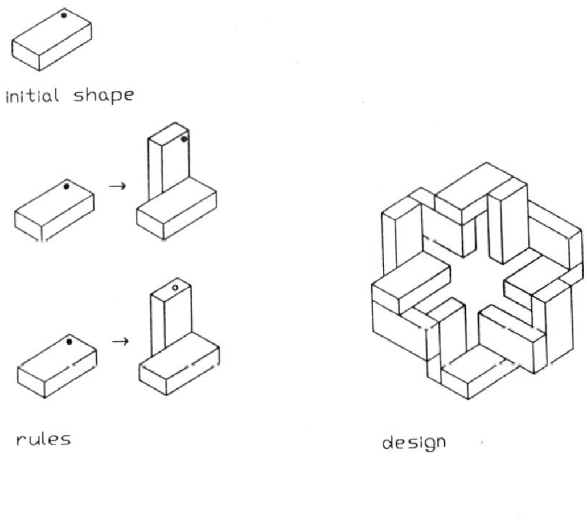

Figure 7. A complex grammar defined from basic grammars (a) and (h) in figure 4.

Another way to elaborate the rules of grammars is to use subtraction rules. Addition rules allow designs to be built up in accordance with particular spatial relations; subtraction rules allow pieces of these designs to be taken away in accordance with particular spatial relations. For instance, figure 9 illustrates a complex grammar that is the same as the grammar of figure 8c, but with one subtraction rule added. The subtraction rule is based on the same spatial relation as the two addition rules above it. It allows a pillar to be extracted from a design only when it is in the specified spatial relation with an oblong.

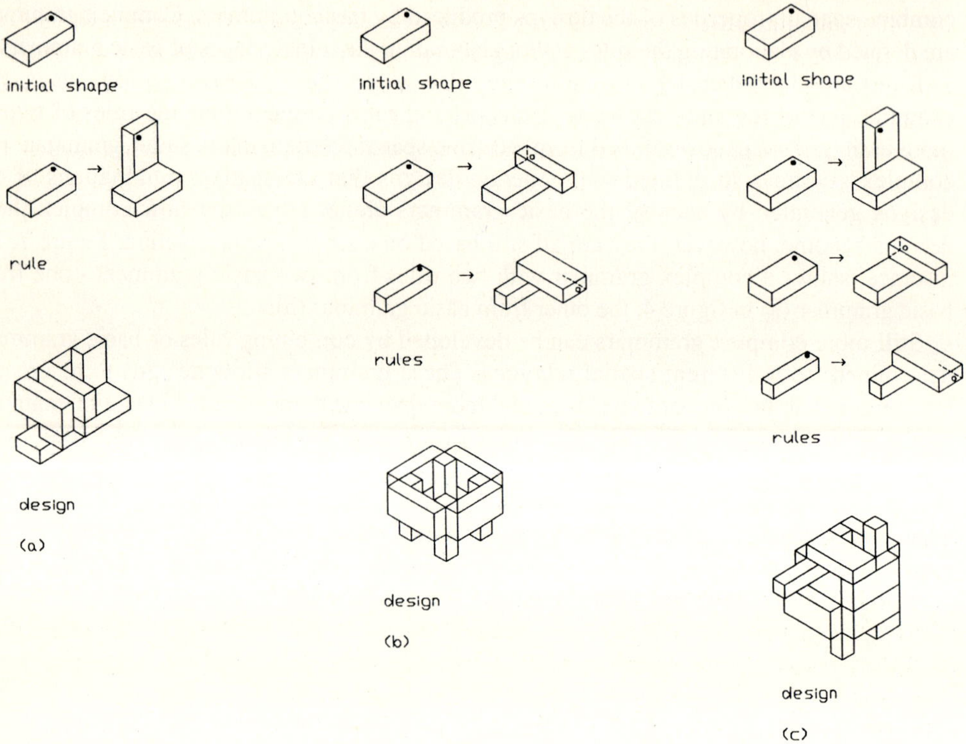

Figure 8. A complex grammar (c) defined from two basic grammars (a) and (b), each determined from a different spatial relation.

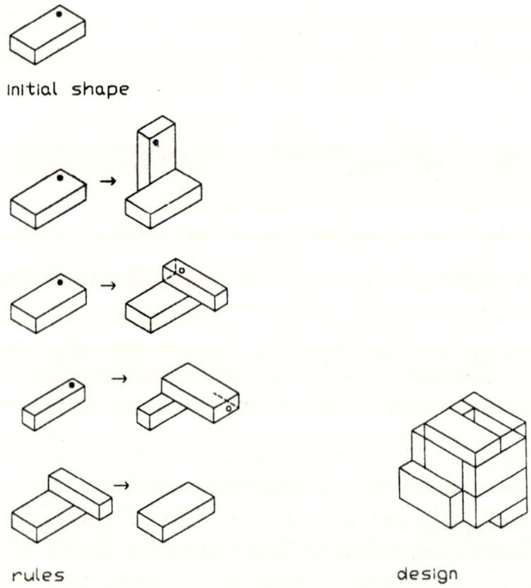

Figure 9. A complex grammar with a subtraction rule.

Complex grammars can be defined not only by elaborating the rules of grammars but also by elaborating the initial shapes of grammars. One simple way of elaborating an initial shape is to elaborate the way it is labelled. Consider, for example, the grammar in figure 10. Except for the initial shape, this grammar is identical to basic grammar (d) in figure 4. The initial shape has two labels allowing the rule to be applied in two different places. Designs generated by this grammar have identical parts that develop from the same initial shape. Compare the design generated by this grammar with the design generated by basic grammar (d) in figure 4.

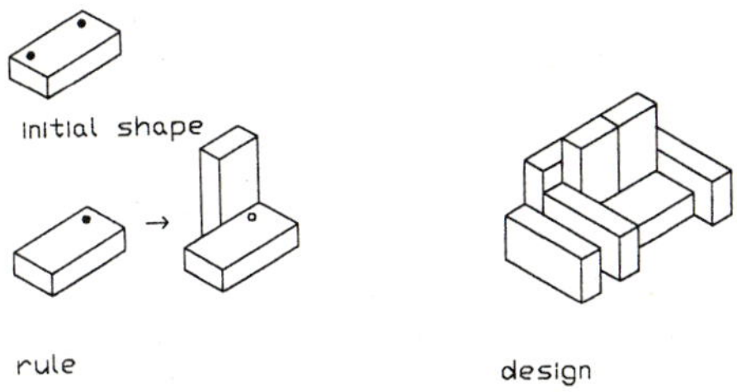

Figure 10. A complex grammar with an elaborated initial shape.

Ways of elaborating the initial shapes or rules of grammars are limitless. Some of the more obvious and simple ways, a few of which were described above, are structured into a sequence of exercises that students carry out in class. In their own projects, students either duplicate class exercises using their own vocabularies and spatial relations, or invent their own elaborations on the basis of class exercises. In beginning projects, students are encouraged to be experimental and to work abstractly - the purpose and context of designs are not a consideration. Once students become more facile with grammars, more advanced projects that respond to specific architectural programmes are undertaken. Figure 11 shows a more advanced student project for an historical museum in the Italian hilltown of San Gimignano.

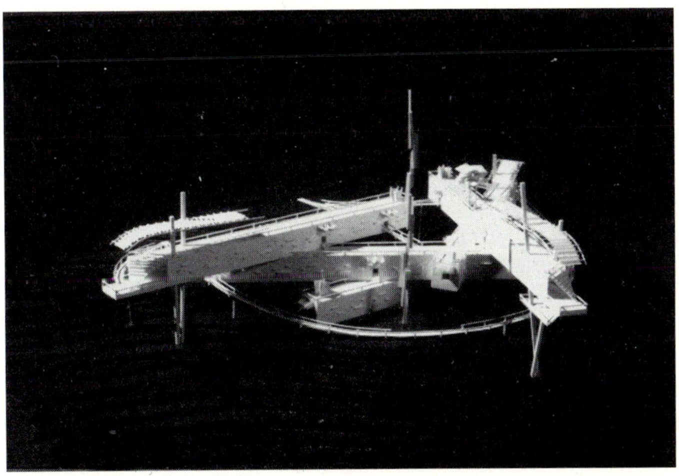

Figure 11. A project for a museum in San Gimignano (Randy Brown).

San Gimignano is probably best known for the many tall defensive towers that once stood throughout the town. Only a few of these towers now remain. The long horizontal corridors of the museum are meant to evoke towers that have fallen down the hillside into a seemingly random heap. The overall massing of the corridors, though, was created with one spatial relation. Figure 12a shows this relation. The massing design of the museum was only one of numerous massing designs explored by the student using basic grammars determined from this one spatial relation. Some of these different massing studies are shown in figure 12b.

While the overall massing of the museum was created with one spatial relation, the details of the museum - for example, the sculptural spire in front of the museum, the display panels, window awnings, and roofing structures - were created with another spatial relation. This spatial relation - between a pillar and a curved rectangular plane - is shown in figure 13a. Some of the many designs created with basic grammars determined from this relation are shown in figure 13b. All of these forms were used in the final design of the museum.

(a)

(b)

Figure 12. A spatial relation (a), and some massing designs generated with it (b) (Randy Brown).

(a)

(b)

Figure 13. A spatial relation (a), and some designs generated with it (b) (Randy Brown).

Designing with Color Grammars

Once the formal details of shape grammars are understood, exercises for developing color grammars are introduced. Color grammars are developed in an analogous way as shape grammars. First, a vocabulary of colored, 3-dimensional shapes is chosen. Next, spatial relations between colored shapes in the vocabulary are defined. Figure 14a, for example, shows a vocabulary consisting of an oblong with red, yellow, and blue faces, and a handed (reflected) version of this oblong. Figure 14b shows a spatial relation between two of these shapes. Except for colors, this spatial relation is the same as the spatial relation shown earlier in figure 2. Addition and subtraction rules can be determined from this or other spatial relations between colored shapes in exactly the same way that they are determined from a spatial relation between uncolored shapes.

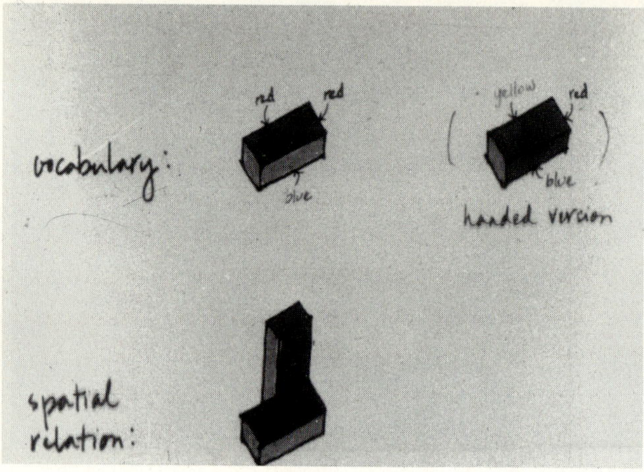

Figure 14. A vocabulary consisting of a colored oblong (a), and a spatial relation between two such oblongs (b).

Given a spatial relation between colored shapes, a set of *basic color grammars* can be defined. Like basic shape grammars, basic color grammars are defined using one or both of the two addition rules defined from the chosen spatial relation. However, basic color grammars not only distinguish all of the simplest, most basic designs that can be generated with a particular spatial relation between colored shapes; they also distinguish all of the different possible *colorings* of these designs that can be generated with the spatial relation.

Basic color grammars are enumerated systematically by *repositioning* the shapes in the addition rule (or rules) defined from a spatial relation. Shapes are repositioned so that the geometric relationship between shapes remains the same, but color relationships change. Different repositionings of colored shapes in a rule are analogous to different positionings of labels on uncolored shapes in a rule, as discussed earlier for basic shape grammars. Both colors and labels restrict the ways that rules apply and thus lead to designs with distinct formal properties.

Different repositionings of colored shapes in a rule are enumerated according to both the symmetries of the shapes with color and the symmetries of the shapes without color. Each different repositioning of a shape in a rule determines a different basic color grammar. (Depending on the symmetries of the colored shapes in a rule, labels may also be needed to distinguish basic color grammars.) Some of these different color grammars generate different designs in terms of both form and coloring. Some generate the same designs in terms of form but with different colorings. In general, the set of basic color grammars determined from a particular spatial relation can be divided into equivalence classes, where grammars in different classes generate different forms, and grammars in the same class generate the same forms but with different colorings. The number of equivalence classes and the number of grammars in each class can be calculated according to the symmetries of the shapes in the spatial relation (Knight forthcoming).

Figures 15 and 16 illustrate some of the basic color grammars determined from the spatial relation in figure 14b. Sixty-four basic color grammars are possible, corresponding to the eight possible repositionings of one oblong in the spatial relation multiplied by the eight possible repositionings of the other oblong. The sixty-four basic color grammars can be divided into eight equivalence classes with eight grammars in each class. Figure 15a shows a basic color grammar from each of the eight different equivalence classes. A design generated by each grammar is shown in figure 15b. Notice that in terms of form, these eight designs are the same as the eight designs determined from the uncolored version of the spatial relation used to determine the designs here. (See figures 2 and 4.)

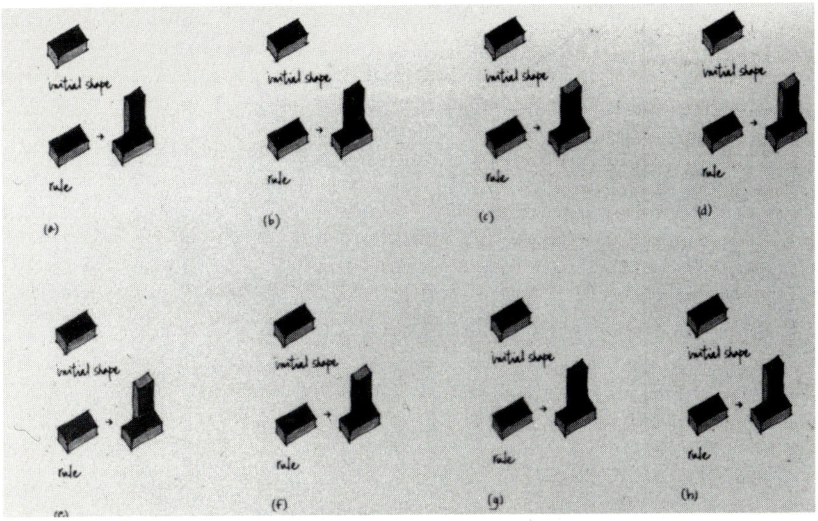

(a)

(b)

Figure 15. Basic color grammars from different equivalence classes (a), and the different designs generated by them (b).

Figure 16a shows eight basic color grammars from the same equivalence class. A design generated by each grammar is shown in figure 16b.

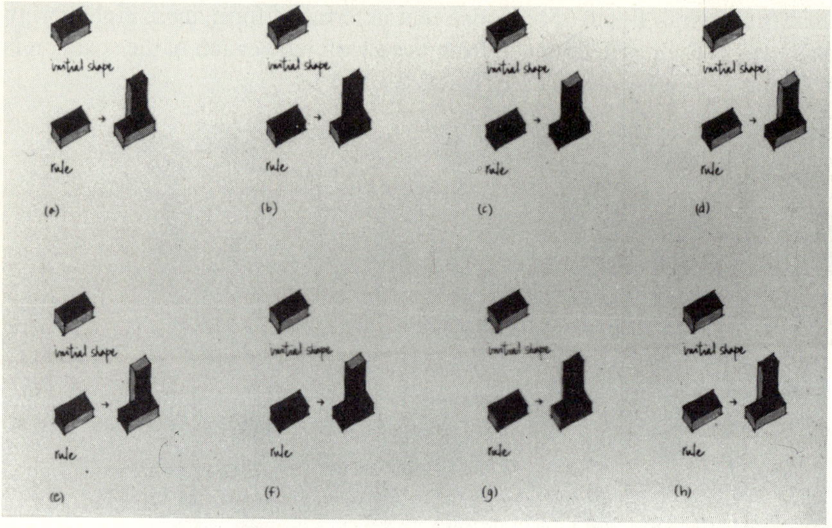

(a)

(b)

Figure 16. Basic color grammars from the same equivalence class (a), and the designs generated by them (b).

Figure 17a shows a student project using basic color grammars. Each of the designs shown is generated by a different basic color grammar. However, each color grammar is based on the same two vocabulary elements - a pillar and a square, each with beige, copper, and blue faces - put together in the same geometric relationship. This relationship is shown in figure 17b. The two different forms shown in figure 17a and the three alternative colorings of these forms are produced simply by repositioning shapes in the rules of the grammars. Many other forms and colorings of these forms, besides the ones shown here, are possible.

(a)

(b)

Figure 17. Two different forms and three alternative colorings of these forms (a) generated with the same vocabulary elements in the same geometric relationship (b).

Once some or all of the designs implied by a particular spatial relation between colored shapes are identified with basic color grammars, more complex color grammars can be developed. These are developed using essentially the same techniques discussed previously for complex shape grammars.

Conclusions

Probably the most exciting aspect of the two series of exercises described here is that starting with simple shapes put together in simple relationships - in other words, starting with simple compositional ideas - many of the possible designs and colorings of these designs that can be generated with the starting shapes and relations can be explored in a systematic and straightforward way. Often, the designs generated this way are ones not likely to be imagined or conceived of otherwise, for example, using the conventional trial and error, studio method of designing. Students are continually surprised not only by the quality of the designs they produce but, just as importantly, by their understanding of these designs.

One difficulty some students experience, though, is the translation of abstract, experimental forms into architectural designs that fit particular contexts or programmes. Often, this results from a student's inability to predict and control the kinds of forms that will be generated from a particular vocabulary and spatial relation. Experience seems to be the best solution to this problem. And, even though grammars are the basis for making designs, aesthetic, functional, and other traditional design decisions must still be made in the usual way. However, since it is now grammars that are being designed, these decisions can be made not at the level of individual designs but at the level of the more fundamental grammars underlying designs.

The work described here is still very new. Continued work and further refinements of the programme promise to lead to interesting, new grammar-based design work.

Acknowledgements

The research reported in this paper was supported in part by a grant from the Academic Senate of the University of California, Los Angeles. Thanks are due to Djordje Krstic, Jeng Tay-Sheng, and Randy Brown for allowing their work to be reproduced here, and to Nirva Fereshetian for her excellent work in preparing the figures.

References

Flemming, U. 1986. "More Than the Sum of Parts: The Grammar of Queen Anne Houses." *Environment and Planning B: Planning and Design* 14, no. 3: 323-350.

Knight, T. W. 1980. "The Generation of Hepplewhite-Style Chair-Back Designs." *Environment and Planning B* 7, no. 2: 227-238.

Knight, T. W. 1981. "The Forty-One Steps." *Environment and Planning B* 8, no. 1: 97-114.

Knight, T. W. 1989. "Color Grammars: Designing With Lines and Colors." *Environment and Planning B: Planning and Design* 16, no. 4: 417-449.

Knight, T. W. "Exercises with 3-D Color Grammars." forthcoming.

Koning, H., and J. Eizenberg. 1981. "The Language of the Prairie: Frank Lloyd Wright's Prairie Houses." *Environment and Planning B* 8, no. 3: 295-323.

Stiny, G. 1975. *Pictorial and Formal Aspects of Shape and Shape Grammars*. Basel: Birkhäuser Verlag.

Stiny, G. 1977. "Ice-Ray: A Note on the Generation of Chinese Lattice Designs." *Environment and Planning B* 4, no. 1: 89-98.

Stiny, G., and W. J. Mitchell. 1978. "The Palladian Grammar." *Environment and Planning B* 5, no. 1: 5-18.

Stiny, G. 1980. "Kindergarten Grammars: Designing with Froebel's Building Gifts." *Environment and Planning B* 7, no. 4: 409-462.

Stiny, G. "Shape: Algebra, Grammar, and Description." forthcoming.

3 Experiments in Architectural Design Development Using CAD

Charles M. Eastman and Jurg Lang

Graduate School of Architecture and Urban Planning
University of California,
Los Angeles, CA 90024-1467, U.S.A.

The need to explore development techniques in computer-based design is reviewed. Some premises are given for design development using computers, including integrating multiple representations, the use of object-based modeling and the importance of visual analysis and 3-D modeling. We then present techniques used in a UCLA design studio that explored methods of computer-based design development based on these premises. The two main methods used were hierarchical object structures and multi-representational coordination. They were applied using conventional CAD systems. Some lessons learned from this class are reviewed.

Introduction

During their professional education, future architects learn in their studio classes alternative processes of design. They learn from their teachers the use of different representations, such as concept sketches, bubble diagrams, circulation diagrams, massing diagrams as a means to analyze certain compositional issues, or the use of wall sections as means to study fabrication and detailing.

In the sequence of assignments, students also learn by example various sequences of design development using these representations. For example, a studio may require circulation and massing studies in the early weeks, followed by a site study, followed by a schematic set of plans and a model. Of course, different faculty utilize different sequences, possibly for different types of projects, but each series of assignments indicates to the student alternative development sequences for the evolving design. After experiencing these imposed processes for a few iterations, they become "natural" and are incorporated into the way architects think about design. In this manner, early teachings become the natural and unselfconscious mode of working in later practice.

This type of architectural education has existed since the beginning of architectural schools. The processes have been refined and have evolved in a natural way, resulting in an effective, though largely uncodified, set of practices.

Notice that most of these practices are intricately woven around the use of paper-based, iconic representations. Plans, sections, isometrics, elevations are intrinsic to these processes and the mode of thinking they build upon. The physical model has been the only important alternative medium of design consideration. Notice also that engineers have strongly moved into algebraic, symbolic representations, quite different from those used by architects. That is to note, other design professions did not follow the architectural path.

Over the last ten years, computers have reached a stage of development and a price where they are thought to serve as alternatives to the more traditional paper representations. It was naively thought by many in the 1970's that computers would quickly replace drawing boards and that new computer-based design processes would quickly evolve. That has not happened. The computer instead has made significant inroads into architecture by providing one-for-one replacements for earlier representations, particularly orthographic drawings, renderings, energy and other forms of analysis, and recently physical models. If one learns computer-aided design (CAD) today, or buys a CAD product, the functionalities provided are those that support a substitution for some existing representation. They are also the main focus of current computer marketing. This kind of one-for-one replacement allows computers to be integrated into design without re-work of the entire process. The informally learned process of design can continue and architects can work in their traditional modes with relatively small adjustments.

The computer however has different operations and different representational strengths from paper or physical models. In the longer run, one can expect quite different processes of design development to evolve. Thus there is tremendous need to actively explore larger re-organizations of this process. Such re-organizations are usually not practical to undertake in architectural practice, when under the fire of deadlines and guaranteed results. Thus the schools of architecture have a major contribution to make in re-thinking the process of design in light of computer based design tools.

Computers are still a scarce commodity in schools of architecture and many students pass through schools today without gaining familiarity with their use. Most schools hope to impart some level of competency in their use through a short sequence, possibly culminating with a single studio emphasizing computational techniques. At the same time, the student still takes six or more studios utilizing paper and cardboard media. The integration of computers in architectural students design processes has barely begun.

Theoretical Premises

Traditional design involves working in multiple representations. These are usually different forms of drawings: plans, sections, elevations, drawn as schematics, design development or construction drawings. Other representations of an architectural design include, physical models, specifications and the data used in various analytical calculations.

The typical process of design involves using one or more of these representations to develop a design concept. After this has been accomplished, the design information is translated into other representations to gain insight with regard to its physical form, functional performance, cost or other issues of interest. Design proceeds with the eventual definition of an array of representations, many generated by specialists, such as structural, mechanical and lighting engineers. Each new representation informs the existing ones. Eventually, all the representations consistently define a single building or artifact that satisfies the various intentions for the project.

From this description, it is clear that an inherent aspect of design activity is the translation between representations. We are most aware of this when we make a physical model from plans and elevations, or when we take data from drawings for input into some form of analysis. Most of the time, these sorts of translations are expensive and time consuming and are therefore done only occasionally. Many representations that could inform the architect on some behavior of the design are not used during design development because of the cost of data translation between representations. These include both computer-based representations, such as energy or lighting analysis, and others that are manual, such as maintaining a physical model of the current design. Most representations are used late in design, as a check that it does not perform badly rather than to inform how the design can be improved.

Visual Analysis

An important architectonic example of this issue is *visual analysis*. What we call visual analysis is the development of a special representation of the design in order to better evaluate its appearance or experiential impact. Studio faculty commonly require physical models and renderings as representations of design work, so students may gain experience in evaluating design in these representations and integrating them in their development processes. Some faculty teach good methods of model refinement and modification. Yet, physical models and renderings are time consuming to generate, and like all others, are typically used toward the end of schematic design.

Computer based visual analysis should be a commonly used capability, given the importance of visual considerations to the profession. Computer modeling of buildings in three dimensions and the generation of high quality images is a well developed capability. Many presentations at CAAD conferences show the stunning results that can be extracted from modern computer workstations running advanced visualization software (Greenberg 1989). When examined, however, most modeling has been done as a rendering, at the end of design, for presentation uses, in a manner replacing a physical model. Exploration of design alternatives have still been done manually, with little or no computer aid.

While there is growing exploration of 3-D modeling and visualization in schools, there has been little application in practice. This is because 3-D modeling typically involves a separate representation from a set of CAD drawing data, and separate development. School studios can encourage design using 3-D modeling exclusively, without considering the need to generate traditional drawings. In the profession, such strategies are not practical. Firms only use 3-D modeling if they can charge extra for defining the model, similar to construction of a physical model (Teicholz 1988). It has not yet become integrated into normal design development practices that produce drawings as the main product. Some computer advocates propose that eventually drawings will disappear and a 3-D computer model will serve as construction information. That will not happen soon.

In detail, there are three issues being addressed here. First is *facilitating the use of multiple representations in design*, by reducing the cost of translation. The computer can make a major contribution to this issue, but it requires new processes of design development. Second, the *integration of 3-D modeling techniques to design development* is central if other geometric data is to be generated for other representations, such as lighting and visualization, energy, acoustics or structures. Only 3-D modeling supports the generation and checking of geometry in a complete manner (Eastman 1976). *Visual analysis, then, is the lead application to integrate 3-D modeling with drawing production*, and opens the door to integrating other applications. Computer based 3-D models and visualization should allow visual analysis to be used throughout the design process, leading to better designs.

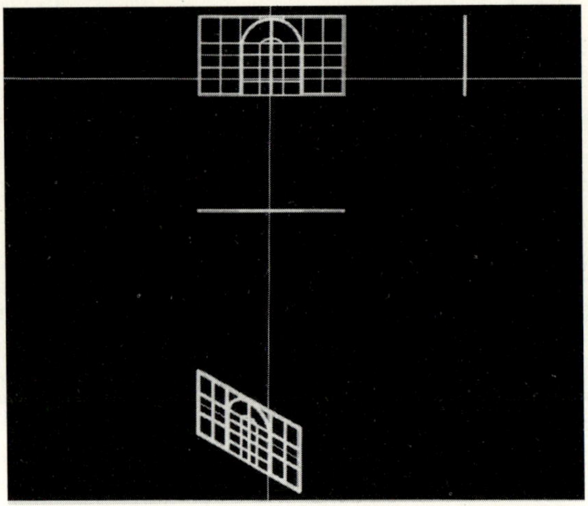

Figure 1. A screen image of the multiple views of a window located on different layers of the window "object".

Object Based Modeling

There has been continuous interest in what we call "object based modeling" of buildings. Object based modeling involves representing a building in terms of the objects that it is composed of. An object is both a unit of composition and a carrier of different information used in multiple representations.

An object may be any unit of composition, ranging in scale from a complete building shell, to a wall, to a window pane. Multiple representations are defined for each object. For example any such object may have a plan, several elevations, and a 3-D model, as well as associated property descriptions, each of which is also a separate representation. An example is shown in figure 1.

Objects are organized hierarchically. Highly aggregated objects, such as an apartment unit has as parts floors, ceilings, walls, stairs and so forth. See figure 6. Each of these objects also have lower level objects. The hierarchical relations may be defined and managed explicitly by the CAD environment. Alternatively they may be managed by the user, who keeps track of what objects are composed into other objects at different levels of abstraction. The window pane is known to be a part embedded in some wall; a wall is part of some building unit and so forth.

A second aspect of object based modeling is the logical structure it suggests as a framework for design development. A design, defined as a hierarchy of objects, can be modified in several ways, each having implications with regard to maintaining the hierarchical structure. A change may be made to any object at any level of detail, with propagation upwards in the hierarchy to more aggregated objects and also downwards in the structure to the detail objects the change effects. See figure 2.

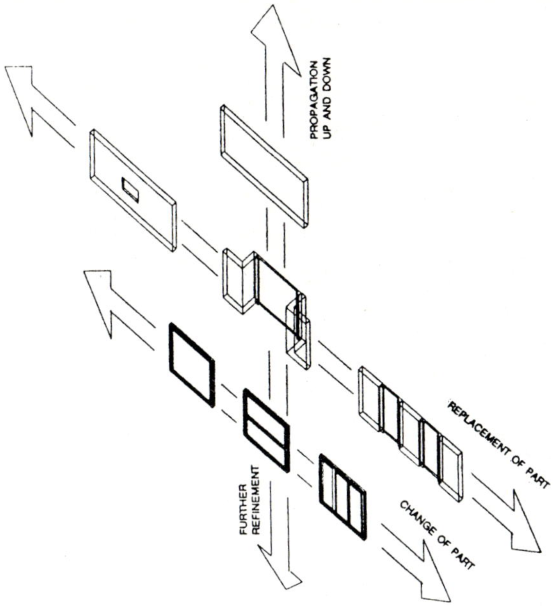

Figure 2. A graphical representation of the different types of actions that are embedded in the object model approach to design.

Three types of development operations are naturally defined:

1. A change to the arrangement of objects can be made at a top or middle level in the hierarchy, resulting in changes to both the higher level aggregated objects of which it is a part and also the lower level components. For example, a different arrangement and shape of walls is defined for an apartment unit, resulting in a change in the area of the total unit, its relations to site, the total building shape and other aggregated properties. It also requires changes to the components making up the wall, i.e. downward, to realize at the detailed level the new shape. These may be achieved automatically, if they simply involve spatial transforms of existing component objects. If shapes or properties are modified, then the designer may have to determine how these changes will be realized at more detailed design levels.
2. A second kind of change is made by replacing one object for another; this change eliminates all the objects below the previous one and replaces them with new ones, if they have been defined. It also propagates upward, resulting in new aggregated properties and/or geometry.
3. Also, an object at the bottom level can be further decomposed and refined further. For example, a wall may be defined in terms of its internal materials, surfaces and molding.

Object based design has a powerful logical structure that can support a variety of development processes. While it is based on a well-defined set of parts, the designer can define and re-define the parts as the design proceeds.

There have been a few examples of object-based CAD systems, both in research: GLIDE (Eastman and Henrion 1977) and Arch: MODEL (Borkin et al 1976), and also commercial systems: GDS, STAR and SONATA. The commercial systems embed most of the capabilities described in an explicit fashion. Object based design provides at least one important design development paradigm for architecture.

Object based modeling can be undertaken, using the traditional CAD structures of symbols[1] and layers (Eastman, 1991). A symbol is used to describe and store an object. An object may be abstract and conceptual, such as a building mass or activity space; or it may be detailed and correspond to a component used to construct the building, such as a door or window.

Using symbols to implement object based modeling requires a different type of layer management scheme from those typically recommended (such as by the American Institute of Architects). It is important to allocate a separate set of layers for use by different classes of representations early in the process and fix them: for example, plan, section, 3-D model and elevation. All symbols will use this structure (as they do with normal layer schemes now). These sets of layers need to be subdivided further to support: various scales of presentation and level of detail, and different design disciplines, similar to good use today. An example layer management structure is shown in figure 3. These allocations are used to manage information in all symbols.

Layers are used to manage graphic information. Another allocation is needed for attributes. In most CAD systems one can define multiple attribute sets for an object, allowing each attribute set to be used in the same way as layers, but for data associated with some form of analysis.

This approach is based on the recognition that, using todays drawing conventions, floorplans and elevations are different from an horizontal section or front projection of a building. Sections of a 3-D solid representation require extensive editing to be used for floorplans: line weights are different, dotted lines show ceiling conditions on the plan, stairs and cabinets are abstracted. These differences are reviewed in detail in (Eastman 1987).

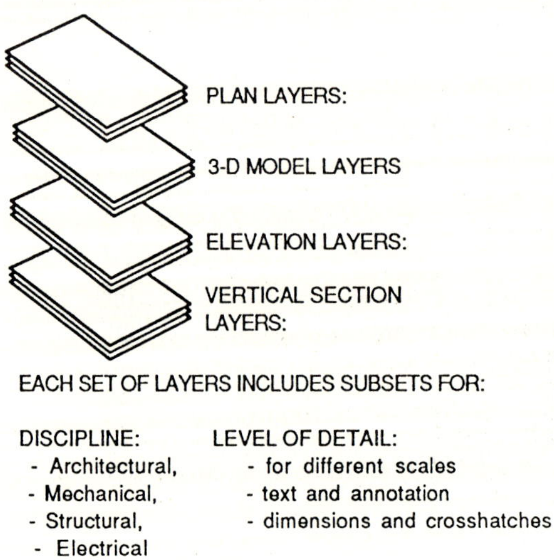

Figure 3. Object modeling using conventional CAD systems requires a different layer management scheme that includes views, as well as discipline and level of detail.

Intention

Like most schools, U.C.L.A. offers a sequence of classes applying computers to design. After two quarters of background classes, students take a studio devoted to design development, emphasizing computer-based representations. These studios present to the student some known methods of design development using computers and allow the students to explore others on their own.[2]

This paper presents the results of one such exploration, developed in the context of a design studio taught in the Spring of 1990. Students were at different levels in their architectural education; some were in the second year of a first professional degree program and others were advanced students taking a second degree specializing in CAD.

The students enrolled in the studio had already taken previous courses in computer use. They had all surveyed the effective use of the standard computer-based representations, especially 2-D orthographic drawings and 3-D modeling for visualization. Some knowledge of managing multiple representations had also previously been presented.

In the spirit of traditional studios, the faculty (the two authors of this paper) presented a design problem for the quarter and then defined a set of required submissions that were based on pre-developed concepts of computer based design development. That is, the sequence of submissions were organized to suggest a development process uniquely useful in the use of CAD for design. Otherwise, the course was approached as a traditional design studio, focusing on architectonic issues.

An important aspect of our studio methodology was to explore how to use 3-D modeling and visualization as an integral design tool, while still producing drawings. At the system level, visual analysis was supported in two different ways: (i) in simple format using the 3-D capabilities of the CAD system; and (ii) by extracting data and sending it to a special visualization computer, allowing realtime walk-throughs of spaces. The first method was used for generating the layout, the second allowed high quality, quickly generated visual reviews.

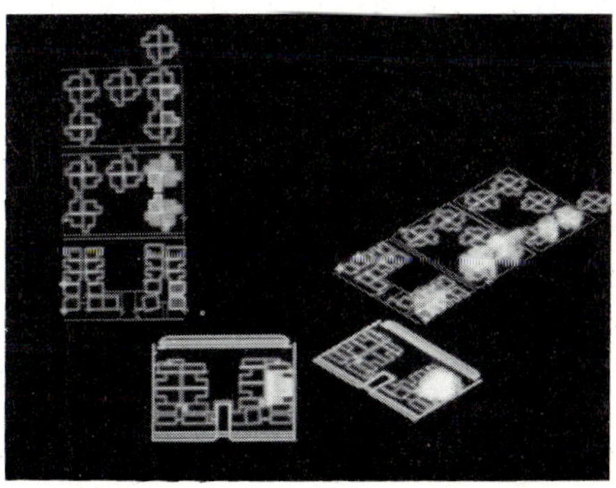

Figure 4. Some of the different plans developed in the studio that reflect different strategies for gaining amenity for each of the residential units.

The conceptual goal is to allow parallel development of the design in multiple representations, so that design actions always set up the data in the various representations to be ready for use in each of them. Visual analysis was considered as a test case for other forms of analysis, such as energy, lighting or structure. If integration could be achieved for visual analysis, the same techniques should transfer to these other forms.

The CAD system used was Computervision CADDS4X running on SUN-3 workstations. 3-D visualization while designing was supported by the surfaces and solids packages of Computervision. Visualization analysis was supported by the Personal Visualizer software developed by Wavefront Technologies running on a Personal IRIS workstation by Silicon Graphics. Translation from Computervision was accomplished by using a CV IGES translator out and Wavefront IGES in.

Examples / The Project

The studio project dealt with medium density housing in Los Angeles. The site is one of the largest remaining tracts of open space within the city of Los Angeles, the old Howard Hughes airport site at Playa del Rey. The site, consisting of about 700 acres, bordered on the south by the Loyola bluffs, on the west by Santa Monica Bay and on the north by Marina del Rey, is currently undergoing development. The developers are attempting to make it a model for new development within Los Angeles. As such, it is of higher density than most housing. It is to include residences for a wide range of income and family types. It includes neighborhood shopping, schools and recreation, at a density that encourages access without using automobiles. It is foreseen that some blocks will have convenience stores and professional offices along one street.

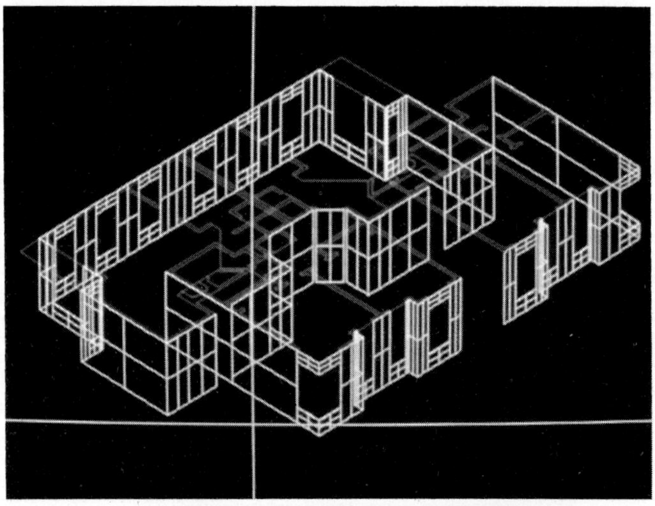

Figure 5. A floorplan of one of the units and the set of walls that bound it.

There were strong design guidelines regarding street widths, sitelines and setbacks. The goals embedded in the guidelines included a strong street facade with a small but significant buffer from the street, wide walking avenues and minimal on-street parking. Most parking was underground. The program implied walk-up units in buildings of two to four stories in height.

Each student took one block as a design and development area, which consisted of between 2.5 and 3 acres. The program density ranged from 35 units to 80 units per acre, with units ranging in size from 900 square foot studios to 1500 square foot two-bedroom condominiums. All student projects involved multiple buildings on the site with one or more interior courtyards.

Multiple Representations

In the previous class, students learned to work in object-based modeling, using traditional CAD systems. In that class, the focus was on de-mountable buildings which had a natural affinity with modular construction. That was not the case in this project.

The bottom level elements of composition used by students in this project were walls and other panels, which could be composed into living units, or else the housing units as a whole. At the unit level, explorations were undertaken regarding how single units could be composed in various ways to gain additional amenities for the units, as shown in figure 4. Pinwheel layouts were tried, as a means to gain private outdoor space, as well as split-level plans, where each unit consisted of two floors, not stacked but staggered diagonally about a central entrance. In this form of layout, the visual expanse is greater than a stacked plan and cross-ventilation is also provided.

After the units were defined, they were made into symbols. The plan was defined on one layer, (shown in red) and the walls were defined in 3-D on other layers, as shown in figure 5. In some student's projects, the interior walls were separated from the outside walls by assigning them to different layers, so they could be turned off when outside images were generated. The result was that each object corresponded to a symbol in the design. Changing the symbol or its location changed its location in all the representations, here, 3-D and plan.

The units were also composed into a building. See figures 7 and 8. Street facades could be evaluated from many angles. Students found that if they took certain elements out of the unit and located them at the building level in the hierarchy, this allowed them to be varied for different units, and respond to the composition of the overall facade in rich and interesting ways.

With the exterior walls defined for each unit, and in some cases, stair and balcony railings and exposed framing, the amount of visual information in the design became quite large. But because each unit or detail was a symbol, only a few instances were stored in full in the project database[3]. Regenerating the design from the database, however, could be tedious.

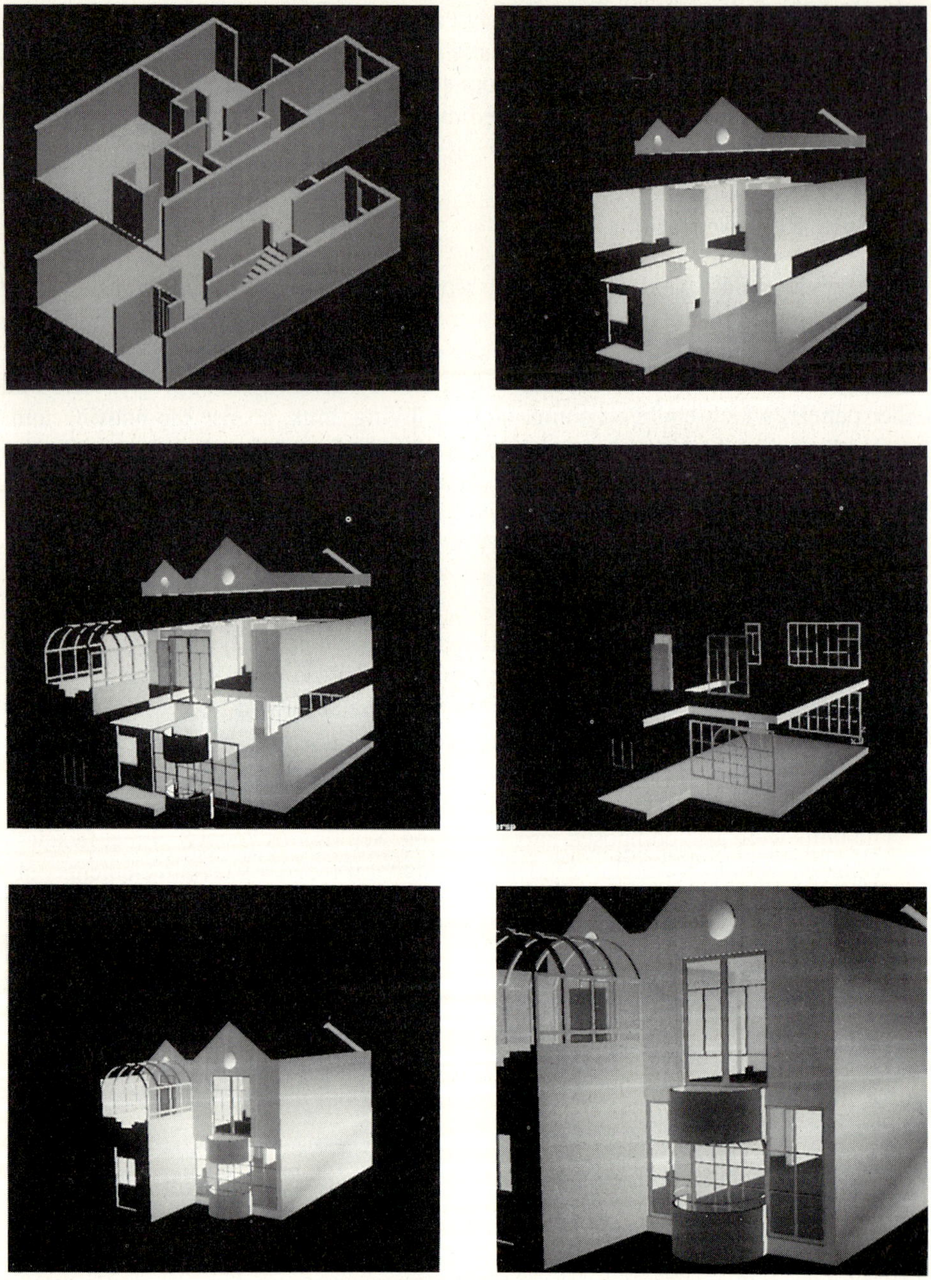

Figure 6. The composition of a unit into a building. The single unit floor and walls had associated facade walls and alternative window units. Atriums were added and the unit composed into a building, which was then composed into the complex (project by Ken Aluko).

Figure 7. The unit developed in figure 6 was composed into a building complex, with varied massing and details (project by Ken Aluko).

Because the composition was composed of symbols and all their layers, it was simply a matter of turning on the appropriate layers to generate the building floorplan, or alternatively, another set of layers for the 3-D model. Alternatively, both could be shown together. See figure 5. Using this process as described, party walls were duplicated. This could have been eliminated by making the potential party walls separate objects and including them or not, as required, within the overall building configuration. In an office environment, additional representations would have been added to the symbols, for elevations or sections.

By grouping the multiple representations of an object within the design on the different layers of a symbol, the coherence of the object data is maintained. It does not eliminate the need to propagate a change made in one representation to the others, but it makes this job easier because all the representations associated with the object are together. And of course, a locational change to an object operates on all views.

The effect of this approach was that students were able to develop their design in a way that produced both drawings and 3-D images throughout the process. Some students used the visualization capabilities of Computervision for quick reviews of their composition. Each view usually took several minutes to compute. Others found that they could translate their data and bring it up on the SGI Personal Visualizer in about the same time. But once in the Personal Visualizer, its Quickshade option allowed any view to be generated in just a few seconds. They could walk through their design (in wire frame mode) select a view and have it shaded in a couple of seconds. One student commented that though he had used CAD previously, this was the first time that he gained significant insights into the design faster than by using paper and pencil.

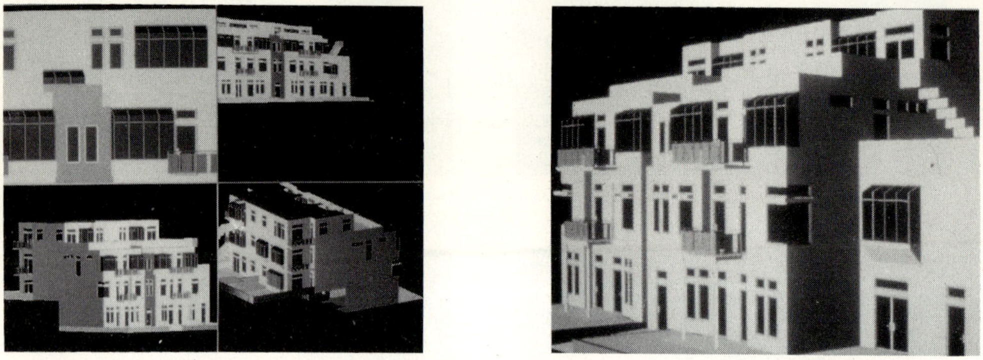

Figure 8. Another design developed for Playa del Rey. Here the student refined the external character of the building over time, and developed a roof garden scheme where each unit had its own garden, on the ground or on the roof of an adjacent unit.

Another effect was the elimination of most of the time traditionally needed for presentation. Most students had practiced generating good rendering quality images as they carried out their visualization studies. As a result, most of the students generated their presentation images in just a few hours, allowing much longer time to refine the design.

Hierarchical Development Strategies

Space savings was not the primary benefit of making the living units and all other objects into symbols. If all objects had been copied rather than instanced, the common heritage between them would have been lost. Changes would have had to be made to them individually. As symbols, however, changes could be made to any one object, and the change later propagated to all instances of the object, as a global update. Symbols carry the heritage relationship.

Walls could be replaced or new window units tried, first in one unit, then propagated to all or some subset of all the units. The symbol structure used in one student's project for a single unit is shown in figure 6. Students learned to work with common elements, allocating them in complex ways to provide variety from a limited vocabulary.

The building compositions were also made into symbols. These also were replicated over the site, resulting in overall designs that had more than one hundred units. Students learned that one building composition could be juxtaposed to a different one with interesting results, as shown in Figures 7 and 8. Later, if design intentions involved changing one or more building compositions, its instances could be easily updated.

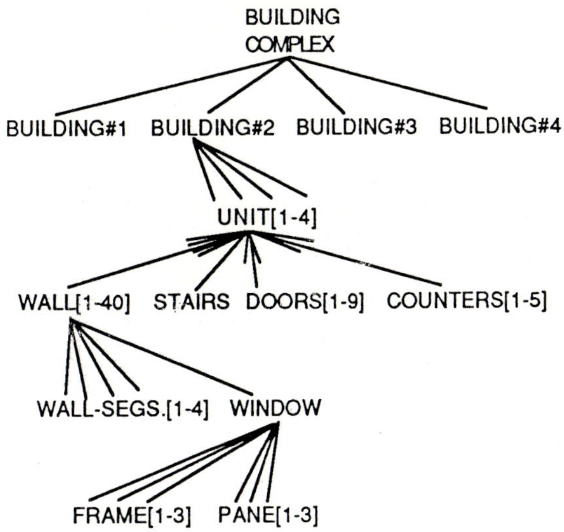

Figure 9. An example hierarchical structure of symbols used in one of the projects.

Design typically proceeds by adding detail, materials, color, detailing of structure, architectural finishes, etc. Such detailing, when followed consistently from the total project downwards, is called "top-down design".

Sometimes changes are not made at the bottom level, however, but within a composed component in the middle of the hierarchy. This type of change is easily accomplished, but requires discipline so as to not lose the heritage relations defined in the object hierarchy.

A change is typically accomplished by exploding a symbol into its components and modifying some objects within it or their composition, then re-making it into a symbol and replacing the change everywhere the old symbol existed. In this way, a change is conceptually made in the middle or top of the hierarchy and propagated downward. The change is also propagated upward to the total design, of course.

These methods of design development provide a structured but highly flexible regime of design development actions. Other designers and teachers have also begun to explore hierarchical structures (Madrazo 1990). The students spoke about this structure in terms of design vocabulary. They viewed their design process as defining a vocabulary of design elements and simultaneously creating a composition from them. Students quickly reached beyond simplistic repetition and explored ways to provide extra amenities, such as rooftop gardens and special views. With experience gained during the course, most students reached a high degree of competence in manipulating their design this way.

Working with the principles of object modeling constitutes a fundamental change in the design process. One has to resist the temptation of making a quick change of a line and instead act within a more disciplined process of isolating the change and encapsulating it as a symbol. Thus the immediacy of the intervention is replaced by a systematic procedure which, depending on the CAD system used, can be quick and easy or rather tedious. The spontaneous single intervention seems quicker, yet in the long run can never offer the structural advantages and the speed of exploration provided by object modeling.

Data Management Issues

These two strategies, based on object-based modeling, utilize many symbols, at many levels in the composition hierarchy. Objects can be nested quite deeply, as shown in figure 9. One object may be part of several others and it also may be made up of others. When a change is made to a object, there is a need to regenerate all the affected objects. There is an obvious need to keep track of which object has which others nested within it.

In addition, as design proceeds, there are multiple versions of each symbol, as one is replaced with another. Memory management also led to multiple copies of symbols, as described below. Thus the names within the symbol lattice change over time and have multiple alternatives.

Traditional CAD systems provide no computerized help in keeping track of symbol versions and users must maintain extensive notes to keep track of their symbol or object structure. We recommended that students keep a notebook with them to record this structure.

After the class, it was recognized that an additional layer could be allocated and assigned to each symbol that could carry the symbol's composition. For example, if a window version was composed of frame version 7 and the mullions were version 3, these identifiers could be kept in a short list with the symbol. Attributes also could be used for this purpose.

Another issue was the size of the display files that were created over time. While the database remained relatively compact, because of the extensive reliance of symbols, the drawing files in CV, which carries information logically equivalent to a display list, grew very large. Manipulation would become extremely slow when the display list started getting swapped in virtual memory. If approached straightforwardly, each symbol has all the relevant design information within it: multiple 2-D projections at all levels of detail, 3-D model, and possibly material properties.

In Computervision, each symbol (in CV called a Figure) is stored on a separate file. A project is a directory and all its sub-files. Thus by splitting a unit symbol into several parts, for example making the inside walls a separate symbol from the outside walls, the outside walls could be loaded alone into the building and the city block complex, eliminating about two-thirds of the original project size.

In CV, it turned out to be very helpful to carry along multiple versions of all the symbols, each with different levels of complexity and size, as layers could not be unloaded from the display list (in CV, the drawing file). The different levels of complexity allowed one to only work with the information they actually needed. The cost, of course, is that one had to manage changes made to one version of the symbol to all the other versions. In many cases, this worked better than turning off layers, which in most systems does not unload them from the display list.

It is clear that CAD systems are still lacking in power and in certain dimensions of data management. One of these is the ability to manipulate large complex databases. Faster machines with more memory is one solution. But another limitation is the lack of object version control techniques. Needed are means to keep track of the component objects defining any other object. Also, needed are means to manage the version aspects of the different views of an object. These and other desired capabilities are described more fully in (Eastman, 1991).

Evaluation

The traditional means to evaluate studio work is a design review and jury. The faculty review of the student projects were impressed with the quantity of work students were able to generate in a ten week studio. The quick rendering capabilities were an obvious benefit. They also commented in a few cases on the spatial quality and level of visual resolution of the design development, which seemed an improvement over what the students had accomplished previously. The thought was that some students benefited from the high level of three dimensional feedback provided by the 3-D representation. The faculty who taught the course were not able to model the site in the system before the class (though this was intended) and negative comments were made about the lack of context for the student's work.

Our studio also encountered several issues of design presentation. Many faculty and students are engrossed by the subtle shading and quality of the renderings generated by high resolution displays and visualization software. But after this is accepted and internalized, we recognized that in many respects computer presentations of design projects are visually meager in comparison with traditional paper presentations. In a traditional jury, a student will hang five to ten different views of his project, with possibly the addition of a physical model. There is a visual richness that allows reviewers to quickly scan a lot of information, to review it in different presentations and scales. In contrast, CAD presentations on a screen present one or possibly four representations.

There is a need to provide the same amount of information with the same or greater richness in CAD presentations. Students should consider using multiple screens and composing multiple projections on screen. The benefits of paper presentation of a design is still strong. The media is not the message.

Early advocates of 3-D modeling suggested that it would soon replace 2-D for the representation of choice in architectural CAD. It has not done so, mostly for the reasons of cost, as an additional separate representation. The multiple representation approach to CAD allows the benefits of 3-D imaging to be integrated with only a small additional cost to normal drawing generation. The results can be distinctly different. It is a practical way for practitioners to take greater advantage of the capabilities of modern CAD systems. The cost of managing both 3-D and 2-D information on different layers is more than just doing 2-D layers alone, but much less than doing both separately.

Another issue emerged during the class regarding information coordination. As configured for the class, the CAD system provided the environment for defining the geometry. After it was generated, the geometry was transferred to the visualization machine. Here a designer would add color texture, lights and other visual details of the design, in support of rendering. The problem was that the design information is dispersed over multiple representations again. If energy analysis was integrated in, some material properties would be defined for visualization in the visualization environment, other material properties for the same materials would be added in the energy program. Any change made to the material properties would have to be remembered and updated to each representation separately. Some of the benefits of CAAD would have been lost.

Currently, the translator into Personal Visualizer assigns material classes according to layer. All the surfaces on a layer must be assigned the same material class. This use of layers is often at cross purposes with other uses. For example, it is usually not desired to put the interior walls of different rooms on different layers; in most cases, they will be assigned common layers. But this forces them to take the same color or material in the visualization system. This led to much revision of layers in the later part of the course, in order to group objects according to materials. Many of the changes violated the earlier developed drawing conventions regarding which representations go on which layers.

To overcome this problem, we are building a material library within the CV and AutoCad environments that hold material properties as an attribute name. These material names will serve as cross references into multiple materials libraries associated with different translators. The unique visualization properties of that material will be automatically loaded when the CAD data is translated into the visualizer (Liggett and Jepson, 1991). Similar loading of energy related material properties will take place when the CAD data is run through the translator for energy analysis. Similar approaches will be used for other translators.

References:

Borkin, H., J. McIntosh, and P. McIntosh. 1981. "ARCH:Model: A Geometric Modeling Relational database System." *ARCH: Model User's Manual*. Architectural research Laboratory, University of Michigan. Michigan: Ann Arbor.

Eastman, C. M. 1976. "General purpose building description systems." *Computer-Aided Design* 8, no.1:17-26.

Eastman, C. M., and M. Henrion. 1977. "GLIDE: a language for design information systems." In *SIGGRAPH'77 Proc. Computer Graphics* 11, no. 2: 24-33.

Eastman, C. M. 1987. "Fundamental problems in the development of computer-based architectural design models." In Y. Kalay (ed.). *Computability in Design* . New York: John Wiley.

Eastman, C. M. 1991. "The evolution of CAD: integrating multiple representations." *Building and Environ.* 26, no. 1: 17-24.

Greenberg, D. 1989. "Light Reflection Models for Computer Graphics." *AAAS Science* 244, no. 14: 166-173.

Liggett, R., W. Jepson, and S. Teodosiadis. 1991. "A stratified approach to the integration of low cost modeling with advanced technology rendering." In G. Schmitt (ed.). *CAAD Futures '91*. Zurich.

Madrazo, L. 1990. "The Integration of Computer Modeling in Architectural Design." In P. Jordan (ed.). *ACADIA'90 From Research to Practice*. U. of Montana: Association for Computer-aided Design in Architecture.

Teicholz, E. 1988. reported in *Progressive Architecture*. January 1988.

---

[1] also called figures and blocks in some CAD systems.

[2] U.C.L.A. is currently revising the CAD part of its program, with a required sequence for all students and broadened integration, both in design and technology classes.

[3] Computervision requires that shaded images use Extended N-Figures, a type of symbol that copies all of the components. Thus symbols do not realize much of a saving when using CV alone. The IGES translator, however, allowed N-Figures to be translated and viewed on the Personal Visualizer, which did allow the savings.

4 DAC or Design and Computers

Alan H. Bridges

Department of Architecture and Building Science
University of Strathclyde
131 Rottenrow
Glasgow G4 ONG, United Kingdom

This paper describes the use of simple computer draughting techniques to explore elements of architectural design theory and suggests that this relatively neglected subject could be liberated by computing to once again play an important part in architectural design education.

Introduction

The question usually posed in relation to computers and the teaching of architectural design is "How can we use computers in the design studio?". Such a question presupposes an existing structure for teaching design and that computers can be made to fit into that structure. A more appropriate question might be "How may we teach design in the computing studio?". To emphasize the precedence of design over computing I have reversed the usual acronym of Computer Aided Design and called this paper DAC or Design And Computers. The full potential of computing in architectural design will only be realized by the creation of new models of the design process appropriate to the new design medium and these new methodologies need to reflect the nature of the design medium being used rather than simply transferring the techniques of the traditional design media to the computer. An analogy with another art - theater - illustrates the point. At the beginning of this century drama was transformed by the introduction of the new technology of the cinema. Actors, directors and producers had to find a way of working in the new medium and, initially, simply carried over theatrical conventions into film. This response to technological change is quite usual; only a few years previously the response to the introduction of the still camera was to imitate painting. Computer aided design is at an equivalent stage of development and programs which automate traditional draughting are well established in practice. However, in the way that we now realize that cinema is not merely theater done with machines, computer aided design is not just architectural design done with computers. This paper describes some explorations of architectural design theory using very simple computing concepts, nothing more than the drawing system as a "design processor" analogous to word processing, showing how design theory can be made live again in a computing environment.

Types of Drawings

Traditional drawings on paper are different to computer based drawings in a number of significant ways. The traditional, Pencil Aided Design (PAD), drawing is, essentially, unstructured - each line is drawn independently of every other line. Thus, if the drawing subsequently requires modification, individual lines have to be erased and redrawn. In a Computer Aided Design (CAD) drawing the elements of the design are represented by a set of "graphic primitives" (such as lines, rectangles, polygons, arcs, circles, etc.) arranged in a two dimensional coordinate system. It is thus possible to globally change a rectangle of one size for a rectangle of a different size (or a quite different shape, say a circle), or make copies of the shape in various ways. The second main difference is the concept of scale. PAD drawings are produced to specific scales, 1:100, 1:50, 1:20, etc. often entailing the redrawing of many elements at a different size with no real difference in their information content. A CAD drawing is stored in the computer at full size and different scale drawings produced by the computer drawing system modifying its fullsize data appropriately.

These two specific features of CAD enable a drawing to be manipulated in a way that relates uniquely to the medium of computing. The ease of modification encourages the exploration of design variation: rather than simply having to accept "preordained" rules from some architectural treatise and being given one or two illustrative examples the student is able to explore unlimited numbers of variations and, equally importantly, contravene the given rule and quickly see the effect. Some of these ideas obviously relate closely to issues being explored with shape grammars and students with a particular interest in computing are able to go on to explore these topics, however, this course is taught as an architectural theory rather than a computing option and the computing element is kept, deliberately, in the background. Only a small section of the course is described here and the examples used are drawn from studios taught at the Faculteit der Bouwkunde, TU Delft and at the Department of Architecture and Building Science, University of Strathclyde.

Shape Definition

As shapes may be made up from graphic primitives we have a choice in the way in which an object is defined. To take a trivial example, a triangle might be seen as a shape consisting of three connected lines or, alternatively, as a three sided instance of the polygon primitive. Mitchell et al (1990) have described the development of a customized CAD system (Topdown) for the exploration of parametric variations building on such concepts and this shell has been used successfully at Delft and Strathclyde as a complementary exercise to the ideas discussed here. This paper simply concentrates on the use of very elementary concepts of computer draughting in the exploration of design theory, making use of the ease of modification of example drawings to investigate topics in architectural theory: as the computing requirements are minimal there is no reason to use sophisticated drawing systems and the class exercises have been carried out using a variety of software. The interest in geometry is a fundamental component of design and computer drawing systems provide a convenient medium for its exploration. Whilst geometry in one form or another exists in all buildings, to use it creatively as a formative generator the student must be aware of a number of underlying principles. The most fundamental level is the use of basic geometrical figures (circle, square, triangle, etc. in two dimensions) to determine the built form configuration. The circle is the most perfect shape and requires “vulgarizing” for use in anything but the most monumental designs. The circle is defined by its center and circumference, but even when the circumference is broken by a number of openings the geometrical identity remains (figure 1). The three dimensional extensions of the circle may be the cylinder (e.g. Botta's Casa Rotonda or Saarinen’s MIT Chapel), the sphere (Boullée's Cenotaph for Newton or Ledoux’s Maison des Gardes Agricoles for the Château de Maupertuis) or, more commonly, the hemisphere (Pantheon, Rome). All of these shapes emphasize the centrality of the interior space. To make this space usable for anything other than monumental ceremony requires the fragmentation of the space by the insertion of parallel walls (Corbusier's Chancellery for the French Embassy, Brasilia) or the fragmentation of the space (Botta).

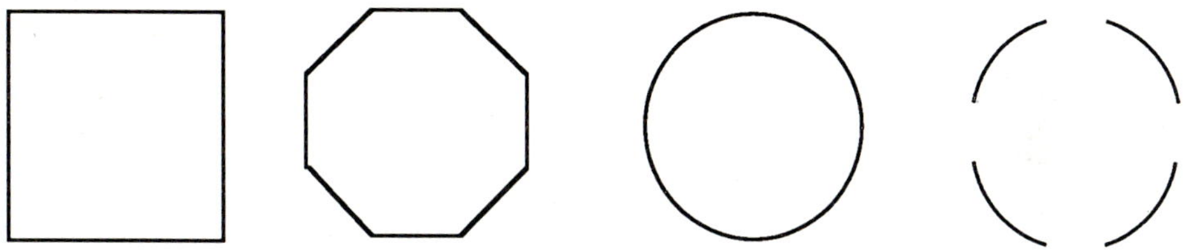

Figure 1. Transformation of Circle into Square and the Problems of Openings in a Circle.

In contrast to the circle the triangle lacks a center as the defining edges have no precise reference. The acute angles between these edges make the triangle an extremely confining space. If openings are made in the sides the center is established by the intersection of the angles and the openings. On the other hand, if the angles are removed the triangle almost disappears; the space is opened up and, depending upon the length of side, may appear to be an implied hexagon (figure 2). The three dimensional equivalents are the prism and pyramid. Examples are rare because of the difficulty of handling space with acute corners: one example is Frank Lloyd Wright’s Vigo Sundt House at Madison, Wisconsin, and another, using implied space, is Borromini’s San Ivo a la Sapienza in Rome (figure 3).

The square contains strong fields of emphasis at its corners, periphery, diagonals, medians and center. Recognition of these properties allows intervention to reinforce or modify its intrinsic characteristics. The square may be modified with respect to internal subspaces or external space. If parts of the edges are removed (the corners remaining intact) there is an implosion of space. If the corners are removed the space explodes outwards (figure 2). This property was exploited by Frank Lloyd Wright in his house designs where, starting from the nucleus of the hearth space progresses outwards. The three dimensional extensions of the square are the cube and tetrahedron or prism. Perfect cube rooms tend not to be strictly equivalent in all directions, but, nevertheless occur in special rooms in great houses. Square plans are attractive because of their compactness. Transformations of the square may be made to give it orientation by, for example, the insertion of walls. The shape may be "eroded" by the placing of openings. In both cases the importance of the center is reduced.

The higher order shapes increasingly move towards the circle, but are important as transitionary forms. Figures such as the octagon are used to form an interface between the square and the circle (figure 1).

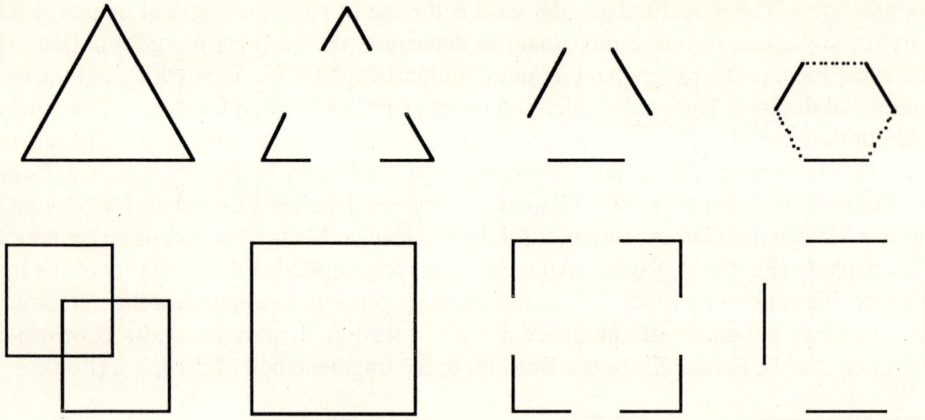

Figure 2. Modifications of the Triangle and Square.

These spatial characteristics of elementary geometric figures are explored, both in two dimensions and in their extensions into three dimensions. Transformations of the basic shapes are investigated: introducing new elements to give orientation or directionality. The different problems and possibilities of forming openings in a square space and a circular space. The "claustrophobic" effects of the acute angles in triangular spaces and the opening up of the triangle by the removal of those corners. Combinations of elements (e.g. a circle and a square) may be used: such figures do not even have to physically exist but may be implied by other figures. Combinations may include different degrees of overlap: one figure may be adjacent to, overlap, or be entirely contained within another figure. These geometrical combinations may themselves then be further combined. Figure 3 shows an example of how an apparently complex plan form is derived from simple combinations of elements and how those elements themselves are modified in the making of the design.

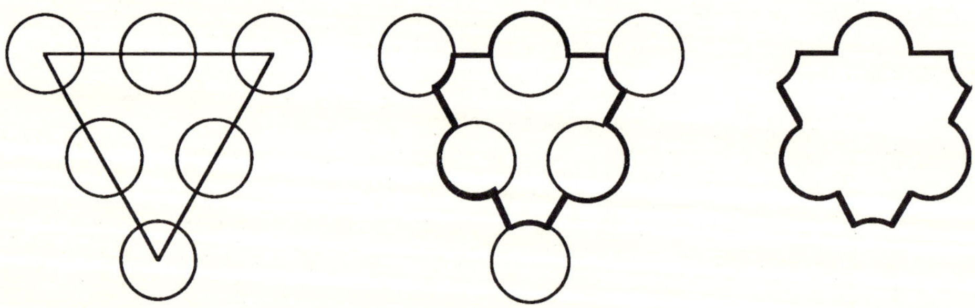

Figure 3. Parties and Diagrammatic Plan of S. Ivo, Rome (1642).

Combinations may be made with similar geometries, for example, two circles, three triangles, etc. of the same or different size. The square is the most commonly used figure, partly because in certain combinations it produces larger versions of itself. The nine-square format assembled from three rows of three squares is one of the classic formative geometries. Durand shows a "formule graphique" using 2 x 2, 3 x 3, 4 x 4, and 5 x 5 square generators.

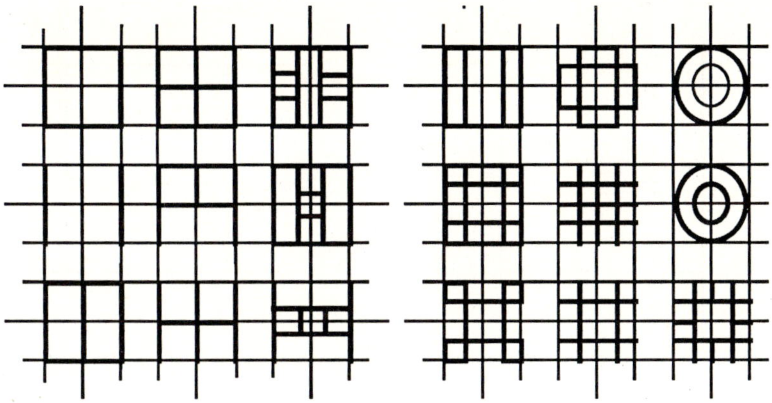

Figure 4. Parties from Durand's "Formule Graphique Applicable aux Edifices Publics Voutés dont les parties sont destinées à des usages différents".

Palladio's villas are based on a nine-square plan, modified by the insertion of extra divisions to make a non-regular 5 x 3 plan. The Palladian Villas all derive from a single partie developed from an analysis of the requirements of an Italian villa: loggias and a large hall in the central axis, two or three livingrooms or bedrooms of various sizes at the sides, and, between them and the hall, space for smaller rooms and staircases (figure 5). The Villa Thiene at Cicogna, built during the 1550's shows the pattern most clearly. The rooms, together with the porticos, are defined by a rectangle divided by two longitudinal and four transverse lines. The Villa Badoer at Fratta, Polesine (c. 1566) (figure 6) follows the same pattern, but with one portico now placed outside the cube of the building. The Villa Cornaro at Piombino Dese (1566) is essentially the same scheme inverted with the two small rooms each side of the hall joined to form larger rooms with their axes at right angles to the hall. The staircases are moved to the wings leaving an almost square hall with the same width as the porticos. When the staircases are brought inside alongside the small rooms the hall takes on the cruciform shape of the Villa Foscari at Mira (La Malcontenta, 1560) (figure 7).

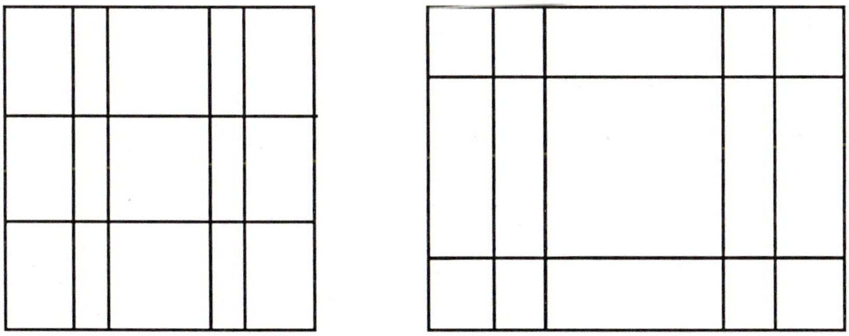

Figure 5. Parti for Palladio's Villas, together with diagrammatic plan of Villa Thiene at Cicogna.

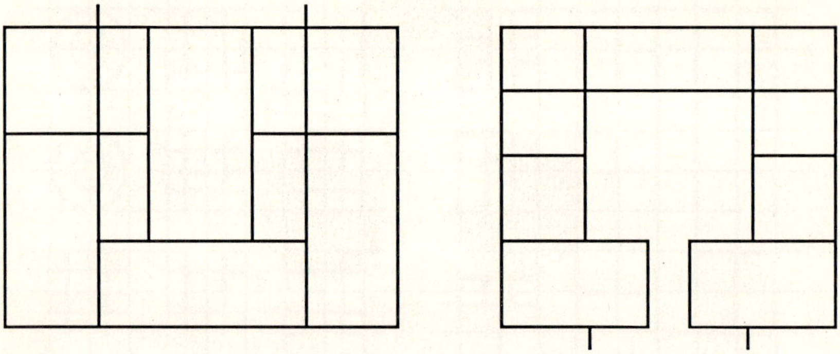

Figure 6. Diagrammatic plans of Palladio's Villa Badoer at Fratta, Polesine and Villa Cornaro at Piombino Dese.

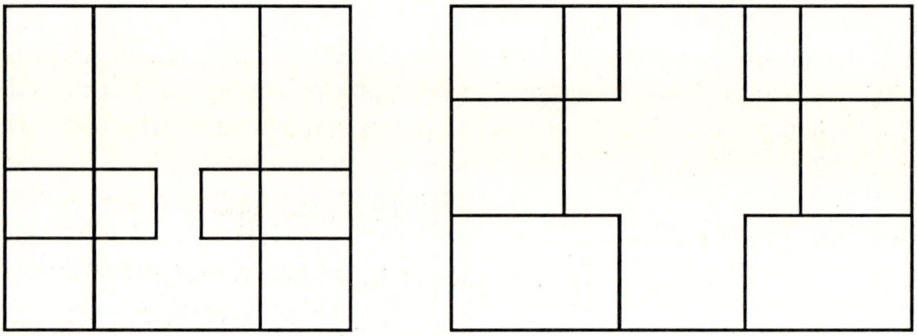

Figure 7. Villa Emo at Fanzola and Villa Foscari (La Malcontenta) at Mira.

Variations may be made on any of these plans by removing certain component parts, modifying the sizes of component parts or substituting other shapes for the squares. Forms may be generated using parts of the basic geometric shape, such as half a circle; or geometries obtained by locating elements at the corners of an implied larger geometric shape. Certain combinations or reductions will result in particular proportions and proportional generating systems may be a subject of study in themselves.

The Readability of Forms

When we draw plans or elevations the forms we are describing are usually defined by their edges. The Platonic Solids are good examples of the importance of edges: simply because they are so familiar the eye almost automatically recognizes the shape and builds the edges, even when they are not explicitly expressed. Several well known optical illusions demonstrate the strong presence of "phantom edges" (figure 8).

Figure 8. Illusionary triangle.

For other shapes it is common to explicitly emphasize edges in various ways: examples from classical architecture may be referred to to show how the base, corners and cornice are accentuated. When we draw a plan we draw the walls (edges of the space) rather than the spaces themselves, but, for designers, it is the space that is important, rather than the defining elements. To emphasize the space instead of the walls a computer paint system can invert figure and ground very simply, but soon the eye simply reads the white lines (which were black before) as a negative plan. An interesting exercise in spatial perception and definition is to "paint" the spaces with tones related to the degree of enclosure of the space or reflecting the relief of the ceiling (figure 9). Axonometric and perspective projections provide other ways of exploring space.

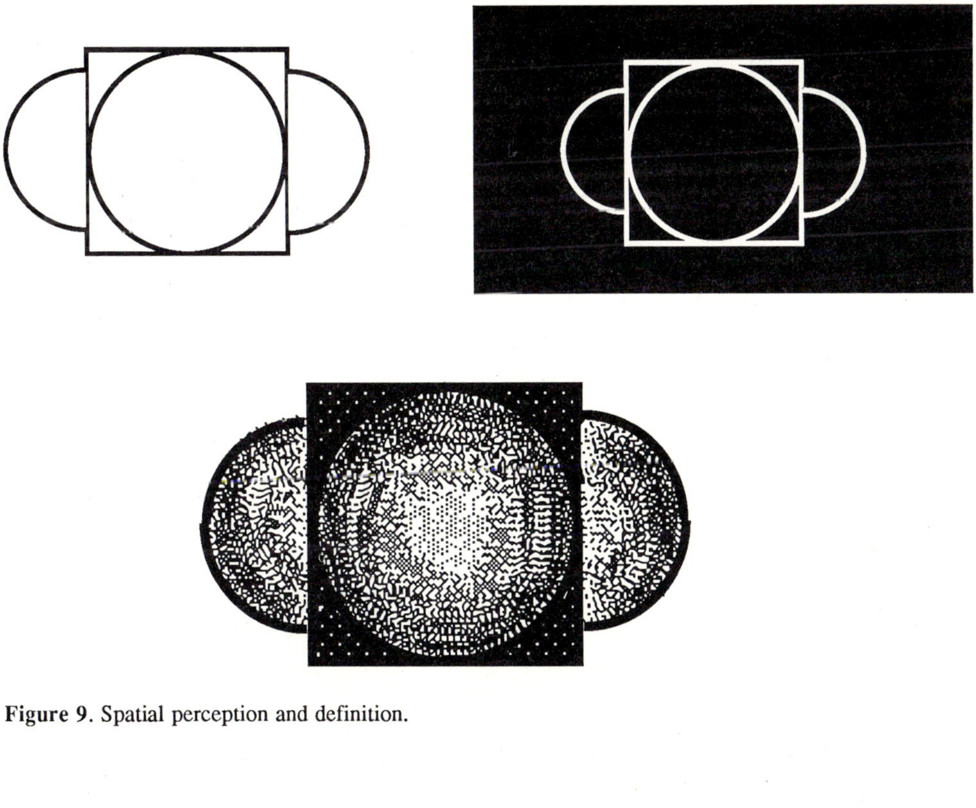

Figure 9. Spatial perception and definition.

Order in Building

The requirements of construction usually restrict designs to fairly simple geometries making use of the repetition of elements that can easily be assembled together. Repetition, alignment and juxtaposition of identical elements impose order regardless, but architectural design acquires its own autonomy by regulating that order in particular ways. Repetition and similarity may be explored, making use of the drawing systems facility to copy and move elements easily. Repetition in design is derived in three different ways: by simply adding similar elements; by dividing the whole; or by making a linked series without a clearly defined form but with elements such as material, scale, proportion, position of windows, etc, in common.

Proximity of elements is important, for elements which are close together are grouped and separated from those that are further away (figure 10). The positioning of windows in facades is used to explore these various "Gestalt Laws" as a means of introducing rhythm and vitality into elevations. The elements of the facade become integrated through common enclosure on a ground and, when the whole is repeated (through alignment and series) linearity and rhythm become important.

Figure 10. Adjacency and Directional Factors Creating Gestalts.

Individual students may explore the possibilities of the first two phenomena and the combination of their work can demonstrate the third. The importance of the proximity of elements may be explored by manipulating facades, grouping elements in different ways. Street facades may be modified to see how linearity and rhythm are important. The evolution of forms, where the intervals or elements in a repetitive structure gradually change their form, size or orientation are explored. The geometrical properties of centrality, axiality, orientation, etc are used to establish hierarchies of forms. A hierarchy implies primary and secondary elements with one or more forms dominating the others. This implied order can act as a powerful unifying factor in design, making it possible to combine disparate elements in more recognizably ordered designs. Dominant and subordinate elements are recognizable not only in facades or massing, but in architectural space as well. The design of house elevations and the combination of the class work into a street facade makes an interesting project insofar as the resulting street never appears to be such a pot-pourri as might be imagined beforehand.

A simpler exercise is based on the design of a modular exhibition stand which is then analyzed using Arnheim's "energy fields" of forms: this makes the design of the space and the circulation paths very explicit. Arnheim (1977) made the suggestion that architects should replace the notion of figure/ground with one of "energy fields" created by objects. The space would then be defined by vectors modified by distances, expansions and contractions (figure 11). These force fields are plotted on a separate layer over the plan and indicate how the spatial organization works and how junctions between spaces may be resolved.

Definition of Space

Space may be defined implicitly or explicitly. The various ways of defining space each have particular consequences in terms of the "spatial field". Spaces may be closed and introverted or open and extrovert. The way in which Frank Lloyd Wright eliminated corners from the plan and distorted spatial geometry by turning parts of the envelope through 90 degrees may be analyzed by modifying spatial enclosures "in the style of FLW" (figure 12).

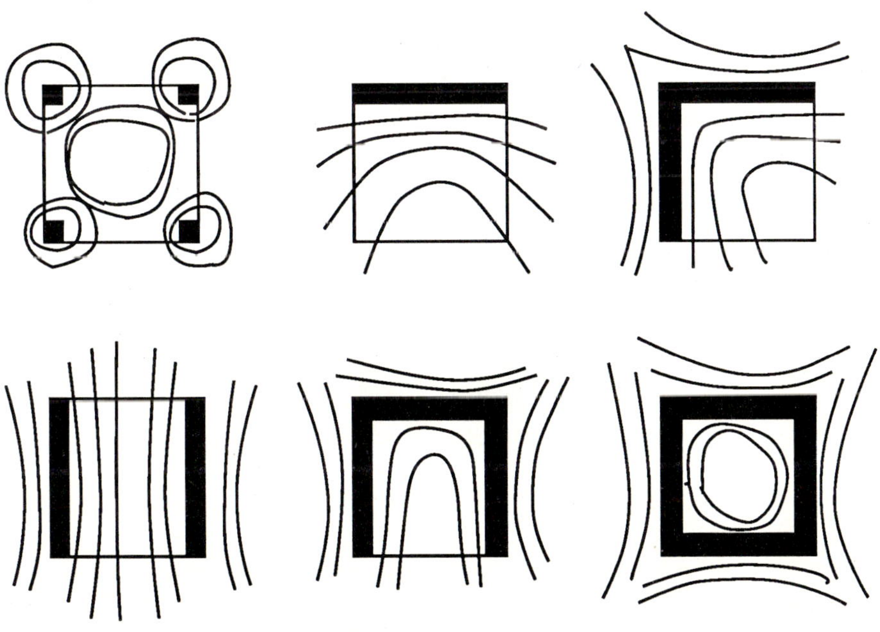

Figure 11. Arnheim's Spatial Fields.

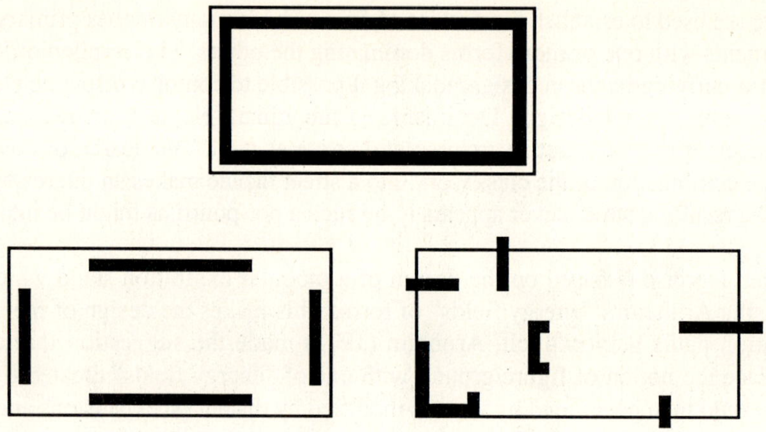

Figure 12. Frank Lloyd Wright's New Spatial Order.

Models are built of famous houses such as the Usonian Houses of Frank Lloyd Wright, Asplund's Villa Snellman, the Rietveld-Schroeder house, Mario Botta's single family houses, Corbusier's Villa Savoye (see figure 13) and their spatial properties analyzed in plan and through various three-dimensional projections. Mies van de Rohe's Barcelona Pavilion is analyzed to explore the definition of space by different forms of boundaries in the manner described in Oxman et al (1987). Students are encouraged to make their own explorations, developing ideas of spatial juxtaposition and interpenetration (figure 14).

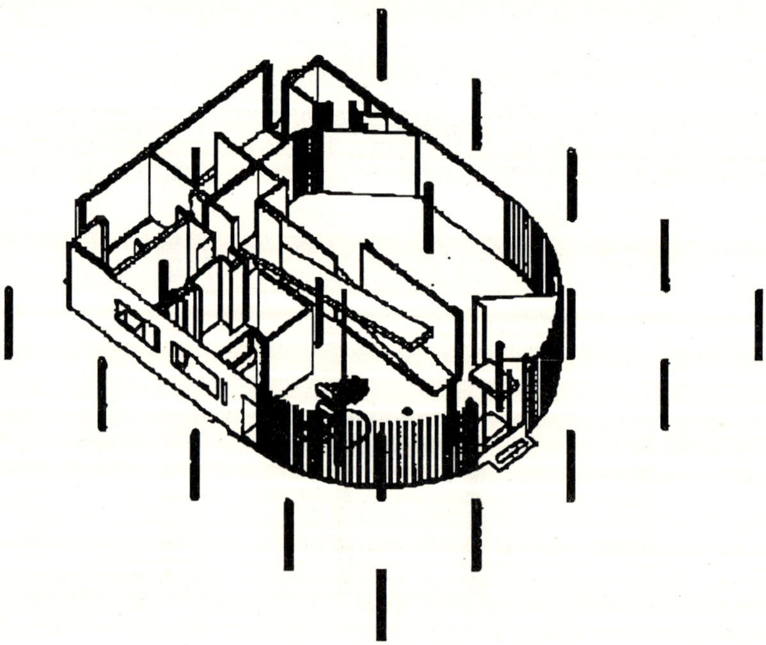

Figure 13. Villa Savoye Analytical Drawing.

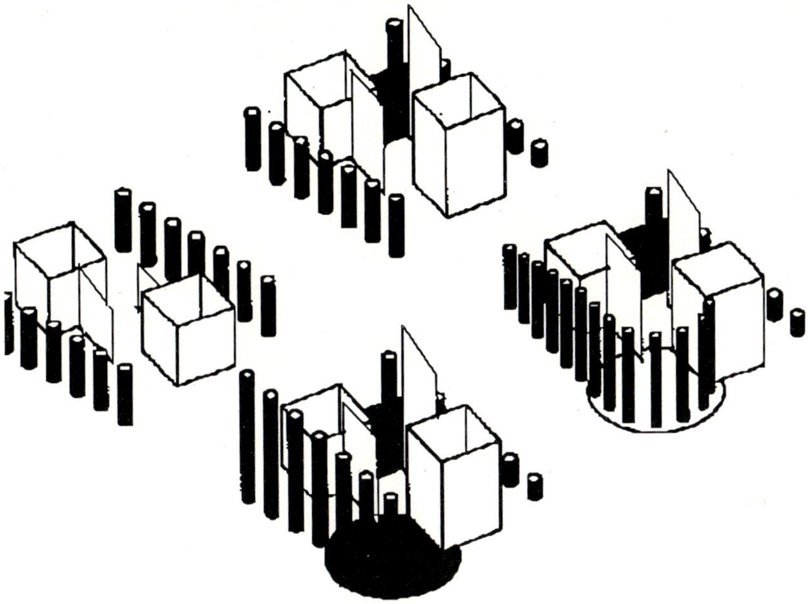

Figure 14. Investigations of Spatial Arrangement.

The Villa Savoye is a disarmingly sophisticated building. The basic organization is so apparently straightforward: regularly spaced pilotis supporting a box within which interior divisions are freely disposed. Le Corbusier formally explores the relationship between organic spatial development and the requirements of external form. A casual reading of the drawings for this house tempts us to see the design in too simple or direct terms without grasping the implications of the formal concepts. The degree of study needed to build the computer model enables some of these points to be appreciated and the attempt to reinterpret those ideas shows the difficulty involved.

Conclusions

The formal teaching of architectural theory and composition has not been very fashionable in Schools of Architecture for several years now. Indeed there is a considerable inbuilt resistance in students to the application of any form of rules or procedures. There is however a general interest in computing and this can be utilized to advantage. The Architectural Theory Course, the introductory part of which is described here, is taught to second year undergraduates at Strathclyde and slightly more senior students at Delft. The format of teaching is usually a forty-five minute lecture followed by a minimum of one hour practical computing. The first lectures cover the basic spatial elements and grids as ordering and generating devices in design. Example illustrations are taken from sources as diverse as Durand, Palladio and Peter Eisenman. Students are then required to make a design arranged on a grid in an explicable way. Everyone works intuitively but some students always begin to make designs which exhibit some internal regularities or structure: symmetry about an axis, repetition with ordered variation, incremental changes of scale, etc. It is then possible to get that student to attempt to explain the rules he or she has in fact used (even if the design was thought to have been developed intuitively). By carrying out the exercise first (after simply showing a number of examples) it is possible to then discuss the resulting designs and show how the best designs tend to have intuitively obeyed the principles we are attempting to teach. Thus an element of learning by discovery is introduced and the student is not simply attempting to apply predefined "rules". Having revealed the formal elements of the design the student is then encouraged to alter those features and discuss the results. The student thus learns by doing rather than by rote. Later classes show how the deliberate breaking of rules or the collision of two or more formal systems can be used as generators of designs. Similarly, other classes illustrate how divergence from the norm, the breaking of symmetry or the distortion of regular patterns may introduce complexity into the design. In all cases it is the ease with which computer based drawings can be modified which makes this form of design exploration possible.

References

Arnheim, Rudolf. 1977. *The Dynamics of Architectural Form.* Berkeley: University of California Press.

Durand, Jean-Nicolas-Louis. 1819. *Précis des Leçons d'Architecture.* Paris: L'Ecole Royale Polytechnique. 1819. Reprinted 1975, Unterschneidheim : Uhl Verlag.

Durand, Jean-Nicolas-Louis. 1821. *Partie Graphique des Cours d'Architecture.* Paris: L'Ecole Royale Polytechnique. 1821. Reprinted 1975, Unterschneidheim : Uhl Verlag.

Mitchell, William J., Robin S. Liggett, and Milton Tan. 1990. "Top-Down Knowledge-Based Design." In Malcolm McCullough, William J. Mitchell and Patrick Purcell (eds.). *The Electronic Design Studio.* Cambridge, Mass.: MIT Press.

Palladio, Andrea. 1738. *The Four Books of Architecture* (Ware's Edition, 1965 reprint). New York, N.Y.: Dover.

Oxman, Robert, Antony Radford, and Rivka Oxman. 1987. *The Language of Architectural Plans.* Canberra: Australian Institute of Architects.

5 Design Education with Computers

Leandro Madrazo

Lehrstuhl für Architektur und CAAD
ETH Zürich
CH 8093 Zürich, Switzerland

This paper summarizes a teaching project carried out by the CAAD Chair in the Department of Architecture at the ETH in Zürich during the last one and a half years. The approach adopted for the design education with computers focuses on two major issues: design representations *and* design strategies. *The alternative representations that computers can provide are discussed in the first part of the paper. The core of this first part is a detailed description of a course in which hierarchical structures were used to teach some of the alternative design representations that are unique to computers. The second part of the paper proposes that understanding design as the interplay of systems is a design strategy which can lead to an effective integration of computers in design. A brief description of the content of another course developed around this concept is included.*

Introduction

Unlike the sculptor or the painter, the architect is detached from the actual artifact he is trying to create. While the work of the sculptor and the painter are results of direct interaction with the object itself, the architect does not create a building through the direct manipulation of real objects in space. Architecture is conceived in a world of abstractions; it is essentially a product of thc intellect, a mental process dealing with symbols that refer to the real world where the building is built.

There are some simple, pragmatic reasons behind the detachment of the architect from the object of his creation, among them, the fact that raising a building represents a collective effort that requires a huge investment of time and money. A more significant reason, however, is that the existence of architecture as a discipline and the position of architects as central figures in the creation of the built environment are intimately related to the division between 'design' and 'construction' as it was established after the Renaissance. Significantly, Alberti started his treatise *On the Art of Building* (Alberti 1452) by describing the division between *lineamenta* and *structura* :

" The whole matter of building is composed of lineaments and structure. All the intent and purpose of lineaments lies in finding the correct, infallible way of joining and fitting together those lines and angles which define and enclose the surfaces of the building. ...let lineaments be the precise and correct outline, conceived in the mind, made up of lines and angles, and perfected in the learned intellect and imagination."

The Abstract and Real Worlds

The architect's realm lies between two worlds: the abstract world in which the building is conceived and the real world in which it is experienced. The abstraction of design by architects has a similar purpose as formulas have for physicists: it allows them to capture some relevant aspects of reality in order to manipulate them in the realm of the intellect. Le Corbusier talked about this similarity in *Vers une Architecture* (Le Corbusier 1923):

"Le plan est la détermination du tout; il est le moment décisif. Un plan n'est pas joli à dessiner comme le visage d'une madone; c'est une austère abstraction; ce n'est qu'une algébrisation aride au regard. Le travail du mathématicien reste tout de même une des plus hautes activités de l'esprit humain".

The ultimate purpose of the activity of the architect is the real object, the creation of space. In this regard, the architect must be aware of the impact that decisions made in the realm of the abstract will have in the real world of the built environment. Le Corbusier was also aware of the link between the two worlds when he wrote (Le Corbusier 1923):

"L'homme voit les choses de l'architecture avec ses yeux qui sont à 1 m. 70 du sol. On ne peut compter qu'avec des buts accessibles à l'oeil, qu'avec des intentions qui usent des éléments de l'architecture".

Conceptual Tools of Design

Abstractions of a design are something more than a link between the individual world of the designer and the outside world; they create a reality of their own. Architecture often becomes trapped in this world of abstractions that was actually meant to represent it. Moreover, some architectural concepts belong exclusively to the abstract world and do not necessarily have a place in the physical world.

The order we try to find in the composition of a facade, for example, may be the result of using a specific orthographic projection to capture some of the properties of the real building.

The mechanisms we use to design a facade (to play with the proportions of openings, to create tensions and balances between parts of the composition) are consistent with the properties of the conceptual tools that we are using to conceive the building. Moreover, the very concept of 'facade' exists because orthographic projections were developed as a way of controlling the geometric properties of real objects before they are built. Therefore, the conceptual decompositions that an architect makes in order to conceive a building are consistent with the design representations that are known to the architect.

The interdependence between *what we can think of* and the characteristics of the tool that we have *to think with* is such that we cannot escape the use of the representations of design that we know, even when we are facing complex design problems that exceed the limitations of those representations.

Alternative Design Representations with Computers

The possibility that computers might provide alternative design representations was recognized in the first applications of computers in architecture. For Ivan Sutherland, the attraction of using computers in design lay in the structured nature of computer drawings (Sutherland 1975):

"To a large extent it has turned out that the usefulness of computer drawings is precisely their structured nature ...... The drawing itself has properties quite independent of the properties of the object it is describing."

The new representation possibilities offered by computers for design inspired Herbert Simon to develop a new theory of design (Simon 1969). In his book *The Sciences of the Artificial*, he explains the relationship between the kinds of representation that can be made of a problem and the solutions that can be found. He concludes that solving a problem simply means representing it so as to make the solution transparent. Following Simon it is possible to imagine that, at some moment, computers will be able to provide new representations that help a designer to better understand the actual complexity of design issues.

Although these alternative representations have not yet been realized in practice, the basic assumptions are still valid. In order to define the role of computers in design, it is not enough to recognize a computer's capability to produce new representations. The critical point is how architects can actually use those representations to conceive and represent design in a different way. Thus, *a clear definition of the role of computers in architectural design cannot emerge until computers offer new representations of design that architects can use to conceive and represent a building.*

Alternative Design Representations: The Reality of Current Systems

Current computer-aided design systems do not provide alternative design representations that the architect can use to conceive a design. The representations of design that we find in today's computer-aided design systems have not broken any new ground (Madrazo 1991). They rely too heavily on the conventional representations that we know through hand drawings and physical models. Because of this, current systems are used to emulate tasks that were previously done manually, for example, creating a set of construction drawings or a three-dimensional model for visualization purposes.

Today, a large gap exists between what a computer should be able to do in order to become an irreplaceable tool for design, and what current commercial systems actually can do. The situation is such, that it is even difficult to justify the term 'computer-aided design' when the capabilities of the available systems are considered. Rather, the use of expressions such as 'computer drafting', 'computer modeling' or 'computer animation' better describe the possibilities offered by computer systems in architecture at this time.

As a result of this situation, educators who are interested in teaching about the unique potential that computers offer for design, face a paradoxical situation: there are no computer tools that prove that computers have a place in architectural design. In this context, the alternatives are whether to adjust design teaching to the capabilities of those systems (which means to teach drafting and modeling with computers and to make students proficient in the use of selected packages) or to create some new conceptual tools that support a specific approach to design (Schmitt 1989).

Computers in Design Education: Teaching New Design Representations

The education of design with computers should concentrate on those aspects of a computer that make it a unique tool for addressing design issues, for example, its different design representations.

The course that took place during the Wintersemester 1990 at the ETH introduced a method of computer representation for design that cannot be implemented with traditional tools. Rather than using a standard system to teach, we created our own environment and tools for the students to use during the course.

Although most of the ideas that were presented in the course belong to the world of object-oriented languages, the task of providing a completely new set of tools outside one of the commercial packages was beyond our possibilities. For this reason, the new tools and their corresponding environment were programmed in AutoLISP and interfaced with AutoCAD (Version 10).

Course Content

The goal of the course was to focus on understanding some of the basic concepts related to the representation of design with computers. We purposely avoided specific architectural references by developing exercises based on the representation of abstract three-dimensional objects. Although we considered the simplification of design issues advantageous for making the basic ideas clearer, it was not intended to suggest that a trivialization of design is necessary in order to bring it into the realm of computers.

Three fundamental ideas served as a basis for the presentation of the capabilities of computers as unique tools for design: *design vocabulary, multiple representations* and *hierarchical structures*.

Design Vocabulary

With the computer, the designer is more aware of the fact that the representation of a design idea takes place within a closed universe of objects. These objects make up the design vocabulary. Because the vocabulary is restricted, more attention is paid to the exploration of spatial relationships between elements of the vocabulary and to the ways in which the existing vocabulary can be enhanced by the creation of new elements.

The concepts of *types* and *instances* are used to explore the representation of design within a design vocabulary. The objects created by the provided functions are extruded shapes made in two steps: first a two-dimensional profile is defined and, second, a complete three-dimensional objects is created within the boundaries of a 1x1x1 unit cube. Instances of these objects are used to create more complex objects thus enhancing the initial vocabulary. The instances also can be assigned different scale values.

Multiple Representations

Typically, each abstraction of a design is an expression of a particular set of issues filtered out of the overall complexity of the design. Working with traditional tools, each abstraction becomes unique. A detailed section of a facade is a separate drawing with no link to the floor plan. Massing studies are done with physical models which have no real link to the drawings. One significant capability that the computer offers is the ability to interrelate the different representations of the same object.

We use different *levels of detail* for the same object to illustrate this idea. Different representations for every type in the vocabulary are created with a function that cuts and adds rectangular sections to a given square. An instantiation menu makes it possible to select an instance of a type and 'increase' or 'decrease' the level of detail according to the structure of the design vocabulary.

Hierarchical Structures

The idea of creating a hierarchical structure of a design is the main objective of the course. Although architects have long been familiar with the concept of hierarchies in design, it is only now, with the computer, that we can actually have a representation of those hierarchies that we can use to design.

The proposed hierarchical structure is the result of *instantiating* the elements of the design vocabulary to create more complex elements. At the top of the structure, the most basic elements are created as single unit types organized according to their levels of detail. The operations to create those types are embedded in the functions that create them. In a second level, new operations are applied to the instances of those objects to create more complex ones.

At every level of the structure, different kinds of *objects* and *operations* are used to create compositions with existing objects or new ones that are then added to the vocabulary. The criteria for creating the most basic objects, for example, is fundamentally different than that of the more complex object. In the first case, the most relevant issue for the creation of simple objects is the operation used to give them form. For more complex objects, however, it is crucial to define the spatial relationships between the instances of the simpler objects. Thus, at every level of the hierarchy different design considerations can be isolated and treated separately.

The most important aspect, however, is the dynamic character of this hierarchical representation of design. The changes performed at the top of the hierarchy (for example, redefining some elements in the first vocabulary) will propagate down through the other levels. Thus, it is not necessary to question the overall design process in order to explore different alternatives of design.

Description of the Exercises

The exercises for this course have been designed to allow the students to progress in the understanding of the basic principles involved in a regulated fashion. In order to complete the exercises, the students need only the provided set of tools and a basic knowledge of the most generic operations of the commercial package.

Exercise 1: Creating Form with the Computer

The first two exercises introduce students to three-dimensional space. In the first, the three-dimensional space is introduced by exploring the relationship between the plane and the vertical dimension.The three-dimensional objects are extruded shapes whose outlines are defined using a 3x3 grid interface (Figure 1).

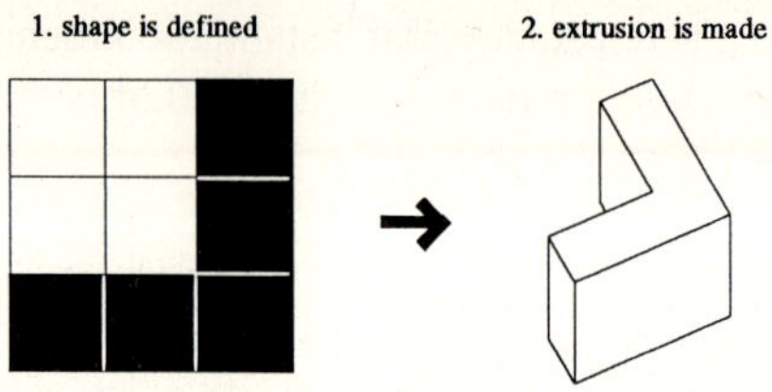

Figure 1. The interface used to create extruded objects.

The function CREATE_OBJECT creates an object with surfaces on all sides (note that in AutoCAD version 10, creating a complete 3d object involves more operations than just a simple extrusion). Within the same function, the resulting object is then defined as a 'block' and a slide of the object made to be used in an icon menu. A series of objects created with this function make up the first *design vocabulary* (Figure 2).

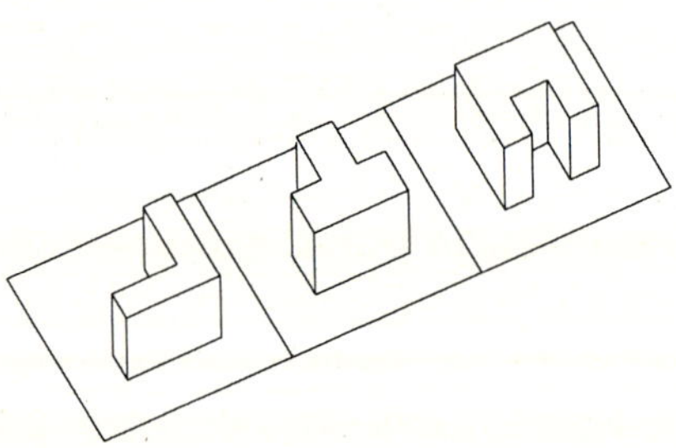

Figure 2. The first design vocabulary.

In the second part of the exercise, different compositions are made by placing combinations of the objects over a plane (Figure 3). When the function INSERT_OBJECT is invoked, an icon menu appears on the screen displaying the existing objects. Each inserted object is an *instance* of the original *type*. Each instance can be individually scaled at the moment of insertion. Special editing functions are provided to modify the position of the inserted object or redefine the scale factor. With X_FLIP, Y_FLIP it is possible to change the orientation of the inserted object with one mouse-click. Z_ROT rotates the object through an axis passing through the center of the section. Z_RESIZE modifies the height of the object.

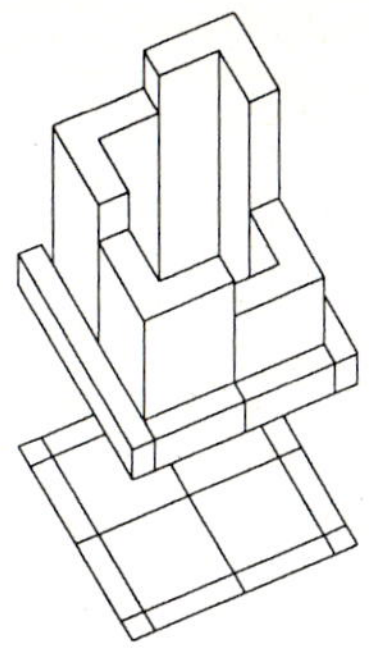

Figure 3. Composition of extruded objects over a plane.

Exercise 2: The Three Dimensions

In this second exercise, the operations that were restricted to the relationship between the plane and the vertical dimension are expanded to all three dimensions of space.

The function INSERT_OBJECT allows one to insert an object with any orientation in space. Similarly, scale factors can be applied to any of the three axes of the object. The editing functions are also enhanced to allow modification in all three dimensions. FLIP, ROT and RESIZE replace their two-dimensional counterparts from the first exercise. The function RESIZE is particularly useful since it circumvents the necessity in AutoCAD of manually deleting and reinserting blocks in order to rescale them. With RESIZE one can select an instance of the block and modify graphically any dimension along the three axes of the block.

The goal of this exercise is to create complex objects out of simpler ones. Every type defined in the vocabulary can be scaled and placed in any position in space. To illustrate the idea, we provide a function that allows the student to build different cube constructions out of one of the types of the vocabulary created in exercise one (Figure 4). With the function CREATE_CUBE, a pop-up menu displays three different cube constructions: a cube defined as a single instance of a type, six instances defining the faces of a cube and twelve instances defining the edges of a cube. A second menu follows which displays the existing objects. After the second selection, the function prompts for some scale factors and the cube is created.

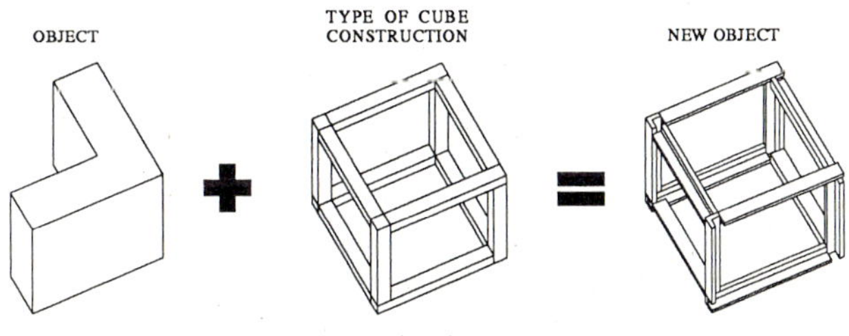

Figure 4. The function CREATE_CUBE creates a cube from a vocabulary type by instanciating it as the twelve edge elements.

In the second part of the exercise, the student uses the new editing functions to modify the configurations of the cubes obtained with CREATE_CUBE (Figure 5). The different transformations are the result of changing the orientation and scale factors of the instances using a few interactive tools (the functions FLIP, ROT and RESIZE).

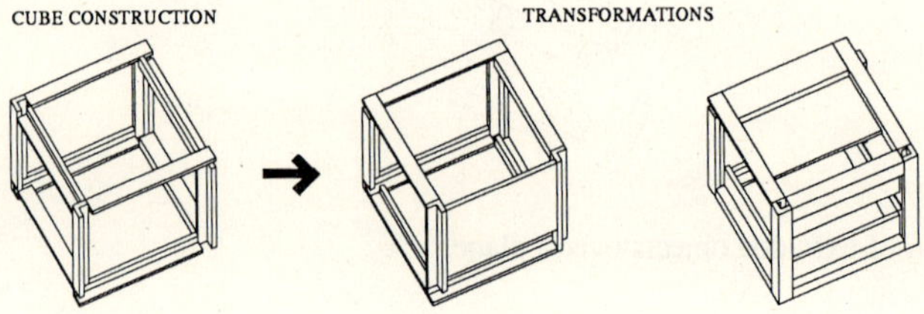

Figure 5. Two different transformations of a cube construction previously created with the function CREATE_CUBE.

Exercise 3: Levels of Detail

After three-dimensional space and the concepts of types and instances have been introduced, the main core of the course begins. In the third exercise, objects can be created with a new function (EXTEND_PROFILE) with which two-dimensional rectilinear shapes can be created by cutting and adding sections to an initial 1x1 square (Figure 6). As in the first and second exercises, the function CREATE_OBJECT automatically extrudes the two-dimensional shape, inserts surfaces on all sides, defines the resulting objects as a block and makes a slide for the pop-up menu display.

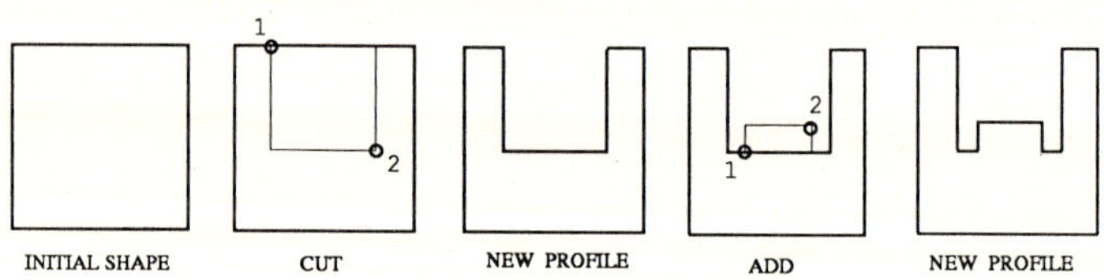

Figure 6. The interface to create two-dimensional profiles with cutting and adding operations.

The concept of *multiple representations* is established and developed with the inclusion of different levels of detail for every object in the design vocabulary (Figure 7). The purpose of the exercise is to complete a table of objects, organized horizontally as a collection of types and vertically according to levels of detail. The table works in combination with an INSTANTIATION menu, which allows the manipulation of the objects when they are inserted. Thus, it is possible to select an instance and 'increase' or 'decrease' its level of detail, or substitute one type with another while maintaining the same level of detail. Also, any modification of the scale factors of an instance at any level of detail are inherited by its replacement.

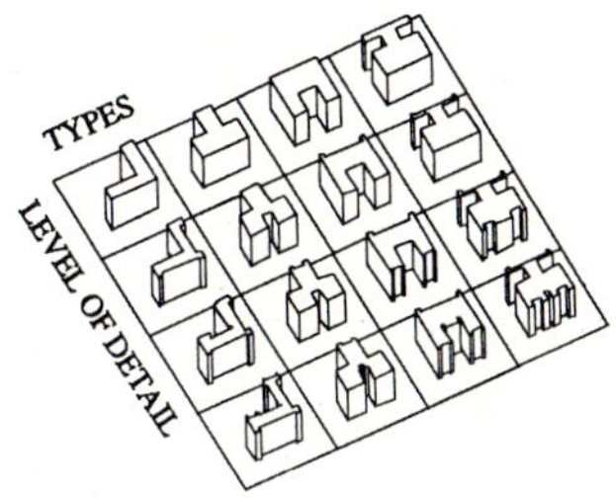

Figure 7. The enhanced vocabulary with types and levels of detail.

Exercise 4: Building a Hierarchical Representation

The goal of this exercise is to explore possibilities for creating new objects within a restricted design vocabulary (Figure 8). New objects are the result of creating combinations of instances of the original single unit types with different scale factors. The spatial relationships between the objects of the first vocabulary determine the characteristics of the more complex ones of which they are a part. The initial vocabulary is then expanded by the new, compound objects.

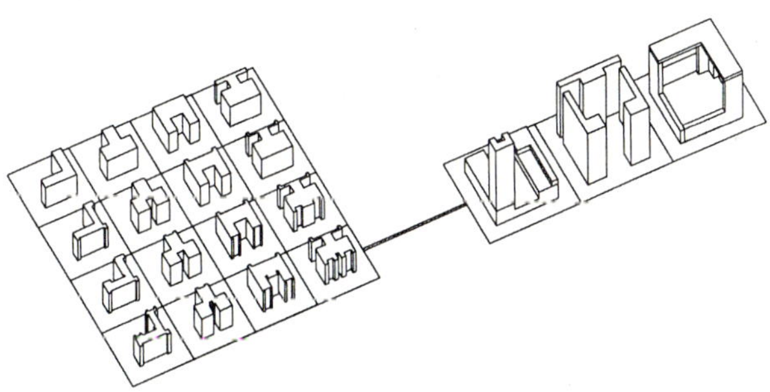

Figure 8. The design vocabulary is enhanced by more complex elements.

The transformation of a simple object into a complex one can be described in terms of the application of an *operator* to an *object*. The objects in the hierarchy are made up of two components: the geometric properties of the object (OBJECT) and the operations that determine the spatial properties of that object (OPERATOR). Recursive application of the operations on the vocabulary results in a hierarchical structure as seen in Figure 9.

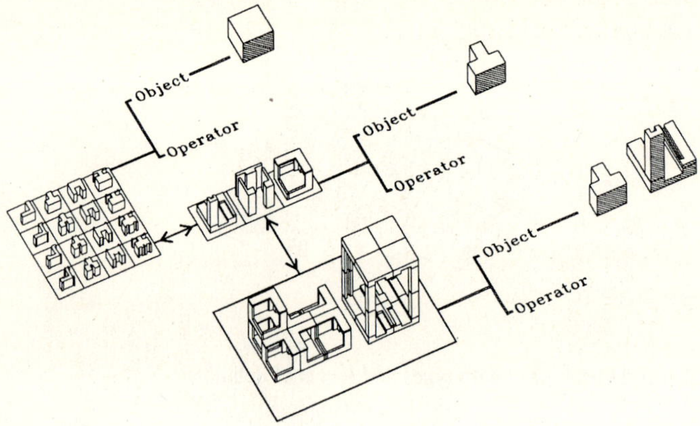

Figure 9. A hierarchical structure based on objects and operators.

It is possible at this point to create a composition with the most simple elements of the first vocabulary, for example, a cube (Figure 10). After having created new complex elements in the vocabulary, the instantiation menu can be used to automatically replace the most simple cubes by more complex ones. In order to explore different formal expressions based on the first volumetric schemes, one must simply select a cube and use the function 'increase' level of detail or 'substitute' types.

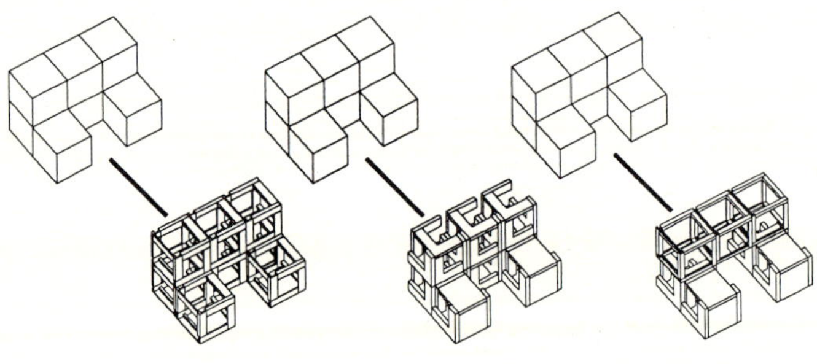

Figure 10. Replacing simple elements with more complex ones.

Exercise 5: Using the Hierarchical Representations

Building up a representation in this way results in a hierarchical structure made up of the objects of the first design vocabulary and objects created by applying operations to them. The purpose of this exercise is to use the concept of *instantiation* to create design alternatives within the hierarchical structure already created. For example, it is possible to go to the top of the hierarchy and redefine one of the types and levels of detail. In Figure 11, the redefinition of the L-shape in the first vocabulary results in the automatic update of all the instances in all levels of the hierarchical structure.

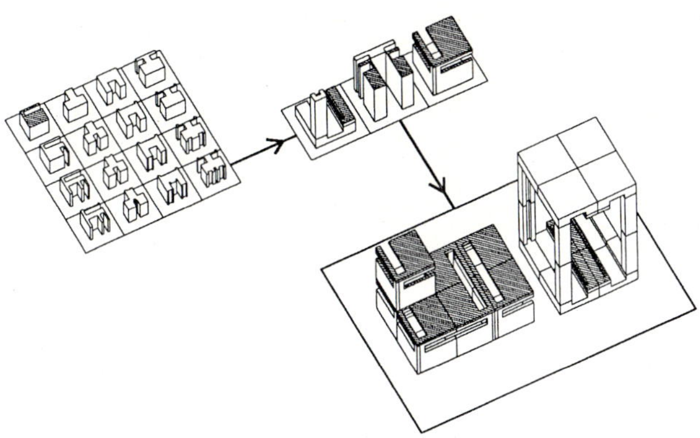

Figure 11. Exploration of design alternatives within the hierarchical structure.

It is also possible to explore alternatives from any level within the hierarchy. A new solution might require the enhancement of the vocabulary at an intermediate level of the hierarchy. At this point, the design vocabulary needs to be enhanced in the upper levels of the hierarchy (Figure 12).

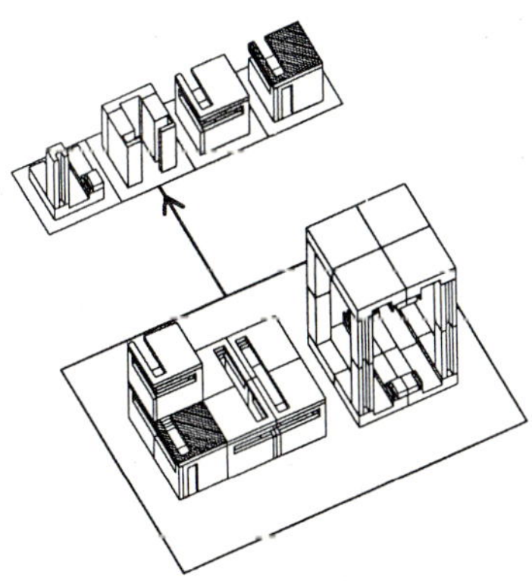

Figure 12. New elements are added to different levels of the hierarchy.

Another way to creatively exploit the representation of design with this hierarchical structure is to create multiple decompositions of a compound object. Figure 13 shows four possible decompositions which are based on different interpretations that a designer might have for a design. In each case, new elements can be created to reflect the concepts behind each decomposition and added to the vocabulary.

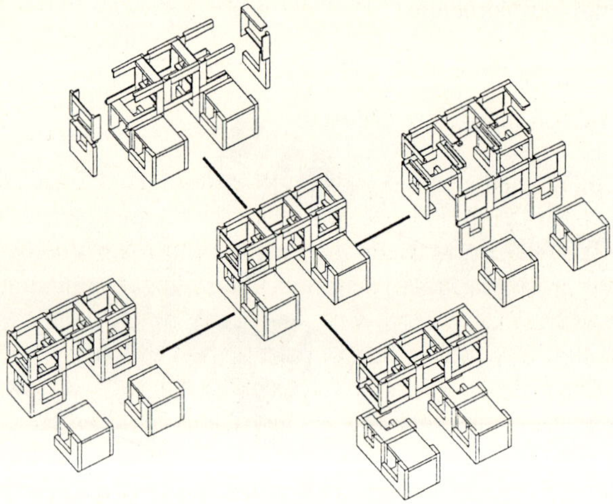

Figure 13. Decompositions reflecting different perceptions of the same scheme.

PART TWO: DESIGN STRATEGIES

The first part of the paper focused on the issue of design representation in isolation from any references to architectural design. This second part specifically addresses the role of computers in architectural design. The central point of the discussion is that architects will need to develop certain *design strategies* in order to use the representations provided by computers to conceive a design. One of those strategies is understanding design as the result of the interplay of systems.

Creation and Representation of Architectural Knowledge

Typically, an architect starts a design with sketches in order to communicate an idea from his or her mind to the outside world. At the early stages of the design process there is a necessity to think freely about a design without much interference from the medium used to represent it. However, such an intimate connection between ideas and tools cannot be achieved with the conventional computer systems. As soon as the architect moves to the computer to continue the design that was started with sketches the tool starts to mediate the ideas. The exact geometry of every element and the level of abstraction of each object have to be defined. The design also has to be broken into parts that can be implemented in the computer as symbols, layers or files. Attributes and names have to be assigned to the elements and groups of elements in the design.

With sketches the architect is creating knowledge; then that knowledge must be transferred to the computer. Although during this transition a new understanding of the original idea may emerge, it is difficult to continue designing working exclusively with the computer. The critical issue is how to enable an architect to create knowledge while working with the computer, rather than simply using it to represent what is already known. In this context, it can be argued that the role of computers in architectural design *is to capture the design logic of an individual architect by representing the design process itself, rather than the output of that process.*

The Dialectic Between Form and Context

According to Christopher Alexander, a design is the result of the dialectic between form and context (Alexander 1964). The architect moves from one to the other in the process of design, establishing the boundaries between the *definition of the problem* (context) and the *formal solution* to that problem (form). Being unable to understand completely all of the complexities of the context in which the form has to fit, the architect begins by making a formal hypothesis. In this way, the form proposed by him becomes the description of the problem and, at the same time, its solution. By acting in this way, Alexander contends that the architect loses the chance to really understand all of the complexities of the problem he is supposed to solve.

The response of the architect to a given problem takes place in the realm of form. Faced with the objective description of the design task (a single family house in the countryside, an office building in front of a public square in an historical district, the design of an exhibition) the architect 'invents' (or reinvents) the problem in order to bring it into a territory in which he can handle it according to his own skills. Once a design problem has entered the territory of individual forms, formal solutions to the problems are created. From that moment, the search for the solution of a problem is mixed with the search for the internal order of the forms.

A computer tool should be able to increase the awareness of the architect about the boundaries between the two worlds, context and form, where design takes place. The representation of the context does not necessarily have to occur in the realm of form. A computer tool could maintain separate representations of the context and the form and make the architect aware of the possible links between them. A project developed for the CAAD Futures '91 exhibition will be used to illustrate the dynamic interaction between form and context in the process of design.

Design as the Interplay of Systems: A Project for an Exhibition

This exhibit, conceived of as part of the CAAD Futures' 91 conference, is the expression of the ideas developed for the courses of the CAAD Lehrstuhl at the ETH in Zürich. The exhibition was to be located in the lobby of the Department of Architecture at the ETH, a residual space where multiple paths to different parts of the building intersect.

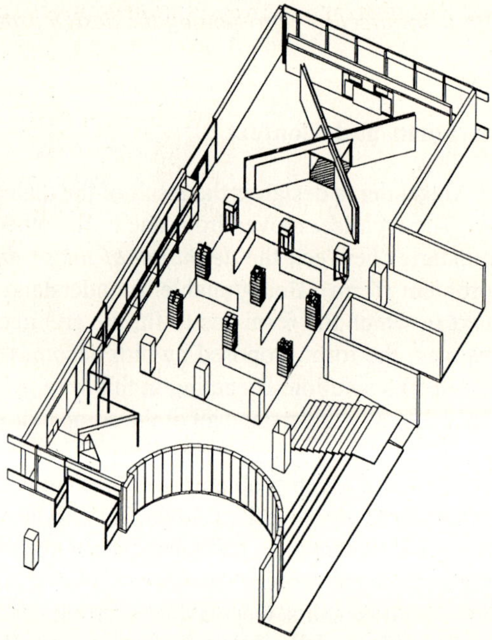

Figure 14. First proposal for the CAAD Futures '91 exhibition. Project by Leandro Madrazo.

As a response to the partitioned character of the space, different systems of elements were introduced that could accommodate the areas delimited by the existing circulation patterns. Figure 14 shows the four basic systems of the design: a 3x4 arrangement of 'columns', a 'portico', a 'cross' and a system of transparent 'panels' hung from the ceiling.

The part of the project that will be used to illustrate the dynamic interaction of context and form in the process of design is the one that deals with the relationship between the system of the 'cross' and the system of the 'columns'. The system of the columns is the materialization of the concepts of design vocabulary and levels of detail that were described in the first part of this paper. The cross divides the end of the room into four spaces, two of which are designed for viewing slides projected on the walls of the room from projection shelves located in the upper part of the center of the cross.

The system of the columns has some well-defined properties. The columns start out as simple boxes. In the second row they acquire the classic decomposition of base, shaft and capital. In the third row, the detailing of the joints and the capitals is more refined. In the last row, however, the columns no longer represent an increase in the level of detailing. The reasoning behind this is that, at that point, the system of columns starts to interact with the system of the cross (Figure 14).

Working at the level of the context, following Alexander's terms, an important consideration was that a visitor moving within the system of columns should perceive the last row as a threshold to the system of the cross. Thus, rather than keeping the criteria of increasing the level of detail for each successive row, the last columns became more transparent, as a way of creating a transition from the column system to the cross system. Formal solutions to the contextual problem 'make a transparent row of columns to mark a threshold with the next system' are numerous. Figure 15 shows two of the alternatives considered.

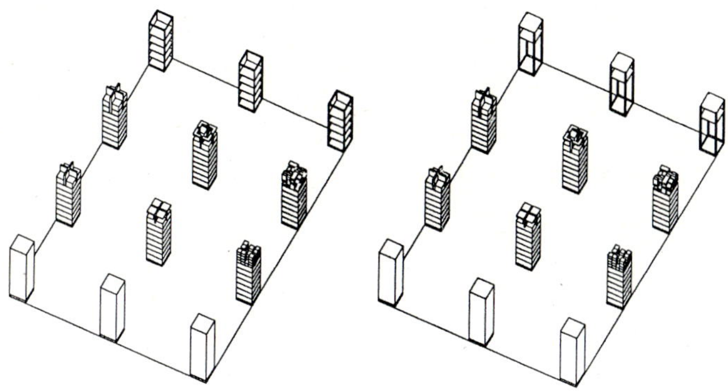

Figure 15. Two formal solutions for the last row of columns.

Other alternatives are possible if, instead of focusing on the geometric characteristics of the columns, the material of the columns is considered. For example, by using glass the columns could remain transparent while at the same time maintaining a progression in the level of detail. The final option transfers some of the geometric attributes of the 'cross' to the columns. Thus, the cross-shape is also reflected in the base and shaft of the columns in the last row (Figure 16).

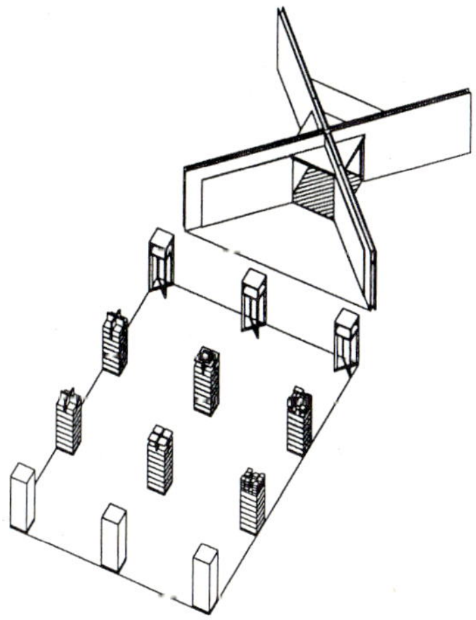

Figure 16. The interaction between the systems of the cross and the columns.

A similar reasoning is behind the formal definition of the 'portico'. Initially, the portico ran parallel to the wall in order to create an intermediate space between the two existing columns, the room and the wall (Figure 14). A relationship was established between the portico and the main entrance to the lobby, which is also the main entrance of the exhibit space. The portico was to grow towards this 'gate' as though being attracted by it. On its way towards the gate, the portico breaks away from the wall, finds an equilibrium and confronts the gate at a 45 degrees angle. The recognition of the gate as an element of the problem is, in this case, part of the context. The portico itself is the system in the design which specifically responds to that contextual problem.

The computer tool used for this simple design was a standard three-dimensional modeling program. The articulation of the design thinking occurred using only the tools that were developed for the course described earlier (the INSTANTIATION menu for instance, was used to modify the levels of detail in the column system). At this point it is interesting to consider what would be the characteristics of the optimal computer-aided design system, for this type of design strategy.

An ideal system for this design problem would have to be able to create a representation of the problems discovered at the level of the context (for example, the representation of the condition 'make a threshold'). Then, the different formal solutions given to that condition would have been recognized in relationship with the representation of the context. In this example, the formal answers to the contextual condition 'make a threshold' were three different formal solutions for the columns (excluding the possibility to making them out of glass, which was discarded as impractical in terms of the budget).

Also, the computer tool should be able to maintain a description of the attributes of every system of elements. This way would have enabled one to transfer attributes from elements and/or systems of elements inter alia, in much the same way that the geometric attribute of the cross was applied to the last row of columns to express the interaction between the system of the cross and the system of the columns.

If such a reasoning could be articulated with a computer tool, then it would be possible to claim that design is taking place within the computer environment. It would be the design process itself that is captured in the computer. The representation of the design using the computer can then allow one to have access to that structure that Sutherland recognized as the genuine value of computer representation.

Design as the Interplay of Systems: A Course in Design Strategies

The implementation of new design representations made possible by computer tools will require architects to create or adopt certain design strategies in order to make effective use of the new tools for design. Thinking of design as the interplay between systems is one of many strategies that could be explicitly supported by future computer tools. In a separate course, a design strategy was introduced based on the interplay of systems, similar to that used to the design the exhibition space described above.

The four systems that the course focused on were: structure, circulation, interior space and exterior enclosure. After an introductory exercise dealing with massing studies, the volumes of the preliminary design were replaced by structural elements made up of columns, porticos and/or walls. The circulation elements were considered next, including among others: stairs, ramps and corridors. Figure 17 shows an intermediate stage of a student project in which the connection between the different circulation elements and the structural frame were of primary concern.

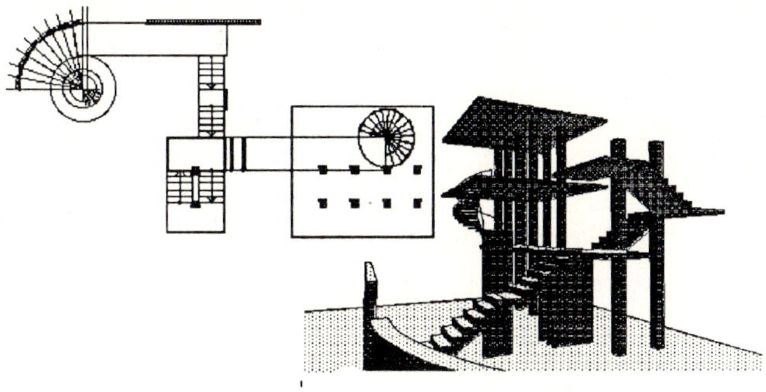

Figure 17. Creating a scheme with the structure and circulation systems. Project by Thomas Kaempfer.

The next stage in the process was to consider the interior spaces that were implicated by the earlier schemes that focused on the structural and circulation systems. Figure 18 illustrates two different spatial compositions by the same student, generated around the scheme that he had developed during the previous exercises. In figure (a) the stair-ramp is enclosed in a new space that becomes a pavilion and other spaces adjacent to the spiral stair (which intersected the rhythm of the structural system) were also defined. In the second example, figure (b), a different approach was taken. Two spaces, one with a square plan and another with a curvilinear wall were located along the spine created by the structural frame.

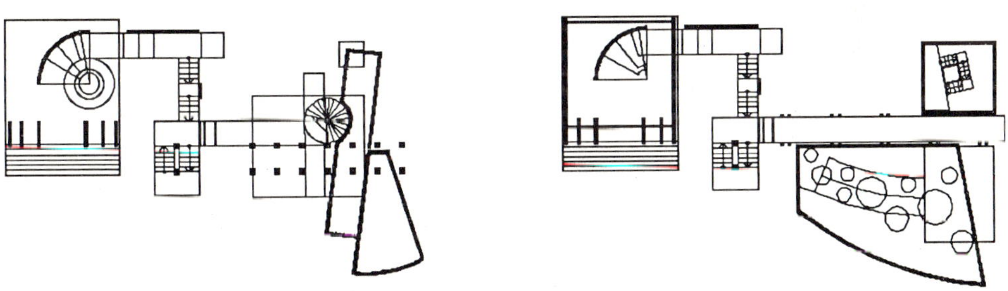

Figure 18. Two different approaches for creating the interior spaces based on the structural and circulation systems.

The quality of the spaces that were being created needed to be taken into account at this stage. Inside the space defined by the curvilinear wall, for example, a relationship between the round openings in the ceiling and the ramp was established (Figure 19). Issues such as light penetration began to be taken into account.

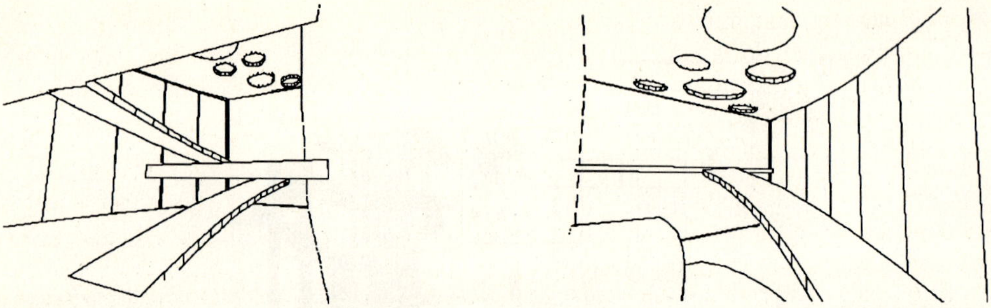

Figure 19. The relationship between the ramp and the openings in the ceiling that allow light to penetrate into the space.

The last stage of this proposed strategy was to look at the building from the outside (Figure 20). The exercise focused on how the existing systems were to be expressed on the outside of the building. In this student project, the pattern of openings cut into the ceiling slab reflect the stair-ramp below. Similarly, a portico was added on the exterior of the curvilinear wall and the tower was given some sculptural characteristics by adding of a balcony and stairs to its top.

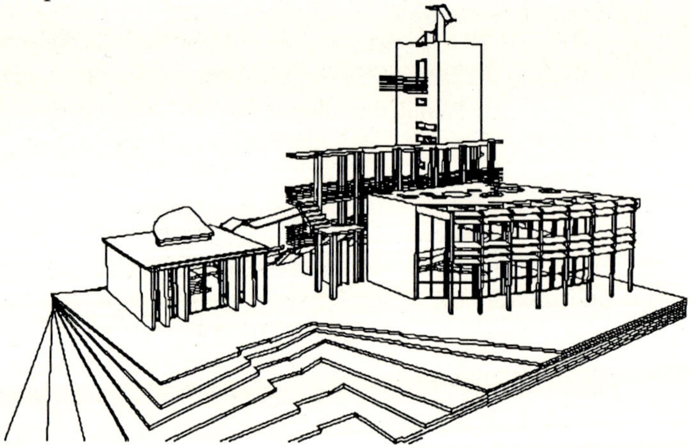

Figure 20. The design continues focusing on the exterior of the building.

Considering design as the interplay between systems gave the students an opportunity to better understand the design logic that was governing the design process. The students were aware of the properties of every system as well as the role of each system in the overall definition of the design.

When a new system was introduced to the design the critical issues included not only the issues specific to the new system, but also how to define the character of the interrelationships between the new and the existing systems, as well as those between all of the systems and the contextual conditions established by the students. As a result of the interaction between systems, hierarchies were established which helped to determine the role of every part within the whole.

By approaching design in this way, we were purposely breaking with some of the conventions of traditional design studios in order to offer students the opportunity to freely explore architectural issues in a context which is unique to computers. The students gained a solid background about some basic principles involving architectural design, which can then be extrapolated upon and used for more 'realistic' design problems.

Conclusions

In order to set up an agenda for the education of design with computers it is necessary to put the current stage of development in this field into context. At the moment, there is little justification for the use of computers in design if we consider the capabilities of the current systems alone. On the other hand, it is precisely the absence of a clear role for computers in design that has become the driving force behind continuous research in the field. The ideas expressed in this paper are meant to contribute to that research.

In the context of a professional program in an architecture school, a main objective for educators involved with teaching design with computers is to break the barriers that cause the subject to be treated as a specialization, closed or even unrelated to other areas of the curriculum. The ultimate validity of ideas developed around the use of computers in design can only be tested when the issues involved become a part of the general architectural debate that occurs in schools of architecture. Along this line, our goal is to use computers as a platform from which a different understanding about architectural issues can emerge.

Acknowledgements

The two courses described here took place in the CAAD Lehrstuhl chaired by Gerhard Schmitt. The programming of the new tools for the course on design representations was the combined work of Hans Uli Matter, Sharon Refvem, Annelies Zeidler and Leandro Madrazo. The design and programming of the instantiation functions was the work of Bharat Dave and Earl Mark. The implementation of the environment and interfaces for the new tools was done by Annelies Zeidler. Additional support was provided by Chen-Cheng Chen and Shen-Guan Shih. My special thanks to Sharon Refvem and Gerhard Schmitt for their many suggestions in writing this paper.

References

Alberti, Leon Battista. [1452] 1988. *On the Art of Building in Ten Books*. Trans. Joseph Rykwert, Neil Leach and Robert Tavernor. Cambridge, Mass.: The MIT Press.

Alexander, Christopher. 1964. *Notes on the Synthesis of Form*. Cambridge, Mass.: Harvard University Press.

Le Corbusier. 1923. *Vers une architecture*. Paris: Les Editions G. Crès et cie.

Madrazo, Leandro. 1991. "Designing with Computers." In *ARECDAO 91* 3d International Symposium on Computer Aided Design in Architecture and Civil Engineering. Barcelona.

Schmitt, Gerhard. 1990. "Classes of Design-Classes of Tools." In Malcolm McCullough, William J. Mitchell and Patrick Purcell (eds.). *The Electronic Design Studio.* Cambridge, Mass.: MIT Press.

Sutherland, Ivan. 1975. "Structure in Drawings and the Hidden-Surface Problem." In Nicholas Negroponte (ed.). *Reflections on Computer Aids to Design and Architecture.* New York: Petrocelli/Charter.

Simon, Herbert. 1969. *The Sciences of the Artificial.* Cambridge, Mass.: MIT Press.

6 Imagining Light: A Visualization of Daylighting Data

Brian Sumption, Bruce Haglund, Alexander Zabrodsky

Department of Architecture
University of Idaho
Moscow, Idaho 83843 U.S.A.

The task of designing effective lighting for buildings requires both artistic and technical competence. In this way it is archetypical of the discipline of architectural design. The interaction of buildings with solar lighting is complex and ever-changing. Added complexity comes with the use of electric lights and their daylight-sensitive control systems. State-of-the-art daylight prediction tools most often provide precision data that is in obscure numerical formats hindering the communication and perception of information hidden within. We are exploring the use of scientific visualization to transform incomprehensible tables of data into images that visually oriented designers will find more accessible. By representing lighting data and their interactions with the environment visually, students and design professionals may be able to "imagine the light" in ways that will help them understand and solve complex lighting design problems.

Introduction

We are concerned with teaching architecture students to design effective lighting with skill and confidence. There are, however, several obstacles to the goal, all related to understanding the complex interactions between the light, the building components, its occupants, and the environment. As architects move through the design process, models of how the lighting will eventually perform in the physical world evolve in the mind's eye. The confidence a designer may have in the validity of these models is to a great extent dependent upon the strategies and tools that are brought to bear on the problem. The state-of-the-art suggests that there are three major approaches to the complex problem of predicting and understanding daylights interactions with buildings: physical models, CAD-based luminance renderings and computer lighting predictors. Both the physical models and luminance renderings can be very effective at providing both artistic and technical insights into daylighting design that can inform the designer. For both, research and development of methodologies has proceeded in a timely manner with significant improvements that aid the designer. Nonetheless, neither methodology is always the ideal. For example, physical models are expensive, time-consuming, and may not give accurate insights into seasonal variances in lighting. A ray tracing rendering program can make very useful images of the effects of lighting, but these are incredibly time-consuming and do not indicate the dynamic nature of light easily. We have recognized the potential of computerized daylight level predictors to fill some of these niches, in spite the fact that presently even the best of them, SUPERLITE, poses some severe liabilities.

The primary problem with SUPERLITE, and most other programs of its kind, is one of making its numerically formatted output more useful to students and designers. Our approach to solving this problem is to apply the principles of scientific visualization to the transformation of output from, otherwise excellent, research tools such as SUPERLITE. By designing appropriate visualizations, the data can be represented in a manner that offers the possibility of giving valuable insight into lighting problems obtainable in perhaps no other way.

The Image of Light

Our efforts center on presenting information about lighting in a medium that will stimulate students' imaginations regarding the relationship between light and space. The luminance rendering tools contain algorithms aimed at the realistic rendition of model surfaces. Simple, flat shading to ray tracing and bump mapping techniques provide a palette which fits the needs of most applications requiring a static understanding of the visual impact of light on a space. As compelling and realistic as the images may be, they still lack many of the dynamic attributes that we deem important. We have chosen to focus on developing visualization techniques which represent light as a natural, dynamic phenomenon that fills a space. When examined in the context of a specific environment, the visualization may reveal patterns or behaviors that are insightful to the student's understanding of the nature of light and space.

The first visualization we designed, LIGHTSCAPES, stressed the idea of light being distributed throughout a space. Standard practice for daylighting and electric lighting calls for lighting levels to be measured at gridded intervals at the work-plane level within the room (figure 1). A multidimensional, mathematical model was chosen to represent the light levels within the room: the x- and y-axes represent the length and width of the room, the z-axis represents the intensity of the illumination. The color and opacity of the model represents the source of the light and reinforces the representation of intensity, and finally, time is represented through animation. This model produces a multicolored spline mesh that hovers and moves within the space. To test this construct we generated a case study of the Farm Credit Bank building in Spokane, Washington. Design features of the facility were used in conjunction with the prediction tool, SUPERLITE, to determine natural lighting conditions within the building with respect to various outside lighting situations.

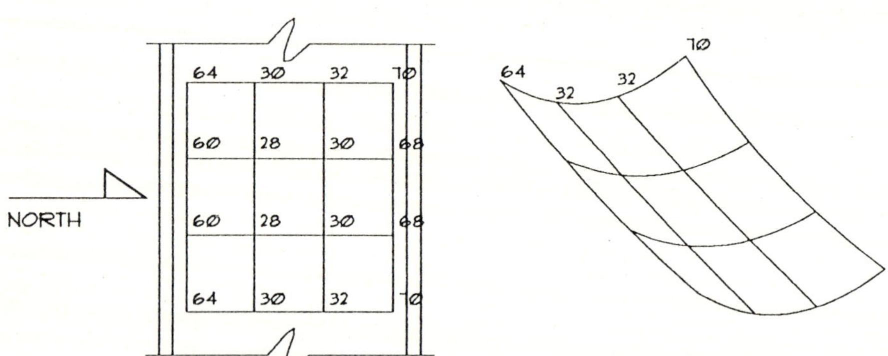

Figure 1. Gridded daylight measurement in plan transformed into three-dimensional spline mesh.

"SUPERLITE, developed by Lawrence Berkeley Laboratory (LBL), can analyze complex room and light source geometries with great precision. SUPERLITE models the effects of both direct and defuse or reflected sunlight. Running time varies with the complexity of the room and external obstructions. Operation of the program is not for the faint-hearted computer novice: Entries must be made item-by-item with a text editor, and the results are a tabular display of numbers. It is useful primarily to researchers and lighting designers who need detailed daylighting analysis."(Lord 1990).

This assessment accurately portrays SUTERLITE as a fine source of technical data, accurately predicting daylight levels at grid points within a space. Unmentioned are the potential advantages it has over physical models and CAD-based luminance renderings. The primary advantage is that a single run of the PC-based version of SUPERLITE takes a few minutes compared to the hours required for a physical model or a single luminance rendering. Moreover, SUPERLITE can be run parametrically to generate data for a typical day or a typical year under different sky conditions or different quality of light can be quickly generated. However, the problem of data representation remains.

Once the lighting conditions data was obtained from SUPERLITE, it was translated into the model parameters of position, color, opacity, and texture in order to isolate important data features. This transformed data was then used to generate both static and dynamic images through the use of rendering and animation software (figure 2). In the case of the animations, time frames were compressed to allow daily or annual interactions to be viewed in a short time.

Producing the Image

The creation of the visualization is comprised of three distinct phases: data generation, data transformation, and image generation.

The data generation phase consists of two discreet processes: creating a computerized image of the building using a CAD system and generating lighting data using the lighting prediction program, SUPERLITE. Pertinent building characteristics, such as geometry and orientation, were defined and encoded using a CAD program. This CAD-generated image was used primarily to establish a visual frame of reference for lighting images.

Data describing building surface material properties such as color, reflectivity, and transmission values, as well as environmental settings that defined latitude, time and date, and sky conditions (such as clear or overcast) were assembled into an input file to provide the contextual world in which light would be modeled. Using this file SUPERLITE was then run parametrically as the predictive tool to generate hourly mathematical descriptions of specific lighting conditions for both clear and cloudy days for each month of the year. Each of these descriptions consists of large tabular arrays of daylighting information including position (x, y), magnitude (illuminance, z), and time and sky condition. We wrote a program to calculate electric lighting levels by "sensing" the daylight levels predicted by SUPERLITE and applying the electric lighting control algorithm used in the building to the electric light level prediction data supplied by the lamp manufacturer. Both electric light levels and composite (electric plus daylight) levels were obtained for each time and position in the parametric SUPERLITE runs. SUPERLITE itself has no method of combining electric and natural lighting levels.

Figure 2 . Illuminance levels, typical floor of Farm Credit Building.

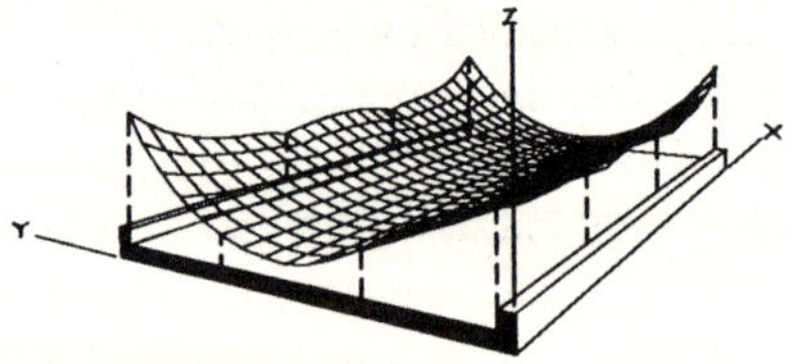

Figure 3. Spline mesh suspended above building platform.

In the data transformation phase lighting data were converted from tabular form to a multidimensional model. We wrote transfer functions to relate the dynamic range of scalar lighting data to image attributes. To create a nonrigid spline mesh to image the lighting data, "x" and "y" coordinates defining the mesh were assigned positional values associated with each datum position in the room. this provided a consistent referencing platform corresponding to the CAD image, upon which additional attributes could be related in a meaningful way. As an example, the mesh's "z" coordinates were given a scalar lighting value in footcandle units. This resulted in an illumination "topography" relating intensity of illumination to the floor plan (figure 3). In addition, each of the vertices of the mesh was assigned a color value to help isolate and reveal patterns and features contained within the data. Color maps were used to reinforce topographic patterns in the surface by associating a color ramp through a look-up table to scalar "z" coordinate data. This is analogous to color-coded topography maps. The color mapping of vertices was also used to indicate the source and character of light. In our case, which is bilaterally sidelighted from the north and the south, we assigned a color ramp from yellow (intense light) to lavender grey (subdued) for south light, and from blue (intense) to lavender grey (subdued) for north light. For electric lighting we assigned a constant light grey. Differences in incandescent, florescent, north and south daylighting color temperatures can be distinguished in this manner.

Transparency values were also assigned to individual mesh surfaces at this time. These modeling attributes were primarily used to allow viewing of overlaying meshes after the rendering sequence. In the Farm Credit Bank study three separate models were created. They represent the independent contributions of electric and daylighting illumination sources and the composite effect of these two sources. By use of transparency values the three meshes could be viewed simultaneously as well as separately (figure 4). The daylighting mesh was assigned a transparency value which would produce an opaque surface to reinforce its importance in our mind's eye. When the electric light was modeled, a grey, highly transparent color value was assigned uniformly, and the composite light, while using the same color ramp as the daylight, was also given a high degree of transparency in order to hover cloud-like above the daylight model's surface. Similarly, recommended illumination levels can be modeled as planes within the space to establish visual thresholds (viewed with the lighting data) against which building performance can be evaluated.

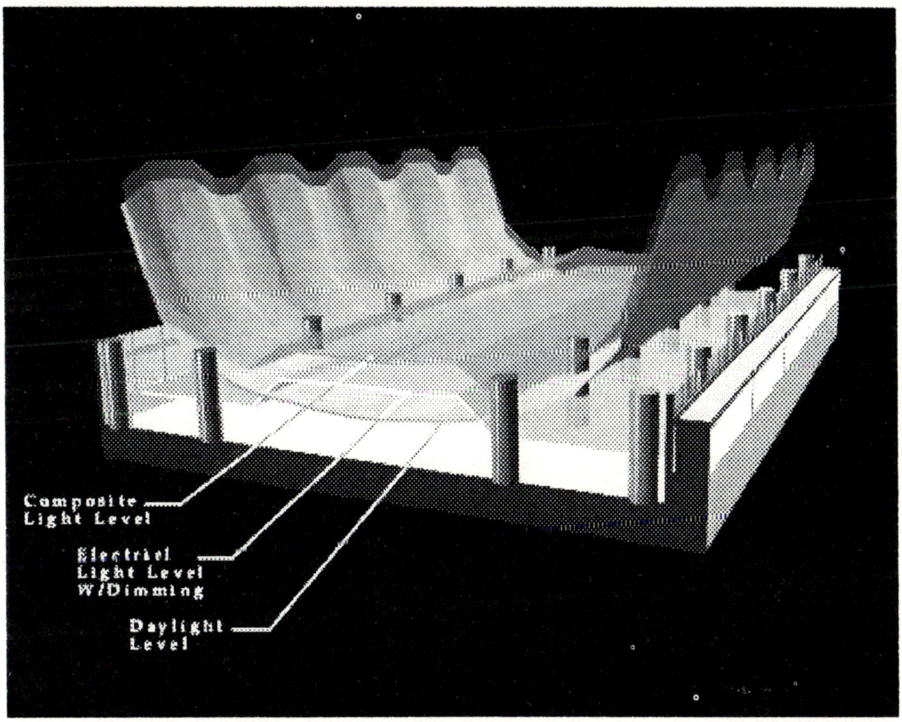

Figure 4. Three lighting meshes viewed simultaneously.

The image generation phase consisted of writing a simple program to translate the data describing the lighting meshes into a file format that was acceptable to a solid modeling program. The CAD-generated model of the building was imported and merged with the lighting model and production variables were created that would allow for the greatest opportunity to see and understand the nature of the daylighting and its interaction within the architectural space. Individual images were assembled into animations to simulate a broader contextual understanding of events (figure 5). For example, animating the surfaces to illustrate daily and seasonal cycles has allowed us to compress greater quantities of data into short time frames which conversely expands information comprehension potential. While this potential is attractive, the computational horsepower required to generate the imagery remains a bottleneck that slows the process of creating high quality images.

Conclusion

At present, each of the three steps of the visualization process is computationally intensive and is run in a noninteractive batch processing mode. It takes patience and skill to create the image, however, the resulting five-dimensional model (x,y position, intensity, time, and source) give a satisfying image of light's complex interactions. The time investment for obtaining this dynamic image is comparable to the physical and luminance rendering techniques. We look forward to the reality of affordable real-time simulation where the average student and designer working on average projects will "pilot" the course of simulations, responding to the dynamics of the situation as they occur. In the interim we are working on incorporating our case studies into Digital Video Interactive (DVI) and Hypercard Technologies and writing general programs so the transformation phase can be accomplished for any existing or imagined building with less effort. The integrated media environments that these technologies present will be both familiar and satisfying as a learning tool for architecturally trained individuals.

Our work has also raised questions that require further investigation. Are there other visualizations that can provide a more satisfying image? We have begun this investigation with a series of visualizations based upon the fact that SUPERLITE can be run parametrically at different work plane levels generating a 3-dimensionally uniform grid of sample data. A number of different transformation functions are being applied to this data to visually extract information about the behavior of light in a space. For example, there are usually constant intensity surfaces embedded in the 3-dimensional scalar data that can be imaged as triangulated spline mesh in much the same way as the previous data was modeled and displayed. To examine the behavior of a range of values within a space a number of options are available. The 3-dimensional scalar data can be seen as a stack of cross-sections normal to any useful axis. Fore-plane clipping can reveal interior sections as topological surfaces. Homotopy, or the metamorphosis from one topological surface to another can be performed by passing the clip plane through the space to examine changes across the volume or the section can remain at one location while lighting or design parameters are altered. Finally, vertices of this 3-dimensional grid can be tested against a variety of variables, such as light levels or visual comfort. Points that meet or fail to meet the test criteria can be assembled into bounded volumes that occupy space. These solids can then be examined across time or condition or further edited with peeling or slicing functions.

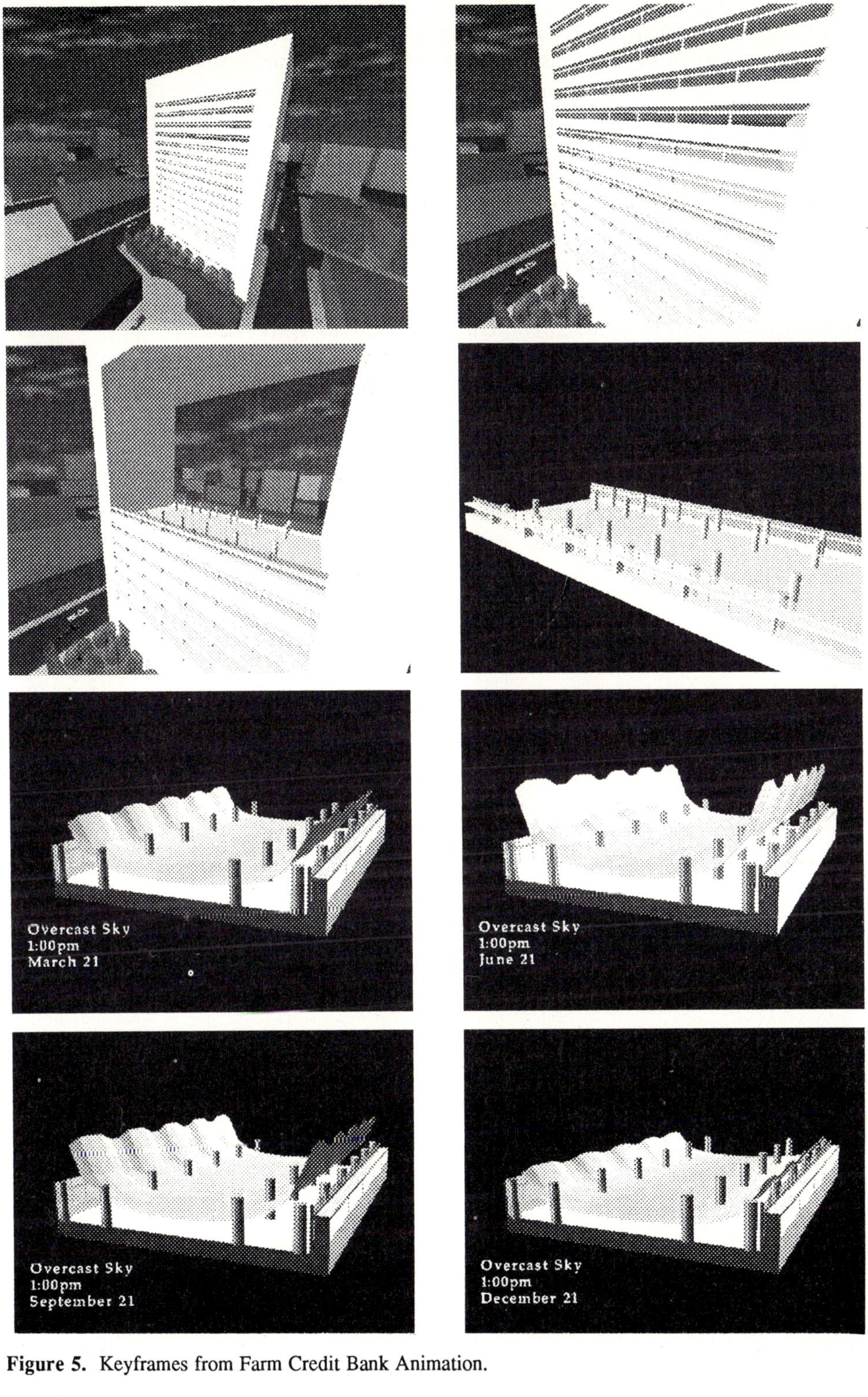

Figure 5. Keyframes from Farm Credit Bank Animation.

These models could provide qualitative views of lighting interactions while the current model primarily provides a quantitative overview of these interactions. We anticipate that the visualization techniques we've used can be applied to other facets of architectural design, since lighting design is archetypical for the discipline of architectural design.

References

Buser, P., B. Radic, and K. Semmler. 1990. "Surface Visualization." In D. Thalmann (ed.). *Scientific Visualization and Graphic simulation*. Wiley & Sons Ltd.

Cox, D. 1990. "The Art of Scientific Visualization." *Academic Computing,* no. 3: 21-24.

Lord, D. 1990. "Computer Aided Lighting." *Progressive Architecture,* no. 11: 126-127.

Milne, M., and T. Labib. 1990. "Tools for Designing Climate Responsive Buildings." In J. Jordan (ed.). *ACADIA 90*. Montana: State University.

7 A Stratified Approach to the Integration of Low Cost Modeling with Advanced Technology Rendering

Robin Liggett, William Jepson, Stephen Teodosiadis

Graduate School of Architecture and Urban Planning
University of California, Los Angeles
Los Angeles, California 90024, U.S.A.

This paper presents a stratified approach to the integration of low cost modeling software (such as AutoCAD) with advanced workstation based rendering systems (such as Wavefront and the Silicon Graphics radiosity renderer). Powerful extensions to the basic modeling system are introduced which greatly reduce the required design effort, while significantly increasing the efficiency of the rendering software.

Introduction

The technology for producing high resolution shaded perspective images and real-time simulated movement through complex scenes is now becoming available within a reasonable price range. Unfortunately such systems are still at the high end of the cost spectrum for computer aided design workstations.

In most cases the sophisticated visualization packages which utilize advanced workstation technology do not include a well developed or comprehensive framework for the creation and management of the 3-dimensional models which are to be rendered. Rather they operate with a simple geometric modeler supplied with the renderer or on geometric databases extracted from other CAD packages. While rendering images can be a time consuming process in terms of machine computation this process can be executed, overnight or as a background task during the day, with little or no human input. The modeling process, however, is time consuming both in terms of person hours as well as in workstation utilization (terminal hours). Models that are to be rendered must also conform to certain requirements if the rendering and lighting models are to work correctly and efficiently.

Ideally, one would like to be able to model effectively on low end (and low cost) machines using industry standard CAD software packages in order to leverage the knowledge and dollar investment which is required for rendering and animation. A designer should be able to easily develop a model on these inexpensive machines, while ensuring that the model developed is in a form compatible with the more expensive and sophisticated rendering systems.

This paper presents the strategy developed at UCLA for combining these two levels of technology. AutoCAD has been selected as the modeling package and Silicon Graphics' radiosity renderer is being utilized as the highend visualization package. The integration of the two packages is accomplished by an intelligent database conversion program. It operates on a DXF file to translate a 3-dimensional AutoCAD model to the form required for efficient rendering by the radiosity renderer. This conversion program is cognizant of the unique requirements which must be met for the radiosity renderer to operate in an optimal fashion. In order to enhance the ability of the designer to model in an efficient and natural way a set of predefined blocks, which make it very easy to build up a coherent 3-d model, have been provided within AutoCAD. These predefined blocks allow the designer to utilize his/her AutoCAD knowledge base to minimize effort by following a simple set of modeling guidelines.

This paper will discuss the requirements of the visualization system, how the translator prepares the data, and the modeling process which provides not only an efficient way to generate a 3-d model of a building (with attributes of color and material) but is able to transparently (to the designer) translate the building data base into the form required by the visualization system.

Rendering Packages

There are currently a number of rendering packages available on the market. These range from personal computer based packages such as AutoShade to sophisticated renderers available on high-speed workstations, e.g. Wavefront.

Differences between rendering packages encompass a wide range of issues such as types of shading algorithms, accuracy of lighting models and "real-time walk-through" capabilities. These issues impact directly the computation and data base requirements of the models.

The simplest type of renderer is one which produces a flat shaded polygonal representation of a scene such as AutoShade. Objects displayed in this manner will be rendered using a simple cosine shading approach and will appear faceted to the observer.

The Wavefront renderer also operates on a polygonal database, but allows faces to be combined into what are called smoothing groups. Interpolation techniques are then used to achieve the desired smooth shaded appearance. Two popular forms of shading are Gouraud and Phong shading. Gouraud shading uses a linear interpolation of the values at the vertices of the polygons. Phong shading interpolates the surface normals using a cosine based approximation to get a smoother appearance as well as more convincing specular highlights.

The basic Wavefront renderer is not intended to produce a quantitatively exact lighting model, rather it utilizes quick "rule-of-thumb" calculations to efficiently simulate environmental effects (i.e. lighting effects) such as specular highlights and reflections. These estimates are based upon what is known as "local illumination", i.e. light that comes directly from the light source to the point being rendered (Foley et al. 1990). The interreflection of light, particularly between diffusely reflecting surfaces is approximated with a single ambient light parameter which is applied equally to all surfaces in this type of lighting model.

In contrast, a "global illumination" model computes the color at a point in terms of light directly emitted by light sources and of light that is indirectly reflected and transmitted (Foley et al. 1990). Two global illumination models which use almost opposite approaches to generating an image are ray-tracing and radiosity. Ray-tracing techniques are only concerned with light that enters the viewer's eye. It calculates specular effects and reflection and is particularly appropriate for environments that contain highly reflective surfaces. Radiosity, in contrast, is concerned with the interreflection of light throughout a scene and is best suited to environments containing mostly matte surfaces (Greenberg 1991).

Radiosity renderers, which are based on thermal-engineering models for the emission and reflection of radiation, assume the conservation of light energy in a closed environment. All energy emitted or reflected by each surface is accounted for by its reflection from or absorption by other surfaces. The rate at which energy leaves a surface, called its "radiosity", is the sum of the rates at which the surface emits energy and reflects or transmits it from that surface or other surfaces (Foley et al. 1990).

Figure 1. Silicon Graphics radiosity rendering, model courtesy of Dr. Fred Brooks, UNC Chapel Hill.

One basic difference you will see between a single frame created by a renderer using a "local illumination model" and one generated by a "global illumination model" is the effect of shadows. The local illumination renderer will create hard-line shadows as the light sources are defined as points. A global illumination model creates soft shadows as area light sources can be defined and reflections of all surfaces are considered. Figures 1 and 2 illustrate the realistic lighting effects achieved by the radiosity method of rendering.

A major advantage (for most architectural applications) of the radiosity model when compared to other types of illumination models is that radiosity determines all light interactions in an environment in a "view-independent" way. Once the luminosity on each surface has been calculated the model is invariant to shift in view. Views can be rendered in real-time (if using a sufficiently powerful workstation), allowing dynamic sequences to be shown.

Recalculations are only needed if the positions of the light sources are changed (or changes are made to the geometry or the surface materials of the model).

Figure 2. Silicon Graphics radiosity rendering, design by Marc Mack Architects, model courtesy of Charles Ehrlich, U.C. Berkeley.

The ideal imaging system would employ a combination of radiosity and ray-tracing techniques. The radiosity model would be used to create the illumination model to light the environment and then ray-tracing would be employed in real-time to render shiny surfaces. This would be possible by making use of advanced multi-processor workstations which are now becoming increasingly popular. These sophisticated workstations are capable of supporting two or more tightly coupled processors each working independently. For example, with a two processor workstation one processor can be used to cull the database, throwing out facets that are not in view, while the other processor is used to render the remaining data. Additional processors could be used to ray-trace, in real-time, any reflective surfaces or to provide additional culling capabilities for display.

Interface Between Modeler and Renderer

While some rendering packages are closely coupled with a CAD package that can be used for the 3-dimensional modeling task (e.g. AutoCAD-AutoShade), most rendering systems do not include a well-developed or comprehensive framework for 3-d modeling. They rely on geometric data bases that are extracted from other CAD systems. Since a rendering system has its own input data requirements, some sort of translator is generally needed to interpret the 3-d data·base into the form needed by the renderer.

RenderMan, for example, is a specification for an interface between a modeler and a rendering package that would allow a 3-dimensional modeling system to pass a scene description to a renderer. It is intended to provide all modelers access to the same rendering solution (Upstill 1989). Renderman specifies conventions for a set of C-callable functions that will accept data in a particular format from the modeler and then translate it into the form required by the specific renderer. Thus each rendering system would modify the contents of the functions to transform data into its particular internal format. On the other side, the modeler needs to invoke these functions, providing the 3-d data in the appropriate form.

All renderers require a description of each surface of the 3-d model which is to be viewed. These surfaces have to be defined according to conventions that indicate which direction the surface normal is pointing (i.e. which way the surface is oriented). In architectural models most surfaces represent the exteriors of solid objects such as walls or of closed rectangular parallelepipeds such as mullions. In these cases the interior surfaces of the objects being modeled are never seen. For efficient operation of the renderer, the interior surfaces (surfaces may be one or two sided) should not be included in the database passed to the renderer. Thus a problem arises. If the 3-d modeler does not follow the correct conventions (particular to each renderer) when modeling, the renderer will be unable to determine the appropriate orientation of the surface (normal direction) and both sides of the surface will then need to be rendered. This can increase the number of surfaces in the model significantly (in many cases it will double the number of polygons in the model).

The simplest type of interface places the burden of providing the data in the appropriate form on the modeler. It requires the modeler to operate in a coherent fashion (i.e. create the model from 3-d surfaces which are defined in a very specific way). For many simple modelers (e.g. AutoCAD) the ability to orient some single sided surfaces in arbitrary directions is either non-existent or it is extremely difficult. The alternative is to create a very inefficient database for the renderer in which both faces of each surface are defined, or to attempt to reorient each surface by editing the database in the renderer. The latter approach, which is taken by the existing translator between AutoCAD and Wavefront, requires the user to interactively specify which direction each surface normal is pointed before rendering. While this capability is useful for specifying the normal direction for a few non-conventional surfaces, it is far too tedious a process to apply routinely to all surfaces. Additionally, since this process happens after translation has occurred the changes made to the database are not transferred back to the modeler and must be reapplied each time the translation takes place.

At the other extreme, one could let the modeler work in any manner desired and leave it to an intelligent translator to convert the model to the form required by the rendering package. While this leaves the greatest degree of freedom for the modeler it isn't necessarily the most efficient approach. It is not possible, in many cases, for the translator to determine what was actually meant by the modeler.

We have opted for an approach which uses an intelligent translator to convert much of the model efficiently, so that requirements of the rendering system are transparent to the designer. In addition we provide an extension to the modeling system which should make it easier for the designer to create 3-d models, which can be intelligently translated.

Requirements of the Radiosity Renderer

We have selected a radiosity rendering package under development by Silicon Graphics Inc. (SGI) as the highend visualization package. Two main reasons for using this renderer are the accuracy of the lighting simulation model and the ability for real-time simulated movement through the scene. We expect, though, that models run through our translator could also be rendered by other packages (e.g. Wavefront).

The SGI radiosity package requires input in the Berkeley Unigrafix format. The Berkeley Unigrafix tools have been developed at U.C. Berkeley over the last several years by Professor Carlos H. Sequin and his students. The Unigrafix language specifies 3-dimensional polyhedral objects in terms of vertices and faces. A face is a planar polygon that may be concave and may have holes. A face is defined by listing a set of vertex names in a counter-clockwise fashion, so that the surface normal is defined as being oriented towards the viewer. Holes (termed voids) in faces are defined by a list of vertices which are specified in a clockwise fashion and are attached to a single face. Figure 3 shows the Unigrafix language specification for a simple face and void.

This method of representing faces and holes in faces is particularly well-suited to the radiosity renderer. To perform radiosity analysis, the environment is divided into discrete surface areas, or patches, for which a constant radiosity is assumed. The integral relationship over the environment is then approximated by a summation over the patches. A set of simultaneous equations can then be generated and solved to obtain the patch radiosities, thus describing the propagation of light energy within the environment (Cohen et al. 1986).

Patches are created by meshing (subdividing) the polygons of a model. The finer the mesh the more accurate and realistic the rendered image. However, computation time increases as the square of the number of discrete surface patches, thus effectively limiting the level of subdivision.

```
v v1  x1, y1, z1;
v v2  x2, y2, z2;
v v3  x3, y3, z3;
v v4  x4, y4, z4;
v v5  x5, y5, z5;
v v6  x6, y6, z6;
v v7  x7, y7, z7;
v v8  x8, y8, z8;

f f1 (v1,v2,v3,v4) (v5,v8,v7,v6) material;
        face            void
```

Figure 3. Berkeley Unigrafix Specification of Vertices, Faces and Voids.

The patches need not be of the same size, and the radiosity algorithm can be used to determine the most efficient meshing. The level of surface subdivision in an environment should reflect the radiosity gradients (changes in luminance). Large patches need to be subdivided only if the radiosity varies greatly across the surface causing illumination inaccuracies. Therefore, to improve image quality the areas of the surfaces with high radiosity gradients (such as shadow boundaries) must be subdivided into finer and finer grids of patches (Cohen et al 1986, 1988).

In order to optimize the implementation of such adaptive subdivision, it is necessary to begin with a model based on the largest possible surface patches. Therefore, defining a wall and window in terms of a surface and void in Unigrafix format is ideal for the radiosity meshing algorithms.

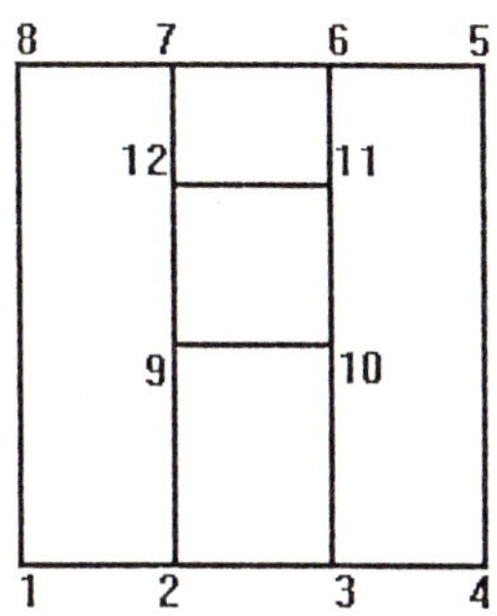


```
v v1  x1, y1, z1;
v v2  x2, y2, z2;
v v3  x3, y3, z3;
v v4  x4, y4, z4;
v v5  x5, y5, z5;
v v6  x6, y6, z6;
v v7  x 7, y7, z7;
v v8  x8, y8, z8;
v v9  x9, y9, z9;
v v10 x10, y10, z10;
v v11 x11, y11, z11;
v v12 x12, y12, z12;

f f1 (v1,v2,v7,v8)    material;
f f2 (v2,v3,v10,v9)   material;
f f3 (v12,v11,v6,v7)  material;
f f4 (v3,v4,v5,v6)    material;
```

Figure 4. Representing an Opening by Partitioning a Surface.

This is in contrast to the use of a renderer such as AutoShade which does not recognize the concept of a void. For these types of renderers an opening in a wall must be created by partitioning the wall into smaller polygons surrounding the opening (see figure 4). This will not adversely effect rendering techniques which apply linear interpolation between vertices to shade a polygon. However, this type of partitioning would constrain a radiosity model's ability to mesh the surface in a way which maximizes efficiency in computing luminosity.

The Berkeley Unigrafix format is also attractive from the modeling standpoint. Its use of definitions of graphic primitives and instances of these primitives closely follows our approach to modeling. This approach emphasizes the hierarchical development of a vocabulary of graphic elements which are instantiated by varying position and size parameters (Mitchell et al. 1987). Unigrafix primitive definitions can be used to pre-specify a set of efficient graphic elements. For example, the cubic cylinder shown in figure 5 is defined by specifying only the outer faces. This cube can be scaled and positioned in a variety of ways to model mullions, columns, etc., and provides an efficient element from the renderer's perspective.

Color and materials in the Unigrafix language can be described in terms of the RGB or the HSL (Hue, Saturation and Lightness) model. Colors can be assigned to primitives, instances of primitives or faces, giving maximum flexibility with regard to modeling techniques.

Lighting can be specified by defining specific point lights as well as surface or area light sources. The point lights are currently used only for preview lighting as the radiosity code does not recognize dimensionless entities. However, these lighting primitives can be interpreted in different ways for other rendering packages. The area light sources are the only radiosity lighting constructs. They are defined by attaching emission values to a geometrically defined surface, again giving a great deal of flexibility in lighting the environment.

Customizing the AutoCAD Modeling Environment

AutoCAD was selected as the modeling environment for a number of reasons. Its availability on low-cost machines and its large share of the current architecture CAD market made it particularly attractive. It is assumed that most architecture firms have access to a CAD system at the AutoCAD level. As an educational institution we needed to provide CAD access to many students. Thus a strategy of modeling on low-end systems, that have the ability feed a few high-end systems, is ideal given financial limitations. In addition, AutoCAD seems particularly useful due to the ease in which it can be modified to fit individual modeling needs. So even though our translator can interpret any 3-dimensional model built in AutoCAD, we have taken advantage of AutoCAD's open architecture to add a subset of modeling tools that can be used for efficient modeling with respect to the rendering process.

Since we are focusing on Architectural models we have chosen to take advantage of the ASG (formerly AEC) package's method of entering walls and windows. Modeling with ASG makes it particularly easy to enter walls of a building quickly with a number of options available for dealing with wall intersections. The use of ASG for entering walls is not required, however. Walls can be built using LINES, PLINES, or the new DOUBLE lines available in Version 11 by specifying a THICKNESS parameter. These entities will be interpreted in the same way as ASG walls. A key feature in our intelligent translator is the ability to identify all pairs of parallel surfaces that are within a specified distance (tolerance factor) of each other. By describing only the outer faces of these surfaces appropriately (in terms of the normal conventions of the radiosity model) the total number of surfaces in the model is significantly reduced (see figure 6).

Openings in a wall are modeled conveniently with ASG. The 3-d installation package should not be used, however, as it inserts the openings by partitioning the wall. A non-installed ASG window is just represented as a line with a position and thickness. The AutoCAD DXF file, then, contains a description of the wall as two lines with thickness and a window as a line with thickness. (Note, in both cases thickness represents the height of the entity). These are easily translated into the surface-void representation of the Unigrafix format.

Modeling walls as surfaces with voids for openings enhances the flexibility of the 3-d modeling process. If a wall has to be partitioned to represent an opening, and an opening is moved or the wall size is changed, the model may have to be significantly altered. Representing the wall as a single surface with openings, makes it easy to resize the wall without changing the openings, or alternatively to modify the openings without changing the wall.

This simple representation of an opening allows easy substitution from a library of more detailed openings that are available on a special window menu (see figure 7). By attaching an attribute to the simple opening representation, the actual substitution need not occur until the translation takes place to the Unigrafix format. While the more detailed model can be viewed in the rendered image, a simplified version of it is used during the modeling phase, significantly reducing the size of the data base AutoCAD must manage.

```
def cubic_cylinder;
        v v1  -0.5,  0.5, 1.0;
        v v2  -0.5,  0.5, 0.0;
        v v3   0.5,  0.5, 0.0;
        v v4   0.5,  0.5, 1.0;
        v v5   0.5, -0.5, 0.0;
        v v6   0.5, -0.5, 1.0;
        v v7  -0.5, -0.5, 0.0;
        v v8  -0.5, -0.5, 1.0;

        f f1  (v1,v2,v3,v4) material;
        f f2  (v4,v3,v5,v6) material;
        f f3  (v6,v5,v7,v8) material;
        f f4  (v8,v7,v2,v1) material;
end;

i (cubic_cylinder material -sx2 -sy2 -sz6 -tx20 -ty10 -rz30);
```

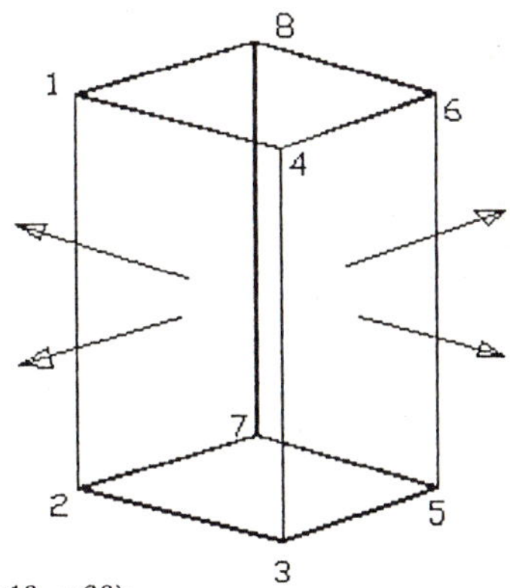

Figure 5. Definition of a Graphic Primitive in Berkeley Unigrafix Format.

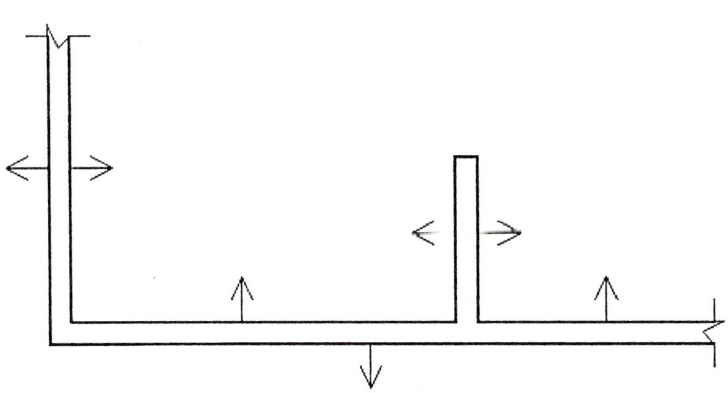

Figure 6. Description of Normals for Surfaces Interpreted as Walls.

The library of detailed 3-d openings can be expanded as the designer builds a vocabulary based upon a combination of a predefined set of openings and a custom set of openings which he/she has created. These custom openings can be generated from the set of efficient elements (provided on a special menu shown in figure 8) which are predefined. The elements are described as "efficient" with respect to the renderer's requirements but also provide significant efficiencies for AutoCAD due to their simplified representation in the overall model. Alternatively users can build their own blocks, following a set of recommendations for efficient modeling. In the worst case, the translator will interpret any model built by the user. However, a major goal of this project is to encourage and teach a particular style of modeling which we feel is efficient from both the modeling and rendering perspective.

All surfaces of a 3-d model are not necessarily modeled as walls. Surfaces can be created in AutoCAD via a number of primitives which include 3DFACE and POLYLINE. Surfaces created in this manner can be interpreted by the translator but may result in an inefficient representation (i.e. both sides defined) unless they fall into the special class of parallel surfaces discussed earlier.

The biggest problem encountered when working with AutoCAD is its internal representation of curved surfaces (which include tabulated surfaces, ruled surfaces, edge surfaces, and surfaces of revolution). Rather than store such a surface in terms of the equations of its defining curves, AutoCAD meshes the surface and stores it as a set of vertices (the original curve definitions are not available in the DXF file). This again constrains the radiosity renderer since knowledge of the defining curves can be used to mesh each surface in the most appropriate manner. It also results in a significantly enlarged geometric database as the coordinates for each facet must be stored. Until a more robust format for the three dimensional database definition is provided, we have to accept the meshing done internally by AutoCAD.

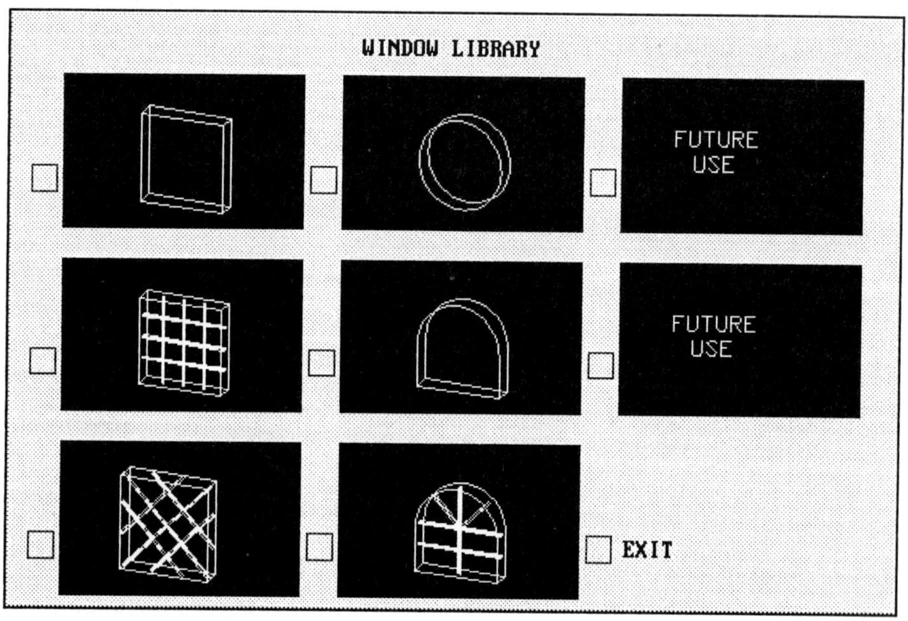

Figure 7. Menu Showing Library of 3-D Openings.

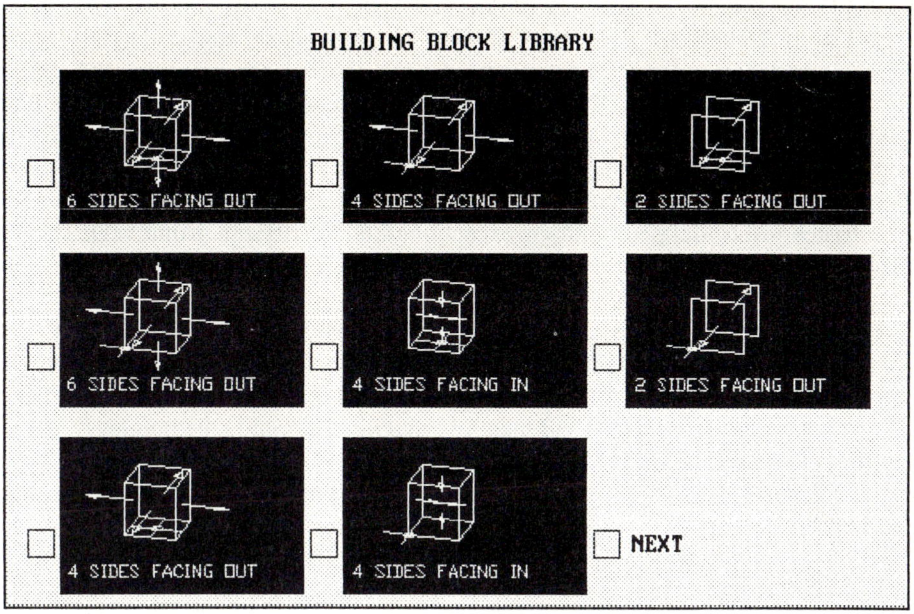

Figure 8. Menu of Efficient Primitives.

Material and color assignment follows AutoCAD's standard conventions. A number representing color can be attached to a layer, a block or an entity. AutoCAD's hierarchical rules are followed for attaching color/material to the entities of the rendered model. The numeric color value matches entries in a table describing available colors or materials which are given in terms of an RGB representation. This table is used as an input file to the translator which attaches the appropriate color specification when interpreting the DXF file. This file can be easily modified by the user to provide a different menu of color/material options.

Lights can be placed in the scene when modeling in AutoCAD. A light menu provides for point and area lights. While point lights will not be seen in the AutoCAD model, they will be included in the DXF file and output to the Unigrafix file (UXF). Area lights will be visible in the AutoCAD model as surfaces.

The Translator

Our intelligent database conversion program operates on the AutoCAD DXF file to translate the 3-D AutoCAD model to the Berkeley Unigrafix format required for efficient rendering by the radiosity renderer. The translator is written in C and can work either on the PC workstation or a UNIX workstation. For large databases it is generally much more efficient to run it on a UNIX workstation.

The translator program can interpret any AutoCAD entities and output them in Unigrafix format. The intelligent feature of the translator, however, is its efficient interpretation of a particular set of objects. The key objects focused on are the walls and windows specified in ASG format and the set of efficient graphic primitives that are included in the customized AutoCAD modeler. There is no efficient graphic primitives that are included in the customized AutoCAD modeler. There is no information in the DXF file actually associating two lines as a wall. As the DXF file is read, all lines with heights are stored in a data structure. Each line is then matched to other lines in the data base to which it is parallel. If the lines are within a specified tolerance factor of each other, they are assumed to represent the interior and exterior surfaces of a wall. Only the exterior side of each surface is listed as a FACE in the UXF file.

The tolerance factor is an input value to the interpreter. If it is set small enough both sides of all surfaces will be defined (with the exception of the predefined primitives). This could be considered the worst case scenario with regard to size of the database passed to the renderer.

The simple windows specified in ASG are also defined in terms of lines with heights and are added to a window data structure as the DXF file is read. Once all walls are interpreted, the wall list is searched to determine which wall contains each window (first by finding all walls parallel to the window line and then by checking the coordinate bounds of the walls and window to determine overlap). The library of openings is then searched to locate the geometric definition of the current window. A void of the appropriate size and shape is inserted into the face of the wall in question and the graphic primitives associated with the requested window are placed into the UXF file. Figure 9a shows the UXF file definition of the primitive inserted to create the head, sill and jam surfaces of a simple window.

As the DXF file is read, any AutoCAD blocks used in the model are interpreted as Unigrafix primitive definitions. Instances of these definitions are inserted into the rendering database as they are referenced in the entity section of the DXF file. Primitive definitions can instance other primitive definitions just as blocks can be nested in AutoCAD. Instance definitions of the graphic primitives that are contained in the menus added to AutoCAD are already specified in the translator program. Thus these blocks need not be retranslated every time. Only blocks that have not been previously defined will need to be translated. This approach allows complex assemblies to be readily substituted for the relatively simple primitives which are initially used during the preliminary design phase. Figures 9b and 9c illustrate the option of substituting more sophisticated openings by instancing more complex primitive definitions.

Any other surface entities in the DXF file are translated appropriately into Unigrafix vertices and faces after they are checked for planarity. An additional check is also made to detect coplanar contiguous surfaces which are composed of the same material. These surfaces are often the result of the faceted approach which AutoCAD uses to represent ruled and tabulated surfaces. Once detected these polygons are combined into one large polyline resulting in a significant decrease in database size (nominally by a factor of six).

If a model is too large to handle as a single AutoCAD drawing, several DXF files can be translated into one UXF file. In this way a complex environment can be created without overtaxing the modeling capabilities of a low-end workstation.

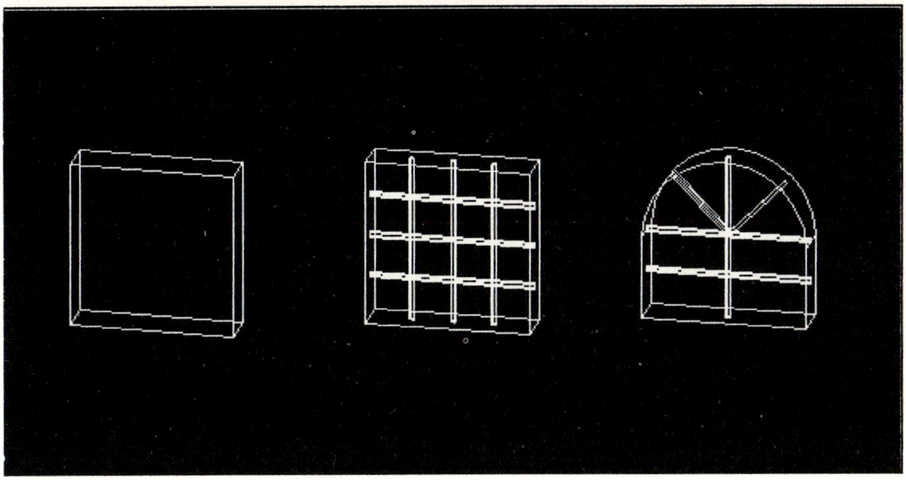

(a) (b) (c)

```
def tube;
        v v1  0,0,0;
        v v2  0,1,0;
        v v3  0,1,1;
        v v4  0,0,1;
        v v5  1,0,1;
        v v6  1,1,1;
        v v7  1,1,0;
        v v8  1,0,0;

        f f1  (v1,v2,v3,v4) material;
        f f2  (v4,v3,v5,v6) material;
        f f3  (v6,v5,v7,v8) material;
        f f4  (v8,v7,v2,v1) material;
end;

i (tube material -sx36 -sy6 -sz36 -tx240 -ty120 -tz36);                    (a)



def wintype1;
        i (tube material);
        i (cubic_cylinder material -sx0.1 -sy0.1 -tx0.25 -ty0.5);
        i (cubic_cylinder material -sx0.1 -sy0.1 -tx0.5  -ty0.5);
        i (cubic_cylinder material -sx0.1 -sy0.1 -tx0.75 -ty0.5);
        i (cubic_cylinder material -sy0.1 -sz0.1 -ty0.5  -tz0.25);
        i (cubic_cylinder material -sy0.1 -sz0.1 -ty0.5  -tz0.5);
        i (cubic_cylinder material -sy0.1 -sz0.1 -ty0.5  -tz0.75);
end;

i (wintype1 material -sx36 -sy6 -sz36 -tx240 -ty120 -tz36);                 (b)
```

Figure 9. Alternative Window Primitives.

Conclusion

A recent Scientific American article by Donald Greenberg (1991) describing rendering methods concluded with the following quote:

"Computer-aided design systems can now produce the kinds of images architects need. The most important issue yet to be resolved is software that makes it easy for architects to create their models."

The approach described in this paper addresses this critical problem of modeling by providing a very powerful three dimensional design editor. During the early stages of the schematic design process, walls may be specified as simple masses without regard to fenestration or other detail. As the design evolves simple openings may be included without regard to detail and without requiring changes to the previously specified walls (unless the walls themselves are changed). During the final design phase of a project, fully articulated doors, windows and other complex assemblies may be readily substituted and/or modified with a minimum of effort and without requiring further changes to the previously defined model. Each of these steps builds upon the last without requiring the designer to invest additional time to undo or substantially modify any of his/her previous efforts.

Figures 10 through 15 illustrate this design process. A 3-d model is developed in AutoCAD with simple opening representations (see figure 10). This model can be previewed on the SGI workstation using hardware shading capabilities to check for inconsistencies in the model (see figure 11). The same model can then be fully articulated with more complex openings (see figures 12 through 15).

This stratified approach which links a modeling package such as AutoCAD with a visualization package such as the Silicon Graphics' radiosity renderer is able to utilize both levels of technology in an optimal fashion. By fully exploiting the unique capabilities of the resources available, the size of the AutoCAD database is significantly reduced and the feasible scale of a project is greatly expanded. This results in an increase in both productivity and capability for an architect working at a PC level workstation. Finally, it provides a system which integrates numerous low-cost workstations using readily available CAD software for the time intensive design function with a smaller number of higher cost super workstations which are used for producing final images and animation.

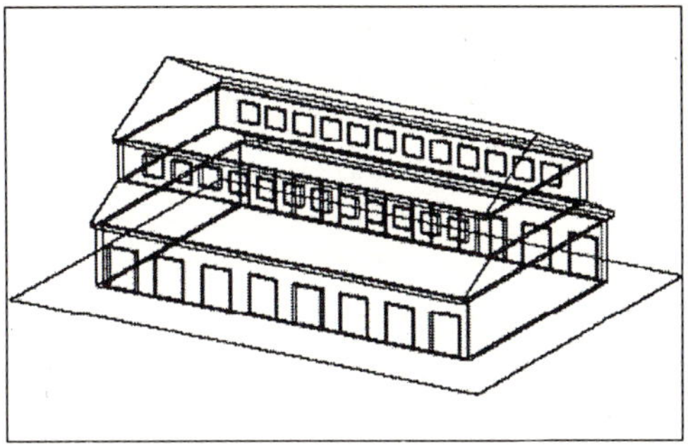

Figure 10. 3-D model developed in AutoCAD.

Figure 11. Flat shaded model.

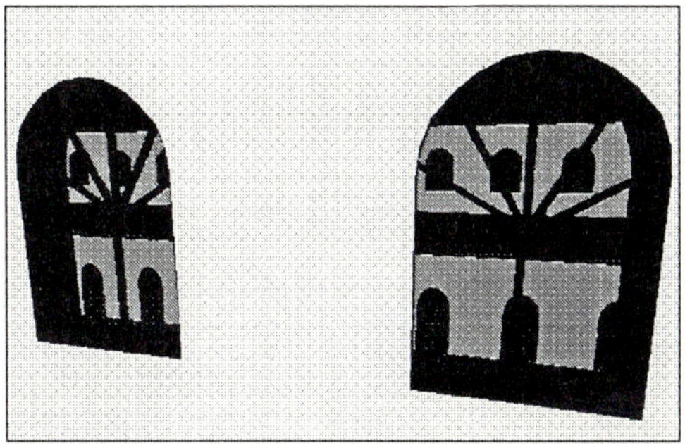

Figure 12. Model articulated with arched openings.

Figure 13. Close up of arched window detail.

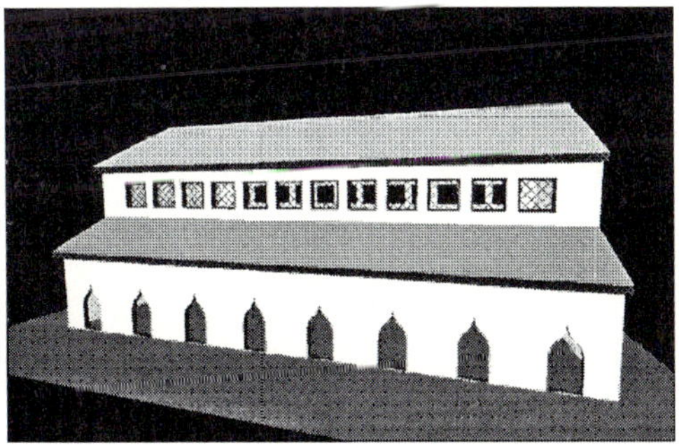

Figure 14. Substitution of alternative opening detail.

Figure 15. Close up of window detail.

References

Cohen, Michael F., Shenchang Eric Chen, John R. Wallace, and Donald P. Greenberg. 1988. "A Progressive Refinement Approach To Fast Radiosity Image Generation." *Computer Graphics* 22, no. 4: 75-84.

Cohen, Michael F., Donald P. Greenberg, and Philip J. Brock. 1986. "An Efficient Radiosity Approach for Realistic Image Synthesis." *IEEE CG&A* March, pp. 26-35.

Foley, James D., Andries van Dam, Steven K. Feiner, and John F. Hughes. 1990. *Computer Graphics, Principles and Practice*. Addison-Wesley Publishing Company.

Greenberg, Donald P. 1991. "Computers and Architecture." *Scientific American*, February: 104-109.

Mitchell, William J., Robin S. Liggett, and Thomas Kvan. 1987. *The Art of Computer Graphics Programming*. Van Nostrand Reinhold Company.

Upstill, Steve. 1989. *The RenderMan Companion*. Addison-Wesley Publishing Company.

8 The Computer-Aided Studio Critic: Gaining Control of What We Look At

John Danahy

Center for Landscape Research, University of Toronto,
230 College Street
Toronto, Ontario M5S 1A1, Canada

This paper presents an approach to teaching that put computer resources in the hands of a studio instructor. A design professor or tutor that is expert in the use of the tool. The studio master used the computer to "study" the propositions of students. This was done as an extension of his current teaching practice. The critic used the computer as another tool additional to discussion, pencil and paper, and working models. Computer walk-throughs and visual representations of concepts were used by the professor to convey his interpretation of the work to students. In this model the students did not have to use the computer. The model recognized the years of experience and expensive equipment required to create an adequate representation of a design scheme and view it in the very short time period available during desk critiques. This approach for studio teaching has not been identified and discussed in any depth in recent literature on CAD studio teaching. The emphasis of papers presented at CAD conferences has been on how to provide students with better software and skills needed to make effective use of computers in their studio work.

An Emphasis in the CAD Literature on Better Training, and Training Methods

A body of knowledge and experience with using computers in design studios is emerging in the conference proceedings of ACADIA, ECAADE and CAAD Futures. The authors of papers in these proceedings are reporting the results of their efforts to use various tools, and methods to introduce computers to the curricula at their schools. It appears that people are very encouraged by their experiments. People are discovering new ways of looking at designs and analyzing them.

This positive outlook is tempered in almost every case with an overwhelming concern that the students skill and the type of problem be carefully matched in order to realize the positive results (1). Today's technology is not automatic nor as easy to master as word processors. Computer aided design is not an easy medium to just pick up and use without training or experience. A consensus exists that if one wants to avoid spending 50% or more of the time in a studio devoted to training activity then one needs to carefully prepare incoming students. McCullough (McCullough et al. 1990) cautions that when the threshold for adapting to computers is too high for students, particularly weak students, they may be overwhelmed by it.

A student's skill level is possibly the most profound variable when trying to use today's technology in a design studio. Rubinger (1988) believes that "To derive the benefits of

CAD, it is necessary to be fluent in its use. But if design studios are about learning to design, it is not productive to try to learn computer applications at the same time. CAD applications must be learned, and learned thoroughly."

The analysis in these papers and most other papers is directed towards the issue of getting students to a level of achievement with the tools that permits them to master the medium enough to use it for creative expression. Zdepski & Goldman (1986) identify several issues they believe must be addressed. Two of the the questions they believe must be asked are;

"what is the start-up time for students to use CAD usefully ?"

"what are pedagogical implications ?"

Jordan (1988) feels that a subtle obstacle to the deployment of computers has been methodological uncertainty. Should one look at the use of computers in terms of "tool-building" or "tool-using". The issue of literacy extends to the wise or appropriate use of a tool in design not just the technical proficiency of the student. Brown (1987) is concerned that pedagogical objectives are too often lost to an apparent lack of fit between the tool and its proposed use. Steinfeld (1988) ran an, "... experimental studio designed to explore how the act of learning the CAD tool could also be educationally valuable. To compensate for the expected decrease in productivity, design studio projects of limited scope can be offered." He established a pedagogical strategy to compensate for the productivity loss.

It also seems that critiques at the computer terminal or at final reviews spend an inordinate amount of time consumed by technical issues rather than the design objectives of the students work (Fox 1990 & Harfmann, Swerdloff, Kalay 1986). Ömer Akin (1990) asks us to look at how the tool changes the way we design. He also feels the computer has the potential to change the student, instruction and the instructor. Discussion about the role of the professor as an active user of the technology in interactive visual debate is largely absent from current papers.

This paper originally set out to review the roles described in recent CAD papers of the studio critic and the critic's skill level. I was unable to find enough to discuss. I noticed that the vocabulary used in the papers is centered on phrases such as; 'the system does .... ', 'the student can ... ', or 'it allows the student to ...'. I never found the words - "the professor showed ..." or " the professor did".

It seems that most of us (including the author's previous articles) are writing about the mechanics of our systems and the syllabi of our courses. There is an amazing lack of discussion about the professors and their activity on computers. We are not looking at our own ability to use the computer to preform our role as studio critic and coach. Based on verbal discussions I have had with these and many other attenders to these conferences and visits to various schools I know that some of the authors are trying to use computers in this way. However, we are not writing about or debating this point formally in the literature on computer-aided design.

A Role Model for Using Computers in Studio Teaching

The following is an attempt to define an alternative role model for computer-aided design teachers that addresses this deficiency.

In conventional teaching practice students are the initiators of most if not all of the visual material used in discussion. Verbiage is the primary representation used to express spatial ideas by reviewers in final presentations. Visual material is often limited to occasional gestures made toward drawings on a wall. Even in desk critiques, verbiage is often the primary medium used to discuss designs. Pencil and paper is used less frequently for very schematic drawing and occasionally a wall or a tree on a working model may be manipulated by the professor to convey an idea to a student. I contend that this normative lack of emphasis on visual language can be ameliorated through the use of computers capable of supporting visual communication as a dialogue.

Computers should add the capability for two way visual dialogue to the review process. We should begin to use computers to foster the use of visual representations as not simply passive devices intended for the delivery of a message. It is time that we use visual representations as a more important part of the professor's language. Computers should be able to provide the capacity to generate pictures as a form of visual "discussion". Desk crits and even final reviews should become two way visual discussions rather than one way visual propositions followed by only talk on the part of the professor.

If as the literature contends, well trained students are able to use computers to improve geometric precision and the turn-around-time necessary to include perspective images or other forms of analysis in their work, then well trained professors should be able to employ computers to be more effective in their role as critics. If a studio teacher is proficient and literate in the use of this medium, why should the professor not bring serious professional tools into their work with students.

This approach seeks to make it possible for the professor to directly communicate and explore a student's design visually. In this model visual material moves from being a passive medium (controlled by the student) to an active participatory medium. If the professor can have active control of what we see and parametric control over some of the critical dimensional factors of the design, the professor should be able to work directly with the student to expose a whole series of design decisions the student has made but does not yet implicitly understand how her or his abstractions are manifested in the design. The balance of this paper will focus on the pedagogical role of professor as computer-aided critic rather than as an instructor of CAD.

The paper traces an experiment in which the author used his own computer tools in a junior design studio he teaches. The author became the computer-aided design critic for a week in the fall of 1990. The success of this test lead to a decision this year to change our curriculum and strategy for computing in Landscape Architecture. The next section will outline the experience in studio teaching at Toronto that lead to this experiment.

The Tools We Use in Studio at Toronto: Seeing & Intuition

We believe that the advances we have been making in research at Toronto are too valuable to be left only to the end of the educational cycle in our senior design studio. We now have a generation of tools that are extremely useful in making three dimensional ideas explicit and understandable to graphically inexperienced people. It is my contention that our research tools may be more profoundly useful in accelerating spatial literacy among our students than they have been in the professional environments where the spatial perception of professional users may be more developed.

The Programme has been fortunate to have a limited number of Silicon Graphics workstations that are made available for teaching during studio hours and off hours by the Center for Landscape Research. Research funding has completely underwritten the efforts to use computers in studio over the last several years. The Center has one silicon graphics 4D-310 VGX workstation capable of drawing 500,000 lit polygons per second, one 4D-70 GT workstation capable of drawing 40,000 lit polygons per second, one 4D-25TG and two 4D-20TG personal irises capable of drawing approximately 20,000 lit polygons per second. We also have a fairly comprehensive set of software tools that we have built to undertake a series of professional projects and previous senior design studios in the Center for Landscape Research.

Our first paper in the ACADIA 89 Workshop identified our premise regarding representational speed and interaction. The goal being to engage a users intuition. We discovered that the optimum threshold for the response of graphics to a users actions was 1/4 to 1/2 second refresh rate and that one could tolerate up to a 1 second refresh rate before the act of exploring a line of thinking in front of the computer had to be preconceived before undertaking an action. At that time, we had to limit the representational budget to 1000 facets or polygons in an integer right rectangular coordinate space. The modeler we developed represented our hypothesis (a 4 dimensional hypothesis that can only be adequately captured on video as an expression for communication). Then in 1989 we began using the Silicon Graphics 4D series workstations. The advent of faster geometry engines and a hardware z-buffer permitted us to transfer our experience with shaded lighting representations of design ideas into an arbitrary polygonal (boundary representation) floating point coordinate space. This technology began with a $40,000 price tag and is now (3 years later) available as a plug-in graphics board for 386 DOS computers in the $3,000 to $6,000 range. We have found that one can effectively represent a massing model or a part of a building design such as a lobby using a representational budget of 5000 polygons. It is very important that one adapt the level of abstraction to fit with the computational budget if one wants to employ the technology for the kind of intuitively driven design exploration we have posited.

The fourth year studio in Landscape Architecture at our School uses computers to help students see their work in a manner that allows students to discover for themselves the merit of a design. This is accomplished through direct observation of the design in perspective. We believe that if students can learn from mistakes that they can compress the amount of time necessary for them to develop an adequate level of experience with a problem. We have successfully applied computer graphics to the problem of improving our students perception of their work. The time it takes a student to achieve this state stands as a major impediment to introducing these very useful tools to students in the early years (Danahy 1988).

It takes fourth year students 3 to 6 weeks of introductory exercises in studio to achieve this level of proficiency. This technical skill in the operation of a computer is not the same as being literate in its application. I find it very difficult to get students to make wise judgements about the abstraction of design ideas so that the representations are useful and also computable in real-time. This skill takes experience and more than 3 weeks introduction to such a totally new medium. I have found that even when I carefully monitor the progress of students, they have a compelling desire to push whatever level of computer they are using past its useful function in the pursuit of more detail. This will often occur even when they have not firmly defined the spatial concept of a scheme. By the end of the term last year, over half of the students were able to develop designs using 3 days of computer time that external reviewers thought represented the work of a 4 to 6 week problem.

I have speculated for some time that this kind of learning about scale and dimension in visual perception would greatly benefit first or second year students. It is the author's feeling that these tools may be even more useful in accelerating the spatial literacy skills of first and second year students.

Learning computer-aided design tools to a level of mastery that permits a user to develop ideas as a direct result of using the computer as a representational medium is a very time consuming process. Papers addressing the subject of developing computer literacy generally present a pedagogical sequence taking from between two and three preparation courses before students are well enough prepared to be able to enter a computer-aided design studio and not have students spend 50 to 100% of their time devoted to learning the tool being used in that studio.

A question raised by this paper is that it may be a better use of resources and professors' time to lead by example. A conclusion could be to put a high-end system in the hands of an expert critic than a few less capable systems in the hands of students.

Teaching Landscape Architecture at Toronto: The Role of Second Year Design

The School of Architecture and Landscape Architecture at the University of Toronto offers Bachelor of Architecture and Bachelor of Landscape Architecture degrees. The first year design studios at the School are intended as a general introduction to design. Architecture and Landscape Architecture attempt to make the first year studios as interconnected as possible. The School has had a mandatory introductory computing course in the third year for several years. Its usefulness in preparing students for senior design studios has been largely non-existent.

In 1990, the School's curriculum committee decided to move the computer course into the first year with the drawing and visual literacy sequence. In the past, the course tried to be all things to all interests and seldom satisfied any one interest's needs. It is generally felt that at least three preparatory courses would be required to cover the range of material that had been given as a mandate for that course. Instead, the time allocated for computers is being incorporated with the first year skills course. This course is related to drawing and visual literacy. The focus of the computer component is on two and three dimensional modelling. This content parallels the principles being addressed in the drawing, physical model making and photography workshops of the course. The School's overall strategy to computing is to use computers anywhere that staff are willing and able to bring it into core courses and selected studios. Landscape Architecture has had the benefit of significant research resources and full-time professors capable of integrating computers in subsequent courses.

Second Year Landscape Architecture Design Studio introduces students to the fundamental types of comprehensive landscape architectural problems. It is also a year that is focused on teaching design process and graphic expression in a variety of mediums. The year is divided into problems characterized by either natural systems or social / human use determinants. Landscape architecture draws a significant percentage if its students from non design areas. Many students are prepared for the natural sciences. Architecture on the other hand, tends to attract a majority of people with strong interests in drawing. Since natural systems are a part of the design/planning palette of the landscape architectural profession, there is a tendency to find a stronger emphasis on design procedures and technique than is found in the pedagogical approaches used in architecture at Toronto. The course aims to develop visual literacy in the use of plan, section, and model-making unique to the development of landscape design ideas. We try to develop the students' capacity to "see" the implications of their designs. The starting point in this process is to help students understand how their 2-dimensional representations translate into experienced 3-dimensional form.

An Experiment with the Computer-Aided Desk Critique

The paper traces an experiment in which the author used his own computer tools in a junior design studio he teaches. The author became the computer-aided design critic for a week in the spring of 1990. The author met with each student for a one hour review. The design concept of each student was digitized and modelled by the professor during the first half of the session from a plan drawing (usually pencil on trace paper, see figure 1) prepared by the student. This proved to be a very efficient use of both the professor's and the student's time. The second half of the time was spent examining and walking through the scheme.

The students developed a better capacity to "see" the implications of their designs. They were able to see in an unambiguous way how their 2-dimensional representations translated into experienced 3-dimensional form. Students were able to see for themselves if a given party translated effectively. Staff and a student's peers were able to more freely challenge and discuss the effect of one party in the space over another because of the comparative and accurate nature of the computer images. We feel this is a powerful form of learning. Students were much less likely to seize upon a party based solely on conventional wisdom. And students that could not see problems with an unconventional party could sometimes see past the bias of their own drawing since they had not crafted it.

The success of this test lead to a decision this year to integrate computer based critiquing as an integral part of second year design for the two problems described previously. These problems are now offered in the spring term after students have had a series of comprehensive site planning problems and greater experience with model making, and plan, section, and perspective drawing. The spring term now adds the use of panorama drawing and computer visualization as described next.

Studio Problem Description

In 1990, the Programme has strengthened the visualization and visual thinking aspects of the course by teaming the author (the computer "expert") and the drawing professor (a proponent of panoramic 360 degree perspective as a design procedure) together as the studio critics. In addition to computing, the author is the faculty member charged with the person-environment relations component of the curriculum. The studio is run parallel to the Social

Factors in Landscape Architecture course. Issues of programming for social interaction and visual perception are part of the studio objectives.

The studio uses three problems beginning with a design in panorama exercise lasting two weeks. This is followed by a four week courtyard problem and a seven week urban plaza design problem. The last two problems are the ones where the author has used the computer as a tool for use in desk critiques.

Problem II: Designing an Exterior Space Delimited by Built Form

The aim of this project is to give the student the opportunity to learn about traditional design procedure and media. This is accomplished through the solution of a landscape design problem that is focused on concern for the human use of a strongly defined, simple urban space already familiar to the student. This project is focused on the design of an exterior space that is primarily delimited by built form. The edges of the space that the student designs in this problem are defined by the walls of the architecture found on the site. The student selects a quadrangle or courtyard in the Earth Sciences Complex of the University of Toronto to design. Students are divided into groups to prepare base material for drawing, physical and computer models during the first week of the problem. (footnote).

Problem III: Designing an Exterior Space Formed by Landscape Elements

The aim of this project is to further refine and demonstrate the student's understanding of traditional design procedure and media. This is accomplished through the solution of a landscape design problem that is focused on concern for the human use of an ill defined, complex urban space already familiar to the student. This project is focused on the design of an exterior space that is *not* primarily delimited by built form. The edges of the spaces that the student designs in this problem are not clearly defined by the walls of the architecture found on the site. A goal is to immerse our students (especially the non design background students) in an extremely rich array of visual representations of their design ideas. We want them to develop and calibrate their capacity to judge scale and perceived composition of design spaces through disciplined procedure. The hypothesis of the approach is that we will be able to accelerate the time frame in which students begin to accurately translate two dimensional diagrams in plan into perceived experience and vise versa in their mind's eye.

Using the Computer to Develop a Visual Dialogue

The same model for critiques that was used in 1990 was followed this year. A base model was prepared for the courtyard problem by three students with previous experience in AutoCAD and the base model from last year's problem was used for the third problem. The students not involved in this activity prepared base drawings and physical models during this period of time. A typical session with the computer began by examining a sketch plan brought to the critique by the student. I would take the base model available in the system and quickly digitize or position (by eye) a schematic placement of vegetation, terrain changes and built elements such as stairs, ramps or buildings to complete a representation of the concept that was sufficient to permit us to discuss the student's ideas.

Once this task was complete, I would meet with the student and spend at least a half hour discussing the project. I would also continue to modify the model as the discussion progressed to address the analytical concerns defined below. This time period often extended to one or two hours if we could afford the time. I would also set up the model for them on one of the Iris computers and show them the basic moves necessary to continue examining the model on their own while I met with another student. We would meet again briefly and make modifications to the scheme. Images were then saved and printed on an 11x17 inch Seiko Colour Printer. These images were used for further sketching or directly in the final presentation.

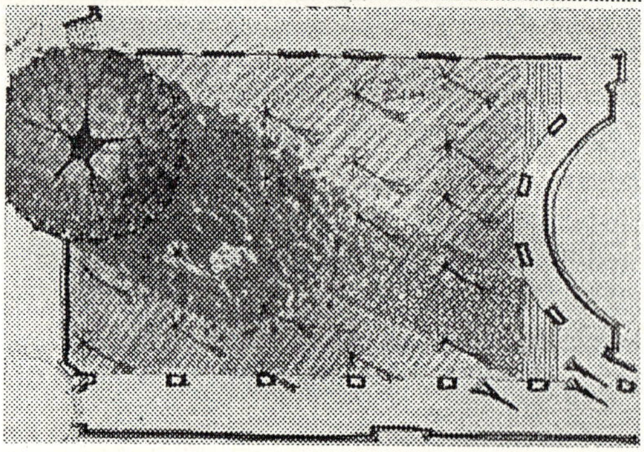

Figure 1. The drawing on the right is a scanned image of a student's concept plan. The perspective images from the computer above showed the student that the textural quality of the plan drawing had nothing to do how the space would appear to users.

Figure 2. In this scheme the student wished to deal with grade change by rising one half of the space and planting trees in the lower half. What was not understood until the computer desk crit was that the branching point for the trees during the first twenty years on the scheme would totally obscure the formal composition of 'hard' elements that the student tried to achieve.

Figure 3. This illustrates the software interface used to parametrically apply leaves in the canopy zone of each tree. this also permitted us to evaluate degrees of transparency and variations in containment that would occur as the season changes.

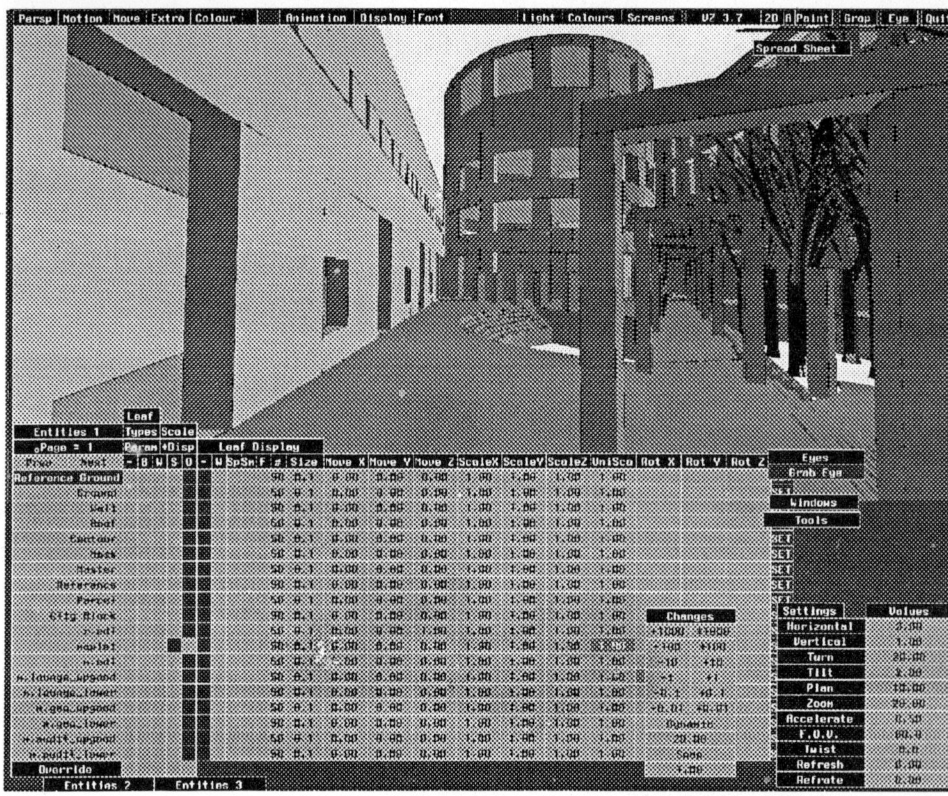

Figure 4. This scheme is a study in the use of a row of columnar trees with two large specimen trees to organize the space.

The educational objectives for the exercise were:

- to bring the power of our visualization tools to studio and better support a heuristic approach to discussion and design development.
- to engage the curiosity of our students for computing in a fun and powerful way so that they can better understand why they need to prepare themselves for its use in the upper years.
- for them to observe an experienced user as a role model and see how to abstract ideas and establish an efficient, computable vocabulary of representations in this medium.

The model I used for these sessions involved two fundamental activities.
The first was a review of the student's concept in terms of the following concerns that I wanted every student to address in their design;

1. Spatial Containment - landscape edge as degrees of containment using semi transparency or filtering one's vision to symbolically create the illusion or feeling of containment.
2. Translation of the design idea from plan into perspective eye-level experience - analyze the percentage of a viewer's cone of vision actually occupied by the geometry of the design elements important to the overall composition of the space.
3. Movement through the space - analyzing the scheme from multiple vantage points to determine if it works from all locations.
4. Scale of the Spaces for Social Interaction - placement of representations of people into a scene - to populate it, furnish it and then ask the student whether they think the design will be used according to the stated design objectives.
5. Scale of Plant material over time - analyze whether the design achieves an adequate degree of containment at various years in the maturation of a landscape.

The second activity was to openendedly explore the model with the student to determine if the students ideas had been met. During a typical session the student and I would explore an aspect of geometric dimension until one of the two of us found a problem or opportunity. Since the student could not explore the scheme through modelling, I was careful to not completely direct the course of the session. I would try to communicate to the student through the evolution of the images or by varying a critical parameter until the student said something. If they liked or disliked the effect we would try to analyze their reaction and the parameters producing their response. In this way, I was attempting to make the student more sensitive to things they had been defining in the design that had remained at a largely unconscious level.

I was able to reach my half of the students in the studio for the second problem and most of the students in the whole class for the first problem effectively within the time limitations for desk critiques. I had hoped that the tools might be fast enough to permit me to have a desk crit with all 20 students in the studio. This limitation implies that as with all other one-to-one teaching methods this techniques can only be employed if the staff have the requisite skills to rapidly model on the computer being used. The problem centered more on the entry of the basic design concept. This model cannot become central to a curriculum until a significant percentage of the professors have developed the skill of using this technology.

The most vexing problem I encountered was trying to keep the complete time to enter an idea and discuss it to within the one hour limit we had set. If a scheme involves complex ground plane geometry it can take more than the half hour allocated to enter the scheme. If the time becomes greater than that it becomes impossible to deal with a whole class and therefore, not viable as general technique in design teaching. Most professors would not be willing or able to spend the extra time necessary to do this work. An alternative would be to hire a graduate student to assist in the process.

Results / Observations

The computer was most useful for those aspects of a design that could be played with in a dynamic manner. Since the model for teaching is concerned primarily with the strategic dimensions in a design that influence visual perception of the intended concept it became very apparent that the requirement for a real-time system extended not just to the representation but also the act of modelling.

Since I was in control of both what we looked at and what we modelled, I was able to control the abstraction of a design in order to focus attention on the organizing principles of the proposed scheme for discussion with the student. In those cases where a scheme was represented simply or with parametric objects we could propose changes to a scheme in seconds. It turned out that sometimes even when a student was able to generate a model on their own prior to the desk critique the way they constructed the model had a great influence on whether we could exploit the computational speed of the machines to engage in visual dialogue.

If one was evaluating the dimensional workability of a concept, I found that it was sometimes better to position design elements on a students plan by "eye" rather than use the digitizing tablet. This task would usually allow the model building phase to stay well within the 1/2 hour allotted and proved to be sufficiently accurate if done while the existing conditions layer of information was turned on for reference. It also showed students the value of very simple abstract visual representations. Many times after digitizing accurate representations of a complex of stairs to determine how altering the number of stairs would influcnce the look of a space we would find that thc basic positioning of the stairs has not yet been resolved. Hence, the time required to digitize the precision of the stairs was wasted.

I also found we could simply place elements such as trees into the model until the desired visual cffect was achieved. We would then go into the 2-dimensional view of the system and analyze what spacing dimension created the desired impression. This approach allowed students to more directly understand the role physical dimensions play in design.

Results from the Final Review

At the end of term reviews a Personal Iris computer was set up in the room during the presentations. I was able to enter the concepts of three students that I had not had an opportunity to work with previously in the project. Their schemes were modelled while the students presented their work. I was able to listen to the presentation, identify a key element or strategic idea in the scheme that was dependent on geometric properties (dimensions) and model a representation of the geometric idea. The representation was then used to confirm the degree to which the design worked in terms of dynamic movement and the growth of vegetation over time. In all three cases, it became clear that the planting strategy that appeared to work in the plan did not in fact produce the desired effect when viewed with the perspective accuracy of the computer. These were students that had not had the benefit of a previous desk critique at the computer (refer to figure 5).

In the final reviews, it turned out that a great many students misrepresented important dimensional aspects of their designs in the hand drawings that were not based on computer printouts. They successfully conveyed intentions for the textural qualities of their proposed spaces with drawings. However, dimensional accuracy was another matter all together. When the actual number of trees proposed were placed into the computer model and given realistic size and age parameters, most schemes failed to achieve the intentions expressed in the plans for creating a strong sense of visual enclosure and containment. The most fascinating thing that became apparent during the use of the computer during the final reviews was that the other professors and guest critics did not notice these problems when all that they had to refer too were the plans, sections, hand drawn perspectives, and the physical models (refer to figure 6).

References

Akin, Ö. 1990. "Computational Design Instruction: Towards a Pedagogy." In M. McCullough, W. Mitchell, and P. Purcell (eds.). 1990. *The Electronic Design Studio. Cambridge.* Mass.: MIT Press.

Brown, J. 1987. "Integrating Computers into the Design Studio; A Critical Evaluation." In B. Novitski (ed.). *ACADIA 87.* Integrating Computers into the Architectural Curriculum. North Carolina: Raleigh.

Danahy, J. 1990. "Irises in the Landscape." In M. McCullough, W. Mitchell, and P. Purcell (eds.). *The Electronic Design Studio.* Cambridge, Mass.: MIT Press.

Danahy, J. 1988. "Engaging Intuitive Visual Thinking in Urban Design Modelling: A Real-Time Hypothesis." In P. Bancroft (ed.). *ACADIA 88* Computing in Design Education. Michigan: Ann Arbor.

Fox 1990. "Integrating Computing into an Architectural Undergraduate Program." In M. McCullough, W. Mitchell, and P. Purcell (eds.). 1990. *The Electronic Design Studio.* Cambridge, Mass.: MIT Press.

Jordan, M. 1988. "Arch 431: Computer-Aided Design." In P. Bancroft (ed.). *ACADIA 88* Computing in Design Education. Michigan: Ann Arbor.

Harfmann, A., Swerdloff, and Y. Kalay 1986. "The Terminal Crit." In Turner, J. (ed.). *ACADIA 86* Architectural Education, Research, and Practice in the Next Decade. Houston, Texas.

McCullough, M. 1989. " Low Threshold Modelling." In M. McCullough, W. Mitchell, and P. Purcell (eds.). 1990. *The Electronic Design Studio.* Cambridge, Mass.: MIT Press.

Rubinger, M. 1988. "Drawing Lessons From Word Processing." In P. Bancroft (ed.). *ACADIA 88* Computing in Design Education. Michigan: Ann Arbor.

Steinfeld. 1988. "Using CAD to Teach Architectural Design." In P. Bancroft (ed.). *ACADIA 88* Computing in Design Education. Michigan: Ann Arbor.

Zdepski, S., and G. Goldman. 1986. "The Computability of Design." In J. Turner (ed.). *ACADIA 86* Architectural Education, Research, and Practice in the Next Decade. Houston, Texas.

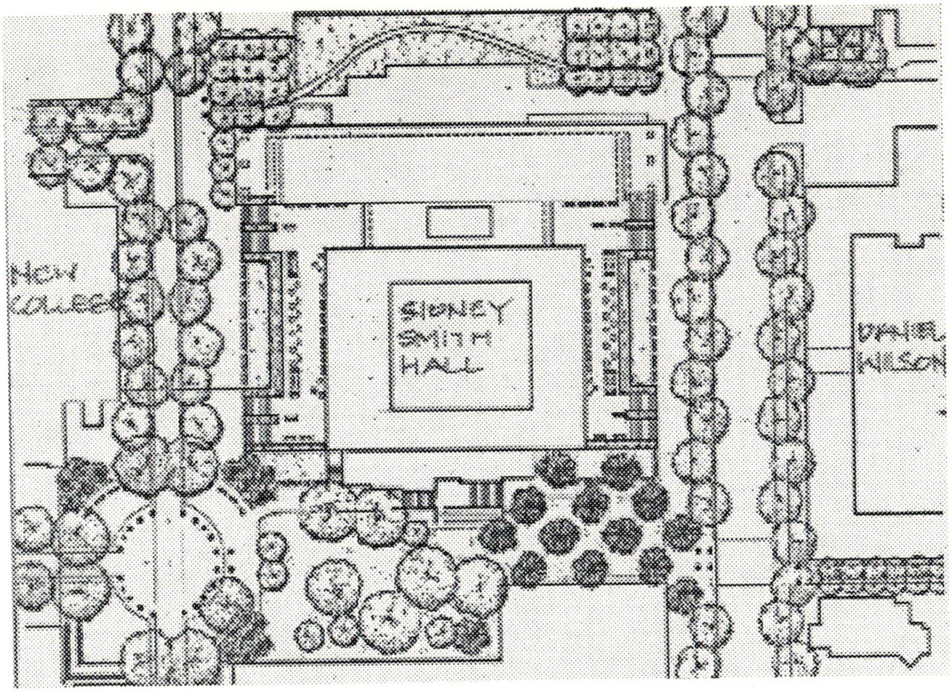

Figure 5. This scheme was modelled while the student presented and was used to provide comment on the planting strategy employed. The scheme did not provide any significant degree of spatial containment for the space for the first 40 years. If a tree were to die then the degree of containment implied by the hand drawn plan would never be achieved.

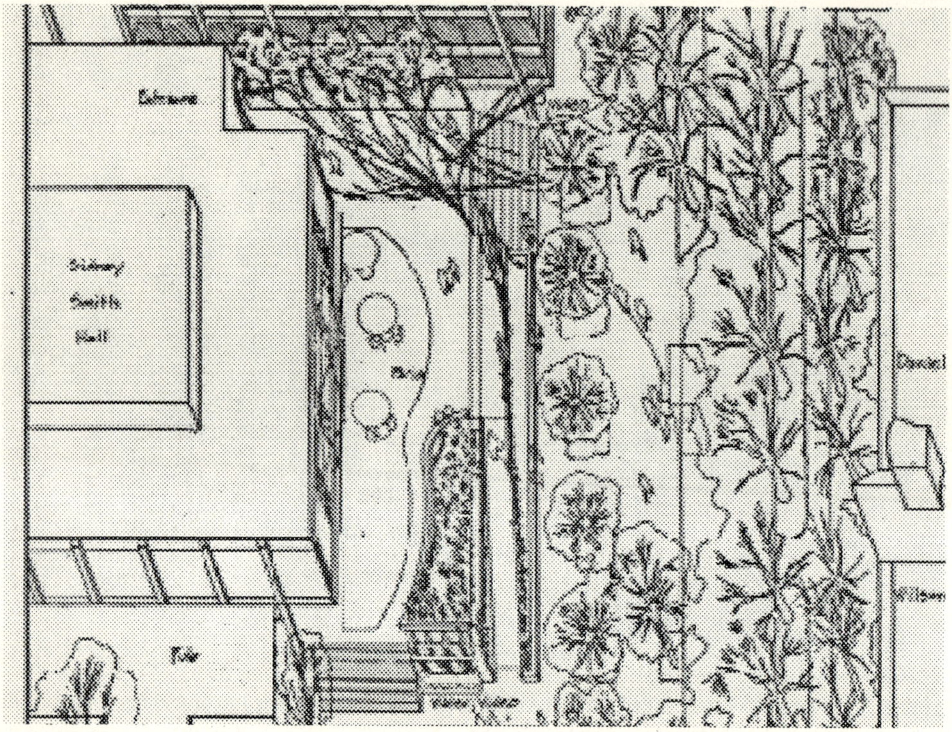

Figure 6. This is another scheme modelled while the student presented and was used to provide comments on the planting strategy employed. The scheme also had problems providing spatial containment for the space for the first 40 years.

Figure 7. The top image shows a template of social fields of view defined by Jan Gehl applied to a student's design below.

Figure 8. The top and bottom schemes are based on strong circular geometries in the plan view. The strength of the idea is not as apparent when viewed in perspective. Vertical elements that do not figure prominently in plan become the dominant spatial geometry.

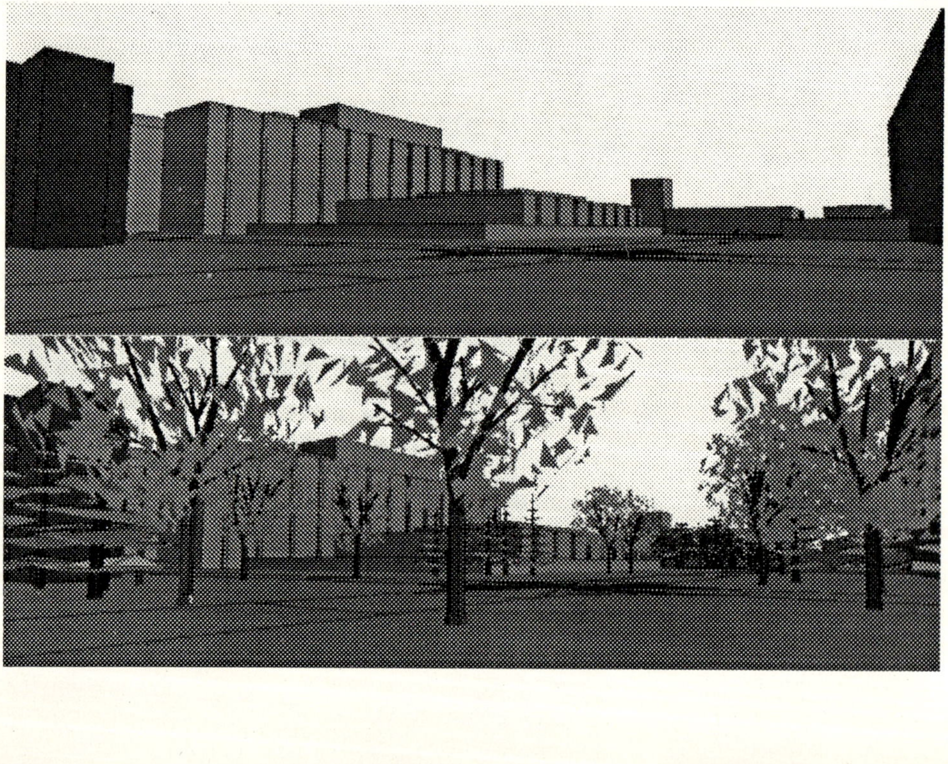

9 An Evaluation Module for "An Interface for Designing" (AID): A Procedure based on Trichotomic Segmentation

Elena Mortola and Alessandro Giangrande

Laboratorio CAAD, Dipartimento di Progettazione Architettonica e Urbana
Università "La Sapienza"
Via Gramsci 53, 00197 Rome, Italy

The paper illustrates a model used to construct the evaluation module for "An Interface for Designing" (AID), a system to aid architectural design. The model can be used at the end of every cycle of analysis-synthesis-evaluation in the intermediate phases of design development. With the aid of this model it is possible to evaluate the quality of a project in overall terms to establish whether the project is acceptable, whether it should be elaborated ex-novo or whether it is necessary to begin a new cycle to improve it. In this last case it is also possible to evaluate the effectiveness of the possible actions and strategies for improvement. The model is based on a procedure of trichotomic segmentation, developed within the MCDA (Multi-Criteria Decision Aid), which uses the outranking relation to compare the project with some evaluation profiles taken as projects for reference. In the paper an example of the application of the model in the teaching field will also be described.

Introduction: Design Process and Evaluation

Under the pressure of social needs and a will to cope with the complex problems of today's world, the 60's and the early 70's witnessed the birth of a number of methods and techniques intended as aids in the design process. In many cases these methods sought to break down the barriers existing among the disciplines and to verify the applicability of the scientific method to the fields of artistic research and design (Alexander 1964, Archer 1965 and 1968, Broadbent 1966, Gregory 1966, Jones 1963 and 1970, Luckman 1967).

The intrinsic limits of the methods proposed together with the decline of interest in a more systematic way of projecting, led architects in the mid-70' to become more interested in the language and form of architecture.

In recent years, however, the widespread diffusion of computer technologies, the emergence of the so-called environmental crisis and the growing complexity of the decision making context have led architects to think about method again as an important tool to manage the design process, both from a technical point of view as well as from an organizational one. In fact, the architect's tasks seem to be growing more and more difficult as time passes. Architects are finding themselves in situations where they have to coordinate multidisciplinary work groups, where they have to identify design actions to protect human and environmental values and yet, at the same time, keep in mind the limits imposed by the decision making context.

A number of methods consider designing a process that consists in a sequence of cycles of analysis-synthesis-evaluation (Archer 1965, Jones 1963, Luckman 1967, Maver 1977 and 1988). Such methods usually differ from each other owing to the number of cycles in the process or owing to the number of steps in each cycle. The basic idea is that every cycle must be repeated several times before completing the project.

This way of conceiving the design process is useful in some kinds of projecting (for example, in mechanical engineering) but it is much less useful in architecture. In fact, the designing of architecture - especially in the early stages - appears as an ill-structured and ill-defined problem, one that is difficult to control. We can encounter alterations both in the sequence as well as in the duration of the various steps in a cycle. A procedure based on successive cycles of analysis-synthesis-evaluation proves to be of a certain usefulness only in the more advanced phases of the design process, when the solution has reached relative stability.

Whereas methods of analysis are fairly numerous and efficient, methods of synthesis are virtually nil: in fact, this step in the cycle depends entirely on the capacity for synthesizing of the individual architect. As for as evaluation is concerned, the methods available refer to very specific aspects of the process. What we are talking about in general, are methods regarding technical control. It would be inexact, in our opinion, to consider them real tools of evaluation, because they do not allow us to evaluate a project from an overall point of view.

In this paper a evaluation method is described that is based on MCDA (Multi-Criteria Decision Aid). This method is particularly suitable for a process with different "actors" (designers, consultants, users, etc.), but can also be used by the individual designer who intends to simulate the decision making context. The method allows us to directly compare the performances related to the building efficiency in terms of environmental comfort, costs, etc, with other intrinsically qualitative aspects such as the relationship between the project and the landscape or the historical and cultural context. The model helps the designer therefore to evaluate the project in explicit and global manner without overlooking qualitative aspects. It aids him in making choices which imply complex tradeoffs between performances of different type.

The method has been used to construct a module of evaluation which is part of a design support system named "An Interface for Designing" (AID), which is in the working stage (Mortola 1988, 1989a, 1989b, 1990, Mortola and Sansoni 1990, Giangrande et al. 1991).

This system, which can be applied to different phases of the design process, has been developed with the aid of Hypercard. It is made up of a number of modules, some of which can be interfaced with other commercial systems and programs, frequently used in CAAD or in the scientific field.

Evaluation and MCDA

In many disciplines such as economics, statistical theory of decisions, operations research, games theory, etc., the rationality of a choice is guaranteed when the decision maker, knowing all the feasible alternatives and their consequences, selects the best alternative on the basis of a single criterion (e.g. the profit maximization).

This paradigm of decision making went into crisis in the 1950's as a result of the studies carried out in the social choice theory (Arrow 1951), in the behavioral sciences and in the organizations theory (March and Simon 1958). These studies have led progressively to a lack of conviction about the possibility of explaining and forecasting decision makers' behavior, according to codes of rationality (Simon 1957). These studies questioned the validity of many classical evaluation models and favoured, from the middle 60's, the development of a new field of research which put to good use the theories of the previous decade: the Multi-Criteria Decision Aid (MCDA) (Jaquet-Lagrèze at al 1978, Roy 1968, 1985). The methods and techniques developed in MCDA furnishes the actor with the tools that help him to make a decision in the light of multiple and often conflicting points of view. According to this approach the term "optimization" loses the meaning: in contrast with some evaluation techniques developed in the field of operations research, such as MOLP (Multiple Objective Linear Programming), the MCDA methods do not lead to the "objectively" best solution, which, in fact, doesn't exist.

In the MCDA the decision is seen not so much as a result, but as a process with different steps, in which one or more dominant points are prevalent of view: the rationality of the decision process is evaluated as "coherence with the objectives of the decision makers" (Sfez 1973). From this point of view it is important that a method allows us to take into account the complex game of interaction between the different elements of the decision making process. The "hard" models of operations research are substituted by "soft" ones (less mathematical but equally rigorous), which allows the actors to interact directly and in easier way with the evaluation tool. In the MCDA some concepts as actor, action and criterion assume particular importance. The actor is an individual (or a group of individuals who participates in an homogeneous and coherent way in the process) and can directly or indirectly influence the decision. By *action* we mean the representation that an actor constructs of a solution (or of an element which helps to obtain a solution). In architectural design the action is the entire project or a design decision that modifies it. By *criterion* we mean a "model" (indicator, objective function, etc.) that allows us to compare more actions and to evaluate their effectiveness in an explicit way.

In MCDA usually more than one criteria are in conflict: in any case the criteria used to evaluate the action (or the actions) must make up a coherent "family", i.e. a set of exhaustive and not redundant criteria (Roy 1985, p.310).

Another fundamental concept is problem formulation. The problem formulations considered in the MCDA are four: α, β, γ, δ (Roy 1985, p.75). The objective of the problem formulation α is to help to choose one action considered the "best" among those studied (selection procedure). In the problem formulation β the objective is to help to sort out all those actions that are "good" (segmentation procedure). In the problem formulation γ the actions are ranked in a decreasing order of preference (ordering procedure). The objective of the problem formulation δ is to analyze the actions and their consequences to aid the decision maker to make a choice. This problem formulation does not lead necessarily to rank the actions, nor to choose the best action(s).

The applications of the MCDA are numerous in the planning and management fields but are less diffuse in the architecture one (Calderaro et al. 1986).

In the following pages we will illustrate the method we used to realize the evaluation module for the AID system and its application to an experiment of architectural design in a didactic context.

The Evaluation Method

The evaluation method is based on problem formulation β (see above). This is the only MCDA problem formulation usable when we need to evaluate an action not according to a set of alternative actions, but with respect to absolute references. In the specific case we used a trichotomic segmentation procedure (Moscarola and Roy 1977, Roy 1981) to establish if the action is good, bad, or uncertain. The procedure assigns the action to one of three categories: K^+ (action accepted), K^- (action rejected) and $K^?$ (the action merits an additional examination). The action is evaluated with respect to n criteria by l actors ("judges"). The n criteria are represented by the same number of semantic differentials (Osgood et al. 1957) which correspond to all those aspects, and only those, which are meaningful to evaluate the project with reference to the design theme, the context and the level of definition of the project itself. A semantic differential consists of one or more pairs of adjectives or statement antonyms. These are the polar terms or factors which have to be used in judging the objects presented. In order to increase precision of responses, a range of choices between each extreme is allowed.

In our case every semantic differential is defined by a scale of 7 levels. The two extreme levels of the scale, 1 and 7, represent respectively the negative and the positive polar terms of the differential. The meaning of every polar term is defined by a sentence and some images, maps or diagrams of exemplary projects. Every judge assigns the project to a level of the scale which will be all the more closer to the positive (or negative) polar term as the project is judged better (or worse) respecting the considered criterion. In this manner the judges define l vectors with n components a_j^k (j=1,2,...n; k=1,2,...l). The j-th component of this vector represents the level of the project on the criterion j in the opinion of the judge k.

In the applications which interest us, the judges can be from time to time the designers and the consultants of a professional studio, the jury of a competition, the components of a building commission, or a board of examining professors.

To guarantee a correct evaluation of the project with respect to all the criteria it is necessary that the jury be composed of experts in different sectors. In a no conflict situation the evaluation of the project can be carried out by the judges in collaboration. In the didactic context, a student can simulate the judgments of a board of examiners to identify the aspects (criteria) where his project is weaker. Every judge assigns afterwards the weights w_j^k (j=1,2,...n; k=1,2,...l) to the criteria. These weights are coefficients which reflect the importance that each judge, on the basis of his own system of values, assigns to the different criteria, considering the design theme and the context. The sum of weights assigned by a judge to all the criteria must be equal to 1.

The procedure asks moreover that each judge defines a pair of vectors with n components: b_j^k, c_j^k, named respectively the upper and the lower profile. These profiles represent two sets of reference projects which discriminate between acceptable and uncertain projects (b_j^k) and between uncertain and unacceptable projects (c_j^k). Therefore, for every criterion, the level of the upper profile must be always greater than that of the corresponding lower profile.

If the project is overall upper profiles (or under the lower ones) the project can be assigned, without hesitation, to the category K^+ (or K^-). If, as often happens, these conditions aren't met, it is necessary to compare the project with all the profiles by the outranking relation S defined as follows: given two actions, a1 and a2, a1 S a2 (a1 outranks a2) if a1 is, at least, as good as a2 (Roy 1985, p.122). To establish if the project a outranks a specific profile p (or vice versa) the indexes of concordance C^k (a,p) (Roy 1968) have to be calculated as follows:

$$C^k(a,p) = \Sigma_j w_j^k c_j^k(a,p), \qquad (k=1,2,...l) \qquad (1)$$

where

$$c_j^k(a,p)= \begin{cases} 1 \text{ if } g_j^k(a) >= g_j^k(p) \\ 0 \text{ if } g_j^k(a) < g_j^k(p) \end{cases} \qquad (j=1,2,...,n;\ k=1,2,...l). \qquad (2)$$

g_j^k (a) and $g_j^k(p)$ are respectively the levels of a and p on the criterion j. The condition $g_j^k(a)>= g_j^k(p)$ is fulfilled if the project is assigned to a level of the semantic differential equal or higher to the level of the reference profile. The index of concordance can vary between 0 and 1: the more this value is near 1, the more is the comprehensive weight of criteria which agree upon the sentence "a is, at least, as good as p". To calculate the "symmetrical" indexes $C^k(p,a)$ it is sufficient change in (1) and (2) a with p. In general $C^k(p,a) \neq C^k(a,p)$.

To assert that a outranks p it isn't sufficient that $C^k(a,p)$ assumes values near to 1. If the difference $g_j^k(p)$ - $g_j^k(a)$ is considerable, also for only one criterion, the outranking couldn't occur, or, eventually, appear not very credible, aside from the value of $C^k(a,p)$.

The procedure asks that every judge assign a veto threshold v_j^k to each criterion (Roy 1978). v_j^k represents the maximum value of difference $g_j^k(p)$ - $g_j^k(a)$ that the judge k could accept for the criterion j in order to attribute to the outranking a Sp a high credibility. The veto thresholds are used to calculate the "fuzzy" indexes $S^k(a,p)$, which represent the credibility degrees of outranking aSp.

To calculate these indexes we must calculate the indexes of discordance D_j^k (a,p), which are defined as follows:

$$D_j^k(a,p) = \begin{cases} 1 & \text{if } g_j^k(p) > g_j^k(a) + v_j \\ 0.5 & \text{if } g_j^k(p) = g_j^k(a) + v_j \\ 0 & \text{if } g_j^k(p) < g_j^k(a) + v_j \end{cases} \qquad (j=1,2,...n;\ k=1,2,...l) \qquad (3)$$

The indexes $S^k(a,p)$ are calculated in the following way:

$$S^k(a,p) = \begin{cases} C^k(a,p) \text{ if } D_j^k(a,p) <= C^k(a,p), \text{V}j \\ C^k(a,p)\, \Pi_j \dfrac{1- D_j^k(a,p)}{1- C^k(a,p)}, \end{cases} \qquad (k=1,2,...l) \qquad (4)$$

where Π_j is extended to all the values of j for which is $D_j^k(a,p) > C^k(a,p)$. In general, the smaller are the thresholds of veto v_j, the lesser is the degree of credibility of the outranking. Comparing the project with all the profiles, upper and lower, we obtain for each judge four indexes: $S^k(a,b)$,$S^k(b,a)$,$S^k(a,c)$,$S^k(c,a)$.

To assign the project to the category K^+ (project accepted), K^- (project rejected) or $K^?$ (the project needs improvement) we use the decision tree shown in the figure 1 (Scharlig 1985, Vansnick 1979).

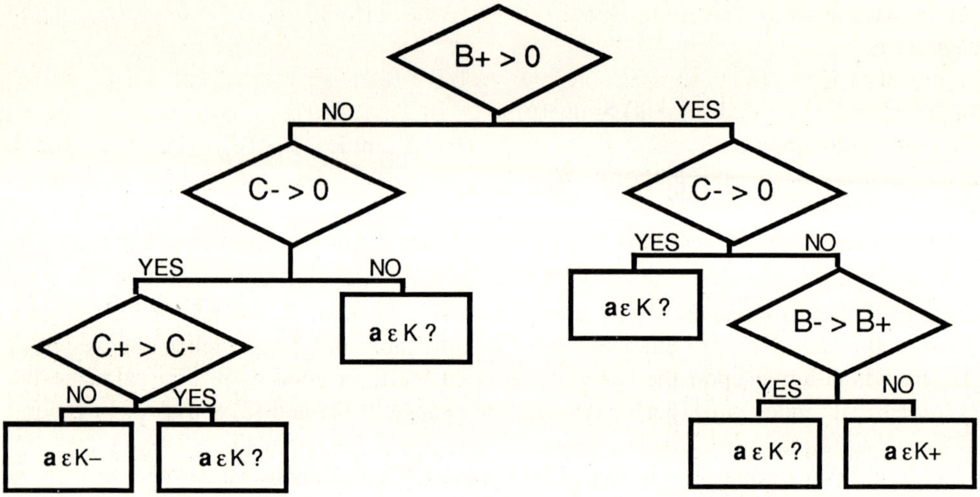

Figure 1. The Decision Tree.

where B^+, B^-, C^+ e C^- represent respectively the number of judges for which the indexes $S^k(a,b)$, $S^k(b,a)$, $S^k(a,c)$, $S^k(c,a)$ exceed respectively a threshold T. This threshold is chosen empirically, considering that the more it grows in value, the more severe the "filtering" of the corresponding index and the fewer the number of judges for which the corresponding outranking relation assumes credibility. Considering that the choice of the threshold is arbitrary, it is necessary to conduct a sensitivity analysis, varying its values in a suitable range (e.g. 0.6 - 0.9) in order to verify the stability of the results of evaluation.

An Application of the Evaluation Model

The procedure of evaluation has been applied, as a didactic experience, to one of the projects of the Italian students who participated in an inter-school competition, proposed by Strathclyde University in Glasgow for European students of architecture.

The theme of the competition was the design of a Media Lover House, a home for the 21st century. This competition intended to celebrate an important event in English architecture: the competition proposed in December of 1900 by the German revue "Zeitschrift fur Innendekoration", for the design of an Art Lover House ("Ein herrschaftliches Wohnhaus eines Kunstfreundes"). One of the participants was the architect

C.R. Mackintosh; his project is now taking shape in Bellahouston Park, on the occasion of the celebration of Glasgow architecture, which marked the European City of Culture for 1990.

The building is intended for habitation with some characteristics connected with the kind of user (a media lover). Especially, it should provide for collateral activities to satisfy professional, social, and cultural needs, to promote hobbies, and to encourage communication and meeting at professional and family level, with the aid of advanced technologies. In addition the project should propose innovative solutions for the management of the building, in order to obtain the energy to be used, from the natural surroundings. The resident group is made up of 6 standing inhabitants, not necessarily linked by familiarities, and of two guests.

The participants to the competition could moreover choose the localization of the house. In the following we shall describe the application of the evaluation procedure to the project developed for this competition and for the "thesis of laurea" by the students Francesca R. Castelli and Anna Gadola (chairman: Prof. Arch. Elena Mortola, co-chairman: Arch. Maurizio Clarotti).

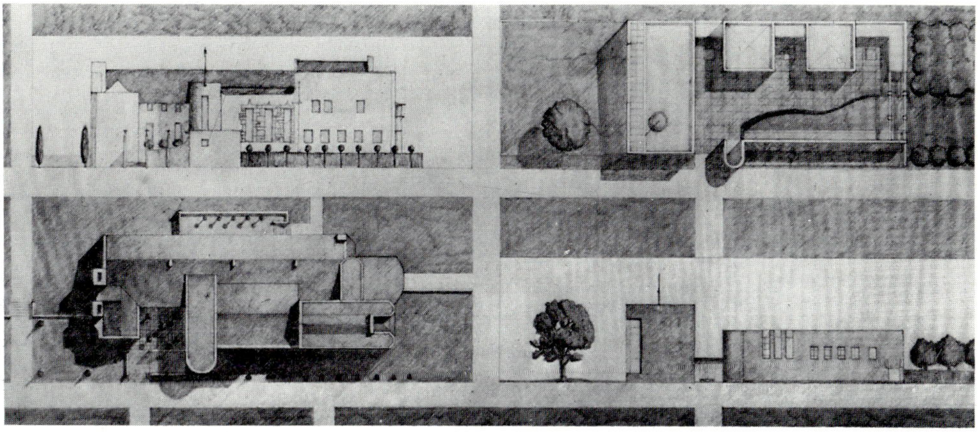

Figure 2. The design of a Media Lover House (Thesis in Design Methods). The project of the students compared with the Art Lover House of C. R. Mackintosh.

The students, in developing their project, used the system AID. The project was emblematically located in Bella Houston Park, in front of the Art Lover House of Mackintosh (figure 2). The evaluation procedure has been applied by the students to the last two cycles of analysis-syntesis-evaluation of the development design phase (figure 3).

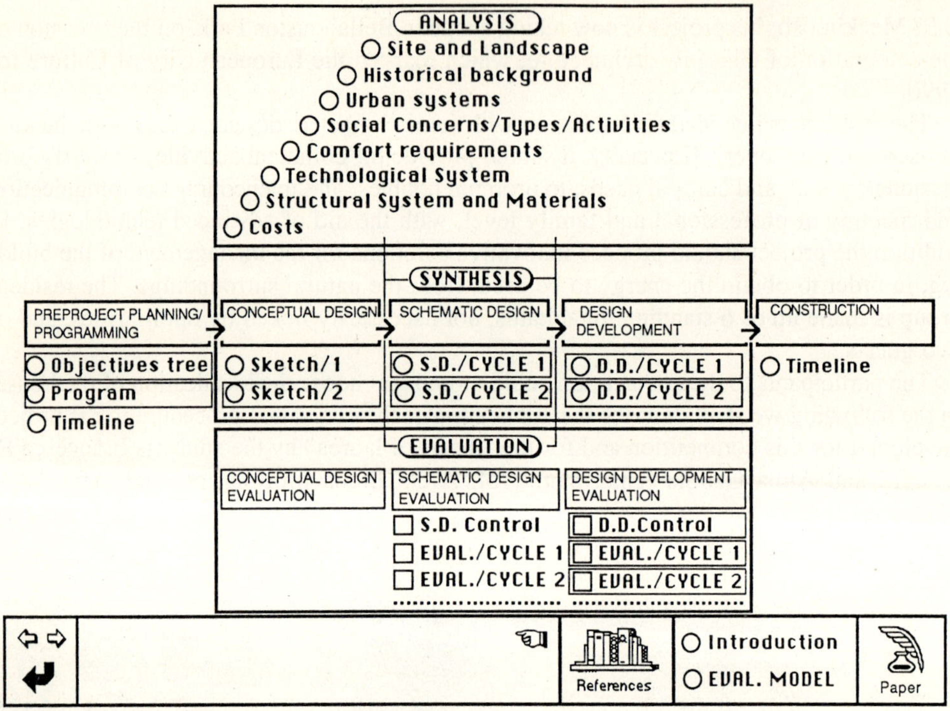

Figure 3. The Menu of An Interface for Designing (AID).

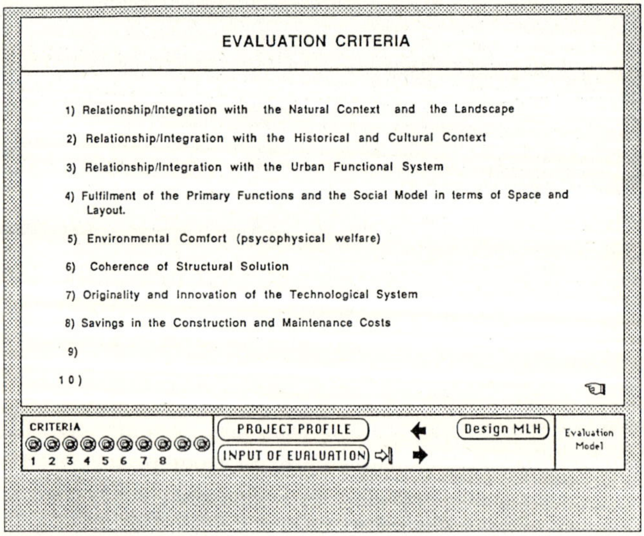

Figure 4. The Evaluation criteria.

With the aid of the procedure, in the last but one cycle, the students defined a strategy to modify the project. A strategy is the prefiguration of a set of design actions which could improve the project with respect to one or more criteria. To evaluate the efficiency of a strategy it is sufficient to apply the evaluation model to the vectors which represent the estimated performances of the modified project. To chose the best strategy the students considered only the actions that do not lead to the total transformation of the project and that allowed the minimum design effort.

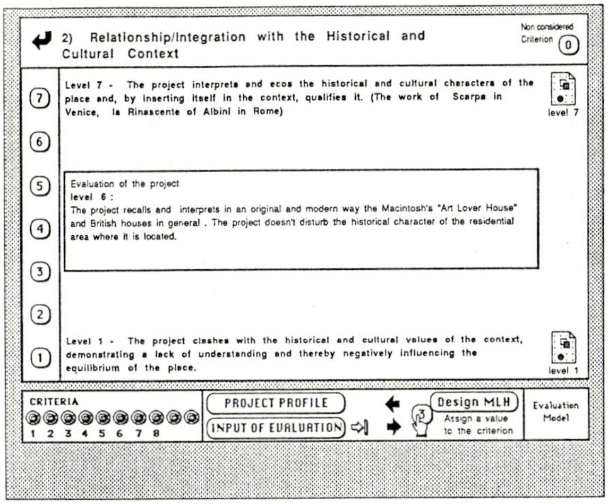

Figure 5a. An example of semantic differential (criterion 2).

Figure 5b. The Architecture of C. R. Mackintosh is the main historical reference of the project.

The choice of the evaluation criteria was done together by the students and by six professors (figure 4) (see Annex). The lack of a criterion on the quality of the formal aspects is justified by the fact that every criterion takes into account this requirement (see, for example, the criterion 5). To choose the examples to be used to better explain the meaning of the polar terms of the semantic differentials, many projects were analyzed and evaluated in relation to the different criteria (figure 5a, 5b and 6).

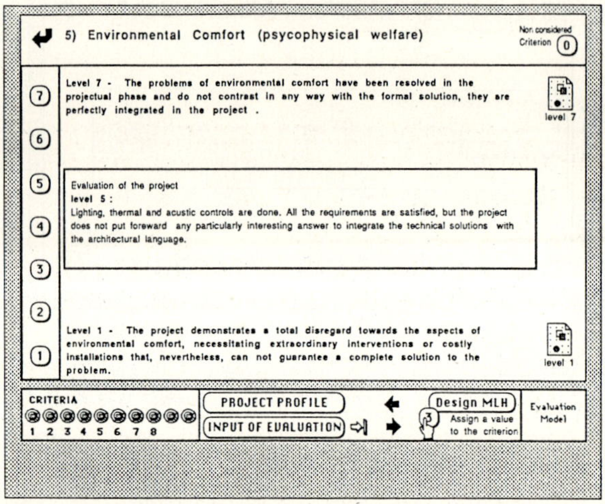

Figure 6. Another example of semantic differential (criterion 5).

This helped to develop in the students a multicriteria mentality, i.e., the capacity of considering together many different aspects of designing. The weights of the criteria were assigned separately by every judge (figure 7), who, successively, evaluated the project in collaboration. This evaluation is a result of a preliminary discussion which makes an agreement between the judges a norm for this procedure.

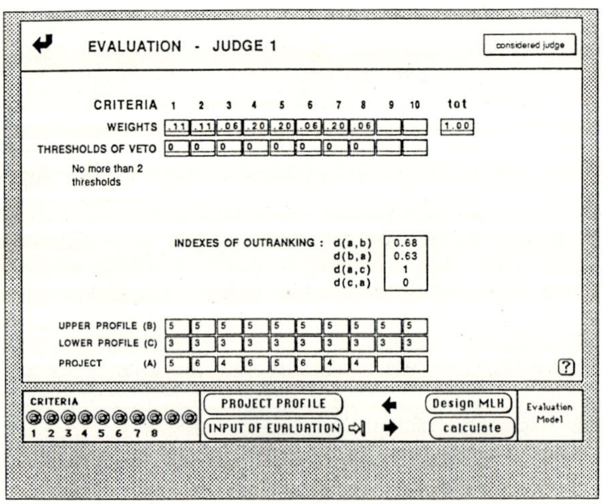

Figure 7. The Evaluation of a judge.

The judges decided to use the same reference profiles, i.e.

$$b^k = (5,5,5,5,5,5,5,5)$$

$$(k=1,2, ...l)$$

$$c^k = (3,3,3,3,3,3,3,3).$$

The profiles are "flat", i.e., the levels are the same for every criterion. At the end of the considered cycle the project is evaluated as follows

$$a = (5,5,4,5,4,4,3,4).$$

Considering the results of evaluation, we deduce that the technological systems are not innovative (level 3) and that the relationship with the urban context (in functional terms), the comfort in the building, the static solution, the construction and maintenance costs cannot be considered satisfying (level 4). The performances referred to the other criteria are sufficient (level 5). The project, evaluated with the trichotomic segmentation procedure, is assigned to the category $K^?$. The sensitivity analysis showed that the evaluation result was stable.

With the aid of the model the students explored some strategies to improve the project. A strategy is the prefiguration of a set of design actions which could improve the project in respect to one or more criteria. To choose the best strategy the students considered only the actions that did not imply a revolutionary transformation of the project and allowed the minimum design effort. A first strategy was developed to improve the projects:

- the originality of the technological solutions, with particular reference to the use of techniques to obtain the energy to be used for the management of the building from the natural surroundings (from level 3 to level 4);
- the relationship with the historical setting, through a study on the English houses and the architectural language of Mackintosh (from level 5 to level 6);
- the layout problems (from level 5 to level 6).

This strategy should improve the project as follows:

$$a=(5,\mathbf{6},4,\mathbf{6},4,4,\mathbf{4},4)$$

The components in bold style indicate the changed levels. These modifications aren't sufficient to change the project from the category $K^?$ to the category K^+. The students decided to explore a strategy which considered other improvements, in addition to those considered previously (figure 8). The new improvements are related to the static solution (from level 4 to level 5) and the comfort conditions inside the building (from level 4 to level 6), i.e.:

$$a= (5,6,4,6,\mathbf{5},\mathbf{6},4,4)$$

The evaluation model, with these performances, assigned the project to the category K^+ (figure 9).

In conclusion, these simulations, achieved with the aid of the evaluation model, allowed to identify paths to be taken in order to improve the global quality of the project. The necessary controls and modifications were conducted successively by the students using the AID system. Some significant drawings of the project generated during the synthesis phase are shown in the figures 10-12.

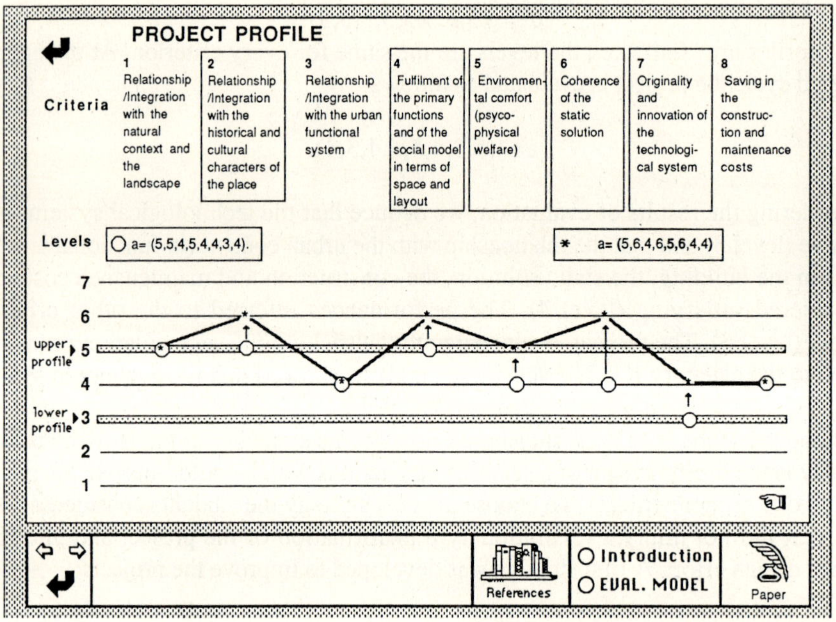

Figure 8. Searching for strategies to improve the project. The actions that do not imply a revolutionary transformation of the project and allow the minimum design effort are considered.

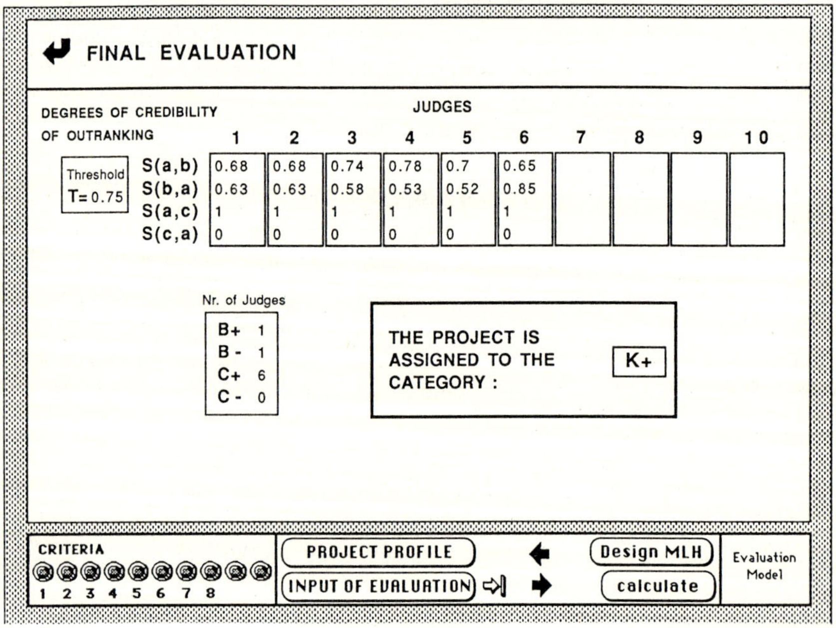

Figure 9. The final evaluation.

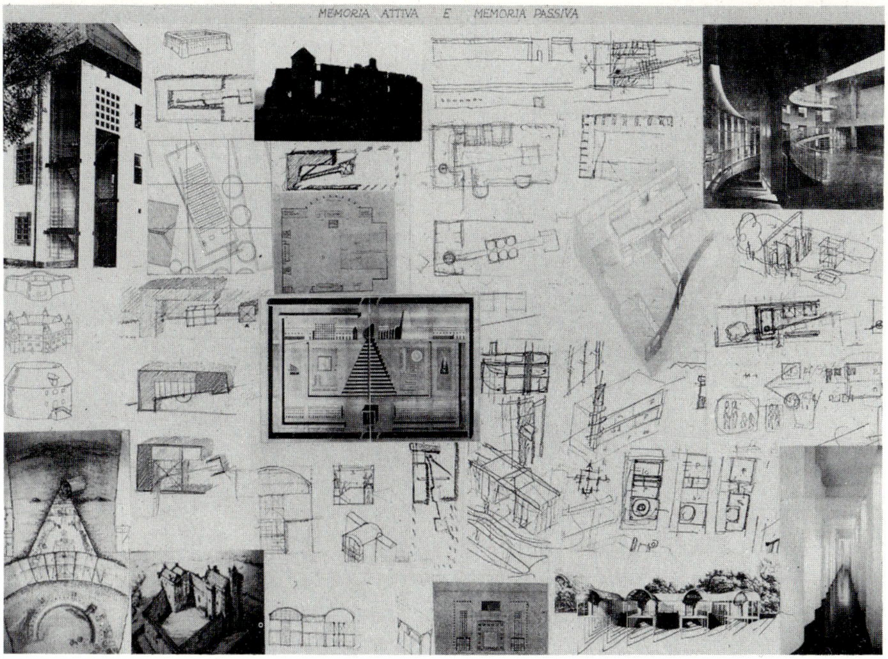

Figure 10. The step of synthesis (conceptual design): The images contained in the designer's memory help produce the first sketches.

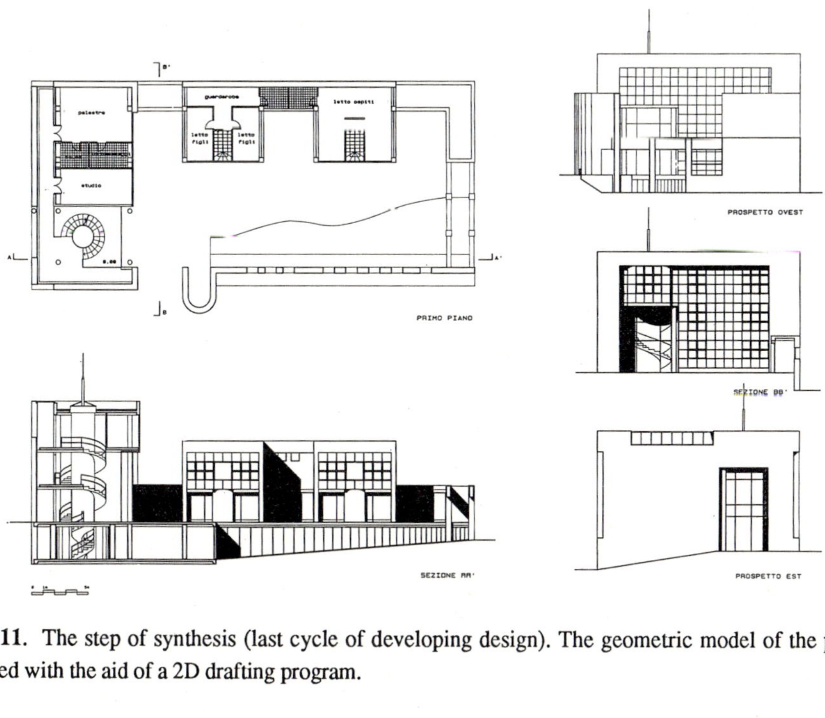

Figure 11. The step of synthesis (last cycle of developing design). The geometric model of the project is elaborated with the aid of a 2D drafting program.

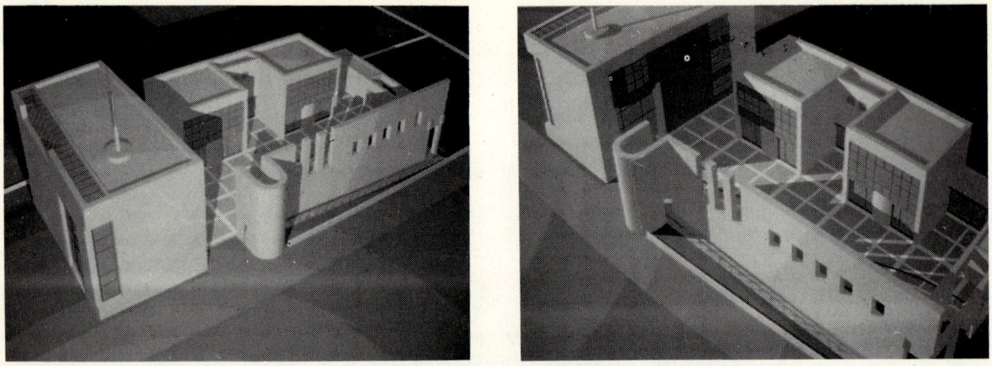

Figure 12. The step of synthesis (last cycle of developing design). A 3D model helps to define volumes, spaces and materials.

References:

Alexander, C. 1964. *Notes on Synthesis of Form*. Cambridge: Harvard University Press.

Archer, L. B. 1965. *Systematic Method For Designers*. London: Council of Industrial Design.

Archer L. B. 1968. *The Structure of Design Processes Thesis,* London: Royal College of Art.

Arrow, K. J. 1951. *Social choice and individual values*. New York: J. Wiley & Sons.

Broadbent, G. H. 1966. "Creativity." In S. Gregory (ed.). *The Design Method*. London: Butterworths.

Calderaro, V., A. Giangrande, P. Mirabelli, and E. Mortola. 1986. "Decision Support Systems (DSS) in Computer Aided Design (CAAD)." *ECAADE*. Roma.

Giangrande, A., A. Magrini, E. Mortola 1991. "Uno strumento di aiuto alla valutazione nel processo progettuale." In Atti del *Convegno Aicographics*. Milano: Mondadori Informatica.

Jacquet-Lagreze, J., J. Moscarola, B. Roy, and G. Hirsch. 1978. "Description d'un processus de décision." *Cahier du Lamsade* no. 13. Université Paris IX Dauphine.

Jones, J. C. 1963. "A Method of Systematic Design." In J. C. Jones, and D. G. Thornley (eds.). *Conference on Design Method*. Oxford: Pergamon Press.

Jones, J. C. 1970. *Design Methods*. New York: J. Wiley & Sons.

Luckman, J. 1967. "An Approach to the Management of Design." *Operational Research Quarterly* 18, 4.

Negroponte, N. 1970. *The Architecture Machine*. Cambridge, MA: MIT Press.

Maver, T. W. 1977. "Building Appraisal." In J. S. Gero (ed.). *Computer Application in Architecture*. London: ASP.

Maver, Thomas W. 1988. "Software tools for the Technical Evaluation of Design Alternatives." In Thomas W. Maver and Harry Wagter (eds.). *CAAD Futures 87*. Amsterdam: Elsevier.

March, J. G., H. A. Simon. 1958. *Organization*. New York: J. Wiley & Sons.

Mortola, E. 1983. "Una esperienza didattica nel settore del CAAD." In Jackson (ed.). *Computer Graphics, elaborazione di immagini*. Milano: Gruppo.

Mortola, E. 1988. "Computer grafica e progettazione: una esperienza didattica." *Pixel*. anno 9 no. 11.

Mortola, E. 1989. "Un' interfaccia per progettare." *Ricerca e Progetto*. vol. 10.

Mortola, E. 1989. "An Interface for Designing." In *ECAADE* Education-Research and Practice. Aarhus, Denmark: School of Architecture in Aarhus.

Mortola, E. 1990. "Computer Grafica e Progettazione." In Cangemi (ed.). *10 Lezioni di Architettura*. Roma.

Mortola, E., C. Sansoni. 1990. "L' insegnamento della Computer Grafica e del CAD nella Facoltà di Architettura di Roma." In D. Marini and L. Moltedo (eds.). *Conoscenza per immagini*. Milano: Il Rostro.

Mortola, E. 1991. "Concorso di architettura per studenti europei: progettare a House for a Media Lover." (A home for the 21st century). *Progetto e Ricerca* 3.

Moscarola, J., B. Roy. 1977. "Procedure automatique d'examen de dossiers fondée sur une segmentation trichotomique en présence de critères multiples." *R.A.I.R.O.* Vol II, no. 2.

Osgood, C. E., C. J. Suci, and P. H. Tannenbau. 1957. *The measurement of meaning*. Urbana: Univ. of Illinois Press.

Roy, B. 1968. "Classement et choix en présence de points de vue multiples (la methode ELECTRE)." *Revue Francaise d'Informatique et de Recherche Operationelle*, vol. 8: 57-75.

Roy, B. 1978. "ELECTRE III: Algorithm de déclassement basée sur une représentation flue de préférence en présence de critères multiples." *Cahiers du CERO* Vol. 20, no. 1.

Roy, B. 1981. "A Multicriteria Analysis for Trichotomic Segmentation Problems." In P. Nijkamp, and J. Spronk. (eds.). *Multiple Criteria Analysis*. Gaver.

Roy, B. 1985. *Methodologie multicritère d'aide à la décision*. Paris: Economica.

Scharlig, A. 1985. *Décider sur plusieurs critères*. Lausanne: Presses Polytechniques Romandes.

Sfez, L. 1973. *Critique de la Décision*. Paris: A. Colin.

Simon, H. 1957. *Models of man*. New York: J. Wiley & Sons.

Annex / Criteria:

1. *Relationship/Integration with the Natural Context and the Landscape*
Level 7 - The project takes into account the characteristics of the place and its natural aspects, itself becoming an important element of the place and/or improving its quality (Wright 's Kaufmann House, some examples of Castles in Scotland or France).
Level 1 - The project contrasts with the landscape, altering its characteristics.

2. *Relationship/Integration with the Historical and Cultural Character of the Place*
Level 7 - The project interprets and recalls the historical and cultural characters of the place and, inserting itself in the context, qualifies it (the work of Scarpa in Venice, la Rinascente of Albini in Rome).
Level 1 - The project puts itself in contrast with the historical and cultural values of the context, demonstrating a lack of understanding and thereby negatively influencing the equilibrium of the place.

3. *Relationship/Integration with the Urban Functional System*
Level 7 - The project matches very well the hierarchical structure of the roads network and urban services. In addition, this integration is plainly rendered in the projectual solution (the Crescent in Bath, l'unité d'habitation of Le Corbusier, some Dutch and German projects of the 1930's).
Level 1 - The project neglects the problems of the urban functional system, hindering its function.

4. *Fulfillment of the Primary Functions and of the Social Model in Terms of Space and Layout*
Level 7 - The layout and dimensioning of the spaces take into consideration the needs of the users. Different activities and possible changes with time of the needs are also forecasted. In addition, the project represents an innovative solution (Existenz minimum of Gropius, Siedlungen of Ernst May and Bruno Taut, the Weissenhof).
Level 1 - The layout and the spaces do not take into consideration the needs of the users, making the carrying out of personal activities difficult and revealing a total absence of spacial flexibility.

5. *Environmental Comfort (psycho-physical welfare)*
Level 7 - The environmental comfort performances are satisfied and do not contrast in any way with the formal solution.
Level 1 - The project does not take into consideration the comfort requirements, necessitating extraordinary interventions or costly installations that, nevertheless, can not guarantee a complete solution to the problem.

6. *Coherence of Structural Solution*
Level 7 - The project points out a precise correspondence between the structural typology and the materials utilized. The static solution, coherent with the formal solution, shows its structural clearness and coherence.
Level 1 - The structural typology is not coherent with the formal solution and contrasts with the materials.

7. *Originality and Innovation of the Technological System*
Level 7 - The project owns the most advanced technological systems (related to construction technology, security, recycling of construction materials, production of energy, management of equipments, etc.) meeting the highest level of quality's needs without altering the architectural image itself.
Level 1 - The project does not take into consideration any innovation concerning technological systems: the systems used are outdated and do not integrate with the formal solution.

8. *Saving in the Construction and Maintenance Costs*
Level 7 - The cost level is contained with respect to the choice of materials and construction elements which take into consideration the obsolescence problems, as well as the security and environmental comfort; in addition, the costs fit the resources of the users.
Level 1 - The project presents elevated costs and low quality because of erroneous solutions from the financial point of view.

Research

10 On Knowing — Feeling and Expression

Aart Bijl

EdCAAD, Department of Architecture
University of Edinburgh
Edinburgh EH1 1JZ, Scotland, UK

The basic assumptions for CAD, and for any use of computers, are re-examined. They refer to how we know things, how we think of knowledge being represented, and the impact of representation techniques on evolution of knowledge. Japan offers stimulating clues on how we might regard the usefulness of computers, and these are explained. Evocative illustrations are presented, to show a direction for future developments.

Introduction

Here follows a plea for something different: a shift of emphasis away from techniques inside computers, and towards thoughts on how we envisage computers being used. After long experience in design and CAD, it is now time to look again at the intended relationship between computers and designers.

The activity of designing employs knowledge in a way which does not rest on fixed demarcations between abilities of a technical kind and our aesthetic sensitivities. As I will try to show later, interaction between persons engaged in designing depends on affinity between each other. Computers are logically determinate machines, materially very different from ourselves, so they are inherently insensitive to *our* knowledge. What, then, do we think about the possibility of designers using computers?

> *Computers do perform useful tasks for people, but do we have to think of them being like people? What different expectations ought persons to have of computers and of other people? Might the differences tell us something about the kind of usefulness we want from machines?*

We are familiar with the strong association between computers and knowledge — the notion of knowledge being represented and acted upon within computers.

We are also familiar with the notion of aesthetics. I use this term to refer to all such human feeling as we are not able to externalize in logical form, as in the form of logically articulated written words, or mathematics. It refers to knowledge in mind, and expressions with evocative intent — normal occurrences indicated by ordinary human behavior. Designers and other persons from the arts quite properly exercise such behavior professionally.

My central question, and it is a very general one, is illustrated in figure 1. Can knowledge within a person be externalized, detached, and realized in a machine, so that it will show intelligent behavior as though from the person? The reference to aesthetics in my figure makes this question very difficult.

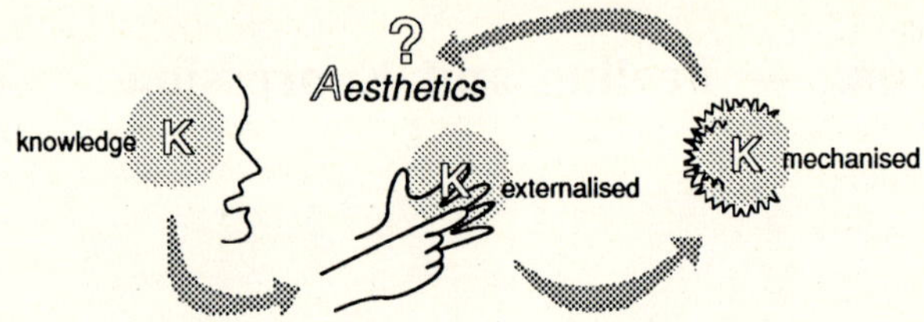

Figure 1. Externalizing Knowledge?

These questions are not helped by partisan arguments over contending representational strategies in computers. Differences at that level, as between classical logic, production systems, frame systems, semantic networks, and neural networks, do not alter the logically determinate nature of computers. Few researchers now claim that we can define a single coherent logic which accounts for our knowledge.

Paradigms such as object oriented systems, hypermedia, and machine learning get closer to these questions. They offer metaphors by which people might gain some appreciation of functionalities available from within computers. But too often these paradigms are accepted too quickly as justification for developing particular computational techniques, based on assumptions hidden from users. They entail assumptions which rest uneasily with people's ordinary knowledge.

More critically, developments aimed at standardization and data exchange, associated with product modelling, imply dangerous assumptions about routine design separated from innovative design. Over time, given unforeseen changes in demand, responses from designers have to be innovative even in 'mundane' fields of design. If innovation is inhibited then designing will not be possible.

Stimulus From Japan

Why do we need to trouble ourselves with these questions? Many people in AI will claim there are different kinds of knowledge, and certain kinds can be realized in machines. That position presumes clear demarcations between kinds of knowledge, which can be explained to users of computers. Knowledge can then be detached from persons and hidden within computers, and computers can be made to act autonomously so as to determine the actions of persons. We ought to consider what all this implies. What can motivate a computer's actions, in whose interests, and with what responsibility? What will be the effect on people's normal evolution of knowledge?

We need to think about knowledge: how it might occur within persons, how it is made evident and shared between persons, and how it is used in the actions of persons. It is on these points that I found my recent visits to Japan very stimulating — there I found a fresh perspective from which to reassess common Western notions about knowledge.

The special quality found in Japan I think is largely attributable to its long period of closure, for over 200 years, up to 1868. That period of closure, of isolation, engendered the homogeneity of its population (the Japanese Spirit), its sense of togetherness, its suppression of individual difference; and closure preserved the Eastern blending of material and spiritual sensitivities. These effects are passed between generations, and they are still evident today. The quality found in Japan is special in being combined with (and providing a necessary basis for?) its material success in accordance with Western standards.

In ordinary day-by-day experience there were some surprises. Contrary to impressions many of us might have from afar, within Japan its people have a light and easy sense of humor, enjoy informality, and avoid conflict. It is true they are always busy, but that is just their way of being alive (not the same as working hard). Japanese people are exceptionally law abiding (no common mugging, theft or extortion, not even tipping), and that also is just part of being alive. They see no point in doing things differently. All this is very comfortable for a visitor.

Central to what I found in Japan is the feeling of togetherness, based on acceptance of the notion of similarity. This refers to Japanese minds being similar; knowing what is in one is in another, and acting together without requiring full and explicit communication. Here we begin to have a clue to a different approach to knowledge.

One might say that all human minds are similar, and different from other species or artefacts *we* make. This similarity is masked by the common Western assumption of individual difference and external reference. From my experience in Japan, coupled with experience in design (Bijl 1989), it is fruitful to consider how this similarity might form the necessary basis to any corpus of human knowledge, and how it is effective without explanation.

Logic and Aesthetics

In my Ohio paper (1991a) I argue that human decisions and actions are largely influenced by aesthetic sensitivities. Aesthetics is usually associated with expressions of *beauty;* but, more generally, this can be taken to indicate any stimulation of any of our senses, and our ability to judge whether it is good. Acceptance of the central role of aesthetics, in this broad sense, is evident in Japan. It is evident in ordinary everyday behavior, politeness, and in most things that are within reach, which can be touched (but not in distant things, such as objects in modern urban space). This acceptance of aesthetics is also evident in the appearance of food, a very important part of Japanese life.

Aesthetic sensitivities determine what we want things to be, and more generally, how we express what we know. Overt techniques and formal logic can be useful for realizing what we want but, deep down, the knowledge on which they rest is aesthetically determined within ourselves.

If formal logic does not determine expressions from human knowledge, how, then, can people expect to benefit from their use of computers?
What can Japan tell us about the act of realizing expressions from aesthetic sensitivities?

Knowledge

In Japan I found that knowledge is recognized only through an association of expression with *position* (of a person). Position is important, and without it an expression is treated as though it were not present. I have developed this view in my Edinburgh paper (1991b). There I concluded that knowledge is seen as some integral combination of whatever constitutes the intelligent party and abstractions it forms from its sensations of other things. Externalized representations or expressions from such knowledge, detached from the intelligent party, cannot be knowledge.

Basically, the understanding seems to be that each one of us can be confident about our ability to know, embracing all ways we have of knowing, including use of all our sensations, our feelings. We have this confidence without explanation. It then follows that we cannot be sure (in a definite and shared way) what it is that each of us knows. We act together by invoking responses from each other's knowledge, and we use language to reach into and stimulate states of such knowledge.

Language expressions can be logically inconsistent, ambiguous, and their effectiveness relies on affinity between persons — the presumption of similarity.

Ambiguity is effective in allowing different and unreconciled interpretations, and in stimulating unexpected and informative responses.

Position is accepted as implying separate but similar truths within persons, with validity determined by responsive behavior of society — the position it grants to a person.

How, then, does Japan view the idea of computers operating on representations detached from human knowledge?
Can we think of computers being artificially intelligent, as machines operating on their representations of our expressions?

Formal Logic

My reassessment of concepts employed in computer technology goes back to fundamental philosophies of thought. These appear to determine (or reflect) our perceptions of ourselves in the world. The dominance of determinate logic in Western philosophy is now being realized in the form of computer technology, and we may have something to learn from the different philosophies of the East.

We commonly think of logic as dealing with how we can know our world, and it sets conditions on what the world has to be so as to be knowable, as indicated in figure 2. This world has to be subject to orderly decomposition in terms of logically distinct and related entities, and resulting representations have to be verifiable outside ourselves, objectively. We have the belief that logical representations can match things as they really are, and when we think they do we say they are true.

A world conditioned in this way can then be recreated in a computer. This is no accident; we have made computers to be logic machines.

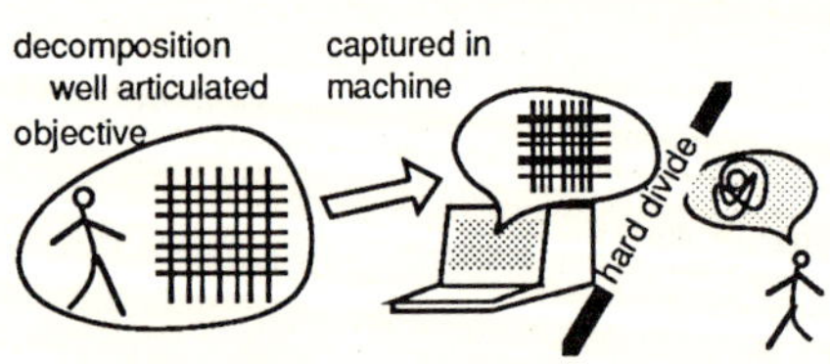

Figure 2. A Logical World.

This line of thought, reflected in our scientific tradition, is evident in our search for singular and exclusive truths, our endeavors to simplify. We do not tolerate contradictory views of the same thing. Difference must be resolved. Only one answer can be right. Resolution is equated with progress.

We can find evidence in social behavior and politics, even amongst scientists. We value competition. Success goes to winners who have destroyed their opposition.

We can also find evidence in religion. We have single exclusive Gods: "I am all... there is no other...".

This 'I' translates into the individuality of persons, their free will, and competition. Interaction between persons is based on an expectation of difference, with resolution calling on external reference... and we have the dictum "knowledge is power".

These might be extravagant observations, but I think they do have some bearing on our attitude towards computers. The expectation of difference between individuals, and belief in the objectivity of logic, may underlie our use of highly articulate and explicit forms of language expression. We think of expressions as conveying knowledge so completely that it does not matter who or what they come from. They can be verified by reference to reality. And computers can be made to use expressions just as well as persons.

Of course I am setting out an extreme position, but its prevalence is evident in the way we give pejorative connotations to words like ambiguous and inconsistent. Too many people (including computer scientists) appear to hold the view that expressions which are ambiguous cannot be referring to knowledge — the condition of classical two-valued logic. Thus we get a hard divide between those people and the more ordinary perceptions of other persons (figure 2) — this divide cuts off many ordinary activities as being beyond knowledge, and it is very uncomfortable for designers.

We need to bracket our understanding of logic in order to broaden its application. In my Edinburgh paper I concluded that we ought more commonly to regard logical truth values as referring to states of expressions, independently of how expressions might relate to our knowledge about the world. By doing so, we should be able to employ logic on any forms of expression serving any human knowledge.

Eastern Philosophy

My understanding of Japanese philosophy of thought (Bijl 1990) has come to me through conversations with professors at RCAST, Tokyo University, and the Universities of Kyushu, Kyoto, Osaka, Tohoku, and Hokkaido. Most of these conversations were with professors of computer science — with some exceptions: an architect, a musician, and a philosopher of science. My interest was to try and explore the relationship between Eastern thought and the kind of thinking which is realized in computers.

Japan offers its own way of knowing the world. This embraces how we know things, but transcends formal logic and religion, without mysticism... employing a distinction between our knowing and the actuality of things. It sets no limits on what the world can be, or on our sense of knowing. This way of knowing is associated with Buddhism, but it is on a plane above religious practices and accommodates the earthly order of Confucianism.

Professor Hori of RCAST described the Buddhist world as being nebulous, chaotic, and full, as indicated in figure 3. To a Western mind, these are vague and difficult terms, and we are inclined to attribute them to woolly thinking or mysticism. However, I came to understand this description as referring simply to a *whole* world extending beyond things that might be captured in a single logical view, and extending beyond human perceptions. It is a whole world which does not presume decomposition into separate things — what we see as the separating spaces in between are no less significant than what we see as things. For a trained Buddhist, philosophical endeavor might be characterized as self-realization of 'full... = empty'.

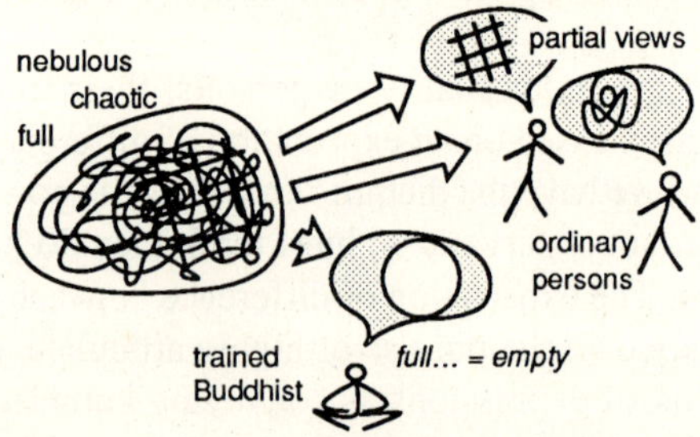

Figure 3. An Eastern World.

The effects of this philosophy on ordinary life are interesting. Truth applies within persons, with no externalized formula for representing truth — so all methods for constructing expressions of partial views of the world are equally legitimate. Different views co-exist in the same space and time, without invoking conflict or the urge to resolve differences.

Evidence can be found in social behavior and politics, in the practice of 'making room', politeness, and in the importance of position over argument.
Evidence can also be found in religion. There we find an accommodation of very many Gods, and the pronouncement of Buddha: "I am nothing... there is all...".

This 'I' translates into suppression of individuality in persons, in the sense that persons do not proclaim their separateness. Instead, as described to me by Professor Murakami of RCAST (the philosopher of science), people have a collective identity and an ability to reach consensus without relying on verbal articulation. The effect can be seen as a spontaneous form of democracy which is said to be at least as representative as Western democracy.

This collective identity is further indicated by the relative lack of structure in language expressions. These expressions are not meant to be explicit, ambiguity is normal, and meaning relies on uniformity of context *within* persons — again, the presumption of similarity. Professor Tanaka of Hokkaido University expressed this well when he described his ambition to me. He wants to work on an approach to language which emphasizes use of "very large vocabularies *not based on anything*" — allowing vocabulary terms to be formal entities (with behavior) which people can use in any way they choose.

As a tentative conclusion which has relevance for computing: Japanese philosophy appears to accept no external reference for determining forms of expression. Formal logic is accepted, but without any priority over other constructions (figure 3). We find, therefore, a softer divide between technically precise knowledge and expressions from human aesthetic sensitivities.

This softer distinction could become the focus of an important contribution from the East, to our understanding of design support systems and, more generally, systems that have to accommodate people's ordinary perceptions of the world, in the West.

Computer Science

It seems clear that scientists and other people in Japan can make innovative contributions to the way we regard computer technology. However, to do so they need to overcome an inhibition induced by their own tradition.

When Japanese scientists present their work to the international scientific community they see that community as one which is already established, which has position. Given the importance attached to position, Japanese scientists see themselves as having to serve their time, 'play a game' according to rules set by people from the West. This game is not just science in isolation. It is a game which draws on all that is embraced by Western philosophy: separateness of individuals, logical articulation, objective reference, competition for the truth. Instead of accepting this entire game, Japanese scientists ought to be encouraged to change some of the rules. Uncritical acceptance of the rules gives credence to common Western assumptions, despite these assumptions feeling foreign within Japan. This I think explains the apparent contradiction of Japanese scientists presenting their work in terms which imply acceptance of external reference and the naive 'real world' assumption, whilst denying that assumption in much of their behavior within Japan.

That assumption is accepted for what it enables scientists to do, alongside contrary assumptions which are useful for doing other things, without sensing conflict. Computers then are not justified by some overwhelming argument about how all things are or should be known — no singular and exclusive view about human knowledge. Computers just are things we make, coexisting with other things, and they offer an opportunity for commercial and scientific success in the international community.

We are still left with questions about how computers should be accepted as coexisting with other things, if they are used and if they exert influence on expressions from human knowledge. It is on these questions that Japanese philosophy might offer useful insights.

Computer applications

The non-scientists with whom I was able to have lengthy discussions, Professor Hara of Tokyo University (the architect) and Mr. Hayama (the musician), both saw the role of computers as a medium for expressions. They envisaged the prospect of being able to realize dynamic expressions in ways which presently are impossible without computers. Professor Hara saw computers as expanding the ways in which persons can imprint their record of life on the world, and evoke responses from other people. Mr. Hayama foresaw a new media oriented society, with a new kind of literacy supported by computers, leading to improved understanding between people.

These views reflect deep consideration of how people communicate, and the evocative role of expressions. Computers are seen as offering an opportunity for enriching contact between persons, as well as the more usual advantage of communication over distance and spreading to many persons.

Our conversations focused on expressions, but with little discussion of the significance of their structures, or their meaning. It was as though such matters are best left to persons who decide what particular expressions are to be, and that might turn out to be a good strategy.

It would be helpful to have more contributions from the design community, and from people engaged in the arts. What is it that such people see themselves doing? What do drawings and other expressions of their work do? What do designers offer which is distinct from the services provided by other persons? In whose interest do they do so, and with what purpose? Given their answers to some of these questions, how do these people think computers can help?

Where This Leads...

The different perceptions I found in Japan offer promising insights into my central question (set out in the introduction). These can now be summarized as follows:

a) a world that is whole, chaotic and nebulous
— not orderly decomposable and objectively knowable;

b) knowledge within persons
— not separable from persons;

c) communication based on similarity
— does not anticipate difference in individuals;

d) expressions sparse, evocative
— not representational, explicit;

e) tolerance of inconsistency across expressions
— not logically resolvable to singular outcomes;

f) soft distinction between technical precision and aesthetic sensitivities
— no hard divide between testable knowledge and human feeling.

Taken together, these points indicate a human centered view of the world, they indicate optimism in persons exercising responsibility, and they favour collective evolutionary progress. They deny any separate external reference as authority for particular actions, and do not favour revolution. This does not preclude innovation, but implies conditions on how innovations come about and how they become accepted.

The notion of knowledge being inseparable from persons, while expressions are accepted as serving communicative intent between persons, provides a clue to a different way in which we might regard computers. The strategy which begins to emerge for CAD, and for any use of computers, then rests on three main premises.

1. Our knowledge remains within and is part of persons, evolving in response to our experience in the world.
2. Expressions are externalizations, artefacts, from our knowledge, used with communicative intent — and computers are artefacts, expressions.
3. Forms used to realize expressions are without meaning, yet are necessary to our recognition of instances, and are durable within cultures.

I know that I am using terms here in a slightly unusual way. 'Without meaning' refers to relationships we feel between ourselves and particulars we sense in the world. Knowledge has to take account of such feeling, even if we cannot explain how this happens. Knowledge considered in this way is important to most human decisions and actions, and evidently so in the case of designers.

On the following pages I present evocative illustrations to show where these premises start and how they might be developed. My illustrations are intentionally evocative since they deal with matters which cannot be contained in one logically coherent argument, but which nevertheless are important to us. I hope they stimulate some useful thoughts on how we might view the further development of computer technology.

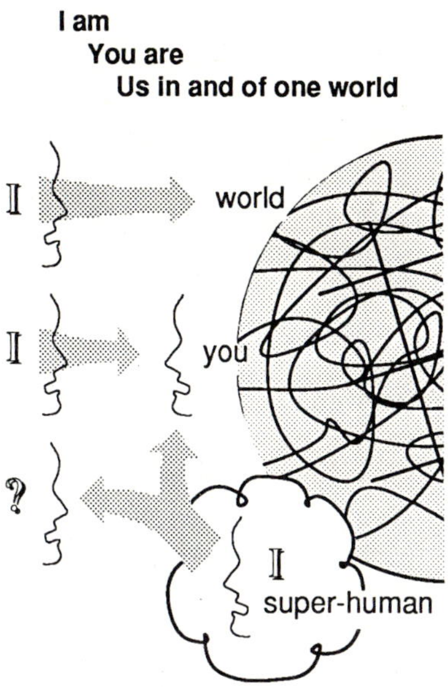

Figure 4. Metaphysics. This figure illustrates a relationship between ourselves within a whole and nebulous world. I sense that 'I' am, I see the 'world', and see 'you' in this world.— but I cannot stand outside myself, which presents problems for my perception of 'us'. These are the problems we face when we program 'our' knowledge into computers — someone has to assume the role of super-human, which is likely to result in conflict.

1. Us

I
My mind sees the world
And I see you
But not myself
To see us
I have to be detached
Super-human
I can tell you what I want
But not what you must do
Not program you
You
What my mind knows
Yours cannot
Yet we know each other
You might know the same
If we know what sameness is
Being both similar and different
We are inside ourselves
And show ourselves
In the world out there
World
The world is
We are in and of it
We know it
Knowledge of the world
Felt within ourselves
Determined by what we are
One world known by all
And many loosely bounded worlds
Felt separately in each of us.

We might think of ourselves as bounded individuals, as discrete things, but to know ourselves within a larger world we have to call on larger systems which include ourselves. That gets us into religion and philosophy.

Notions of 'us' imply some super-human (or metaphysical) external reference: "something else, which we have no way of sensing, must be out there in order to preserve the coherence of what we know from experience". So we get sub-atomic particles in physics, 'dark mass' in astronomy, and 'necessity' in logic. And we have religious deities whom we call upon to preserve social order.

Is such external reference really necessary? To put this question more gently, do we have to explain and agree a singular external reference? Alternatively, we can accept that such references come from within ourselves, moderated by each of us being part of the same whole.

These references have to be fixed, to provide adequate support for what we do, and they have to be loose, to accommodate new knowledge… including design innovation.

Whenever any one of us believes he or she has the authority to tell someone else what to do, we invoke some metaphysical position. And that is the case when we develop computers as a means of programming other persons… with the attendant danger of inhibiting innovation.

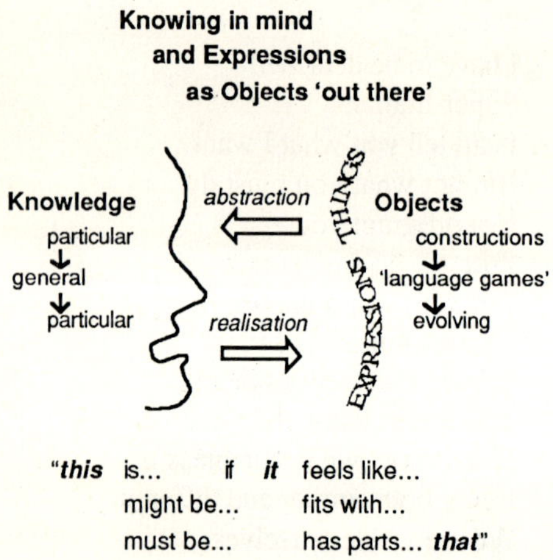

Figure 5. Knowledge and Expressions.

2.Out There

Knowledge
Our abstractions
From our sensations
Held as meanings within ourselves
Exercised on expressions
And other things in the world
Entailing recognition and prediction
Accommodates feelings
As determinants of actions
Without explanation
Objectivity
We share particulars
Only by what we show outside
Outward expression
To respond to expressions
To act with each other
We invoke detached authority
We have logic and mathematics
Poetry and painting and music
Christianity and Buddhism
Reality
They give us forms
Turning our insides out
Shaping our outward reality
Forms of expression
Invite more expressions
To sustain our shared reality
We have many realities
Realized in different expressions
Joined within ourselves.

Figure 5 illustrates a relationship between knowledge and expressions, as set out in my Edinburgh paper (1991b). Knowledge refers to states of mind, partly innate and partly abstractions from our sensations of the world. Abstractions give us particulars which we generalize, to produce further particulars which get realized as our expressions. Expressions are objects of the world, ready to be subjects for further knowledge.

This explanation draws a distinction between knowledge as an integral part of persons (or other dissimilar things, but we would have difficulty appreciating their knowledge), and expressions as realized objects produced with communicative intent. Knowledge here accommodates feelings as determinants of actions.

I am looking for an explanation which accounts for everyday knowledge, and which does not exclude any expressions from within persons. I mean to include aesthetic expressions, coming from feelings included in knowledge, which determine expressions about things not verifiable by overt systems of logic. I see this non-logical knowledge as essential to ordinary human behavior, and as the foundation of specializations which offer 'technical and testable' knowledge.

Knowledge cannot be externalized in some definite and shared way, and formal logic is no exception. In this view, logical expressions cannot be the same as knowledge of logic: what makes our logic useful remains inside and part of us.

In putting forward this view, I am not advocating the idea that knowledge is mysteriously idiosyncratic in different persons. We can see ourselves as materially and mentally similar, linked within one world, so we can assume similarity in knowledge. We can do so without explanation.

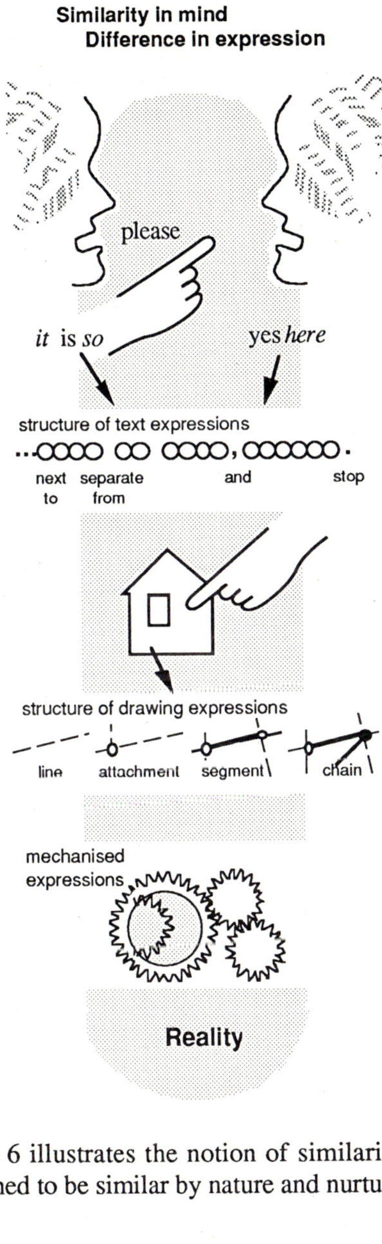

3.Acting Together

Homogeneity
No one form works alone
They all are mediated in us
Conditioned by what we are
Ourselves unrevealed
Instruments of knowledge
Excluded from expressions
Sharing any reality
Presumes similarity in us
Without explanation
Expressions
What we show of ourselves
Serves to stimulate responses
From knowledge in each other
Richness in expression
Ambiguity and contradiction
Stimulates unforeseen knowledge
Poverty in expression
Singularity and consistency
Produces a dead reality
Machines
Realizations of just one form
Overt logical determinacy
Sustaining mechanical action
Bounded in their inner worlds
Their artefactual internal consistencies
Blind to the outer world
Action
Without knowledge
And no responsibility.

Figure 6. Similarity.

Figure 6 illustrates the notion of similarity and how it relates to expressions. Minds are presumed to be similar by nature and nurture, as compared with the materially very different things *we* make. The things we make are expressions — the purpose we associate with them is to move our physical and mental states.

This view of expressions, and their purpose, covers all artefacts. They are used without us having to know (in any definite and shared way) what is actually in our minds or exactly how they are similar. We make things and observe the responses they evoke from other persons and, indeed, from other objects in the world. We accumulate knowledge from these responses to condition further things we make.

We have theories for how we exercise knowledge: by deduction, induction, and abduction. None of these theories explain what is actually happening in our minds, or why we produce particular expressions.

Through long use, certain forms of expression become recognizable to us, and they show regularities which we find effective in evoking desired responses. Thus we have text as a form of language expression, overlaid with conditions to make them satisfactory expressions in given contexts. Logical conditions might be included, if the expressions are thereby thought to be more explicit in the contexts of dissimilar persons — and if similarity is presumed then form without logic might be more important.

Other forms of expression include drawings, similarly overlaid with conditions. We can extend our examples to include painting, poetry, and music. Expressions can be mechanized, governed by an internal logic which produces external behavior. Such behavior then serves to evoke responses from other persons or other objects. Remembering that these are our expressions, not our knowledge, they include computers.

Taken together, all these expressions are our reality. They are a dynamic reality reflecting our changing perceptions — representing what we know about the world. In developing computer technology, we ought to take great care not to destroy this complex relationship between expressions and knowledge: we should not try to turn expressive artefacts into knowledge. As a diversion (to fill this space between illustrations), let us look at what an artist has said about representation and expression. Nikolai Tarabukin was a Russian philosopher of art from the early part of this century, and part of the Constructivist Movement, (quoted in Duval 1981):

"While old art, from naturalism to early Cubism, is a 'representational' art characterized by the connection between the pictorial forms and those of the real outside world, the new art breaks off this connection, this dependent relationship, in order to create autonomous objects. And while the art of the past was opposed to the real world... the new art is in a sense immanent to the world of reality: it creates objects, and no longer pictorial copies (naturalism) or arbitrary compositions (Cubism)... Pictorial art is not a 'vision'; this would enormously restrict the artist's work and limit its pictorial and philosophical meaning in the extreme. Just as music is not an art of imitating real sounds, so the art of painting is not 'knowledge', for the domain of knowledge lies chiefly in science. Art is 'fabrication' and action... before all else a voluntary function, for it establishes the primacy of creation... Painting is not called upon to 'represent' the things of the outside world, but to fashion, make and create objects. It is not a 'representational' art but a 'constructive' art. It is a voluntary impulse... valuing intuition in the highest degree."

Here we see a challenge against art expressions as representations that imitate reality (irrespective of what reality might be) or as reproductions of visual stimuli. Art expressions are autonomous objects in their own right, and are immanent or inherent to reality. The objects are fabrications or constructions in our world of experience. Creation of these objects is seen as a voluntary or independent function, not determined by overt knowledge. An interesting distinction is drawn between pictorial and philosophical meaning of art objects, and knowledge as a domain of science — the latter probably refers to a restricted notion of knowledge being verifiable by scientific method, implying some separate scientific reality. The "primacy of creation over knowledge" then calls on some whole human sense of knowing which is invoked by art.

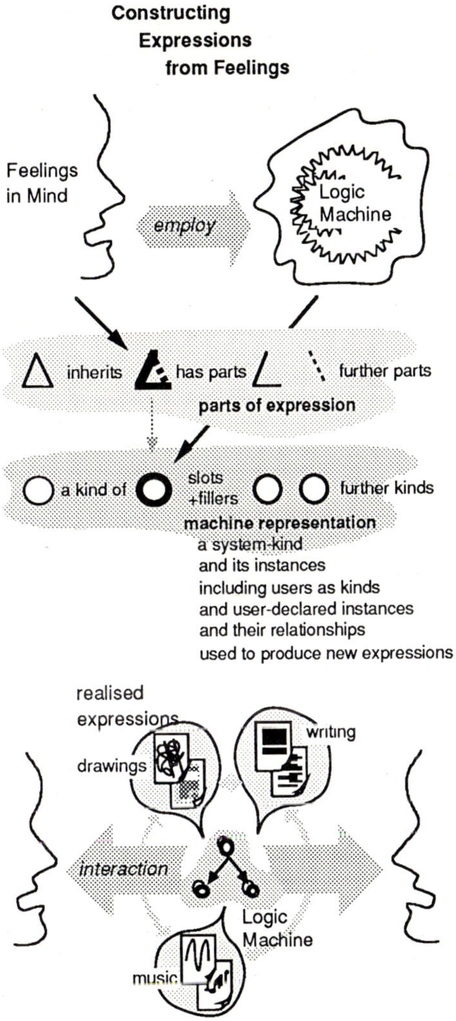

4.Information Technology
Computers
Logic machines
With artificial intelligence
Used to process our expressions
Dealing with forms in expressions
Not determined by things out there
Understood and used by us
Used to construct further expressions
To stimulate our interaction
And extend our reality
Disaster
Machines with hidden assumptions
Presumed fixed reality
Obscured responsibility
Computers that are 'easy to use'
Institutionalize repetition
Stop us thinking
Autonomous machines
Dictating instances of expression
Limiting what we can say and do
Hope
'Meaningless' machines
Offering logical mechanisms
For making evocative expressions
A formal logic
Realized outside knowledge
For non-logical human expressions
A new literacy
Employing that logic
In our whole and dynamic reality

Figure 7. Machines for Processing Expressions. This figure indicates how we might view the usefulness of future computer systems. They might be used as logic machines operating on expressions, to realize expressions from feelings persons have in mind. We want them to operate on expressive forms without knowing what expressions might be about.

Art, as in the form of drawing and painting, is sensed visually, and the stimulus invokes meaning. We feel and know art invokes meaning even if we cannot articulate and re-express this meaning in some other form, as in words. These expressions serve communication between persons, just as the writings of authors of novels or poetry communicate with other persons. The meaning we derive from art contributes to our knowledge and influences our actions. Where I differ from the position indicated by this quotation from Tarabukin, is that I am trying to reduce the distinction between expressions from art and science. Science might employ *different* abilities within ourselves (which we cannot see) but, in both art and science, expressions can be viewed as immanent to our world of experience, constituting our realty.

A system should offer correspondences between the different parts of users' own expressions and the machine's differentiated instances of its representational entities (called kinds in the figure) — without those entities being like user-expressions, or being seen by users. Users should then expect to have control over the machine's behavior, thereby controlling the machine's operations on arrangements of its entities, in order to produce new instances of users' own expressions. Evaluations by the system refer to states of its representation, and not the world outside the machine. Usefulness is to be seen in terms of machine-support for person-to-person interaction.

5. Examples

Numbers

A little fun with plus 1
take primes
divisible by no numbers
other than themselves and 1
3, 5, 7, 11, 13, 17...
to each add 1
you get primes
31, 71, 131...
or products of primes
51, 111, 171...
or you get evens
3 + 1 = 4,
5 + 1 = 6,
7 + 1 = 8...
except for 2
2 + 1 = 3 ...distinctly odd

A form of expression
For which we have arithmetic
Which tells us 'right from wrong'
Numbers come from us
We cannot sense them out there
But use them to show what we know
We manipulate numbers
According to our formalism
But what makes this system right?

Figure 8. Sameness and Similarity.

Numbers are our notation for quantities (of units of measure: length, volume, and numbers of instances...). Arithmetic is our formalism for associating and performing operations on numbers, independently from anything else to which we apply numbers.

The two responses to adding 1, in the above figure, indicate different perceptions of these numbers. One sees them as numerals, objects which are the numeric expressions, which depict numbers; to which a further numeral is added. The other sees them as numbers which are eligible for operators from the formalism of arithmetic; to which the + operator is applied. In both cases the results can be assessed arithmetically, in terms of primes and evens.

The first case results in further primes or products of primes, arising from a function that does not come from arithmetic. Yet the results present a certain order which has arithmetic properties. Is this purely chance?

The second case does employ an arithmetic function and it points to the number 2 as posing a question. Here we have a function and value applied to 2 which produces a result that is different from the results of the same function and value applied to all other primes. This might make us consider sets of primes, and we might think of one set containing 2 and another set containing all other primes. What then is the use of a set containing only one member? Ought we to reconsider whether 2 really is a prime?

These cases illustrate numbers as coming from us, and show how fragile our notion of numbers is — there is nothing 'out there' to tell us what numbers must be. The second case illustrates our general difficulty in knowing from what points of view things can be considered to be the same, as when they are primes. How different can things be before they are no longer the same? — the old problem of differentiating between types and instances.

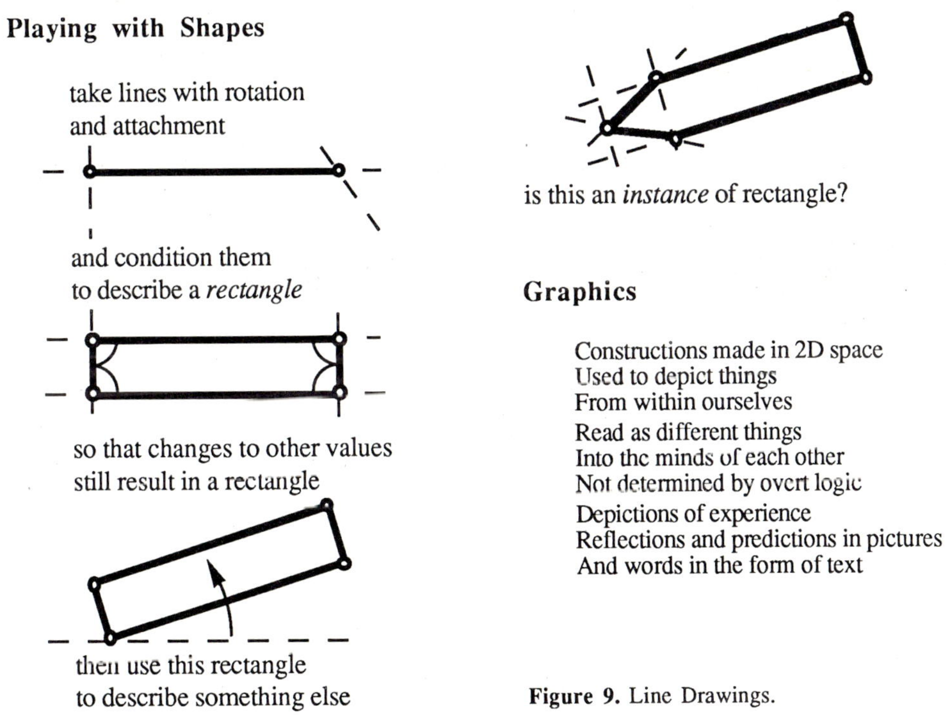

Figure 9. Line Drawings.

As with numbers, lines are not seen in the world, other than those we make. Unlike numbers, we have no general and agreed system for manipulating and reading arrangements of lines. They can be ambiguous and evocative, which makes them effective.

Like arithmetic applied to numbers, we sometimes apply geometries to arrangements of lines, and those lines depict our geometries. We also produce arrangements of lines not determined by geometries, just as we express sequences of words not determined by grammars. Where do those lines come from, within us? Why do we use them?

When we try to show ourselves being logical in our use of lines, we face odd difficulties. We do not have external criteria for our geometries, and geometries do not tell us how they should be applied to depictions of other things.

So the question posed in the above figure can be rephrased more generally, just as in the previous example of numbers. For something to be an instance of something else, to what extent must it be the same? In the present case it might be misleading to call the pointed shape a rectangle. But it might be useful to do so if we want to preserve its inherited rectangular properties in any further manipulations of this shape.

Expression / Shaped from Stone

Figure 10. St. Giles Cathedral, Edinburgh.

Figure 11. Rietveld's House, Utrecht.

Architecture

Constructions made in 3D space
Used to express human aspirations
With money as a measure of priorities
Designs for non-existent things
Drawing on inner human sensitivities
And realized through use of logic
Buildings evoke responses
They are seen as functioning practically
And judged aesthetically

These two examples from architecture illustrate the role of aesthetic sensitivities in human decisions and actions, and in the value attributed to results.

The first, St. Giles Cathedral, is an expression from the 12th Century, intended to reach many people. It expresses spiritual aspirations and a sense of place in the world. These are functions for which we have no calculations or other explicit methods of explanation. The form was determined by aesthetic sensitivities from within persons. The effectiveness of this expression is evident in responses it has evoked from many people through time, including destructive acts indicating conflicts.

The building has served as a focus for interaction between persons, and its importance as an expression is indicated by the energy which people have continued to expend on it.The second example, Rietveld's house, closer to our time, has survived some 70 years. It has been through a period of neglect, and has been restored to be a show-piece of Dutch architecture. Why? It is not particularly noteworthy in fulfilling the practical functions of a house. Its sole justification is as an aesthetic expression. We value what we see of someone in the past giving expression to his perception of a changing world: a reconciliation between man and a modern technological world.

This house makes us feel good about the prospect of a vigorous new reconciliation with our newer technology. We might still ask why has this and other older examples of architectural expression proved to be so durable, while present-day examples are pushed into oblivion by a rapid and bewildering succession of still newer buildings? Might the answer be that our current architectural expressions fail to touch deep aesthetic truths within people?

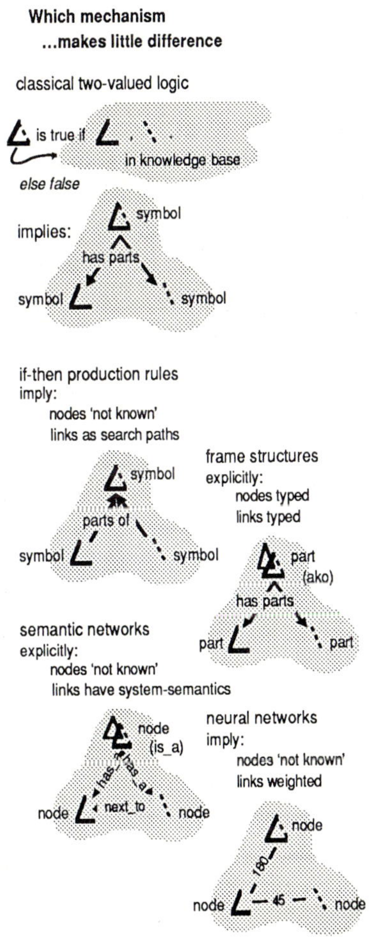

Figure 12. Logic.

6.Where Next

Discovering Forms
Properties of expressions
Serving communicative intent
Durable within cultures
Laws of forms
Observed and obeyed
So we can know expressions
Dynamics of forms
Which can be realized in machines
To support people's interaction
Logic
Focus on structure of forms
Parts and relationships
Including conditions
Truths in logic
Reference within ourselves
Revealed by our use of forms
Forms interposed
Between man and machine
Displaying human responsibility
Applications
All forms of expression
Realized as artefacts
Outside persons
Mechanized operations
Used to express knowledge
Technical and aesthetic
Integration of science and art
Industry and politics
Without boundary

Logic now becomes strongly associated with 'mechanisms' operating within perceiving parties. For us, it includes all relationships as we are able to comprehend, irrespective of what else might be 'out there'.

When we make machines and intend them to behave as perceiving parties, we do so by devising logic mechanisms which govern their internal operations, as in the above figure. All these mechanisms are 'blind' in that they are unable to share our sensations for particulars in the world, and we ought therefore to be cautious in regarding them as being intelligent.

Such mechanisms might be used to construct models, conceived as logical abstractions showing relationships between our knowledge and observed phenomenon. Showing then entails some partial realization in the form of an expression. However, the point I am trying to illustrate is that a machine cannot know it is realizing a model, and it cannot assess relevance to observed phenomena outside itself. Such knowing has to be exercised by persons using the machine, and for that purpose it might make little difference which variant of logic the machine employs.

Positions of Others

Readers of my writing ask: How do I fit within the spectrum of AI's critics? This question is not easy to answer. It supposes clear comparisons between distinctly different positions, and when we look into them we meet qualifications which point to similarities.

I have presented a personal view. It reflects my own experience, including influences from cursory readings of Russell (1912) and Wittgenstein (1953), with welcome assistance from Pears (1985), and of Steiner (1978) on Heidegger, and Kripke (1980), Putnam (1981), and Magee (1987). My view on logic seems quite compatible with those of many logicians, including Wittgenstein's in both his early and later works. Divergence occurs when people use logic to validate correspondence between their expressions and other things as-they-actually-are.

Referring to work more directly connected with computing, I will now risk gross misrepresentation. Hubert Dreyfus (1979) is well known for condemning AI's preoccupation with 'toy systems', arguing that they do not display intelligence, and making them bigger and more complex will not make them intelligent. Following the path of Heidegger, he claims formalizations involve regression, and they cannot account for our sense of being-in-the-world. We cannot make autonomously intelligent systems that can deal with our real everyday tasks. Dreyfus' position is sometimes criticized, unfairly I think, for implying that computers cannot be made to do anything useful. His position seems to me to be acceptable if we see it as an attack on artificial human intelligence.

John Searle (1984) criticizes the notion of artificial intelligence by identifying aspects of human beings and claiming they cannot be replicated in machines: focusing on aspects such as intentionality. Interestingly, he adopts a 'hard realist' and reductionist stance, arguing that we can know (definitely and in a shared way) what people actually are, and we can know how machines are different. This is interesting because if such knowledge were to be possible we might then have a specification for humanly intelligent logic machines. That would appear to undermine Searle's own criticisms of AI.

Winograd and Flores (1986) have attracted the interest of the AI-in-design community. They question the realist and reductionist position, also citing Heidegger. They argue that "language cannot be understood as the transmission of information... [but rather] as interlinked patterns of activity... [based on] commitment" (pp 76). I would agree that this refers to a kind of commitment which cannot be found within computers. However, their conclusions seem odd: advocating 'co-ordinator' systems, as ready-to-hand tools, "whose use leads to better domains of interpretation... convey a kind of 'coaching'... train people to improve their effectiveness... reveals for people how their language acts..." (pp. 179) — presuming proper knowledge about language acts, detached from participants who make and use them. This is odd because Winograd and Floris appear to recognize knowledge in persons in a manner which questions such detachment.

My conclusions differ in that I am advocating 'simple' tools for constructing expressions, disconnected from knowledge we variously might associate with particular expressions. Here my distinction between expression and representation is important, regarding representations as occurring within intelligent parties and not in expressions themselves. I envisage people using computers to construct expressions which invoke meanings variously within themselves, supporting evolving patterns of person-to-person interaction — the notion of computer literacy.

Conclusions

In this paper I have discussed knowledge including meaning and intention, and separately we have expressions including machines. Meaning and intention are included in knowledge in the sense that they link ourselves with particulars of things we observe in the world — constituting what we know and determining our actions.

Expressions are tangible things we use to prod and invoke states of knowledge in ourselves and each other. They are subject to formal conditions which are necessary to our recognition of the presence of expressions: how else do we distinguish music from other noise, visual art from other manipulations of light, and architecture from other heaps of matter?

Forms used in expressions are neutral (or meaningless) in the sense that they are not determined by varying particulars of things we observe in the world; we can accept that they are meaningful only in the task of realizing expressions, not in determining what instances ought to be. In this sense, forms might include geometry used in architecture, tonal scales in music, and meter in poetry.

Durability of forms used in expressions depends on their being meaningless, as in the example of our treatment of numbers detached from other things numbers might be used to describe.

The dynamics of expressions then constitutes our reality, on which we exercise our knowledge. The emerging strategy for using computers, then, is to target machines at manipulations within and across forms, and to give persons full control of forms they decide to use in their expressions.

We need to become clearer about the nature of forms, their durable properties and the ways in which they are used. We can then expect to target computer technology at forms so that computers can be used by many people to construct interrelated expressions from a broad spread of human knowledge. We can expect to do so without determining what knowledge actually is, and we might find that suitable computational systems can be quite simple.

We want computational systems which know nothing about their users' knowledge. The abstract formal systems they support should be apparent in their surface behavior, resting on minimal machine-functionality applied to a minimal set of representational entities and relationships. Machine-representations then refer to parts and links in users' expressions, and that ought to be enough to be useful to people constructing their own expressions.

My plea is that we ought to put more effort into research on forms of expression, beyond formal logic and mathematics, and independently from computers and particular applications. We want to discover how forms in general cohere, and how they are used to evoke human knowledge. If we can become clear about our use of forms then we will have a sound target for widely useful computer systems.

References

Bijl, A. 1989. *Computer Discipline and Design Practice - Shaping Our Future.* Edinburgh: University Press.

Bijl, A. 1990. "Formality in Design: Logic and What Else...?" In *International Symposium on AI in Engineering,* as part of the Pacific Rim International Conference on AI '90. Nagoya, Japan.

Bijl, A. 1991a. "Logic in ICAD and Use of Logic in Design." Submitted to *IFIP Working Conference on Intelligent CAD.* Ohio, US.

Bijl, A. 1991b. "Defining Intelligent CAD - What Computers can Know and Do." Accepted for International Conference on AI in Design '91. Edinburgh, UK.

Dreyfus, H.L. 1979. *What Computers Can't Do: The Limits of Artificial Intelligence.* With introduction to revised edition. NY: Harper Colophon Books.

Duval, J.-L. 1981. *Avant-Garde Art 1914-1939.* SKIRA Macmillan.

Kripke, S. 1980. *Naming and Necessity.* Blackwell.

Magee, B. 1987. *The Great Philosophers: An Introduction to Western Philosophy.* BBC Books.

Pears, D. 1985. *Wittgenstein.* (with postscript). Fontana.

Putnam, H. 1981. *Reason, Truth and History.* Cambridge: University Press.

Russell, B. 1912. *The Problems of Philosophy.* Oxford (9th impression 1980).

Searle, J. 1984. *Minds, Brains and Science.* Reith Lectures, BBC Publication.

Steiner, G. 1978. *Heidegger.* Fontana.

Winograd, T., and F. Flores. 1986. *Understanding Computers and Cognition: A New Foundation for Design.* New Jersey: Ablex Publishing Corporation.

11 An Intelligent Simulation Approach in Simulating Dynamic Processes in Architectural Environments

Filiz Ozel

School of Architecture
New Jersey Institute of Technology
Newark, NJ 07102, U.S.A.

The implications of object-oriented data models and rule-based reasoning systems is being researched in a wide variety of application areas ranging from VLSI circuit design (Afsarmanesh et al 1990) to architectural environments (Coyne et al 1990). The potential of this approach in the development of discrete event simulations is also being scrutinized (Birtwistle et al 1986). Such computer models are usually called "expert simulations" or "intelligent simulations". Typically rule-basing in such models allows the definition of intelligent-objects that can reason about the simulated dynamic processes through an inferencing system. The major advantage of this approach over traditional simulation languages is its ability to provide direct reference to real world objects and processes.

The simulation of dynamic processes in architectural environments poses an additional problem of resolving the interaction of architectural objects with other objects such as humans, water, smoke etc., depending on the process simulated. Object-oriented approach promises potential in solving this specific problem. The first part of this paper addresses expert simulation approach within the context of architectural settings, then the second part summarizes work done in the application of such an approach to an emergency egress simulation.

Introduction

The simulation of dynamic processes in architectural settings requires the representation of objects that have spatial and temporal qualities. Such objects are usually highly structured and are composed of other objects, many of which have properties that vary in time and space. Simulations in architectural settings must deal with the physical environment as well as other objects such as humans that are located in such environments.

In representing complex objects, a number of studies have proposed extensions to conventional record-oriented data models (Lorie, R. A. and Plouffe, W. 1983), but a more widely implemented approach has been the development of entity- or object-oriented data models (Lochovsky 1986; Coyne et al 1990). Researchers have also begun to explore the implications of object-oriented data structuring methods in simulating dynamic processes (Adelsberger 1986), where knowledge about dynamic processes are represented as rules that allow inferencing. While expert systems aim at reasoning <u>about</u> the objects represented in a system, object oriented simulation environments aim to define intelligent objects that can reason about their environment, their relationship to each other and to the changing conditions in the simulated process. This paper focuses on the implications of object oriented data structures and rule-based simulation environments on the simulation of dynamic processes in architectural settings. An emergency egress model will be used as an example in the second half of the paper.

The representation of architectural knowledge solely as rules, is often found to be inadequate, since reasoning about architectural artifacts requires "method calls", i.e. procedures that extract knowledge from an existing data base. Thus, architectural expert systems usually call for a mixture of rule-based and procedure-based reasoning mechanisms. Simulation languages are traditionally procedure-based, and they tend to process real world objects in a highly abstract manner. On the other hand, architectural environments do not usually lend themselves to the level of abstraction expected and supported by traditional simulation languages such as GPSS (Schriber 1974), etc. The configurational aspects of such environments must usually become constraints in spatial processes, thus abstraction limits the accuracy and the realistic representation of the real world event under study. Therefore, a programming platform is needed that simultaneously allows accurate descriptions of architectural settings and the simulation of dynamic processes in such settings.

Expert Simulation Systems

Among the advantages of expert simulation approach cited by Robertson (1987) are: a) the ease of describing intelligent agents (objects in a simulation), b) the creation of the simulation by the application of 'small chunks of knowledge' through an inferencing system, which means that the structure of the simulation is dynamically generated by the inferencing mechanisms and not explicitly by the programmer.

Robertson refers to the ability of an expert simulation to appeal to one's intuitions about the real world so that the rules that define the real world can be used in the simulation and vice versa as "Referential Transparency". Traditional simulation languages tend to create and use operational mechanisms that do not necessarily have real world counterparts. This leads to the problem of using mechanisms that do not appeal to our intuitions about the real world. In fact referential transparency afforded by Expert Simulation Systems is one of the major advantages of using expert system approaches in simulating dynamic processes in architectural environments.

Rule based systems are relatively high level tools for capturing the descriptions of the behavior of systems. In addition they can also encompass computational interpretation. For the purposes of rule based simulation languages, it is necessary that the system under study allow structuring of data and operations into object and relation descriptions. Forward chaining systems additionally provide the means to couple operations with the objects that make up the domain of the operations.

Object oriented programming refers to a data structuring approach that is based on real world objects and their properties. Several programming languages support such data structuring environments. Smalltalk, Simula, Ross, KBS and Orient84/K are only some of these languages (Adelsberger 1986). For example Ross, which stands for Rule Oriented Simulation System (Khlar, Faught & Martins 1980) was developed specifically for war game simulations and military air battles. It represents real world behavior/ knowledge by rules and by incorporating knowledge in hierarchically arranged objects. Objects in the system have names, parents, properties and behaviors (as messages) associated with them. Smalltalk (Goldberg et al 1983) is considered to be the hallmark of object oriented programming languages. Its philosophy is to define abstract objects and classes, and operations that may take place on those objects. The class of an object defines what properties its objects can have and their associated operations. Thus when a class object is instantiated, it inherits all the properties and operations of its class. KBS, Knowledge Based Simulation, was developed at Carnegie Mellon University for the Intelligent Management System project. The underlying database is similar to Ross, and was specifically designed as a knowledge based simulation environment.

There is some consensus in the use of the following terminology among researchers interested in the development of intelligent simulations:

Object : This refers to a class of objects in the simulation that represents a real world counterpart. Objects can be simulated entities such as people, or architectural components such as walls, doors, windows etc. Specific instances of an object in a simulation are generated from its type (or class description). In terms of data structuring, objects are data systems which request, send, and receive data via sub-routines called messages.

Simulation Knowledge Base : However, it is not enough to define and create the objects in a simulation, one must also describe the inter-connectivity of objects.The interconnectivity of components is defined as the interdependence of objects to each other within the context of the dynamic process simulated and can be represented by Artificial Intelligence software engineering concept called rule basing. Oren (1986) defines knowledge in the domain of computer simulations as facts and rules, procedures, methods about objects (projected to the instances of objects) and their relationships with each other and with their environment. A rule can reside in an architectural data model along with actual components and can be executed by an inference engine. Function of a component can also be stored as an object and get associated with a component.

Each object needs to be associated with: a) its initial state in the simulation, b) logic rules that govern its operation, and c) how it can change state. These rules include all of the other objects or processes that affect its operation. As the simulation proceeds, each object is associated with new states of the system, where a time stamp is used as a reference. The simulation logic rules express propositions about objects, since the researcher aims to test hypothesis about their behavior in a simulation. As a result, all objects in the system are logically interconnected with each other and with the processes that could influence their behavior.

Agent : This refers to an instance of a particular Object specification. These are the active objects in a simulation. In the simulation of dynamic processes in architectural settings, a distinction must be made between active and passive objects. While the former actually generate the simulated dynamic process, the latter usually act as constraints (such as architectural elements acting as barriers), or wait for a scheduled time to become active (such as the arrival of fire fighters in an emergency egress simulation).

Behavior : This refers to the history of actions taken by an agent. Since these are sequences of actions, they can be subdivided into smaller behavior chains. Behavior can also be described as the actions taken by an agent between two simulated times.

Graphic interface : This refers not only to an iconic representation of the agents, but also to the configurational description of architectural settings. When the behavior of agents heavily rely on the interaction with the environment (as it is in spatial behavior of people, cars, robots etc.), the interaction with a graphic database becomes a major component in a simulation. Usually traditional simulation languages do not support graphic interfaces or provide very limited support.

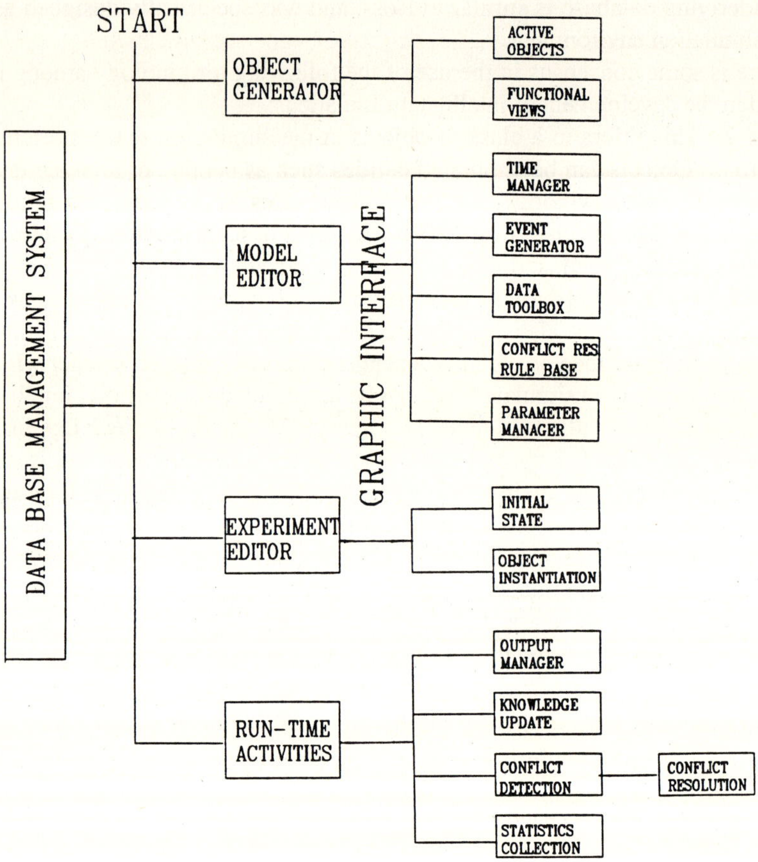

Figure 1. The Structure of Intelligent Simulations in Architectural Settings.

While existing CAD systems can be the basis for a graphic interface, other graphic tools such as virtual reality software can be very powerful. In fact, the simulation of dynamic processes in architectural environments can be reflected to the user within a very realistic virtual setting. For example, the graphic interface of a fire spread simulation can show smoke and fire spread in a virtual reality environment.

The Structure of Expert Simulations

Functions in an expert simulation environment can be divided into those that are related to the description of real world events and objects, and those that are related to an experimental setup. Simulation of dynamic processes is actually an experimentation technique, where the parameters of a real world event are explored by means of the output data produced by the simulation. In essence, setting the experimentation is the instantiation of the system developed. In non-deterministic simulations (i.e. stochastic ones), each instance of the system generates a different set of output data which need to be further analyzed. The parts of an object oriented and rule based simulation environment can be seen in figure 1.

a) Object Generator Module

This allows one to generate the objects in a simulation independent of the context in which they will be used. The nature of the objects in architectural settings and the architectural environment itself allow a hierarchical structure. Parts (or components) are related to each other in a hierarchic manner.

One must also make a clear distinction between the object representation of architectural environments and the representation of active objects. While the former can be part of a more general object description and data base system, the latter needs to be more specific. The process of extracting functional views from an architectural object data base for simulation purposes is not any different than the process of retrieving functional views for expert system purposes. (A functional view is defined as a data model that is extracted from a more extensive object data base to meet the specific requirements of an expert system application). On the other hand, simulation-specific objects need not only be defined within their own type hierarchy, but their relationship to the extracted functional view of the architectural setting also need to be established. Furthermore, in a multi-purpose simulation environment, one needs to provide facilities to generate new types as well as the instances of these types. Thus, this module must encompass a type generator as well as an instance generator.

The Object generator must have an interface which could at times be graphics that would allow one:

- to define the configuration and location of active objects (possibly through a Computer Aided Design system, i.e. a graphic data base to define the configuration of objects),
- to position objects on the screen,
- to modify their location, size, and configuration,
- to specify the properties of the objects,
- to specify the relationship between objects,
- to specify the constraints on the objects,
- to establish class-instance relationships where instances inherit the characteristics of the class they belong to.

Since simulations are highly procedure-based, there is a also a clear need to create a system where "methods" as well as properties are inherited by the instances of objects. Manola and Dayal (1990, p.211) solve this problem by treating stored as well as computed properties as functions, i.e. the system they have developed uses a function-inheritance system.

b) Model Editor Module

This module helps to establish the rule base of the processes simulated, define the relationship between objects in time and space, and define the functional relationship between them. Among the tools that are needed to build the model are:

i. Time Manager

Two traditional approaches to time management in simulations are the time-increment method and the event scheduling method. Time managers in expert simulations will have to provide both options. Furthermore, tagging of objects with a time stamp can help with statistical data collection. Temporal properties of the objects in a simulation, such as first_action_time, current_action_time etc. need to be part of the object data structure. An additional issue in time management is the condition of an object at different times during the simulation. This can be resolved either with a version control facility, where different versions of an object at different time frames are stored, or those properties of objects that have changed over time are time stamped and a record of these is saved.

ii. Event Generator and Scheduler

This is the process of creating the rule base of the events in the system. Major transactions in this section are :

a) Establishing the relationship between objects and events;
b) Determining the parametric relationship between objects;
c) Defining the method associated with the execution of each event.

Several researchers propose a "goal driven" event-execution system within the intelligent-simulation environments. Adelsberger and Shannon (1986, pp.110) use the term "goal-directed simulation", and Robertson (1986, p.13) refers to "goals" as he discusses a bank-queue simulation where people have goals but detailed actions are molded by the environment. BGRAF, the emergency egress simulation developed by this researcher also uses a "goal driven" event driver. In defining intelligent-objects, goal-oriented behavior can allow the objects in the system to reason about their environment, and choose an action strategy.

The mechanics of each event needs to be defined as a method. This can be irrespective of the objects it will act upon, such as moving an object at a given speed irrespective of whether it is a car or a human being. Most spatial events can be defined as generic methods, while the interaction of different objects needs to be more specific.

Subdividing the objects into affecting and affected agents can start defining the relationship between objects through a method. Rather than embedding the object_relationship (except for spatial relationship) into object_type hierarchy, it can be made part of the event description and the associated method that will act upon these agents. This helps to identify a wide variety of relationships specific to an expert_simulation without necessarily providing this data in the object data base. In a sense, events are also treated as objects through this structure.

iii. Parameter-base Manager

Determines the parametric relationship between objects and events, which is established by factors such as size, proximity, density etc. The Event_selection process can rely on such parametric relationships. This is usually a general rule base that is checked by objects prior to the selection of new action strategies.

iv. A Numerical Data Tool Box That Can Generate Random Numbers and Different Distribution Functions

Random number generators are used in simulating the chance parameters in stochastic simulations. In the development of stochastic expert simulations, Robertson (1986) proposes an "uncertainty factor", where a percentage of certainty is embedded into the rule base. This allows the intelligent-object to select among a number of alternatives and to reason about the immediate circumstances. For example in an emergency egress simulation:

IF smoke_density greater than 10mg/cubic feet*
THEN fire is located at current_floor (75%)*
IF smoke_density greater than 10mg/cubic feet*
THEN turn back (60%)*
(* The numbers are given for demonstration purposes)

Among other tools needed during model building are the interface between the rule base managing language and the object data base generating language, an on-line knowledge update facility, and an on-line documentation.

- Conditions of conflict resolution

The Model generator must also provide a rule base to resolve conflicts.

c) Experiment Editor

While model building environment refers to the creation of the hypothesis of the researcher about the real world event, experimentation refers to the instantiation of the model built. This requires the instantiation of the objects in the system and the specification of different parameters. Intelligent agents inherit the properties, relationships and method associations from their type. Therefore, while the model building step establishes the types of objects, experimentation step instantiates these objects. Furthermore, simulations aim to generate knowledge about the states of a given system, thus there is a need to describe the initial state of the system. Thus the parts of an experiment generator can be identified as follows:

- Initial state generator for each experiment,
- Object instantiation,
- Specification of termination conditions
- Statistical output manager
- Definition of interrupt conditions
- Specification of the parameters of the simulation state manager which keeps track of the states of the simulation.

d) Run Time Activities

Among the run-time activities are display and output management, collection of data about the states of the objects in the simulation and hardcopy generation. Error and conflict detection need to be done during run-time, so that they can be resolved using the rule base of conflict resolution. Forward and backward chaining processes help to drive the simulation. Updating of the knowledge base during run-time represents the learning process. Therefore, intelligent agents in the simulation can learn during the course of the simulation by updating the rule-base.

Object Base of the Emergency Egress Simulation

In the past, researchers have studied dynamic processes in architectural environments by the development of discrete event simulations, such as fire spread models (Jones 1986) and emergency egress models (Stahl 1979, Ozel 1987 etc.). These models usually rely on procedural languages such as Fortran and are based on a variety of representations of architectural environments, none of which are object oriented. For example, in BFIRES (Stahl 1979) walls, doors and people are only allowed to occupy grid locations on a building plan, and BGRAF uses the data base of a CAD system called CAEADS (Turner et al 1984). In BGRAF, Fortran was preferred to more specific simulation languages such as GPSS (Schriber 1974), due to the need to incorporate graphical interface and the need to access a CAD data base.

Conceptually, the development of object data systems helps to build a simulation where simulated objects directly relate to their real world counterparts. This allows ease at tracing the performance of the model, the nature of the objects in the model and the states of the model within a given time period. Furthermore, object oriented data structures help to establish the relationship of architectural and non-architectural objects much more clearly.

In defining the structure of the objects, it is important to differentiate between those objects that are passive in the system and those that are active. Typically, passive objects are the architectural elements in the system, and active ones are those that participate and create the dynamic process. Therefore, while passive ones do not necessarily have a "behavior" associated with them, active ones must have one or more behaviors associated with them, some of which may include relationships with passive objects. Within the scope of this paper, the data structure of passive objects, i.e. the architectural environment will not be addressed, since it has already been addressed by this researcher in a jointly authored paper (Ozel & MacKellar, 1991). The extraction of functional views from a single data model, and the details of the relationship between passive and active objects will be reserved for a future paper. Active objects in BGRAF-II are structured as follows:

name	-	object name
parents	-	names of the superclasses to which this object belongs
properties	-	description of object characteristics
behaviors	-	rules describing the object's function and behavior characteristics

Examples of BGRAF-II objects:

name	-	Occupant group
parent	-	People
properties	-	Location, walking_speed, mobility, sleep_status, smoke_tolerance, tolerance_to_stress, noise_tolerance, current_action, current_goal, safety_status, initial_action_time, safe_exit_time, current_time.
behavior	-	Goal structure of the object and the methods associated with actions
name	-	Alarm
parent	-	Fire safety system
properties	-	Loudness, location, sounding_time, current_time, alarm_switch
behavior	-	IF sounding_time EQUAL current_time, THEN increase alarm_switch by one. IF alarm_switch EQUAL one, THEN increase information_buildup factor.
name	-	Extinguisher
parent	-	Fire safety system
properties	-	Location, type, assigned_person, in_use, etc.
behavior	-	IF in_use ON, THEN decrease fire_spread_rate. IF assigned THEN set in_use ON.

The Event Base of the Emergency Egress Conceptual Model

a) Event Generator of the Model

BGRAF was visualized as a tool where different conceptual models of emergency egress behavior can be tested. This was achieved by differentiating "goals" of the simulated people from their actual "actions". An "action" had the potential to be associated with a variety of "goals". The stochastic component was incorporated into the model at the "next goal" selection process. Actions were associated with a goal by the model user.

BGRAF can function as a general purpose emergency egress simulation by means of a rule based system, since model users can identify their hypothesis about the behavior of people during fires by accessing and modifying this system. The dialogue with the model user can aid in the modification of the rule base. Data from real world fire incidents indicate that people show different response patterns in different types of occupancies, therefore the ability of emergency egress simulations to allow change in the rule base is very critical in processing a wide variety of theories about human behavior in fires.

The decision process concerning the relationship of the individual with the environment, with other people and with the event-specific elements (i.e. fire and smoke spread) establishes the rule base of the model. This is in fact the reflection of the relationship of active and passive objects to the rule base. In the original version of BGRAF, these were built into the procedural knowledge base, and did not allow forward and backward chaining.

Affecting agent	-	Person
Affected agent	-	Door
Constraints	-	Affected and affecting agents be within 2 ft. of each other Affected agent be closed Smoke level at the adjacent space not exceed the tolerance level of the affecting agent Affecting agent not_incapaciated
Associated method	-	Set door status to open and update the graphic display

Action name	-	Wake person
Affecting agent	-	Person
Affected agent	-	Person
Constraints	-	Affected and affecting agents must be in the same space Affected agent asleep and not_incapaciated Affecting agent not_asleep Affecting agent not_incapaciated
Associated method	-	Set sleep_status of the affected agent to "awake"

This can be extended to as many actions as needed. The advantage of object-oriented and rule-based approach is the ease with which new actions can be added to the simulation, since actions need not be built into the code as it is in the case of other programming approaches. Furthermore, actions can be more systematically defined, thus new actions can be defined consistent with the existing ones, and the role of each action can be traced more easily during run time for statistical purposes.

For example, in the original version of BGRAF, rescue was not an action defined in the event library. To add this action, one needed to know the data and programming structure of the model, and there was no readily available method to upgrade the library. Whereas in an object oriented environment, since the structure of each action is clear and there is referential transparency, one can easily add new actions. A "rescue" action will be as follows within the structure identified above:

Action name	-	Rescue
Affecting agent	-	Person
Affected agent	-	Person
Constraints	-	Affecting and affected agents must be within the same space Affecting and affected agents must be within 1 ft. of each other The mobility of the affected agent must be nil (i.e. either handicapped, ill, drugged etc.) OR the safety_status must be nil (i.e. the person is incapacitated due to smoke etc.)
Associated method	-	Move the affecting and affected agents together towards exits

b) Goal Generator

As discussed earlier, among the properties of rule based object oriented simulations, Adelsberger and Shannon (1986, p.110) cite "Goal directedness" as a method that can augment the experimentor and provide automatic modification to the simulation model. BGRAF also uses a goal-driven simulation approach. Within this structure, the model user was able to identify several deterministic alternative action strategies that will lead to the same goal.

Objects are related to goals within a Has_goal relationship, and the behavior of active agents are identified with this relationship. Has_goal relationship of each object has an associated uncertainty factor.

On the other hand, each goal is associated with a set of actions with a Has_action relationship, which also entails an uncertainty factor, i.e. each action has a likelihood of leading to a selected goal. The weight of this factor may change from one condition to another. The constraints in the rule base of each action determine whether the conditions are appropriate for the execution of a selected action. Originally in BGRAF, action selection was deterministic, but the goal selection process was stochastic, and environmental constraints contributed only to the goal change process. Whereas when intelligent agents respond to changing conditions in a dynamic process, they should select an action strategy that would best fit the given conditions. Therefore, deterministic action strategies can be replaced by inferencing mechanisms.

c) Goal Modifiers

Goal modifiers act as conditions that will affect a goal change, i.e. change the behavior of an agent. Some of the approaches to the management of knowledge base of goal modification are:

a) Providing a rule base embedded into the behavior of the object, which controls the response to method calls.

b) Creating a local knowledge base independent of the methods that define the behavior of objects as in Orient84/K object oriented language (Adelsberger et al 1986).

c) Providing a general knowledge base, which is checked by every object-type, whenever a method call is activated.

The second approach has the potential to reduce processing time, since only those rules related to a specific object are checked. On the other hand it may result in the repetition of certain rules for different objects. The decision between the second and the third options depends on the number of different objects needed in a simulation and the amount of redundancy in the rule base, therefore it must be decided upon on a case by case basis while developing intelligent simulations. At this point in this study, rules exist in a general rule base, since emergency egress simulations do not have a wide variety of active objects.

Rules for goal modifiers can be time-dependent or local-condition-dependent. While the former requires a scheduling process expressed within the bounds of the simulated time, the latter requires reasoning about objects and/or checking the existence of certain conditions. These can best be expressed in terms of IF-THEN rules, and can use pre-stored or calculated parameters.

Some of the time dependant modifiers are:

1. IF alarms go_off, THEN activate agent and choose goal.
2. IF Smoke_detectors sound, THEN activate agent and choose goal.
3. IF fire_fighters arrive, THEN rescue action,
4. IF fire_fighters arrive, THEN alert action. etc.

Examples of condition dependent modifier rules are:

1. IF noise-level .GT. noise_tolerance, THEN wake person
   constraint: limit on the proximity of the person to the source of the noise
2. IF density_of_smoke .GT. smoke_tolerance of individual, THEN inactivate person
   constraint: consider only the smoke_density of the current location of the person
3. IF fire exists in the current_room, THEN add onto the information buildup factor (that may modify the current_action or goal)
   constraint: current_goal must not be fight fire
4. IF current_room ventilated, THEN increase tolerance_to_stress
   constraint: person must not be already incapacitated
   person must be in the ventilated room
5. IF current_room_ventilated, THEN reduce the smoke_level of current_room
6. IF fire extinguished, THEN increase tolerance_to_stress
   constraint: person must not be already incapacitated
7. IF tolerance_to_stress .GT. information_build_up_factor, THEN activate action change
8. IF asleep, THEN no_action
9. IF mobility nil, THEN no_action etc.

Currently, the project summarized above is under development. There are plans to access an object-oriented data model that is being developed using INGRES data base system with an interface to AutoCAD as part of a code analysis expert system (Ozel & Mackellar, 1990).

Summary

Object-oriented, rule based simulation environments provide the possibility of simulating dynamic processes in architectural environments with direct reference to real-world counterparts. The process which is sometimes termed as "referential transparency", has several advantages, among which are the ease with which the model user can trace the processes in the model, the clear identification of the logic of the system as a set of logical rules, the potential to describe new objects and add new rules to the simulation knowledge base, and the possibility of distinguishing architectural objects from objects located in such environments which resolves the problem of representing the interaction of dynamic objects with the environment. Furthermore, such simulation systems have the potential to access the data base of more general purpose architectural object data models, and extract functional views as required by the specifics of the simulated process.

The distinction between architectural expert systems and expert simulations lies in the fact that the former aims at aiding the architect in reasoning about architectural objects, whereas the latter tries to simulate how intelligent objects reason about processes in such environments. Due to this reasoning mechanism, intelligent objects can modify their behavior and choose alternate strategies that will lead to the same goal. While, traditional simulation environments were able to provide such alternatives only by strictly defining available strategies, theoretically intelligent agents can generate alternate strategies from the rule base by means of an inferencing system.

The potential of intelligent simulations is only beginning to be tapped by researchers from a variety of disciplines. Architectural researchers need to focus more on this potential, since they tend to deal with issues related to computer simulations very often due to the fuzziness of the line between architectural expert systems and architectural performance simulations.

References

Adelsberger, H. Helmo, and Robert E. Shannon. 1986. "Rule based object oriented simulation systems." *Intelligent Simulation Environments*, pp. 107-112. San Diego, CA: Simulation Councils Inc.

Afsarmanesh, H., D. Knapp, D. McLeod, and A. Parker. 1990. "An extensible Object Oriented Approach to Databases for VLSI/CAD." In S. Zdonik and D. Maier (eds.). *Object Oriented Data Base Systems*, pp. 607-618. San Mateo, CA: Morgan Kaufmann.

Balci Osman. 1987. "Methodology and Validation." In Balci Osman (ed.). *Conference on Simulations*. San Diego, CA: The Society for Computer Simulation.

Birtwistle, Graham, and John Kendall. 1986. "A View of LISP." *Intelligent Simulation Environments*, pp. 157-161. San Diego, CA: Simulation Councils Inc.

Coyne, R. D., M. A. Rosenman, A. D. Radford, M. Balachandran, and J. S. Gero. 1990. *Knowledge-Based Design Systems*. New York, NY: Addison-Wesley Co.

Goldberg, Adele, and David Robson. 1983. *Smalltalk-80: The language and its implementation*. New York, NY: Addison Wesley Co.

Jones, W. 1986. *FAST: A Fire and Smoke Spread Model*. NBS, Center for Fire Research Publication.

Klahr, P., W. S. Faught, and G. R. Martins. 1980 "Rule Oriented Simulation." In *International Conference on Cybernetics and Society*, pp. 350-354.

Lochovshy, F. (ed.) 1986 "Database Engineering." Special Issue on *Object oriented Systems* 8, no.4.

Lorie, R.A., and W. Plouffe. 1983. "Complex Objects and their use in design transactions." In *ACM Engineering Design Applications*. San Jose, CA.

Luker, Paul, and Heimo Adelsberger (eds.). 1986. "Intelligent Simulation Environments." In *Conference on Intelligent Simulation Environments*. San Diego, CA: Simulation Councils Inc.

Manola, F., and U. Dayal. 1990. "An Object Oriented Data Model." In S. Zdonik and D. Maier (eds.). *Object Oriented Database Systems*, pp. 209-215. San Mateo, CA: Morgan Kaufman Publ.

Oren, Tuncer. 1986. "Knowledge bases for an advanced simulation environment." *Intelligent Simulation Environments*, pp. 16-22. San Diego, CA: Simulation Councils Inc.

Ozel, Filiz. 1987. "The Computer Model BGRAF: A Cognitive Approach to Emergency Egress Simulation." Doctoral Program in Arch. Dissertation. University of Michigan, MI: Ann Arbor.

Ozel, F., and B. MacKellar. 1991. "An Integrity Constraint Approach to Verifying Building Designs." Research Paper accepted for presentation and publication at the *First International Conference on Artificial Intelligence in Design*. Edinburgh, UK.

Robertson, P. 1986. "A rule based expert simulation environment." *Intelligent Simulation Environments*, pp. 9-15. San Diego, CA: Simulation Councils Inc.

Schriber, Thomas J. 1974. "Simulation Using GPSS." New York, NY: John Wiley and Sons.

Stahl, F. I. 1979. "Final Report on the BFIRES/Version 1, Computer Simulation of Emergency Egress Behavior During Fires: Calibration and Analysis, NBSIR 79-1713." Washington DC: National Bureau of Standards, Fire and Life Safety Program.

Turner, J., Ted Hall, and Lynn Borema. 1984. *CAEADS: User's manual*. University of Michigan, Architecture and Urban Planning Research Lab., MI: Ann Arbor.

Zdonik, Stanley, and David Maier (eds.). 1990. *Object Oriented Data Base Systems*. San Mateo, CA: Morgan Kaufmann.

12 Intelligent Systems for Supporting Architectural Design

Gianfranco Carrara(*), Yehuda E.Kalay(**), Gabriele Novembri(***)

(*)Department of Building Techniques and Environmental Control,
"La Sapienza" University, Rome, Italy
(**) School of Architecture and Planning,
State University of New York at Buffalo, Buffalo, NY, USA
(***) Cartesiana Consortium, Rome, Italy

Design can be considered a process leading to the definition of a physical form that achieves a certain predefined set of objectives. The process comprises three distinct operations: (1) definition of the desired set of performance criteria (design goals); (2) production of alternative design solutions; (3) evaluation of the expected performances of alternative design solutions, and comparing them to predefined criteria. Difficulties arise in performing each one of the three operations, as well as in combining them into a purposeful, unified process. First, it is difficult to define the desired performance criteria prior to and independently of, the search for an acceptable solution that achieves them, since many aspects of the desired criteria can only be discovered through the search for an acceptable solution. Furthermore, the search for such a solution may well alter the definition of these criteria, as new criteria and incompatibilities between existing criteria are discovered. Second the generation of a design solution is a task demanding creativity, judgement, and experience, all three of which are difficult to define, teach, and otherwise capture in some explicit manner. Third, it is difficult to evaluate the expected performances of alternative design solutions and to compare them to the predefined criteria. Design parameters interact with each other in complex ways, which cause effects and side effects. Predicting the expected performances of even primary effects involves extrapolating non-physical characteristics from the proposed solution's physical organization, a process which relies on a host of assumptions (physical, sociological, psychological, etc.) and hence is seldom a reliable measure. A fourth problem arises from the need to coordinate the three operations in an iterative process that will converge on an acceptable design solution in reasonable time. Computational techniques that were developed in the past to assist designers in performing the above mentioned activities have shown limitations and proved inadequate to a large degree. In this paper we discuss the work in progress aimed at developing an intelligent support system for building and architectural design, which will be able to play a decisive role in the definition, evaluation and putting into effect of the design choices.

The Methodological Approach

Current design practice calls for the constant presence and the reciprocal close integration of an ever growing number of different disciplinary competences of rapidly evolving scientific, technological and organizational content. Such specialization and integration include significant problems, due both to the need for a constant, widespread professional updating, and to the increasing difficulty in communicating between experts in different fields, even when they are often closely related. Furthermore the increased "intrinsic" difficulties of the field are exacerbated by other difficulties, often no less imposing, derived from the methods of implementing the building process, that is, the procedures governing all the phases of designing, constructing and managing the building asset.

Faced with these situations, all the parties concerned and the operators in the field feel the need for formulating building information in a clear and technically flawless manner provided in a timely fashion. It must meet the information needs of the building process phase in which it is used, and be verifiable, modifiable, and updatable in real time, so it can optimize the solution and respond to the complex ensemble of variables, while enabling the solution to be compared with other solutions.

It has been shown (Carrara et al 1985, Kalay 1985) that the development of software systems to support design must be based on a thorough analysis of the methodologies and the logical procedures of the design process itself, aimed at identifying those activities that can or should be computer supported.

Researchers responding to this challenge demonstrated the importance of the techniques of representing knowledge, and incorporating it in CAAD tools (Carrara et al 1985, Carrara et al 1986, Novembri 1989, Kalay 1985). They have also demonstrated the close co-pooling between the concepts of prototype refinement, prototype adaptation on one hand and between prototype generation and Routine and Creative Design (Gero et al 1988) on the other. Routine and creative design are applied alternatively by the designer. Situations can in fact occur in which, starting with existing solutions, it might become necessary to define new partial solutions, while a new design solution can to be perfected and completed in all its parts to arrive at the final design.

Different methods have been proposed to implement the process of seeking design solutions (Shaviv 1979, Woodbury 1987, Swerdloff et al 1987, Flemming 1987, Stiny 1980). Each of these systems has shown interesting potentials but also strong limitations emerging clearly if the results they produce are compared to the real situations in which the designer works. This makes these systems basically merely theoretical and therefore of limited use.

In actual design work, many factors concerning the design process are unknown to the designer and would not seem to be determinable a priori. Rather, the search for a design solution is a learning process, through which facts, possibilities and compromises are discovered, which can influence and modify choices and decisions already made, as well as radically change objectives that have already been set.

Moreover, design solutions cannot be defined separately from the process that determines their viability, since it is the evaluation of the choices that were made, that leads to achieving the objectives (Simon 1969). The difficulty of forecasting all the effects and consequences of the choices that were made precludes planning of the process, except at the most abstract level. Rather the designer must weigh the positive or negative effects of all the solutions adopted and to derive operational indications from this evaluation. The choices must be assessed not only also in relation to achieving the objectives, but also in the light of the choices that were made earlier.

The difficulties of formalizing and fully understanding the mechanisms of learning, creativity, and the critical capacities necessary to develop an activity such as designing, seem to be (under current conditions) insurmountable. These processes are the exclusive prerogative of humans, and will remain so for a long time to come.

Recognizing these difficulties and at the same time faced with the real necessity of producing tools capable of helping the designer, led some time ago to the definition of a different approach aimed at producing software instruments that able to facilitate design work as a whole without attempting in any way to supplant it. This approach is based on the fact that designers are capable of handling extremely complex problems and processes, and have, in the course of the centuries, achieved results that are there for all eyes to see.

Perhaps, to improve the quality and the reliability of the responses supplied by the designer, it is not necessary to think of automating the design process at all levels. It seems more prudent and worthwhile to consider producing tools that are able to establish a symbiosis between the capabilities of the designer and those of the machine.

Developing such a system is still a task of outstanding difficulty, requiring the identification of the operations that can in reality be carried out by the computer and, among these, the choice of the ones that a design system must or should carry out, while at the same time defining the procedures of integration and dialogue with the designer.

The following pages illustrate the structure of a Knowledge-Based Assistant (which we call KAAD), which is being developed within the framework of a combined research project of the CAD laboratory of "La Sapienza" University's Faculty of Engineering - Rome , the Cartesiana Consortium and the State University of New York at Buffalo.

The purpose of this research is to produce a software system that can establish an effective working symbiosis with the designer by making a complex, articulated representation of building objects, simulate their behavior and verify the design choices. The proposed system will be able to cooperate with the designer in:

- guaranteeing the rational nature of the design solutions;
- fostering the competence of the action and the quality of the proposal;
- permitting the updating of technological and organizational solutions;
- making an "historical memory" of solutions elaborated earlier and of the assessments of their behavior with respect to the requisites laid down as the basis for any subsequent development.

The system can attribute a class (and hence a meaning) to every graphic note used by the designer, thereby enabling the semantic interpretation of sketches. Every declarative phase is matched by a series of deductive processes intended to determine all the consequences of the declarations made with the objective of defining a correct integrated representation of the design solution and determining the compliance of the choices made with regard to the assumed set of constraints. This process entails the determination of all the quantities necessary for the purpose. The designer is able to modify interactively the definitions given both at the level of the general scheme and regarding aspects of detail, observing the variations that these modifications entail in the quantities concerned. Choices not in keeping with the system of defined constraints are pointed out to the designer.

The system operates on a knowledge base aimed at producing a complex model of the objects as the designer defines them. The knowledge base enables knowledge of the objects to be represented by defining classes of concepts and instances. The classes are defined by prototypes which correspond to an intentional representation of the objects involved in the design activity (Bobrow et al 1975). Implementation of the system is based on the formalism of frames implemented in the Common Lisp language and it uses a hybrid object-oriented programming paradigm.

The representation of the design goals is performed by expressing their objective aspects (requirements) and by defining their allowable values (performance specifications). The resulting system of requirements defines the set of all the possible building objects consisting of the set of characteristics (attributes and relations) which are considered relevant to represent the particular kind of desired building object with respect to the consistency check against the designer goals.

Generally speaking, there is no single object corresponding to an abstract representation but the whole class of the building objects that are equivalent with respect to the values assumed by the considered characteristics. The more we increase their number and their specifications, the smaller becomes the membership of the class, until it coincides with one single object (given that the assessed specifications are fully consistent). Moreover, the corresponding representation evolves up to the total prefiguration of the building object.

It is not possible, therefore, to completely define a building object deductively in advance, since it is inferred from the considered goals and is itself a result of the design process. All that can be established in advance in that the characteristics assumed to represent any building object are hierarchical, topological, geometrical and they have functional relations between the parts of the object - at any level of aggregation, as components, as space units, as building units, or as the whole building (Carrara et al. 1990).

The system comprises four modules: the knowledge base, the evaluator system, the design goal database and the user interface and design control system.

The functional scheme of the proposed system is illustrated in figure 1.

The Knowledge Base (KB)

The KB is the system software component making it possible to construct a conceptual model of the building organism and of its evolution at the necessary level of detail in the various phases of the design process. The KB contains three categories of objects which together create the representation which in the future will be termed prototypes, instances or objects and groups, respectively.

Prototypes

The KAAD system's knowledge base has been created by implementing a set of prototypes, slots and calculating procedures. The system of prototypes is a basic component of a frame-based knowledge representation system because it guides the inferential process of the system through the slot filling process.

Prototypes represent the generalization of a group of objects in the design sphere and constitute the knowledge base of the system (Gero et al 1988). In this work it has been assumed that the type of information the designer normally uses derives from a vision of reality of intentional type (Bobrow et al 1975, Hofstadter 1979). The representation adopted is therefore based on a discrete number of attributes, relations and "methods" made up of rules of the IF - THEN type or of calculation procedures.

The description of the characteristics of the objects is made by pairs of slot-facets. Each slot represents a particular characteristic of the object, while the facets represent the set of the values that can be assigned to that characteristic. It is possible through the definition of appropriate slots to represent information such as default values or maximum and minimum values.

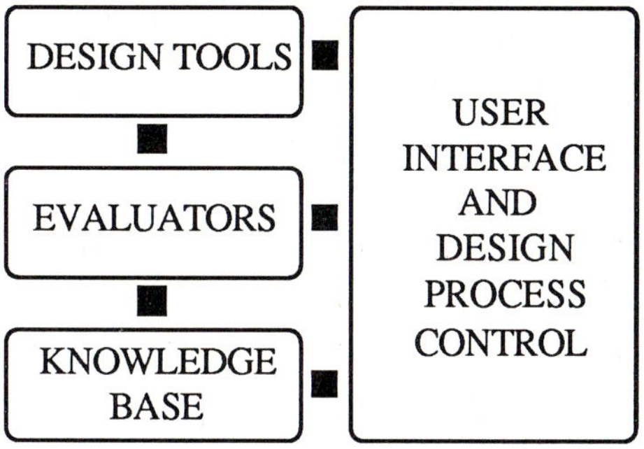

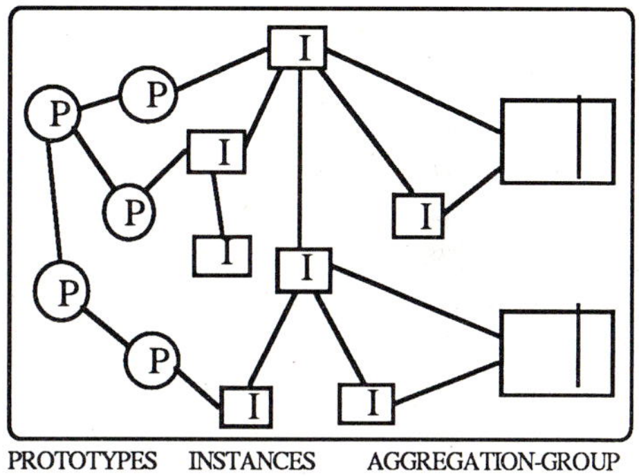

Figure 1. General structure of the system.

Figure 2. Internal structure of the Database.

A large number of prototypes relating to physical objects or existing spaces together defining a building organism have been pin-pointed and made operative in the KAAD system. To describe the results achieved it is necessary to first set out certain definitions. In the following, a building will be considered as a structured set of spaces created by a structured set of physical elements. We will define a space unit as an equivalence class of spaces intended for the performance of the same activities for which the same environmental and dimensional characteristics are required. A building unit (B.U.) is an equivalence class of structured sets of spaces which recursively corresponds to a structured set of Building Units and Space Units (Carrara85).

A functional element (F.E.) is an equivalence class of physical objects (Building Elements) able to play a role in delimiting and classifying the space, in achieving an adequate level of safety, environmental comfort and visual perception. A Functional Subsystem (F.S.) is an equivalence class of structured sets of Physical Objects (Building Subsystems) which recursively corresponds to a structured set of Functional Subsystems or Functional Elements.

The Space Unit Prototype

The Space Unit prototype is made up of SLOTS and FACETS which stem in part from the definition of the formalism adopted. Through the ISA and AKO slots (Winston 1984,

Bobrow et al 1975, Carrara et al 1985) a hierarchical organization of the prototypes is made, corresponding to different levels of generality of knowledge.
In addition to the slots and the facets foreseen by the formalism, further characteristics have been defined which derive from the nature and the particularity of the application that has been made thereof. In the case of the SPACE UNITS, the following slots are considered:

- IMS (immediate successor): this identifies the objects that together define the one under examination. The type of objects that can be contained in this slot are only functional elements. corresponding to the IMP slot, a facet termed all (allowable set) is defined, identifying the ensemble of values admissible for the slot considered. In the case under examination the only values permitted are frames of the functional element type.
- IMP, which identifies the building units that the space unit considered helps to make. As in the preceding case, an "all facet" has been defined which specifies only frames of building unit type as admissible values.
- ADJ ("Adjacent"), which relates the unit considered with other environmental units making up the Building Organism. In this case a function is supplied in the prototype enabling the system to calculate the list of ADJ of the space unit considered on the basis of the arrangement of the constituent elements. This procedure, which within the context of frames formalism takes the name of procedural attachment, calculates the above values using the inheritance procedure activated by the inquiry functions. Each functional unit which contributes towards defining the space unit considered is "requested" for the list of the IMPs from which the space units adjacent to the one considered are obtained.

Those defined are only some of the possible relations of hierarchical and topological type that generally come into play in the definition of a building object. Generally, in fact, all flows of information, of persons, energy or things lead to the consideration of a high number of complex relations whose detailed description falls beyond the scope of the present paper.

ISA	VALUE	S.U.
AKO	VALUE	PROTOTYPE
IMS	VALUE	Some Functional subsystems
IMP	VALUE	Some Functional subsystems
SHAPE	VALUE	Some LISP procedures
	TO-CALC	Some LISP procedures
ADJ	VALUE	Some adjacent space units
	TO-CALC	Some LISP procedures
NETSUP	VALUE	14.50 Mq
	TO-CALC	Some LISP procedures

Apart from characteristics such as those referred to above, which we could define as being of "relational" type, physical characteristics of the objects have also been defined such as for example, net and gross areas, net volume and gross volume, and dispersed heating power. These characteristics are mainly represented by calculation procedures which, however, thanks to the procedural attachment allowed by the frames formalism, are handled by the system in the manner of data. All the procedures defined base their functioning on cooperation with other objects of the knowledge base.

Thus for example the procedure that determines the dispersed power simply asks for the necessary heat characteristics, through a series of functions, from the various functional elements which together define it. Each functional element is able to answer this type of request because it too possesses procedural attachments permitting this type of procedure. This type of approach, called object oriented (Tello 1989), offers countless advantages and in the case under examination it enables a highly flexible system to be produced.

The Building Unit Prototype

A building unit, as stated in the definitions, is made up of a structured ensemble of space units. As the space unit prototype, the building unit prototype foresees the isa, ako and ims slots. In this however the admissible values for the imp slot are only frames of building unit type, while those for the imp slot may be of space unit and building unit type.

In the case of building units, too, all the construction characteristics such as shape, high and squ (area) are defined by procedural attachments which, contrary to those relating to the space unit, do not directly calculate the relative values but only "request" and summate the corresponding values of the elements hierarchically subordinate thereto. By definition, a building unit does not in fact possess form and dimensions of its own, these deriving from the respective characteristics of the subordinate elements.

FLAT-F1		
ISA	VALUE	BU
AKO	VALUE	PROTOTYPE
IMS	VALUE	- Some space units and/or building units

Functional Subsystem Prototype

The Functional Subsystem prototype is structurally similar to that used to represent building units. In this case, too, the IMS and IMP slots define, respectively, the objects that compose them or that the functional Subsystem helps to define. On the basis of the definitions given, each functional element may be made up either of Functional Subsystem or of Functional Elements.

FS		
ISA	VALUE	Functional Subsystem
AKO	VALUE	PROTOTYPE
IMS	VALUE	- Some space units and/or building units

The Functional Element Prototype

The prototype that represents a Functional Element is from a conceptual stand-point wholly similar to the one relative to space units. Whereas the space unit represents the "minimum" element of what is generally defined as space sub-system, the Functional Element may be thought of as the basic element of the technological sub-system. Contrary to what happens for the space unit prototype, in this case no IMS slot is foreseen. That is, the Functional Element is regarded as a directly available physical object or in any case not requiring any specific design measure except in the definition of the ways whereby it helps to define more complex physical objects. The IMP slot contains the indication of the functional elements which the building element helps to define.

FE		
ISA	VALUE	PROTOTYPE
IMP	VALUE	Some Functional Subsystems
SHAPE	VALUE	Some Views

Views of Objects

In the functional element prototype the geometrical characteristics of the objects represented are considered. In fact the slot that contains an indication of the views that define the physical shape of the object is called the shape slot. The views are flat parametric views (In section or 3-dimensional) of the building elements. Each view is provided with conditions of activation and with one or more procedural attachments which have the advantage of displaying the geometry of the objects. The views are defined in a system of local coordinates and are repositioned in space every time an instance of the building element prototype to which this said view is linked is defined. The procedural attachment present in the view is accommodated in the shape slot and is constituted by a lisp function that contains the calls to the functions of the graphic subsystem which enable the object to be drawn. The graphic functions which the user can use are all operators defined on the hybrid edge data structure (Kalay). Formally every shape is a function of P1....Pn points in the space and of an unlimited number of parameters. Although the views are mainly accommodated by functional elements, the possibility has nevertheless been foreseen of giving their own shape also to objects of the knowledge base which, at least from a logical stand-point, do not possess this as functional elements, space units and building units. In this way, these objects of the knowledge base can be seen globally through a simple graphic interaction.

View		
Isa	Value	Prototype
Shape	Value	
	To-Calc	- Calls to the functions of the Graphic Subsystem

Groups

A further prototype that has been defined in the knowledge base is the group prototype. A group is made up of the list of the objects which together define the group. When the list defining the group includes instances, it is the single object that becomes a member of that particular group. If instead a prototype is included in the list, the whole class of objects depending on it, becomes part of the group.

Group		
Isa	Value	Prototype
Elements	Value	- Some Prototypes or Instances of Objects

Definition of the groups takes on great importance, because often the specification of certain characteristics is supplied precisely by using aggregations of objects which follow a different logic from that on the basis of which the prototypes of the knowledge base have been defined.

The Evaluator Subsystem

It has been shown in the preceding pages how, through the potentials offered by the procedural attachment, it is possible to represent a number of aspects of the building objects which imply the determination of new values based on the information contained in the knowledge base. There are however situations, for which this type of approach cannot be followed. Many of the indications that are normally necessary in design activity have for the most part already been codified in efficient, reliable calculation codes. Therefore it does not appear realistic to think of rewriting them in the context of a new more general system because such an effort would be prohibitive.

In addition to the preceding considerations, which we could call operative in character, there exist also methodological type motivations. The use of a complex calculation code always implies on the designer's part a schematization of the problem that it is intended to tackle. The schematization of the problem is in fact another design activity calling for all the designer's critical capacity and experience. It does not therefore appear possible to crystallize the carrying out of this process in a calculation procedure or method, otherwise there would be the risk of obtaining results that would be formally correct but absolutely senseless.

Goals

One of the aspects characterizing the proposed system is the possibility of defining constraints that have to be respected by the choices adopted during the course of the design activity. Two types of constraints have been considered: constraints of natural type and those of design type.

Constraints of natural type define limits of variation dictated by common sense, and their purpose is to guarantee the general coherence of the knowledge base. A natural constraint is represented by means of the introduction into the prototypes of specific facets relating to the characteristics on which it is intended to place a constraint. In the following example natural constraints (max and min range) are defined for some characteristics of the apartment Flat-F1.

Flat-F1		
Isa	Value	Bu
Elements	Value	Some Prototypes or Instances of Objects
Sup	Value	Actual Value
	Max	Max Value
	Min	Min Value
℃	Range	Range Values

The "design constraints" (which we call requirement) are on the other hand defined by the designer in order to establish performances required of the building object, and they may be represented by special frames. Design constraints may be external, if due to cogent normative, and internal if defined directly by the designer. Design type constraints enable the designer to define complex relations among the objects of the knowledge base. The use of this mechanism makes it possible for example to specify constraints relating to the objects which together define the spaces subsystem (space units and building units) and the physical elements subsystem (functional elements and building elements). Thus for example conditions can be defined which establish that a given building unit must consist of a given ensemble of space units and building units or that a given group of building elements must be correlated on the basis of a given system of rules.

Req-11		
Isa	Value	Requirement
Subject	Value	-Some Prototypes or Instances of Objects
Sup	Max	Max Value
	Min	Min Value

The definition of the constraints of design type assumes great importance in defining the modalities whereby the objects of the knowledge base interact together at the level of both prototypes and instances.

The requisite prototype foresees the definition of two slots, the first of which defines the field of application of the requisite or, in other words, the ensemble of objects to which it is applied, while the second one establishes which characteristic is to be constrained, and the values there should be for this.

The definition of a constraint requires the specification for a given slot, of the fields of variation of the values that this can accommodate. To this end the frames formalism offers the possibility of defining facets dedicated to this purpose. A number of examples of slots are set out below.

- Range. The range facet permits the definition of a continuous variation interval of the values associated with a slot. in the range facet the minimum and maximum values of this interval are therefore stored.
- Set. The set facet serves instead to define a discrete variation interval of the values. If a value is specified for a certain characteristic, the program will thus have to compare the given value with the ensemble of those permitted.
- Class. The introduction of a class facet is in answer to the need to define that a value belongs to a given class of values. If a number of classes are specified, the programme, beside accepting the values specified, will make provision also for their classification with respect thereto.
- Max, min. The max and min facets define the maximum and minimum thresholds of acceptance for the values of the slots. This is the simplest type of constraint among those considered because it asks the program to control only the acceptability or otherwise of the values introduced.

The User Interface and The Control System

The user interface is responsible for communications between user and system and it enables the functioning thereof to be controlled. The interface has been made using development instruments based on the use of dialogue windows and pointing systems such as the mouse and the graphic panel.

The designer can use the system in various ways. He can, through a traditional graphic subsystem, make preliminary layouts of the object which he defines without initially specifying any information as to the nature and type of the signs that have been drawn. At any moment, it is possible to go over to a declaration phase in which the geometrical entities being drawn are declared to belong to a class of objects already defined in the system, which the designer has previously defined or whose definition and creation are simultaneously carried out. Whenever the system possesses sufficient data to identify clearly an object as belonging to a given class, automatically, through an inheritance process, the object concerned inherits all the characteristics specified for the prototypes on which it depends. Through this process, the ensemble of the natural and design constraints defined is propagated to the single instances. The type and the number of characteristics that the system controls, are chosen however, by the designer who can define monitoring windows. This type of entity present in the knowledge base simply makes provision, and shows up at every designer-system interaction. Alternatively if specifically requested by the designer, it can evaluate the aspect/s whose monitoring has been requested. If the goal contains a procedural attachment that must be activated in the event of a non- respecting of the conditions specified (as in the case of goals relating to geometrical aspects) it is automatically activated by the system.

Conclusions

The above system is proposed as the first result of the definition of a different approach to the problems of designing and of Computer Aided Design in particular, stemming from an analysis of the experiments made earlier within the CAD context. On the basis of the definitions given, the formal structure of a support system for building and architectural design has been defined.This is able to simulate the behavior of building objects and to enable the designer to work on them in a natural way, i.e. without influencing his design methodology.

Although experimental, the prototype constructed on the basis of the foregoing considerations has given evidence of interesting potentials which will be analyzed and further studied in the on-going research activity.

References

Aksoylu Y. 1982. *Two different Systematic Approaches to Design*. Technical report. University of California, Berkeley, CA.

Bobrow D. G., and A. Collins. 1975. *Representation And Understanding*. New York, NY: Academic Press.

Carrara G., and G. Novembri. 1986. "Constraint Bounded Design Search." In A. Pipes (ed.). *CAAD Futures*. London: Butterworths.

Carrara G., and G. Novembri. 1985. "KAAD: a Knowledge Based Assistant for Architectural Design." In *eCAADe* 4th European Conference on Research and Teaching Experiences. Roma.

Carrara G., and G. Novembri. 1990. "Knowledge Assistant in the process of Architectural Design." *Building And Environment* vol. 25, no. 3. Pergamon Press.

Carrara G., A. Fioravanti, and G. Novembri. 1989. "Towards a New Generation of Computer Assistant For Architectural Design: An Existing Scenario." In *eCAADe Conference*. Aarhus, Denmark.

Gero J. S., M. L. Maher, and W. Zhang. 1988 . "Design Knowledge and Representation." In J. S. Gero (ed.). *Artificial Intelligence in Engineering an Design*. Elsevier.

Gero, John S. 1985. "Knowledge Based Design Systems In Architecture." In *eCAADe 4th European conference on Research and Teaching Experiences*. Roma.

Hofstadter, D. R. 1979. *Goedel, Escher, Bach : An Eternal Golden Braid*. Basic Books Inc.

Kalay, Y. E. 1987. *Computability of Design*. New York, NY: John Wiley & Sons.

Kalay, Y. E. 1985. "Redefining the Role of Computers in Architecture: From Drafting/Modeling to Knowledge Based Assistants." *Computer Aided Design*.

Novembri, G. 1989. *Progettazione Edilizia e Tecniche della Knowledge Engineering*. Universita di Roma, La Sapienza.

Shaviv, E., and D. Gali. 1979. "A Model of Space Allocation in Complex Building." *Building International*. June.

Simon H. A. 1969. *The Sciences of Artificial*. MIT Press.

Stiny, G. 1980. "Introduction to Shape and Shape Grammars." *Environment and Planning* 1980 B 7: 343-351.

Swerdloff, L. C., and Y. E. Kalay. 1987. "A Partnership Approach to Computer Aided Design." In Kalay (ed.). *Computability of Design*. New York, NY: John Wiley & Sons.

Tello, E. R. 1989. *Object-Oriented Programming for Artificial Intelligence: A Guide to Tools and System Design*. Addison-Wesley.

Winston, P. H. 1984. *Artificial Intelligence*. Addison-Wesley.

Woodbury. 1987. "Strategies for Interactive Design System" In Kalay (ed.). *Computability of Design*. New York, NY: Wiley & Sons.

13 Solid Modeling of Architectural Design with PLASM Language

Alberto Paoluzzi, Claudio Sansoni***

(*)Dip. di Informatica e Sistemistica, Università "La Sapienza"
V. Buonarroti 12, 00185 Roma, Italy
(**)Dip. di Progettazione Arch. e Urb., Università "La Sapienza"
V. Gramsci 53, 00197 Roma, Italy

PLASM (Programming LAnguage for Solid Modeling) is a prototype, high level, user oriented, functional design language currently being developed at the University of Rome "La Sapienza". A PLASM "program" is the symbolic definition of a complex of variational polyhedra depending on some unbound variable, and therefore allows for the description of a whole set of geometric solutions to a design problem. In our view the language should be used, possibly with the assistance of a graphical user interface, both in the first steps of the design process as well in the detailed design. In the paper the guide-lines are shown for the preliminary definition of the syntax of the language. The paper also contains the definition of some new and very powerful solid operators.

Introduction

PLASM is an experimental design language which allows us to define and evaluate the expressions of a special "calculus on polyhedra". It is a pure functional language, where expressions contain operators which map some complexes of polyhedra into other complexes of polyhedra. The language is inspired by the style introduced by the Backus's languages FP (Backus 1978, Williams 1982) and FL (Backus et al. 1989) for programming at function level. PLASM allows us to symbolically describe parametric architectural shapes, but the language can also be used for other applications, e.g. to describe the robot, the motion and the environment in the off-line programming of robots (Bernardini et al. 1991).

As the objects and expressions are parametric, the language can generate complex "variational" objects, as well perform the automatic mapping between design representations at different detail levels. For example, PLASM can be used to define the 2D parametric layout of a building, as well to automatically generate a 3D solid model. In particular, the language introduces some powerful new operators for *product*, *power*, *offset*, etc., of complexes of polyhedra. A key concept is the introduction of an extension of the *traversal* operation (typical of PHIGS-like graphical systems), which allows us to describe structured solid objects fully without specifying all low level geometry details. We note also that the PLASM operators are *dimension independent*, since they are defined for polyhedra of a generic dimension (and not only for 2D or 3D objects). The operators are *abstract*, as their evaluation does not depend from the representation of arguments.

PLASM is planned to be used both by application programmers, who can define new high level operators by writing language *scripts*, and by designers, who can evaluate pre-defined functions in library packages or interactively instanciate language constructs with the aid of a user-oriented graphical interface, which must allow for bidirectional echoing between a language window and a graphical window.

In an imperative language a program is a sequence of instructions which implement a mapping between input and output data. To program design methods and algorithms in an imperative language may be very hard to do, in a general case, so that problem-oriented languages are needed for design. Various languages (Steele 1975, Borning 1981, 1986, Leler 1985, 1988) were developed to solve design problems in engineering areas quite far from architecture (e.g. in the design of mechanisms or electrical networks), and these work by solving a set of simultaneous constraints. In such languages a "program" is simply a description of functionality and a sequence of constraints (expressed algebraically).

PLASM's aim is to give support for the description of geometrical solutions to shape design problems (in general by producing "solid" models) and to allow for automatic transformation between design descriptions at different levels of detail. A "program" is in this case a parametric shape description, given as a set of definitions (with or without some unbound variable). When the program is applied to specific values as parameters, then a geometric model for the designed shape is produced. A natural choice was to adopt an applicative style of programming, and obtain from the right side of each definition the result of the evaluation of an expression of a special "calculus" over polyhedra.

The development of PLASM is one of the research lines of the CAD group at DIS. After having developed the polyhedral solid modeler MINERVA (Paoluzzi et al. 1989) we are currently working on methods for the representation and manipulation of polyhedra of generic dimensions (Ferrucci et al. 1991). Such an approach allows us to treat several geometric problems in an unified manner (Bernardini et al.).

The paper is organized as follows. First, some main approaches to the use of computers in design are recalled and compared with the programming approach proposed here; then some guide-lines about the language syntax and operational semantics are given, showing the applicative style of the language and some low-level pre-defined functions. A strong emphasis should be given to the fact that most of PLASM functions are reducible to the evaluation of the `STRUCT` function, i.e. to the traversal of a structure. Some new high level operators on polyhedra are then introduced and some simple examples are discussed, with the aim of giving some flavor to the expressive power of the language. In the conclusion some critical issues and open problems are outlined.

Geometric Modeling and Building Design:

Current Systems vs. Programming Approach

The current systems used in architectural design can be classified into two broad categories:

- 2D drafting systems: the main aid they give is the possibility of organizing the design hierarchically into groups and levels. Such systems are the most diffuse in the professional ateliers because they do not essentially change the classical practice of the architect's work;
- 3D editing and rendering systems: These are used to perform 3D projections, produce hidden surface removed views and, more recently, realistic rendering of the design volumes and of the external envelopes, as well to realize electronic walks-through. 3D systems are

quite weak from the modeling point of view, as they need a lot of data and of human work in order to define the model to be rendered. So they are used mainly in the final stage of the design process, since by then any change in the model may become very expensive and hard to do.

The best current systems are highly interactive, and use data structures which are transparent to the user. In our approach we want conversely to offer a programming environment to the architect, allowing him to symbolically define the design shape, as well to trace any (geometrical) decision which influenced the generation of that shape. The use of a special purpose language makes the user free from emulating the drafting process; furthermore, this may stimulate the architect's creativity, as it allows him to explore several design solutions quickly.

The Standard Top-down Approach

A building can be seen as a container of spaces, where the internal partitions determine the configuration of inner spaces, while the external envelope determines the volume as a whole. Hence the designer needs to have contemporary control of both empty and full subsets of spaces.

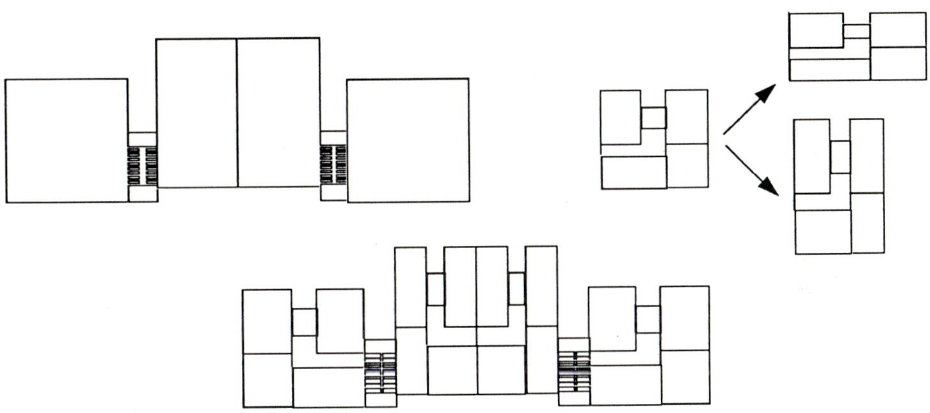

Figure 1. Design development by top-down refinement with an extensive use of affine transformations.

In the first design stages it is common to choose a top-down approach and to work by successive refinements. For example, when the object as a whole is already defined as a set of possibly interpenetrating volumes, and the external constraints are satisfied, it is possible to define the internal subdivisions by hierarchically partitioning the parent volumes and by using an adimensional geometry approach (see Figure 1). In this case, the designer attention is dedicated to the shape as a whole: the need is evident for tools to be able to manipulate the shape by affine transformations and set operations, without explicitly requiring the complete specification of the geometry of the internal partitions. March and Steadman have shown in (March et al. 1971) how since the early seventies the affine transformations are often applied to the architectural design. Such approach can be easily modelled by allowing the design language to contain a structure definition mechanism analogous to that given by the PHIGS graphics standard (PHIGS 1987).

Variational and Rule-based Approach

The use of rules in architecture is very ancient; the rules which control the ratios between the parts of temples as a function of the column diameter are an eloquent example (Chitham 1985). In the same way, in the age of modern architecture, Le Corbusier used his "Modulor" (Le Corbusier 1965) and based shape ratios on the golden section and Fibonacci's series in order to obtain a harmonic control of proportions.

A parametric representation, also denoted as "primitive instancing" in (Requicha 1980), is defined as a procedure which generates a shape instance depending on the values of a predefined set of parameters. Often it is necessary to modify a previously defined object, where the change must affect (recursively) all the adjacent objects. A solution to this problem is given by variational geometry (Gossard 1988), originating in the mechanical design domain, by assuming geometrical constraints between object parts. The explicit definition of the shape, usual in current graphical systems, needs the enumeration of the (either absolute or relative) position of object vertices. Conversely, the variational approach is implicit, as it contains constraints and not (only) coordinates. So, a variational definition makes the objects have some explicit degrees of freedom. This representation is a very powerful design aid, as a parametric definition easily allows us to explore the consequences on the whole object that are induced by a change in a part of it.

"Design by constraint" is an important rule-based design methodology (Barford 1987) where whole classes of design solutions are implicitly defined. The front view and the structural grid of a building are two examples of shapes where the final configuration can be defined with dimensional rules. It is possible to introduce in a variational PLASM definition many "rules of composition" both as conditional constructs `IF:<cond,expr1,expr2>` and as relational or logical or type constraints that the objects or the parameters must satisfy, and which express positional or dimensional relationships between the parts of a structured object.

In the following example we use the term "variational" object to denote an expression where either affine transformations or component objects or both may depend on some parameters, and where explicit constraints between parameters may be given and, in this case, are satisfied by any object instance. As will be shown in the paper, the symbolic representation contained in a PLASM script can be considered as a variational machinery any time it contains a set of unbound parameters (at the left side of definitions).

The PLASM Approach

PLASM (Programming LAnguage for Solid Modeling) is an experimental language for the symbolic description of parametric polyhedral complexes. The language domain is restricted to linear polyhedra, as curved objects can always be approximated by piecewise-linear polyhedra. Several operators are specialized for the architectural design domain. Using pre-defined operators, the user can develop his own higher-level architectural operators. For example, it is possible to implement several compositions of symmetry and series, as well as operators which result, when applied to specific data and evaluated, in specific parts of the building fabric (like the staircases or the structural grid).

The geometry of a PLASM object is described by instancing pre-defined operators, either contained in external libraries or user-defined. A complex object is defined by building a new definition. This can be done in several ways, e.g.: (a) by specifying a 1D complex (which is a graph containing vertices and edges); (b) by specifying a 2D parametric complex (which is the plane partition induced by a 1D complex); (c) by evaluating the boundary of the cells of the 3D complex generated by the extrusion of a 2D complex; and (d) by defining a structure containing operators, elementary objects and affine transformations of substructures.

With PLASM it is possible: to work in a traditional way by developing plan and section drawings (and then to automatically generate a 3D model of the building, by using some specialized operators, as will be described in this paper); to directly assembly 3D solid components; to integrate the two techniques depending on the problem and on the chosen design style.

In our view, PLASM may constitute the kernel of specialized macro-languages for different areas of architectural design (housing, hospitals, architecture of interiors, etc.), it might also be used to produce personalized packages where recurrent choices and styles of the designer are registered. We notice that such an approach is coherent with the tendency to define special purpose languages in areas where application programs were used before. The reason is that such languages make the user able to build specific applications in a much more powerful and flexible way. Examples of this trend are the Postscript language for the description of high quality text pages, TeX (Knuth 84) and LaTeX (Lamport 1986) for electronic typesetting, Mathematica (Wolfram 88) for symbolic computation, RenderMan (Pixar 89) for realistic rendering, and many others.

Summing up, we believe that the programming approach with PLASM language may provide a very flexible and powerful aid to design development. In particular, both a bottom-up approach, based on component assembly, and a top-down approach, based on model refinement, as well any kind of mixed strategies of design development which can be freely chosen by the designer.

Syntactical Notes

A PLASM *expression* may contain *operators*, *sequences*, *atoms* and parenthesis (to make explicit or modify the order of evaluation of the expression). A PLASM *script* is a sequence of *definitions* separated by commas. A definition may concern expressions or operators. Both contain a left and a right part separated by a symbol "=". The right part of a definition always contains an expression. A definition may also contain an optional script, which has the definition as scope.

Atomic objects belong to simple types. Simple types are the Booleans `BOOL`, the reals `REAL`, the integers `INT`, the affine transformations `TRANSF` and the polyhedra `POL`. Sequences are ordered multi-sets of PLASM objects or expressions, enclosed within pair of angle delimiters "<" and ">". Structures are applications of the `STRUCT` operator, defined on ordered sequences of transformations and polyhedra:

$$\texttt{STRUCT: (TRANSF} \cup \texttt{POL)*} \rightarrow \texttt{POL.}$$

The types `TRANSF` and `POL` are partitioned in subtypes of objects with a given dimension, denoted by a positive integer. i.e. transformations and polyhedra may be 0,1,2,3, ..., n-dimensional. The `0D` cells of a polyhedron in $\Re^n$ are nD points, which are represented as sequences of `n` reals. A nD affine transformation in $\mathtt{TRANSF}^n$ is a (n+1)(n+1) non singular matrix, internally represented (when the dimensions are given) as a sequence of reals.

An operator is a mapping from the product set of parameter domains to the output domain. The language contains a special form for the definition of operators, consisting of: (a) the reserved word `Def`; (b) the operator identifier; (c) an optional expression, usually a sequence of integers, which gives a further specification to the operator, enclosed within single or double braces; (d) the optional sequence of unbound parameters, enclosed within parenthesis; (e) the reserved symbol "="; (f) a PLASM expression used to evaluate the operator; (g) an optional script, enclosed between the reserved words `Where` and `End;` (h) the optional sequence of default values for parameters, between the reserved words `Default` and `End`. The single or double braces around the optional parameters specify the reduction rule that must be used when the operator is applied with more than one optional parameter.

Application Rules and Combining Forms

An operator (a function) is normally invoked in prefix form by applying its identifier to an actual parameter. Application, denoted as `expr1:expr2`, apply the value of `expr1` (a function) to the value of `expr2`. Infix form is allowed for binary operators. Actual parameters must usually coincide in order and type with formal parameters given on the right side of the definition of the operator. Some parameters may be not given in the actual parameter sequence (but given the corresponding comma pairs). In this case the default values of such parameters are used in the evaluation process. Expressions or names of expressions within the current scope can be used in the application.

When a *binary* operator is applied to more than two arguments it is recursively evaluated using the follow equivalence:

```
op:<x1,..., xm, xn> = op:<op:<x1,..., xm>, xn>
```

Unary operators (defined as applicable to atoms), when applied to a sequence of arguments, evaluate to the sequence of applications to the elements of the sequence:

```
op:<x1,..., xn> = <op:x1,..., op:xn>
```

According to FL, two special combining forms are used (a) to apply a sequence of functions to the same argument and (b) to apply a function to every element of a sequence argument:

```
[op1, op2,..., opn]:x =  <op1:x, op2:x,..., opn:x>
    α:op:<x1,x2,...,xn> = <op:x1,op:x2,...,op:xn>
```

The `α:op` function (apply-to-all) evaluates to error when applied to an atom.

Some operators have been defined by using an optional sequence of integers enclosed within single or double "{" and "}" parenthesis, which usually specify the subset of coordinates affected by the operator. In this case the evaluation process can be regarded as follows:

```
op{i1,...,in} is equivalent to op{i1}:op{i2,...,in}
```

if op has ben defined with Def op{{i}}; else if op has been defined with Def op{i}, then the following reduction rule applies:

```
op{i1,...,in} is equivalent to [op{i1},op{i2},...,op{in}]
```

The first reduction rule applies, e.g., to the transformation functions T, R, S, H or to the center function defined in the next sections; the second applies, e.g., to the functions min, max, med. When the definition was Def op{i1,...,in}(y) = Body, the reduction equivalencies expressed in Body are applied. Notice that in the application of a sequence of optional parameters, only the single brace pair is used. In order to make the PLASM expressions easier to read, binary composition of functions is allowed. An infix symbol "∘" must be provided in this case:

```
op2 ∘ op1:x = op2:(op1:x)
```

Transformations

The elementary affine transformations, i.e. translation "T", scaling "S", rotation "R" and shearing "H", could be seen as maps (REAL)* × $POL^n \rightarrow POL^n$, where POL^n denotes the set of polyhedra of dimension n. In PLASM instead they are considered as maps from a space of real parameters to the space of squared invertible matrices. e.g., the translation in the direction x_n, which depends on one real parameter, is represented by a squared matrix of unknown dimensions (which are fixed only at traversal time). Such an object is syntactically expressed as T{n}:a, where the positive integer n denotes the n-th coordinate and the real a is the transformation parameter. Transformations are applied to polyhedra by using structures, described in the next section. e.g., the translation T{n}:a is applied to the polyhedron P by evaluating the expression STRUCT:<T{n}:a,P>. The effect of the evaluation of such an expression is that of summing the real number a to the n-th coordinate of P vertices. Pre-defined operations on transformations are the binary composition "∘", the unary inverse and the standard identity ID:x = x (which applies to PLASM expressions of any type).

Polyhedra

A *polyhedral complex* P is defined as a set of polyhedral cells such that: (a) if p ∈ P, then any face of p is in P; (b) if p, q ∈ P, then either their intersection is empty, or coincides with both the intersection of their boundaries and the union of a P subset. We denote as $\mathcal{P}^{i,n}$ the set of polyhedral complexes of intrinsic dimension i embedded in $\Re^n$. Intrinsic dimension of a polyhedron is the dimension of the maximal simplices contained in it; the dimension of the embedding space coincides with the number of coordinates of vertices. The type polyhedron "POL" is the set of all polyhedral complexes, together with a set of operators and a set of constants.

Pre-defined operations on polyhedra are (a) the regularized set operations (operators are overloaded): *union* "+", *intersection* "&", *difference* "-", defined in a dimension independent way (Bernardini et al. 1991); (b) the *extrusion* "EXTR" (Ferrucci et al. 91, Bernardini et al. 1991), defined as

$$\underline{\mathrm{EXTR}}: \mathcal{P}^{m,n} \rightarrow \mathcal{P}^{m+1,n+1}$$

where EXTR{d}:P maps to the cartesian product P × [0,d], where [0,d] is an interval of the real axes. The expression with default specification EXTR:P instead evaluates to P × [0,1]; (c) the specialized operators described in the next sections. Pre-defined constants are: the empty polyhedron EMPTYP; the standard simplices s{n}, where s{n} is defined as the convex combination of the n+1 points

<0,0,...,0>, <1,0,...,0>,..., <0,0,...,1>.

In PLASM there is no external (symbolic) representation of polyhedra with special language constructs. Each polyhedron in POL can be generated by evaluating some language expression. Some pre-defined operators allow the input/output of polyhedra from/to external text files using a suitable format specification, i.e. the "winged representation" described in (Paoluzzi et al. 90; Ferrucci et al. 91). The internal representation of polyhedra in PLASM is planned to be decompositive, where each polyhedral cell is represented as a set of quasi-disjoint convex sets. Other internal representations are possible, e.g. simplical decompositions either of the boundary (Paoluzzi et al. 1989) or of the interior (Paoluzzi et al. 90) or boundary recursive (Rossignac et al. 89).

Some Pre-defined Operators:

Basic Functions

Following FL, we have that:

```
                  f:x if p:x = true;
IF:<p,f,g>:x =
                  g:x if p:x = false;
```

s1, s2, ..., sn select the first, second and n-th element of a sequence; SEL applied to a sequence of integers evaluates to the sequence of corresponding selector functions: SEL:<1..n> = <s1,s2, ...,sn>, where the primitive infix function .. is the integer interval constructor:

<i1,in> = <i1,i1+1,...,in-1,in>.

NOP is a function which has no effect, i.e. returns nothing, for any argument; `ID:x = x`, for any `x`, is the standard identity function. K is the constant function, defined as `K:x:y = x` for any `y`; CARD gives the integer cardinality of a sequence. CONS is the usual sequence constructor, TAIL removes the first element of a sequence:

```
CONS:<x,<x1,...,xn>> = <x,x1,...,xn>
   TAIL:<x1,...,xn> = <x2,...,xn>
```

MKSEQ and MKPOL are sequence and polyhedra constructors, respectively. The first, when applied to an atom of type `POL` (polyhedral complex), returns the sequence of its higher order cells; the second, when applied to a sequence of quasi-disjoint polyhedra of the same order, returns the corresponding complex as an atom.

Structure & Traversal

Structure is our denotation for the expression `STRUCT:expr`, where STRUCT is a predefined function and `expr` is a sequence of structures, transformations and polyhedra. The evaluation of a STRUCT function is called the *traversal* of a structure. The result of a structure traversal is a polyhedral complex, possibly non-connected or even empty. Each polyhedral component of the sequence is called *substructure*. The STRUCT operator allows us to define hierarchical objects. The domain of such an operator is very close to the set of PHIGS structures, with two main differences. First, all the substructures must have the same dimension; e.g., to mix polylines with polygons is not allowed. Second, an implicit Boolean operation (progressive difference) is introduced between the substructures. In particular, the default evaluation of the polyhedron `P = STRUCT:<x1,x2,...,xm,xn>`, where `x1,..,xn` are polyhedral expressions, is

```
P = STRUCT:<x1,x2,...,xm,xn> =
= MKPOL:<x1,-:<x2,x1>,...,-:<xn,xm,...,x2,x1>>
```

where the minus function denotes a Boolean difference operation. When some transformations `Ti,Tj,...,Tk` are contained in the sequence to which the STRUCT function is applied, the following reduction rules apply:

```
STRUCT:<Ti,xp,...,Tj,xq,...,Tk,xr,...,xs> =
= STRUCT:<Ti,xp,..,STRUCT:<Tj,xq,..,STRUCT:<Tk,xr,..,xs>>>
STRUCT:<Tk,xr,...,xs> =
- STRUCT:<STRUCT:<Tk,xr>,...,STRUCT:<Tk,xs>>
```

Finally we have, with `xr,xs POL` and Tk in `TRANSF`:

```
STRUCT:<Tk,xr> = xs; STRUCT:<Tk> = NOP; STRUCT:<xr> = xr;
```

Notice that this evaluation mechanism *has the same semantics as the traversal of PHIGS structures* or than other popular handling mechanisms of local coordinates in similar graphics systems. Commands like `pushmatrix` or `popmatrix` in the Silicon Graphics GL library are e.g. implementable in PLASM simply by opening or closing a `STRUCT` application.

Structures have a central role in the PLASM language. In particular:
(a) Structures do not allow the interpenetration of solids. Hence, if used smartly, they allow the user to define complex geometrical objects without explicitly defining the low-level geometrical details, as can be seen in the Figure 2, which contains the object resulting from a STRUCT function evaluation, after the execution of implicit differences between substructures. Notice that a different order in the sequencing of substructures may result in a very different evaluated object (see Figures 2b, 2c). This characteristic can be very useful to the designer;
(b) They give the language the same expressive power of PHIGS, because (i) the parts of an objects can be defined in local modeling coordinates; (ii) the object parts can be instanced many times in different locations by simply inserting their name after proper transformation matrices (the traversal can also be implemented as a Depth-First-Search, by maintaining the matrices in a stack and computing a current transformation matrix, which is applied to polyhedra during a structure traversal);
(c) Both the previous properties result in a very natural and powerful way of modelling the building objects, which are always strongly structured and with some amount of shape iteration.

Some examples of the use of structures are given in the following sections. Other examples can be found in (Paoluzzi 1990).

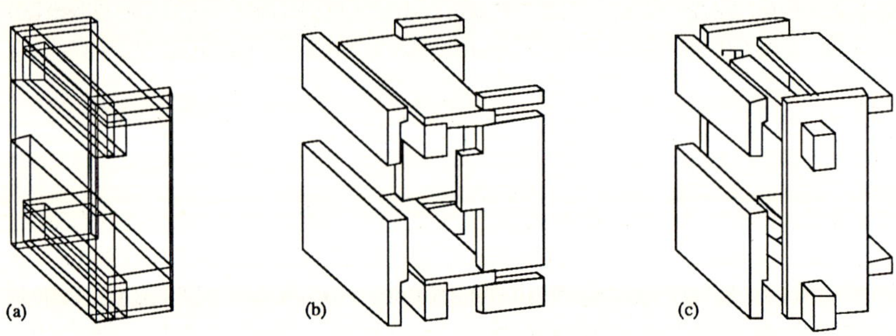

Figure 2. An evaluated structure defined by four objects, each one containing two parallelepipeds. (a) Structure definition as a sequence of isothetic (interpenetrating) parallelepipeds; (b) PLASM evaluated expression, assuming that each substructure is given in world coordinates `STRUCT:<Beams,Roofs, Enclosures,Partitions>`; (c) PLASM evaluated expression `STRUCT:<Beams,-Partitions,Enclosures,Roofs>`.

Sizing and Positioning

In this subsection some primitive and non primitive operators are discussed. The latter are of general usefulness, and therefore will be stored in PLASM permanent packages. The appli-

MAX{i1..in}:x, MIN{i1..in}:x, MED{i1..in}:x

cations evaluate to the sequence of the maximum, minimum or medium coordinates of the argument x. The default forms MAX:x, MIN:x and MED:x evaluate to the full sequence of coordinates of the specified x point. The function SIZE, which returns the sequence of measures along a specified subset of coordinates (remember the application rules with optional integer parameters), is defined as

```
Def SIZE{i} = -:[MAX{i},MIN{i}]
```

The function BOX is defined as follows, where the result is an object of type POL:

```
Def BOX{i1..in} = Struct:[T{i1..in}:MIN{i1..in},*:α":SIZE{i1..in}]
```

where α"<x1,...,xn> = <"x1,"x2,...,"xn> generates a sequence of 1D polyhedra corresponding to some edges of the containment box. The " constructor and the "*" product function are described in the next sections. When BOX is applied to a polyhedral expression, i.e. we have BOX{i1..in}:x, the minimal nD parallelopiped, oriented as the reference frame, is returned which contains the projection of x in the subspace of coordinates x1,...,xn. The application

```
CENTRE:x
```

applies a translation to the argument, in such a way that its results refer to an origin located at the centroid of its containment box. This function can be defined as:

```
Def CENTRE{{i}} = STRUCT:[T{i}:-MED{i}, ID]
```

The application of the binary operator ALIGN{<i,MAX,MIN>}:<x1,x2> is equivalent to the traversal of a structure constituted by the two argument expressions, with a translation in between, which relocates x2 with respect to x1, according to the location directive given in the optional argument sequence. For the function to work properly, x1 and x2 must be embedded in the same space (same number n of coordinates), and i must range between 1 and n. Each alignment directive must have the form <i,Pos1,Pos2>, with Pos1,Pos2 ∈ {MIN,MAX,MED}, and must specify the relative location of Obj1,Obj2 along the i-th coordinate direction, according to the following definition:

```
Def ALIGN {{<i,Pos1,Pos2>}} (Obj1:IsPol,Obj2:IsPol) =
STRUCT:<Obj1, T{i}:(Pos1{i}:Obj1 - Pos2{i}:Obj2), Obj2>
```

The expressive power of the function ALIGN in architectural composition can be very high, especially when used within hierarchical expressions. The Figure 3 shows the result of the application of this function in a simple building front, made with a wall and a window. Note that with the suitable use of such a construct, any kind of score can be obtained.

Notice also that the function works properly when applied to a sequence argument with more than two elements.

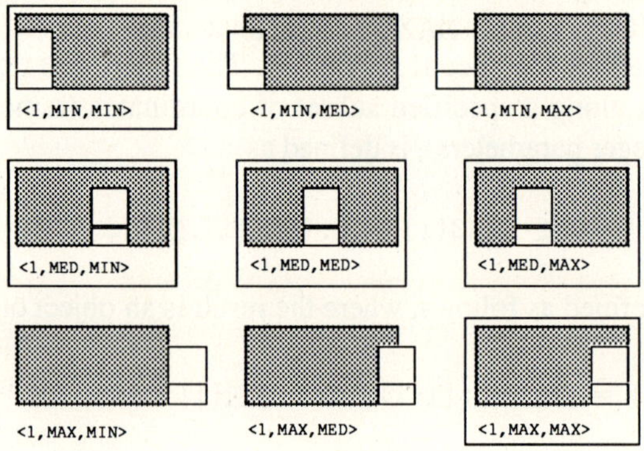

Figure 3. Front object for different values of the alignment directive along the x direction. The most useful of these are highlighted by enclosing them in a box.

Repeat Patterns

Two repeat binary functions #:<n,x>, ##:<n,sequence> (or n#x and n##sequence) can be used with the aim of replicating a PLASM expression or sequence an integer number of times. They can be particularly useful within an " operator instance (discussed in the following) or within structures. The repeat operators establish the following equivalences:

```
<2 # <1,2>,3> = <<1,2>,<1,2>,3>
      <4 # 1> = <1,1,1,1>
<2 ## <1,Fun:x>> = <1,Fun:x,1,Fun:x>
```

If Step is a polyhedron given in local coordinates, then a stair operator with a variable n number of steps and a variable shape of step can be defined as follows:

```
Def Stair (n:isInt, Step:isPol) =
    STRUCT:< STRUCT:<S{3}:(3/4), Step>,
    (n-1) ## STRUCT:<T{1,3}:<(3/4)a, (3/4)b>, Step> >
    Where a = SIZE{1}:Step, b = SIZE{3}:Step, 1 ≤ n, n ≤ 20 End
    Default n = 10, Step = MKBOX{1..3}:<28,80,16> End
```

isInt and isPol are two pre-defined predicates, used for the type-checking of unbound objects. MKBOX (with 3 optional integer parameters) is used as the constructor of a 3D box polyhedron. Default values for n and Step are given in the definition, to be used when the parameters are not instanced, or evaluate to error or exception. Default values are also used to perform the graphical echo of function definition. The resulting polyhedral complex is shown in Figure 4.

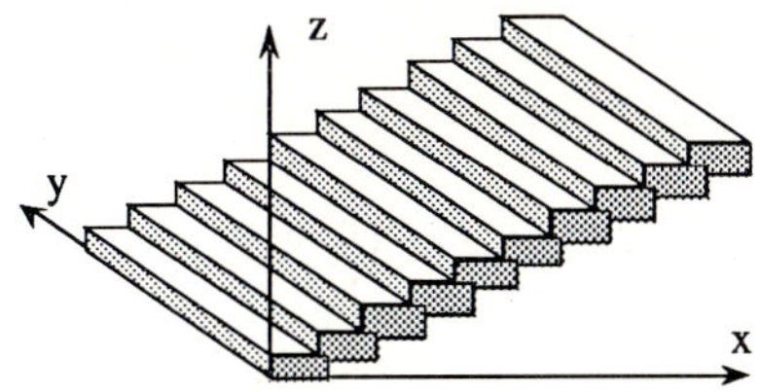

Figure 4. The complex resulting from the evaluation of both the expressions `Stair:<10,Step>` or `Stair`.

High Level Operators on Polyhedra

Boundary

The boundary operator `@` is a mapping:

$$@: \mathcal{P}^{n,m} \rightarrow \mathcal{P}^{n-1,m}, \qquad 1 \leq n \leq m.$$

E.g., the boundary of a 3D polyhedron is a complex of 2D polyhedra whose support space (union of cells) coincides with the set of points which do not belong either to the interior or to the exterior of the polyhedron; the boundary of a 2D polyhedron is a 1D complex, i.e. a set of line segments (see Figure 5b). The boundary of a structure STRUCT:<x1,...,xn> may be obtained by evaluating the expression

@:STRUCT:<x1,...,xn>.

Skeletons

The r-skeleton K^r of an n-complex $P \in \mathcal{P}^{n,m}$ ($n \leq m$) is the maximal regular subcomplex with implicit dimension r. We call *r-extractor* the mapping

$$@r: \mathcal{P}^{n,m} \rightarrow \mathcal{P}^{r,m}, \qquad 0 \leq r \leq n$$

such that `@r:P` is the r-skeleton of the polyhedral complex `P`. So, `@0:P` and denotes the set of `P` vertices, `@1:P` the set of vertices and edges, while `@2:P` is the set of vertices, edges and faces. In Figure 5 is shown the result of the expression -:[@,@1]: Plan which is equivalent to @:Plan - @1:Plan. In this context the function "-" denotes a Boolean difference between sets of points having intrinsic dimension 1D, i.e. less than the dimension of the embedding space (2D). Such objects cannot be considered "solids". A set operation between non-solid objects is computed as the union of the results of the same operation between pairs of "solid" subcomplexes lying in the same subspaces.

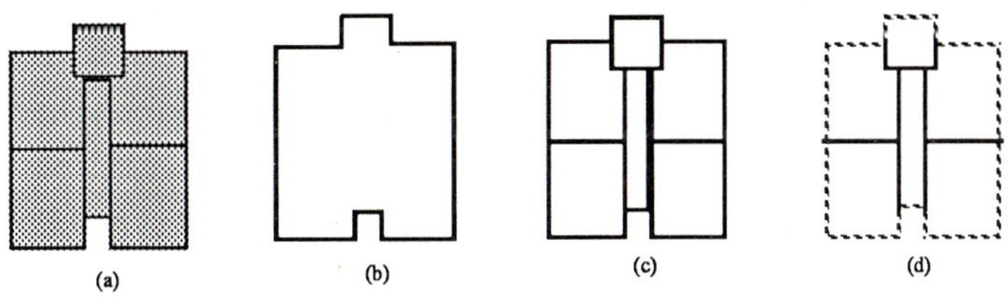

Figure 5. (a) The 2-complex `Plan`; (b) the 1-complex `@:Plan`; (c) the 1-complex `@1:Plan`; (d) the complex `-:[@,@1]:Plan` (solid lines).

Generation of 1D Polyhedra

The operator " is used to define, easily (using local coordinates) and compactly, 1D polyhedra embedded in the 1D space. Such polyhedra are then used as sets of linear measures by other PLASM operators. Such "dimensioning" operator " is defined as a mapping:

$$": (\Re - \{0\})^* \rightarrow \mathcal{P}^{1,1}.$$

A special form of the syntax allows us to write `"x` instead that `" : x`. Negative parameters are used to introduce empty intervals in the evaluated complex. The semantics of such an operator are, once again, a reduction to a structure traversal :

```
Def " = STRUCT:α:(IF:<isPos, 1##[STRUCT:[S{1},K:s{1}],T{1}], T{1}:->)
```

We remember that `s{1}` is the standard 1D simplex, i.e. the line interval `[0,1]`, so that `STRUCT:[S{1}, K:s{1}]:x`, with `x ∈ REAL`, evaluates to the 1D polyhedron which covers the interval `[0,x]` of the real line. In Figure 6 two 1D polyhedra generated by applying " to two sequences of real expressions are shown. Some more examples of such an operator are given later in the paper.

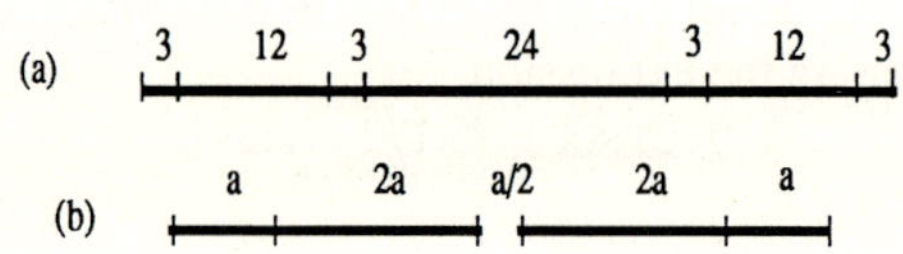

Figure 6.1D polyhedra generated by "quoting" sequences of real expressions: (a) `"[s2,3*s1,s2,6*s1,s2,3*s1,s2]:<4,3>`; (b) `"[ID,2*ID,-ID/2,2*ID,ID]:a`

Product of 1D Polyhedra (Grid Generation)

Starting from a sequence of n polyhedral complexes in $POL^0 \cup POL^1$, the *product* operator produces a complex of intrinsic dimension $r \leq n$, where r is the sum of intrinsic dimension of the arguments:

$$*:\langle x1,x2,\ldots,xn\rangle = x \in POL^r, \qquad x1,x2,\ldots,xn \in POL^0 \cup POL^1$$

It is permissible to write the application of this operator in infix form, since the following equation holds

$$*:\langle x1,x2,\ldots,xm,xn\rangle = \langle *:\langle x1,x2,\ldots,xm\rangle \; ** \; xn\rangle$$

where ** denotes the power operation described in the next section (The true reason is that the mathematical definitions of the two operations coincide). The cells of the output complex of the expression `X1 * X2` are generated by computing cartesian products between any pair of cells of the argument complexes:

$$X1 * X2 = \{x \mid x = x1 \times x2,\ x1 \in X1,\ x2 \in X2\}$$

e.g. the line segments of a 3D grid with cubic cells of side `a` can be generated as `GridEdges:a`, where the definition of the function `GridEdges` follows (see Figure 7).

```
Def GridEdges = @1:*[x,y,z]
    Where x = "[4 # ID], y = "[5 # ID], z = "[4 # ID] End
```

Similarly, the arrangement of polygons shown in the exploded view of Figure 7c is obtained as

```
Def GridFaces = @2:*[x,y,z]
    Where x = "[2 # 2*ID], y = "[3*ID], z = "[3 # ID] End
```

It can be useful to trace the evaluation process of the expression `GridFaces:a`

```
GridFaces:a =
    = @2:*:[x,y,z]:a =
    = @2:*:<x:a,y:a,z:a> =
    = @2:*:<"[2 # 2*ID]:a,"[3*ID]:a,"[3 # ID]:a> =
    = @2:*:<"[2*ID,2*ID]:a,"[3*ID]:a,"[ID,ID,ID]:a> =
    = @2:*:<"<2*ID:a,2*ID:a>,"<3*ID:a>, "<ID:a,ID:a,ID:a>> =
    = @2:*:<"<2a,2a>,"<3a>, "<a,a,a>> =
    = @2:*:<STRUCT:<STRUCT:<S{1}:2a,s{1}>,T{1}:2a,
                 STRUCT:<S{1}:2a,s{1}>,T{1}:2a>,
            STRUCT:<STRUCT:<S{1}:3a,s{1}>,T{1}:3a>,
            STRUCT:<STRUCT:<S{1}:a,s{1}>,T{1}:a,
                       STRUCT:<S{1}:a,s{1}>,T{1}:a,
                       STRUCT:<S{1}:a,s{1}>,T{1}:a>> =
    = @2:*:<STRUCT:<L2a,T{1}:2a,L2a,T{1}:2a>,
            STRUCT:<L3a,T{1}:3a>,
            STRUCT:<La,T{1}:a,La,T{1}:a,La,T{1}:a>> =
    = @2:*:<STRUCT:<L2a,STRUCT:<T{1}:2a,L2a>>,
            STRUCT:<L3a>,
            STRUCT:<La,STRUCT:<T{1}:a,La,STRUCT:<T{1}:a,La>>>> =
    = @2:*:<P1^1, P2^1, P3^1> = @2:P123^3 = P123^2
```

where: L_{2a}, L_{3a}, L_a respectively represent (in local coordinates) the 1D segments of length `2a,3a,a`; $P_1{}^1, P_2{}^1, P_3{}^1$ are complexes of 1D polyhedra which contain `2,1` and `3` relocated instances of L_{2a}, L_{3a}, L_a, respectively; $P_{123}{}^3$ is the 3D complex with solid parallelopiped cells generated by the product of $P_1{}^1, P_2{}^1, P_3{}^1$; and finally $P_{123}{}^2$ is the 2-skeleton of $P_{123}{}^3$ (see Figure 7c).

A combined use of the operators " and * is shown in the following. The 2-complex `Plan` contains four squares of side `a`, two squares of smaller side `b`, and a rectangle with sides `b` and `2a-2b = 2(a-b)`. The four bigger squares can be defined as

`"<a,-b,a>*"<a,a>.`

The central part of the object is given, in world coordinates, as

`"<-a,b>*"<-b/2,b,2(a-b),b>.`

The whole parametric definition may be given, using local modelling coordinates, as:

```
Def Plan (a:isReal, b:isReal) =
    STRUCT: <"<a,-b,a>*"<a,a>, T{1,2}:<a,b/2>, "<b> *"<b,2(a-b),b>>
    Where 0 ≤ b, b ≤ a End
    Default b = 24, a = 48 End
```

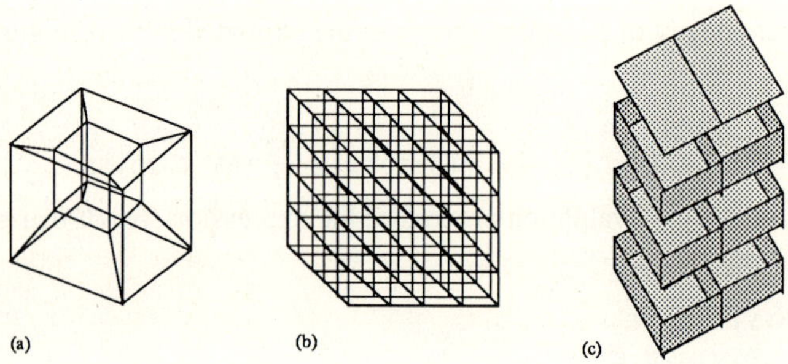

Figure 7. (a) Perspective view of the edges `@1:*:<4 # "1>` of the 4D standard hypercube, which can also be described as `@1:("1*"1*"1*"1);` (b) axonometric view of the object `GridEdges:1` defined in the text; (c) exploded view of the arrangement of polygons in $\Re^3$ obtained by evaluating the expression `GridFaces:a`

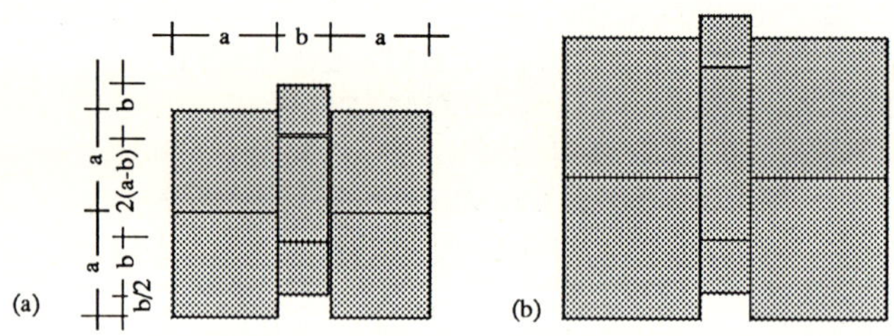

Figure 8. Two instances of the parametric complex `Plan`, corresponding to different values of the parameter `a`.

Power of Polyhedra

The power of polyhedra is defined as a mapping from pairs `<Basis,Exponent>` of polyhedra to polyhedra. The `exponent` argument must have either dimension `0` or `1`. The power operator `"**"` extrudes the polyhedron `Basis` $\in \mathcal{P}^{n,m}$ into $\Re^{m+1}$ if the polyhedron `Exponent` is in $\mathcal{P}^{1,1}$, otherways simply embeds `Basis` into $\Re^{m+1}$. In particular, if `Basis` and `Exponent` are two polyhedral complexes with proper dimensions, and $b \times e$ is the point set obtained as cartesian product of two polyhedral cells, we can write:

$$**: \mathcal{P}^{n,m} \times \mathcal{P}^{i,1} \rightarrow \mathcal{P}^{n+i,m+1} \qquad i \in \{0,1\},$$

Basis ** Exponent = $\{p | p = b \times e, b \in \text{Basis}, e \in \text{Exponent}\}$

In Figure 9 two examples of power application with basis `Plan` are given, showing both a multiple embedding one of the 2D object `Plan` in 3D (depending on the real cells of the 0D exponent) and one of the generation of a multiple instance of a solid (3D) version of `Plan` (depending on the cells of the 1D exponent). A more complex and interesting example is shown in Figure 10, where the power operator is combined with the 2D skeleton extractor function.

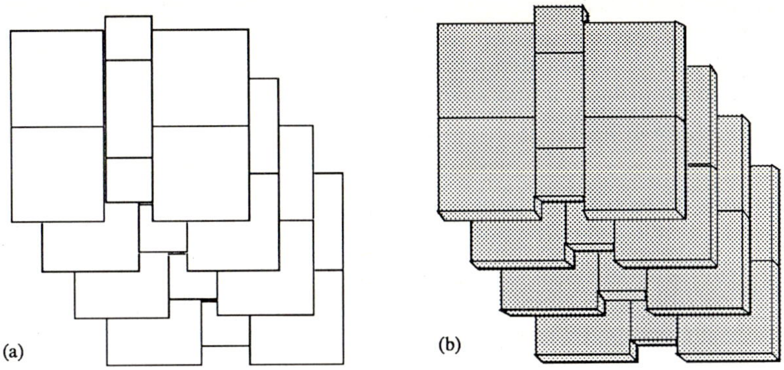

Figure 9. (a) The polyhedron Plan ** (@0:"<h,h,h>). (b) The polyhedron Plan**"<w,-(h - w),w,-(h - w),w,-(h - w),w>; the result is a solid complex whose connected components have width w and are located at distance h-w.

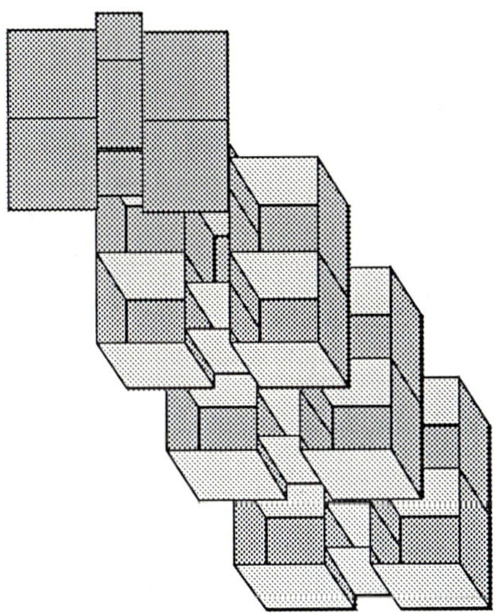

Figure 10. A graphical representation of the 2-complex in $\Re^3$ generated by evaluating the expression @2:(Plan ** "<h,h,h>), where h is the distance between adjacent floors. The function can be abstracted with respect to h and to the number n of floors: @2:**:[K:Plan,":#:[s1,s2]]:<n,h>. A more useful abstraction is @2:**:[s3,":#:[s1,s2]]:<n,h,Plan>, and a new operator Def Block (x1:isInt,x2:isReal,x3:isPol) = @2:**:[x3, ":#:[x1,x2]] can be defined, such that the model in the figure can be generated as Block:<3,h,Plan>. Obviously, for different values of Plan or h a completely different 3-floor model may be obtained.

An extended form of the power operator, which applies parametric transformations to the cells of the resulting complex, is defined in (Paoluzzi 1990). An example of the generation of a circular stair using two nested instances of the (extended) power operator is also given there.

Intersection of Extrusions

The intersection of extrusions, denoted with the symbol "&&", is an operator from sequences, with length at least 2 and at most n, of polyhedral complexes in $\mathcal{P}^{n-1,n-1}$ to the polyhedral complexes in $\mathcal{P}^{n,n}$

$$\&\&: (\mathcal{P}^{n-1,n-1})^{m} \to \mathcal{P}^{n,n}, \qquad 2 \leq m \leq n$$

The arguments of such an operator will be usually called *sections*. The infix form is allowed only when applied to two arguments, as the operator is not associative. The effect of the evaluation of the && operator is a polyhedral complex whose cells are obtained by intersecting, in all possible ways, the cells of the straight infinite extrusions of the arguments. Such extrusions are computed after having embedded the arguments into coordinate hyperplanes of the embedding space of the result.

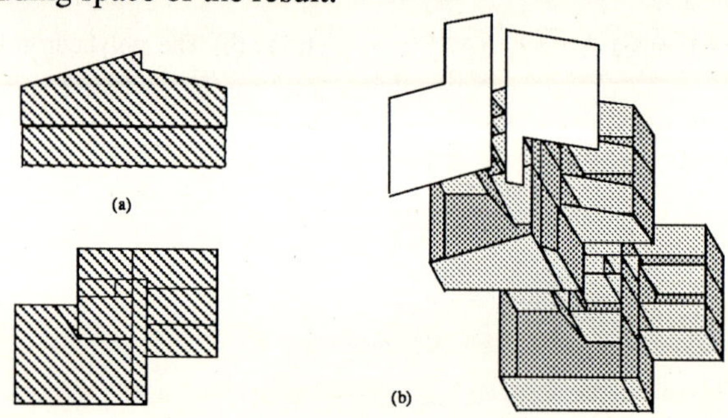

Figure 11. (a) The arguments `Section` and `Plan` of a `&&` operation; (b) exploded view of the 2D complex generated by the expression `@2:&&{1,3}:<Section,Plan>`.

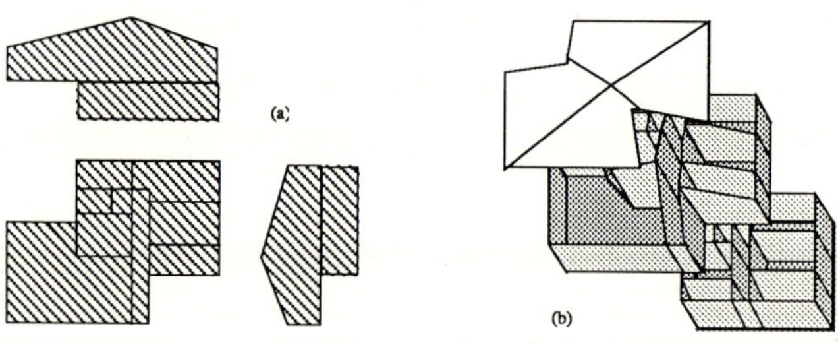

Figure 12. (a) The arguments `Section1`, `Section2` and `Plan` of a `&&` operation; (b) exploded view of the 2D complex generated by the expression `@2:&&:<Section1,Section2,Plan>`.

E.g., the expression `&&{3,1}:<plan,section>`, where `plan`, `section` $\in \mathcal{P}^{2,2}$, is evaluated as follows: the `plan` argument is embedded in the plane `x3 = 0` of the 3D space and indefinitely extruded in the `x3` direction, while the `section` argument is embedded in the plane `x1 = 0` and indefinitely extruded in the `x1` direction. The 3D solid polyhedral complex resulting from this operation is finally computed by intersecting the extruded cells in all possible ways. The 2-skeleton of such complex, i.e. the set of 2D boundary faces of the 3D cells (and the set of their edges and vertices), is graphically represented in Figure 11.

Lattice of Objects

The "`Lattice`" binary operator, used for relocating a set of instances of the same object, optionally dependant on the elements of a Boolean array, is useful to define the structural grid of a building or the set of windows in the building front. The operator is applied as:

`LATTICE{BoolArray}:<x1, x2>`

and can be written also in a special infix form:

`x1 ${BoolArray} x2`

where the vertices of `x1, x2` ∈ `POL` must have the same number of coordinates. The semantics of this operator is that of generating a set of instances of the `x2` argument, each one having as a relative origin, one of the points (0-cells) in `x1`. The optional argument `BoolArray`, nD array of Booleans with a one-to-one mapping with the `x1` 0-cells, controls the existence of the `x2` instances, depending on the truth value of the corresponding `BoolArray` elements. In more formal terms, we can write that a `LATTICE` function is equivalent to the structure given in the following, where, as usual, the underlined words represent functions or keywords pre-defined in the language.

```
Def LATTICE (BoolArray, x1:isPol, x2:isPol) =
    STRUCT:a:(IF:<s1,INSTANCE,NOP>):PAIRS
    Where     INSTANCE = STRUCT:[T{1..CARD:s2}:a-:s2, K:x2]
              PAIRS = a:a:[1 ## SEL:<1..LAST>]:<BoolArray,@0:x1>
              LAST = MIN:<CARD:BoolArray,CARD:@0:x1>     End
```

Restricted Offset

The "`OFFSET`" operator "`++`" generates a polyhedral complex in $\mathcal{P}^{n,n}$ starting from a polyhedral argument in $\mathcal{P}^{n-1,n}$, called *basis* of the operator, and from a real number, called *width* of the operator:

$$++:\ \mathcal{P}^{n-1,n} \times \Re \rightarrow \mathcal{P}^{n,n}.$$

The `OFFSET` operator is used to increase the intrinsic dimension of the argument, i.e. to make it solid. It is also possible to use an extended form

$$++:\ \mathcal{P}^{n-1,n} \times \Re \times \Re \rightarrow \mathcal{P}^{n,n},$$

where the two real arguments are called *right width* and *left width*, with respect to the internal orientation of the (highest order) cells of the basis polyhedron.

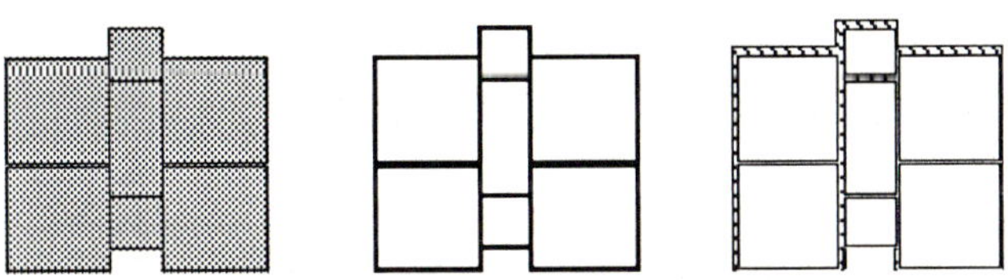

(a) (b) (c)

Figure 13. (a) The 2D polyhedral complex `Plan`; (b) the 1D complex `@1:Plan`; (c) the polyhedron generated by the expression `++:@1:Plan`.

It is very easy to compute the `OFFSET` function when the base argument is the n-1 skeleton of a solid complex `P` $\in$ `POL`^{n}. It is possible to show that in this case the function can be computed as a Boolean difference between the object `+:MKSEQ:P`, where the expression represents the Boolean sum applied to the sequence of `P` cells, and `MKSEQ:P`, after having suitably enlarged/shrunk the objects, with a method described in (Paoluzzi 1991). This can be done very efficiently way when the internal representation of polyhedral cells is a boundary representation.

```
Def OFFSET (P:isPol{n},width:isReal) = -:CONS<
    MoveVert{width/2}:+:MKSEQ:P, MoveVert{-width/2}:MKSEQ:P >
```

Replacement

According to (Mitchell 1991), we notice that in design development by top-down refinement it can be very useful to have a special function to quickly explore the consequences of refinement decisions, without loosing either the previous definitions, or the corresponding compiled objects. Such a function may be applied as follows:
REPLACE:<ScriptName, NewScriptName, OldExpr, NewExpr>

The effect of such a special function (notice that it is not a standard PLASM function) is that of generating a temporary instance of the definitions in `ScriptName`, without the object in `OldExpr` and with an instance of the evaluated `NewExpr`, mapped in the same containment box of `OldExpr`. `REPLACE` is hence an operator over PLASM scripts; its semantics can be outlined as follows:

(a) select the script corresponding to `ScriptName`, and make a copy called `NewScriptName`;
(b) replace in `NewScriptName` all instances of `OldExpr` with `ScaledNewExpr`;
(c) insert within a clause `Where End` in `NewScriptName` the definition
Def ScaledNewExpr= STRUCT:<MAP:BOX:<NewExpr,OldExpr>, NewExpr>
(d) evaluate `NewScript`.

where `MAP` is a Pre-defined PLASM binary operator which takes as arguments two cuboids with the same intrinsic dimension, and gives as a result the transformation matrix which maps the first argument into the second. Remember that a unary function (like `BOX`), when applied to a sequence of arguments, evaluates to the sequence of applications.

Conclusions

In this paper the current status of development of the new design language PLASM have been presented. In particular the most significant decisions about syntax and semantics of the language has been discussed. Some important features of the language concern its dimension independent approach to the modelling, its general approach to variational geometry, the introduction of some new and powerful domain-oriented solid operators, the use of local coordinates for each object definition, and the reduction of most functions to the traversal of a structure.

The PLASM language is inspired by the very powerful applicative style introduced by the Backus's languages FP and FL for programming at function level. When the language is used at low-level, it may appear a bit cryptic, but it is intended as the kernel for specialized high-level macro-languages, to be used in different areas of architectural design (e.g. housing, hospitals, architecture of interiors, etc.). A more verbose version of the syntax might be useful for non-technical user.

We believe that a key point for the successful acceptance of this language will be a well designed graphical user interface. Such an interface should symbolically trace any graphical action of the designer on the currently selected shape (picking, grouping, cutting, pasting, dragging, etc), in addition it should provide a graphical echo of expression evaluated in the listener window. Furthermore, the language should be considered as a component of a very high level graphical environment, with solid modelling, rendering and real time visual simulation subsystems. Our aim is to provide standard interfaces toward such subsystems, and at the same time to provide a complete independence of the language, so that it will be possible to exploit the future hardware and software developments.

A huge computing power is required for using this language in practical cases, but next generation graphics workstations (the G-machine with more than 50 Mflops for $ 10,000 (Van Dam 1991)) are at the door, and parallel machines are already here.

Acknowledgements

This work has been supported in part by the "PF Edilizia" of the Italian Research Council, under the contract CT CNR 90.01702PF64. We would like to thank Claudio Gori Giorgi and Ettore Zambelli for their encouragement and help in starting the project; Chanderjit Bajaj, Luigia Carlucci Aiello and Michael O'Connor for useful discussions and advice; Lorenzo Saladini for his help in revising the language syntax and making it more close to FL; the referees for their comments and suggestions. Ours is the responsibility of any errors and imprecision (e.g. the applicative style used in a naive way) in the paper, which must be considered as a work progress report. Some figures have been produced with the solid modeler MINERVA, developed by the CAD Group at DIS.

References

Backus, J. 1978. "Can Programming Be Liberated from the Von Neuman's Style? A Functional Style and its Algebra of Programs." *Communications of the ACM*, ACM Turing Award Lecture.

Backus, J., J. H. Williams, E. L. Wimmers, P. Lucas, and A. Aiken. 1989. *FL Language Manual, Parts 1 and 2*. Research RJ 7100 (67163), Computer Science, IBM Almaden Res. Center.

Barford, L.A. 1986. *Representing Generic Solid Models by Constraints*. Dept. of Computer Science, Cornell University, Tech. Rep. 86-801, Ithaca, NY.

Borning, A. H. 1981. "The Programming Language Aspects of Thing Lab, a Constraint-Oriented Simulation Laboratory." *ACM Trans. on Programming Languages and Systems* 3, no. 4: 353-387.

Borning, A.H. 1986. "Defining Constraints Graphically". In *CHI'86 Conference*, pp. 137-143.

Chitham, R. 1985. *The classical orders of architecture*. London: Architectural Press.

Bernardini, F., V. Ferrucci, and A. Paoluzzi. 1991. "Working with Dimension Independent Polyhedra." Tech. Report TR-07-91, Dip. di Informatica e Sistemistica, Univ. "La Sapienza", Rome.

Flemming, U. 1990. "Syntactic Structures in Architecture: Teaching composition with Computer Assistance." In M. McCullough, W. J. Mitchell, and P. Purcell (eds.). *The Electronic Design Studio.* Cambridge, MA: MIT Press.

Ferrucci, V., and A. Paoluzzi. 1991. "Extrusion and boundary evaluation for multidimensional polyhedra." *Computer Aided Design.* 23, no. 1: 40-50.

Ferrucci, V., and F. Bernardini. 1990. "Simple_X^n: User Manual and Implementation Notes. Parts 1 and 2." Tech. Report, Dip. di Informatica e Sistemistica, Univ. "La Sapienza", Rome.

Gossard, D. C., R. P. Zuffante, and H. Sakurai. 1988. "Representing Dimensions Tolerances, and Features in MCAE Systems." *IEEE Computer Graphics and Applications* 8, no. 2: 51-59.

Goguen, J. A., and T. Winkler. 1988. "Introducing OBJ3." Res. report, RSI-CSL-88-9, Menlo Park, California.

PHIGS, (Programmer's Hierarchical Interactive Graphics System). 1987. *Draft Standard ISO dp9592-1.* International Standards Organization, Geneva.

Kalay, Y. E. 1989. *Modeling Objects and Environments.* New York, NY: Wiley Interscience.

Kalay, Y. E. 1989. "The hybrid edge: a topological data structure for vertically integrated geometric modeling". *Computer Aided Design* 21, no. 3: 130-140.

Knuth, D.,E. 1984. *The TeXbook.* Reading, MA: Addison Wesley.

Lamport, L. 1986. *LaTeX.* Reading, MA: Addison Wesley.

Le Corbusier. 1965. *Le Modulor.* Boulogne: Editions de l'Architecture d'Aujourd'hui.

Leler, W.M. 1985. "Constraint Languages for Computer Aided Design". *SIGDA Newsletter* 15, no. 2: 11-15.

Leler, W.M. 1988. *Constraint Programming Languages.* Reading, MA: Addison-Wesley.

March, L. and P. Steadman. 1971. *The geometry of environment.* London: RIBA Publ.

Mitchell, W. J.. 1990. *The Logic of Architecture.* Cambridge, MA: The MIT Press.

Mitchell, W. J., R. S Liggett, and T. Milton. 1990. "Top-Down Knowledge-Based Design". In M. McCullough, W. J. Mitchell, and P. Purcell (eds.). *The Electronic Design Studio.* Cambridge, MA: MIT Press.

Paoluzzi, A. 1990. *A set of new solid operators, with CAAD examples.* manuscript.

Paoluzzi, A. and C. Cattani. 1990. "Simplicial based representation and algorithms for multidimensional polyhedra." Submitted paper. A preliminary version appeared as: C. Cattani and A. Paoluzzi. "Solid Modeling in Any Dimension." Dip. di Informatica e Sistemistica, Univ. "La Sapienza", Tech. rep. 02-89, Rome, 1989.

Paoluzzi, A., M. Ramella, and A. Santarelli. 1989. "Boolean Algebra over Linear Polyhedra". *Computer Aided Design* 21, no. 8: 474-484.

Pixar. 1989. *The RenderMan Interface Specification.* San Rafael, California.

Requicha, A. A. G. 1980. "Representations for Rigid Solids: Theory, Methods and Systems." *ACM Computing Surveys* 12, no. 4: 437-464.

Rossignac, J. R., and M. A. O'Connor. 1990. "SGC: A Dimension-independent model for pointsets with internal structures and incomplete boundaries." In M. J. Wozny, J.U. Turner and K. Preiss (eds.). *Geometric Modeling for Product Engineering.* Proc. of the 1988 IFIP/NSF Workshop on Geometric Modelling, pp. 145-180. Rensselaerville, NY. North-Holland.

Schmitt, G. 1990. "Classes of Design - Classes of Tools." In Malcolm McCullough, William J. Mitchell, and Patrick Purcell (eds.). *The Electronic Design Studio.* Cambridge, MA: MIT Press.

Steele, G.L. 1975. "The Definition and Implementation of a Computer Programming Language Based on Constraints." PhD. Thesis. Stanford (Published as Comp. Sc. Dpt. Report STAN-CS-75-499).

Williams, J. H. 1982. "Notes on the FP Style of Functional Programming", In J. Darlington, P. Henderson and D.A. Turner (eds.). *Functional Programming and its Applications.* Cambridge: Cambridge Univ. Press.

Wittkower, R. 1949. *Architectural Principles in the age of humanism.* London: Academy Editions.

Wolfram, S. 1988. *Mathematica.* Redwood City: Addison Wesley.

14 Use of Data Modeling in the Conceptual Structuring of Design Problems

Charles M. Eastman

Graduate School of Architecture and Urban Planning
University of California,
Los Angeles, CA 90024-1467, U.S.A.

An approach is presented for defining the information needed or used in a design task, based on data modeling techniques. Called EDM, it allows representation of the information complexity imposed both from the performances or technologies involved as well as imposed criteria, such as aesthetic intentions. Here, EDM is applied to the design of chairs, a design domain with highly diverse technologies and information structures. The relation is shown between the information considered and the class of designs possible. Also shown is the complexity of different design structures and the implication of information structures for conventional and creative design.

Introduction

In all fields, design involves the *management of complexity*. The complexity may be *internal*, imposed by performance requirements or the construction technology, as in aerospace vehicle and space station design. Alternatively, the complexity may be imposed *externally*, as a set of design intentions and aesthetic rules, as in certain avant garde architecture. Complexity of a design, as meant here, is different from visual complexity; a visually simple design may have a significant underlying structural complexity. Today, designers can only consider complexity intuitively, in the experience of a particular problem. There has been no way to represent it or measure it.

This recognition suggests a serious shortcoming in existing capabilities for representing design problems. There is a long history of development of representations of *design solutions*, through drawings and specifications, and more recently, through the use of computer tools such as surface and solids modeling. But these representations only depict the resulting form, not the contextual conditions, the expected performances or the intentions imposed upon the design by its designers. Thus they do not depict the design's structure.

There have been some previous attempts to depict the structure of design problems, for example:

- Alexander's pattern language in architecture and urban planning (Alexander, 1977),
- Karnopp's development of Bond Graphs in mechanical and electrical system design (Karnopp and Rosenberg, 1975).

Neither of these tools has had an impact on professional design. Both have been influential, however, in the education of designers, as early (and recently resurrected) means to explicate the nature of design problems and ways of solving them.

The need for better ways to represent the full structure of design problems has been only a theoretical and pedagogical concern until recently. The development of computer databases for design has led to renewed interest in defining the structure of information about a design. The motivating need is to specify a database structure for use in a particular design context, so that the database can respond to the problem with the same generality and flexibility as paper and pencil.

Ad hoc efforts to develop integrated design databases that cover a variety of functional criteria, support data needed for fabrication (and possibly testing and assembly) and that provide some level of knowledge-base or expert system advice, have been developed in different product domains. These generally have been very expensive to develop, do not respond well to the actual design problems, impose severe restrictions on the scope of design allowed and require constant re-implementation when technological or functional knowledge changes (Encarnaçao and Krause, 1982). These problems suggest that better tools, possibly based on formal methods to define the structure of design information, could be extremely helpful in developing more powerful CAD systems.

Data Modeling

The complexity encountered in the early days of general database research led to the development of data modeling techniques (Jardin, 1974). The intention was to develop very high level languages, close to the application, that could capture the nature of the enterprise being modeled. Several data models have been developed, some out of the database research field such as the entity-relationship model (Chen, 1976) and NIAM (Van Griethuysen 1983), others later out of the expert system, knowledge base and artificial intelligence fields (Peckham and Maryanski, 1988).

Recently, data modeling has been applied to engineering and architecture, as a tool to help address the complexity of data organization for design databases. Most of these efforts have applied data models to capture certain complex semantic issues, such as certain relations between form and function (Batory and Kim, 1985), (Hartzband and Maryanski, 1985). Others have compared the use of different data models in engineering (Shaw et al, 1989). International standards efforts, PDES and STEP, have started defining product models using data modeling, in order to define standards for translation between CAD systems (Smith, 1986). Here, architecture is one product area and some draft product models have been defined (Gielingh, 1988), (Turner, 1988).

Recently, work has been undertaken by the author and his colleagues to develop data modeling techniques specifically tailored to deal with design knowledge. This work is based on the recognition that design knowledge has a different logic and structure from traditional databases. For example, design data is incomplete for most of design, lacks integrity, may carry multiple alternative descriptions and includes procedural as well as declarative knowledge (Bond, Eastman and Chase, 1991). Responding to these distinctions, the author's group developed a new data model, called EDM. The development of EDM is based upon the following goals (Eastman, Bond and Chase, 1991a):

1. representation of function as well as the form and physical properties of the product;

2. support for multiple levels of abstraction and for the various phases of the product life cycle;
3. representation of semantics sufficient for all uses;
4. ability to determine the integrity of information, as needed by a particular application;
5. extensible semantics, supporting the addition of new functional evaluations, new technologies and new conceptual generalizations.

The intention has been to define a small set of structures that capture the semantics of design and engineering information. For defining these structures, we chose as a neutral but powerful meta-language set theory and predicate logic.

The lower level primitives are based on the premises that all design data can be represented as sets of data and relations over the sets. The relations are defined by and come from many sources, including: (i) definitions of measurements, i.e., mass/volume = density; (ii) physical laws, e.g., single occupancy of regions in space-time; (iii) issues of representation, e.g., well-formedness rules for solids modeling or the consistency of indices with the list they refer to; (iv) functional criteria, i.e., rules of composition for pipes, structures or walls; (v) performance measures, such as fluid flow or sound transmission; (vi) dimensional fit, e.g., sizing conditions for pipes and other components that join; (vii) trade practices, such as tolerances for poured concrete, grout spacing, and (viii) design intent, such as dimensional spacing, form relationships and aesthetic criteria (Bond, Eastman and Chase, 1991). We use *constraints* to define all such relations and dependencies between data. Here, a constraint is an expression over a set of data that evaluates to true or false. Our premise is that constraint relations in design vary from being simple to highly complex. It is their aggregate organization, however, that makes design problems especially difficult.

Based on these primitives, EDM provides a small, well-defined set of forms which is used to define a product model. These forms provide various scopes for constraints. Thus they organize the relations between data. We consider the management of these relations to be a central issue in design information management. Our effort has been to package constraints into structures in a form that makes their behavior both apparent and tractable. The forms allow definition of both abstract, conceptual design information as well as low level production based information.

In previous papers, the concepts of EDM have been formally defined (Eastman, Bond and Chase, 1991c), (Bond, Eastman and Chase, 1991) and have been applied to various areas of design knowledge (Eastman, Bond and Chase, 1991b), (Eastman, 1991). These previous papers have laid out the formal foundations for the approach. They also tested in a limited way the range of knowledge EDM is able to depict. In the previous papers, the emphasis was on using EDM for defining design databases.

In this paper, we extend the range of design knowledge being investigated and apply these tools more directly to the issue of design knowledge. The intent is to gain a better understanding of the structure of design knowledge. Making the structure of design information explicit is a powerful step in addressing the intuitive issues of complexity.

In this paper, the EDM data model is applied to a highly unstructured design area, where many diverse creative designs have been developed and where re-formulations have led to highly diverse results. The product area considered here is the design of *chairs*. Chairs respond to a single primary function and have been produced by almost all civilizations.

Given available materials and technology, a great variety of chairs have been designed, some of them ingenious and creative. Today, new designs for chairs evolve primarily from externally imposed structure. Even in such a simple product, the complexity of relations can be quite high.

Chairs are particularly interesting because of the wide range of structure they may incorporate. Chairs may have articulated parts or be of a single molded form. They may rest on a floor or hang from some support. This range challenges most work on design and information structures because of its diversity.

By making the information structures explicit in the design of different classes of chair, the effects of design assumptions can be seen and the limitations of concepts exposed. That is, we can see how different knowledge structures lead to different designs. Also, by investigating data modeling issues in such an unstructured and creative product area, insights into the use of data modeling in more internally complex areas can also be gained. By considering the information re-structuring issues used in previous innovations, clues are offered regarding how future innovations might be developed.

An underlying assumption of this work, not investigated here, is that the information needed to structure and explore designs in an external storage medium is not different from the information used by humans in the intuitive solving of design problems. The knowledge structures developed in the following sections may be relevant for understanding design, whether by man or machine. The processes used to design with, using this information, may be very different, however. Arguments supporting this assumption can be built from work in cognitive science and the psychology of design (Akin, 1986), (Lawson, 1990).

The EDM Structures

EDM Elements

Below are the primitive structures from which the higher level forms are constructed. We start with:

domain(Dname,{Values})

a name and a set of possible values. The value set may be explicitly enumerated (for example, color names) or denoted implicitly by lower and upper bounds over some rational scale (for example, weights). A domain roughly corresponds to the computer language concept of type. Domains are grouped into aggregations, where:

aggregation(Aname1,{Variable:Dname1 | Variable2 = Aname2})

a named aggregation and a set of variable - domain name pairs (bars (|) denote alternative subsets). A variable may denote a domain or another aggregation. Each variable identifies a particular use of a domain in some context. In traditional parlance, an aggregation is a record or relation type. Relations between variables (in aggregations) are denoted using constraints:

(i) a *constraint definition* has the form:

constraint(Cname,Exp,[Evariables])

where the expression *Exp* is a predicate definition evaluating to true or false. *Evariables* are simply the list of variables occurring in the expression Exp. The *Evariables* occurring in the *Exp* must be uniquely identified.

(ii) a *constraint use* includes the path variable definitions and correspondences to Evariables, in the context of its use.

Ccall ::= Cname[Pvariables]
where Pvariable ::= Fename.Pvariable | Aggname.Pvariable | Variable

A constraint definition is similar to a procedure definition and a constraint call is similar to a call of the procedure.
These primitives, domain, aggregation and constraint, allow us to construct high level forms that package data and constraints, eg. design knowledge, in ways that are easy to interpret and manage.

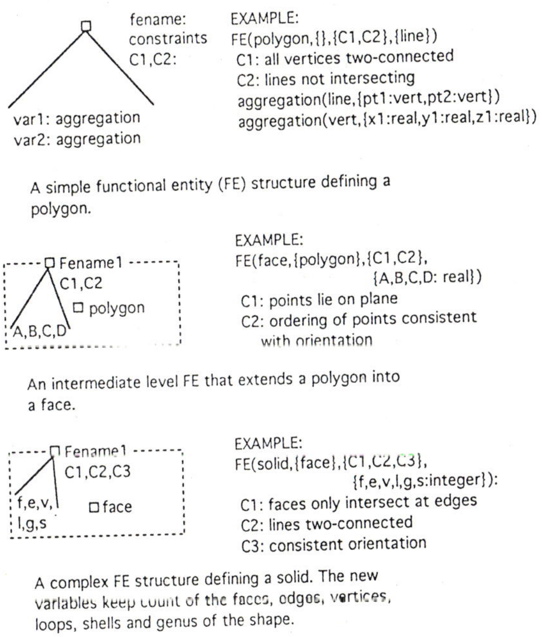

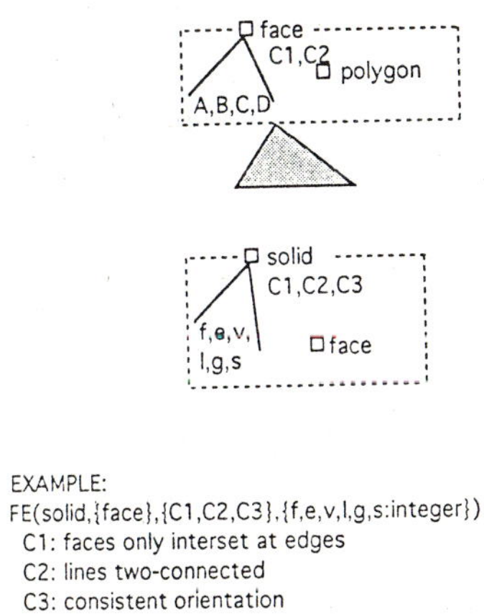

Figure 1. The example FEs, a simple one with only an aggregation and two others that inherit FEs to define a boundary representation solids model.

Figure 2. A generalization structure allows one FE to inherit the semantics of another. The filled inverted cone designates that the FE is specialized by another.

EDM Forms

Given the above elements, the four EDM structures are defined below.

Functional Entity

The singular data object within EDM is the Functional Entity (FE). It defines an aggregation and a set of embedded FEs. Constraints apply to variables in both the embedded FEs and aggregation. It has the form:

FE(Fename1,{Fename2},{Cname[Pvariable1]},Aname1)

a composite structure with the name *Fename1* and is made up of a set of FEs, *{Fename2}*, an aggregation *Aname1*, and a set of constraint calls *{Cname[Pvariable1]}*. The *Pvariables* of the FE constraint must be a subset of the aggregation variables of the component FEs or the aggregation.

Figure 1 diagrammatically depicts both a simple FE, consisting only of an aggregation, and its sequential embedding in more complex cases, where the FE is made up of both FEs and variables in an aggregation. Aggregation variables are graphically depicted by the enclosing funnel lines. In the first case, a set of lines satisfying two constraints define a polygon. The constraints require that the polygon is well-formed: that its vertices are all two-connected and its lines non-intersecting. In the second case, the polygons are extended with a surface definition, to define a bounded surface. Constraints here make the polygon lie on the plane and order the polygon points. The bounded surfaces are then arranged into a boundary representation solids model (Mantyla, 1988). The arrangement of faces is restricted by three constraints: allowing faces to only touch at edges, making all edges two-connected, and making faces consistently oriented. In figure 1, the set *{Fename2}* consists of only one subFE; in other cases there may be several.

Most often, an FE is a set of properties: a shape model or a set of material properties. These are composed into other FEs to define composite definitions corresponding to physical objects. Thus some FEs correspond to physical objects.

Generalization and Specialization

Generalization is broadly recognized as an important form of data abstraction (Shaw et al,1989). In (Bond, Eastman and Chase, 1991), we introduced a new definition of generalization which is a partial order relation between two EDM forms. In general, one form is a generalization of another if it has fewer variables or its constraints allow a greater space of alternatives. The generalization relation is denoted A<<B.

Specialization is the inverse relation to generalization. It is not defined as a separate relation, but is embedded in the FE definition:

*FE(Fename1,{Fename2},{Cname[Pvariable1]},Aname1) => Fename1 << Fename2*for all Fename2.

Thus the previously defined FE form is also sufficient for carrying the generalization-specialization relation. Through specialization, the variables and constraints within a FE may come from many different FEs, which have been specialized into a lattice of FE definitions. We graphically depict a generalization as shown in figure 2. Parent FEs are identified by an inverted filled funnel. The specialized FE carried within another FE, is identified by name within a box denoting the other FE.

Generalization is the means to organize conceptual classes of objects and instances of those objects. Instead of making a strict distinction regarding class and instance, as found in most programming languages, we recognize that in design specifications can be made at any level of specificity and shared across multiple sub-classes or across instances of physical objects.

An intuitive example is shown in figure 3. Here, a wall opening is defined at the top, possibly with height, width and reference wall as variables. There are three specializations of wall opening: door, window and arch, each with different variables and possibly constraints that specialize them. Windows, for example, have a light transmission coefficient and an area. Doors have a type: pocket, sliding, hinged. These definitions are then specialized further. Glass doors is the merging of both the properties of window and door. Also, no specification is an instance; it can always be specialized by adding new variables or constraints. Thus the window size is partially specified, possibly for one side of the building, then members created from this partially determined size. The intent that all windows on one side of the building are to have the same height is captured by the partial specification. New aggregations or FEs could be added even to base FEs, which have all variables constrained to single values (not shown here). These capabilities are all supported by our definition of generalization-specialization.

Accumulation

Another information structure in design involves the relation between detailed functional information and its more aggregated forms. This relation covers those between disjoint FEs. This structure is:

Accumulation(Accname,Fename1,{Cname1[Pvariable1]},{Fename2},{Cname2},[Pvariabl e2]})

a relation named *Accname*, defined by a set of constraints *{Cname1}* over *Fename1* and a the set of FEs, *{Fename2}*. The accumulation defines a one-to-many relation between the variables within the FEs defined. In addition, an accumulation includes a constraint set *{Cname2}* that defines the preconditions that the FEs must satisfy. That is, these constraints define the necessary relations between the members of *{Fename2}* if they are to possess the function or intent characterized in the expression in *Cname1*.

Figure 4 diagrams an accumulation. It graphically shows a relation (in other cases the algorithm could be a complex algorithm) over FEs, possibly nested within other FEs. In this example, the relation defines the relation of forces in a set of members incident to a joint and the forces within them.

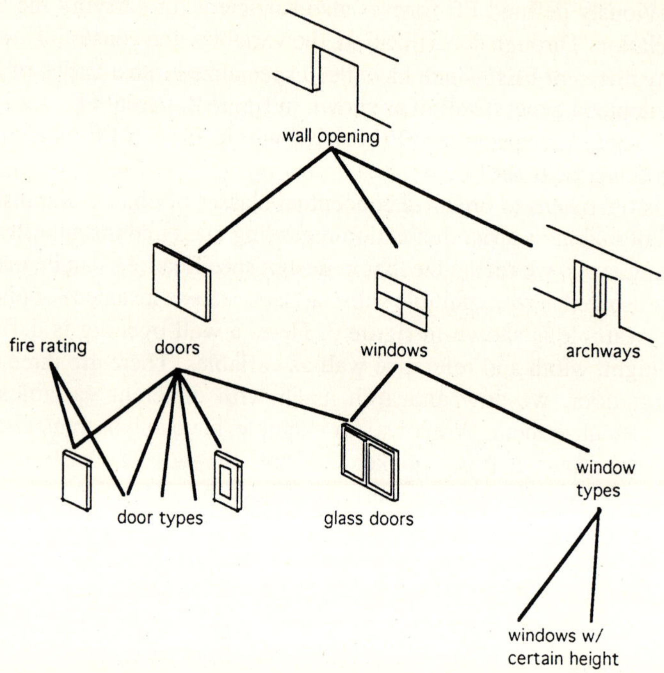

Figure 3. An example generalization-specialization lattice.

This relation must sum to zero for a static truss. The general interpretation of an accumulation is that it defines a one-to-many relationship between disjoint FEs. The relation may involve any type of relation: property accumulation for some particular functioning or performance, for construction, for aesthetics, etc. Analyses are typically defined as accumulations and determine the performance of the set *{Fename2}*; the result is assigned to *Fename1*. Design decisions typically operate top-down, from a single aggregate definition to components.

An accumulation also includes restrictions on allowed FE values, in the form of constraints, that must be satisfied if the functions associated with the accumulation are to be realized. The constraints {Cname2} in the figure define the well-formedness of the structural system, i.e. that they are connected as a graph, with loads only imposed at joints. In other cases, they would define the well-formedness of walls or the size constraints between the parts of an assembly, for example.

Composition

The last product information structure deals with the compositional aspects of products:

composition(Comname,Fename1,{Fename2},{Accname})

a named relation between one FE and a set of FEs that compose it. The composition has the functions or performances specified by the set of accumulations, *{Accname}*. See figure 5.

A composition is equivalent to a set of accumulations that all apply to the same set of FEs. The set *{Fename2}* can be considered the replacement to *Fename1*, defining it in more detail. The information gain of the composition is that the constraint sets may be reduced to a much smaller set than those defined by the accumulations separately.

In figure 5, the joint accumulations for all joints are combined with another for shape to define the composition for a whole truss. The shape relation defines the relation between the aggregate shape of the truss and its component parts.

Compositions group a set of accumulations that apply to a common one-to-many structure of FEs. In figure 5, the parts of the composition are members and joints and the whole is a truss. A composition typically corresponds to what is intuitively thought of as a technology, an assembly with a range of specified performances.

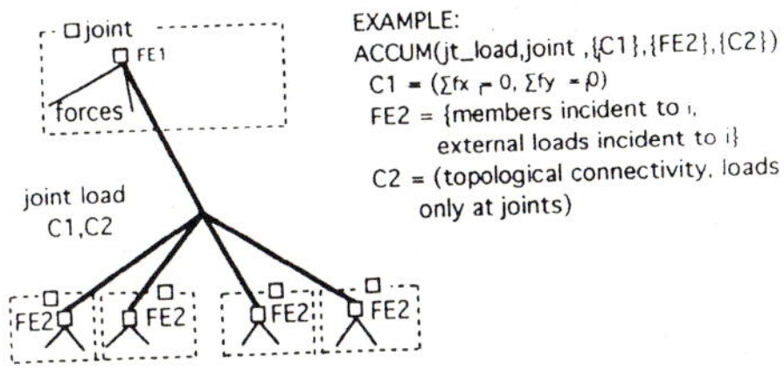

Figure 4. The depiction of an accumulation, which relates disjoint FEs in a one-to-many relation. In the example, the sum of the forces about a joint are derived.

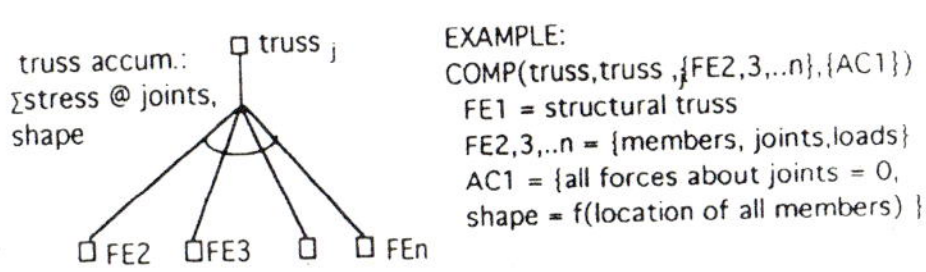

Figure 5. The depiction of a composition, which integrates multiple accumulations.

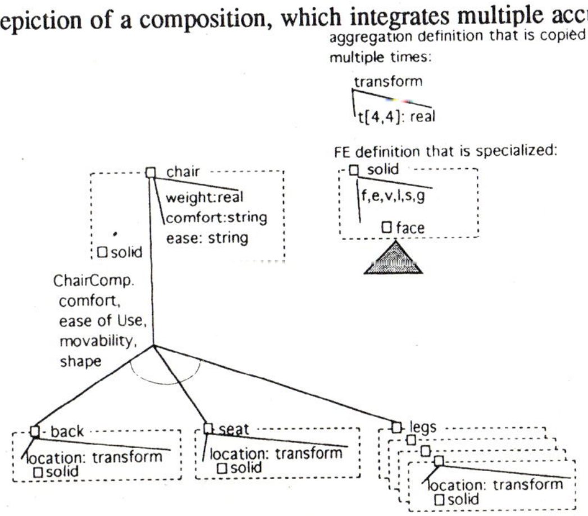

Figure 6. The simple conceptual definition of a chair, based on the dictionary definition.

Thus a box truss is an alternative composition having similar functions and capabilities. A composition can be considered as the efficient encoding of the set of accumulations over a set of FEs. The inverse of composition is part-of (but without accumulations or constraints):

part-of(Ptname,Fename2,Fename1) =>
composition(Comname,Fename1,{Fename2},{Accname})
(for all Poname2)

Composition and part-of have been proposed structures in most other product models (Shaw et al, 1989). Part-of relations, defined separately and without a composition, lose much of their semantic meaning. Thus we always derive Part-of from Composition.

When these forms are used in design, it is assumed that organized arrangements of forms will be pre-defined as knowledge structures that can be retrieved and applied within a general design environment. These then become available as knowledge-bases to be incorporated into particular design projects.

There are at least three different ways in which EDM structures might be used to define a CAD database. Designers may retrieve high level EDM structures that define typical structures used for products and design with them. This use would result in *conventional design*, the most common case. Alternatively, designers may select pre-defined low level structures and arrange them together in a possibly unique higher level structure in which to design. Here, the result may be an *innovative design*, resulting in new arrangements of standard components and functions. For example, existing low level FEs and constraints may be arranged to define new high level FEs. As a third alternative, designers may define new semantic structures using the EDM forms, that is new knowledge not currently within an available knowledge-base, and use this to design with. In this case, the design reflects new knowledge. It is only this case, that I would call *creative design*. These definitions are based upon the information structures used in design and the space or set of designs they imply.

Unique knowledge structures may be defined within EDM for a single design. This is accomplished by modifying existing or adding new EDM forms to define new semantic relations. Thus EDM supports creative design. The decisions regarding how the new information forms link to accumulations and satisfy constraints corresponds to the design issues of determining how functions will be supported and performances satisfied. Thus the definition of an arrangement of EDM forms corresponds to the structuring and formulation of a design task. At the same time, it delimits the set of forms possible and has associated ranges of performance capabilities. It is in this manner that EDM provides insight into the structure of design tasks. An emphasis of EDM is the normalized structure of design knowledge, allowing it to be encoded and modularized for re-use.

The Design of Chairs

Probably the best way to evaluate EDM's ability to encode design knowledge is by considering an example. For the example, I approach product knowledge informally, close to the way it is traditionally understood by designers. Then I will show how this knowledge can be encoded in the EDM structures. I will rely on EDM's graphic syntax for depicting the information, rather than the textual one.

Simple Chairs

A *chair* is defined as (Oxford English Dictionary, 1971):

> *"a seat for one person, implying comfort and ease, that is an article of furniture, four-legged, with rest for the back."*

A *seat* is defined to be:

> *"for sitting, which is a posture in which the weight of the body rests upon its posterior."*

Furniture is defined as:

> *"movable articles in a dwelling house."*

The dictionary definition of chair provides some basic knowledge needed to conceptually design examples. The definition, with the supporting definitions of seating and furniture, includes its function (for sitting) and parts of its form (four-legged, back). Qualities are implied (comfort and ease). Taken at this level, the knowledge regarding the concept chair can be diagrammed as shown in figure 6. It consists of a high level FE called chair, which has some basic attributes defined in its aggregation. This FE is decomposed into at least six component FEs: seat, back and four legs. Here, each subFE is assumed to have a shape and location. The solid FE defined earlier is used to define shape (see figure 1) and is inherited through the specialization relation. The transform is assumed to be defined as an aggregation and is copied into the forms that need it.

Four accumulations are implied for this composition, based on the dictionary definitions: for evaluation of ease of use, comfort, movability and for accumulating the total shape from the shape of the component parts. This last accumulation is used for visual review, planning of packing and shipping, etc. An intuitively obvious constraint that can be used to accumulate properties for movability is summation of the chair's weight. The constraint for deriving the complete shape of the chair from its parts is intuitively obvious as the union of all the individual part shapes. Ease of use and comfort could be intuitively dealt with by building a prototype and trying it out. Each of these accumulations has an evaluation value in the top-level chair FE. These values are what the accumulations define in relation to the component properties.

Many people consider design to be easy, because common cultural knowledge allows one to partially structure some design problems in a way that allows simplistic solutions. The given cultural definition of chair has been outlined above. The importance of such definitions should not be underestimated, because they are what most users apply. But like most culturally defined design definitions, this one is incomplete. Necessary performances are omitted, particularly structural rigidity, and the accumulations for comfort and ease of use are limited. Many chairs feel acceptable upon initially sitting in them, but become uncomfortable after a few minutes. Thus more technical definitions are needed for serious design. Such knowledge is part of the technical and craft knowledge in the various design domains.

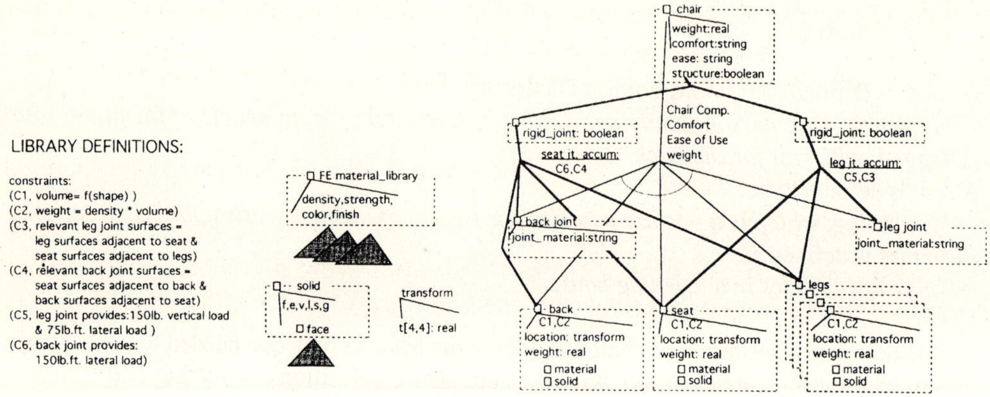

Figure 7. Definition of a more complex chair, based on a library of properties and constraints.

To be more complete, the knowledge structure for designing chairs requires means to define the joining between the leg and seat and between the seat and the back, allowing the structural relations between these parts to be considered. These are shown integrated into the original structure in figure 7. Pre-defined library knowledge is shown on the left. The joint conditions are defined as accumulations over the multiple parts involved, with rigid structural joining being the overall property. A joint FE is added to the overall chair composition, defining the joint material, such as glue, weld or bolt. The structural criteria have been defined very explicitly, in constraint C5, with specific loads the joint must tolerate. The joint uses a precondition constraint, (C3), to identify the surfaces making up the joint. The identified surfaces, together with the joint FE, allow a variety of tests to be defined, including empirical testing of a prototype or finite element analysis.

The joint accumulation for the back similarly identifies a performance criterion, C6, and a pre-condition to identify the relevant surfaces. It may apply to the seat and/or the legs, depending upon the nature of the joint. Notice also that compositions and accumulations may overlap, as happens in figure 7. This is because any accumulation may relate subsets of variables describing features that may be overlapping. The rigid joints are first shown separately for legs and back. Combining the rigid joints is another accumulation that checks for the structural soundness of the overall design.

Material has been added as an inherited FE for each part of the chair. Here, a material library is pre-defined with the desired properties specialized into the different chair parts. The accumulation for deriving the weight of the chair has been included also. The derivation takes several steps. First, the volume of the shape must exist. This is checked in constraint C1, which checks that the volume value is consistent with the solid shape, for each chair component. The volume is then multiplied by the material density to derive the weight. The density is assumed to be a property of the material of each part. The weights are then summed for each part of the chair (joint materials are assumed to be too small to affect the computation).

This EDM data model is schematic, without support for detail design. Only the weight and structure accumulations have been defined. Yet given this structure, defining to some level of detail the conceptual structure of a class of chairs (a fairly limited set, I should add), one could begin to design within the class defined, that is, to create specializations of this structure.

Figure 8 presents example chairs within this class. All the chairs have the same major compositional structure: four legs, a seat and a back. They vary in dimensions, curvature, angles, and also in whether they have arms or bracing. Technically, this range of designs can be generated by varying the parameters of a single family of designs. Such a range of designs seems similar to that allowed by prototypes, as used in expert systems (Maher, 1988).

Figure 8. A sample of chairs allowed by the simple concept definition.

The difference between figure 6 and figure 7 is the difference between the cultural knowledge of chairs and the addition of a minimal amount of more specialized design knowledge. Comfort has still not been considered, nor has any externally imposed stylistic or aesthetic relations.

A More General Definition of Chair

The dictionary definition of chair is unnecessarily restrictive. It eliminates pedestal chairs, as designed by Charles Eames and the bent tube Breuer chairs, among others. In addition to other forms of legs, there are chairs without legs at all, such as basket and other forms of hanging chairs. A unique variation of a chair is the "bean bag chair", filled with any of a variety of irregular, small grain filling.

How can this range of chair designs be embedded into a design knowledge structure? One elaboration involves eliminating the FE form called "leg" in our definition and replacing it with a more abstract functional definition that the seat must be supported off the ground.

Then this functional requirement can be responded to by several alternative compositional structures. For example, in figure 9, three are shown: constructed frames, single element structures and hanging structures. Each of these would have a different set of components and different rules of composition. Disjoint alternatives are graphically denoted by a line with diagonal dashes. Chairs thus have different structures and no single structure can carry the detail information needed for designing. Figure 9 assumes the availability of the same library as figure 7.

In a manner similar to *support_structure*, the back and seat can also defined as a single functional unit, allowing them to be defined by one or more components (not shown). Various seat-back compositions can be defined to depict different families of solution: wicker on a frame, leather stretched between the seat and the back frame, molded fiberglass seat-back, etc. Each of these define disjoint families of seat-backs. Together, these revisions allow a wider range of chair forms to be defined.

Some chairs do not even have the same high level structure defined in the dictionary definition. But if one tries to define a single general product model for this range of chairs, it would be too general to hold the specific information needed to design with. Some alternative combination of structures seems mandatory. In most areas of design, it is necessary to consider different classes of composition, each having different model. For example bean bag chairs have a different data model from most chairs, with different components and attributes. Such a technology can be defined to include all types of fillers, such as beans, sand, water (both very heavy) or air (inflated chairs). In figure 9, on the left is shown this alternative structure.

Each composition defines a different set of components that can make the same assembly, with different forms responding to the fixed, given set of functions. A system of components that, when composed, provide a set of functions is here called a *technology*. Thus the filled bag chair is a technology. Alternative technologies exist for seat-backs and also for support_structures.

One kind of basic knowledge involved in design, as demonstrated here, is the knowledge of alternative technologies/compositions. Here, each composition refers to a parameterized family of forms that satisfy a known set of functions. Knowledge of a different technology adds a new family of designs to the possible set. The larger the set of alternative technologies for some part of a design, the larger the space of alternative designs.

Evaluation of Chair Designs in Terms of Comfort

A large amount of ergonomic research has studied the stress on the back resulting from various seating postures and also subjective assessments of extended sitting in chairs with different seat and back contours. Some tests have assessed posture with different tasks, such as reading, writing and relaxing. Many of these studies are summarized in Grandjean (1973).

The dictionary definition and our elaboration distinguished back from seat. If these are taken to be physical elements, then we have seen that the definition is too restrictive. They need to be considered *features* that are sets of surfaces within the form of the chair. The comfort and ease of use accumulations apply to the relevant surfaces, even though there is not a seat and back part per se.

The angle of the chair seat and its height from the floor interact. Too shallow or horizontal seats result in sliding forward. Too steep angles result in difficulty in getting up. In some studies, angles of 5° to 7° from horizontal appear to be preferred for most activities (Keegan, 1962), (Akerblom, 1948). Other studies show larger angles are more relaxing, up to 26° (Yamaguchi, 1970). The seat height found most comfortable in various studies ranged from

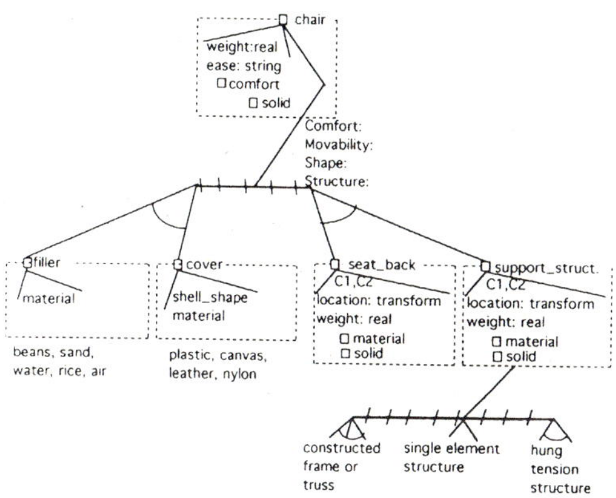

Figure 9. Elaboration of the chair concepts.

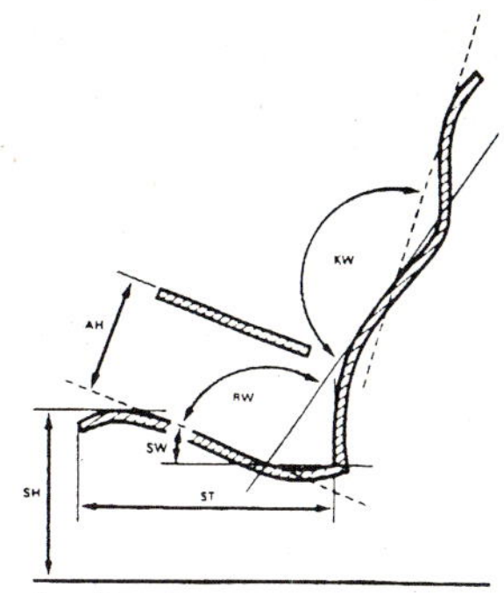

Construction Detail:

	Healthy person		Persons w/ back ailments	Compromise
	Reading	Resting	Rest	Read and Rest
Angle of seat	23	26	20	23
Slope at backrest	103	107	106.5	107
Seat Height(cm.)	40	39	41.5	40
Depth of seat(cm.)	47	47	48	48
Height of lumbar pad above seat(cm.)	14	14	9	8-14
Height of arms(cm.)	26	26	26	26

Figure 10. Ideal seating for people without and with back ailments, from (Grandjean et al. 1967).

32 cm. to 42 cm., with most centering around 39 cm. These studies have been made with different cultural groups, whose body stature varies. Lower seats require a greater seating angle. Seat depths of 43-44 cm. seem preferable for most people (Keegan, 1962), (Akerblom, 1948). More angled seats lead to deeper preferred seating, up to 48 cm. for relaxation at 26° (Grandjean,1973, pp. 120-122).

The preferred seat-to-back angle also varies according to the angle of the seat. Larger seat angles lead to smaller back angles. Different studies suggest angles between 100 and 120°, with larger angles for resting and smaller angles for reading and writing (Grandjean, 1973, pp. 106-114).

These results suggest a set of constraints, with regard to the seat height, the seat angle from horizontal and the angle of the back to the seat. The constraints can set limits within which a reasonable level of comfort will be achieved.

But seating typically involves not flat surfaces but curves. The comfort of a chair responds subtly to gradations in contour. Figure 10 reproduces an ideal contour developed by Grandjean et al. (1967) from extensive empirical studies. The grey area indicates stiff by Grandjean et al. (1967) from extensive empirical studies. The grey area indicates stiff latex above a hard shell, indicated by the black line. The latex allows even distribution of pressure over the seating surface (as does all padding, on the seat or the person's posterior). Lumbar support in the lower back should be 8-10 cm. above the point where the back and seat join.

None of the work on seating comfort has been defined quantitatively, in a manner easily processed on computer. Most existing studies have attempted to define a single fixed contour that is comfortable to the largest segment of the population. Existing data appears to be sufficient to provide ideal contours from which deviation could be measured. I have found no work that would calibrate the degree of discomfort resulting from such deviations.

Figure 11 presents a later study's ideal contour (Grandjean, 1973, pp. 118-119). This contour could be defined within the comfort accumulation. Deviations from this ideal could be computed at constant intervals with the equivalent cross section of a designed chair. The differences between the two contours, stored in a vector is one measure of the comfort of the chair. Such an accumulation is shown in figure 12. The seat and back contour are extracted using the accumulation pre-condition constraints. These are then compared to the ideal contour and differences identified.

In the author's experience with chairs, the lateral contour of the seat, from side to side and the contour of the back, also affect seating comfort. No information has been found, however, with regard to these issues.

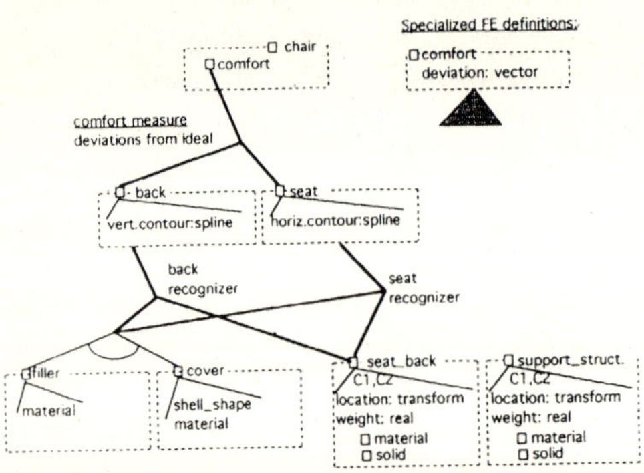

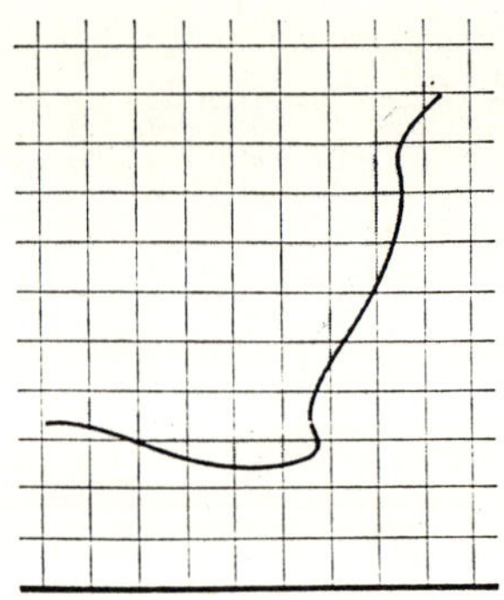

Figure 11. The contour derived by Grandjean in a later study of ideal seating (Grandjean, 1973).

Figure 12. The comfort accumulations applied to the chair concepts. Seat and back are recognized features, then evaluated.

Thus any measurement based evaluation of alternative chair designs, in terms of comfort, is currently limited. Because of the lack of data, it is still mandatory that construction of a prototype and test of its comfort be undertaken. This, of course, only allows determination of its acceptability, comfort wise. It tells us very little about its relative comfort.

Figure 13 updates the joint and structural evaluation. The rigid joint conditions needed for checking the structural soundness must address different conditions in the different compositional structures. Supports made by frames have different joint conditions than those in hanging chairs. Part of the special knowledge about a composition is how to evaluate different functions within it. This becomes more apparent when we consider the definition of a composition as a set of elements related by accumulations.

Aesthetic Considerations in the Design of Chairs

I turn now to an issue of external complexity. There are many ways to develop an aesthetic approach to the design of furniture and it may be based on quite varied philosophical bases. Here, we consider aesthetic considerations to be those that are outside of the function of the product and that influence its cultural interpretation, particularly stylistically.

Historically, one important influence on the aesthetic aspects of chairs has been the materials used. Different styles have associated materials: steam bent woods for the modernist style of Alvar Aalto, fiberglass for the chairs of Charles and Ray Eames, the tubular steel of the various European architectural modernists: Corbusier, Breuer, and Mies. Recently, avant garde Italian design is producing chairs made from flat steel stock, which have their own distinctive style. Each material has ways for bending and joining it, which defines a vocabulary of forms. Many of these styles evolved from the exploration of production ways of working a material. Thus in many cases, the aesthetic issues of a chair design are determined by the choice of materials and the set of forms the material defines, using current production methods.

Associated with a particular material may a range of methods for working it. In these cases, other issues may be applied. In figure 14, I show a simple exploration of the change of scale of the whole chair design and also its component members. In the example, it is shown that oak may be used to define a mission style chair, by using flat wide elements and wide overall proportions. By narrowing the overall proportions, the same material and design may be used to create other chairs, such as a Scandinavian style chair. In these cases smaller rounder elements are selected. In the last case, one slat is removed from the back.

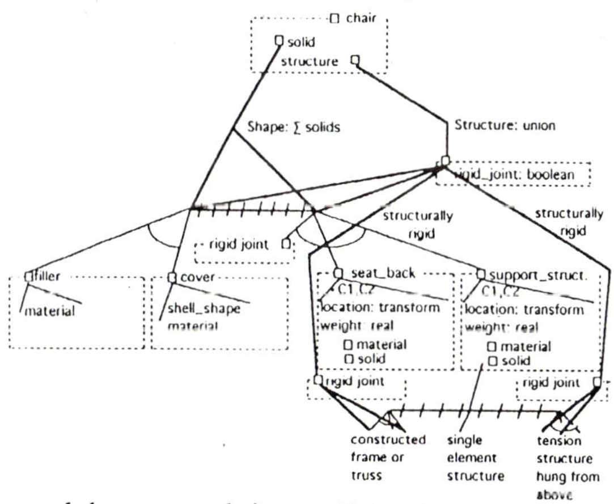

Figure 13. The structures and shape accumulations applied to the more general chair concept. Alternative structures are connected with a line crossed with dashes.

These issues are captured within EDM in different ways. The aesthetic issues associated with a material are captured by restricting the set of materials, geometry and joining of materials to a restricted set or range of alternatives. The overall proportional issues could be captured in the shape accumulation, which could have constraints added that eliminated certain overall proportions. The component material proportions could be restricted by imposing constraints on the set of shapes allowed for defining the component designs. These issues only scratch the issues associated with aesthetic concerns.

Use of an EDM Structure for Design

The EDM structures laid out here define a conceptual model of the product being designed, in this case a chair. We have discussed how the definition of this conceptual structure affects the class of designs allowed. We assume that a designer both generates chair conceptual structures, as defined here, and further constrains the structures by selecting materials, colors and other properties that determine the final design of a chair

The analysis of design information used in chair design has not proceeded to the level of detail needed to actually construction. In particular, the information needed to develop a detail design within a particular technology has nor been defined, though we have given some hints about its contents. Such information would be needed to support detail design, to the fabrication level.

Discussion

Most of the efforts to structure design knowledge have relied on simple, well-defined forms. Until now, design knowledge in intuitive and open-ended design domains has not been attempted. Part of this avoidance has been the paucity of adequate tools.

I have attempted to show here how an open-ended and ill-structured design domain may be recorded. In particular, I have generalized various classes and sub-classes of knowledge in a way that they can be used by others. These knowledge structures are not the only ones possible; there may be more elegant means to represent the same or an expanded domain of chair design knowledge. Elegance will only come after mastery of the concepts.

Most of the names of things used in design, both whole products and components, have both an associated function and a form. The information structures defined here imply both. Probably the most common method of design creativity is to redefine an existing component as a function and find new ways to support that function. An example is the re-definition of seat and back to be seat and knees in the new posture chairs recently introduced to the market. This change of definition was based on original studies of comfort and support.

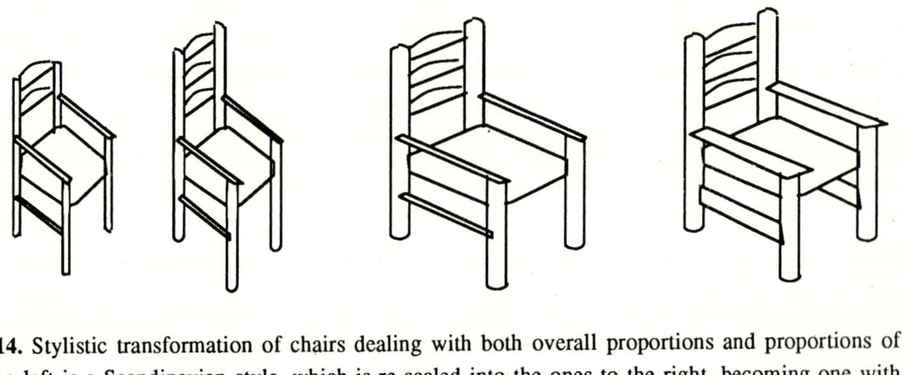

Figure 14. Stylistic transformation of chairs dealing with both overall proportions and proportions of parts. The left is a Scandinavian style, which is re-scaled into the ones to the right, becoming one with mission style. The number of back slats was also reduced.

Innovation may come from identifying an alternative technology for any one of the structures defined. For example, the support provided by a hammock, strung between two trees, might be the basis for generating a new support technology for a chair design. Alternatively, one might attempt to develop and use a hovercraft air-cushion. Each technology has a range of geometry and other properties that affect the total valuation of a chair design. We usually do not worry about the noise a chair might make, but this would become an issue if an air cushion is used.

New forms of chair easily arise out of this type of analysis: inflatable chairs, as a modification of a bean-bag chair; hovering and hammock chairs, defined by identifying new alternatives for the support function, as defined in figure 9, or new forms of seat-backs, such as a potato chip chair.

As these examples are presented, it should be apparent to the reader that the focus of EDM is not to define specific designs, though that is possible, but rather to define design knowledge.

The application of data modeling has clear implications for the definition of design tools. As CAD technology moves toward systems that include more intelligence about a product domain, data modeling suggests the limits of a particular data model. The chair definitions here could be used as an initial specification for the development of a chair design system.

Acknowledgements

The author acknowledges the contribution of his associates, especially Alan Bond and Scott Chase, to the ideas developed here. This work has been supported by the National Science Foundation, grant number DDM-8915665.

References

Akerblom, B. 1948. *Standing and Sitting Posture.* Stockholm: Nordiska Bokhandeln.

Akin, Omer. 1986. *The Psychology of Architectural Design.* London: Pion Press.

Alexander, C., S. Ishikawa, and M. Silverstein. 1977. *A Pattern Language.* New York, NY: Oxford University Press.

Batory, D. S., and W. Kim. 1985. "Modeling concepts for VLSI CAD Objects." *ACM Trans. on Database Sys.* 10, no. 3: 322-346.

Bond, Alan H., C. Eastman, and S. Chase. 1991. "Theoretical Foundations of EDM Product Models." *Design and Computation Report.* UCLA: GSAUP.

Chen, P. 1976. "The entity-relationship model: towards a unified view of data." *ACM Trans. on Database Sys.* 1, no. 1: 9-36.

Eastman, C. M., 1991. "A data model analysis of modularity and extensibility in building databases." *Environ. and Building.* (to appear).

Eastman, C., A. Bond, and S. Chase. 1991a. "A formal approach for product model information." *Research in Engineering Design* 2, no. 2: 65-80.

Eastman, C. M., A. Bond, and S. Chase. 1991b. "Application and evaluation of an engineering data model." *Research in Engineering Design* 2: 4, (forthcoming).

Eastman, C. M., A. Bond, and S. Chase. 1991c. "A data model for engineering design databases." In *Artificial Intelligence in Design.* Edinburgh, Scotland.

Encarnaçao, J., and F. L. Krause (eds.). 1982. *File Structures and Databases for CAD.* New York, NY: North Holland Press.

Gielingh, Wim. 1988. *General AEC Reference Model (GARM), ISO TC184/SC4*. Document 3.2.2.1 (Draft). October. TNO-IBBC.

Grandjean, E., A. Boni, and H. Kretszchmar. 1967. "Entwicklung eines Ruhesesselprofils für gesunde und rückenkranke Menschen." *Wohnungsmedizin* 5: 51-56.

Grandjean, E. 1973. *Ergonomics of the Home*. London: Taylor and Francis.

Jardine, and Donald (ed.). 1974. *Data Base Management Systems*. 1973. In *SHARE Working Conference*. New York, NY: North Holland Press.

Karnopp, Dean, and R. Rosenberg. 1975. *System Dynamics: A Unified Approach*. New York, NY: John Wiley and Sons.

Keegan, J. J. 1962. "Evaluation and improvement of seats." *Industr. Med. Surg*. 31: 137-148.

Lawson, Bryan. 1990. *How Designers Think*. 2nd Edition. London: Butterworth Architecture.

Maher, M.L., 1987. "Engineering design synthesis: a domain independent representation." *A.I. in Engr. Design and Management* 1, no. 3: 207-213.

Mantyla, M. 1988. *Introduction to Solid Modeling*. Rockville, MD: Computer Science Press.

Oxford English Dictionary. 1971. Oxford University Press.

Peckham, J., and F. Maryanski. 1988. "Semantic data models." *ACM Comp. Surv*. 20, no. 3: 153-190.

Shaw, N. K., M. S. Bloor, and A. de Pennington. 1989. "Product data models." *Research in Engineering Design* 1, no. 1: 43-50.

Smith, B. 1986. *A Report on the PDES initiation effort*. (May 20) Gaithersburg, MD: National Bureau of Standards.

Turner, J. A. 1988. "A systems approach to the conceptual modeling of buildings." In P. Christiansson. (ed.). *CIB Conference on Building Data Models*, TC 5.2 and 7.8. Lund, Sweden.

Van Griethuysen (ed.). 1983. *On Conceptual Schema*. ISO Report TC97/SC5/WG3.

Yamaguchi, Y., and F. Umezawa. 1970. "Development of a chair to minimize disc distortion in the sitting posture." unpublished paper reported in (Grandjean, 1973).

15 A Framework for Modeling and Communicating Abstractions of Constructed Facilities

M. Kiumarse Zamanian, Steven J. Fenves

Department of Civil Engineering and
Engineering Design Research Center
Carnegie Mellon University
Pittsburgh, PA 15213-3890, U.S.A.

Management of information about constructed facilities in a computer-integrated environment is a challenging task because this information evolves from, and is viewed by many different disciplines throughout the facility's lifecycle. We present a general framework for modeling and reasoning about the components of a constructed facility at any desired level of abstraction, and communicating the information across disciplines at any stage in the lifecycle of the facility, as well as across stages. Our research has been motivated by an objective similar to that of STEP, which intends to establish an international protocol for the exchange of CAD data. The descriptive information about a facility is divided into two separate but linked groups: spatial and non-spatial attributes. The primary emphasis of this research is to provide a single, uniform representation and reasoning paradigm for dealing with the various spatial abstractions of the facility components regardless of their geometric dimensionalities.

Introduction

The domain of constructed facilities constitutes a large part of the Architecture Engineering and Construction (AEC) profession. This domain involves many different disciplines, e.g., architecture, structural, mechanical and electrical engineering. Each discipline has its own view of the facility and uses different levels of detail and representation schemes for modeling the facility components during the various phases of the facility's lifecycle. As a result, a large number of specialized computer programs have been developed for drafting, design, visualization, analysis, construction management, cost estimation, and facility management, each with its own specialized representation of the facility. Apart from IGES (Initial Graphic Exchange Standard) (IGES 87), which is widely used for exchange of computer-generated drawing data and the recent international efforts for the development of the IGES's successor STEP (STandard for Exchange of Product model data) (Gielingh 88), very little work has been done on defining a general interchange format for the domain of constructed facilities. While some users have decided to purchase only the products of a specific vendor, such as AutoCAD with its DXF protocol (DXF 87), others have been forced to use the low-level drafting primitives of the IGES standard to deal with the issues of data exchange among different CAD/CAE programs. Consequently, the problem of "intelligent" exchange of facility information between different CAD/CAE program still remains a challenge to researchers in industry and academia.

The desire of the CAD/CAE profession to move from "islands of automation" to massive integration, the trend towards a "paperless" office environment, the recent advances in information modeling and management, and the successful use of high-level information exchange protocols in other domains, such as electronics (EDIF 88, Lipsett et al. 86), are the motivations for our present effort in developing a framework for modeling and communicating facility information in a computer-integrated environment. Because the spatial information of facility components, i.e., their geometric attributes and topological relationships, constitute the most important and often most challenging type of information to be dealt with, this work primarily concentrates on the issues of representing and reasoning about the spatial information of the facility components. The non-spatial information of the facility components and their linkage to the corresponding spatial information are also addressed; however, due to extensive efforts of other researchers in dealing with the non-spatial information, we have limited our efforts in this area to issues which are only of direct relevance to our overall framework.

Proposed Approach

All existing data exchange standards use a file for communicating information from one CAD/CAE system to another. The contents of this file are respectively written and retrieved by special-purpose pre- and post-processing modules of the CAD/CAE system based on a specific format established by its corresponding standard committee. The level of sophistication of this format and the type of data it can describe varies greatly from one standard to another. For example IGES (IGES 87) has a very primitive flat format with no high-level constructs, while VHDL (Lipsett et al. 86) provides a high-level data definition language suitable for expressing various characteristics of complex integrated circuits. Regardless of how sophisticated and elaborate the format of the data exchange file is, the pre- and post-processing modules of the CAD/CAE programs must still directly deal with the raw information in the exchanged file. This approach exposes detailed data to all users and therefore prevents data encapsulation on the one hand, and severely restricts future modifications and extensions to the format on the other. Furthermore, storing and retrieving certain types of information, such as complex geometric models, into and from a file requires much more knowledge than simply the format of how the data is stored in a file; therefore, this approach is not particularly suitable for exchanging high-level spatial information.

In our approach, we propose to provide a standard functional interface as the protocol for defining and retrieving various types and levels of information about constructed facilities. This approach is similar in nature to standard languages, such as SQL (Date 88), defined for interfacing with relational databases; however, this interface and its underlying data model and programs that manipulate the information are specifically designed and selected for the particular domain of constructed facilities. A similar but somewhat general architecture has been proposed by Howard (Howard 86) for interfacing databases and knowledge based systems in the structural engineering domain. However, to the best of our knowledge, to this date the uniform and consistent modeling and communication of the information pertaining to the domain of constructed facilities, specifically the geometric data and the topological relations, in a computer-integrated environment has not been exclusively addressed by any other research group.

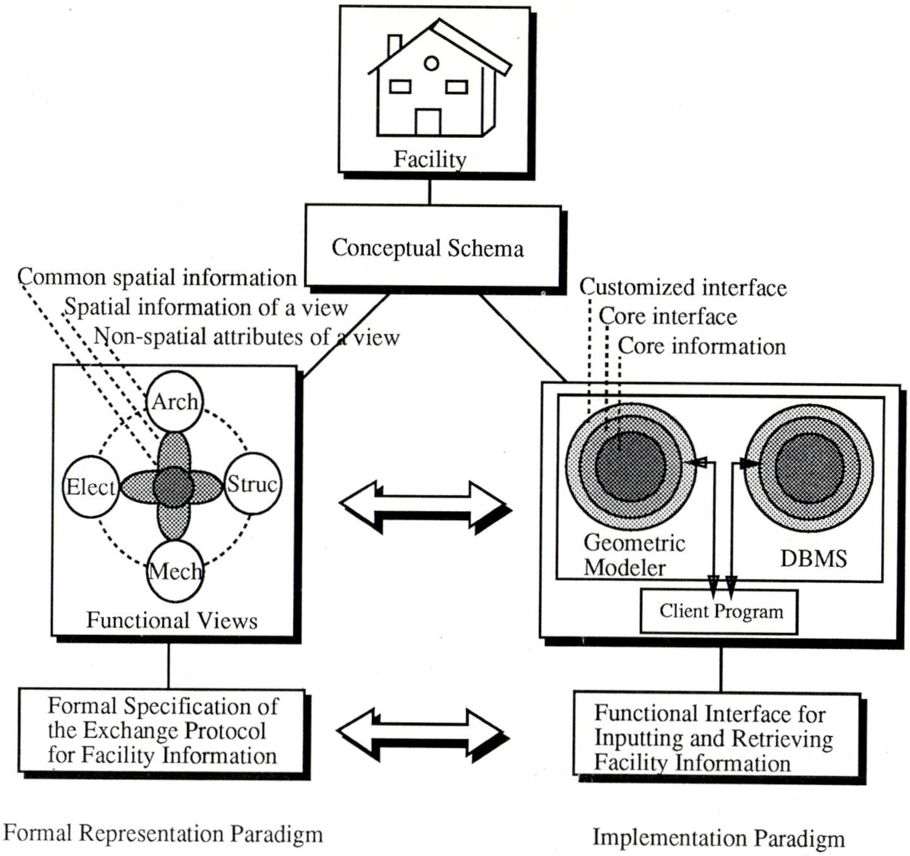

Figure 1. A Framework for Modeling and Communication of Facility Data.

Figure 1 presents the overall structure of our approach. In this figure we define several functional views for a constructed facility (e.g., architectural, structural, electrical and mechanical for the design stage), where each view consists of a set of common and discipline-specific elements, their spatial attributes, and the discipline-specific non-spatial attributes of the elements used in that view. The spatial information is mapped onto a conceptual schema representing the union of all spatial information. Thus the system can, in principle, respond to queries such as: "find all architectural rooms supported by at least one structural beam whose grade of steel is the same as that of the structural column located at the north-west corner of the HVAC zone K3." The spatial attributes of the facility components are handled by a geometric modeling system, while the non-spatial attributes are dealt with in a separate database management system (in our case a relational database). A client program, designed and implemented specifically for storing and retrieving the facility information, interacts with the geometric modeler and the database management server programs and therefore encapsulates the underlying representation schemes and the functional behaviors of the two server programs. This client program consequently provides a functional interface with which users can specify new information and query existing information about a facility to be respectively stored in, and retrieved from, the server programs. Each of the server programs, as well as the client program, has its own data representation scheme, and it is the client program's responsibility to coordinate the translation between these different representation schemes. Formal specification of the functional interface to this client program in turn establishes the proposed information exchange protocol for constructed facilities.

Organization and Representation of Facility Information

Constructed facilities can be thought of as assemblies of components that are put together to perform specific functions for a variety of disciplines, such as architecture and structural engineering. An important characteristic of these components is that they can be represented as abstractions of data that demonstrate different behaviors to different applications of a facility. These abstractions can in turn be classified, based on their behaviors and specific attributes, into various types. Although these types and abstractions are not as well defined and distinct as those of assemblies used in other domains, such as electrical circuits, they provide a basis for establishing the formal information models of constructed facilities.

A majority of the existing information models use a hierarchical scheme for organizing the components of a facility (Turner 88, Powell et al. 88, Lavakare et al. 89). Although a hierarchical scheme is suitable for the high-level decomposition of a facility, it fails to model the complex relationships between the low-level components. Therefore, this work proposes to use a more general organization scheme that combines a hierarchical structure for the high-level components of the facility with a network representation that models the decomposition at each level of this hierarchy (Keirouz 88, Bjork et al. 89).

In addition to the organization of a facility, formal representation of various attributes of each component of the facility is an important information modeling issue. Two major types of information must be dealt with in modeling the components of a facility: descriptive that consists of spatial and non-spatial attributes, and functional (Keirouz 88). This paper deals solely with the descriptive type of information. The spatial attributes pertain to the component's geometry and topology (e.g, a room is a cuboid of certain dimensions adjacent to a set of walls, floors, and ceilings), while the non-spatial attributes are all the other properties of the component (e.g., the thermal conductivity of a wall, the color of a face of the wall, etc.). Furthermore, different disciplines may use different abstractions, aggregations, and spatial subdivisions of the components of interest. Every component of a facility, physical or abstract, is in turn a collection of these types of information and is represented by an "object" (Keirouz 88, Bjork et al. 89) in the information model. An object provides an abstraction for a component and can be viewed differently by various disciplines. For example, a wall may be viewed as a partitioning element by the architect, as a load bearing component by the structural engineer, or as a routing agent by the mechanical or electrical designer; meanwhile each of these disciplines may have one or more geometric abstractions and discipline-specific attributes associated with the object "wall", as illustrated in Figure 2. The geometric representations associated with each object also depend on the level of detail and type of information required by a specific discipline at a particular phase of the facility lifecycle. The geometric representations therefore may vary from simple wireframe to complex solid models. Dealing with the mixed-dimensional geometric abstractions and the topological relationships of the facility components are of particular interest in this work and are discussed extensively in the next section.

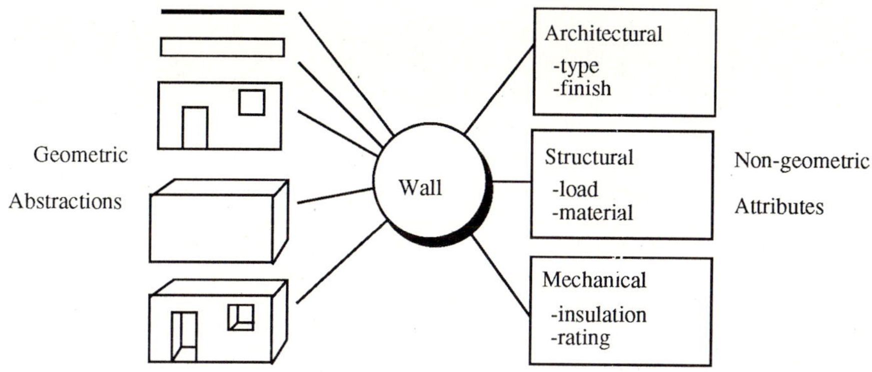

Figure 2. An Object Representation of a Facility Component.

Facility Spatial Information

While the majority of the non-spatial attributes of facility components can be represented using relational databases or other traditional data modeling techniques, other, more specialized representation schemes are needed for dealing with the spatial attributes. Presently, many CAD/CAE systems provide a geometric modeling system that offers a variety of representation schemes, such as wire-frame, surface, and/or solid modeling; however, these schemes are generally disjoint and have entirely different internal data structures and algorithms. This limitation prevents users from modeling and reasoning about various spatial abstractions of a facility in a single, uniform framework. For example (as in Figure 2), a wall may be represented as a line during the preliminary design phase and by a planar surface or a cuboid for the detailed design or analysis phase. Representing these different abstractions in a single geometric modeling paradigm is presently not supported by any AEC CAD/CAE system, primarily due to the lack of support for the more recently developed non-manifold geometric modeling techniques (Hoffmann 89). Our research has heavily utilized this new representation paradigm, specifically the vertex-based, non-manifold geometric modeling system, Noodles, developed by Gursoz (Gursoz et al. 90).

Several major issues have been identified in our research for dealing with the spatial information of constructed facilities; these include:

- overall spatial organization,
- spatial decomposition and aggregation,
- compositional polymorphism,
- topological polymorphism, and
- reasoning about implicit topological relationships.

These items are briefly described in the following paragraphs:

Overall spatial organization. The organization of components (or objects in a general data modeling sense) in a constructed facility can be conceptually viewed as a directed graph structure whose nodes correspond to the objects and whose links describe the spatial relationship between related objects (Zamanian et al. 90). As an extreme example, a fire zone can be linked to a HVAC duct via the "contains" relationship. This graph structure can potentially contain all the spatial information about all the facility components; however, it is too general and contains too much data (objects and relationships) for any one particular discipline to deal with. Therefore, it is necessary to provide each discipline with its own, more specialized organizational scheme of the components while maintaining consistency between these discipline-specific models and the primary model. Consistency is achieved by making each specific spatial model a discipline-specific (or functional) "view" of the primary (or conceptual) model, in the same sense as used in database management systems. For example, architects may wish to deal with spaces such as floors which contain suites which in turn consist of rooms that are separated by walls. This organization of spaces is simply a specialized view of the primary model containing the spatial information about all the spaces in the facility, which may include rooms, pipes, walls, beams, etc.

Spatial decomposition and aggregation. Although different disciplines have their own special arrangements of objects in a constructed facility, in most cases they deal with the spatial decomposition of the facility in a hierarchical fashion, i.e., given a particular object, they subdivide that object into smaller subobjects by defining either partitions or individual subobjects, or both. This process is in fact initiated by modeling the constructed facility itself, either by defining its bounding envelope or directly via its topology and geometry, where the three-dimensional physical universe is partitioned into objects corresponding to the "inside" and the "outside" of the facility. Once this "inside" object is defined, it can be recursively decomposed into disjoint subobjects until the desired level of granularity has been reached for any particular discipline. During this process, it is also possible to decompose a union of several objects instead of limiting the decomposition technique to the leaf nodes of the hierarchical tree. It is important to note that although the decomposition methodology described here is the same for all disciplines, it does not imply that the level of decomposition or the arrangement of objects must also the same. In other words, each discipline is free to arrange its own spatial organization; meanwhile, it can also use the objects generated by other disciplines for defining its own objects.

Compositional polymorphism. Based on the above discussion, one of the major objectives of this work is to allow any discipline to define and retrieve the spatial information of the components of a constructed facility at any desired level of abstraction or detail. By using a non-manifold geometric modeling paradigm, representations of different dimensionality can harmoniously coexist in the same model. Furthermore, an application can exploit any level of spatial composition of the objects, via the proposed functional interface of the client program, regardless of the level of dimensionality used for representing those objects. One of the main advantages of this approach is that objects of lower-level dimensionality can generally be extended to higher-levels of dimensionality by producing their approximate enclosing envelopes from the available geometric attributes. For example, the line representation of a girder, often used in simple structural analysis programs, can be extruded to a two-dimensional rectangle by using the specified height of the girder and the direction of extrusion. The rectangular representation of the girder can in turn be used for interference checking with distribution elements, such as pipes or ducts. Furthermore, the girder stiffeners can be represented as nodes on the one-dimensional, or line segments on the two-dimensional, representation of the girder, respectively. Finally, the girder flanges can be represented as additional two-dimensional rectangles, or the entire girder can be represented as a three-dimensional solid. Thus, depending on the level of approximation at which the spatial information is available or needed, various abstractions with different dimensionalities of the facility components can be composed.

Topological polymorphism. The representation of a spatial abstraction of an object is merely a mathematical approximation of the actual geometry of that object. The degree of approximation used for representing a particular object is generally determined by the level of detail needed for dealing with that object. Furthermore, in order to be able to retrieve the desired topological relations between spatial abstractions of different dimensionality, it is necessary to make these relations invariant with respect to the dimensionality of geometric entities used to represent those abstractions. For example, one must be able to retrieve topological relations, such as intersection or part-of, between an HVAC piping network that is represented by either a connected set of one-dimensional lines or a set of solid objects and the structural floor systems that are modeled by either planar rectangles or three-dimensional cuboids. The use of a non-manifold geometric modeling scheme addresses the topological polymorphism issue when one deals only with the explicit topological relations between the entities of the geometric model. Handling the implicit topological relationships that are perceived by various disciplines at higher levels of abstractions than those represented in the geometric model is a much more complex task and is somewhat domain dependent. This issue is discussed next.

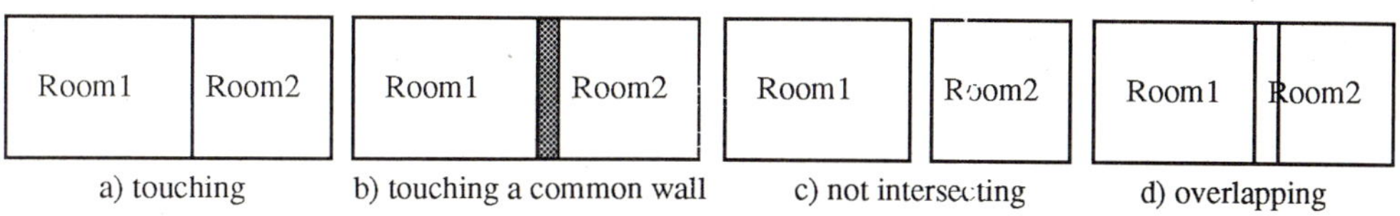

Figure 3. Topological Relationships of Two Rooms.

Reasoning about implicit topological relationships. The explicit topological relationships of the geometric representations of the facility abstractions are readily available in the non-manifold geometric modeling paradigm used. However, most disciplines often perceive topological relationships, e.g., "part-of", "intersects" or "adjacent-to", that differ from the explicit topological relationships represented in the geometric model of the facility. For example, consider the topological relationships of two rooms illustrated in Figure 3. For simplicity, the two rooms are represented by two rectangles in all four cases, since the dimensionality and type of geometric entities used are not important. The two rooms in all cases of this example are perceived to be adjacent or next to each other by the architect or the HVAC designer; however, it is only in case (a) that the two corresponding rectangles explicitly share one edge and thus are said to be explicitly adjacent. For the remaining three cases, there is simply not enough information in the geometric model to directly provide this implicit topological relationship. To resolve such implicit topological relationships, we first proposed to augment the spatial operators of the geometric modeler to construct a tolerance envelope around the desired geometric entities based on some user defined tolerance value (Zamanian et al. 90). After further studying the problem, we concluded that the tolerance envelope approach is only appropriate for very simple cases and becomes extremely complicated in more general cases. Therefore, we decided to deal with this problem at a higher level of abstraction than that provided in the non-manifold paradigm, and subsequently devised a new representation scheme on top of the non-manifold paradigm for representing and reasoning about various abstractions of constructed facilities regardless of the dimensionality and type of geometric entities used. This representation scheme is described next.

A General Spatial Representation Scheme

The need for reasoning about implicit topological relations and for a high-level symbolic language to define and query the spatial information of constructed facilities motivated the development of this general spatial representation scheme. Some existing geometric representation techniques used in the architectural and the structural engineering domains (Fenves et al. 76, Stiny 80, Coyne et al. 90) have been studied throughout this work, but none of these techniques provides a sufficiently general scheme for dealing with the mixed-dimensional spatial abstractions of facilities in a single, uniform fashion. This section provides a formal description of this representation scheme and discusses its relationship to the non-manifold representation scheme used as its implementation basis.

Two types of spatial representation schemes are identified in this work: a minimal representation scheme corresponding to that of the the vertex-based, non-manifold geometric modeler adopted, and a maximal representation scheme developed in this work. The minimal scheme is based on a boundary representation scheme that uses four disjoint, atomic geometric elements, i.e., vertex, edge, face, and solid, and a number of internal topological elements, e.g., shell, loop, etc., for modeling geometric models with possible "dangling" elements while guaranteeing closure under all Boolean operations. The maximal scheme uses special geometric entities referred to as "superior elements," such as planes, lines, or points, to define geometric entities of appropriate dimensionality with which the boundaries of a spatial configuration or any of its spatial subsets can be identified. The two representation schemes are consistent (Requicha 80); however, there is only a unique mapping from the maximal representation to the minimal representation, and not *vice versa* (this is similar to the relation between CSG and B-Rep solid models(Requicha 80)). Although the superior-element representation scheme can theoretically handle non-linear configurations, due to limitations of the existing geometric modeling techniques (Hoffmann 89) our research is limited to linear spatial configurations. This limitation is not severe, because the majority of constructed facilities have linear geometry and their curved segments can be accurately approximated as piece-wise linear segments.

An n-dimensional ($1 \leq n \leq 3$) spatial configuration S is a subset of E^n and can consist of various m-dimensional ($0 \leq m \leq n$) spatial subsets. In the 2-dimensional spatial configuration illustrated in Figure 4a, the spatial subsets correspond to all possible two-dimensional spaces (spaces are n-dimensional) and the one- and zero-dimensional partitions separating those spaces. The set A, consisting of disjoint, atomic elements corresponding to the minimal representation of this configuration, is shown in Figure 4b, and set the B, shown in Figure 4c, contains the superior lines (superior-elements are n-1-dimensional). Figure 4d illustrates two spatial subsets of this spatial configuration and their corresponding minimal and maximal representations. It is important to note that the concave (a concave geometric entity has internal angles greater than 180 degrees and possibly cavities or dangling parts of the same or lower dimensions) subsets of a spatial configuration can not be uniquely represented by the superior-element scheme but are representable by applying Boolean operations on convex subsets, which in turn are uniquely represented by the maximal scheme.

The superior-element representation scheme can be formally described by the following syntax:

$S \equiv A$

$S ::= (e_1 ... e_n)$

$e_i ::= (C\ (b_i, ... ,b_m))\ |\ (\mathrm{BOOL}(e_j\ e_k))$

$C ::= \mathrm{NULL}\ |\ \mathrm{E}\ |\ b_i\ |\ (b_i \,.\, b_j)$

BOOL ::= UNION | INTERSECTION | DIFFERENCE

$b_i \in B$

Here S is a n-dimensional ($1 \leq n \leq 3$) spatial configuration that is comprised of various possible m-dimensional ($0 \leq m \leq n$) spatial subsets e_i and its minimal representation is the set A. Each convex subset e_i is defined by a m-dimensional "carrier" (the notion of "carrier" is borrowed from (Hoffmann 89)) model C that spatially contains e_i and a list of superior elements that uniquely contain all the boundaries of e_i. C, depending on the dimensionality and type of e_i, can be NULL (when m=0), the Euclidean space E^m, a superior element, or the intersection of two superior elements. Each concave spatial subset is in turn defined by a Boolean operation and two other spatial subsets (concave or convex). Finally, the n-1-dimensional superior elements b_i corresponding to S are members of a set B specified by the user.

Spatial Decomposition, Selection, Composition, and View Creation

As discussed earlier, constructed facilities can be modeled as assemblies of various objects that represent different abstractions of the facility components (e.g., rooms, zones, girders, and pipes). In the top-down definition of these objects, objects corresponding to higher abstractions are recursively decomposed to create lower-level objects of desired abstractions. Similarly, for the bottom-up definition of the objects, lower-level objects are grouped to create the high-level abstractions needed for other objects. Furthermore, it is often desirable to create views by collecting information from one or more facility objects. These issues are extensively addressed in some of the recent data models of constructed facilities (Fenves et al. 90, Eastman et al. 90, Bjork et al. 89, Gielingh 88, Keirouz 88, Powell et al. 88, Law et al. 90) mostly for dealing with the non-spatial attributes of the facility components. In this work, we use our proposed superior-element representation scheme as the basis for specifically addressing the management of the facility spatial information. The spatial operations proposed in this work are closely related to similar operations used in database management systems for developing appropriate taxonomies and groupings of information. Our initial findings suggest that there exist parallel hierarchical structures in the geometric model and the database organization of a constructed facility.

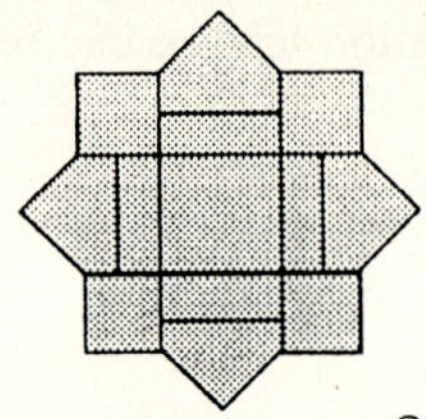

a) Spatial Configuration S

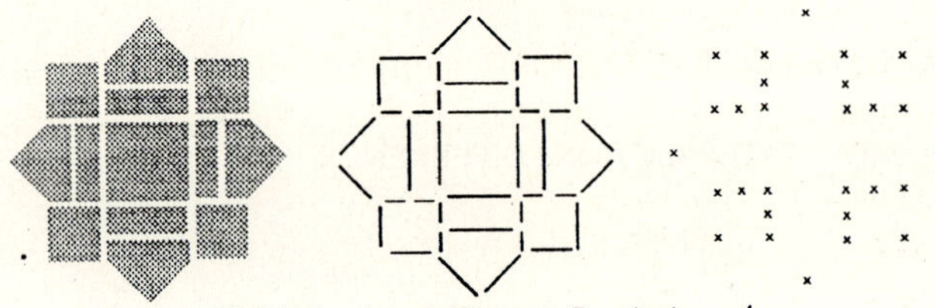

b) Disjoint, Atomic Elements Constituting A

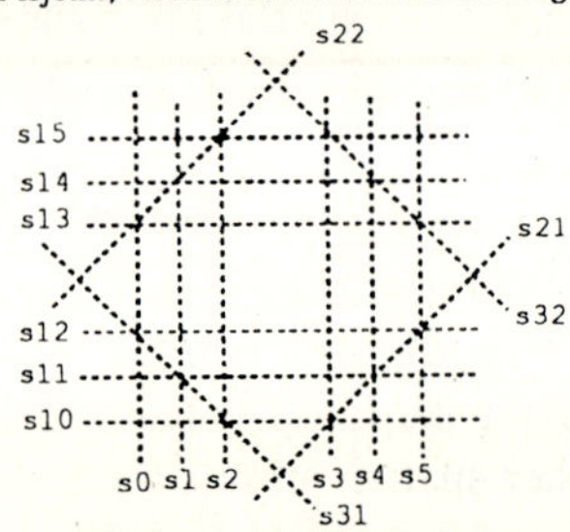

c) Superior Elements Constituting B

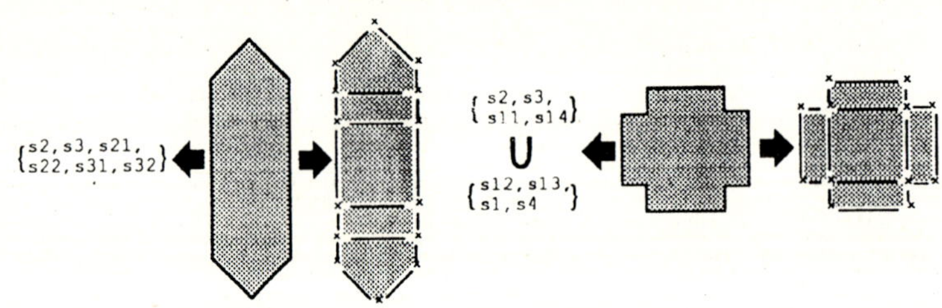

d) Representation of Convex and Concave Spaces

Figure 4. An Example of a Spatial Configuration.

Decomposition. Based on the above description of the proposed maximal representation scheme, a recursive spatial decomposition technique is developed. This technique is formally described as follows using the above nomenclature:

$$C_i \supset S_i$$

$$C_i \equiv E \mid a_{(i-m)k} \mid \{ a_{(i-m)k} \ldots a_{(i-n)l} \} \quad (1 \le m,n \le i)$$

$$S_i \equiv A_i$$

$$a_{ij} \in A_i$$

$$a_{ij} ::= \text{vertex} \mid \text{edge} \mid \text{face} \mid \text{solid}$$

$$b_{ij} \in B_i$$

$$C_i \oplus B_i \Rightarrow A_i$$

This formalism basically states that a spatial configuration S_i (with S_0 representing the starting configuration) is created by partitioning its carrier model C_i with a set of superior elements b_{ij} in B_i via the $\oplus$ operator. The carrier model is equivalent to either the Euclidean space (often used to initiate the decomposition process), an atomic element, or a composition of the atomic elements created in the previous decompositions, i.e., from a_{i-n} $(1 \leq n \leq i)$. This recursive process is continued with a new set of superior elements, which may have a different dimensionality than the dimensionalities of sets used in the previous steps, until the desired level of spatial granularity is reached.

Selection. Specific atomic elements created during the decomposition process can be selected based on some given criteria. Here we define a binary selection operator $\ominus$ and its two operands as sets A_i and D_{ik} corresponding to the specified sets of atomic elements and selection criteria, respectively. The result of a selection operation, A_{ik}, is consequently a subset of A_i, i.e.,

$$A_{ik} = A_i \ominus D_{ik}$$

Note that the second subscript in the above equation indicates the possibility of multiple selections from the same set of atomic elements. The function $\ominus$ is similar to the "select" operation used in relational databases, with A_i being analogous to a relational table and D_{ik} representing the constraints imposed on the attributes of selected tuples.

The elements in D_{ik} can be of three types:

1. geometric class of elements in A_i ,
2. superior elements in B_{ik} defining the spatial extent of D_{ik}, and
3. a list of labels of labeled elements in A_i.

The selection criteria in D_{ik} are combined through the logical connective "AND" in order to satisfy each criteria and return only those selected elements that satisfy all the given criteria.

Composition. Selected atomic elements generated via the decomposition process can be put together to compose new subsets of their corresponding spatial configuration. The composition operation, indicated by the binary operator $\otimes$, therefore creates a new set of atomic elements from two other sets that are generated via the decomposition, selection, or composition operations. Because the atomic elements of any spatial set must be disjoint, overlapping elements from the two sets in a composition operation are split into their corresponding disjoint atomic elements. As shown in Figure 5, the composition operation distinctly preserves the overlap of its operands by creating new elements that can also be represented and identified by the superior elements associated with the composed set.

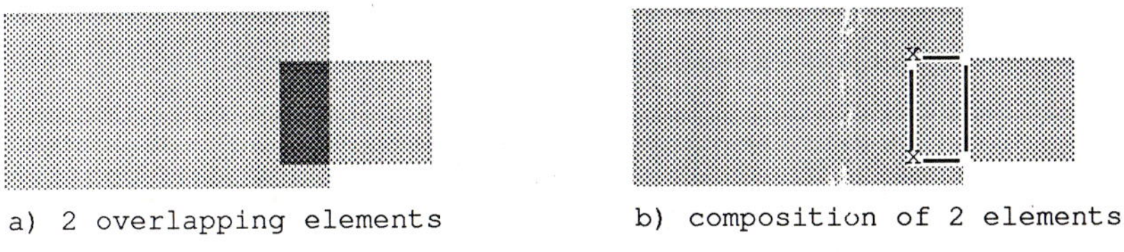

Figure 5. Composition of two Overlapping Elements.

View creation. Discipline-specific views (or functional views) of a spatial configuration are represented by spatial subsets of that configuration in a way that those subsets contain only the information needed by their corresponding disciplines. Views are created using the selection and the composition operations described above.

Labeling of spatial elements. Although the superior-element representation scheme can be used for identifying the elements of a spatial configuration and its subsets, this scheme may appear cumbersome and not very efficient. Therefore, a mechanism is provided for attaching user-defined labels to spatial configurations and their elements or subsets when they are created or when later identified by the superior-element representation scheme.

Using the spatial configuration from our previous example in Figure 4, the spatial operations and the labeling mechanism discussed above are used to create this configuration and subsequently several of its spatial subsets, as illustrated in Figure 6. A graph structure representing the sequence of operations used to create the configurations in Figure 6 is shown in Figure 7.

Linkage between Non-spatial and Spatial Information

As briefly mentioned earlier, management of the non-spatial attributes of the facility components in a computer-integrated environment is as important as dealing with the spatial attributes. Much work has been done in the area of data modeling and information management for the domain of constructed facilities, primarily for dealing with the general organization of the facility representation and of the non-spatial attributes (Fenves et al. 90, Eastman et al. 90, Bjork et al. 89, Powell et al. 88). The contribution of the present work is to provide a linkage between the spatial and non-spatial attributes of the facility components while maintaining separate data models and representation schemes for each of the information types. The major advantage of separating the management of the spatial and non-spatial information is that data representation schemes and algorithms that are most appropriate for the particular type of data being considered are used. On the other hand, there is a performance price to pay when data is partitioned across different server programs and has different representation schemes. The proposed system, illustrated in Figure 1, involving separate server programs for the spatial and non-spatial information is intended to minimize excessive performance costs by capitalizing on three assumptions:

1. The hierarchical operations of decomposition, selection, and composition pertain equally to non-spatial and spatial attributes of facility components (for non-spatial attributes, composition is limited to assemblies of disjoint (non-overlapping) elements). In other words, the discipline specific (or functional) organization of non-spatial information follows the same hierarchical decomposition as that of the spatial information.

2. All non-spatial attributes of interest in a view are keyed or indexed to some spatial element in the decomposition hierarchy. The unique identifier attached to each spatial element (user-defined label or system-generated internal identifier) also serves as the key to the non-spatial attributes of that element in every functional view.

3. Unlike the spatial information, which is likely to exhibit commonality across views (at least at the higher levels of abstraction), it is anticipated that most non-spatial attributes will be specific to one functional view only. Therefore, separation of management actually imposes beneficial segregation of the non-spatial attributes by function.

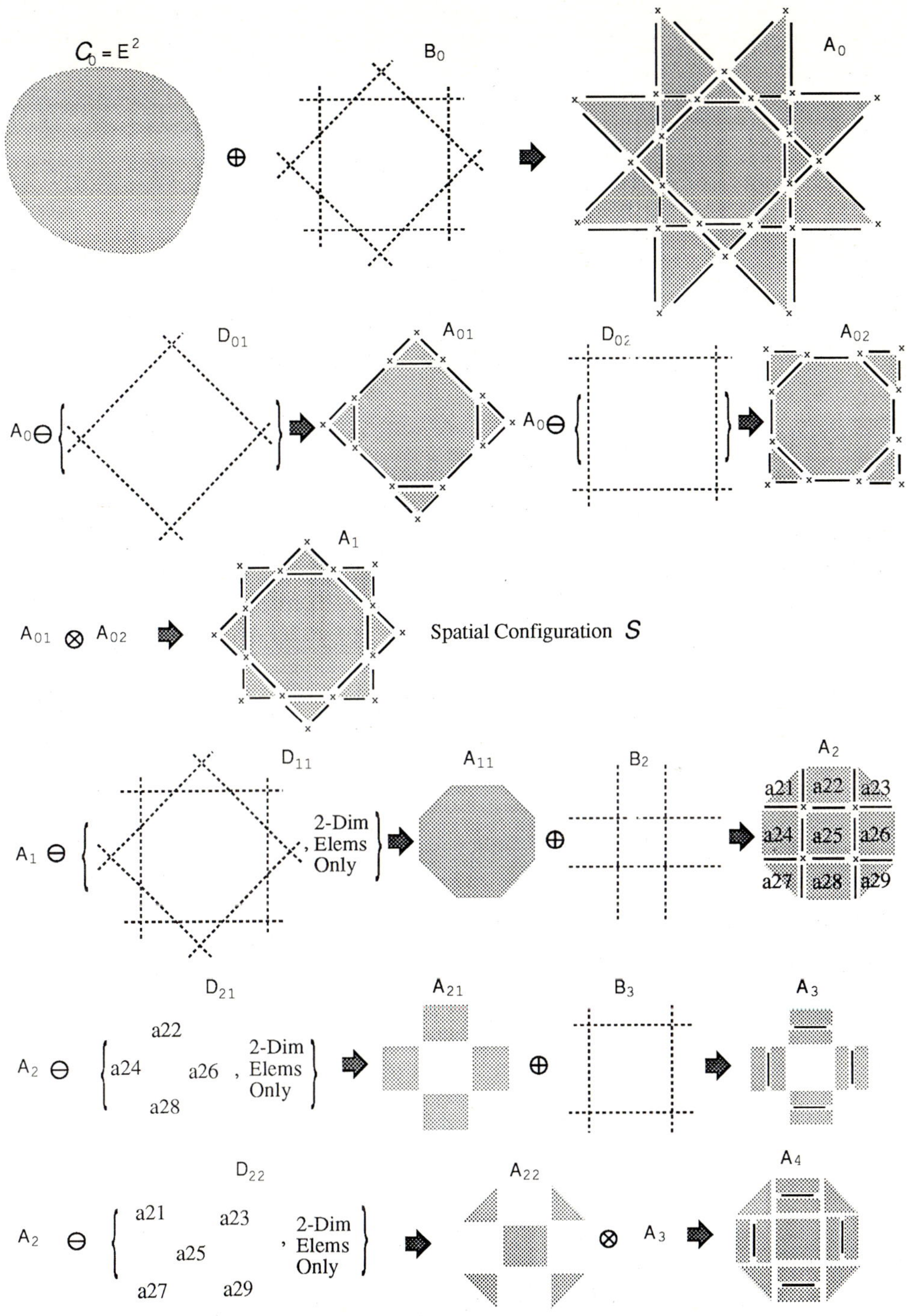

Figure 6. An Example Usage of the Proposed Spatial Operations.

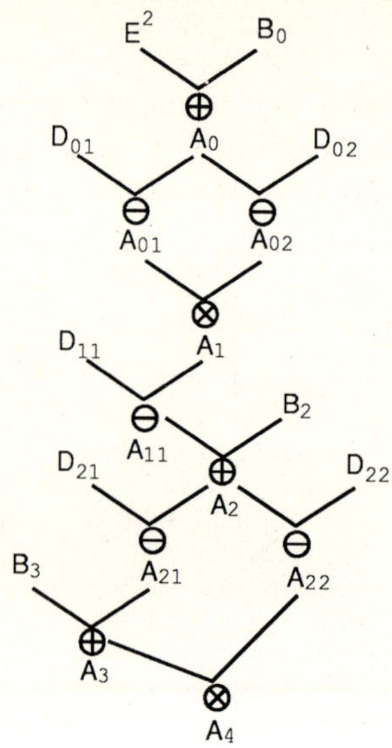

Figure 7. Graph Illustrating the Operations Used in the Example.

The third point above does not preclude retrieval of non-spatial attributes across functional views; it simply capitalizes on the common spatial information that unites the multiple functionalities of facility components. To illustrate this point, let us consider the hypothetical query used in above, i.e., "find all architectural rooms supported by at least one structural beam whose grade of steel is the same as that of the structural column located at the north-west corner of the HVAC zone K3." This query can be broken into several subqueries issued to the geometric modeler and the database manager as follows:

1. locate north-west corner of zone K3 in the HVAC view (spatial);
2. find a column in the structural view at the location found in 1 (spatial);
3. retrieve the grade of steel for the column found in 2 (non-spatial);
4. retrieve all beams in the structural view with grade equal to the value found in 3 (non-spatial);
5. find all rooms in the architectural view such that each room is supported at least by one of the beams found in 4 (spatial).

Implementation

The current partial implementation of the proposed framework shown in Figure 1 links the Sybase relational database (Sybase 89) with the Noodles non-manifold geometric modeler (Gursoz et al. 90). A menu-driven prototype client program with interactive graphic viewing capability has been developed in order to define the facility components by mixed-dimensional geometry of any desired abstraction, and optionally to attach non-spatial attributes to these components. The linkage to the relational database enables users to automatically transfer data from or to the database via the client program without the detailed knowledge about the underlying table organizations or the SQL commands issued. Every component is uniquely identified by its user-defined name and functional view. Furthermore, a unique internal identification is attached to every component once it is defined, and the spatial attributes (represented in terms of the geometric entities of Noodles) and the non-spatial attributes (represented in terms of the tuples in relational tables) of a component are linked together via this internal identification. The object-based client program encapsulates the underlying data representations and functional interfaces provided by the geometric modeler and the relational database, thus providing a higher level of abstraction for dealing with the facility information.

Two of the future facilities to be incorporated in the prototype client program are best illustrated in connection with Figure 6.

1. The introduction of a "level" attribute as part of the component identification. Thus if both $A2$ and A_3 are part of the same functional view, the higher-level elements in A_2 can be differentiated from the lower-level elements in A_3, and different non-spatial attributes associated with elements of each level.

2. The automatic generation of hierarchical, topological, and geometric attributes in the non-spatial database in response to user requests, to facilitate processing by application programs. Examples of these types of attributes are:

- spaces in A_4 that are subdivisions of spaces in A_2(hierarchical);
- end vertices of edges or edges of faces(topological); and
- coordinates of vertices, lengths of edges, areas of faces, or volumes of solids (geometric).

It must be noted that if the user chooses to include spatial information in the non-spatial database, it is his/her responsibility to maintain consistency between this information and its corresponding data in the geometric modeler.

Conclusions and Future Work

This paper discusses issues with regards to the representation of mixed-dimensional spatial abstractions of the components of constructed facilities. These issues are of great importance for the development of the proposed framework for modeling and communicating all facility information in a computer-integrated environment. A general representation and identification scheme is developed to deal uniformly with the topological relationships between mixed-dimensional geometric abstractions of components used by different functional views throughout the lifecycle of a constructed facility. This scheme is based on a maximal boundary representation technique that is provided on top of the minimal boundary representation of the underlying non-manifold geometric modeler. This maximal (or superior-element) representation scheme provides a symbolic way of representing and identifying the implicit topological relationships in a spatial configuration and its subparts consistently and uniformly regardless of the dimensionality of the configuration's geometric entities.

Several issues will be studied closely and possibly implemented in the remaining time frame of this research. These issues include: associating multiple, mixed-dimensional geometric representations to a single component while providing consistent topological relationships between components; expansion of lower-level geometric entities to higher-level ones to deal with the evolution of the facility throughout its lifecycle; additions and enhancements to the existing object-based client program that manages the interactions between the two server programs handling the spatial and non-spatial attributes of the facility; and, formal specification of a data exchange protocol for specifying and retrieving facility information via the functional interface of the object-based client program.

Acknowledgments. This research has been supported under the cooperative agreement number ECD-8943164 by the Engineering Design Research Center, an NSF Engineering Research Center at Carnegie Mellon University.

References

Bjork et al., B., and H. Penttila. 1989 "A scenario for the development and implementation of a building product model standard." In *Current Research and Development in Integrated Design, Construction and Facility Management*. CIFE, Stanford University. Stanford, CA.

Coyne, R. F., and U. Flemming. 1990 "Planning in design synthesis: abstraction-based LOOS." In *Artificial Intelligence in Engineering, AIENG 90*. Boston, MA.

Date, C. J. 1988. *A Guide to SQL Standard*. Reading. MA.: Addison-Wesley.

"DXF." *AutoCAD Reference Manual*. Sausalito, CA: Autodesk Inc. 1987.

Eastman, C. M., A. Bond, and Chase, S. 1990 "A formal approach for product model information." *Research in Engineering Design*. (in process).

Introduction to EDIF. 1988. 2001 Eye Street, N. W., Washington D.C. 20006: Electronic Industries Association.

Fenves, S. J., U. Flemming, C. Hendrickson, M. L. Maher, and G. Schmitt. 1990 "Integrated software environment for building design and construction." *CAD* 22, no. 1: 27-36.

Fenves, S. J., and S. A. Liadis. 1976 "A data structure for computer-aided design of buildings." *APEC*, pp. 14-18.

Gielingh, W. 1988. *General AEC reference model (GARM)*. Technical report. AEC committee of ISO/STEP, P.O. Box 49, 2600 AA Delft, The Netherlands.

Gursoz, E. L., Y. Choi, and F. B. Prinz. 1990 "Vertex-based representation of non-manifold boundaries." In M. J. Wozny, J. U. Turner, and K. Preiss (eds.). *Geometric Modeling for Product Engineering*, pp. 107-130. IFIP WG 5.2/NSF, New York, North-Holland.

Hoffmann, C. M. 1989. *Geometric and Solid Modeling: An Introduction*. Morgan Kaufmann.

Howard, H. C. 1986. *Interfacing databases and knowledge-based systems for structural engineering applications*. PhD thesis, Pittsburgh, PA: Carnegie Mellon University.

Initial Graphic Exchange Specification (IGES) Version 3.0. 1987. Gaithersburg: National Institute of Standards and Technology.

Keirouz, W. T. 1988. *Domain modeling of constructed facilities for robot applications*. PhD thesis. Pittsburgh, PA: Carnegie Mellon University.

Lavakare, A., and H. C. Howard. June 1989. *Structural steel framing data model*. Technical report. Stanford University, Stanford, CA: Center for Integrated Facility Engineering.

Law, K. H., T. Barsalou, and G. Wiederhold. 1990. "Management of complex structural engineering objects in a relational framework." *Engineering with Computers*, no. 6: 81-92.

Lipsett, R., E. Marschner, and M. Shahdad. 1986. "VHDL - the language." *IEEE Design and Test*, April, pp. 28-40.

Powell, G. H. and R. Bhateja. 1988 ."Data base design for computer-integrated structural engineering." *Engineering with Computers*, no. 4: 135-143.

Requicha, A. A. G. December 1980. "Representations for rigid solids: Theory, methods, and systems." *Computing Surveys* 12, no. 4: 437-464.

Stiny, G. 1980. "Introduction to shape and shape grammars." *Environment and Planning* B, no. 7: 343-351.

Sybase SQL Server Reference Manual. 1989. Sybase, Inc. Emeryville, CA.

Turner, J. July 1988. *AEC Building System Model, ISO TC184/SC4/WG1 doc. 3.2.2.4*. University of Michigan. MI.: Ann Arbor.

Zamanian, M. K., and S. J. Fenves. 1990. *An information exchange protocol for constructed facilities*. Technical Report 12-37-90, Engineering Design Research Center (EDRC), Carnegie Mellon Univ., Pittsburgh, PA.

16 Mutation and Analogy to Support Creativity in Computer-Aided Design

John S. Gero, Mary Lou Maher

Design Computing Unit
University of Sydney
NSW 2006 Australia

Creative processes in computer-aided design are identified as those that introduce new design variables into the design process. This paper describes the ideas behind the development of a computational model of creative processes in design. This computational model is founded on the use of mutation and analogy processes working in tandem using design prototypes as the representation schema.

Introduction

Creative design while highly valued is not currently supported by computer programs used during design. Research in design and artificial intelligence shows potential for improving our understanding of design and establishing computational models for creative design. Research in computational processes for design has been primarily concerned with routine design which has not provided much insight into the adequacy of these processes to support creative design. The distinction between routine and creative design is subjective but an operational definition can be given. Routine design is the result of making design decisions in the context of a design situation where all the decision variables are known a priori. Thus, in routine design the designer operates within a defined, closed state space of possible designs where the differences between designs can be characterized largely by the values selected for the design variables. To a lesser extent it can be further characterized by the selection of which variables to include in the design from a predefined range of variables. Creative design occurs when new design variables are introduced in the process of designing. Thus, in creative design the designer operates within a changing state space of possible designs; a state space which increases in size with the introduction of each new variable, Figure 1.

This paper describes the ideas behind the development of a computational model of creative processes, where creative processes in computer-aided design are identified as those that introduce new design variables into the design process thus providing the opportunity for novel designs to result. Two computational processes being explored are mutation and analogy working in tandem, where mutation involves the use of mutation operators to produce new variables and analogy finds similar situations and extracts knowledge from them to assist in the incorporation of the new variables into the current situation.

Analogy and Mutation as Computational Processes

Analogy is a particularly useful approach for solving an unfamiliar new problem without adequate or directly applicable knowledge. Various forms of analogical reasoning in computer systems is an active research area in artificial intelligence and its application (Prieditis 1988). Based on the nature of the knowledge transferred from previous experience to the new problem, the analogical reasoning approach can be classified into two categories: transformational analogy and derivational analogy (Carbonell 1982, 1983, 1986). Transformational analogy adapts the solutions to the past problems for the new problem. Derivational analogy applies the past problem solving processes or methods to solve the new problem. By analogy, the relations between the new problem and some past experience or knowledge about a particular phenomenon can be found. This experience or knowledge can be placed in the new situation so that the new problem can be better understood or a new plan for solving the problem can be generated. An example of an implementation that uses analogy to improve the efficiency of the search for alternative designs is reported in (Zhao and Maher 1988). An example of a knowledge based system for creative mechanical design, EDISON (Dyer et al 1986), uses analogy as a mechanism for invention.

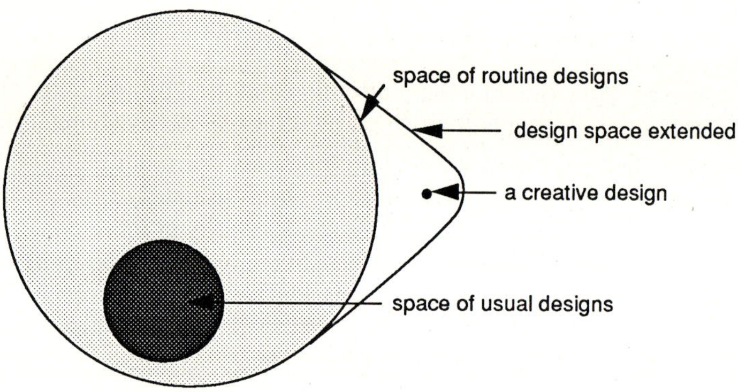

Figure 1. State space of routine and creative designs.

Mutation is the deliberate action of changing features or attributes of an object or a concept in an unconventional manner. By unconventional manner we mean that the change is not restricted by the common rules and constraints. The purpose of mutation is to produce new properties, functions and meanings of an old object or concept by changing some of its basic features. Mutation can be performed in many different ways. Some variations of mutation are multiplication, division, addition, subtraction, and substitution operations performed on the features, functions and mechanisms of concepts. Computerization of mutation has been successful when the representation was appropriate; AM (Lenat 1982, Lenat and Brown 1983) is an example of applying simple mutation in the domain of mathematics. In complex representations computers still do not have adequate knowledge and it is difficult to obtain meaningful mutation operations. This may often make mutation seem somewhat arbitrary. Without appropriate guidance, its nature is to some extent opportunistic and success can not be guaranteed.

Supporting Creativity in Computer-Aided Design

In order to make use of analogy and mutation to support creativity in computer-aided design, three issues have been identified:

(i) the representation of design experience,

(ii) the identification and application of mutation operators, and

(iii) the development and application of analogical reasoning.

Representation of Design Experience

Design experience provides the source of knowledge for both mutation and analogy. For mutation, experience provides a typical design which forms the basis of mutation. For analogy, design experience provides various design situations from which an appropriate analogy can be drawn. To distinguish the representation of previous design experience from the current design situation, we introduce the terms *source* and *target*. Source knowledge is a representation of previous design experience in a particular domain, such as building design. This is in contrast to a target design space which provides a representation of the current design problem and its context.

The representation to be used for the source space is the schema *design prototypes* developed at the University of Sydney (Gero 1990). A design prototype is a generalization of groupings of elements in a design domain which provides the basis for the commencement and continuation of a design process. The design prototype thus represents generalizations of previous designs from which new design solutions applicable to the current situation can be derived. To facilitate design reasoning and support mutation and analogy, a design prototype generalizes previous designs according to the following categories:

- Functions are the design goals that can be achieved by using the design prototype. The functions of a design prototype are a primary consideration in determining whether it is suitable for a particular design context. In architectural design this may include, within a particular context, style, type of building, purpose and intent.
- *Structure* information describes the design in terms of its physical existence or the conditions for such existence. Structure is described in terms of decision variables whose values will be determined during the design process. In a building this may include the topology of the spaces, their geometry and the materials of construction of the bounding elements to those spaces.
- *Behaviors* are the expected responses of the design in the current design context. In architectural design, for example, some behavior characteristics are efficient circulation, adequate lighting, thermal comfort, and cost.
- *Dependency knowledge* provides the relations between function, behavior and structure. For example, the behavior cost may be related to the structure material.

This explicit representation of design knowledge can support creativity because it goes beyond the representation of only decision variables as is customary in mathematical models of design processes (Radford and Gero 1988). The mapping from function to structure represents available heuristics for producing design solutions using knowledge-based expert system approaches. The mapping from structure to behavior is explicitly available through analytical processes. The dependency knowledge provides the basis for reasoning about the associations and potential values of related variables within a design context. Figure 2 illustrates a generalized dependency network where the progression from left to right represents the relations between functions (F), behaviors (B), behavior variables (BV), structure variables (SV) and structures (S). An example of part of a dependency network for a design prototype representing generalized double hung windows is shown in Figure 3.

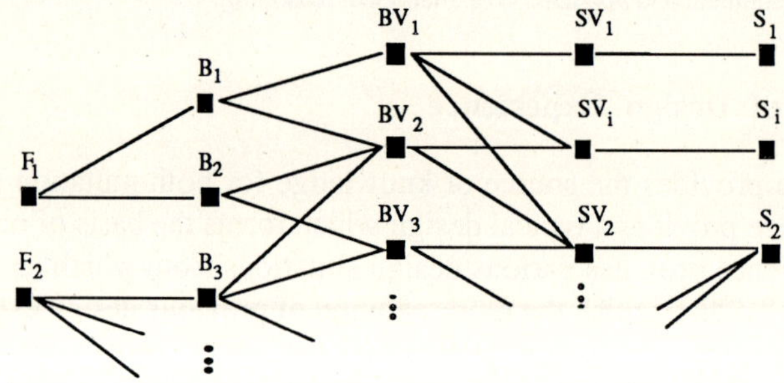

Figure 2. A dependency network in a design prototype showing the relationship among function, behavior, behavior variables, structure variables and structure.

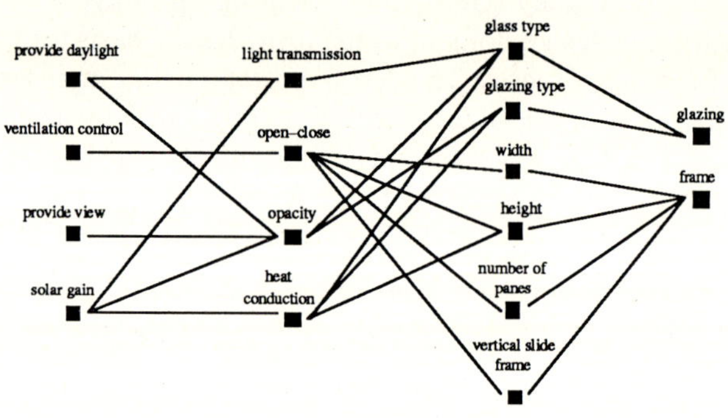

Figure 3. Part of the dependency network for the design prototype concerned with double hung windows.

Mutation Operators for Creative Design

Mutation operators are used to introduce new decision variables in the target space. Such mutation operators might be multiplication, where a decision variable becomes two variables of the same nature; or addition, where a decision variable of a different nature is introduced.

Mutation operators are applied to structure decision variables and are used to introduce one or more new variables into a design. There are two classes of mutation operators:

(i) homogeneous, i.e., those which produce new variables of the same type as the variable being mutated, and

(ii) heterogeneous, i.e. those which produce new variables of a different type.

Homogeneous operators include division where a single variable, X, is divided into two variables, X1 and X2, thus introducing a second variable of the same type as X. As a result new structures can be produced. The issue of homogeneity is important since homogeneous variables can use the existing dependency information in the design prototype from its precursor variable, Figure 4. Other homogeneous operators include multiplication and exponentiation, although only division has been reported in Cagan (1990). In the dependency network of the window prototype, a homogeneous mutation could be the division of the structure variable height into height1 and height2. The relations in the dependency network are modified as shown in Figure 5.

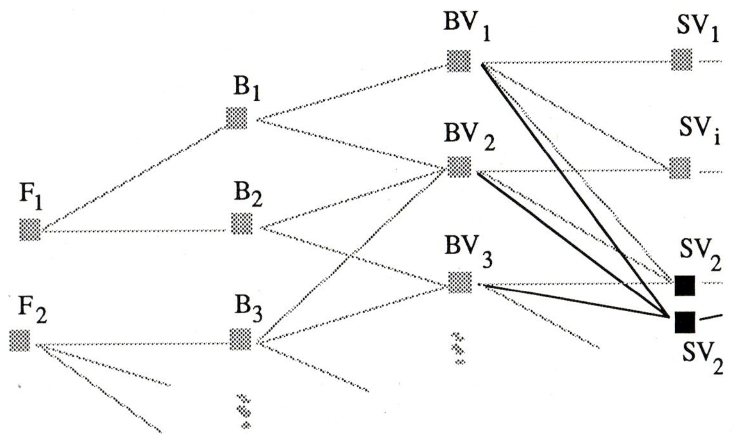

Figure 4. Modified dependency network after a homogeneous mutation operation on SV2 where SV2 has been divided into {SV21, SV22}.

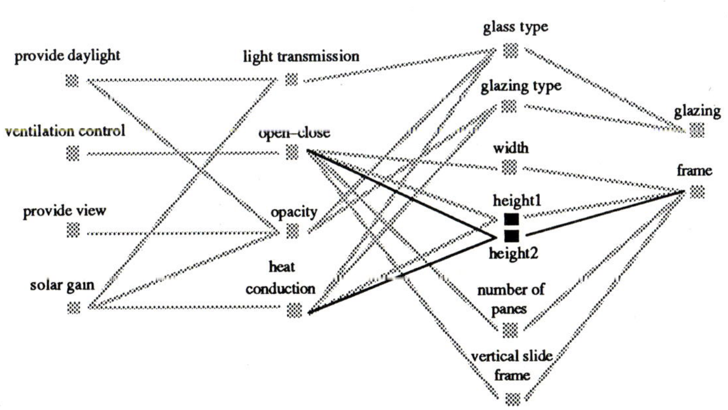

Figure 5. Modified dependency network for the double hung window design prototype after a homogeneous mutation operation.

Heterogeneous operators include addition and the set operations of union and intersection in general. An example of using addition as a mutation operator is to select the structure variable length and add as a new variable the variable angle to it. This results in a length that can be rotated where previously it was fixed in direction. Heterogeneous variables, however, require additional dependency information for their inclusion in the design prototype since no such information currently exists in the design prototype, Figure 6. In the window design prototype, the use of an addition mutation operator to produce the rotation variable is illustrated in Figure 7.

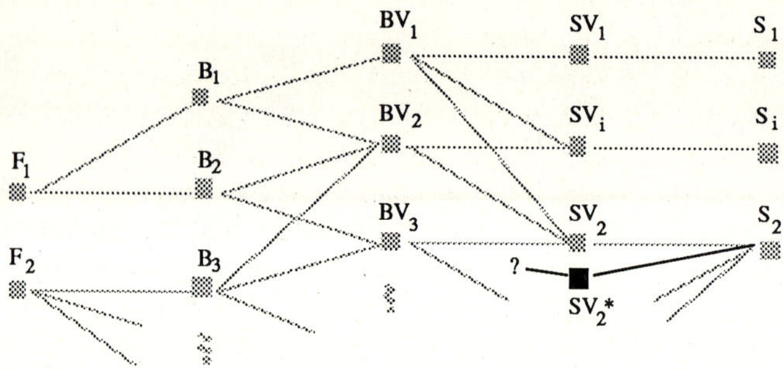

Figure 6. In a heterogeneous mutation a new variable SV2* is introduced through an addition mutation process and has no behavior dependency knowledge available.

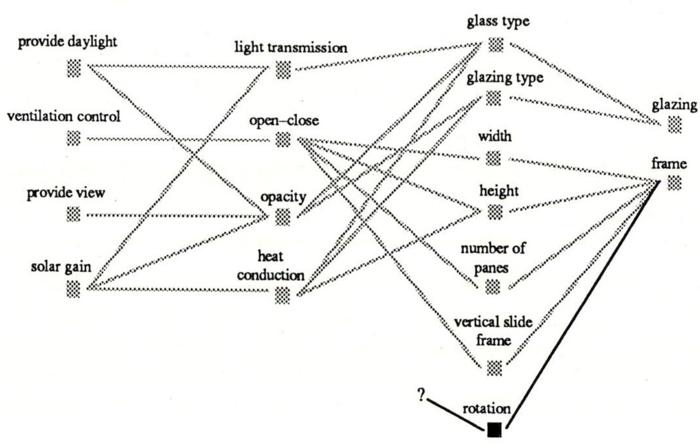

Figure 7. The dependency network of the double hung window design prototype after the addition of the rotation variable.

Analogical Reasoning for Creative Design

Analogical reasoning tasks are identified for finding relevant knowledge in the source space to accommodate a new heterogeneous design variable in the target space. Once a new variable has been introduced the issue of how to integrate it into the current situation arises. Here we use existing techniques and approaches for analogical reasoning to identify relevant design prototypes which potentially contain knowledge appropriate for the integration of that new variable. Analogical reasoning can be considered in two major steps: finding an analogous situation and using the knowledge from the previous situation in the new situation. The techniques derived from research in artificial intelligence that are relevant to supporting analogical reasoning in creative design processes are memory indexing and transformation.

Memory indexing. Memory organization is important when attempting to make associations between design prototypes that may be very different except for a few shared attributes. Indexing is used to facilitate information flow across contexts, on which analogical reasoning is based. Design prototypes are grouped and retrieved according to their similarities of characteristics through indices. The indices are related to specific manifestations of the design prototype knowledge categories, i.e. functions, structures and behaviors. To support the mutation of a prototype, the dependency networks of the source prototypes are used. If a structure variable is introduced, the dependency networks are indexed by their structure variables. For example, the introduction of the variable, rotation, in the double hung window requires finding previous experience in which rotation is a structure variable. The search for relevant design prototypes in this example may result in the retrieval of a revolving door design prototype. Figure 8 illustrates the dependency network of a revolving door design prototype.

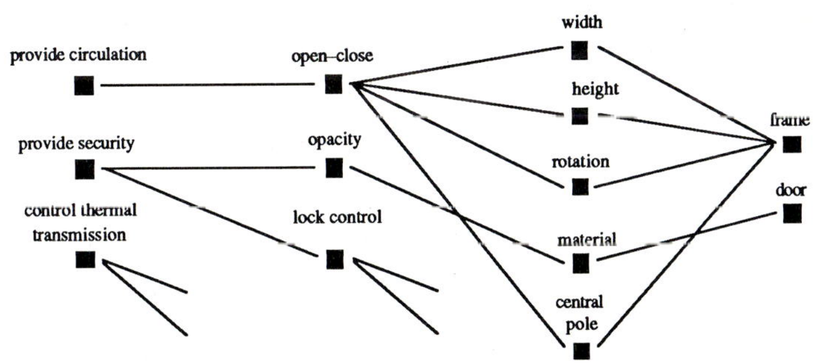

Figure 8. The dependency network of the revolving door design prototype.

Transformation. Once a potentially appropriate source design prototype is identified, a transformation of that design prototype's knowledge is needed to establish its relevance to the new design context. In the model for creative design being used here, the current context is defined by the selected design prototype in the target space, for example, the double hung window. The source knowledge for accommodating the introduction of a new variable in the target space is the retrieved design prototype, for example, the revolving door. The transformation from the source space to the target space requires selecting the relevant parts of the dependency network and combining this with the dependency network in the target space, Figure 9.

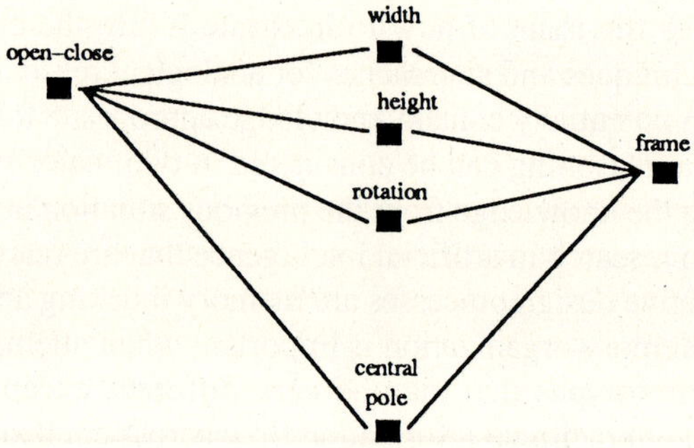

Figure 9. Part of the dependency network of the revolving door design prototype retrieved in the search for another design prototype containing the structure variable rotation.

This can be executed using the structure-mapping approach of Falkenhainer et al (1989/90) where the indexed structure variable acts as a focus and the related structure and behavior variables are mapped from the source design prototype onto the target design prototype. Clearly, there must be a map to part of the structure otherwise the new variable is not part of the structure. However, new behavior variables may result which are part of existing behaviors. Alternately, new behavior variables may introduce new behaviors which may or may not be part of existing functions. If they are not a part of existing functions then a new function is introduced. For the window example, the combined dependency network is illustrated in Figure 10. This 'new' window operates in manner similar to that of a revolving door and is reflected in the dependency network by the introduction of the new nodes 'rotation' and 'central post'.

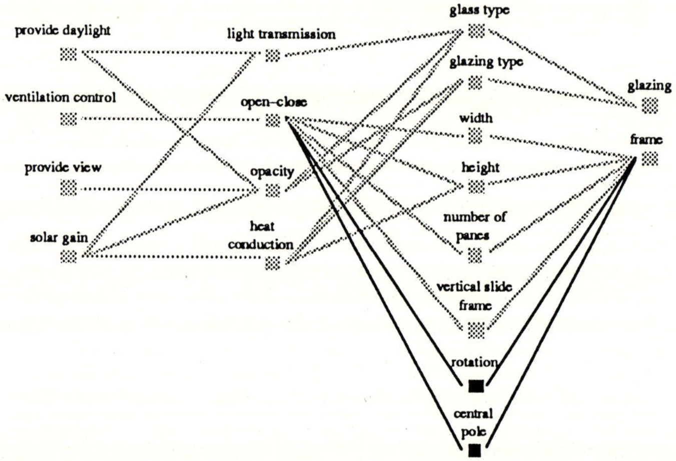

Figure 10. Combining the relevant part of the dependency network of the revolving door design prototype with the existing window design prototype, where the bold relations and nodes represent the knowledge imported from the revolving door to create a new window design.

Discussion

The ideas in this paper have been partially implemented. The dependency networks and associated design prototypes have been implemented to support routine design at the University of Sydney and for creative design at Carnegie Mellon University. The implementations have not progressed as far as the ideas described here. As the implementations proceed, the need for more knowledge in the dependency networks and the implications of the application of mutation operators on the dependency networks becomes more explicit.

The computational processes of mutation and analogy provide approaches to supporting creative design but their application is strongly dependent on the representation of the source and target spaces. In our model we use a representation centered on the concept of design prototypes because they provide a rich environment for organizing design knowledge. The explicit representation of function, behavior, and structure as attributes and dependencies facilitates mutation and analogical reasoning. A different representation of design knowledge, such as logic, rules, or design grammars, may invalidate much of the effectiveness of the application of mutation and analogy as described in this paper.

Acknowledgements

The authors wish to thank Fang Zhao, Jun Jo and Lena Qian with whom they have had fruitful discussions.

References

Cagan, J. 1990. *Innovative Design of Mechanical Structures.* PhD Thesis (unpublished), Department of Mechanical Engineering, University of California, Berkeley.

Carbonell, J. G. 1982. "Towards a computational model of metaphor in common sense reasoning." In *Fourth Annual Meeting of the Cognitive Science Society.*

Carbonell, J. G. 1983. "Learning by analogy: formulating and generalizing plans from past experience." In R. S. Michalski, J. G. Carbonell and T. M. Mitchell (eds.). *Machine Learning: An Artificial Intelligence Approach.* Palo Alto, California: Tioga.

Carbonell, J. G. 1986. "Derivational analogy: a theory of reconstructive problem solving and expertise acquisition." In R. S. Michalski, J. G. Carbonell and T. M. Mitchell (eds.). *Machine Learning II: An Artificial Intelligence Approach.* Los Altos, California: Morgan Kaufmann.

Dyer, M. G., M. Flowers, and J. Hodges, 1986. "EDISON: an engineering design invention system operating naively." In D. Sriram and R. Adey (eds.). *Applications of Artificial Intelligence to Engineering Problems.* Berlin: Springer-Verlag.

Falkenhainer, B., K. D. Forbus, and D. Gentner. 1989/90. "The structure-mapping engine: algorithm and examples." *Artificial Intelligence* 4, no. 1: 1-63.

Gero, J. S. 1990. "Design prototypes: a knowledge representation schema for design." *AI Magazine* 11, no. 4: 26–36.

Lenat, D. B. 1982. "An artificial Intelligence approach to discovery in mathematics as heuristic search." In R. Davis and D. B. Lenat (eds.). *Knowledge-Based Systems in Artificial Intelligence.* New York: McGraw-Hill.

Lenat, D., and J. S. Brown. 1983. "Why AM and Eurisko appear to work." *Proc. AAAI-83*, pp. 236-240.

Prieditis, A. 1988. *Analogica*. London: Pitman/Morgan Kaufmann.

Radford, A. D., and J. S. Gero. 1988. *Design by Optimization in Architecture and Building*. New York: Van Nostrand Reinhold.

Zhao, F., and M. L. Maher. 1988. "Using analogical reasoning to design buildings." *Engineering with Computers, no.* 4: 107–119.

17 Computational Modalities of Evaluation and Prediction in Design

Yehuda E. Kalay

Computer-Aided Design Research Center
State University of New York
Buffalo, New York 14214, U.S.A.

Evaluation can be defined as measuring the fit between achieved (or expected) performances and stated criteria. It is complicated by the multi-criteria and multi-level modalities of design, where an overall balance of performances is preferred to maximizing the performance of a few characteristics, and where evaluation must be performed at different design phases, each characterized by a different informational profile. Each design modality requires a different approach to evaluation: the Multi-Criteria modality requires evaluation of a proposed solution at a particular design phase from multiple points of view, while the Multi-Level modality requires the evaluation of a particular performance characteristic at several different design phases. This paper discusses the multi-modal nature of evaluation and prediction in design, exemplified by some of the approaches that have been proposed to support them computationally. It then argues for the need to develop an integrated, multi-modal design evaluation paradigm.

Design is a discipline that formally recognizes our ability to influence the future and our responsibility to do so in the "proper" way. The process of design, therefore, is the purposeful and conscious specification of the actions that ought to be taken in order to achieve some desired conditions. Specifying the actions that will lead to achieving some desired human wants or needs by complex systems such as buildings is, however, difficult, because it involves political, psychological, social, economic, environmental, technical and many other variables. There is seldom a formula that can be used to specify the desired performances of any one of these variables, let alone specify a desired combination of their effects and interactions. Rather, the process of design can be likened to *exploratory search*, where alternative courses of action are hypothesized and their effects are predicted and evaluated by comparing them to the objectives. The evaluation may find that the predicted effects achieve the objectives, thus validating the proposed course of action. More often, however, the predicted effects do not achieve the objectives, or they conflict with each other. In such cases the actions must be modified so that they will achieve the objectives, or the objectives must be revised to match the predicted effects. The design process can thus be said to comprise three major tasks, performed iteratively: (a) defining a set of objectives that the proposed actions should achieve; (b) specifying actions that, in the opinion of the designer, will achieve the objectives; (c) predicting and evaluating the effects of the proposed actions to verify that they are consistent with each other and that they will achieve the objectives.

This discussion focuses on the third task, whose centrality to the process of design stems from the fact that prediction and evaluation are the "glue" that binds the other two components of the triad: specifying the actions that achieve a set of objectives cannot be separated from predicting and evaluating the expected effects of these actions, because the evaluation guides the generative process toward achieving the stated objectives, uncovers opportunities to be explored and indicates tradeoffs that must be made in order to improve the overall quality of the solution.

Prediction and evaluation are, therefore, important means for defining and clarifying the objectives of the design process, as well as for guiding it toward achieving them. They rely on the designer's ability to predict the environmental, psychological, social, economic and other effects that will ensue from executing the specified actions, evaluate the desirability of these effects and derive operational conclusions from the evaluation. To evaluate the correspondence between the effects of the proposed actions and the specified objectives the designer must translate between two different representational schemes: the *physical* representation that is used to describe the designed artifact, and the *functional* representation that is used to describe the design objectives. For example, to evaluate the coherence, or "readability" of the proposed but yet non-existing building (i.e., its functionality), the designer must predict the psychological effects of the floorplan (i.e., the physical representation of the building), on the mental disposition of the average user. The derivation of functional assessments from the building's physical representation is error-prone, because it relies on assumptions and generalizations about the effects of the physical environment on the behavior of people, which is complicated by considerations such as memory, prior experiences and capacity for learning, in addition to being context- and time-dependent.

To alleviate these difficulties, the search for methods that can predict the effects of design decisions began in the 1960's, seeking a synthesis between the designer's creative and rational faculties. These methods, comprising a series of logical and mechanical operations, would (according to their early proponents) free the designer from the tedious evaluative aspects of his work to the great advantage of his creative powers (Jones 1980). They would provide instant feedback on the effects and side effects of decisions made through his creative skills and allow him to adjust these decisions to achieve the objectives. Furthermore, a rational and deductive approach to the processes of prediction and evaluation would make it possible to identify a certain number of operations that could be automated. Consequently, proponents of such evaluative and predictive methods tried to model them in a way that would also take full advantage of the potential offered by computers (Cross 1977).

Three decades of research have, nevertheless, failed to realize this aspiration. In fact, the considerable knowledge gained in predicting and evaluating specific aspects of design (e.g., energy, behavior in space, etc.), remains largely unutilized in everyday architectural design practice and most building projects do not enjoy the fruits of the considerable expertise gained in similar design enterprises (Carrara et al 1991). This failure is due, to a large extent, to the *isolation* of the study of evaluation from the other components of the design process and, subsequently, our failure to integrate seamlessly the ensuing evaluation methods and tools with the other components of the design process. In fact, it is the position of this author that the centrality of evaluation to the design process actually *precludes* its study (and the implementation of computational methods that result from it) independently from the study of the design process as a whole.

Recently some methods have been developed that recognize the complexity of evaluation and its dependency on other components of the design process. To understand the motivations behind these methods and how they can be integrated into a comprehensive, computational framework, we must better understand the role and the process of evaluation itself, and how it is used in the design process. This understanding will further not only design evaluation research, but also computer-aided design in general.

What is Evaluation?

Evaluation is a term that has many meanings and is subject to many interpretations, ranging from measuring the performance of buildings (or other artifacts) to measuring the performance of the people who design them (Goldschmidt 1991). They also range from interpreting evaluation as *retrospective diagnosis*, in the sense of post-occupancy evaluation of completed projects (Jockusch 1991), to interpreting evaluation as a process of *dynamic transformation*, in the sense of mapping between different representational schemes (Manning and Mattar 1991). In between these extremes we find the "usual" meanings and interpretations of evaluation, as the counterpart of generating design solutions and as critique of the decisions that lead to their completion.

Evaluation can thus be understood as a process that compares what *has been* achieved (or is *projected* to have been achieved) to what *ought to be* achieved. Evaluation, therefore, can be defined as *measuring the fit between achieved or expected performances and stated objectives.*

Evaluation is a proactive, operational term, not only because its accomplishment requires considerable effort, but also because it is a dynamic component of the design process itself (as well as of other processes, such as medical diagnosis). Evaluation is called for when a given state of affairs is known to be or is suspected to be deficient in some non-obvious way (e.g., the patient is sick, but the cause for his illness is not known), and while there is still hope and desire to improve it. The purpose of evaluation, like the purpose of medical diagnosis, is to establish what could and should be done to improve the current state of the designed artifact, and possibly to determine what steps ought to be taken to accomplish the improvement. Conversely, if the solution is known to be optimal (because it was, perhaps, generated by an algorithm that guarantees optimum), or if we are resigned to the fact that it cannot be improved (e.g., in the case of a terminally ill patient), then there is no need to evaluate.

The process of evaluation can, however, only be applied to a given, specific set of performance characteristics, such as the form, composition and location of a building, much like medical diagnosis can only be applied to the physical condition of a patient. When evaluating hypothetical design alternatives where performances are not yet in evidence and cannot, therefore, be measured directly, evaluation must be preceded by *prediction*. Prediction is the process whereby the expected performance characteristics of buildings (or other artifacts) are simulated, hypothesized, imagined, or otherwise made tangible, and can be subjected to evaluation. For example, the rate of heat loss through a given building envelope must be predicted, often by way of simulation, before an evaluative procedure can determine whether this rate is acceptable. Likewise, a building model must be subjected to earthquake simulation before its non-elastic behavior can be evaluated.

In practice, prediction and evaluation are so inseparably tied to each other that they are often considered to be one and the same. Energy analysis by means of heat loss simulation has been, for decades, considered the undisputed method of "evaluating" the energy performance of buildings, as has been cost and structural evaluations. Moreover, implicit evaluations are often confused with prediction, such as in the case of appraising the suitability of a building to support different stages in a family's life-cycle. Yet, it is the opinion of this author that evaluation and prediction should not be confused, so they can be studied independently, for each has its own characteristic methods and distinctive knowledge bases.

Prediction, in most cases, is domain-specific. Although different predictive simulations may rely on similar techniques (e.g., queuing models, stochastic methods, and other forms of linear programming), predicting the loss of energy through the building envelope, for example, is not similar to predicting way-finding in a building (Gross 1991, Jog 1991, Kalisperis 1991, O'Neill 1991). Evaluation, on the other hand, is much less context-dependent. Since it basically measures the difference between *achieved* performance and *desired* performance, evaluation can be regarded as a neutral process, and general methods to perform evaluation can be developed (Simon 1969). Nevertheless, to draw operational conclusions from a specific evaluation it must be combined with domain-specific information.

A discussion of evaluation and prediction in design, therefore, cannot be separated from a discussion of the design process itself. In particular, the partitioning of the design process into discrete "phases", or levels of abstraction on one hand, and the domain-specifity of design decisions on the other, define a framework for studying evaluation in design: different modalities of design require different modalities of evaluation and prediction.

The Modalities of Design

It was stated earlier that design can be viewed as a process that results in specifications whose physical or organizational implementation will produce a solution that meets certain pre-defined objectives. Architectural design usually must meet a wide range of design objectives. Each objective has its own technological, environmental, social, economic and other requirements, and each has been the subject of intensive study, and even specialization, over the years. For example, the objective of making buildings energy-efficient has enjoyed great popularity since the late 1970's, because of the worldwide energy crisis. Likewise, work in the area of earthquake tolerant structures has become the focus of considerable research efforts at the national level.

These individual objectives, however, are not independent of each other: when they are combined in the context of the built environment, design decisions that are intended to meet one objective may support or interfere with the achievement of another objective. For example, to achieve optimal energy efficiency, buildings have been earth-sheltered. But this design solution interferes with accessibility objectives, creates many technological problems and may have psychological drawbacks. The designer must, therefore, achieve the stated individual objectives while reconciling their conflicting effects and side-effects to the benefit of the design solution as a whole.

The difficulties induced by these conflicting demands are further exacerbated by the hierarchical nature of the design decision-making process: broad and general solutions are contemplated first, and are gradually refined as the design progresses. Alternatively, designers combine desired details into new wholes. In both cases, constraints are propagated "up" and "down" different levels of the abstraction hierarchy: high-level organizational decisions constrain lower-level details, while decisions that concern details limit the designer's freedom in selecting high-level organizational schemes (Liggett et al 1991). Design theorists refer to different levels in the design abstraction hierarchy as "design phases." Such phases typically include feasibility studies, conceptual design, design development, detailing and design documentation. While the exact definition of each phase varies among researchers, their existence has been widely accepted since the early 1960s (Asimow 1962, Gregory 1966, Broadbent and Ward 1969).

It is but a small step now to recognize that hierarchical stratification is a characteristic not only of the design process as a whole, but also of its individual components. For example, a circulation system in a building is typically first planned schematically (using such terms as *circular*, *linear*, *radial*, etc.), then refined and articulated gradually into a hierarchy of major and minor traffic zones, which are further refined into a hierarchy of public and private circulation spaces. These are later detailed by adding doorways, fire zones, means of egress, and so on.

Taken together, the composition of design processes can be said to consist of two separate *modalities*:

1. The modality in which the designer focuses on *one* abstraction level, searching for a *composite* solution that achieves multiple design objectives.

2. The modality in which the designer moves between *different* levels of abstraction, searching for a solution to a *particular* design objective.

Figure 1 depicts (schematically) this dual modality: each horizontal "band" represents a particular design phase, while each vertical "band" represents a particular design objective. The bands are overlaid to show the close coupling between the two modalities.

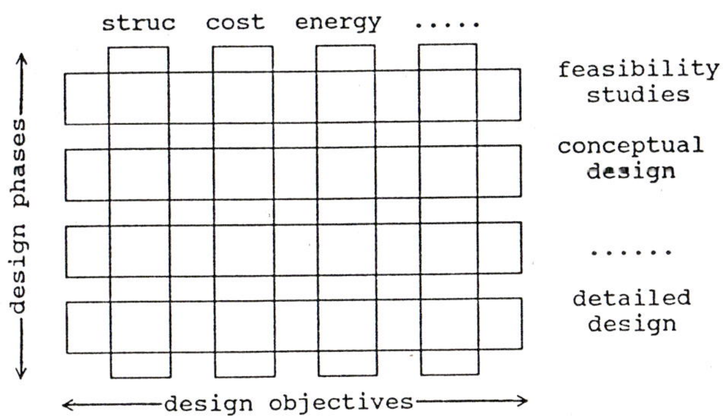

Figure 1. The dual modality of design.

Designers engage both modalities alternately and in parallel: it is often difficult to engage one modality without, at the very least, being cognizant of the other (although the experts whom the designer consults are typically oblivious to design objectives other than their own). Nevertheless, for the purposes of understanding the design process and its evaluation, the distinction ought to be maintained. Furthermore, as will be demonstrated later, the distinction between the two modalities is acknowledged, at least implicitly, in most software systems that were developed to support computationally the design process.

The Modalities of Evaluation

Given the different modalities of design, and given the centrality of evaluation to the design process, it should come as no surprise that the *evaluation* of design solutions follows closely the modalities of the design process itself. Hence, we distinguish between *Multi-Criteria* evaluation and *Multi-Level* evaluation.

The Multi-Criteria evaluation modality examines a given design solution from *several different* points of view (e.g., energy, cost, structural stability, etc.). Because it evaluates a *particular* design solution this modality is limited to a single design phase. Hence, it corresponds to a horizontal band in Figure 1.

The Multi-level evaluation modality examines how the design solution, or a succession of design solutions, satisfy a *particular design objective* (e.g., energy). Given its narrow focus, the same single-criterion evaluation is applied at *different phases* of the design process. It corresponds, therefore, to a vertical band in Figure 1.

Multi-Criteria Evaluation

Proposed design solutions, as well as realized design projects, exhibit many performance characteristics and must meet many objectives. The individual performance characteristics rely, nevertheless, on common physical attributes (e.g., layout, materials, budget, etc.). Attempts to maximize the performance of one characteristic influence, therefore, the performance of others. The designer must consider all (or at least many) of the building's performance characteristics together in order to maximize the overall performance of the solution and to avoid inadvertently diminishing the performance of some characteristics due to overachieving others.

When the evaluation shows that all design objectives have not been equally well satisfied the designer must establish the relative importance of competing or conflicting objectives. Such priorization will allow him to determine the overall merit of the design solution and compare it to other candidate solutions. The designer must also determine the marginal returns of relaxing certain criteria in order to gain in others. For example, when the budget that was established for the purpose of constructing a single family house requires choosing between a third bedroom and a family room, which one of the two will the client prefer to have?

Multi-Level Evaluation

The difficulty in designing large and complex artifacts such as buildings necessitates the use of hierarchical abstraction and stepwise refinement methods as means of partitioning the design process into discrete, manageable "chunks," called *design phases*. Typically, a design solution is first conceived schematically, then further developed and detailed in subsequent design phases. The emerging design solution must, therefore, be evaluated at different levels of resolution: early in the design process it may not be sufficiently well articulated to allow the application of detailed evaluation procedures, nor would it be meaningful to do so even if it were possible. Rather, a generalized appraisal of the designed solution may be called for to verify that the approach chosen by the designer is at all correct. Conversely, in later phases of the design process it may be possible and desirable to perform detailed evaluation of the performances of the proposed solution. In intermediate design phases, where the design solution is only partially developed, it may be prudent to use evaluation methods that can operate with whatever information is available to them, and provide results that are meaningful for the particular design phase. In other words, different evaluation methods are needed to perform evaluation of specific criteria at different design phases.

Additionally, partitioning the design process into discrete phases also means that some decisions must be made prior to others, hence before all the details that may affect them, or are affected by them, are known. It may be very useful to know in advance the implications of early design decisions on the solution in later phases of the design process, before much effort is spent on their adaptation to the particular conditions of the project and before other decisions that rely on them have been made. However, while it is possible to consider multiple different aspects of the designed artifact at a particular phase of the design process, it is virtually impossible to consider *all* aspects at *all* phases. It is possible, however, and even desirable to consider *individual* design characteristics in depth, from top to bottom, anytime in the design process. In early design phases such consideration will help select approaches that are likely to prove productive later on, while later design phases will benefit from reflection upon the reasons for adopting a particular approach rather than another, thereby helping the designer to select details that better support the chosen approach.

Software Implementations of Different Evaluation Modalities

Software systems that perform Multi-Criteria or Multi-Level evaluation of design alternatives have been under development for many years. Recently, some evaluation programs that demonstrate a range of possible approaches to modality-conscious computational evaluation have been developed. In the following, we shall discuss a few examples of each.

Multi-Criteria Evaluation Tools

When designing a software system that operates in the Multi-Criteria evaluation modality one is often faced with the choice (and the desire) to use existing evaluation tools that were developed by experts in their respective disciplines. Typically, each evaluation program requires different input parameters, presented in a particular format and producing output in its own unique way that makes comparing its results to those of other evaluations difficult. This makes the use of existing evaluation tools difficult, often to the extent where it is deemed easier to redesign each and every evaluation to fit the integrated system. Obviously, while redesign solves the integration problem, it necessitates rewriting each evaluation program from scratch.

Another problem faced by designers of Multi-Criteria evaluation software is weighing the performance of different characteristics in order to derive the overall performance measure of the design solution. It can be argued that the overall value of a design solution is a subjective measure it is, nevertheless, what designers (and their clients) are expected to do when faced with the need to choose among multiple options.

Wiezel and Becker have chosen an integration approach with relatively-weighted individual performance criteria, utilizing a database generated by a commercial CAD system (ARC+™) to describe the building at some given design phase. They developed their own set of evaluation procedures, which provides feedback on the thermal, acoustical, fire safety and lighting performance of the building (Wiezel and Becker 1991).

In contrast to this approach, a group of Carnegie Mellon University researchers preferred to rely on a host of existing evaluation programs and developed a common architecture that provides the necessary data for the application of these evaluators (Fenves et al 1991). Evaluations are performed by sending data to each evaluation module. The results from the modules are collected in a central blackboard, for use in subsequent design operations. The blackboard provides a shared memory for both the evaluation and the synthesis modules. Each module is a self-contained knowledge-based system that performs both evaluative and generative tasks in its particular domain of expertise. For example, a module called ARCHPLAN (Schmitt 1988), assists in the development of a design concept. A module called CORE (Flemming et al 1988), evaluates and generates layouts of elements in the service core of the building. The overall architecture of the system allows each process to maintain its own identity and to follow its unique approach, while providing mechanisms for integration that steer these processes towards a common goal.

A hybrid approach that combines the advantages of both integrated evaluators with stand-alone ones was developed by Hacfoort and Veldhuisen (1991). Their system, called COSMOS, provides a quick, sketchy evaluation of a building using built-in, integrated evaluation tools. It also allows the user to request in-depth evaluation of the same criteria using stand-alone, external evaluation modules developed elsewhere.

Most of these (and other) Multi-Criteria evaluation systems strive to provide the designer with an overall measure of the performance of the design solution. While recognizing that such a singular measure is meaningful only for comparative purposes, it is useful, nevertheless, to show the designer how improving certain aspects of the solution may hurt (or enhance) other performance aspects.

Wiezel and Becker have assigned a weight factor, determined through the study of typical urban population sample (Becker 1985), to each design criterion (Figure 2). The degree of satisfying each criterion, as reported by the corresponding evaluator, is multiplied by the weight factor of that criterion, and added to the weighted degrees of all other criteria, thereby providing an overall measure of the performance of the particular design solution.

Hacfoort and Veldhuisen chose to establish the effects each design criterion has on other criteria by using one of two methods to describe the binary relationships between the different performances. The first method is based on linear least-square equations generating a scattergram that shows the criteria that are most seriously affected (both positively and negatively) by the proposed design actions (Figure 3a). The second method is based on a contingencies table that shows the degree to which each design criterion is affected by specific design parameters (Figure 3b). The use of these two kinds of measurements allows them to express different kinds of relationships between the design parameters (ratio, interval, ordinal, and nominal). For example, the relationship between costs per cubic meter and the mean thermal insulation of the building can be expressed through the least-squares method, while the relationship between the quality of the view and the acoustic insulation (in Db(a)) can be expressed by means of the contingencies table method.

Another solution to the problem of comparing the results of different evaluations without actually computing an overall measure of performance was proposed by Schmitt (1987), who used a pie-chart like visual presentation method based on dividing a circle into a number of equal sectors that correspond to the evaluation criteria (Figure 4a). The circle's radius represents the normalized threshold for acceptability of the performances of the different criteria: for criteria such as first cost, heating, cooling and the use of electricity, it represents the preset budget. For criteria such as structural stability, circulation, visual and contextual orientation, it represents the minimum standard of acceptability. If the radius of a particular sector is larger than the radius of the circle then the criteria it represents performs better than the acceptability threshold (e.g., the energy consumption is lower than the established energy budget). If, on the other hand, the radius of the sector is smaller than the circle's radius then the criteria it represents performs more poorly than the acceptability threshold (e.g., the circulation area is excessive). When the performance of some criterion is not quantifyable, Schmitt uses a rule-based system to determine the circle's and the sector's radii. This method of visualization also allows for representing weighted differentiation between the criteria by varying the degree sizes of the sectors that represent them (Figure 4b).

	Building parameter	Enhancing criterion (in terms of "Prevention of)	Wn(%)
1	Acoustic insulation of the external envelope	noise penetration from the outside	8.5
2	Thermal insulation, and resist. to fungi of int. coverings	mould growth due to condensation in the dwelling	8.5
3	Acoustic insulation of inter-dwelling partitions and floors	noise penetration from neighboring dwellings	7.6
4	Balance between thermal insulation and TTC[1] of envelope	excessive expenditures for cooling during summer	7.4
5	Fire endurance of external envelope	fire penetration into the dwelling from outside	7.4
6	Medium TTC of external envelope	excessive heat at noon during summer	7.4
7	Low fire spread of interior coverings	fire spread in the dwelling	7.2
8	Location of thermal insulation close to the inside	excessive cold in the evening during winter	7.2
9	Low TTC of the envelope	excessive heat in the evening during summer	7.0
10	Thermal insulation of external envelope	excessive cold at night during winter	7.0
11	Thermal insulation, and high TTC of envelope	excessive expenditures for heating during winter	6.6
12	Location of thermal insulation close to the inside	excessive cold in the morning during winter	6.3
13	Acoustic insulation of intradwelling partitions	noise penetration between rooms within dwellings	6.1
14	Acoustic insulation of intradwelling partitions	being heard in other rooms (privacy)	5.9

Figure 2. List of building parameters and their weighting factors (Wiezel and Becker 1991).

Multi-Level Evaluation Tools

The major problems in developing software that can assist designers in performing Multi-Level evaluation of individual design characteristics stem from the different informational characteristics of the design phases they must span. They include the propagation of constraints "up" and "down" the design abstraction hierarchy and the selection of software tools that are most suitable for performing the evaluation at each design phase.

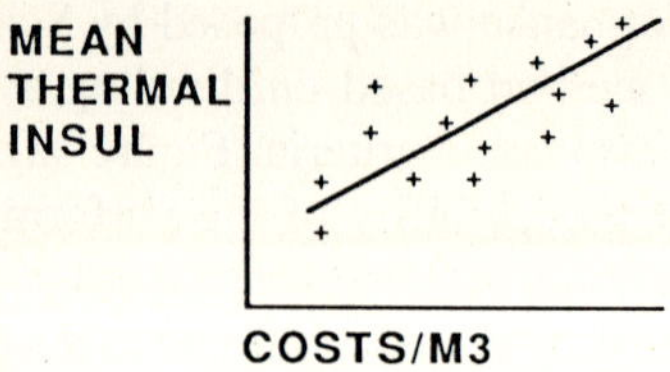

Db(A)	VIEWS 1	2	3	4	T
30 - 39		4		1	5
40 - 49	3			2	5
50 - 59			7		7
60 +			10		10
TOTAL	3	4	17	3	27

Figure 3. (a) Scattergram; (b) Contingencies table (Hacfoort and Veldhuisen 1991).

The propagation of constraints across different levels of the abstraction hierarchy involves *translations* of design constraints between the different representational languages that are used at each abstraction level. Each abstraction level typically uses a particular symbolism to represent its informational content. Schematic design phases, for example, tend to use single line drawings and "block" symbols to denote such information as walls, rooms, or even the style of a column. Detailed design phases, on the other hand, use multiple lines to denote walls, rooms are typically furnished and columns are fully articulated. The transition from one level of abstraction to another is not merely syntactic, but rather a semantic process, since the symbols convey different amounts and even different kinds of information: while the line representing the wall in the schematic phase

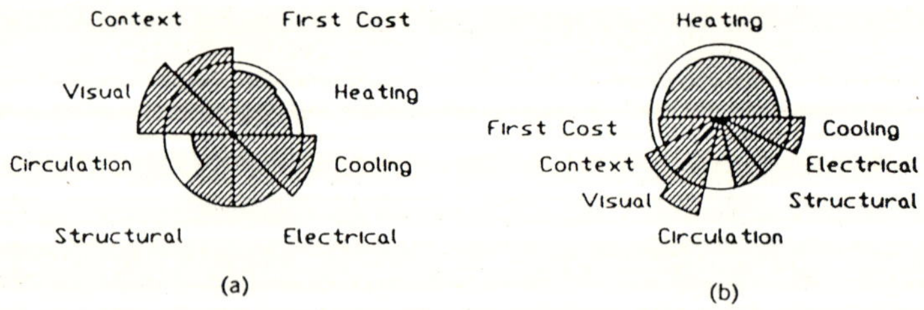

Figure 4. Building criteria visualization: (a) unweighted; (b) weighted (Schmitt 1991).

may convey only the intent of partitioning the space, the fully articulated wall in a detailed design phase conveys both the commitment to partitioning the space as well as the means to be employed for that purpose (dimensions, materials, finishes, etc.). An evaluation tool that can operate across multiple abstraction levels must be capable, therefore, of interpreting the semantic information conveyed by each level and applying it properly.

The different informational characteristics of different abstraction levels also determine the kind of software tools that can be used to perform the evaluation. Early design phases may not contain sufficient information to support energy or structural simulation of the designed artifact, because they lack information concerning materials, finishes, or even exact dimensions. The use of defaults to fill-in missing information may actually be misleading if the building does not conform to the averages from which the defaults were derived (Shaviv and Kalay 1991). Nor is it meaningful to perform such evaluation and to provide the designer with "exact" heat loss information or precise sizing of structural elements even if it were possible to calculate them precisely. Rather, the designer may be interested only in the effects that the orientation of the building will have on its general energy consumption, and whether the chosen structural schema is plausible. On the other hand, if the information needed to perform detailed evaluation is available, chances are that a detailed answer is expected.

Several systems were developed that perform Multi-Level, single criterion evaluation of design solutions. A system developed by Liggett et al (1991), called TOPDOWN, deals with the functional interpretation of architectonic shapes, such as columns and floorplans. It allows the designer to check the degree to which the evaluated element fulfills its desired function (e.g., floor area, structural support, etc.) in any phase of the design process. TOPDOWN deals with the problem of translating the semantics of the design solution between different levels of the abstraction hierarchy by employing shape grammars that tell the system how to refine an abstract, high-level subsystem into a specific arrangement of detailed, lower-level subsystems and how to assemble a set of detailed, lower-level subsystems into higher-level ones (e.g., how to detail a schematic column into a combination of base, shaft, and capital, as depicted in Figure 5).

A default-based approach to Multi-Criteria evaluation has been proposed by Johnson (1991) to calculate the cost of a building at different phases of its design process.

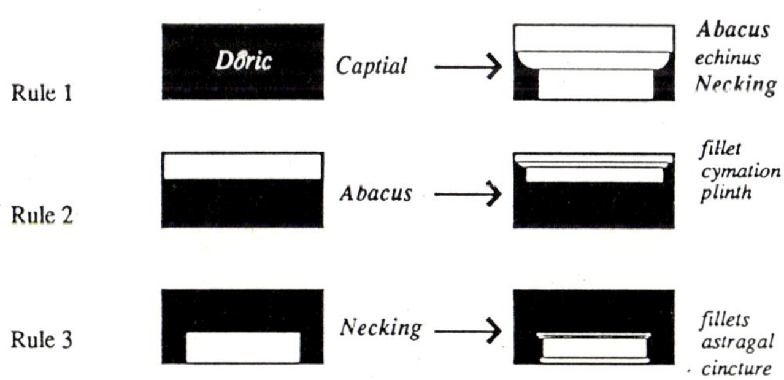

Figure 5. Rules for top-down refinement of a schematic design (Liggett et al 1991).

His method handles the different informational profiles of the design solution at different phases of the process by arranging the defaults in an hierarchical object database, where lower levels of the hierarchy correspond to more detailed design solutions. The system can thus apply general floorprint area calculation in early design phases to compute gross cost per square foot. This estimate is refined by adding more accurate dimensioning and material costs as the design solution becomes more detailed over time.

The reliance on defaults for evaluating design solutions in early design phases was criticized by Shaviv and Kalay (1991) as potentially misleading when the design solution does not conform to the standardized cases from which the defaults were derived. Instead, they proposed to use a combination of rule-based expert systems and simulation modules for evaluating the thermal properties of a building. Expert systems can be used in early design phases to provide a gross, "rule of thumb" evaluation of the proposed solution's thermal properties. In intermediate design phases expert systems can help select appropriate default values for use in simplified thermal properties simulation models (LCR and SLR). In later design phases, accurate thermal analysis software can be used to calculate precise thermal performance (figure 6).

The system deals with the different informational levels of the design solution in different design phases by relying on a knowledge base in which the effects of each building parameter on the thermal behavior of the building as a whole have been stored according to the design phase during which it is first considered and the phases in which it is reconsidered (Figure 7). The knowledge base also contains rules constraining the selection of subsequent building parameters given the decisions that were made earlier. These rules, operating bi-directionally (i.e., top-down and bottom-up), can be used to inform the designer of the con-

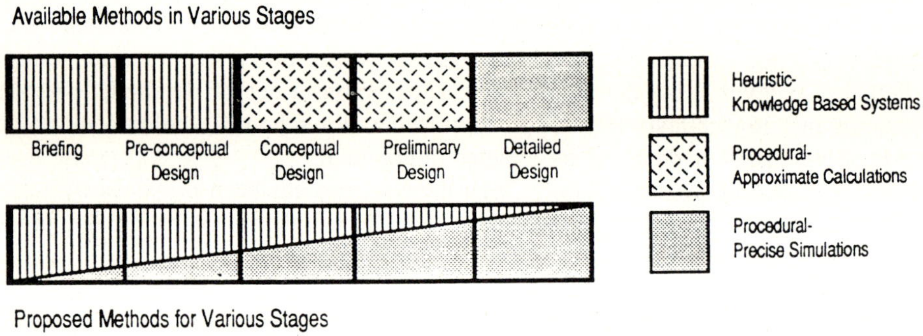

Figure 6. Schematic comparison of the use of available vs. proposed thermal properties evaluation tools in different design phases (Shaviv and Kalay 1991).

sequences (if any) certain design choices will have on the thermal performance of the building. The simulation models, in turn, validate the defaults suggested by the rules and help derive new rules for non-standard design cases.

Conclusion

This discussion presented and established the multi-modal nature of evaluation and the ensuing differences in software tools that support each evaluation modality. These differences stem not only from the different needs that each modality fulfills, but also from the kinds of knowledge it relies upon: the Multi-Criteria modality relies on broad-based knowledge and upon generalized methods for its application, whereas the Multi-Level modality relies upon deep knowledge and specialized methods.

Designers, however, engage both evaluation modalities alternately and in parallel throughout the design process. Furthermore, they shift within each modality from top-down to bottom-up methods, and within the same design phase from one design objective to another. Therefore, they ought to be able to use different design and evaluation methods interchangeably.

DESIGN PHASE	a.	b.	c.	d.	e.	f.
TOTAL FLOOR AREA	◆		+	+		
VOLUME OF BUILDING		◆	+	+		
NO.OF EXTERNAL WALLS			◆	+		
AZIMUTH OF REFERENCE WALL			◆	+		
AREA OF INTERNAL MASS				◆	+	
HEAT CAPACITY OF INTERNAL MASS					◆	
INITIAL TEMP. DISTRIBUTION		◆				
HEAT GAINS: CONSTANT	◆					
HEAT GAINS: SCHEDULE	◆					
HEATER: SCHEDULE; TEMP.SET		◆			+	
COOLER: SCHEDULE; TEMP.SET		◆			+	
VENT: TYPE, SCHEDULE, ACH: DAY; NIGHT		◆			+	
WALL NO 1						
NUMBER OF LAYERS				◆	+	
MATERIALS (c, λ, d)				◆	+	
" " "						
" " "						
WALL: AZIMUTH, INCLINATION			◆	+		
AREA OF WALL			◆	+		
WALL:ALBEDO, EMISSIVITY					◆	
WALL:SC-SUMMER, WINTER				◆	+	
NO OF WINDOWS AND SOLAR ELEMENTS			◆	+		
WINDOW: AREA			◆	+		
WINDOW: TYPE				◆	+	
WINDOW: SC-SUMMER, WINTER		◆			+	
U WINDOW: DAY; NIGHT				◆	+	
U WINDOW: SCHEDULE		◆			+	

Figure 7. Phase-specific classification of energy-related design parameters: ◆ first considered; + reconsidered; (a) briefing, (b) pre-conceptual, (c) conceptual, (d) preliminary, and (e) detailed design phases (Shaviv and Kalay 1991).

The fundamental differences between the computational paradigms that support each evaluation modality make it unlikely, however, that a single evaluation tool could be constructed to support both modalities simultaneously. Such a tool would, by definition, have to include both broad and deep knowledge bases concerning all the relevant performance criteria at each phase of the design process. Such a mammoth knowledge base could hardly be conceived as a monolithic entity, much less be programmed as one.

Rather, computational frameworks for availing different evaluation tools to the designer and facilitating dynamic shifts between the modalities they support, are needed. Such frameworks will include a plethora of specific evaluation tools, many of which have already been developed. They will differ from the integrated models discussed earlier in that they will also include a knowledge base that can be used to select and invoke the right tool at the right time, triggered by both the design phase and the design objective under consideration. Such frameworks will resemble more closely the knowledge of the architect himself, rather than the knowledge of the specialists he relies upon, without sacrificing the specialists' particular knowledge. Hopefully, the discussion presented here will stimulate the research toward developing integrated computational frameworks of this kind.

References

Asimow, M. 1962. *Introduction to Design.* Englewood Cliffs, NJ: Prentice Hall.

Broadbent, G., and A. Ward (eds.). 1969. *Design Methods in Architecture.* London: Lund Humphries.

Carrara, G., Y.E. Kalay, and G. Novembri. 1991. "A Computational Framework for Supporting Creative Architectural Design." In Y.E. Kalay (ed.). *Evaluating and Predicting Design Performance.* New York, NY: John Wiley & Sons.

Cross, N. 1977. *The Automated Architect.* London: Pion Ltd.

Fenves, S.J., U. Flemming, C. Henderson, and M.L. Maher. 1991. "Performance Evaluation in an Integrated Software Environment for Building Design and Construction." In Y.E. Kalay (ed.). *Evaluating and Predicting Design Performance.* New York, NY: John Wiley & Sons.

Flemming, U., R. Coyne, T. Glavin, and M. Rychener. 1988. "A Generative Expert System for the Design of Building Layouts - Version 2." In J.S. Gero (ed.). *Artificial Intelligence in Engineering: Design.* New York, NY: Elsevier.

Goldschmidt, G. 1991. "Criteria For Design Evaluation: A Process Oriented Paradigm." In Y.E. Kalay (ed.). *Evaluating and Predicting Design Performance.* New York, NY: John Wiley & Sons.

Gregory, S.A. (ed.). 1966. *The Design Method.* London: Butterworth.

Gross, M.D., and C. Zimring. 1991. "Predicting Wayfinding Behavior in Buildings - a Schema-Based approach." In Y. E. Kalay (ed.). *Evaluating and Predicting Design Performance.* New York, NY: John Wiley & Sons.

Hacfoort, E.J., and J. Veldhuisen. 1991. "A Building Design and Evaluation System." In Y.E. Kalay (ed.). *Evaluating and Predicting Design Performance.* New York, NY: John Wiley & Sons.

Jockusch, P.R.A. 1991. "How Can We Achieve A Good Building?" In Y.E. Kalay (ed.). *Evaluating and Predicting Design Performance.* New York, NY: John Wiley & Sons.

Jog, B. 1991. "Evaluation of Design Using CAD Systems." In Y.E. Kalay (ed.). *Evaluating and Predicting Design Performance.* New York, NY: John Wiley & Sons.

Johns, C. 1980. *Design Methods.* New York, NY: John Wiley & Sons.

Johnson, R.E. 1991. "Design Inquiry and Resource Allocation." In Y.E. Kalay (ed.). *Evaluating and Predicting Design Performance.* New York, NY: John Wiley & Sons.

Kalisperis, L.N., M. Steinman, and L.H. Summers. 1991. "A Human Thermal Comfort Response Design Model for Non-Orthogonal Surfaces." In Y.E. Kalay (ed.). *Evaluating and Predicting Design Performance.* New York, NY: John Wiley & Sons.

Liggett, R.S., W.J. Mitchell, and M. Tan. 1991. "Multi-Level Analysis and Optimization of Design." In Y.E. Kalay (ed.), *Evaluating and Predicting Design Performance.* New York, NY: John Wiley & Sons.

Manning, P., and S. Mattar. 1991. "Strategy and Tactics, Prediction and Evaluation: A Preliminary to Development of Expert Systems for Total Design of Entire Buildings." In Y.E. Kalay (ed.). *Evaluating and Predicting Design Performance.* New York, NY: John Wiley & Sons.

O'Neill, M. 1991. "A Neural Network Simulation as a Computer-Aided Design Tool for Evaluating Building Legibility." In Y.E. Kalay (ed.). *Evaluating and Predicting Design Performance.* New York: John Wiley & Sons.

Schmitt, G. 1987. "Expert Systems in Design Abstraction and Evaluation." In Y.E. Kalay (ed.). *Computability of Design.* New York, NY: John Wiley & Sons.

Schmitt, G. 1988. "ARCHPLAN - An Architectural Planning Front End to Engineering Design Expert Systems." In M.D. Rychener (ed.). *Expert Systems for Engineering Design.* New York, NY: Academic Press.

Shaviv, E., and Y.E. Kalay. 1991. "Combined Procedural and Heuristic Method to Energy Conscious Building Design and Evaluation." In Y.E. Kalay (ed.). *Evaluating and Predicting Design Performance.* New York, NY: John Wiley & Sons.

Simon, H.A. 1969. *The Sciences of the Artificial.* Cambridge, MA.: MIT Press.

Wiezel, A. and R. Becker. 1991. "Integration of Performance Evaluation in Computer-Aided Design." In Y.E. Kalay (ed.). *Evaluating and Predicting Design Performance.* New York, NY: John Wiley & Sons.

18 What's in a Case: The Use of Case Bases, Knowledge Bases, and Databases in Design

M. A. Rosenman, J. S. Gero, R. E. Oxman[*]

Design Computing Unit
Department of Architectural and Design Science
University of Sydney NSW 2006 Australia

[*]Department of Architecture
Technion Israel Institute of Technology
Haifa 32000 Israel

Design experience can be classified into generalized or compiled knowledge and specific knowledge. Generalized design knowledge has been introduced into computer-aided design in the form of rules, frames and more recently, design prototypes. Case-based reasoning is a well-defined paradigm in artificial intelligence and has obvious scope for its use in design reasoning. This paper explores case-based reasoning in design and argues for the integration of both specific and generalized design knowledge. This integration allows for characterizing what is in a case by drawing upon the schema developed for design prototypes. Finally, the paper argues that the addition of precedent knowledge, in the form of case bases, to knowledge bases and CAD databases will further extend the experience-based capabilities of design systems.

Introduction:

Computer-Aided Design

Computer-aided design has been identified with the uses of databases. These databases contain syntactical information regarding the topological and geometrical properties of the artefacts under consideration. Occasionally, they contain other syntactical information such as material properties. They may allow for the description of classes of objects as well as instances. All semantic information is implicit and is obtained by users' interpretation of representations of the database using their own interpretive knowledge. Recently, knowledge bases have been introduced into computer-aided design as a means of representing generalized or compiled design knowledge (Balachandran et al, 1990). These knowledge bases augment rather than displace databases by providing the semantic information missing from CAD databases. This paper intends to show that case bases add specific precedent knowledge and, by augmenting rather than displacing knowledge bases, further extend the capabilities of such integrated systems.

Modeling Design Experience

Experience plays an important role in design reasoning. Experienced designers use previous designs to solve current situations, as in the use of standard details. One of the great challenges of knowledge-based design has been to develop models of reasoning processes based upon experiential knowledge in order to support routine and non-routine design. Current approaches to design reasoning are based upon the representation of compiled knowledge employing rules, frames and schemas such as design prototypes (Gero, 1987; Rosenman and Gero, 1989). However, the knowledge of specific design histories may have significance in adaptive design.

Compiled knowledge is that knowledge in which several like experiences are generalized into rules or rule-like procedures wherein the details of the specific experiences are usually lost. This compiled or generalized knowledge covers a range of situations rather than a specific situation and its application is contingent on focussing onto a specific situation.

Case or specific knowledge is that knowledge in which specific experiences or episodes are kept and reasoning is based on retrieving the most appropriate experience rather than repeating the process to create it. Case-based reasoning from precedents is well understood in the field of law and is a well-defined paradigm in artificial intelligence (Riesbeck and Schank, 1989; Kolodner, 1987). There are obvious parallels to the use of precedents in design.

The cognitive significance of the relationship between generalized knowledge, such as the design prototype and the detailed knowledge of specific experiences is a current theme in artificial intelligence research (Alterman, 1986).

Towards an Integrated System

This paper explores the role and significance of case-based reasoning in design. It commences with a short discourse of what is involved in the design process and specifically in knowledge-based design. It follows by discussing what is entailed in design using compiled knowledge drawing upon the schema developed for design prototypes. The strengths and weaknesses of this approach are discussed. The paper goes on to discuss knowledge-based design using case knowledge. It argues that both specific and generalized knowledge are required for a design system and that what is in a case is best achieved by drawing upon the design prototype schema.

Finally, an argument is put forward for a heterogeneous knowledge-based computer-aided design system which incorporates CAD databases, compiled knowledge and case knowledge. While the examples are drawn from the architectural field, it is suggested that the approach is more general in its application.

Design Knowledge

Design

The role of design is to abduct specific solutions to given problems. This process entails the translation of a design problem given in functional terms to a design description given in structural terms. In most cases this process involves first describing the behavior required from an artifact since structure/behavior relationships are easier to determine than function/structure relationships except in well-understood situations. This process of translating goals to means is a process of going from the general to the specific, that is to a defined instance.

The Role of Experience in Design

Function is a human construct and therefore no inherent relationship between function and structure exists. However, the relationships between behavior and function are more amenable to interpretation through teleological processes. Given a known structure, its behavior can be interpreted (analyzed) using processes as in qualitative physics (Bobrow 1984, DeKleer and Brown 1984, Kuipers 1984). Hence, knowledge about relationships between structure and behavior and function can be derived and stored. In order to translate function into structure, known structures which relate to that function can be retrieved and manipulated. Design is thus a matter of experience, that is, of acquiring sufficient knowledge about a variety of relevant structures and their behaviors and functions.

Compiled Knowledge and Case Knowledge

Compiled or general knowledge is knowledge obtained from a number of individual experiences. This knowledge may be thought of as rule-like in which a 'rule' exists which is general in nature covering all the individual experiences but without the specific details which make the experiences individual. This knowledge is obtained usually through an abstraction process although it may be learnt directly. For example, one can learn (from books, lectures, etc) that flashing is required under window sills without necessarily undergoing various undesirable experiences. Although one may learn the reasons why this general knowledge is applicable, the 'rule' itself usually does not carry the explanation. Moreover, this general knowledge does not carry with it any particular solution. A particular situation has to be fitted to a general 'rule' and the general conclusion applied. There needs be knowledge on how to apply the conclusion to any particular situation. For example, the flashing in a cavity brick wall is different to the flashing in a timber-framed wall. Examples of compiled knowledge forms are procedures and formulae as used in computational approaches, rules as found in rule-based expert systems or decision tables and decision trees and schemas such as design prototypes which chunk in one representation several elements of general knowledge.

Specific or case knowledge is knowledge in which the actual experience or episode is stored including all relevant details regarding the situation. When a similar experience is faced, all the relevant parts of previous episodes are retrieved and this knowledge is then applied to the situation at hand. This knowledge includes reasoning and justifications as well as the goals and means. Examples of case knowledge include precedents in law, and specific design examples.

Design Using Compiled Knowledge

Compiled knowledge is knowledge of a general form covering a range of situations. The generalization is divorced from any particular instance which may have formed the generalization and thus from any history of its creation (Riesbeck and Schank 1989). As such, knowledge of specific situations is not encoded therein although more specific situations may be covered by more specific compiled knowledge and/or computational procedures.

Rules

Rules are examples of compiled knowledge. In knowledge-based systems, rules take the form of

IF <conditions> THEN <consequents>

where some consequents ensue whenever some set of conditions are met. These conditions apply to a class of instances and the consequents may include actions to be carried out as well as factual inferences. Expert systems use such rules usually of a heuristic nature or using 'rules of thumb'. Examples of rule-based expert systems in design are RETWALL (Hutchinson et al 1987) and SOLAREXPERT (Rosenman and Gero 1989).

```
                                ROOM
TYPOLOGY
    a_type_of:   space
    types:       living_room, bedroom, ...
FUNCTION
    Goals
      provide sufficient space:    for activity
      provide usable space:        for activity
      ...
    Objectives
      provide sufficient natural light
      provide sufficient ventilation
      ...
BEHAVIOUR ATTRIBUTES
      size, natural lighting, natural ventilation, ...
BEHAVIOUR VARIABLES
      floor area, window/floor area ratio, ...
STRUCTURE ELEMENTS
      walls, floor, ceiling, door, window, furniture
STRUCTURE ATTRIBUTES
      shape
STRUCTURE VARIABLES
      ...
CONTEXT
      type of building
KNOWLEDGE
    R1  IF      size OF room IS satisfactory
        THEN  provide sufficient space: for activity FUNCTION_OF room IS satisfied
    ...
```

Figure 1. Example of 'room' design prototype.

Schemata—Design Prototypes

Schemata are separate modules of general compiled knowledge. They have been described as 'an organized framework of knowledge about the world' (Sowa 1984). The schema concept has been implemented in artificial intelligence variously as frames (Minsky 1975, Fikes and Kehler 1985); schemata (Rumelhart 1980); and scripts (Schank and Abelson 1977, Schank 1982).

Design prototypes are schemata chunking together knowledge regarding a class of design experiences. They contain knowledge about function, behavior and structure properties of a class of design elements as well as knowledge regarding the relationships among these properties and between the design elements and their context as well as knowledge regarding the relationships between design prototypes. Part of this knowledge includes the necessary procedures for the generation of an instance, i.e. a design solution from a given design problem specification.

Design prototypes are structured in a hierarchical organization from general to specific, with specific design prototypes inheriting properties from the more general. Figure 1 shows an example of a design prototype while Figure 2 shows an example of a hierarchy of design prototypes.

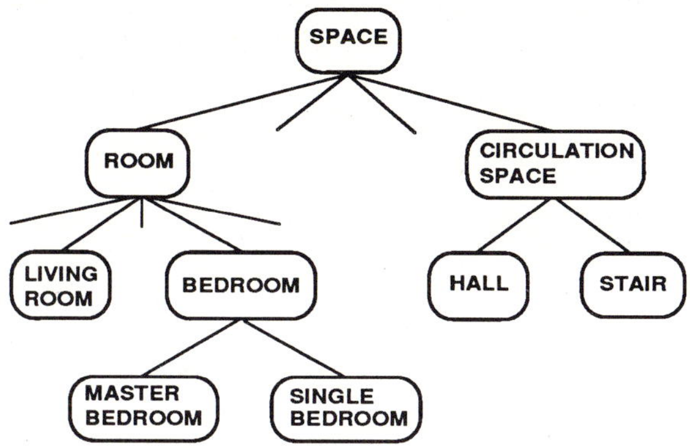

Figure 2. Design prototype hierarchy.

Designing with Design Prototypes

Designing with design prototypes entails the generation of a specific instance in response to a given design problem. A design problem is usually given in terms of some function(s) to be satisfied although it may be given in terms of required behavioral performances, constraints regarding the behavior and/or structure properties or any combination of these. Since design prototypes are structured hierarchically, the process of designing with design prototypes entails the selection of the most specific design prototype, its further specialization by selecting the appropriate structure variables and finally the instantiation of these variables by finding the values which will produce a design satisfying the given requirements.

The knowledge encoded in design prototypes in the form of generative rules supports a refinement schema and can be used efficiently in routine design (Oxman and Gero 1988, Oxman 1990) although suggestions have been made as to their use in non-routine design (Rosenman and Gero 1989). In routine design, the process is as described above. The matching of design prototype to the design requirements is carried out from its function and/or behavior properties and the description of the design prototype is sufficiently complete to carry out the specialization and instantiation processes. In non-routine design, no single design prototype exists which allows this process and the task will involve such processes as the merging of design prototypes, making analogies to design prototypes in another domain and creating new design prototypes from first principles (Rosenman and Gero 1989).

Issues Concerning Generalized Knowledge Schemata

Designing with design prototypes, as with all generalized schemata, is computation oriented and repetitive. There is no learning of previous design experiences and the same problem given again is solved by using the same processes as before. Moreover, the fact that compiled knowledge deals in generalizations means that the refinement processes of prototype instantiation cannot always deal with specific situations, which may in fact be exceptions to the general rule.

As with all generalization schemata, there is the difficulty of constructing generalizations. It is not generally accepted, in cognitive psychology for example, what the correct form of a category (generalization) is. There is no universal agreement as to what comprises a category and what model of categorization to use. All attempts at actually constructing generalizations have met with great difficulty except for well-defined and limited domains. No generalization constructed seems to be able to cover all the members of that generalization. In addition there has been much criticism about the applicability of any predetermined system with regards to their use by different designers with different viewpoints.

Design Using Case Knowledge

Case-Based Reasoning and Case-Based Design

Case-based reasoning is a well-defined paradigm in artificial intelligence (Riesbeck and Schank 1989, Kolodner 1987, Hammond 1986). It is based on the premise that humans reason from specific experiences rather than by following a set of general guidelines. For example, reasoning from precedents is one of the basic methodologies in law. Case-based reasoning relates a current situation to the closest most specific experience in memory and uses that experience to solve the problem at hand. It is thus a memory-based approach rather than a computation approach, whereby solutions to problems already solved need only be retrieved rather than computed again. The key factors in case-based reasoning are the storage of cases as complete patterns of experiences including the reasoning process, the ability to be reminded of the most appropriate case and the application of that case to the current situation. Application of the case may either be a direct application if the current situation and that of the case match exactly, or there may be a need for some modification of the case. This modification may be of various degrees of severity. Case-based reasoning uses the strategies of modification and repair to effect such modifications. New cases are thus produced either as variations on the previous case or, in extreme situations, as new cases. Case-based reasoning thus incorporates a learning capacity in the form of new cases being incorporated into a dynamic case base.

Searching for a case is based on indexing cases with regards to various factors, e.g. goals and attributes. The more efficient the indexing, the more efficient the search. Retrieval is a matter of pattern matching, i.e. matching a required pattern of requirements to an existing set. This match may be exact or partial. In the case of partial matches, some criteria are required to determine the 'best' partial match. Matches may be made to parts of several cases and a new case results from combining elements from these cases, if consistency is satisfied.

Case-based reasoning has been applied to various tasks such as classification (Kolodner 1987), planning (Hammond 1986, Alterman 1986), legal reasoning (Bain 1986), speech recognition (Bradshaw 1987) and pronunciation (Lehnert 1987). While there are many similarities between planning and design, planning differs from design in that the problem of planning is essentially that of scheduling a set of actions. In design, the form of the elements themselves is often unknown and the problem involves topological, geometrical and physical properties and relations between them. Hammond (1986) compares the CHEF program to design problems in architecture but the analogy is relevant only to systems buildings where the range and type of available components is well-defined and design involves an additive process of components.

```
                    SMALL_SINGLE_BEDROOM

TYPOLOGY
   a_type_of:   single_bedroom
FUNCTION
   Goals
      provide minimum space:   for sleeping activity
   Objectives
      ...
BEHAVIOUR ATTRIBUTES
      size
      ...
BEHAVIOUR VARIABLES
      floor area
         range:    7.5 to 9.6
      ...
STRUCTURE ELEMENTS
      ..., corners, ...
STRUCTURE ATTRIBUTES
      shape
         value:    rectangle
STRUCTURE VARIABLES
     length                          width
         range:    3000 to 4000         range:    2400 to 30000
     location of door
         range:    ONE_OF corners
CONTEXT
      ...
KNOWLEDGE
      ...
```

Figure 3. Example of Small_Single_Bedroom design prototype.

Design Cases

Design cases are specific design episodes of previous design experience serving as examples or precedents for future design problems. They contain an entire design episode, i.e. the problem, the solution and the process for arriving at this solution. The problem contains those requirements that had to be satisfied, including goals and constraints, i.e. function, behavior and structure as well as any contextual information. The solution contains a description of all the instances of elements necessary as well as their relationships to each other and to the design as a whole. The design process contains information regarding the knowledge, both procedural and declarative, used in making decisions and the justifications for making those decisions. These justifications may include both successes and failures including other alternatives considered but not selected plus information as to what conditions may lead to their selection. This process information is termed the history of the design case. This history is of extreme importance in guiding the adaptation process when modifications to a design case are necessary. Unlike generalized knowledge, wherein a range of solutions is implied, a case contains a description of a design solution in terms of variables instantiated to specific values. However, while the case may contain various instance descriptions, it is, in itself, a holistic description, a pattern of a total experience.

Specific Generalization vs Instance vs Design Case

In a generalized schema, such as the design prototype schema, the hierarchical structure allows for very specific descriptions, see Figure 3. The more specific the design prototype, the more specific its description, especially its structure description. The design prototype, 'vehicle', may have function and behavior information but can have little specific structure description, whereas the design prototype, 'beetle', has much more specific structure description. However, some information is still be general so as to be able to produce a number of instances of specific 'beetles'. As such, those behavior properties associated with those general structure properties will also be general or have expected values. An instance of a 'beetle' would have all its variables instantiated to a specific value, i.e. color red, cloth seat covering, with air-conditioning, etc. The instance of an artefact includes all instances of elements forming part of that artefact instance, see Figure 4. An instance will have its behavior properties instantiated to actual values or these can be derived from the structure. These actual values can be compared to the expected values and the performance of the instance evaluated. An instance may be derived from a design prototype through refinement in a top-down fashion or, alternatively, an instance may be described unrelated to any such generalization.

```
                    SMALL_SINGLE_BEDROOM.1
TYPOLOGY
   Instance_of:  small_single_bedroom
FUNCTION
   ...
BEHAVIOUR ATTRIBUTES
      size
          value:    satisfactory
      ...
BEHAVIOUR VARIABLES
      floor area
          value:   9.6
      ...
STRUCTURE ELEMENTS
      wall.1,..., wall.4, ..., door.4, wind.4, cnr.1, ..., cnr.4, bed.1, cpd.1, ...
STRUCTURE ATTRIBUTES
      shape
          value:    rectangle
STRUCTURE VARIABLES
      length                             width
          value:    4000                     value:   2400
      location of door.1                 ...
          value:    cnr.1
CONTEXT
      type of building
          value:    low_cost_house
```

Figure 4. Example of Small_Single_Bedroom instance.

Like a design prototype and unlike an instance, a design case is a total description of design experience. However, a design case differs from a set of design prototypes in that its structure description, i.e. its design solution description, is specific as for a set of instances. What differentiates a design case from design instances is that a design case contains a history of the design experience, i.e. it is not merely a description of the artefact itself but also of the problem, processes, and justification for decisions taken. An example of a design case with its constituent instances is given in Figure 5. Since a design case is the encoding of a particular design along with its salient aspects of its episodic design history, it serves as an exemplary mapping maintaining the semantics of its creation. A unique design case might be recorded as the successful design response to an unusual requirement or a particular constraint.

Designing with Design Cases
Designing with design cases involves the use of a previous like experience to solve a given design problem. As in designing with design prototypes, the closest matching experience must be found, however unlike designing with design prototypes, no specialization or instantiation is involved. The design solution exists as a stored description and, if the design situation is sufficiently similar, can be directly appropriated. An example of this, is the use of standard details in a design office, or even 'standard' designs for building types. In some cases, minor modifications may be necessary, e.g. some change in dimensions while in other cases more major modifications may be necessary, requiring some redesign. The processes involved in case-based designing are problem anticipation, search, match, retrieve, select, modify, repair and store.
Problem anticipation. It is usual for design problems to be given with incomplete information. As in the example of menu planning by Kolodner (1987), the problem specification does not mention the possibility of some of the guests being vegetarian. Since this problem had occurred previously (and having led to a failure of the plan was noted by the system) the system, JULIA, asks the planner if there are any vegetarian guests. Similarly, in design problems, in order to avoid inappropriate design cases being accessed through lack of initial information, it is desirable for a system to try and ascertain as much relevant information as possible.

Search. Given a problem description of requirements including functions to be achieved, required behavior performances, the design environment and even constraints on values of structure variables, the case base must be searched to find an appropriate design case. The utility of case-based designing is strongly dependent on the efficiency of the search procedure. Searching could be sequential, parallel or direct using an indexing mechanism. Indexing must be done on the function, behavior, structure and context features.

Match. An appropriate case for consideration is found with regards to the matching of above mentioned features. Perfect matching, i.e. where the required features are found exactly in a case, is unusual. Partial matching occurs when some of the features are matched or the features are matched to some degree.

Retrieve. A case which matches to some defined degree needs to be retrieved for consideration. This may or may not involve display of these cases to the users for perusal and consideration.

Select. A selection of a single case as the basis for determining the design solution has to be made. Alternatively, if only part of a design case is required, then several design cases may require to be selected, and the necessary parts of each extracted. In either situation, the 'best' matching design case should be selected. Selection of the 'best' design case can be on the basis of the most similar or the most useful match (Kolodner 1989). Selection can be carried out by the system or by users after consideration of an appropriate set of candidates

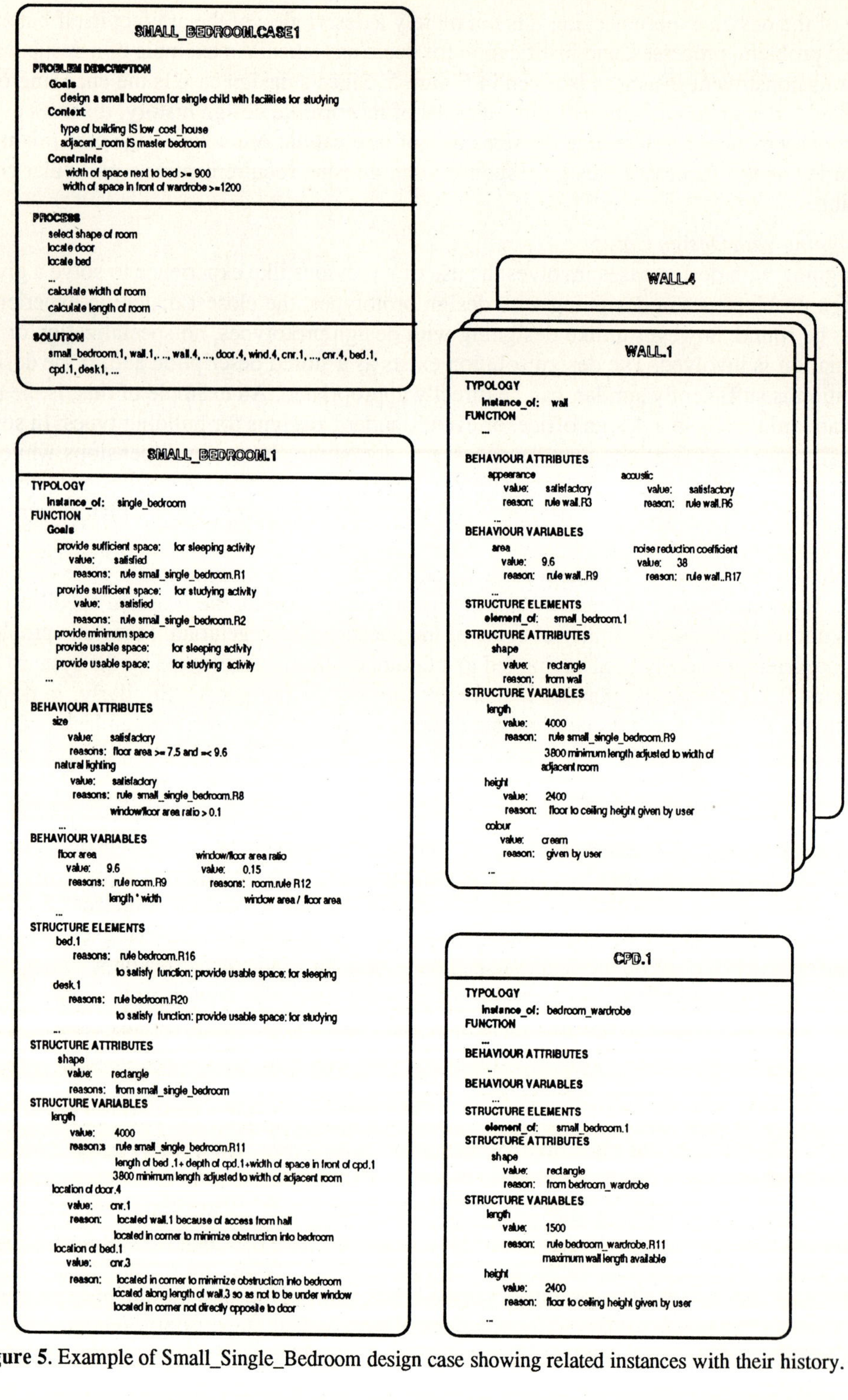

Figure 5. Example of Small_Single_Bedroom design case showing related instances with their history.

retrieved by the system. Selection by the system based on partial matching entails such factors as the importance of the features matched as well as how close they are matched. A similar problem has been addressed in the specialization of design prototypes (Rosenman 1990).

Modify. Where a design case is selected which does not match the design requirements sufficiently, some modifications will be necessary. This may involve the replacement of variables with other variables or simply the alteration of some values of variables.

Repair. In many situations, a modification to an existing design case based on substitution of variables or modification of values will cause some performance failure in some other behavior or function. For example, decreasing the cross-sectional area of a column to satisfy some new spatial requirement may cause buckling. Other modifications may be considered but none may be satisfactory. One of two directions now needs to be taken. Either an alternative design case is selected based on the new information known regarding the necessity for modifications and the effects of modifications or the current selected design case is modified in such a way as to make it acceptable. This latter process is known as the process of repair in case-based reasoning.

Store. After a design case has been modified or repaired, a new design case has been generated. If this new design case is considered to be sufficiently important as a design experience different to existing design cases, then it must be stored in the case base with appropriate indexing. Where the failure of solutions is seen as an important piece of information to the anticipation of future problems, this must be noted in the design case.

What's in a Design Case?

So what is in a design case? Firstly, a description of the design problem including the noting of critical problem areas which need be anticipated. Secondly, a description of the design solution in terms of structure, actual behavior and functions achieved and thirdly, and most importantly the design history.

Issues Concerned with Case-Based Design

Number of design cases

The first issue is the question of when is a design experience sufficiently relevant or important to become a design case. That is, what makes an episode worthwhile to be stored as a design case. What degree of difference is required between design cases to make it worthwhile to store rather than to derive from another design case through modification. This is obviously related to the degree of difficulty of the modification but more importantly to a distinct 'lesson' that a design case serves. That is, each design case must help to solve some distinct problem so as to serve as an example of likely types of design problems. The differences between the various design cases should not be too great or else there will be a great deal of modification and repair necessary and there will be little advantage over a generalized design approach. Yet the difference cannot be so small as to be too trivial and as a consequence the size of the case base be so enormous and detailed that the search and match procedures become extremely inefficient.

Description of case
What features are relevant for a design case? What should the organization of such features be? How can a feature in one design case be related to another feature in a different design case which are related in an abstract manner? For example, if a description of one design case involves the description of a chair that has legs whereas another has a description of a chair with a pedestal, how is the relation between these legs and the pedestal made? How can these questions be resolved without recourse to a generalization, such as 'chair support'?

Organization of case base
In a large case base, there will be many design cases where a large number of features will be the same. For example, in the description of design cases dealing with chairs, many features, such as the chair seat, seat back may be the same in many cases, with some other varying features, such as armrests, legs, pedestals. For efficiency's sake, rather than storing every design case individually in its entirety, a hierarchical approach may be required. In case-based reasoning, Schank's theory of dynamic memory (Schank 1982) provides an organization with knowledge structures called Memory Organization Packets (MOPs). Kolodner's CYRUS system (Kolodner 1984) was the first implemented case-based reasoning system founded on Schank's MOPs. Kolodner's memory organization uses structures called Episodic Memory Organization Packets (E-MOPs). E-MOPs index similar episodes by their differences.

Generalizing from cases
Although there may exist knowledge relating one episode to another, case knowledge is specific to the case or episode. For example, a case may describe a window detail of a some aluminium sliding window on a brick-on-edge sill in a brick cavity wall. If the new situation is to design the same aluminium window in a timber-framed wall the knowledge regarding this situation does not reside in the case. When a different situation is faced, yet a similarity is found to an existing case recourse must be made to some generalization process to apply the lessons of one situation to the new situation.

Modification knowledge
Only some very limited and specific knowledge regarding modification and repair of a design case can be in the design case itself, since future problems cannot be anticipated. In order to take care of a wide range of possible situations this type of knowledge must be of a general nature. Also there needs to be some evaluation of modification strategy, such as, is it better to modify or in some situations is it better to start from a new design case.

Integration of Generalized and Specific Knowledge

The design prototype and the design case represent two different approaches to knowledge-based design. Design prototypes are efficient in their process of design generation and refinement. Design cases are powerful because of their richness of specific detail and history. Case-based design is founded on the use of memory to retrieve specific experiences and utilize specific detailed solutions when the direct experiences are sufficiently close to be of use. However, case-based design lacks the power of generalized knowledge to deal with situations somewhat removed from a specific experience. Case-based design can potentially supplement design prototype-based design with its retrieval, adaptation and repair facilities. An integration of both approaches would use the strengths of both. That is, when direct experience is available it can be used, otherwise recourse can be made to general principles. That is, case-based design can be used when a suitable design case exists, otherwise recourse can be made to the generating functions of a suitable design prototype.

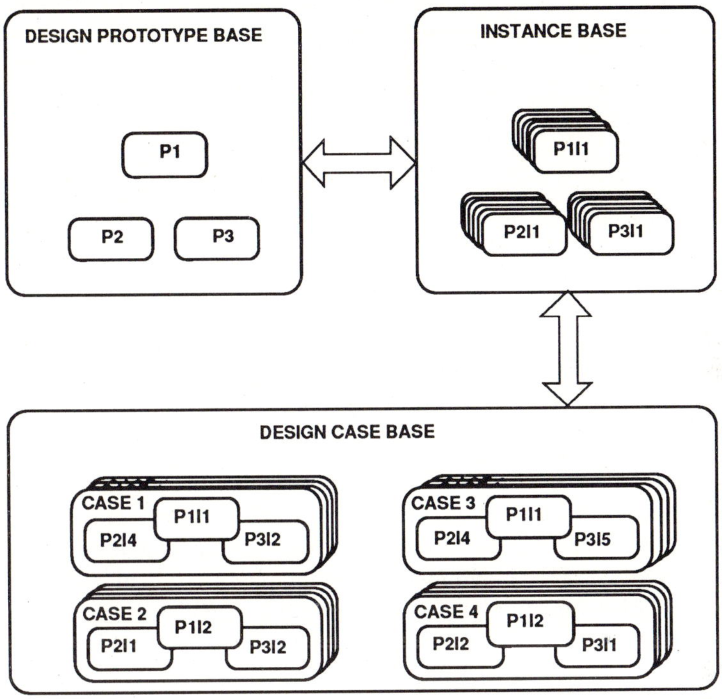

Figure 6. Relationship between design prototypes, instances and design cases.

A system founded on design cases alone means that each case is a unique representation of a total design experience. A design case dealing with the design of a bedroom may be separate to one dealing with a dining room. Yet many problems, decisions and solutions of the two rooms, will be similar, if not the same. For example, the need for natural ventilation, natural light and for access, will result in the inclusion of a window and a door, not to mention elements such as walls, ceilings and floors. The use of a generalized schema allows for the abstraction of like experiences allowing for the formation of higher level concepts, such as 'room' in the above example. This allows for relationships between features in design cases based on a higher level concept rather than on some list of properties. Moreover, basing case descriptions on the representational formalism of the design prototype, answers the 'chicken and egg' question of how to extract relevant features for a design case and where generalizations come from, since both are formulated with respect to each other. In such an approach, general knowledge resides in the design prototype and the design case is seen as providing detailed specific knowledge regarding a situation or an exception to the general 'rule'. The design case contains the problem description, the process used and the set of instances which constitute the solution. These instances contain the information as to which design prototypes and which sources of knowledge were used (and why) to derive attributes and values.

The integration of design cases with the design prototypes representation allows for the modification and repair of a design case through the generating and instantiating capabilities of the design prototype. If a design case retrieved is not identical to the required situation modification may be required involving a change in the value of some variables, e.g. the length of a room. Because a design case encodes its history, including which design prototypes and knowledge are associated with the derivation of values, the respective design prototype can be accessed and the respective knowledge re-run to provide a new instantiation through value modification.

When a newly derived value is unsuccessful in adaptation (and no such modification is successful), then new variables must be generated. Repair involves a change in the variables. This requires access to a higher level abstraction, namely the design prototype, for the construction of a new structure to satisfy behavioral and functional requirements.

This integration of the design prototype and design case formalisms allows for the generation of design cases from design prototypes. Figure 6 shows the relationship between design prototypes, instances generated from design prototypes and design cases.
There are three different types of design cases which may be generated in this way. The first type is the design case in which all the variables and their values are derived through the generating process of the design prototype system. The second type is the design case in which the user selects some of the values of the variables and the third type is the design case in which the user selects some of the variables as well as some of their values. The first type occurs when a defined situation can be matched exactly by a design prototype and all variables and their values are catered for. Re-running the same situation would result in exactly the same set of instances being generated. With the second and third types, re-running the same situation may not result in exactly the same instances being generated, as users may vary their selection of variables and values.

Computer-Aided Design

CAD and CAD Databases

Computer-aided drawing (CAD) systems use databases which solely represent structure properties and traditionally only topology and geometry although other properties, such as material, may be described. Depending on the system, the representation may be of purely graphic elements, i.e. points and lines, or two- and three-dimensional shapes, such as rectangles, circles, prisms, spheres. Labels may be attached to such shapes so that these shapes can be referred to as objects with given properties. Basically, such databases describe instances of such objects although they may also have the ability to create a class descriptions of objects which are stored in object libraries.

Integration of CAD Systems with Knowledge Bases

Lately, there have been moves toward the integration of generalized knowledge bases with graphic systems using CAD databases. Such knowledge bases provide the means of relating semantic information to the purely syntactical information in the CAD databases. These knowledge bases take the form of rule bases of expert systems or hybrid forms of rules and frames. More recently, there has been work on the integration of design prototypes as the general domain knowledge to enhance the integration of such CAD databases with expert systems which deal with specific application knowledge, such as design codes (Balachandran et al 1990). The further addition of case knowledge will increase the ability of design systems to provide support for designers.

In the situation of generating designs, a design problem may be related to a previous design case, rather than to the general domain knowledge. This design case would also include that information related to a CAD database description and would enable the design artefact to be visualized or perhaps, sent to some application program for further evaluation. Modification of the artefact after visual evaluation, by graphic manipulation or direct modification of the database could serve to generate a new design case. In the situation of design evaluation, a design modelled graphically could relate the information thus given in its database to that of an existing design case and certain conclusions drawn that may not be available in the general domain knowledge. For example, building regulations may have general provisions to the effect that a single-dwelling house may not have a rise of more than two storeys except in special circumstances as allowed by Council. The general knowledge does not know, indeed cannot know in advance, all the particular set of circumstances which may lead to Council permitting a particular three-storey house design. However, there may exist a specific design case in a situation similar to the current one where a three-storey house was permitted. The matching of the designed house and the design case will be done through the information in the database plus other specific descriptive information as required. In such examples, a specific design precedent is used rather than a general set of rules which cannot cover every possible situation.

Conclusions

This paper has argued that both generalized knowledge, in the form of design prototypes, and specific knowledge, in the form of cases are valid and important sources of design knowledge. They, not only need not be used exclusive of each other but rather, should be unified into an integrated system so as to utilize the strengths of each. An important result of such an integration is the structure imposed on the design case by the design prototype formalism as well as the ability to access higher level abstractions where necessary.

While, at this stage the focus of this paper is towards routine design, some aspects of non-routine design can be approached using case-based design especially since the processes of modification and repair correspond to those of adaptation or mutation. However, since case-based design is founded on the use of specific experiences it is difficult to see how designs that are new in kind can be generated without recourse to generalizations.

Acknowledgments

This work is supported by a continuing grant from the Australian Research Council.

References

Alterman, R. 1986. "An adaptive planner." *Proceedings of AAAI-86* 1: 65-69.

Bain, W. M. 1986. "A case-based reasoning system for subjective assessment." *Proceedings of the National Conference on Artificial Intelligence*, pp. 523-527.

Balachandran, M., M. A. Rosenman, and J. S. Gero 1990. "A knowledge-based approach to the automatic verification of designs from CAD databases." *Working Paper*. Design Computing Unit, Department of Architectural and Design Science, University of Sydney, Sydney.

Bobrow, D. G. 1984. "Qualitative reasoning about physical systems: an introduction." *Artificial Intelligence* 24: 1-15.

Bradshaw, G. 1987. "Learning about speech sounds: the NEXUS project." *Proceedings of the Fourth International Workshop on Machine Learning*, pp. 1-11.

DeKleer, J. and J. S. Brown 1984. "A qualitative physics based on confluences." *Artificial Intelligence* 24: 7-83.

Fikes, R. and T. Kehler 1985. "The role of frame-based representation in reasoning." *Communications of the ACM* 28, no. 9: 904-920.

Gero, J. S. 1987. "Prototypes: a new schema for knowledge-based design." *Working Paper*. Architectural Computing Unit, Department of Architectural Science, University of Sydney.

Hammond, K. J. 1986. "CHEF: A model of case-based planning." *Proceedings of AAAI-86*, 1: 267-271.

Hutchinson, P. J., M. A. Rosenman and J. S. Gero 1987. "RETWALL: an expert system for the selection of and preliminary design of earth retaining structures." *Knowledge-Based Systems* 1, no. 1: 11-23.

Kolodner, J. L. 1984. *Retrieval and Organizational Strategies in Conceptual Memory: A Computer Model*. Hillsdale, NJ: Lawrence Erlbaum.

Kolodner, J. L. 1987. "Extending problem solver capabilities through case-based inference." *Proceedings of the Fourth International Workshop on Machine Learning*, pp. 167-178.

Kolodner, J. L. 1989. "Judging which is the 'best' case for a case-based reasoner." *Proceedings of Workshop on Case-Based Reasoning*, pp. 77-81.

Kuipers, B. 1984. "Commonsense reasoning about causality: deriving behavior from structure." *Artificial Intelligence* 24: 169-203.

Lehnert, W. 1987. "Case-based problem solving with a large knowledge base of learned cases." *Proceedings of the National Conference on Artificial Intelligence*, pp. 301-306.

Minsky, M. 1975. "A framework for representing knowledge." In P. H. Winston (ed.). *The Psychology of Computer-Vision*. New York: McGraw-Hill, pp. 211-277.

Oxman, R. E. 1990. "Design shells: a formalism for prototype refinement in knowledge-based design systems." *Artificial Intelligence in Engineering* 5, vol. 9: 2-8.

Oxman, R. E. and J. S. Gero 1988. "Designing by prototype refinement in architecture." In J. S. Gero (ed.). *Artificial Intelligence in Engineering V: Design*. Amsterdam: Elsevier/CMP, pp. 395-412.

Riesbeck, C. K. and R. C. Schank 1989. *Inside Case-based Reasoning*. Hillsdale, NJ: Lawrence Erlbaum.

Rosenman, M. A. 1990. "A qualitative evaluation approach to the specialization of design prototypes." *Working Paper*. Design Computing Unit, Department of Architectural and Design Science, University of Sydney, Sydney.

Rosenman, M. A. and J. S. Gero 1989. "Creativity in design using a prototype approach." *Preprints Modelling Creativity and Knowledge-based Creative Design*. Design Computing Unit, Department of Architectural and Design Science, University of Sydney, pp. 207-232.

Rosenman, M. A. and J. S. Gero 1989. "SOLAREXPERT—an expert system for evaluating passive solar energy designs." In B.H.V. Topping (ed.). *Artificial Intelligence Techniques and Applications for Civil and Structural Engineers*. Edinburgh: Civil-Comp Publications, pp. 131-139.

Rumelhart, D. E. 1980. "The building blocks of cognition." In R. J. Spiro and W. F. Brewer (eds). *Theoretical Issues in Reading Comprehension*. Hillsdale, NJ: Lawrence Erlbaum.

Schank, R. C. 1982. *Dynamic Memory: A theory of Reminding and Learning in Computers and People*. Cambridge: University Press.

Schank, R. C. and R. P. Abelson. 1977. *Scripts, Plans, Goals and Understanding: An Inquiry into Human Knowledge Structures*. Hillsdale, NJ: Lawrence Erlbaum.

Sowa, J. F. 1984. *Conceptual Structures*. Reading, MA: Addison-Wesley.

19 Case-based Representation and Adaptation in Design

Shen-Guan Shih

Lehrstuhl für Architektur und CAAD
ETH Zürich
CH 8093 Zürich, Switzerland

By attempting to model the raw memory of experts, case-based reasoning is distinguished from traditional expert systems, which compile experts' knowledge into rules before new problems are given. A case-based reasoning system processes new problems with the most similar prior experiences available, and adapts the prior solutions to solve new problems. Case-based representation of design knowledge utilizes the desirable features of the selected case as syntax rules to adapt the case to a new context. As a central issue of the paper, three types of adaptation aimed at topological modifications are described. The first type - case-based search - can be viewed as a localized search process. It follows the syntactical structure of the case to search for variations which provide the required functionality. Regarding the complexity of computation, it is recognized that when a context sensitive grammar is used to describe the desirable features, the search process become intractable. The second type of adaptation can be viewed as a process of self-organization, in which context-sensitive grammars play an essential role. Evaluations have to be simulated by local interaction among design primitives. The third type is called direct transduction. A case is translated directly to another structure according to its syntax by some translation functions. A direct transduction is not necessarily a composition of design operators and thus, a cross-contextual mapping is possible. As a perspective use of these adaptation methods, a CAD system which provides designers with the ability to modify the syntactical structure of a group of design elements, according to some concerned semantics, would support designers better than current CAD systems.

Introduction

Regarding the psychological phenomenon of reminding in human thinking (Schank 1982), case-based reasoning was considered as a problem solving paradigm in which prior solutions are reused to solve new problems. For problems involving combinatorial search, the reuse of an existing near-hit solution might save a large amount of the computation in finding a solution for similar problems. For many domains where design knowledge is difficult to acquire and may not be objectively applicable, the case-based paradigm provides a model for the acquisition, organization and reuse of specific knowledge. Applying to design problems, case adaptation is chosen among several important issues in the case-based approach to be the focus of this paper. As an operational model of case adaptation, case-based representation of design knowledge is introduced as the basis for discussion.

Adaptation, explained as "a change in structure, function, or form to conform to the environment", is an act which appears repeatedly in the process which brings a design from being conceived to being mature. Current computer aided design systems provide only primitive tools for the modification of designs. To support the adaptation of designs, we clarify the motivation so as to provide designers tools for modifying the syntactical structure of a group of design elements according to some concerned semantics. The task can be further divided into three levels: to discover alternations of the given design in the same context, to modify the given design for the accommodation of new constraints, and to adapt the given design to solve a new problem. Such a system can be defined as a function which takes design descriptions as well as evaluations to be input and then generates designs which comply with the given evaluations.

Following the principle of problem solving, it is assumed that such a design adapting system consists of a generator, which defines the problem space, and an evaluator, which verifies solutions. To enable the discussion, both generating and evaluating processes are assumed to be performed by production systems. By "production systems", we mean those systems that can be defined by N. Chomsky's Phrase Structure Grammar (Chomsky 1957, 1963) or its subsets such as context-free grammar. There exists some kind of mapping between strings of symbols and any representational model of design since the manipulation of strings is the only way that computations can take place at the very primitive level. Accordingly, the generator and the evaluator can be viewed as two grammars, each of which defines a language.

The Integration of Synthesis and Analysis Knowledge

From the computational point of view, synthesis and analysis, the two classes of intelligent activities involved in design process, are performed by the generator and the evaluator respectively. The generator, which defines the vocabulary and the syntax of design, embeds synthesis knowledge. The evaluator, which verifies the semantics of design, embeds analysis knowledge. In the following discussion about the integration of synthesis and analysis knowledge, we use the classifications of constraints defined by C. Eastman (Eastman 1988). Representing analysis knowledge, constraints can be divided into three groups: universal, associated, and unassociated. Universal constraints can be embedded in the design representation in order to reduce the size of the problem space without losing its generality. The integration of universal constraints implies that the vocabulary of the generator is mapped to design elements of a higher structure. Associated constraints can be embedded in design operators, or in other words, in productions, to reduce the size of the search space. Sometimes, this increases the complexity of the grammar of the generator, and increases the difficulty of computation. Unassociated constraints which can be defined with computer programs, exist only if we restrict the grammar to being context free. Since the composition of primitive recursive functions is still primitive recursive and the composition of Turing computable functions is still Turing computable, and thus, the full integration of a generator and an evaluator is possible under the consideration of either solvability or computability.

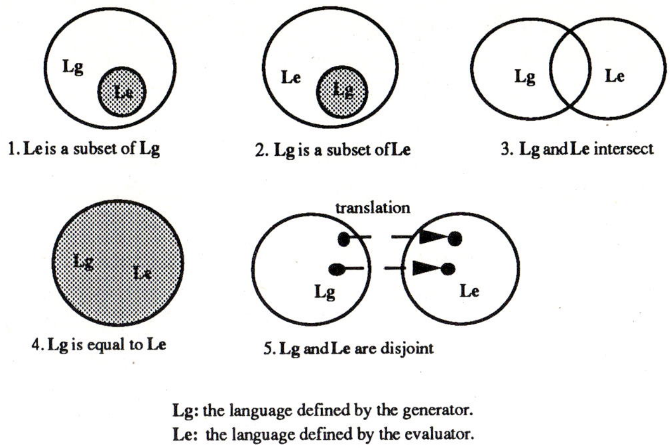

Figure 1. Possible relationships between the two languages defined by the generator and the evaluator.

The degree of integration of synthesis knowledge and analysis knowledge can be defined as the degree to which the language defined by the generator approximates to the language defined by the evaluator. The first case in figure 1 illustrates an example of partial integration. One way to increase integration is to embed more knowledge which is not really universal into the design vocabulary and inevitably, to sacrifice some generality. This could result in one of the variations shown in the second and third diagrams. Another method is to increase the expressive power of the grammar in order to accommodate more associated constraints. This reduces the size of the search space without losing generality, but it may cause the complexity of the grammar to increase. Carrying this approach to an extreme, the fourth diagram shows the full integration of the generator and the evaluator. Except for some relatively easy problems, it would become very difficult for the production system to reach a terminal state. The last diagram illustrates non-integration. In this case, the problem space does not contain any members which can be recognized by the evaluator as solutions. The generator possesses absolutely no knowledge about the evaluation which identifies the goal state. The generator and evaluator might represent two different domains such as shoe making and building evaluation. Searching within such a problem space will not lead to any solution, but there could be cross-contextual translations which provide meaningful connections between the two, seemingly unrelated domains.

Design and Dynamic Systems

Mathematical systems can be categorized as either static or dynamic. A static system is not concerned with the passage of time; whereas a dynamic system evolves over a period of time and can be formulated as the following format: $f_n = f(f_{n-1})$. Along with some other conditions, such systems may behave chaotically. For a numerical function, if there is a nonlinear relationship between the input and output of each operation, the result of the recursive applications may approach one limit, or may be oscillations of different sizes, or in other cases, be totally unpredictable. When the system is stable, it can be analyzed and predicted. When the system behaves chaotically, it can only be simulated but not analyzed.

A design generator can be viewed as a function which recursively uses its own output as the input of the next operation, and thus it can be categorized as a dynamic system. Design evaluators may be static systems in some cases. But in some design problems, they can be dynamic and can only be simulated but not analyzed. For architectural design, such problems include elevator waiting times, dynamic thermal behavior, and pedestrian circulation (Mitchell 1977).

In a generative design system, when the generator presents a chaotic behavior, it is impossible to predict what the design state is going to be after a number of operations without actually performing the operations. When the evaluator presents a chaotic behavior, it may not be possible to recognize a solution in a limited time bound. Returning to the view of generators and evaluators as production systems, whether the behavior of the system is predictable or not is a important factor which decides how effectively a heuristic search can be carried out. To discuss the behavior of production systems, it is helpful to recognize the computational complexity of the grammars which define them. Context-free grammar is an important class of grammars in the paradigm of formal languages. According to the definition of context-free grammar, all productions in the grammar must have exactly one non-terminal on its left hand side. Therefore, the applicable derivations of each non-terminal are constant. Context-sensitive grammar is a super class of context-free grammar. It allows us to have more than one terminal or non-terminal in the left hand side of productions. The applicable derivations of each non-terminal in a context-sensitive grammar are dependent on its context. Taking into account the other observations of these two classes of grammars which are addressed in the following sections, we speculate that those production systems defined with context-sensitive grammars may behave chaotically and those which are defined with context-free grammars do not.

The Problems of Using Compiled Knowledge for Design Synthesis

In the development of a generative system, the definition of design operators is very important. It implies a way of design decomposition which is beyond the level introduced by design vocabulary. When the decomposition is compatible to that which is required for the design evaluation, the search for a solution can be carried out in a effective way, and causal relationships among operations and evaluations can be established. For many design problems, a consistent decomposition of design structures which complies with the requisites of various evaluations may not exist. This is a problem of systems which introduces a pre-defined generator to embed synthesis knowledge.

In some fields of design, knowledge which is objectively applicable may not sufficiently justify all design decisions. Architecture, which is considered as one of the three types of art, has rejected all attempts to describe it with general and logical formalisms. Subjective preferences and intuitions often play important roles in the design process. In such cases, there exists knowledge which is meaningful only at a specific time, and for specific designers. To encode such knowledge and to decide when and where it should be applied is not practical. However, without such kind of knowledge, the search for a solution can not be done efficiently.

Case-based Representation of Design Knowledge

By attempting to model the raw memory of experts, case-based reasoning is distinguished from building expert systems, which compiles an expert's knowledge into rules before new problems are given. A case-based reasoning system processes new problems with the most similar prior experiences available, and adapts the prior solutions to solve new problems. This might avoid the inefficiency of solving problems from scratch every time, as well as the difficulty of deriving generalized knowledge from experts. At the same time, it also provides a way to improve its own performance by learning from new experiences.

To represent architectural design knowledge, B. Faltings proposed a model of case-based representation (Faltings et al 1991), which utilizes the desirable features of the selected case as syntactical rules to adapt the case to a new context. Given a design problem, a case which was designed for a similar context is selected from the case library. The selected case is then adapted to the new context through proper modifications which resolve the conflicts caused by differences between the original and the new context. A case is defined as a complete and precise description of a previous design solution for a specific situation. In addition to the design description, desirable features, the invariant that must not be changed during the process of modification, are to be provided in terms of verification methods. Applying this definition to our discussion about generators and evaluators, the desirable features can be described as a grammar and thus, define a language, which includes all possible designs that have the same features. Furthermore, the case serves as an initial state of the search for solutions which are supposed to have similar structures. That is to say, the selected case and the desirable features play the role of a generator in solving the new design problem. Theoretically, if the desirable features can be described in a computer program, then they can be converted into an equivalent grammar, which can produce design alternatives by applying its productions. A more detailed discussion of this can be found in the sections about case adaptation.

The use of cases as generators avoids the necessity of defining a general generator which is supposed to be applied to all given problems. If the desirable features of the selected case are essential to the perspective solutions, we can focus on each specific problem to define a good generator for the specific situation. The effectiveness of the generator will therefore rely on the adequacy of the selected case and the desirable features. Of course this does not reduce the difficulty of the problem at all. Some difficulties are simply shifted to the sub-process of case retrieval.

The dividing of the problem solving process into case selection and case adaptation provides human designers with a way to express their intentions explicitly, implicitly, and subjectively through the selection of cases. The explicit intentions are described in terms of verification methods. The implicit intentions are hidden inside the case and some of them can be detected by generalized knowledge. The fact that designers often use cases to communicate with each other when both have senses in common implies that generalized knowledge can be used to derive some of the desirable but implicit features. Designers can also select the case according to their preferences.

Case-based representation of design knowledge avoids the problem of using a fixed decomposition to find solutions for different problems. It makes use of cases to provide a more efficient way of searching. Furthermore, designers can express their intentions and can contribute their experiences in a way which they are more familiar with - case selection.

Case Adaptation

When a case is selected for application to a different context, proper modifications of the case are required in order to recover the discrepancy caused by the differences between the new and the original contexts. The modification requires two types of operations: geometrical and topological. The required geometrical operation determines the dimension of each design element according to a set of numerical constraints which maintains the integrity as well as the required functionality of the design. In our development of a prototype system, the technique of dimensionality reduction is used to derive independent parameters which are essential to the resolution of discrepancies caused by the differences of context. Detail discussion can be found in a previous paper (Faltings et al 1991). Topological operations are required when the change of dimensions alone can not successfully adapt the case. In the following figure, the U-shape case used for adaptation is shown at the left and the output of our prototype system after adaptation are shown at the middle and the right.

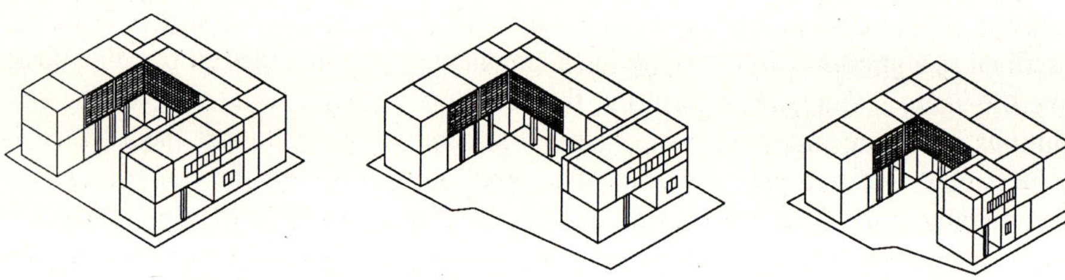

Figure 2. left: the case used for adaptation
middle: the result of topological and geometrical operations
right: the result of only geometrical operation

In this case, the U-shapedness is defined as a desirable feature. The building at the right hand side is a result of pure dimensional modification which resolves the discrepancy caused by the change of the site. The result is not satisfactory because some spaces are reduced to unusable sizes. The system ignores some constraints in order to resolve the over-constrainted problem. The building in the middle of the figure shows the result of both geometrical and topological operations. The adaptation changes the locations of some spaces but maintains the U-shapedness and most functional relationships.

In the following sections we focus on the discussion of topological operations for adaptation. Three types of adaptation under different levels of computational complexity will be discussed. The three types are case-based search, self-organization, and direct transduction.

Context Free Grammar and Case-Based Search

The first type - case-based search - is basically a localized search for the intersection of the two languages defined by the generator and the evaluator. Suppose that a case has been selected, which is represented by **C**, and its desirable features can be verified with a grammar **E1**. Therefore, **C** is a member of **L(E1)**, the language defined by **E1**. There is another grammar **E2**, which defines the goal. The design solution **D** has to be verified by **E2** and thus **D** is a member of **L(E2)**. The purpose of adaptation is to modify the case **C** such that it becomes a member of **L(E2)** without losing the desirable features defined by **E1**. It is supposed that the case is selected properly such that **E1** specifies syntactical structures which are essential to the resolution of **E2**.

The grammar **E1** can be used as a generator if its instances can be derived efficiently. This would require that the derivations do not lead to too many dead-ends or loops. An ideal case occurs when the derivations of the grammar can be described as a tree with all of its leaves in terminal states. In such a case, any derivation sequence will eventually lead to an instance of the language. The selected case serves as a focal point from which the system starts to search in nearby branches for a design alternative which is also a member of **L(E2)**. In this circumstance, the derivation sequence which leads to the generation of **C** is required to enable backtracking.

When the grammar of the generator is context free, the search space can be described as a tree if some priorities of operations are introduced. Ambiguity in the grammar can be avoided by introducing priorities or can be handled by including all possibilities. We can parse the selected case to derive the path which generates the case. By backtracking the path, we are able to search the neighboring branches and test for solutions. Since the relationships between design components are fixed after they are established in a context free grammar, branch and bound search can be effective for some evaluations and thus, reduce the search space to a more tractable size. The terminal nodes being realized can be used to determine the lowest bounds of the search since they will not be removed afterwards.

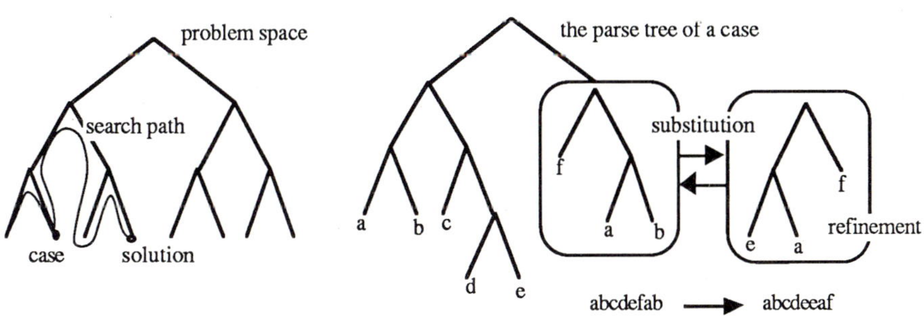

Figure 3. a. case-based search in a hierarchical problem space.
b. the substitution and partial refinement of a parse tree.

The diagram in figure 4a shows a search path from a case to a solution. Each node of the tree represents a design state. Each edge represents an operation performed on a design state. When causal relationships between operations and evaluations can be established, it is possible to identify the part of the design which causes discrepancies between the selected case and the new problem. The trouble maker can then be replaced and refined. The diagram in Figure 4b shows the decomposition of a case as a parse tree. The adaptation of the case appears as a process of substitution and refinement of a part of the design.

Although context-free grammars have relatively limited expressive power, their tractability may overcome this drawback. Context-free grammars may not be able to describe complicated features, but a larger language can be defined that encompasses them and a filter used to filter out the unwanted. If we make an analogy between programming and designing, a programming language is like the syntax of a class of designs, and a program is like a design. The grammar checks the correctness of the syntax, but the semantics is handled mainly by the programmer and has to be tested by its input and output. The unsolvable halting problem implies that no grammar can fully guarantee the correctness of a program. In design, we should not expect the grammar to be able to guarantee the quality of the design either, therefore designs have to be tested by required evaluations. Considering that the syntax of most programming languages are defined with a subset of context-free grammar, it might be more appropriate to have also a context-free grammar for design in which the interpretation of design description can be more tractable.

Making up for its poor expressive power, the tractability of context-free grammar provides the possibility of performing analytical operations on design descriptions. Since a generator is constructed according to desirable features, a context free grammar allows one to decompose the selected case, or the derived design, to various levels in a hierarchy for analytical purposes. Such an advantage is used in the design of some compilers, where some of the semantics of programs such as type checking and variable declaration can be checked efficiently within compilation. Optimization or reuse of programs is also possible.

It has been shown that desirable features can be derived by learning from examples. Tree automata (Thatcher 1967, 1973) can serve to derive common features of syntax tree of context-free grammars. In the work of C.A. Mackenzie (Mackenzie 1989), methods of grammatical inference were used to recognize Palladian-like villa plans based on relational grammar by inferring from 10 examples. Thereby, the desirable features of cases could be derived from multiple selections, and the knowledge which is specific to cases could be acquired automatically.

Case-based search can be more efficient than search from scratch if there are solutions in the nearby branches of the selected case. The tractability of the search relies on the complexity of the grammar. When the grammar is context-free, the decomposition of a design description can be derived for back tracking, desirable features can be inferred from multiple selection of cases, and heuristic search strategies can be more reliable.

Context Sensitive Grammar and Self-Organization

When the generator is defined with a context sensitive grammar, the problem space will be more complex, though it can more precisely approximate the solution set. There is no general way to parse a selected case in order to find the derivation sequence which generates the case, because such languages can not be recognized in a limited time bound. If case-based search is to be used as a strategy for case adaptation under context-sensitive grammars, a full description of the case needs to include the derivations which generated the case itself, to enable a search for close instances. The search would be inefficient because of the existence of ambiguity, loops and dead ends. The branch-and-bound algorithm is not applicable because the relationships between design elements might change after they are established. The decomposition of a design would then be ambiguous. An example is shown in the following figure.

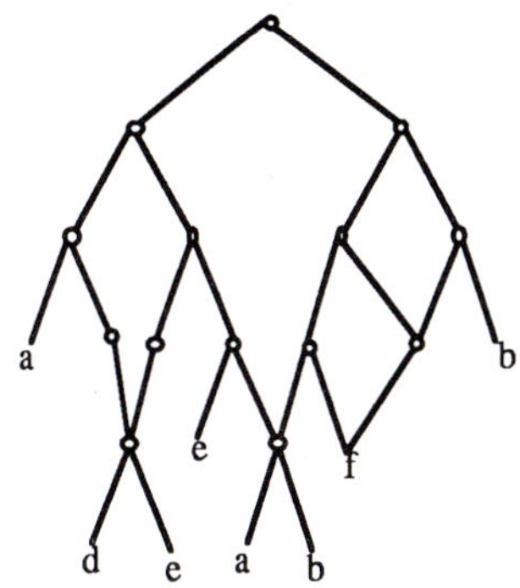

Figure 4. Possible derivations which generate the string "adeeabfb" with a context-sensitive grammar.

Based on the above observations about context free and context sensitive grammars, it is suspected that a generator defined with a context-free grammar has a stable behavior and is thus more or less predictable. A generator defined with a context sensitive grammar may behave chaotically and is unpredictable. For a specific generator and evaluator, it may be possible to define a specific strategy for resolving the intractability of a specific context-sensitive grammar. With a case-based reasoning approach, the generator is not defined ad hoc, and thus, the search process is left to be intractable. In such cases, a case-based search will not be feasible for case adaptation.

The second type of case adaptation comes from the concept of self-organization. It requires that evaluations be approximated by knowledge about local interactions among primitive elements and that they be fully integrated into the generator. Such systems can be viewed as systems of self-organization and can be adaptive to their environments. The growth of an embryo, ants' construction of an ant hill, or the development of an urban area, are all natural phenomena of self-organization. Each case can be viewed as a result of a self-organizing activity. If it is possible to replay the process with a new context initialized, a system might demonstrate an adaptive behavior.

The difficulty is the approximation of global evaluations with local interactions. It is more proper to simulate only localized adaptive behavior. Context-sensitive grammar plays an essential role in this type of adaptation. The grammar defines the derivation of each design element according to the immediate context of the element. For computational purposes, cellular automata (Von Neumann 1966) and interactive Lindenmayer grammar (Lindenmayer 1968) are potential models for the simulation of self-organizations. Achievements have been shown in this way in various fields such as biological simulations, fluid dynamic simulations, and urban development. J. Gero's Prototype (Gero 1987) can be used as a model for the simulation of localized adaptation in design domains. Prototypes, as abstractions of design elements, define possible derivations of the elements with domain knowledge. If a prototype is linked to the design context, domain knowledge can be used to match contextual situations to find if any action can take place to further refine the prototype. The refinement may then trigger chain reactions of other prototypes.

Direct Transduction

The third type of adaptation is direct transduction. Through a proper translation function, a case can be translated directly into the language defined by the evaluator without search or simulation. The transduction is not necessarily a composition of design operators and thus, may exceed the range of the problem space. A meaningful transduction has to embed the semantics, which are usually verified by the evaluator.

Syntax directed translation is one simple example of such transductions. Syntax directed translations can be derived from the permutations of non-terminals and substitutions or alterations of terminals of each production in the grammar. In such transductions, design elements can be substituted by other elements, and the syntax structure of the design may be altered as well. An example is illustrated as below:

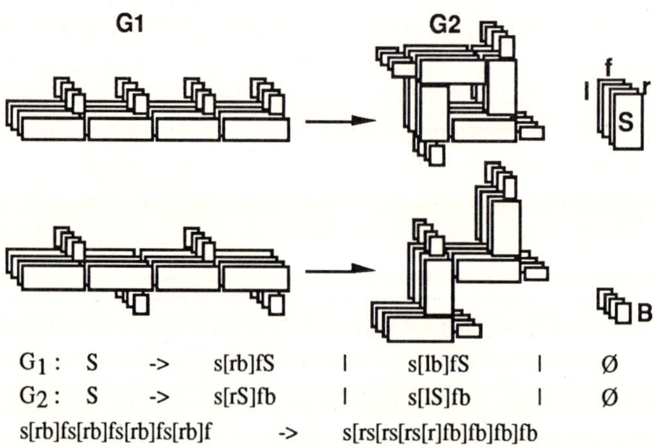

G_1 : S -> s[rb]fS | s[lb]fS | Ø

G_2 : S -> s[rS]fb | s[lS]fb | Ø

s[rb]fs[rb]fs[rb]fs[rb]f -> s[rs[rs[rs[r]fb]fb]fb]fb

s[rb]fs[lb]fs[rb]fs[lb]f -> s[rs[ls[rs[l]fb]fb]fb]fb

Figure 5. An example of syntax directed translation.

Here we use a notation which originated in logo turtle and was used in Lidenmayer grammar to map a string of symbols to graphics (Lidenmayer 1968). In grammars G_1 and G_2, the letters ***s*** and ***b*** represent the design elements shown in the figure. These elements are placed by a imaginary turtle according to its current position and orientation, the symbols ***r***, ***l***, and ***f*** represent the transformations required to move the turtle to the right wing of *s*, left wing of *s*, and front of ***s*** respectively, the symbols *[* and *]* pushes and pops the state of the turtle to and from a stack.

This type of adaptation enables cross-contextual mapping between designs. It means that a design solution might be found by applying cross-contextual mapping to another design for a different design domain. Sycara and Navinchandra indicated in their study (Sycara and Navinchandra 1991) that cross-contextual reminding is one of the two processes of using cases creatively. After such a reminding has been done, cross-contextual mapping would be a necessary process to finish this creative use of case.

Conclusion

By introducing cases, the search for a solution to a design problem is divided into case selection and case adaptation. Concerning the selected case, desirable features, which are defined explicitly by the designer or detected by generalized knowledge, define the space of possible solutions. In the first type of adaptation discussed in this paper, the case serves as a starting point for the search of design solutions. To search for similar design alternatives, the derivations which generate the case have to be derived by parsing when the grammar is context free, or be given when the grammar is context sensitive. The search for a new solution will be more tractable when the generator is defined with a context-free grammar. When the generator is defined with context-sensitive grammar, the behavior of the system can be chaotic and unpredictable. In such cases, a goal directed search or heuristic search strategy will not be reliable. Consequently, case-based search can not be carried out effectively.

Simulation of self-organization is the second type of case adaptation, in which context sensitive grammar plays an essential role. The coding of global evaluations into local interactions can be very difficult to realize. Therefore, it is more adequate to simulate localized adaptation with this approach. It can be combined with the other types of adaptation. Case-based search and direct transduction can be used to modify topological relationships of design elements; whereas self-organization is used to conform each element to its immediate context.

Direct transduction is a kind of short cut when the mapping of the two languages defined by the generator and the evaluator is known or can be derived by inference from examples. When cross-contextual reminding and mapping are applied properly, this may be a key to creativity because it can exceed the range of the problem space. The three types of adaptation can be distinguished by the embedding of semantics defined by the domain knowledge. In case-based search, semantics are examined by the evaluator. In self-organization, semantics of design are fully integrated into the generator and become a part of the syntax. In direct transduction, semantics are embedded in the translation function.

It is expected that the study of case-based representation and adaptation may lead to a change in computer aided design systems so that CAD systems become a tool in making modifications on complete solutions instead of composing pieces. More explicitly, case adaptation can be applied to the evolution of design from one version of a solution to another, to the accommodation of new design constraints, or in the reuse of a prior design for a new design problem. Besides, case selection can become a process which enables designers to express their intentions by choosing cases, without going through the whole process of knowledge acquisition and knowledge engineering.

Acknowledgement

This paper describes ongoing research being carried out as part of a project in the Swiss National Research Program in Artificial Intelligence (NFP 23).

The work is a result of collaborative research with the Laboratoire d'Intelligence Artificielle, and the Institut de Construction Metallique (ICOM) of the EPFL Lausanne. Discussions with the collaborators of this project have made the development of the ideas possible. Special thanks to my advisor Prof. Gerhard Schmitt, to Prof. Boi Faltings, and to my colleagues Chen-Cheng Chen and Sharon Refvem for their advice.

References

Chomsky, N. 1957. *Syntactic Structures*. Mouton, The Hague.

Chomsky, N. 1963. "Formal properties of grammars." In D. Luce, E. Bush, and E. Galanter (eds.). *Handbook of Mathematical Psychology*, no. 2: 323-418. New York: John Wiley.

Eastman, C. 1988. "Automatic Composition in Design." In *1988 NSF Grantee Workshop on Design Theory and Methodology*, pp. 158-172.

Faltings, B., K. F. Hua, G. Schmitt, and S. G. Shih. 1991. "Case-based Representation of Architectural Design Knowledge." In DARPA *Case-Based Reasoning Workshop 1991*.

Gero, J. S. 1987. *Prototypes: A New Schema for Knowledge-Based Design*. Architectural Computing Unit, Department of Architectural Science, University of Sydney.

Lindenmayer, A. 1968. "Mathematical Models for Cellular Interactions in Development." Parts I and II. *Journal of Theoretical Biology* 18: 280-315.

Mackenzie, C.A. 1989. "Inferring relational design grammars." *Environment and Planning B: Planning and Design*. 1989, vol. 16: 253-287.

Mitchell, W. J. 1977. "The computer's role in design." chapter 2 in: *Computer-Aided Architectural Design*, New York: Van Nostrand Reinhold Company.

Schank, R. C. 1982. "Reminding and Memory." Chapter 2 in: *Dynamic Memory - A Theory of Reminding and Learning in Computers and People*. Cambridge: Cambridge University Press.

Sycara, K. P., and D. Navinchandra. 1991. "Influences: A Thematic Abstraction for Creative Use of Multiple Cases." In DARPA *Case-Based Reasoning Workshop 1991*.

Thatcher, J.W. 1967, "Characterizing Derivation Trees of a Context-Free Grammar through a Generalization of Finite-Automata Theory." *Journal of Computer and System Sciences 1*: 317-322.

Thatcher, J. W. 1973. "Tree Automata: An Informal Survey." In A.V. Aho (ed.). *Currents in the Theory of Computing*, pp. 143-172. New Jersey: Prentice-Hall.

Von Neumann, J. 1966. *Theory of Self-Reproducing Automata* (edited and completed by Arthur Burks), Univ. of Illinois Press.

20 Refinement and Adaptation: Two Paradigms of Form Generation in CAAD

Rivka E. Oxman, Robert M. Oxman

Faculty of Architecture and Town Planning
Technion, Israel Institute of Technology
Haifa, 32000, Israel

Within a transformational paradigm of form generation, refinement and adaptation are presented as two distinct concepts which can provide formalisms for encoding design knowledge. Refinement and adaptation are treated as syntactical models of form generation. Computational formal analysis is proposed as a method for the study and modelling of refinement and adaptation in design. Employing the analytical method we demonstrate that formal transformations are dependent upon their membership in classes of architectural designs. Computational issues in form generation through refinement and adaptation are identified.

Introduction: Modelling Design Generation

The generation of form in architectural design is one of the significant research areas in design computing. Prominent among models of design generation, which provide a basis for the computational generation of form, are transformational models which are founded upon symbolic processing. Shape grammars are a well-known application in which symbols of shapes are represented and transformed (Stiny 1980a). The formalism has proven to be useful in the modelling of form generation in art, design and architecture (Mitchell 1990). The work described in this paper, is part of the research tradition which investigates formal representations and transformational models in encoding design knowledge and in the computation of design generation.

Within a transformational approach to form generation, refinement and adaptation are proposed as two models which may provide computational formalisms for generation. Refinement and adaptation are relevant to form generation in design, since they are considered as two distinct ways in which formal knowledge in architectural composition is employed by designers through *typological* and *precedent-based* design. In refinement processes a generalized schema is transformed into a specific design; in adaptation, a specific precedent is transformed into a new design. The current research has focused upon these two models of form generation, their formalization, and their potential role in the computation of generation in design.

Computational formal analysis is proposed as a method for the study of refinement and adaptation operations. Employing this analytical method we demonstrate that formal transformations, which have been previously exploited to model refinement, can potentially be used to model adaptive operations in design. The analytical method is employed to formalize

syntactical steps in architectural composition. It provides a basis for categorizing and formalizing various strategies of refinement and adaptation in design. Both refinement and adaptation operations appear to be influenced by membership in *formal classes of architectural designs*. Such formal classes have been previously defined according to *architectural syntax* (Flemming 1990; Oxman and Oxman 1989, 1990).
The objectives of this research were:

- development of a formal analysis method in the study of refinement and adaptation

- modelling form generation in refinement and adaptation as transformational operations

- identification of computational issues in form generation within the two models

In addition to these primary goals, we have undertaken a preliminary explanation of *formal classes in architectural syntax*. In this paper we demonstrate two classes through the use of case studies.

Form Generation in Architectural Composition through Refinement and Adaptation

Form generative processes in architectural composition have been modelled as transformations of syntactic representations of designs. In such models of generation, design knowledge is encoded as transformation rules. The application of rule-based formalisms to encode syntactical knowledge of architectural designs is well founded in CAAD. Architectural designs have been represented through hierarchical rule sets in the Palladian Grammar (Stiny and Mitchell 1978); multiple rule sets in the Queen Anne Grammar (Flemming 1986), and replacement rules (Weissman Knight 1981). These models are based upon a refinement process of a generic representation of the design. However within the syntactic paradigm, adaptive processes which are based upon the modification of specific architectural precedents, have so far received little attention.

Several distinct approaches to form generation can be identified and can be divided into two main groups. The first, including construction and refinement, is based upon a generic representation of a design which has been generalized from past experiences of many designs. The second, including adaptation, is based upon the modification of specific precedents from past design experience. These approaches are elaborated below.

Construction: Transformation as Assemblage

Construction is the sequential generation of a design in a bottom-up fashion in which a general constructive principle is applied to a vocabulary of elements. The transformational rules for construction are defined as operations without reference to an underlying schema. That is, the rules define element to element relations without specifying underlying organizational concepts. This bottom-up application is exemplified in the Kindergarten Grammar (Stiny 1980b). In distinction to such grammars, building designs are complex formal constructs which may require multiple rule sets for their representation. In the case of multiple rule sets, the existence of an underlying schema may be required to establish the relationships among the rule sets.

Refinement: Transformations upon a Generalized Schema

Refinement is generation through transformation in a top-down fashion. The generic representation of a design schema underlies the refinement process. Refinement is form generation through sequential particularization of designs. Refinement steps specify the transformation from a schematic state to a specific state.

In accomplishing this, refinement instantiates sub-types from a given generic representation of a design. The representation is generic in the sense that it captures the salient attributes of the class of designs. These may include an underlying reference system, such as a grid or axial system, which constitutes the referential system for particularization. These concepts are illustrated in the well-known sequence of drawings, plate 21, of Durand's Leçons in which the initial representation of a spatial order of plan composition is refined. In the accompanying plate 20, Durand provides a range of sub-types for the class of square-based, concentric, dual axis plan compositions. Substitution may be regarded as a method for transforming the generic to the specific representation. This is, in fact, the approach exemplified by Durand. The skeletal syntax of the plan provides the framework for the substitution of detailed column arrangements, partition arrangements, porches, courts, stairs and building masses. Through substitution the schema is elaborated in a top-down fashion. The Palladian Grammar (Stiny and Mitchell 1978) and the Top-Down System (Mitchell, Liggett and Tan 1988) exemplify approaches to generation through refinement in architectural computing.

Adaptation: Transformations upon Design Precedents

Adaptation is a process for modifying an existing design to generate another design. A precedent represents an existing design selected from a precedent repertoire of past experience. In comparison to generic design, a precedent may be regarded as a specific design. Adaptation is defined as modification through transformations upon particularized design descriptions. The use of precedents in design was well established methodologically within the Classical tradition and Beaux Arts theory (Szambien 1982). Among the functions of the 'analytique' in the Beaux Arts method was the selection and study of past precedents which were relevant to a current design situation (Crowe and Hurtt 1986). In these historical examples, precedents as complete designs are adapted in order to create a new design.

Modelling Form Generation in Refinement and Adaptation

Historically, adaptation has been considered to be a significant model for design. Building a repertoire of designs is one potential basis for encoding design knowledge which may be employed in generation. However, until now adaptation has been little explored in architectural design computation. Reasoning in adaptation is a current research subject in artificial intelligence. Case-based reasoning addresses research questions which are relevant to generation through the adaptation of a precedent repertoire. Work in case-based reasoning

(Kolodner 1988) in indexing, selection and repair of the case-base may provide concepts and methods which are relevant to generation through adaptation in design.

In the current research, we have employed formal analysis as a basis for modelling transformation operations in refinement and adaptation. The concept of syntactical classes of designs has been found to be relevant in these models, since types of operations in refinement and adaptation appear to be characteristic of these classes. The method of study has been to analyze a cycle of designs in the work of selected architects, which constitute a sequence of designs within a distinct syntactical class. In the following sections operations in refinement and adaptation and their relationship to syntactic classes will be illustrated.

In this section we propose an approach to modelling refinement and adaptation as transformational operations within the context of architectural syntactical classes. What is a syntactical class? A design world has been defined as a world that is characterized by it's shape vocabulary and operators (Mitchell 1990). According to this view, a syntactical class is a *generalized design world*. Architectural syntax is the formalization of knowledge of general classes of designs (Oxman and Oxman 1990). The concept of grammars has been employed to formalize general syntactical classes in architecture (Flemming 1990). Classes may be based upon morphological principles of two and three-dimensional design which characterize compositional styles. Centralistic-concentric layered designs, and grid-based designs exemplify such general classes.

In our analyses, it appears that in generation, formal operations function in a way characteristic of the syntactic class. Five basic formal operations - instantiation, deletion, transformation, combination and replacement - have been identified (Mitchell 1990). Composition is, therefore, a characteristic set of operations within a specific class of designs.

Refinement of Formal Classes in Design

In design the term schema is often used to indicate the properties of a formal structure which specify the general properties and omit specifications irrelevant to the class of designs. The concept of the schema may be employed to represent generative knowledge which supports an hierarchically structured top-down refinement process. This includes an initial abstracted representation of a design (the schematic, or generic state), which contains the salient elements and relationships of the type. Refinement particularizes this initial state of the schema. The generative refinement process of a syntactical class is a specific set of refinement operations which transform representations from higher-level to instantiated representations. This establishes a state-action tree of specified descriptions of the class.

Design refinement is considered as the sequence of formal transformations upon the initial schema representation. Within formal classes of designs characteristic sets of refinement operations may be defined. These can be represented as part of a design schema. A *generative schema* (Oxman 1990) contains a form design description generator which derives the properties of each level of the refinement tree according to design principles and characteristic operations of the class.

Figure 1 illustrates the basic concept of design generation as transformation operations upon formal representations.

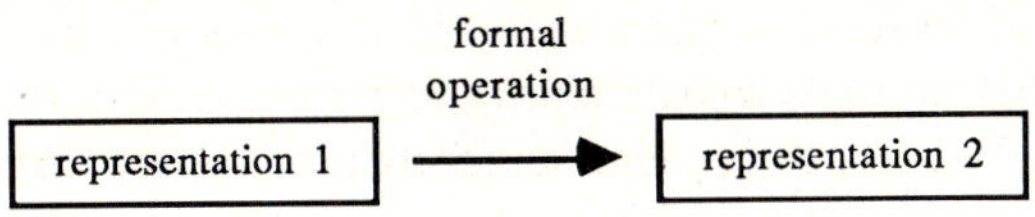

Figure 1. Design generation as a transformation upon a design representation.

Figure 2 illustrates refinement as a process of transforming a schematic description into a specified design. This is a mapping process between a high-level, abstracted representation and its successive specified descriptions. In the computational refinement of the class of designs, inheritance can be employed as a technique to maintain class characteristics. Operations may contain specifications of elements, their attributes, variables and parameters. Representations illustrated in figure 2 are numbered according to their level of refinement.

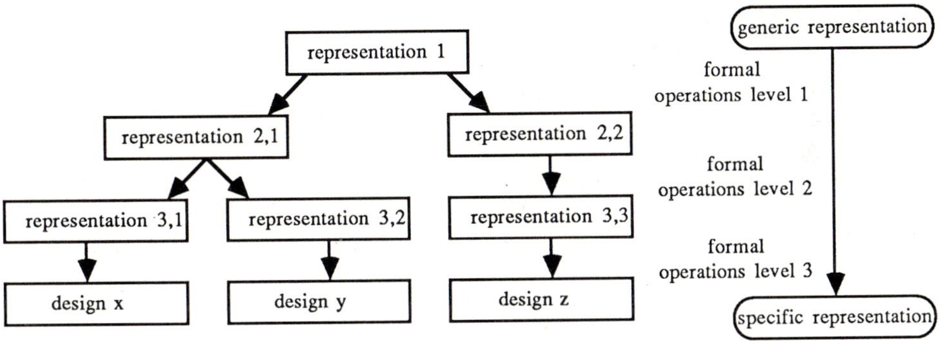

Figure 2. The refinement of a schema as formal transformations of representations through characteristic sets of formal operations.

A rule-based formalism provides computational means to achieve refinement. This is illustrated in figure 3 which is a rule-based representation of the refinement tree. The rule sets of the refinement steps provide alternatives within levels.

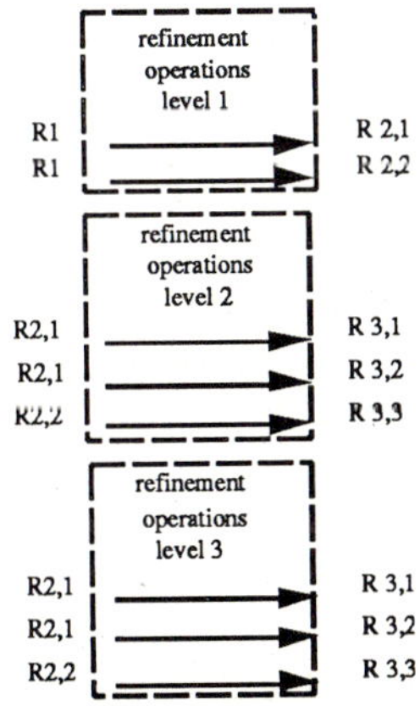

Figure 3. Sets of transformational rules within a formal class.

A simple example of refinement operations within a class of centralistic designs is illustrated in figure 4. In this example a particularization of the core is specified through substitution rules. Thin lines indicate the generic representation, heavy lines indicate a particularization.

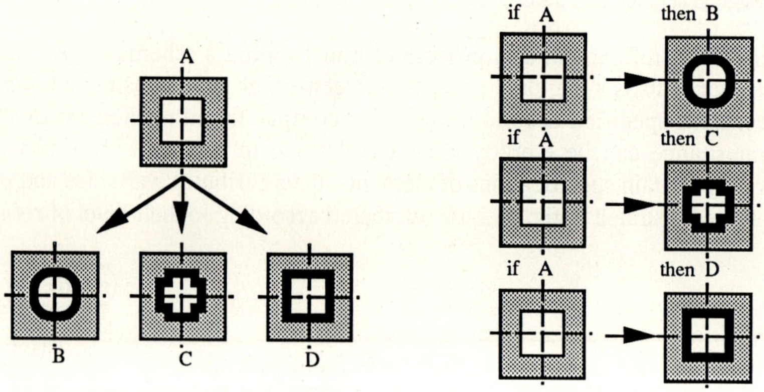

Figure 4. Tree representation and a comparable substitution rule representation for sub-type generation.

In design computation various formalisms support the encoding of refinement. Grammars are the most well-known formalism which can be employed in transformational models of refinement. Grammars are powerful in encoding syntactic descriptions for generation through refinement (Stiny and Mitchell 1978). The formalism of the design prototype (Gero 1987) supplements this syntactical knowledge through the representation of other kinds of knowledge. The design prototype is a conceptual schema for representing a class of generalized design knowledge. It represents and integrates three kinds of descriptions: functional, structural and behavioral descriptions as well as the relations between them. The use of such a formalism provides mapping between structure, (which can be considered the syntactical description of a design) and behavior and function, (which can be considered the semantics of a design).

Adaptation of Formal Classes in Design

Refinement is a model of design generation which is established in the literature and has a substantial body of research in design computation. However, refinement does not explain another significant cognitive style in design, designing with precedents. In contrast to refinement which employs a generic representation as an initial state, adaptation can be regarded as a manipulation process of a specific precedent, or prior design. Adaptation may be defined as the process of transforming a precedent, or precedents, into a new design. The existing design provides an entire solution which is represented and transformed.

Adaptation appears relevant to the modelling of form generation in architectural design. There are various strategies of adaptation in design. We suggest that among these, three classes of strategies can be identified: elemental adaptation, schema adaptation, and hybrid adaptation.

Elemental Adaptation

This is the basic strategy of design adaptation. It is achieved through transformational operations upon the elements of a prior design. The strategy maintains the topological integrity of the existing design schema. The form and geometry of the elements may be modified while the integrity of the scheme is preserved. Figure 5 illustrates a replacement operation in this strategy. The basic operations of elemental adaptation can exist within each of the other strategies.

Figure 5. Elemental adaptation by a replacement operation.

Schema Adaptation

The precedent design suggests an entire schema. Schema adaptation modifies this schema. Certain of its topological characteristics are maintained. Figure 6 illustrates an example of a schema adaptation. In this example, the schema is extended by addition. The insertion of new elements within the existing design extend the number of elements of the schema while maintaining essential characteristics of the composition. Schema adaptation may be exemplified by the design method of the Ecole des Beaux Arts in which specific design precedents were frequently adapted to achieve new designs (Szambien 1982).

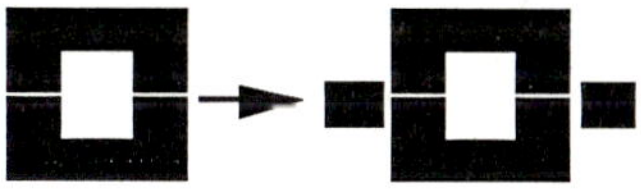

Figure 6. Schema adaptation by the addition of elements.

Addition of elements is the simplest form of schema adaptation. A more complex form of schema adaptation is the transformation of the high-level description which underlies the schema. For example, this may be a modification of the axial system underlying the design illustrated in figure 6.

Adaptation depends upon the interpretation of the precedent's schema. In this context it is interesting to mention the phenomenon of 'emergent form' which has been identified by Stiny (Stiny 1990). The significance of 'non-discrete' interpretations of existing representations is raised as a source of creativity. Ambiguity in interpretation of design representations may be a means of transcending the rigidity of the schema concept. A non-discrete interpretation of the existing design may suggest an adaptation unrelated to the topology of the schema.

Hybrid Adaptation

In elemental adaptation, the element vocabulary is modified. In schema adaptation, the schema is modified. In hybrid adaptation more than one precedent is employed and multiple precedents are incorporated into a new design. Hybridization may maintain, or modify, the existing schema of each of the precedents resulting in an eclectic schema.

Refinement models utilize generic knowledge, which may be encoded by rules. Adaptation models in design computation raise the issue of how to represent and compute with specific cases. In order to develop computational formalisms for adaptation in design, we require a medium for representing design cases in a computer system and, potentially, for reasoning with the knowledge of these cases. Various research efforts have begun to address the relevance of cased-based reasoning for design generation using precedent knowledge. This research may contribute to the development of formalisms which integrate diverse knowledge in reasoning about generation through adaptive strategies with large precedent repertoires of designs. These issues are currently being addressed in the development of integrated CAD databases, general compiled knowledge and case-based knowledge (Rosenman, Gero and Oxman 1991).

Formal Analysis of Transformations in Refinement and Adaptation Analysis of Refinement through Formal Analysis of Case Studies

We have proposed the modelling of refinement as a successive particularization which begins with a generic representation of a design as an initial state. A *formal analysis of refinement* consists of defining a series of operations which transform a specified representation back to the schematic representation. The analysis reconstructs the refinement tree by working towards the generic representation. The objective is to identify and categorize the operations of particularization starting from specific designs and working to their source. Figure 7 illustrates the analysis process.

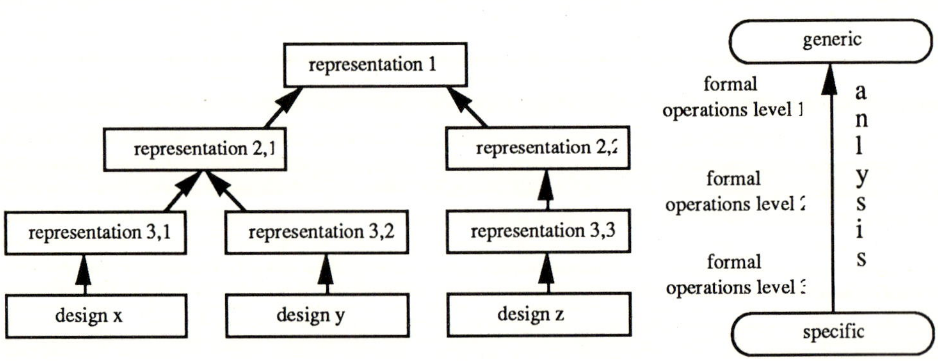

Figure 7. Method for analysis of refinement schema within a class of designs.

The Ring Cycle: Refinement in Kahn's Concentric Layered Designs

In the case studies we have selected designs of various architects which constitute a set of designs within a compositional class and have analyzed the transformations. We have found that transformational operations appear to be characteristic of the class of compositions. In the first series we have analyzed centralistic organizational schemes and have attempted to define the characteristic operations within this class of designs.
The refinement analyses employs the concept of a *general refinement schema in architectural design*. The model proposes an order of design particularization which starts from spatial-organizational representation and ends with a specified physical representation. The refinement model incorporates the following levels: schematic spatial organization, particularized spatial organization, partitioning, boundary conditions, thematic structural elements, non-thematic elements, detailed elements.

In the work of the architect Louis Kahn the recurrent examples of concentric layered designs provide an interesting class of designs which can be analyzed as refinements. Kahn is a fitting source for such an analysis. In his use of the concepts of *form*, as the generic representation which initiates design, and *design*, as specific particularized design, Kahn defined design as a refinement process (Scully 1962). In the series of designs which we have analyzed, Kahn appears to have developed a unique approach to the formal syntax of centralistic organization in ringed layers. It is interesting to observe the continuities in this class of compositions in a tradition including Durand and Ledoux. Kahn maintained certain salient characteristics of this compositional tradition, while extending others.

How might Kahn employ schema-driven refinement within a class of centralistic designs? We selected for study the Goldenberg House of 1959, the Unitarian Church of 1959-1967, and the Phillips Exeter Library, 1967-1972. An illustration of the refinement process as analyzed is given in figure 8 and figure 9. The steps of refinement include: establishing of the spatial scheme of rings, the syntactic subdivision of the ring zones by particularizing a sub-structure of axes and additional rings, the elaboration of the physical structure, etc. Characteristic of Kahn's refinement of this schema is the relationship between the central cross axes and the diagonal axes, which also occurs frequently in Durand. Unique to Kahn is the multiple, hierarchical subdivision of the major rings, sub-themes of asymmetry within the axially symmetrical scheme, and the high degree of formal particularization of the external ring.

The refinement model in the analysis of Kahn's concentric schemes includes the following levels:

- schematic spatial organization: the ring scheme
- elaborated spatial scheme: axial system
- particularized spatial organization: sub-axial scheme and syntactic elaboration
- partitioning and boundary elements: boundary and corner conditions
- thematic structural elements
- non-thematic elements and detailed elements

These categories of the model of refinement have been sub-divided into two groups. The first, illustrated in figure 8, consists of the definition of the spatial syntax of the ring scheme. The second grouping of refinement processes, illustrated in figure 9, includes the physical elaboration of the spatial scheme. Each of the steps within the levels of refinement can be further elaborated according to the formal operations which achieve the refinement.

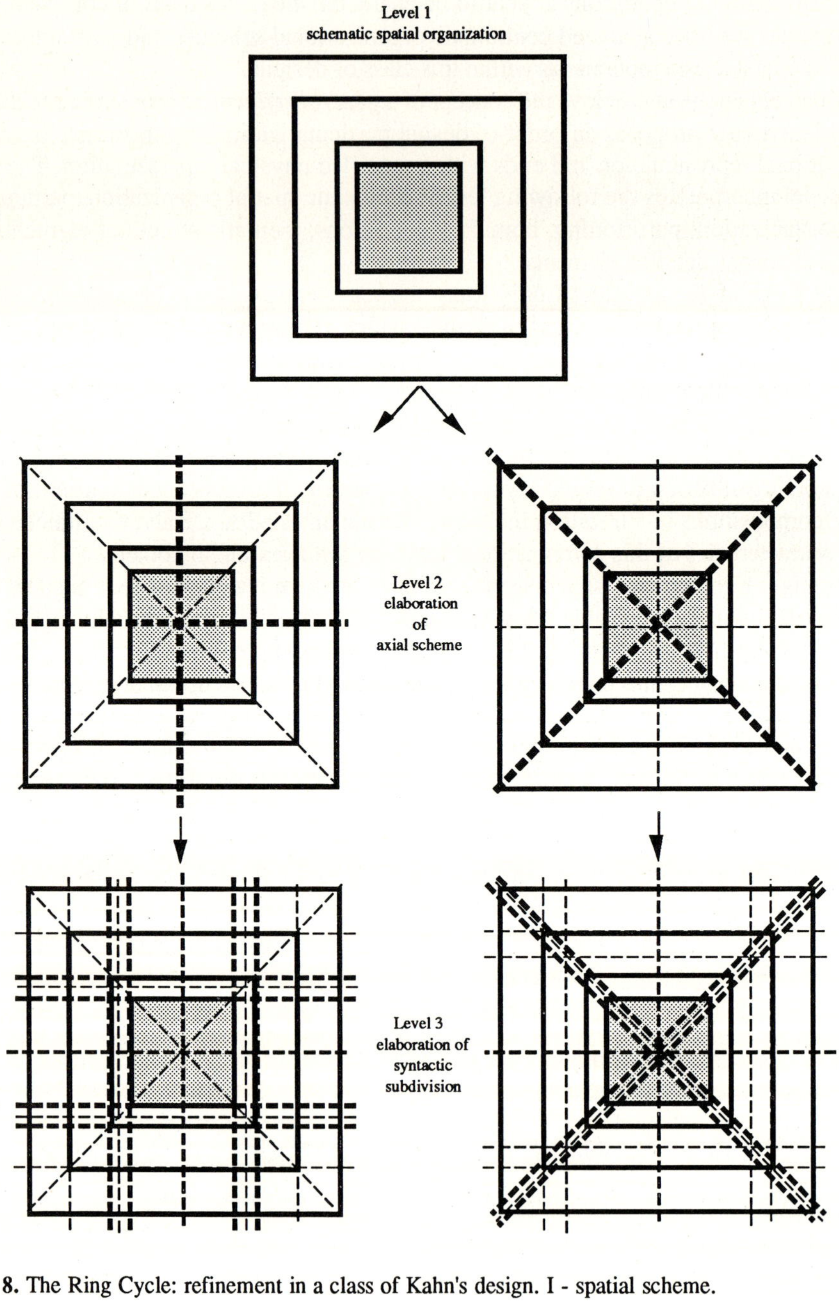

Figure 8. The Ring Cycle: refinement in a class of Kahn's design. I - spatial scheme.

The formal analysis of transformational operations in a class of designs may be applied to the study of facade designs. We have analyzed Kahn's refinement of the syntax of facades within a recurrent facade schema. Figure 10 illustrates the syntactic particularization of facade designs, all of which have a common tri-partite governing scheme. Operations in elevation display the high level of particularization which also characterized Kahn's refine-

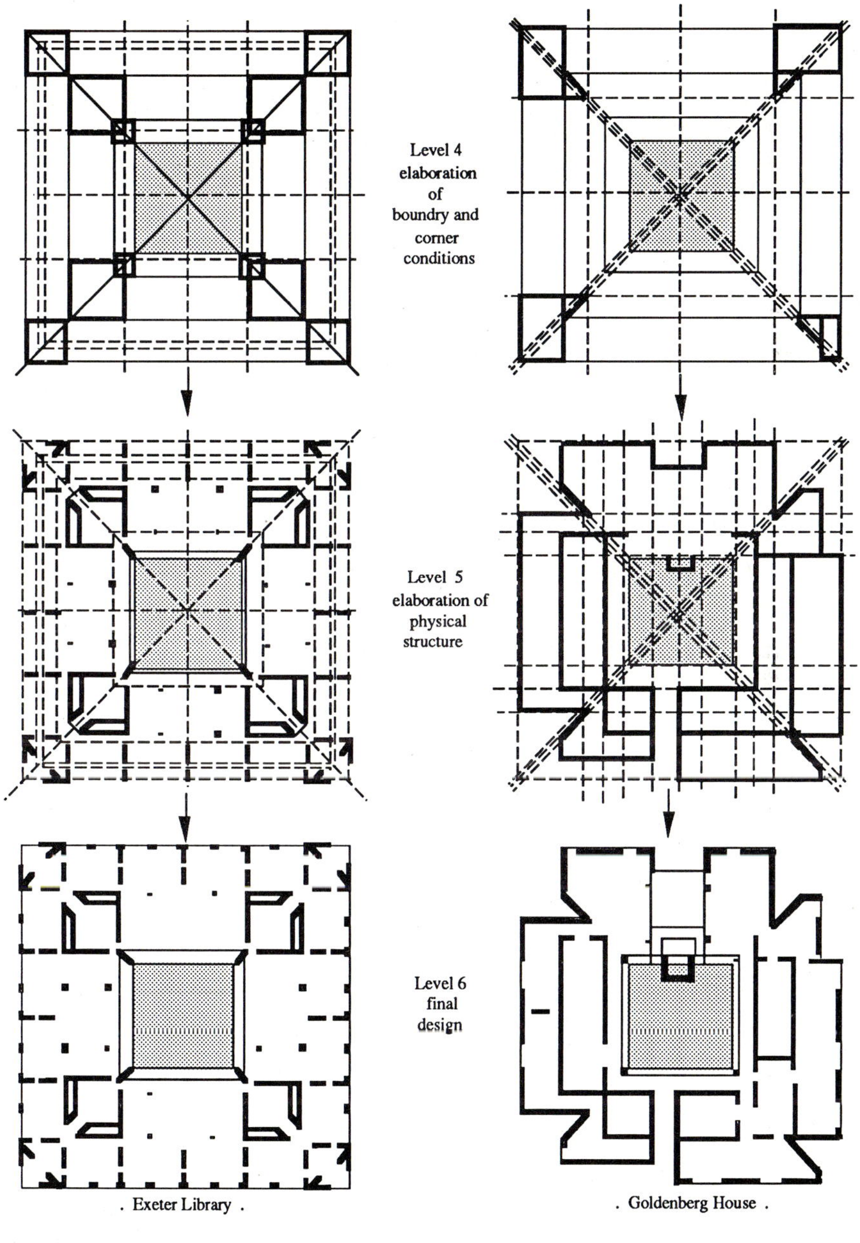

Figure 9. The Ring Cycle: refinement in a class of Kahn's designs. II - physical elaboration.

ment of plans. The highly syntactic nature of operations, the significance of ordering devices such as axial schemes, the tendency to hierarchical order within the scheme are among the high-level principles which underlie the refinement operations of this class of designs.

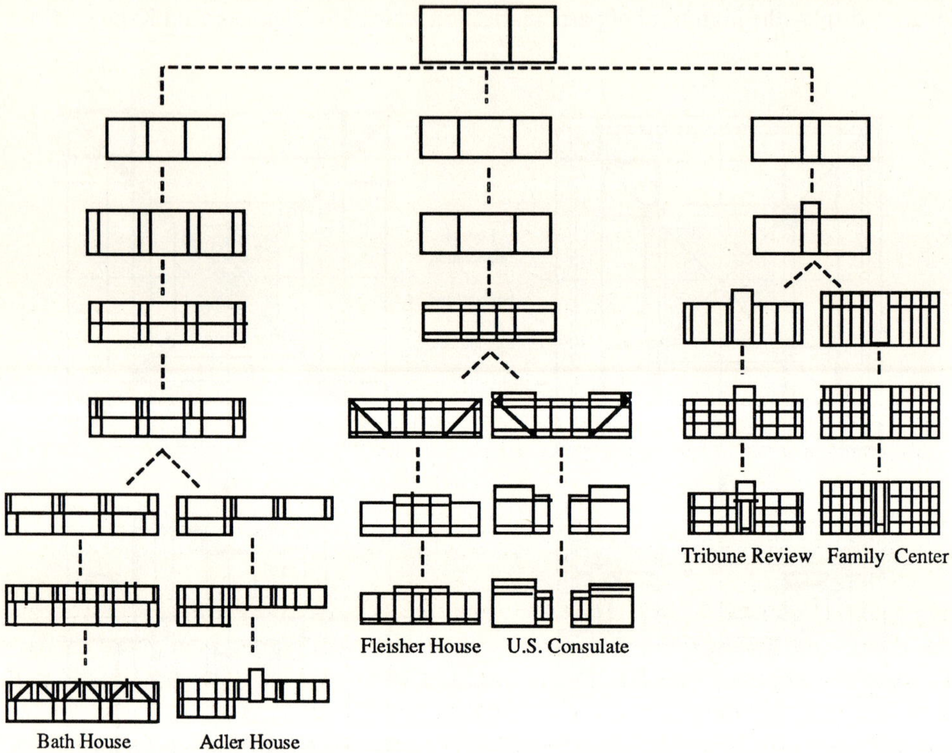

Figure 10. A refinement tree of six facade designs of Kahn.

Analysis of Adaptation through Formal Analysis of Case Studies

Generation through adaptation can be modelled as a series of transformations upon a specific design. Our approach to the analysis of adaptation is the mapping of one precedent into a related precedent in the same class of designs. This mapping is a reconstruction of the operations of adaptation which transform one specific design into another specific design. In the analysis, precedent is mapped into precedent as a sequence of transformation operations. Each step in the sequence identifies an operation of adaptation. These operations and sequences of operations of adaptation may be characteristic in classes of designs.

As in the case of refinement, we have employed sets of related designs as the basis for analysis. A case study of adaptation has been analyzed in the villa designs of Palladio. The mapping between the Villa Rotonda and the Malcontenta provides an example of schema adaptation in which a bi-lateral axial scheme (Rotonda) is mapped into a preference of one of the axes (Malcontenta). Figure 11 illustrates the mapping of adaptive operations. The two designs are superimposed. The dotted lines (Rotonda) are the state to be modified. The solid lines (Malcontenta) are the modified design.

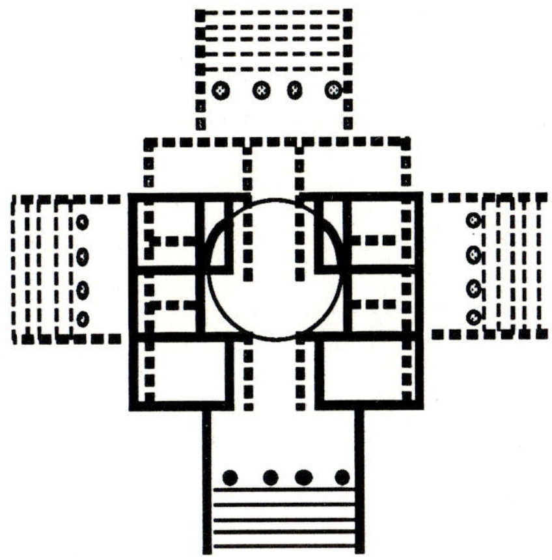

Figure 11. Mapping adaptation in two villas of Palladio.

The Ticino Cycle: Adaptation in Botta's Villa Designs

Botta's cycle of villa designs including Pregassona, 1979, Massagno, 1979, Viganello, 1980, Stabio, 1980, and Origlio, 1981 is a set of related designs with certain common formal characteristics. The source scheme at Pregassona is a bi-axial, nine-square spatial form. An exterior thematic space is incorporated in the spatial diagram within the nine-square form and creates a major element on the main facade. The masses, element vocabulary, roof shapes, treatment of fenestration and the way of introducing natural light share common formal characteristics in all of the villas. They provide an interesting case study of the mapping of one design into another as a process of adaptation.

Figure 12 illustrates an adaptive mapping of Pregassona into Massagno. The adaptive process exemplifies two strategies of adaptation, elemental adaptation and schema adaptation. The increase in length of the diagonal elements (step 2) and the replacement of the stair type (step 3) are examples of elemental adaptation. In schema adaptation, the schema is modified while certain of its other characteristics are preserved. For example, the transverse niche has been transformed into an internal forecourt (step 4). The emergence of this interior-exterior space as the main focal space of the house is the major transformation of the schema. The bi-lateral symmetry of this court is then adapted (step 5). Despite the compression of the square plan base into a rectangle, the remaining schematic characteristics are similar in the two villas. Similar mappings between other pairs of Botta villas in this series were undertaken in the research. Adaptation, at least in this class of designs, appears to be strongly controlled by the discipline of the compositional class.

Adaptive mappings of precedent-based designs have also been studied in the work of architects of different historical periods. For example, the mapping of Schinkel's Altes Museum into Stirling's Staatsgalerie was analyzed, employing the technique of adaptive transformation represented as successive mappings.

Computational formal analysis has provided a means to analyze and model both refinement and adaptation. The computer programs employed (geometrical modelling and animation) have given us a *dynamic mapping* of one design representation into another. This has provided a unique medium for simulating refinement and adaptation as design processes. Furthermore, computational formal analysis has proved to be an effective method for knowledge acquisition in design research and as a medium for teaching concepts of design by means of computer modelling.

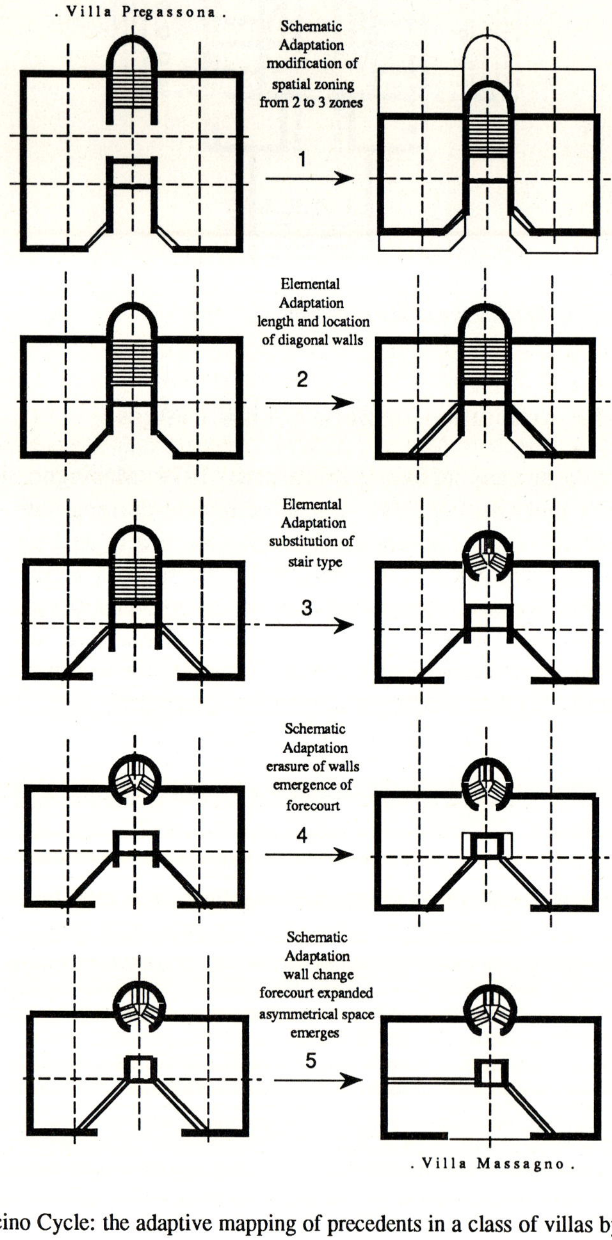

Figure 12. The Ticino Cycle: the adaptive mapping of precedents in a class of villas by Botta.

Conclusions

Refinement and adaptation have been proposed as two distinct approaches to design generation which have relevance for design computation. Representing and reasoning with generalized, typological knowledge, which we have referred to as generic design, and design with specific design precedents, which we have referred to as case-based design, are two paradigms which should be addressed in future research in knowledge-based CAAD.

The formal method which was utilized in the analysis of case studies has proved to be useful as a technique of design research in the study of refinement and adaptation. Additional research is currently being undertaken in the analysis of work of other architects in order to justify our conclusions regarding the general relevance of refinement and adaptation as models of design generation. The research has raised various issues with respect to the formalization of syntactical knowledge as a body of knowledge which we have referred to as architectural syntax. Much work in CAAD is dependent upon modelling this knowledge, and the formalization of syntactical knowledge for CAAD appears to us to be a significant research priority.

Through formal analysis a general model of refinement was elaborated. Applying this general model, we have demonstrated that specific refinement operations are characteristic of architectural syntactic classes. It appears that refinement is related to the high level formal principles of the syntactical class. Exploiting this characteristic in design computing, these high level principles can be represented as a design schema. In knowledge-based CAAD, the representation of transformational operations of refinement may be encoded as part of the design schema. The formalization of schemata for knowledge-based design is dependent upon our understanding of the general compositional principles in architectural design.

Adaptation has so far received little attention in the architectural context. The utility of the transformational model to represent adaptation is one of the research questions addressed in the current work. In our analyses we have employed transformation to model adaptation. In the model we have distinguished between higher level adaptation strategies, termed schematic adaptation, and lower level, specific adaptation strategies, termed elemental adaptation. Adaptation operates directly on a representation of an existing design and results in the direct modification of specific designs. However, in order to achieve a non-trivial adaptation, design reasoning may transcend the detail of the specific design and access a generic level. There appears to us to be an integral relationship between generalized and specific knowledge in design thinking. In this view a design reasoner in knowledge-based CAAD systems should have a capacity to work with both pre-stored specific cases and the general schema.

The concept of a case base which provides access to a precedent repertoire appears to be a promising direction for research and development in CAD and knowledge-based design systems.

Acknowledgments

The research has been funded by the H. Kieval Research Fund through the V.P.R. Fund of the Technion. The authors gratefully acknowledge this assistance. The work illustrated is part of on-going research at the Technion into architectural syntax and the computation of architectural knowledge. Student works were done in the framework of the course, *The Computation of Architectural Knowledge* taught by Rivka E. Oxman. The analysis of the Kahn facades was done by M. Shmuelovitch; the mapping of Palladian villas by U. Lehrman and M. Ben Dor. The concept of the Palladian analysis is based upon Lerup (Lerup, 1989). The analyses were done in Mac Architrion documented in Studio 8 and Gallery.

References

Crowe, N. A. and S. W. Hurtt. 1986. "Visual notes and the acquisition of architectural knowledge." *Journal of Architectural Education*, vol. 39, no. 3: 6-16.

Flemming, Ulrich. 1986. "More than the sum of the parts: the grammar of Queen Anne houses." *Planning and Design* 14, no. 3: 323-50.

Flemming, Ulrich. 1990. "Syntactic structures in architecture." in Malcolm McCullough, William J. Mitchell and Patrick Purcell (eds.). *The Electronic Design Studio*. Cambridge, MA: MIT Press.

Gero, John S. 1987. "Prototypes: a new schema for knowledge-based design." *Working Paper, Architectural Computing Unit*, Department of Architectural Science, University of Sydney.

Kolodner, Janet, L. 1988. *Case-based Reasoning*, Proceedings of the Workshop on Case-Based Reasoning, Florida: DARPA.

Lerup, Lars. 1989. "On Eden, the geography of villas and Dolf Schnebli's Villa Meyer." *Architecture and Urbanism* 2.

Mitchell William J. 1990. *The Logic of Architecture*. Cambridge, MA: MIT Press.

Mitchell, William J., Robin S. Liggett, and Milton Tan. 1988. "The Top Down System and its use in teaching: an exploration of structured knowledge-based design." In Pamela J. Bancroft (ed.). *Proceedings of ACADIA*: Ann Arbor.

Oxman, Rivka E. 1990. "Architectural knowledge structures as design shells.". In Malcolm McCullough, William J. Mitchell and Patrick Purcell (eds.). *The Electronic Design Studio*. Cambridge, MA: MIT Press.

Oxman, Robert M., and Rivka E. Oxman. 1989. "The joy of syntax: the secrets of architectural composition as elucidated through computer graphics education." In *proceedings of ECAADE CAAD-Education Research and Practice*. Aarhus, Denmark.

Oxman, Robert M., and Rivka E. Oxman. 1990. "The computation of architectural knowledge." In Malcolm McCullough, William J. Mitchell and Patrick Purcell (eds.). *The Electronic Design Studio*. Cambridge, Mass.: MIT Press.

Rosenman, Michael, John S. Gero, and Rivka E. Oxman. 1991. "What's in a case." In Gerhard Schmitt (ed.). *Proceedings of CAAD Futures '91*. Zurich.

Scully, Vincent Jr. 1962. *Louis I. Kahn*. N.Y.: Braziller.

Stiny, George. 1980a. "Introduction to shape and shape grammars." *Environment and Planning B*, vol. 8: 343-351.

Stiny, George. 1980b. "Kindergarten grammars: designing with Froebel's building gifts." *Environment and Planning B*, vol. 7: 409-462.

Stiny, George, and William J. Mitchell. 1978. "The Palladian grammar." *Environment and Planning B*, vol. 5: 5-18.

Stiny, George. 1990. "What designers do that computers should." In Malcolm McCullough, William J. Mitchell and Patrick Purcell (eds.). *The Electronic Design Studio*. Cambridge, MA: MIT Press.

Szambien, W. 1982. "Durand and the continuity of tradition." In R. Middleton (ed.). *The Beaux Arts*, Cambridge, MA: MIT Press.

Weissman Knight, T. 1981. "Languages of designs: from known to new." *Environment and Planning B*, vol. 8: 213-238.

21 BAU: A Knowledge-Based System for the Investigation of a Basic Architectural Unit

Herbert Kramel, Chen-Cheng Chen

Department of Architecture
Swiss Federal Institute of Technology, ETH Hönggerberg
CH 8093 Zurich, Switzerland

The control of incremental complexities within an evolutionary design process has been a serious concern in both architectural education and practice. One method of examining this problem is to first define a "basic architectural unit" and a design environment which is composed of multiple units. Different levels of detail will be added to the unit as the design process continues. Secondly, a related computer program called BAU is introduced, which demonstrates that a computer is a meaningful tool for helping the architect to investigate the consequence of a design problem. Thirdly, both the domain expert's and the knowledge engineer's experiences during the development of BAU are described. Finally, the future direction of this research will be discussed.

Introduction

The notion of anonymous architecture (Moholy-Nagy 57) together with the concept of self-organizing processes (Alexander 79) as basic phenomena in architecture have changed the perception of architecture in the 20th century in a rather unobtrusive yet very fundamental way. A further expansion of these basic notions took place when the observation of basic types, and the consequent development of typology, were introduced into the field of anonymous architecture. Together, self organization and typology form powerful concepts for the understanding of human habitat and its settlement patterns as well as the generic processes of both phenomena.

The idea of a small, low key research test project, relating to anonymous architecture came into existence during a chance meeting of a group of people involved in CAAD. A suggestion that concepts developed in AI techniques may be useful for exploring aspects of anonymous architecture guided us in the initial formulation of this research project. It was assumed that similar to cells in a living organism, basic units could be defined in anonymous architecture which again like cells in an organism form clusters or aggregations of larger functional entities such as a house or habitat (Alexander 77, Steadman 79).

Starting with this notion, we defined for our own work a "basic architectural unit" in the form of a cube, since the cube is both in quantitative as well as qualitative terms highly defined and relates well to the CAD environment. In addition to this, the total number of units[1] in an aggregation, their functions - or attributes, as well as the environment (as a geometrically structured field) were defined. Following the definition of basic conditions, a process was set in motion which can be seen either as a design process based on AI methodologies or as a simulation of a process leading to a typologically defined "population" of aggregates (comparable to the habitations we find in ecological niches, such as islands or mountain valleys).

If the goals set out at its inception (described above) are pursued to their logical conclusion, this project will provide additional insight into the nature of self-regulating processes in architecture. It will provide a better understanding of the processes which generate the human habitat. Furthermore it will inform us about contemporary housing problems in developing nations since they can not be seen in the framework of a traditional projects environment. In an "architecture without architects" (Rudofsky 88) the principles of "classical" or "formal" architectural design do not apply. Finally, it can be expected that the project will provide new insights into the nature of possible CAAD application in an area which does not compete with the architectural profession but rather fills a gap where architecture is needed but the architect can not be afforded.

It is quite clear that there are no easy solutions. Yet we believe that this modest research project points in a direction in which, up to now, very little intellectual energy has been applied. The computer with its power of simulation could make substantial contributions in this area. Additionally, this project could show us a new direction in design education where, until now, only the area of "Architettura Maggiore[2]" has been addressed. "Architettura Minore" or Anonymous Architecture is the kind of architecture that concerns the majority of the urban population in developing nations today.

Methodology

Although design has been classified as a complex human activity, it is only recently that concepts and methods for capturing, organizing, and using design expertise have emerged from research in artificial intelligence and cognitive psychology. To generate new insights into the design process, this research incorporates *knowledge engineering* techniques (Rychener 88) to investigate the architectural design process. The primary purpose of this study is to explore the incremental complexity within a design process, the secondary purpose to specify the knowledge that the architect used for solving a design problem and the utilization of that knowledge in a design system (Hayes 83). BAU is a computer-aided design system which has been developed for these purposes.

Design has been modelled within the framework of a general theory of problem-solving[3] (Newell 72). Several prescriptive models related to *design computation* have been proposed, such as, *near decomposable hierarchical systems* (Simon 69), *design model of functional reasoning* (Freeman 71), *generative systems* (Mitchell 77), *general design theory* (Yoshikawa 87), and *prototype refinement* (Gero 88). According to these approaches, design problem-solving can be characterized as a process of searching through alternative states of the representation in order to discover states that satisfy specified criteria. BAU is related to the idea of design problem-solving (Kalay 85). The development of BAU is aimed at defining a proper knowledge representation with which to manipulate the process of transforming a design problem into solutions.

This research is also related to *shape grammars* (Stiny 80), and *space synthesis systems* (Eastman 75), however, this research will only be described according to the knowledge engineering paradigm. In this section, we introduce the basic architectural design object, and our methodology for controlling and investigating the design process within the BAU design environment.

The Basic Architectural Units

We defined a "basic architectural unit" as a cube that is initially 3 x 3 x 3 meters. A unit is a conceptual building module. The four vertical faces of the defined cube can be thought of as four walls, the bottom face as the base, and the top face as the roof of a building module. The allowable combinations of the units are governed by a set of geometric cubic relationships and design rules defined by the domain expert. As the levels of abstraction increase, the variations generated by the units becomes an extremely large set of design alternatives, too numerous for a human designer using traditional methods to produce. BAU has been developed in order to assist the architect in the selection of satisfactory alternatives based on the design rules he defines, and to help him control the incremental complexity of the design process. The design process incorporated in BAU is a reflection of the domain expert's preferences. BAU is developed as a *rule-based design system* (McDermott 80). The development of BAU incorporates the following three alternate processes:

1. Possible design alternatives are generated, based on the knowledge available about the current unit.
2. The domain expert's design rules are applied to the generated alternatives, and only those solutions, which comply to the rule are retained.
3. The unit is redefined as a more sophisticated unit for the next generation.

In the first phase, BAU generates configurations of basic units according to geometric relationships which allow units to be located, removed, or replaced within the design environment. At higher levels of development, the allowable combinations of units are governed by sets of design rules defined by the domain expert. Detailed operations are described in the following sections.

BAU: System Overview

To examine the complexities within a design process, we should discuss at least two basic phenomena of design: *design process* and *design object* (Simon 75). An architectural design process involves the transformation of one physical situation to another, which is a large sequence of smaller design processes. The sequence could conceivably never be complete. The efforts of these transformations focus on the "design object", which is the result of the design process.

Broadly speaking, BAU has been developed as a *top-down refinement* paradigm. Since the problem space generated by BAU is large and complex, it has to be decomposed into pieces or subproblems which are small enough to solve. Solutions to subproblems have to be integrated into an overall solution. The idea of top-down refinement is to start with the highly abstract initial problem specifications and to refine them by adding details and by decomposing them to the point at which primitive operators are available to complete all of the subtasks that are required (Dixon 89). However, because *generate-and-test* cycles are also necessary for each intermediate subtask, *bottom-up composition* is incorporated at the local level of the BAU process.

The design process of BAU can be considered as a state-space search process in which the designer attempts to locate satisfactory choices within an extremely large set of design alternatives. A hierarchy is established at the uppermost level and the general functional requirements for the design units are stated. The abstract refinement process is pre-compiled into a standard structure of parameterized components, and the design process consists of reasoning about constraints in order to determine appropriate parameter values.

Development of BAU

BAU involves a whole sequence of generate-and-test cycles. The first process generates certain design objects that are candidate solutions or components of solutions. The second process tests whether or not a given candidate satisfies a design constraint. In such a generate-and test process, the design is assembled component by component. Each generated component is added to the previous assembly and the new structure then tested.

BAU contains four subtasks, BAU.I, BAU.II, BAU.III, and BAU.IV. BAU.I designs two-dimensional configurations for BAU. BAU.II extends a unit into a three-dimensional unit which contains wall elements, slanted roofs and interior level changes. BAU.III introduces modularized elements to the units and associated construction rules to the environment BAU.IV constructs four bau-houses in a small housing cluster. The following describes what each of BAU's subtasks involves.

Subtask I (BAU.I)

We begin by positioning the units on a plane. The chosen environment (building site) for this study, in order to be compatible with the concept of the "basic architectural units", is a 3 by 3 square grid, with each square measuring three meters by three meters (Figure 1.A).

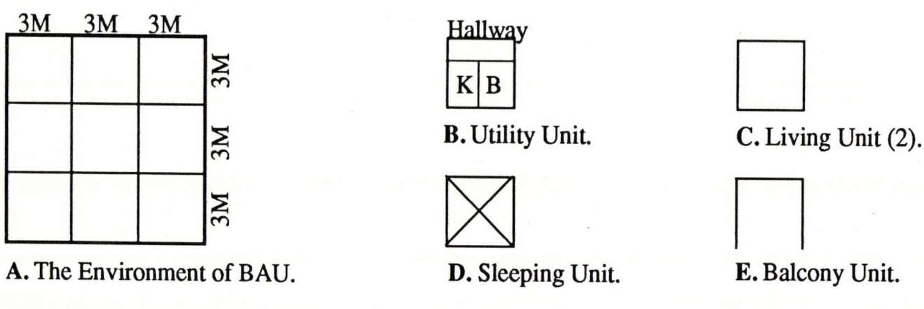

Figure 1. The Basic Architectural Units and their environment.

The unit is only considered as a two dimensional square in BAU.I. Four types of functional units, each three meters square, are chosen: a utility unit, consisting of a kitchen, bathroom, and hallway, represented by the U-Unit shown in Figure 1.B, a living unit, a sleeping unit, and a balcony unit, represented by the L-, S-, and B-Units in Figure 1. C-E respectively. There are eight possible U-Unit configurations, which can be obtained by rotating the standard U-Unit and its symmetric equivalent in ninety degrees increments. (Correspondingly, there are four possible B-Unit configurations.) The design task is to locate one U-Unit, S-Unit, and B-Unit, and two L-Units in the 3 by 3 grid.

Table 1. Rules for describing the BAU environment.

Rule BE-1:
Each unit must be located exactly on a single cell of the 3 by 3 grid

Rule BE-2:
Two connected units must share an edge.

Rule BE-3:
All units must be connected.

The relationships between the units and their environment are governed by the three fundamental rules described in Table 1. Rule BE-1 and BE-2 confine the search space of BAU into a manageable size. Rule BE-3 imposes a basic formation on the house as a response to changing weather. Based on these three BE rules, the architect develops more sophisticated two-dimensional design rules for BAU.I. The design rules of BAU.I are classified into three categories. There are rules for internal connections, external orientations, and ranking.

Rules for Internal Connections

The first category of design rules is "rules for internal connections", which specify the functional relations between units. Table 2 lists seven rules for internal connections. The sequence of these rules is determined by first the simplest units (L-Units), in order to reduce the search space of BAU.I. Rule IC-1, IC-2, and IC-3 specify spatial relations between units. The architect's contention is that a hallway between the living units and the sleeping unit necessary for a house is the basis for Rule IC-4 and IC-5. Rule IC-6 and Rule IC-7 are imposed by the definition of the B-Unit.

Table 2. Rules for internal connections.

Rule IC-1:
The two L-Units have to be connected.

Rule IC-2:
The B-Unit has to be next to an L-Unit.

Rule IC-3:
The kitchen has to be next to an L-Unit.

Rule IC-4:
The hallway has to be next to the S-Unit.

Rule IC-5:
The hallway has to be next to an L-Unit.

Rule IC-6:
The openning of the B-Unit should not be connected to an L-Unit.

Rule IC-7:
The openning of the B-Unit should not be connected with an S-Unit or a U-Unit.

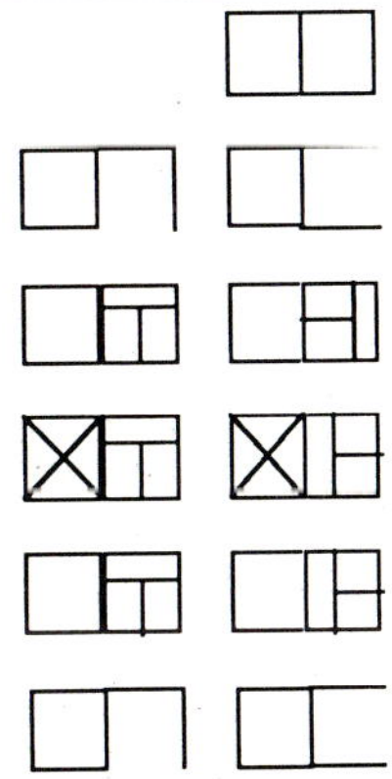

Rules for External Orientations

The second category of design rules for BAU.I, "rules for external orientation", are listed in Table 3. These two rules specify the possible orientations of the balcony. The architect's reason for Rule EO-1 is that a balcony facing north cannot get any sunlight in winter. Rule EO-2 is based on the idea that proper orientation of the balcony will reduce undesirable noise from the street.

Table 3. Rules for external orientations.

Rule EO-1: The opening of the B-Unit should not face to north.	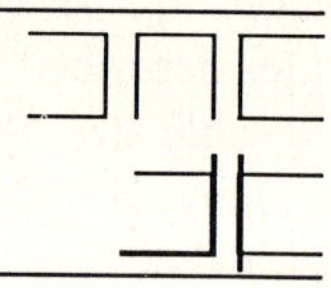
Rule EO-2: The opening of the B-Unit should not face the street.	

Ranking Rule of BAU.I

BAU.I produces a number of solutions. The development of ranking rules enables the architect to judge these configurations based on his own criteria. One of the ranking rules is shown in Table 4. Instead of specifying what should or should not be, this rule describes what would be better. This rule has been translated into a set of ranking values shown at the right side of Table 4. The program sums up the ranking values of empty cells, a configuration with a higher score indicates it is more proper according to the architect's criteria. The score ranges from 7 to 11. Moreover, multiple ranking rules could be applied to BAU, and optimal solutions could be found based on the architect's preferences (weighting factors and objective functions) for each ranking rule. However, as we do not intend to investigate the problem of optimization in design, we'll leave the problem at this point. At the consecutive stages of BAU, different levels of detail will be added to the units based on the results of BAU.I.

Table 4. Ranking rule of BAU.I.

Rule RK-1:
Locating garden at the south of site will be better.

2	1	2
2	2	2
3	3	3

Results of BAU.I

A tic-tac-toc like algorithm is applied to produce the first set of configurations based on the BE Rules. The total number of this set of configurations is 49. Figure 2 illustrates 14 representative configurations.

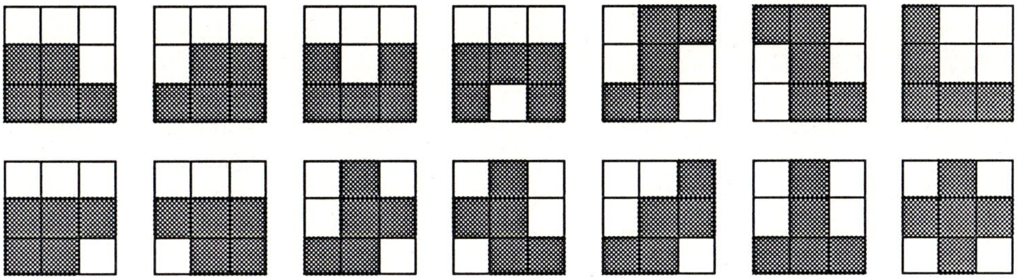

Figure 2. 14 representative configurations generated by the BE rules.

A *significant configuration* is a combination of five units, representing the four functional units and the B-Unit, located on the 3 x 3 grid according to the internal-connection and external-orientation rules that were specified by the domain expert. BAU.1 generates 216 significant configurations, the first 72 of them are shown in Figure 3. Part of the results of Rule RK-1 are shown in Figure 4. The configurations at the top of the figure, which have a higher score (11), are ranked higher than the configurations at the bottom.

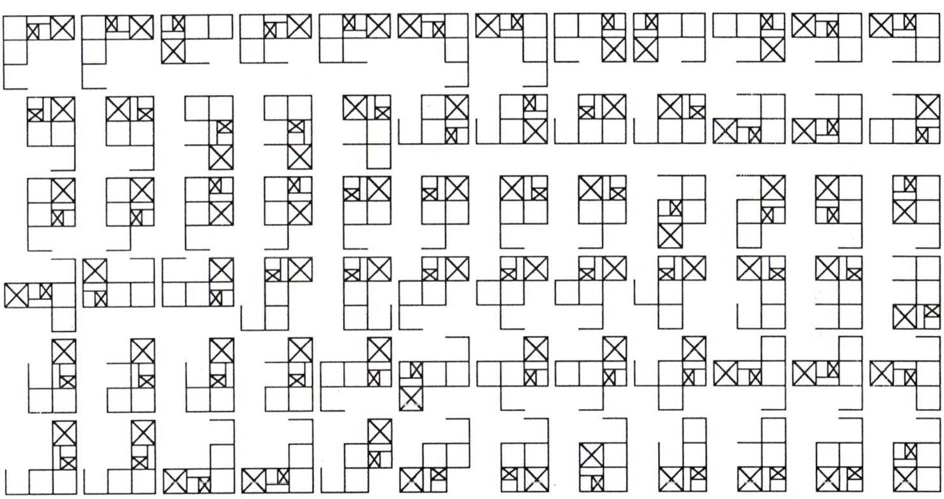

Figure 3. 72 of 216 significant configurations generated by BAU.I.

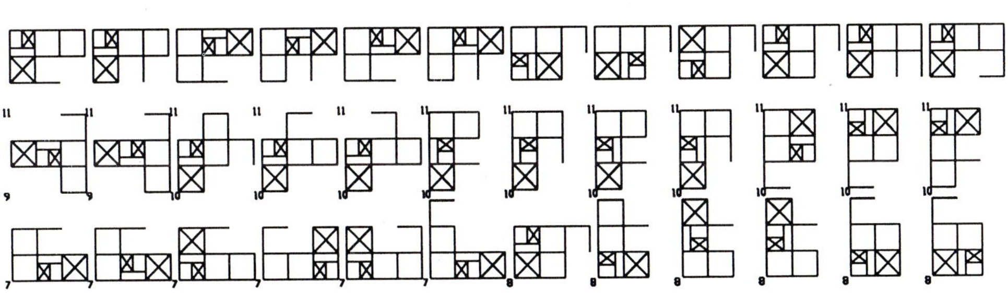

Figure 4. 36 of 216 ranked configurations based on Rule RK-1.

Subtask II (BAU.II)

The next step, once an effective method of generating significant two-dimensional configurations had been developed, was to establish another set of design rules which would allow us to explore the significant configurations in three dimensions. In BAU.II, the unit is extended into a three dimensional cube. The interior level changes and slanted roofs are introduced to define a second type of unit, which is shown in Figure 5.

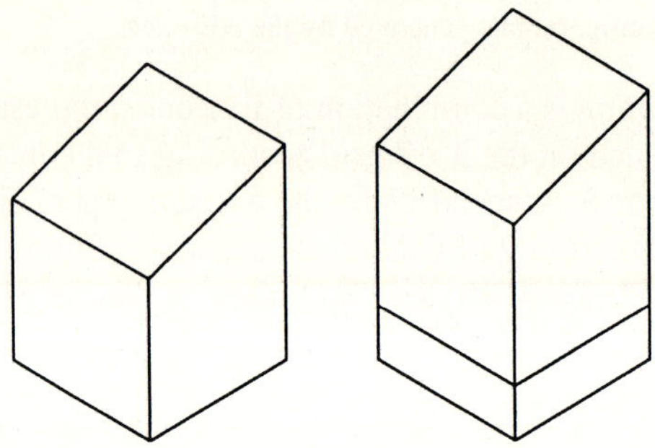

Figure 5. Second type of basic architectural unit.

There are eight possible configurations for this set of units, which can be obtained by rotating the standard unit by ninety degree increments and shifting between the interior level changes of one meter and none. The interior level changes make the interior space and the design problems for BAU more interesting.

Rules of BAU.II

The complexities of a unit increase dramatically when the design tasks move from a two-dimensional plane to three-dimensional space. There are a few important repercussions resulting from the transformation into 3D. First, the problem space BAU encounters becomes extremely large. Each single significant configuration of BAU.I has 1024 (4^5) alternatives for roof combinations. Secondly, we are able to discuss the semantic level of the design problem, e.g., the visual impact of the design, which is no longer restricted to a syntactic level. Thirdly, the rules for satisfactory combinations of roofs are much more difficult to describe and to derive, and translation of the design rules into computer code becomes more complicated. These issues also suggest that design in the third dimension is one of the most significant aspects of architectural design. These implications are explored in the following subsections.

This set of rules is based on the need to provide satisfactory water run-off between roofs and visual appearance. These rules are not easy to describe. During the *knowledge acquisition* of BAU.II, the domain expert (Prof. Herbert Kramel) drew these rules graphically in order to explain his ideas to the knowledge engineer (Chen-Cheng Chen). To make the rules more comprehensible, a notation about the second type of unit is provided at the top of Table 5.

Table 5. Design rules for roofs.

Notations of 2nd type of bau.

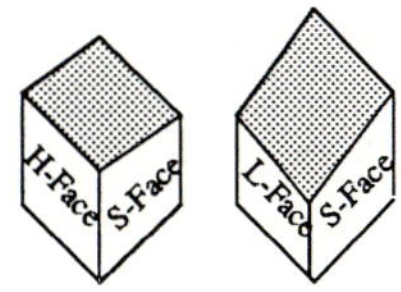

Rule RF-1:
If two units are adjacent, then the L-Face of one unit should not attach to the L-Face or S-Face of another unit.

Rule RF-2:
If three units are in a row, then the L-Face of the middle unit should not attach to the H-Face of another unit, and the H-Face of the middle unit should not attach to a L-Face of the other unit.

Rule RF-3:
If two units are adjacent and one unit's L-Face is attached to another unit's H-Face, then the first unit should be raised 1 meter.

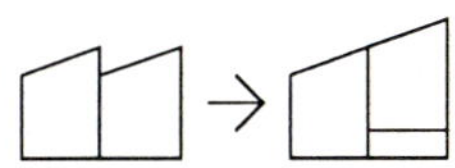

Rule RF-4:
If two adjacent roofs have the same height, then they should share either an H-Face or an S-Face.

Results of BAU.II

After the completion of the cycle related to Rule RF-3, each single significant configuration of BAU.I has about 100 to 200 alternatives for roof combinations. Partial results of Rule RF-3 are shown in Figure 6.

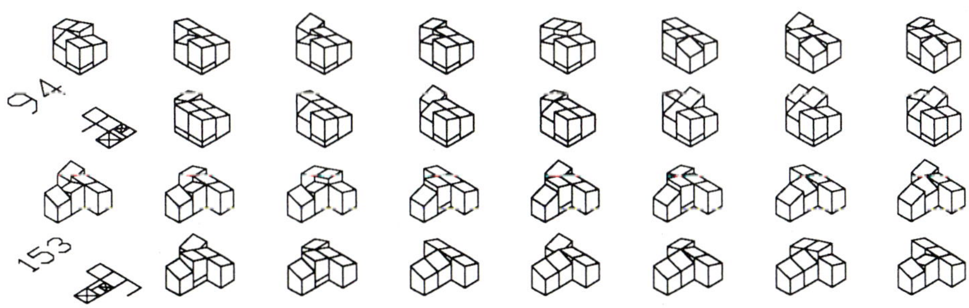

Figure 6. Partial results generated by Rule RF-3.

Although Rule RF-4 is stated quite succinctly, it was the most complex and difficult rule to translate from the domain expert to the knowledge engineer and then to the machine. The architect knew what represented satisfactory and unsatisfactory roof combinations, but had trouble distilling a complete rule to describe his criteria. We worked a couple of weeks to solve this problem, and to derive Rule RF-4.

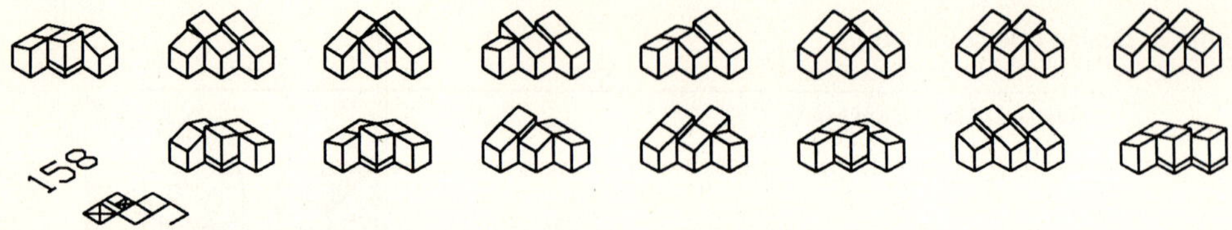

Figure 7. Results of configuration No. 158 generated by Rule RF-4.

In Figure 7, only 15 significant roof combinations are generated out of 1024 possible combinations. The architect could contrast these results with the two dimensional configuration produced in BAU.I (lower-left configuration in Figure 7) to derive the next level of design logic. The research, however, has not continued to this level. This problem will be investigated in our future research.

Subtask III (BAU.III)

The third type of unit is extended into a more complicated and comprehensive building unit, which has different types of windows, interior walls, exterior walls, base, columns, and roofs, depending on the different functional types of the units. One of these unit types is shown in Figure 8.

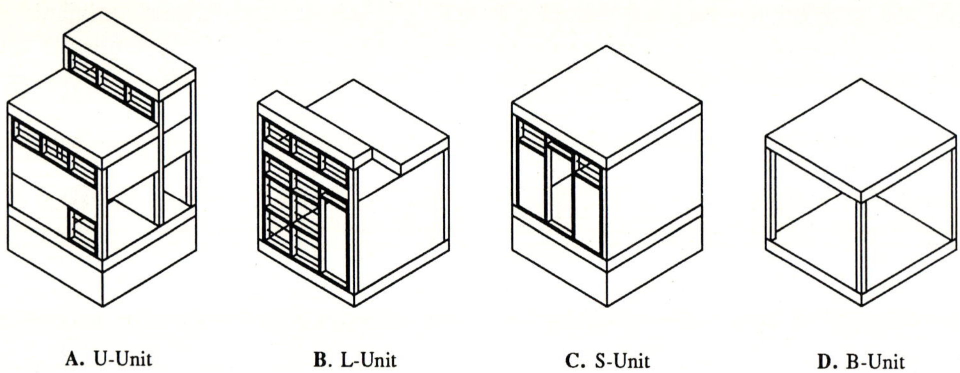

Figure 8. Third type of basic architectural unit.

The major difference between BAU.II and BAU.III is that the units have been pre-compiled into a set of parametric objects in BAU.III. The primary effort of BAU.III is focused on first parameterizing the units, then reasoning about the relations among different parameters of the units. Since the third type of unit contains more building components, the parametric objects are pre-stored in a graphical database. BAU.III generates a descriptions of bau-houses based on the relationships between units defined by the architect. The generated description activates some parameters of the component units and produces results, which can also be used for the structural analysis, cost analysis, and the prediction of energy consumption or for further design analysis.

Rules of BAU.III

Rules for BAU.III address the relationships between adjacent walls. The design decisions are based on the internal circulation and the locations of windows, doors, and interior walls.

Table 6. Design rules for adjacent walls.

Rule AW-1: Two adjacent L-Units have to share an S-Face.
Rule AW-2: U-Unit has to share an S-Face with an L-Unit
Rule AW-3: The opening of the S-Unit should be across from the face attached to the U-Unit.

Results of BAU.III

For each significant configuration of BAU.I, 1 or 2 three-dimensional combinations are generated by BAU.III. In the first phase of BAU.III, we were interested in developing different types of roofs and skylights. Figure 9 presents part of the generated results.

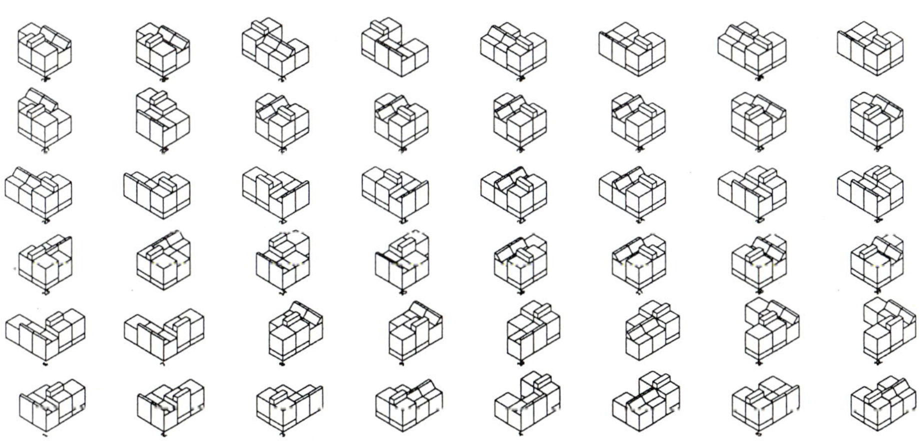

Figure 9. Partial results generated by BAU.III.

In the second phase of BAU.III, detailed information is added, e.g., columns, beams, stairs, doors, and windows. Figure 10 presents four representative combinations.

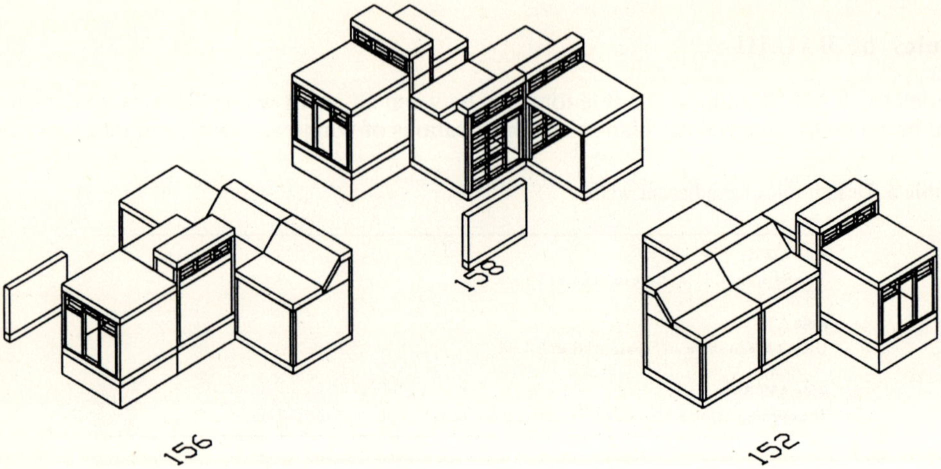

Figure 10. Detailed bau-house samples generated by BAU.III.

Different Levels of Abstraction

We have shown the sequence of how a basic unit is transformed from a two-dimensional square into a three-dimensional building object, and the compositions of different levels of units in the design environment. Although the units have been compiled into a complicated building block, different levels of information about each unit have been stored in different layers during the design objects compilation. This information is available to the architect, and it allows the architect to examine the design object taking advantage of various levels of abstraction.

Current Development of BAU (BAU.IV)

Our current research interest is the investigating of the concept of "a basic architectural unit" in a larger scale design environment. The design environment of BAU.IV is defined as a 9 by 9 grid, and the design task is to locate four generated bau-houses on the grid. This extension emphasizes the relations among multiple bau-houses. In addition, new design elements are introduced, e.g., compound walls, trees, streets, street lamps, fountains, etc. The development of BAU.IV enables us to re-examine the potentials and limitations of our methodology. Retrieval and combinations of bau-houses are the most crucial parts of this stage of work.

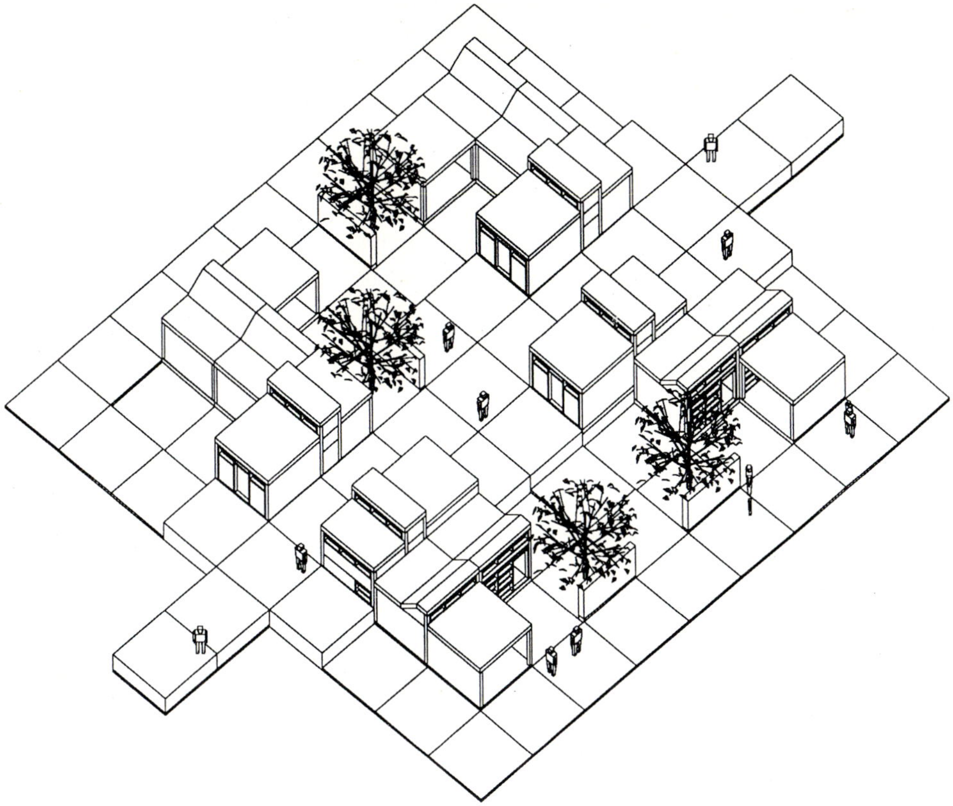

Figure 11. Current development of BAU.IV.

Since BAU.IV is still under development, only partial results of BAU.IV are presented in this paper. Figure 11 shows a bau-cluster generated by BAU.IV.

Experiences Related to BAU

The present section discusses our experiences in the development of BAU. Knowledge representation, control strategies, programming hardware and software, and the project history of BAU are addressed.

Knowledge Representation

The units and their relationships which comprise the design environment are defined explicitly and can therefore be translated easily into descriptions which a computer can manipulate. Two types of information are important for BAU. In order to express the information about the units at different levels and the relationships between the units, a declarative form of representation is necessary. Additionally, a uniform representation for symbolic and graphical representation is an important issue. *List* representation is selected because of its flexibilities in knowledge representation.

Each configuration of BAU is represented as a list containing nine elements. The first element of a bau-list occupies the south-west corner of the environment, and the last element of a bau-list occupies the north-east corner of the environment. At the primitive level, each element of the bau-list contains a binary number, 0 or 1, "0" indicates an empty cell and "1" indicates an occupied cell. As the process continues, each element which is "1" in the bau-list is replaced by the symbol "B", "L", "S", or "U" to indicate that the occupied cell has been replaced by a functional unit. In the later refinement process, each symbol can be extended into a more complicated sub-list which contains more information about the unit.

Table 7. Knowledge representation of the basic architectural unit.

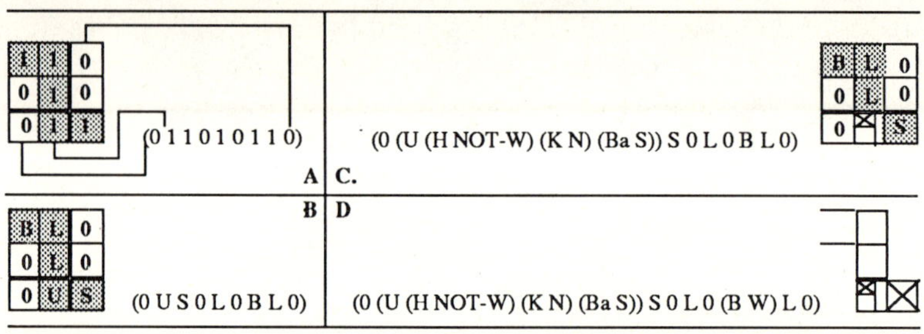

Table 7 presents the manipulation of a bau-list during a BAU.I cycle, for a two-dimensional configuration. The graphical routines read in the bau-list and display the graphical results on the screen (Table 7.D). The same concept of list representation can be extended to the third dimension, information about roofs, and columns, etc, is added to each sub-list. The knowledge representation of BAU also imposes rules about how an abstract design element can be converted into a real building entity and visualized.

Control Strategy

BAU separates knowledge according to the way it is to be processed. Two sorts of knowledge are retained: knowledge for generation and knowledge for testing. Both types of knowledge can be expressed by rules: constructive and restrictive rules, corresponding to generators and filters (Takala 87). The first kind of knowledge is important for maintaining and handling the additional information as the levels of detail increase. The second kind contains the heuristics of the domain expert. The distinction between these two types of knowledge is similar to the distinction between the working memory and production memory elements of a production system[4]. A generate-and-test method is applied to generate the new working memory element and then to test it against the production memory. It is, however, uneconomical to use an exhaustive method to generate the problem space, especially when each problem state contains not just a single symbol. To avoid an exhaustive generate-and-test process, a more efficient search for the significant results is obtained by imposing constraints on the intermediate stages as they are generated. The application of constraints is the most significant part of this project.

Problem Space and Solution Sets

Although it is hard to estimate how much information an architect should maintain within a design process and how complex a design problem is, the systematic investigation of BAU may allow us to examine these problems based on the generated problem space and derived solution set.

The possible problem space[5] of BAU.I is ((9! / (5! x 4!)) x (5! / 2) x 8 x 4), (= 241,920). The number of acceptable solutions for BAU.I (according to the rules defined by the domain expert) is 216, the acceptable solutions represent a percentage of 0.089% (1 / 1,120). The possible problem space of BAU.II and BAU.III is (241,920 x 4^5 x 2), (= 495,452,360). The number of acceptable solutions for BAU.II is 5,765, representing a percentage of 0.00116% (1 / 85,941.43). The number of acceptable solutions for BAU.III is 270, which is 0.0000055% (1 / 1835008.74). It is surprising that an architect can find a design solution in such a huge problem space, and how quickly the constraints prune down the search tree into a manipulable size.

Table 8. Problem space generated by BAU.1.

Rules	No. of Solutions	Rules	No. of Solutions
Rule-BE-1	C (9,5) = 126	Rule-IC-4	608
Rule-BE-2	102	Rule-IC-5	224
Rule-BE-3	49	*B-Unit is assigned.*	224 x 4 = 896
Units are assigned.	49 x (5! / 2) = 2940	Rule-IC-6	896 x (3 / 4) = 672
Rule-IC-1	1272	Rule-IC-7	592
Rule-IC-2	840	Rule-E0-1	444
U-Unit is assigned.	840 x 8 = 6720	Rule-EO-2	216
Rule-IC-3	2048	Rule-RK-1	216

Software and Hardware

Before BAU was developed, it would have been difficult to estimate accurately the problem space and the proper knowledge representation. There is a trade-off between using a procedural language (C Programming Language) and a declarative language (LISP), the former has its advantages in terms of computational efficiency and the latter is good because of its flexibility in knowledge representation. Since incremental complexity is the most significant factor in our problem, LISP was chosen.

The design kit for BAU was first developed using COMMONLISP. AutoCAD and AutoLISP, the computer graphics software system currently being used for the second phase of our development, enable the programmer to define instances, create modules by combining transformed instances, and display the results in two or three dimensions. BAU runs on both IBM RT and SUN4 workstations, under the UNIX operating system. The results of BAU.IV are sent to a special 3D graphics program called STALKER written with the GL graphics library for Silicon Graphics Workstations. This allows the architect to study the volume, material, and color of bau-houses, and to "walk through" the building site in real time.

Project History

We started the discussion of this project in March 1990. Since then, we have had weekly meetings between the domain expert and knowledge engineer. Each meeting lasted about one hour. During the meetings, the domain expert drew his ideas on paper, and explained his ideas to the knowledge engineer. After the meetings, the knowledge engineer tried to translate the domain expert's ideas first into rules, and then into computer code. Each subsystem of BAU took approximately two to three months to develop.

An earlier project (Rogers 78) had first addressed some issues relevant to this project. Two major conceptual problems in the approach taken earlier were (1) generation of the problem space, and (2) acquisition, formalization, and integration of domain knowledge.

Conclusions

BAU has proven that the computer is a meaningful tool for investigating design problems which can be specified by well-defined objectives operating on pre-determined variables or features. Through the development of BAU, the design process becomes directly accessible for detailed examination. It also suggests that there could be a possibility for architectural education to incorporate systematic research-based theory and technique within the studio system. Research and education are linked by an exchange in which the researcher offers theories and techniques applicable to practical problems; and the educational environment, in return, offers researchers new problems as well as practical tests of research results. There are several important lessons that we have learned from BAU:

1. There are some areas of architectural design, in which problems could be clearly defined, goals could be relatively fixed, and phenomena lend themselves to the categories of available theory and techniques.
2. The design requirements for solutions can be expressed by some combination of constraints (design rules) and criteria (design goal). In this case, the design problem-solving process can be viewed as a state-space search process.
3. In design, an exhaustive search can be avoided through a proper ordering of constraints. This is an important factor of design expertise.
4. Through the study of the architect's problem solving behavior, the acquired design model and strategies can be used in automating part of the design process.

There are several questions that remain unanswered in this research: How does a designer accept a design solution in such a large problem space? How can a designer turn a mediocre design scheme into a good design solution? How does a designer structure his design problem before he starts his design problem solving? What are the differences between experts and novices (students) in solving this type of design problem? How does a novice learn design? How does one develop a general design tool for this type of design tasks? These questions are interesting and probably could be examined by incorporating BAU with cognitive psychology studies of design.

There are several possible directions for our future work with BAU. Aside from combining several bau-houses in a larger environment, the indexing and retrieval of existing results of BAU is important. Additionally, we'll introduce 2 by 4 standard wooden structures into the BAU system, to investigate BAU at more detailed levels. Moreover, as part of the techniques of system architecture, computer-aided manufacturing can be incorporated into BAU.

The final consideration is how to extend the acquired experiences of BAU to other design problems. In this regard, two problems should be addressed: First, given a design problem, the issue arises of utilizing solutions of previous problems which are known to be similar to the current problem. Secondly, once a solution for a specific design problem has been found, the question of how to apply and process this knowledge to a class of similar design problems appears (Mostow 85). *Analogical* and *inductive reasoning* are suggested respectively for these two problems in our future research of knowledge acquisition and machine learning in BAU.

The results of this investigation demonstrate some of the possibilities offered by computers for exploring more fully the consequences of design decisions. We anticipate that BAU can be augmented to address new research issues in the incorporation of knowledge-based design systems in architecture, computer-aided architectural manufacturing, and robotic task planning.

Acknowledgements

We wish to express our sincere thanks to Prof. Gerhard Schmitt, Bharat Dave, Sharon Refvem, and Shen-Guan Shih for their recommendations during the development of BAU. This research is supported by the Department of Architecture, at the Swiss Federal Institute of Technology.

References

Alexander, C., S. Ishikawa, and M. Silverstein. 1977. *A Pattern Language*. New York: Oxford University Press.

Alexander, Christopher. 1979. *Notes on the Synthesis of Form*. Cambridge: Harvard University Press.

Dixon, John R. 1989. "On Research Methodology Toward A Scientific Theory of Engineering Design." In S. Newsome, W. R. Spillers, and S. Finger (eds). *Design Theory '88*. New York: Springer-Verlag.

Eastman, Charles M. 1975. *Spatial Synthesis in Computer-Aided Building Design*. London: Applied Science Publishers.

Freeman P., and A. Newell. 1971. "A model for Functional Reasoning in Design". In *Proceedings of the Second International Joint Computer Conference on Artificial Intelligence*. British Computer Society, London.

Gero, J., M.L. Maher, and W.G. Zhang. 1988. *Chunking Structural Design Knowledge as Prototypes*. The Architectural Computing Unit. Department of Architectural Science. University of Sydney, Sydney.

Hayes-Roth, F., D. A. Waterman, and D. B. Lenat. 1983. *Building Expert Systems*. Reading: Addison-Wesley Publishing Company.

Kalay, Yehuda E. 1985. "Redefining the Role of Computers in Architecture: from Drafting/Modelling Tools to Knowledge-Based Design Assistants". *Computer Aided Desig*, vol. 17, no. 7, September.

McDermott, J. 1980. *R1: A Rule-Based Configurer of Computer Systems*. Tech. Rept. CMU-CS-80-119, Department of Computer Science, Carnegie-Mellon University, Pittsburgh.

Mitchell, William J. 1977. *Computer-Aided Architectural Design*. New York: Petrocelli/Charter.

Moholy-Nagy, Sibyl. 1957. *Native Genius in Anonymous Architecture*. New York: Horizon Press.

Mostow, Jack. 1985. "Toward Better Models of the Design Process." *The AI Magazine*, Spring.

Newell Alan, and Herbert A. Simon. 1972. *Human Problem Solving*. New Jersey: Prentice-Hall, Inc.

Rogers, Gary. 1978. *BAU/2*. Technical Report. Department of Architecture, Swiss Federal Institute of Technology, Zürich.

Rudofsky, Bernard. 1988. *Architecture without Architects: A Short Introduction to Non-Pedigreed Architecture*. NM: University of New Mexico Press.

Rychener, Michael (ed). 1988. *Expert Systems for Engineering Design*. New York: Academic Press.

Simon, Herbert A. 1969. *The Sciences of the Artificial*. Cambridge: The MIT Press.

Simon, Herbert A. 1975. "Style in Design". In Eastman, Charles M. (ed). *Spatial Synthesis in Computer-Aided Building Design*. London: Applied Science Publishers.

Stiny, George. 1980. "*Introduction to Shape and Shape Grammars*." Environment and Planning B7:343-351.

Steadman, J. P. 1979. *The Evolution of Designs: Biological Analogy in Architecture and the Applied Arts*. Cambridge: Cambridge University Press.

Takala, Tapio. 1987. "Theoretical Framework for Computer Aided Innovative Design." In Yoshikawa, H. and Warman, E. A. (eds). *Design Theory for CAD*. Amsterdam: North-Holland.

Yoshikawa, Hiroyuki. 1987. "General Design Theory and Artificial Intelligence". In T. Bernold (ed). *Artificial Intelligence in Manufacturing*. Amsterdam: North-Holland.

---

1 From now on, we will use "unit" to indicate the "basic architectural unit".

2 The term is used here as employed by Stanislaus Von Moss in 1964.

3 Problem-solving is a process in which one starts from an initial state and proceeds to search through problem space in order to identify the sequence of operations or actions that will lead to a desired goal.

4 A production system is a database of production rules and some control mechanism that selects applicable production rules to reach some goal states.

5 All the possible states that could occur as a result of intersections between the elements and operators within a problem-solving process.

22 Reading Architectural Plans: A Computable Model

Sally McLaughlin

Department of Architectural and Design Science
University of Sydney
NSW 2006, Australia

A fundamental aspect of the expertise of the architectural designer is the ability to assess the quality of existing and developing proposals from schematic representations such as plans, elevations and sections. In this paper I present a computable model of those aspects of the evaluation of architectural floor plans that I believe to be amenable to rule-like formulation. The objective behind the development of this model is twofold: 1) to articulate a belief about the role of simple symbolic representations in the task of evaluation, a task which relies primarily on uniquely human capabilities; and 2) to explore the possible uses of such representations in the development of design expertise.

Input to the model consists of a specification of a design proposal in terms of walls, doors, windows, openings and spaces together with a specification of the context in which the proposal has been developed. Information about context is used to retrieve the goal packages relevant to the evaluation of the proposal. The goal packages encode information about requirements such as circulation, visual privacy and thermal performance. Generic associations between aspects of a plan and individual goals are used to establish if and how each of the goals have been achieved in the given proposal. These associations formalize relationships between aspects of the topology of the artefact, such as the existence of a door between two rooms, and a goal, in this case the goal of achieving circulation between those two rooms. Output from the model consists of both a graphic representation of the way in which goals are achieved and a list of those goals that have not been achieved. The list of goals not achieved provides a means of accessing appropriate design recommendations. What the model provides is essentially a computational tool for exploring the value judgements made in a particular proposal given a set of predefined requirements such as those to be found in design recommendation literature.

Introduction

A fundamental aspect of the expertise of the architectural designer is the ability to assess the quality of existing and developing proposals. The knowledge intensive nature of this exercise is evident when we consider the nature of the kinds of comments that may be elicited during the course of an examination of a residential floor plan: comments such as "this room will be open and sunny"; "I don't like the relationship between the kitchen and dining room"; or "I don't think having the entry here is going to work"? How is the designer to know that a particular room will be open or sunny? What information allows him to recognize a good or bad relationship between kitchen and dining areas? Finally, how is he able to focus upon particular aspects of the plan and to recognize the contribution that they make to the overall quality of the proposal?

Whilst the ability to perform such evaluations is integrally linked to the designer's ability to create rich, personal simulations of a proposal (Foz 1973), there is a sense in which rule-like expressions may be employed. Consider the following information extracted from a summary of research relating to the quality of planning in family housing (Zeisel and Welch 1981):

When living rooms are used formally by families, they tend to dislike having the main unit entry directly into that formal area. To them it means unnecessarily invading this place in the home.

A number of points may be made in relation to this passage that I believe apply to design recommendation literature in general. First, the passage indicates a particular configuration to be avoided, an entry opening directly into a formal living area, but it is not prescriptive, there are many configurations that would satisfy this requirement. Second, an attempt has been made to convey something of the perspective from which the recommendation is being made, the configuration is disliked because residents feel it allows unnecessary intrusion into formal living areas. This kind of information is important in constructing a perspective from which the rich simulations necessary to the evaluation of an architectural proposal may take place. Finally, the recommendation implicit in the passage should not necessarily be universally applied. The appropriateness and priority given to the considerations expressed have to be assessed in the context of individual proposals, there may be situations where considerations such as a tightly constrained site or the desire to create an immediate feeling of spaciousness upon entering may override the privacy issue.

In this paper I present a symbolic representation of rule-like information extracted in part from design recommendation literature. A computable model is developed that supports the application of these "rules" whilst attempting to respect the nature and limitations of design recommendations as outlined above. The model consists of two components: first, a database of the packages of goals that a designer may bring to bear in the assessment of a proposal in a given context; and second, generic associations between aspects of the plan representation and goals. The objective in developing the model was to apply the rules based on design recommendation literature to individual proposals in such a way as to expose the tradeoffs, the value judgements, that have been made in the course of developing those proposals. In addition, a means of conveniently accessing recommendations so as to fill out the perspective from which the appropriateness of these decisions may be determined, was sought.

Goal Packages

It is well recognized that a designer exploits his knowledge of building types as a basis for proceeding with the development of a design proposal (Foz 1973, Darke 1979, Hillier et al. 1972). Similarly the divisions that occur in design recommendation and design code literature indicate that knowledge of building types is important in the evaluation of design proposals. For example, it is not uncommon for planning information to be organized under categories such as family housing, housing for the elderly, semi-detached housing, home units, office buildings, and buildings for various categories of environmental conditions. In developing a representation of design "rules" based on an interpretation of the design recommendation literature discussed here, I found it useful organize information into sets of constraints indexed under such categories. A group of constraints indexed under a particular context description will be referred to as a goal package. The goal package indexed under the context description *building type = residential, occupants = family* is listed in Table 1. The goal package for the context *goal = optimize_thermal_environment, climate = temperate* is listed in Table 2. The principle advantage of grouping constraints into packages is that it allowed many assumptions about the nature of the artefact to which the constraints would be applied to be made.

```
entry(X)
living(X)
family(X)
dining(X)
# Circulation is required between the entry and the main access to the house. The route will
be used by the residents and both formal and informal visitors. #
goal = circ_reln(X,Y, (residents,formal_visitors,informal_visitors))
   where entry(X) and outdoors(Y) and primary_access_from(Y)
goal = circ_reln(X,Y,residents)
   where outdoors(X) and access_from(X) and
   for all Y where store(Y) and contains(outdoor_equipment,Y)
# Circulation is required between the entry and informal areas. #
goal = circ_reln(X,Y,(residents,informal_visitors))
   where entry(X) and
   for all Y where room(Y) and part_of(zone_informal_living,Y)
goal = circ_reln(X,Y,(residents,formal_visitors,informal_visitors))
   where entry(X) and living(Y)
goal = circ_reln(X,Y, (residents,formal_visitors,informal_visitors))
   where living(X) and dining(Y)
goal = circ_reln(X,Y, (residents,formal_visitors,informal_visitors))
   where bathroom(X) and for all Y where [living(Y) or dining(Y)]
goal = circ_reln(X,Y,residents)
   where bathroom(X) and for all Y where bedroom(Y)
goal = circ_reln(X,Y,residents)
   where laundry(X) and for all Y where outdoors(Y) and
   [ contains(outdoor_clothes_drying,Y) or contains(cleaning_equipment,Y) ]
goal = circ_reln(X,Y,(residents,informal_visitors))
   where kitchen(X) and for all Y where outdoors(Y) and
   [ contains(outdoor_play,Y) or contains(cleaning_equipment,Y) ]
goal = visual_barrier(X,Y)
   where entry(X) and for all Y where room(Y)
goal = visual_barrier(X,Y)
   for all X where store(X) and for all Y where room(Y)
goal = visual_access(X,Y)
   where kitchen(X) and for all Y where outdoors(Y) and contains(outdoor_play,Y)
```

# Informal parts of the house should not be able to be viewed by formal visitors #
goal = visual_barrier(X,Y)
where room(X) and room(Y) and part_of(zone_informal,X)
and for all Y on_circ_path(formal_visitors,Y)
# Normal activities of residents should not be able to be viewed by formal visitors #
goal = visual_barrier(X,Y)
where room(X) and room(Y) and part_of(zone_formal,X) and
for all Y on_circ_path(residents,Y)

Table 1. Goal package for context: building type = residential, occupants = family. This information has been developed primarily by interpreting the recommendations outlined in Zeisel and Welch [1981].

# Minimize heat loss to outdoors and heat gain in summer #
goal = thermal_barrier(X,Y) for all X where room(X) and for all Y where outdoors(Y)
# Minimize heat loss between rooms. #
goal = thermal_barrier(X,Y) for all room(X) and heated (X) and for all room(Y) and !heated(Y)
goal = sunny(X,winter) for all X where room(X) and part_of(zone_living,X)
goal = sunny(X,winter) for all X where bedroom(X)
# not high priority - bedrooms don't need to be as warm as living areas #
goal = not_sunny(X,summer) for all room(X)
goal = wind_barrier(X,Y) for all X where room(X) and for all Y where winter_wind_source(Y)
goal = wind_access(X,Y) for all X where summer_wind_source(X) and direction(Y) and
opposite(X,Y)
goal = construction_type(X,Y) where heavy_weight(Y) or insulated_frame(Y)
for all X where room(X)

Table 2. Goal package for context: goal = optimize_thermal_environment, climate = temperate. Information derived from an interpretation of NSB 21 [1971] *House design for temperate climates.*

part_of(zone_informal_living,X) :- bedroom(X) or kitchen(X) or family(X)
part_of(zone_informal,X) :- bedroom(X) or kitchen(X) or family(X) or laundry(X) or store(X)
part_of(zone_formal,X) :- living(X) or dining(X)
on_circ_path(X,Y) :- variable_member(Proof(circ_reln(A,B,L)),Y) and member(X,L)
part_of(zone_living,X) :- living(X) or family(X) or dining(X) or kitchen(X)
part_of(zone_winter_living,X) :- kitchen(X) or dining(X) or winter_living(X) or winter_family(X)
summer_wind_source(X) :- location = Sydney and [X = NE or X = E]
winter_wind_source(X) :- location = Sydney and [X = NW or X = W or X = SW or X = S]
opaque(X) :- room(X) or wall(X) or door(X)
window(X) :- glazed_window(X)
object(X) :- room(X) or wall(X) or door(X) or window(X)

Table 3. Background knowledge required to interpret goal packages in Tables 1-4. This information is stored in frames.

In this section I wish to consider the relationship between some of the constraints contained in the goal package listed in Table 1 and the design recommendation literature on which they were based. Consider the following extract from Zeisel and Welch [1981] in their summary of research relating to the design of housing for families:

In their home, residents tend to designate separate places for more formal behavior such as entertaining and showing off special furniture or a console TV, and places designated for informal activity such as eating breakfast, children playing, and sitting around when a casual friend drops in. Formal areas may usefully be thought of as "front stage" areas where residents present their "best side" to others; informal areas as "back stage" where residents let down their hair.

The recommendations suggest a need for formal and informal living areas. This is represented in the goal package by proposing that there should be three separate living areas, *living(X), family(X)* and *dining(X)* and by associating individual rooms with the zones *zone_informal, zone_informal_living* and *zone_formal* (see Table 3). The effect of asserting the existence of specific room types within the goal package is that if rooms of these types cannot be found in the design proposal to which the goal package is being applied, a message about the absence of such a room in the proposal will be posted. For example, if the goal package listed in Table 1 were applied to a plan not containing a room of type *living* then the violated constraint *living(X)* together with the appropriate design recommendation would be displayed:

Housing evaluation studies show that many residents prefer to have a living area in their homes that they can use as a "showcase living room" separable from other areas of the dwelling unit, especially where children play.

The effect of associating room types with particular zones is evident when we consider the representation of recommendations such as the following:

The access to living rooms should by-pass dining/den so visitors would not have to pass through a messy all-purpose room.

This recommendation is generalized in the goal package to incorporate the idea that none of the informal parts of the house should be able to be viewed by formal visitors. This objective is represented as follows:

```
goal = visual_barrier(X,Y)
   where room(X) and room(Y) and part_of(zone_informal,X)
   and for all Y on_circ_path(formal_visitors,Y).
```

The predicate *on_circ_path(formal_visitors,X)* (see Table 3) is established by identifying all those rooms that must be passed through by formal visitors in their normal patterns of circulation. The normal patterns of circulation of formal visitors is established by reference to the following constraints:

```
goal = circ_reln(X,Y, (residents,formal_visitors,informal_visitors))
   where entry(X) and outdoors(Y) and primary_access_from(Y)
goal = circ_reln(X,Y,(residents,formal_visitors,informal_visitors))
   where entry(X) and living(Y)
goal = circ_reln(X,Y, (residents,formal_visitors,informal_visitors))
   where living(X) and dining(Y)
goal = circ_reln(X,Y, (residents,formal_visitors,informal_visitors))
   where bathroom(X) and for all Y where [living(Y) or dining(Y)].
```

The first statement represents the fact that circulation is required between the outdoor area that is the principle access to the house and the entry. The second statement conveys the fact that circulation is required between the entry and living room and so on. The effect of defining a *circ_reln* is to specify that two rooms should be fairly close to each other, the goal will not be considered to be achieved if circulation from one room to the next cannot be achieved by passing through only a limited number of rooms. In the examples discussed in this paper this limit will be set to three. Returning to the constraint representing the objective that none of the informal parts of the house should be able to be viewed by formal visitors, this objective will be considered to be violated if there is not a visual barrier between each room associated with zone_informal and any room on the circulation path of formal visitors, i.e. the circulation path between outdoors and entry, entry and living, living and dining and dining/living and a bathroom.

Representation of Artefact and Context Information

An important objective in developing a representational scheme for the floor plans has been to limit the assumptions made about the nature of relevant features at the time of inputting a representation of the artefact. This objective has to be balanced with that of providing a means of supporting simple and unambiguous input. The floor plans employed are represented in terms of walls, doors, windows, openings and spaces. Rooms are a special type of space. Various restrictions are imposed in relation to these entities at the time of input: doors and windows must be inserted into a wall; openings must span from one wall to another; spaces are defined by nominating the walls, doors, windows and openings that bound the space, and these elements must define a closed space. Information about artefacts is stored in frames.

A number of higher level features can be determined from these low level features. For example, the relation next_to(X,Y) can be determined for two spaces X and Y by determining if these spaces share either a door, window, wall or opening. These higher level features are determined as required. Other features may be determined by asking the user to nominate relevant information. Procedures for acquiring additional and higher level features are associated with *if-needed* slots in the relevant frames.

Context information is represented as lists of feature-value pairs. For example, the fact that the building is located in a temperate climate is represented by the feature-value pair *climate = temperate.*

Abstracting Aspects of an Artefact Relevant to the Current Context

In this section I will introduce a set of qualitative associations between the goal predicates used to define the goal packages and the predicates used to describe the topology of a floor plan. The purpose of these associations is to allow the means by which individual goals are achieved within a specific floor plan to be identified. The associations embody knowledge such as the observation that, in the Southern hemisphere, North facing windows create the possibility that a room will be sunny in winter.

The associations are in the form of rules describing the state of the environment that can be achieved given a specific topological configuration and an initial state of the environment.

Rules are selected by working back from the goal specification as follows: first, expanding the goal specification into an initial and final state specification; second, selecting a rule that will reduce the difference between those states; third, attempting to instantiate that rule, identifying the topological features potentially relevant to achieving the goal in the process; and finally determining whether the application of the rule did in fact achieve the final state from the initial state. If the final state has not been achieved an intermediate state is proposed and breadth-first backward chaining is employed.

Before exploring this process in more detail I wish to discuss the nature of the goal specification conversion to an initial and final state, and the form of the rules employed. The information required to convert the goal predicate *circ_reln* into an initial and final state specification is given in Table 4. This information is indexed in a goal conversion table under the index *circ_reln*. The information should be interpreted as the conversion of the requirement that *circulation be provided between spaces X and Y* to a requirement that *if in the initial state there is a person in space X*, that is the circulation pressure in X is positive, *it should be possible to achieve a final state where there is a person in space Y*. While the introduction of the notion of circulation pressure, or *circ_pressure*, is somewhat cumbersome it eliminates the need for recursive rule definitions.

```
Goal:
   circ_reln(X,Y,_)
Conversion:
   Initial_State: eq(circ_pressure(X),+)
   Final_State: eq(circ_pressure(Y),+)

Goal:
   visual_access(X,Y)
Conversion:
   Initial_State: eq(vis_pressure(X),+)
   Final_State: eq(vis_pressure(Y,+)

Goal:
   visual_barrier(X,Y)
Conversion:
   Initial_State: eq(vis_pressure(X),+)
   Final_State: eq(vis_pressure(Y),-)
```

Table 4. Goal conversion for predicates *circ_reln*, *visual_access* and *visual_barrier*.

The form of the rules is derived from that of the rules employed by Forbus [1984] to accomplish qualitative reasoning in the domain of physics. The names of some of the categories have changed and the *influences* section of the original rules has been dropped. The rule connecting the topological feature of adjacent spaces with an opening between them to the facilitation of allowing a person to move from one space to the other is given in Table 5. The first part of the rule, the *individuals* section, specifies the type of the topological features relevant to the rule. In this case variables A and B must be spaces and variable X a door or opening. The second section, the *topological relations* section, specifies the relations between those features that must hold if the rule is to be applied. In this case spaces A and B must be adjacent to each other, and a single door or opening X must be in both spaces. The separation of *individuals* and *topological relations* is necessary for efficient identification of appropriate instantiations of the rule. The topological relations significantly restrict the number of instantiations that need to be considered. The information in the *individuals* section is applied only after potential instantiations have been identified, as a final check on type. The *conditions* section specifies the value of state variables that must exist if the rule is to be applied. In this case the circulation pressure at A must be greater than the circulation pressure at B. This condition is necessary to ensure that rule sequences are constructed in an appropriate order. The *direction* section specifies the way in which the values of state variables will change as a result of the application of the rule. In this case application of the rule will cause a decrease in *circ_pressure* at space A and an increase in *circ_pressure* at space B. In other words, the rule is essentially a simulation of passage from space A to space B. The values 0, + and - are qualitative values: 0 indicates a steady state, + an increase in the value of a variable, and - a decrease in the value of a variable. The rule is indexed in the rule table under the index *circ_pressure*. Each rule is also indexed under a direction predicate. This is to ensure that the construction of a rule sequence proceeds in a single direction.

```
Direction:
   eq(circ_pressure(B),+)                          # circ_pressure(B) increasing #
Rule:
   Individuals:
        space(A)
        space(B)
        door(X) or opening(X)
   Topological Relations:
        next_to(A,B)
        in(A,X)
        in(B,X)
   Conditions:
        gt(circ_pressure(B),circ_pressure(A))      # A > B #
   Direction:
        eq(circ_pressure(A),-)                     # circ_pressure(A) decreasing #
        eq(circ_pressure(B),+)
```

Table 5. Rule indexed under predicate *circ_pressure*.

Some other rules are listed in Table 6. The first relates the presence of windows or openings along a straight line between two spaces to the possibility of visual access between the two spaces. The second relates the presence of an opaque object on a straight line between two spaces to creating a visual barrier between the two spaces.

```
R1
Direction:
   eq(vis_pressure(B),+)
Rule:
   Individuals:
        [space(A)]
        space(B)
        space(C)
        [opening(Xi) window(Xi)]
   Topological Relations:
        next_to(A,C)
        in(C,Xi)
        in(A,Xi)
        straight_line(A,B,all(Xi))          # a straight line must run from A to B through all
the Xi #
   Conditions:
        vis_pressure(A) > vis_pressure(B)
   Direction:
        eq(vis_pressure(B),+))
        eq(vis_pressure(A),-))

R2
Direction:
   eq(vis_pressure(B),-)
Rule:
   Individuals:
        object(X)
        space(A)
        space(B)
   Topological Relations:
        straight_line(A,B,X)
        opaque(X)
   Conditions:
        eq(vis_pressure(A),+)
   Direction
        eq(vis_pressure(B),-)
```

Table 6. Rules indexed under predicate *vis_pressure*.

The rule application algorithm is specified in Table 7. Notable features of this procedure are as follows.

1. A separate goal is set up for each valid instantiation of a *for all* clause. For example, the goal statement:

goal = visual_barrier(X,Y)

where entry(X) and for all Y where room(Y)
applied to the plan represented in Figure 1 would be expanded as follows:
goal = visual_barrier(entry,living)
goal = visual_barrier(entry,dining)
goal = visual_barrier(entry,kitchen) ...

2. Separate goals are temporarily set up for each valid instantiation of the remaining variables. The appropriate instantiation is determined by breadth first search - the first goal achieved is maintained and the rest discarded. For example, the goal statement:
goal = circ_reln(X,bed1,residents) where bathroom(X)
in the context of the plan represented in Figure 1 would be expanded to:
goal = circ_reln(bath1,bed1,residents)
goal = circ_reln(bath2,bed1,residents)
Application of the rules would determine that the goal *circ_reln(bath1,bed1,residents)* could be achieved in a single step, so this goal would be held and the goal *circ_reln (bath2,bed1,residents)* would be dropped.

3. Lists of each potential rule sequence associated with a goal are maintained. When the goal is finally achieved the list of rules that led to the achievement of the goal are stored with the goal. The remaining rule sequences are discarded. As we have already noted search is breadth first so the first rule sequence identified will be that which satisfies the goal in the least number of steps possible.

The rules actually convey very little information. It is the identification of the *individuals* involved and the relations that must exist between these individuals in order for the goal to be achieved that is important. The instantiation of each rule is stored with that rule. Once an appropriate rule sequence has been identified, information as to how the goal has been achieved may be displayed as in Figure 2.

4. Rules are indexed under both predicate and direction. Determination as to an appropriate direction is made by reference to the relation between the required value of a variable in the initial state and the current value of that variable. See Step D'4 of the Rule Application Algorithm.

5. Intermediate states are constructed on the basis of the current value of a variable and the direction of change of that variable associated with the rule applied. See Step 3 of BACK PROPAGATE.

6. It is necessary to constantly monitor the intermediate states being generated in order to ensure that the current rule sequence has not lead to a state that has been achieved by a more efficient means. This is accomplished in Step F1 of the Rule Application Algorithm. Rule sequences that lead to an already identified intermediate state are pruned from the search tree.

7. Topological relations are sorted in INSTANTIATE REMAINING (Step B3) so as to minimize the number of instantiations that need to be investigated.

8. Some predicates may not be specified in the current representation of the plan specification. In this case the user is asked to specify such information (Steps B1 and C2).

9. A limit is placed on the number of rules that can be chained together in order to achieve a goal. This limit is user defined. See Step D'1 of the Rule Application Algorithm.

A1. FOR each *goal* on *goal_queue*:

B1. Expand any *for all* clauses. Set up a separate goal for each instantiation justified in the current context. Ask for any predicates not already available.

B2. FOR each of the expanded goals:

C1. Set *current_goal* to current goal.

C2. Expand any *where* clauses of *current_goal*. Set up temporary goal for each instantiation justified in the current context. Ask for any predicates not available.

C3. Set up *rule_sequence_queue*:

ie. FOR each of the expanded goals:

D1. Convert goal into an initial and final state specification.

D2. Associate an empty rule sequence elt with the goal. Set state of the rule sequence element to the final state obtained in D2.

D3. Add to rule sequence queue.

C4. Set *current_sequence* to first element in rule sequence queue. WHILE there are still elements on rule sequence queue:

D'1. IF number of rules in sequence = UPPER LIMIT

THEN

Set *required_sequence* of *current_goal* to nil and GO TO B2.

D'2. Set *current_state* to the intermediate state associated with the last element on the rule sequence.

D'3. Find a predicate in *current_state* that has a value that differs from its value in the initial state. Note that predicates not specified in the initial state are assumed to be set to 0.

D'4. Determine the direction that the unsatisfied predicate has to change in. Values are given in the table below:

Value of variable in current state	Value of variable in initial state	Required Direction
+	0	+
-	0	-

D'5. Retrieve rules of appropriate predicate name and direction from rule table.

D'6. FOR each rule retrieved:

E1. Establish appropriate binding of constrained individual. Initialize list of *current_bindings* to this. Set sequence_elt to CHECK_BINDINGS(*current_bindings, rule, sequence_elt*).

If CHECK_BINDINGS fails GO TO D'6.

E2. Set up list of remaining bindings.

ie.. Set *current_bindings* to INSTANTIATE_REMAINING(*current_bindings, rule*)

E3. FOR each element on current_bindings list:

F1. IF initial state is satisfied

THEN Set *required_sequence* of *current_goal* to current sequence and GO TO B2.

ELSE

IF intermediate state achieved through instantiation with current binding is not equal to any intermediate state already achieved in pursuing current_goal
THEN copy the current sequence, add *sequence_elt* and append to the end of the rule sequence queue.

D'7. Set *current_sequence* to next element on rule sequence queue.

CHECK BINDINGS (*bindings, rule, sequence_elt*)

1. Check that bindings are of appropriate type as specified in the list of individuals associated with the rule.
2. Check any topology relations involving just these variables and variables for which values have already been established.
3. BACK PROPAGATE(*binding, sequence_elt, rule*) for each element in bindings list. Check any environment conditions involving just these variable and variables for which values have already been established.
4. If the bound variable is a global variable add to list of global bindings associated with current sequence.

BACK PROPAGATE (*binding, sequence_elt, rule*)

1. Look up value of variable in current state.
2. Look up direction of variable in rule.
3. Back propagate the value of the variable as follows:

Current Value	Direction	Initial Value
+	+	0
0	-	+
-	-	0

If there is no constraint on the direction of the variable then the value of that variable will remain constant.

4. Maintain record of state achieved as part of the intermediate state specification to be associated with this application of the rule. Associate with *sequence_elt.state*.

INSTANTIATE REMAINING (*rule, sequence_elt*)

A1. Set *current_bindings* to *sequence_elt.bindings*. FOR each element on *current_bindings*:

B1. IF there are no remaining uninstantiated variables
THEN RETURN(*current_bindings*)

B2. Set *future_sequences* to nil.

B3. Sort topological relations in order of the number of uninstantiated variables (least to most).

B4. Set *relation* to the topological relation with the minimum number of uninstantiated variables and (secondarily) maximum number of total variables.

B5. Find any sets of values that will satisfy the uninstantiated variables in that relation.

B6. FOR each set of variables found:
IF variables pass CHECK BINDINGS(*bindings,rule, sequence_elt*)

THEN
C1.Set *temp_elt* to CHECK BINDINGS and append current set of variables to *temp_elt.bindings*.
C2.Set *temp _sequences* to INSTANTIATE REMAINING (*rule, temp_elt*)
C3. IF *temp_sequences*, THEN append to *future_sequences*.
A2. RETURN (*future_sequences*).

Table 7. Rule application algorithm.

Sample Application

In previous sections I have introduced goal packages, artefact descriptions and a mechanism for mapping between the two. In this section I wish to consider the nature of this mapping process in the context of criticizing an architectural plan. The procedure is essentially as follows: an artefact description is presented for analysis, the goal packages relevant to that artefact are retrieved, and an attempt is made to establish a link between aspects of the artefact

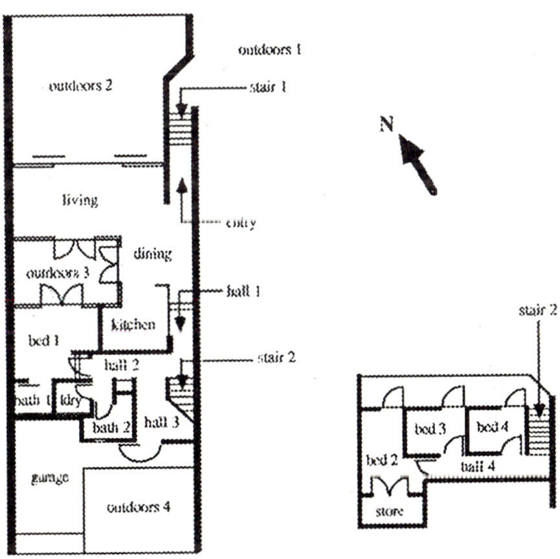

Figure 1. Sample floor plan.

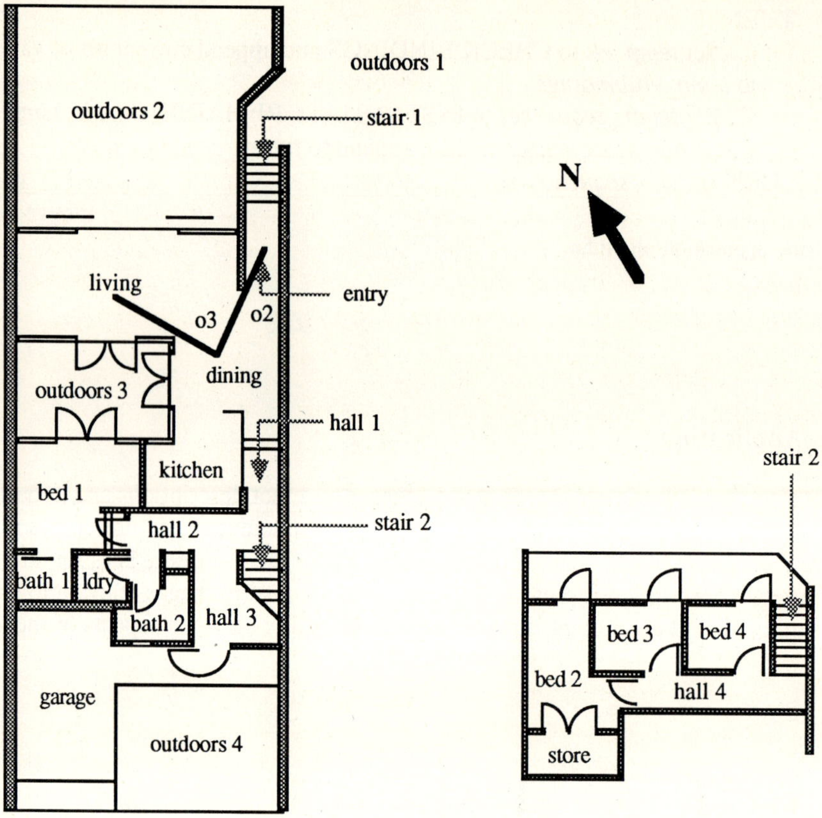

Figure 2. Diagrammatic representation of the features of the plan illustrated in Figure 1 relevant to achieving the goal *circ_reln(X,Y) where living(X) and entry(Y)*. The dark lines connecting entry and dining, and living and dining indicate *next_to* relations between these rooms. The labels *o2* and *o3* are the identifiers associated with the openings that allow passage between each of these pairs of rooms.

and each of the goals in the relevant goal packages. The outcome of this process is a representation of the goals achieved together with an indication as to those aspects of the artefact relevant to the achievement of these goals, and a list of the goals not achieved together with design recommendations pertaining to those goals.

Consider a situation where the plan illustrated in Figure 1 and the following contextual in formation is presented:

context = inner_city, medium_density
building type = residence
climate = temperate
goal = maximize_visual_privacy
goal = optimize_thermal_environment
occupants = family

The goal packages indexed under the indices *building type = residence, occupants = family* (Table 1) and *goal = optimize_thermal_environment, climate = temperate* (Table 2) would be retrieved. Application of inference rules such as those described in the previous section would yield the fact that a number of the goals contained within the goal packages retrieved are satisfied in the current plan. For example the goal *circ_reln(X,Y) where living(X) and entry(X)* contained within the goal package *building type = residence, occupants = family* is determined to be achieved by a) identifying the fact that there is a room labelled living that satisfies *living (X)* and a room entry that satisfies *entry(X)*; b) converting the goal *circ_reln(living,entry)* into an initial state *eq(circ_pressure(living),+)*, and final state *eq(circ_pressure(entry),+)*; and c) applying the rule indexed under the predicate *circ_pressure* (Table 5) twice, once to obtain an increase in the *circ_pressure* associated with the room *dining* from 0 to +, and a second to obtain the required increase in the *circ_pressure* associated with the room *entry* from 0 to +. The individuals and topological relations determined to be relevant to the achievement of the goal are listed in Table 8. A diagramatic representation of the features and relations that are relevant is illustrated in Figure 2. This diagram is intended to summarize the fact that it is the adjacency of the rooms entry and dining, and dining and living, and the existence of a means of passing between each pair of rooms that allows the goal *circ_reln(X,Y) where living(X) and entry(X)* to be achieved. A more comprehensive representation of the features of the plan relevant to the achievement of the goals contained in the two goal packages is illustrated in Figure 3. For simplicity's sake only the constraints imposed by the goal types *circ_reln*, *visual_access* and *sunny(_,winter)* have been displayed.

room(entry)
room(dining)
room(living)
opening(o2)
opening(o3)
next_to(entry,dining)
next_to(dining,living)
in(entry,o2)
in(dining,o2)
in(dining,o3)
in(living,o3)

Table 8. Symbolic representation of the features of the plan illustrated in Figure 1, relevant to achieving the goal circ_reln(X,Y) where living(X) and entry(Y).

It is envisaged that the principle advantage of such a display is that it would provide a compact representation of those aspects of the plan that are desirable and that the designer may wish to attempt to preserve if modifying the original plan. The utility of such a display would undoubtedly rest on the provision of facilities for grouping and ungrouping the constraints that arise from each goal. For example, the diagram in Figure 3 represents only a subset of the constraints identified in the context of the two goal packages retrieved, those displayed have been selected by goal type. Furthermore the overlay of information in Figure 3 obscures the association of particular features with a particular goal, much more clearly illustrated in Figure 2.

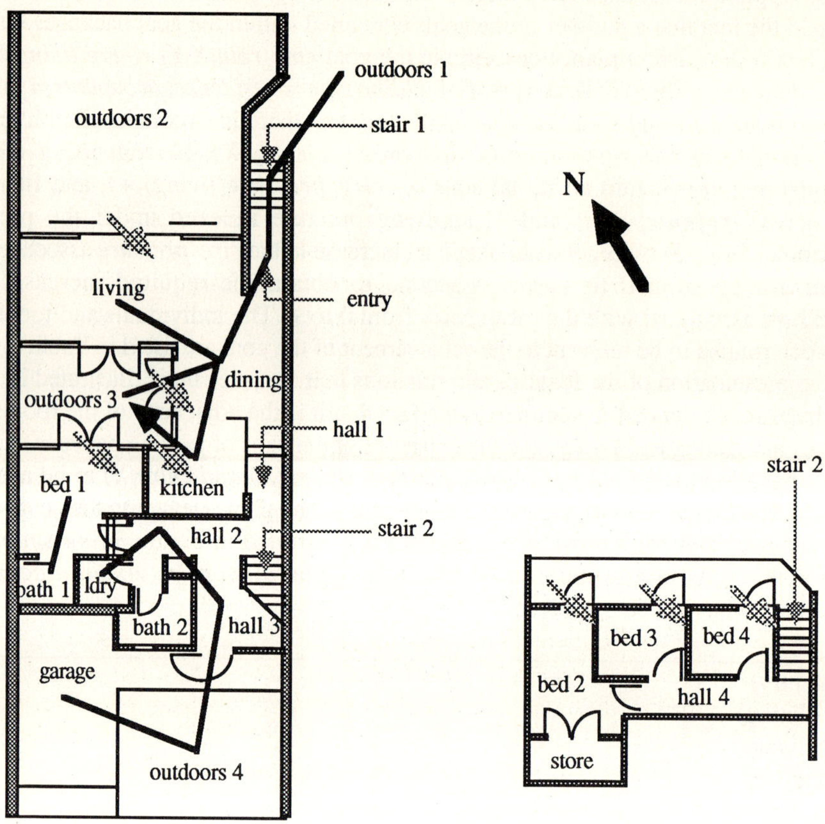

Figure 3. Diagrammatic representation of constraints gleaned from goal packages building type = dwelling, occupants = family and goal = optimize_thermal_environment, climate = temperate. Only the constraints imposed by circ_reln, visual_access and sunny(_,winter) are shown in order to keep the diagram simple. As in Figure 2, heavy lines between two spaces indicate a next_to relation. The dark arrow between the kitchen and outdoors 3 indicates the straight line access through the kitchen window required to create a visual relation between the two spaces. The grey arrows indicate windows or openings that permit the admission of winter sun to rooms where winter sun is required.

Perhaps more useful than information relating to the achievement of particular goals is a determination as to the goals that have not been achieved. Such a determination allows the relevant design recommendations to be presented to the designer for consideration. Returning to the plan illustrated in Figure 1, the initial classification of rooms is such that the goal *room = family(X)* is not satisfied. The following recommendations associated with this goal would be retrieved:

Residents need a separate living area to accommodate informal family activities -T.V., games, children's play, teenager's entertaining, and so on - which otherwise impose on more formal rooms. Research indicates a need for two separate living areas - an informal "sitting room" den and a formal "parlor" living room...In smaller units, increasing the size of the eating area within the kitchen may achieve the same end...Dimensions of the user

need for informal living areas include the fact that the equipment for some of these activities needs to be left in place over time, and other activities want to take place simultaneously with those going on in more formal living areas.
From here the designer has the option of ignoring the recommendation, modifying the plan so as to include a family room or nominating an existing room, for example, the dining room, as a dual purpose room, intended to house the activities associated with both dining and family areas. If this latter course of action is taken other goals that refer to the family room will have to be evaluated in the light of this new information.

A second example of a goal determined to be violated is the goal *goal = circ_reln(X,Y, (residents,formal_visitors,informal_visitors)) where bathroom(X) and for all Y where [living(Y) or dining(Y)]* in the case where Y = living. An upper limit of three is set to restrict the number of rules that are chained together in attempting to achieve a goal. The goals:

circ_reln(bath1,living, (residents,formal_visitors,informal_visitors))
circ_reln(bath2,living, (residents,formal_visitors,informal_visitors))

are determined to be violated on the basis that a rule sequence of three or fewer members could not be found that reduced the difference between the states indicated by either of these goals. Violation of these goals leads to the retrieval of the following recommendation:

The bathroom must service the frontstage and backstage without privacy invasion of either stage...a visitor must be able to get from the sala to the bathroom without passing through the family room, kitchen, or bedrooms or any other private area.
The recommendation refers primarily to privacy requirements and the designer may decide that the relationship between *living* and *bath 2* is satisfactory. Alternatively an attempt may be made to create a more convenient relationship between the two types of spaces.

Conclusion

Much contention continues to surround claims as to the utility of computational tools in the development of architectural design proposals. This is due, at least in part, to the recondite nature of the processes employed by human designers in design development. In this paper attention has been focussed upon a circumscribed aspect of the expertise of the architectural designer, the evaluation of a proposal, and has where possible drawn on information explicitly available to assist in this task, namely design recommendation literature and plan drawings of existing artefacts.

Whilst the focus of this work was established by reference to a particular aspect of the expertise of the human designer, the simple symbolic model developed is not intended to simulate human capabilities in this area. The means by which a human designer determines the adjacency of two rooms, for example, is clearly much more sophisticated than the method described here. The goals considered are pragmatic, they are not sufficient to define the objectives of an architectural designer, but they do represent considerations that should not be ignored. Finally, no attempt has been made to evaluate the appropriateness of tradeoffs between goals, the objective has simply been to expose such tradeoffs.

In one sense the model proposed may be viewed as an attempt to articulate the role of rule-like expressions in the task of evaluating architectural floor plans. From this perspective several points are worthy of note. First, the application of the rules is context dependent, and an appreciation of context is integrally linked to the designer's ability to construct rich personal simulations of artefact and context. An attempt has been made to respect this fundamentally human capacity by simply exposing value judgements rather than attempting to automate the execution of these value judgements. Second, the rules employed by individual designers may be idiosyncratic. Emphasis must be placed on allowing a designer to construct personal goal packages. Third, the rules are not prescriptive, the implications of the rules can only be assimilated in the light of their application to particular artefacts in particular contexts. Fourth, the information that may be gleaned from application of the rules is modest in comparison to yielded by simulation of the proposal. On a more practical level, it is anticipated that the model may provide a basis for the following types of application:

1) A tool for student designer's to explore the tradeoffs made in existing plans, to develop a feel for the appropriateness of the application of various rules within specific contexts.
2) A critic integrated into a design environment. As outlined in the sample application, the model provides a means of conveniently applying and retrieving qualitative design recommendations as well as highlighting desirable aspects of a proposal and indicating relations that a designer should attempt to preserve. Such information may be of use to the novice designer who is still in the process of integrating information such as that contained in the goal packages into a perspective from which they can evaluate developing proposals.

Finally a point should be made about the role of evaluation in architectural design activity in general. It is the view of the author that evaluation is not simply an activity that occurs after a candidate has been proposed, but that evaluation of existing artefacts is fundamental to the proposition of a candidate artefact. Future work will involve using the methods described here to identify those aspects of a plan relevant to the achievement of particular goals, then using similarity based generalization methods in an attempt to identify consistencies across the forms of the resolution of these goals in particular contexts. Such an approach may be seen as an attempt to exploit the value judgements inherent in existing artefacts in order to isolate material that will provide a basis for an initial proposal appropriate to a given context.

References

Darke, J. 1979. 'The primary generator and the design process." *Design Studies* 1, no. 1: 36-44.

Forbus, K.D. 1984. "Qualitative process theory." *Artificial Intelligence* 24: 85-168.

Foz, A. 1973. "Observations on designer behavior in the parti." *Design Research and Methods* 7, no. 4: 320-323.

Hillier, W., J. Musgrove, and P. O'Sullivan. 1972. "Knowledge and design." In Mitchell, W.J. (ed.). *Environmental Design: Research and Practice*. University of California.

Zeisel, J. and P. Welch. 1981. *Housing Designed for Families: A Summary of Research*. Cambridge, MA: Building Diagnostics.

NSB 21 (1971). *House design for temperate climates*. Australian Government Publishing Service.

23 Intra-Medium and Inter-Media Constraints

Stephen M. Ervin

Department of Landscape Architecture
Harvard Graduate School of Design
Cambridge, MA 02138, U.S.A.

Designers work with multiple representations in a variety of media to express and explore different kinds of knowledge. The advantages of multi-media in design are well-known, and exemplified by the current interest in 'hyper-media' approaches to knowledge exploration. A principal activity in working between views in one medium (e.g. plan, section and perspective drawings), or between different representations (diagrams, maps, graphs, pictures, e.g.) is extrapolating decisions made in one view or medium over to others, so that some consistency is maintained, and implications can be explored. The former kind of consistency maintenance (intra-medium) is beginning to be well understood techniques for constraint expression, satisfaction and propagation are starting to appear in 'smart CAD' systems. The latter kind of consistency maintenance (inter-media) is different, less well understood, and will require new mechanisms for constraint management and exploration. Experiments, hypotheses, and solutions in this direction will be central to any effort that seeks to explain, emulate or assist the integrative, synthetic reasoning that characterizes environmental design and planning. This paper examines some of the characteristics and advantages of intra- and inter-media constraint exploration, describes a prototype "designers workstation" and some experiments in the context of landscape planning and design, and lays out some directions for development of these ideas in future computer aided design systems.

Introduction - Constraints among Multiple Representations

Designers work in a variety of media to express and explore different kinds of knowledge. A principal activity in working between views in one medium (e.g. plan, section and perspective drawings), or between different media (diagrams, maps, graphs, pictures, e.g.) is extrapolating decisions made in one view or medium over to others, so that consistency of representation is maintained, and the many implications of any decision are explored. In practice, this consistency cannot be absolute, and the exploration of implications cannot be exhaustive. Designers depend on the conventions and organization of the design-build community enterprise to identify errors and inconsistencies that make it through the design stage. Similarly, designers are often surprised (pleasantly or not) by some unanticipated effect in a built environment. No effort in computational support or artificial intelligence applied to design will likely overcome the complexity and consistency problem of any real-world design problem, especially at the scale of, say landscape planning or urban design. Nor should any such effort seek to limit the possibility for fortuitous delight and discovery. We might well want, however, to improve the chances of error detection and extend the range of possible design explorations. Computer assisted design in its proper sense, seeks to assist, not replace, designers. To that end, we are concerned with understanding the processes of designing, and the forms and dimensions of support required.

In this regard, the general domain of environmental design offers a rich field for exploration and discovery. Problems are often large and complex, solutions are varied, some rules are clear and constant, others as ephemeral as the tracing paper on which they are expressed. One obvious characteristic of such design, whether in practice, education or research, is the heavy reliance on multiple forms of representation, in multiple media. Designers and planners use text, reports, charts, diagrams, maps, plans, details, sketches, photographs, movies, computer simulations and animations, and more, to explore their problems and tell their stories. This paper is based on the simple observation that designers and planners use multiple representations, and explore constraints among them, all the time. Why not provide computational support for these processes?

Graphic Knowledge Representation: Diagrams, Maps, Graphs and Pictures

Multi-media technologies for designers are increasingly available, and their appeal is exemplified by the current interest in 'hyper-media' approaches across disciplines (Delisle 1986, Jonassen, McAleese 1989, Nielsen 1990). The hyper-media movement, which builds on the original ideas of hyper-text (Nelson 1984) , multi-media technology (Katzen 1981) and database theory (Date 1981) , seeks to integrate representations and media in an interactive environment, linking sounds, images, text and numbers with a computer-controlled interface. The principal idea is 'linkage' between items of information. The nature of these links is the subject of active speculation and research, ranging from simple 'buttons' providing static cross-reference to operating systems that support 'hot-links' between applications. The increasing availability of large-volume storage devices (CD-ROM, optical disks, video disks, e.g.), revolutions in signal compression, and available hardware for sound and other output, as well as multiple forms of input, have made both hardware and software developments for hyper-media attractive and possible. The technology has been developed and is in place for publishing and entertainment markets; similar environments for designers are not very far away.

Like the technological approach to computer aided design, it is possible to approach multi-media as a problem of management and hardware. The proliferation and incompatibility of standards, capabilities, new directions and technological improvements make this side of the question a full time job. The concern for researchers in design theory, however, is an alternative question: how do media and forms of representation enter into and effect design reasoning; how are they incorporated into or reflective of, design knowledge? Advances along all technological dimensions are bound to continue to occur exponentially. As designers and design researchers we are confronted with the much more difficult problem: what to do with all the technology?

Choosing representation media is not just a cosmetic choice. Representations are value-laden; every drawing, indeed every CAD system, contains a set of assumptions, biases and normative positions. Knowing as we do that even 'photo-realism' is an abstraction, we must choose representations for rhetorical purposes, to support design arguments, to display design knowledge. The push in computer graphics to achieve ever higher numbers of pixels, finer resolution, truer color, more realistic radiosity and illumination models, is a technically challenging, but epistemologically empty pursuit. In design practice, it is often the case that the simpler the drawing, the richer the design reasoning. Simple line drawings tend to be more full of 'propositional' content, which can be argued about; 'pictorial' representations leave little room for argument, other than 'I (don't) like what I see'. Diagrams and back-of-the-envelope sketches are the chosen media during early design stages, full of content and complexity; perspective renderings come at the more sterile presentation stage. Diagrams and sketches are made for real communication, with ourselves and others; renderings are for final adjustments, and sales pitches.

Representation - graphic and otherwise - in the service of reasoning has been explored by art historians, psychologists, and AI researchers (Arnheim 1969, Bertin 1983, Larkin & Simon 1987, Newell & Simon 1972, Tuftie 1990). One conclusion is that switching representations may often be a key to problem solving. In the case of diagrams, for example, just the act of converting from a verbal, mathematical or logical problem into one of two-dimensional space often serves to clarify relationships and to direct design development or problem solving. Knowledge representation in general is recognized as a critical component of problem-solving and AI approaches (Brachman 1985) , and is the foundation of a body of work in architecture and environmental design (Coyne et al. 1990). Graphical representations, both as containers of and media for exploration of knowledge, are particularly important in design, and have not received as much scrutiny as other symbolic forms.

In design practice, (at least) four essentially different kinds of graphic representation can be found at different times and places, and used for different purposes. *Diagrams*, *maps*, *graphs* and *pictures*, all instances of two-dimensional graphical representation, are here taken as distinct media, both for exploration and communication. The underlying data, in form and content, and the graphic representation (ditto) are different and somewhat incompatible from one medium to the next. (I'll argue later on that they are <u>not</u> just different projections from a single database.) All of these media are essential to the reasoning processes - including visual inference - in design, and all are interconnected in common use. The nature of those interconnections is a pressing research question for the next generation of CAD tools.

Diagrams

Diagrams are those schematic, abstract, and usually simple drawings used to express and explore structural relationships among parts. They are distinguished from maps by being essentially not to scale, and not true to shape (Bertin 1983) ; and from pictures by being concerned with propositional content (ideas) more than appearance. Like maps, and pictures, they are used for visual inference, so their shapes, scales and appearance are important. In the following discussion I use the vocabulary of (Ervin 1989).

'A-Diagrams' - the most abstract ones - are used to express high-level organizational intent. A city may be described as 'radial' or 'grid-based', for example; a path as 'linear' or 'branching'. The use of these diagrams is often in communication, as a visual reminder of some essential property of a proposed plan. 'B-Diagrams' - less abstract - are perhaps more common, as they begin to express form as well as concept. Branching may be alternate or opposite, regular or irregular, hierarchical or network-like. These diagrams give rise to particular shapes and forms when plans are drawn, and their use in visual inference is to explore generic and geometric properties of the class of form, without yet reference to the particular details of the problem at hand. Such diagrams have been called 'form-diagrams' (Milne 1966).

All diagrams have the essential characteristic of conveying, and containing, expressions of constraint which are to be maintained as design development progresses. Design alternatives may be produced within a single diagrammatic context; shifting to another diagram is a qualitatively different change, at another level of abstraction (Ervin 1987, Liggett et al.1990) Used in this way, diagrams are constraints on further refinement, and so on other representations.

The inferential purpose of diagrams is primarily for testing high-level abstract concepts (types and relationships of objects) and beginning to explore spatial arrangement, but without commitment to size, shape, or other refinements. The cognitive processes associated with reading diagrams are more like analogy and association than the more literal readings given to other graphics, such as the three described below.

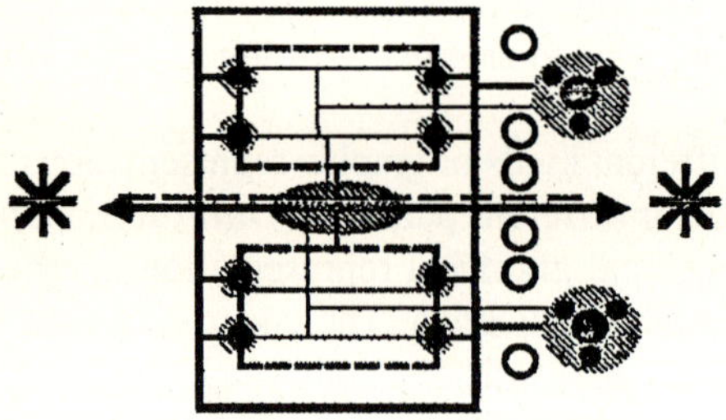

Figure 1a. A-Diagram.

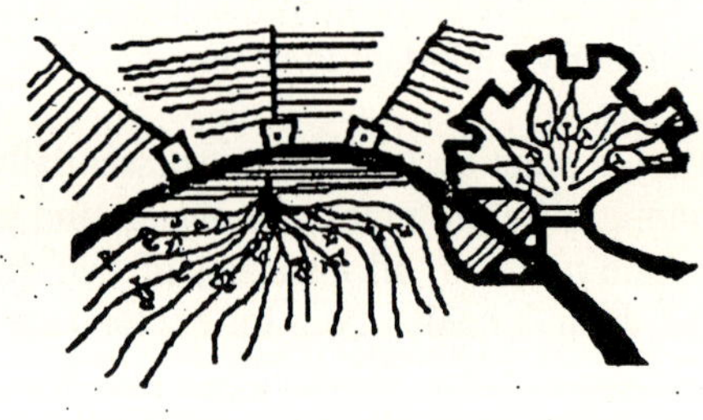

Figure 1b. B-Diagram.

The production of diagrams is still largely unsupported by computer software, except as simple line-graphics in vector drawing systems. The knowledge-based production and exploration of diagrams remains a largely unexplored area deserving more research.

Maps

Maps include any <u>scaled</u> representation of some features across some region of a coordinate space, at any size from regional to backyard. I include traditional plans and sections in this category; they are just maps at different levels of resolution with different cutting planes, or points of view. Their inferential use depends largely on our ability to relate elements of one map to another through some consistent scale and coordinate system conversion, and our ability to relate from the map to the territory. Maps are of course abstractions, like other representations, but their element of scaled-reference makes them distinct.

The inferential purpose of maps (and plans etc.) is primarily for testing dimensions and spatial relationships including coincidence. Their use is primarily by 'identity', that is, a one-to-one mapping is made from the representation to (some aspect of) the world, a more literal reading than the the reading given to diagrams. GIS and CAD software provide ready-made tools for the production and limited analysis of maps, plans and other drawings, but little opportunity to embed design knowledge into the representations.

Graphs

Graphs include all sorts of quantitative displays including tabular and graphic (pie charts, scatterplots, histograms, bar graphs, etc.) They are associated with data that is often represented as rows and columns (or n-dimensional arrays) of related information, and hence most commonly with spreadsheet and data-base management software. Their use in planning and design includes both quantitative comparisons between alternatives and depictions of trends. Spreadsheet software and other mathematical, statistical and quantitative modelling tools provide powerful assistance in numerical exploration, but offer little integration with other software or forms of representation except through limited specially tailored interfaces or cumbersome data interchanges.

Many models and algorithms may be included in this category since many approaches to describing relationships or interactions depend on a matrix or equivalent network representation. Economic input-output models, for example, systems of difference equations including exponential growth and decay models, and other systems describing constraints and relations among parts are conveniently represented in tabular and array form. The inputs and outputs of such models, of course, may be from maps and text, for example, and need not be limited to tables and/or graphs.

Charts and graphs are the most obvious way to present much numeric data visually; the human eye remains the most powerful pattern recognition and trend-spotting apparatus designers and planners can call upon. The inferential purpose of graphs is primarily for testing qualitative relationships among numbers - pattern recognition by eye. The mechanism is more primitive and less 'cerebral' than the reading of maps or diagrams: recognition of clusters, slopes, edges, outlines, etc. are likely very low-level visual abilities.

Pictures

Pictures or images is the term reserved for those graphic representations whose primary characteristic is 'impression', 'expression', or 'realism'. Photographs, sketches, etc. are still abstractions, but in a sense the least abstract of the set of representations considered here. Montages and other results of image processing and 'painting' are included; these include purely digital as well as combined digital/analog representations. CAD and Image Processing software provide the typical tools for computational manipulation of pictures, but the integration of image processing into a comprehensive design workstation is an effort with little theoretical underpinning to guide it.

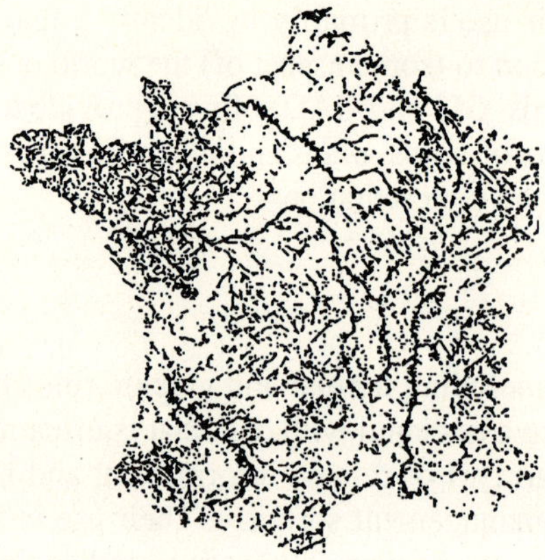

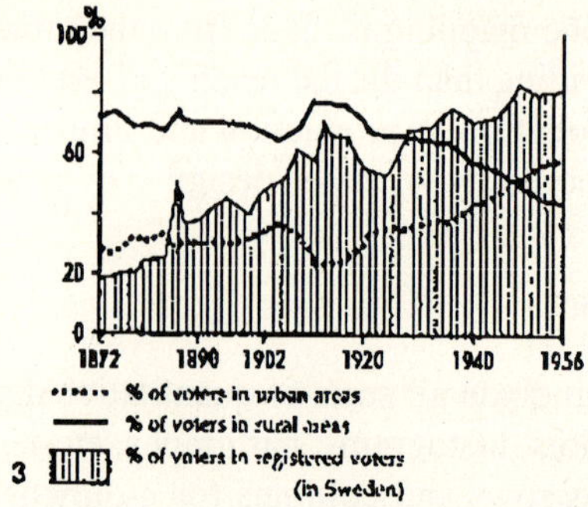

Figure 2. a) A Map. **b)** A Graph.

Figure 2. c) A Picture.

The inferential purpose of pictures is primarily for qualitative and often inarticulate judgements - such things as visual preference, overall form, proportion, balance, etc. These characteristics may be computable, but no designer or planner can well-enough describe her criteria to abdicate responsibility for looking. These readings may be intensely analogical in nature, or extremely literal - visual images and their knowledge-based interpretation remain a mystery and an intriguing if formidable research area. Pictures have the added unique characteristic that they are used, and judged, both for form and substance. We are most likely to be concerned with the 'surface' characteristics as the 'inner' content of pictures when designing, often in ways that are inexplicable but real.

Constraint Management

Constraint management in design is an established research area (Fleisher et al., Gross et al 1987, 1988) turning into an established technology. Expressing, propagating and satisfying numeric and logical constraints is beginning to be well understood, and appearing in production software, typically in mathematical, electrical and mechanical engineering fields (Robinson 1989). The basic formalism is to declare a variable value as falling within some constrained range, usually as some function of other variables' values. Confronted with a network of such constraints, the problem is to find some solution such that all the variables have values and a minimum number of constraints are violated (ideally, of course, none.) Optimization, numerical approximation, simulated annealing, constraint relaxation and other techniques have all been developed for dealing with the problem. Part of the appeal is the ability to explore alternatives -"What results or conflicts appear from variations in base parameters?". Constraint satisfaction systems represent next-generation spreadsheets, with features such as symbolic solvers and interval values, that serve to extend their functionality. Techniques for constraint expression, satisfaction and propagation are also starting to appear in 'smart CAD' systems (Borning, Freeman-Benson, Gross, Nelson 1985).

Designers, of course, have been engaged in 'what-if' analyses and generation of alternatives for a long time. For budgets and pro-forma analyses it is fairly clear how to identify all the elements that contribute to the bottom line; for design problems much less so. Even supposing we can identify a large number of the elements we are concerned with in a design, and identify the relationships between the elements, we are for the most part lacking computer software that can help with simulations of interactions and other aspects of graphic knowledge representation and reasoning.

Constraint satisfaction systems have been shown to be valuable in well defined engineering disciplines; they have yet to be shown effective in complex environmental design situations, although speculation and optimism can be found in the literature (Gross et al.1988) I present here some more speculation in the hopes of furthering the research and development of the technology in the direction of multi-media.

In general, in multi-media or multi-view systems, constraint satisfaction and propagation mechanisms should provide for automatic linkages, so that changes in one medium or view are reflected in other media or views. What the details of that 'reflection' operation might be, and how such reflections are used by designers, is the research agenda that this paper advocates. Since each medium, or representation, may serve as input or output, and since each depends on its own database(s), it is tempting to think of media as isolated and somewhat incompatible, requiring different approaches to information exploration and management. It is easy to imagine both superficial linkages and more substantive ones that multiply the power and the potential of individual representations.

Superficial linkages take the form of simple cross-reference pointers (for example, associating a chosen illustration with a particular paragraph in a report.) These 'hyper-links' provide a skeleton over which to travel between pieces of information in the system; this skeleton may be based on *a-priori* knowledge and constraints, but is bound to be modified during the processes of exploration and annotation.

More substantive links -constraints - take the form of dynamic relations between pieces of information, controlled by explicit models developed by designers. For example, a planner may recognize a relationship between public expenditures on infrastructure and resultant private development of residential and commercial real estate. In such a model, increasing a value in a spreadsheet as part of a gross budget should result in a change in a map - more (or less) residential development in specified parts of the region. Conversely, changes in a map of residential density should trigger revisions to a spreadsheet model predicting energy demand, or sewage production, or transportation loads. Through these dynamic links, complex models that can be viewed as maps, as graphs, or even as pictures, may be developed. Some possibilities for - and problems with - constrained linkages (six in all) between each of the four representations - diagrams, maps, graphs and pictures- are discussed below.

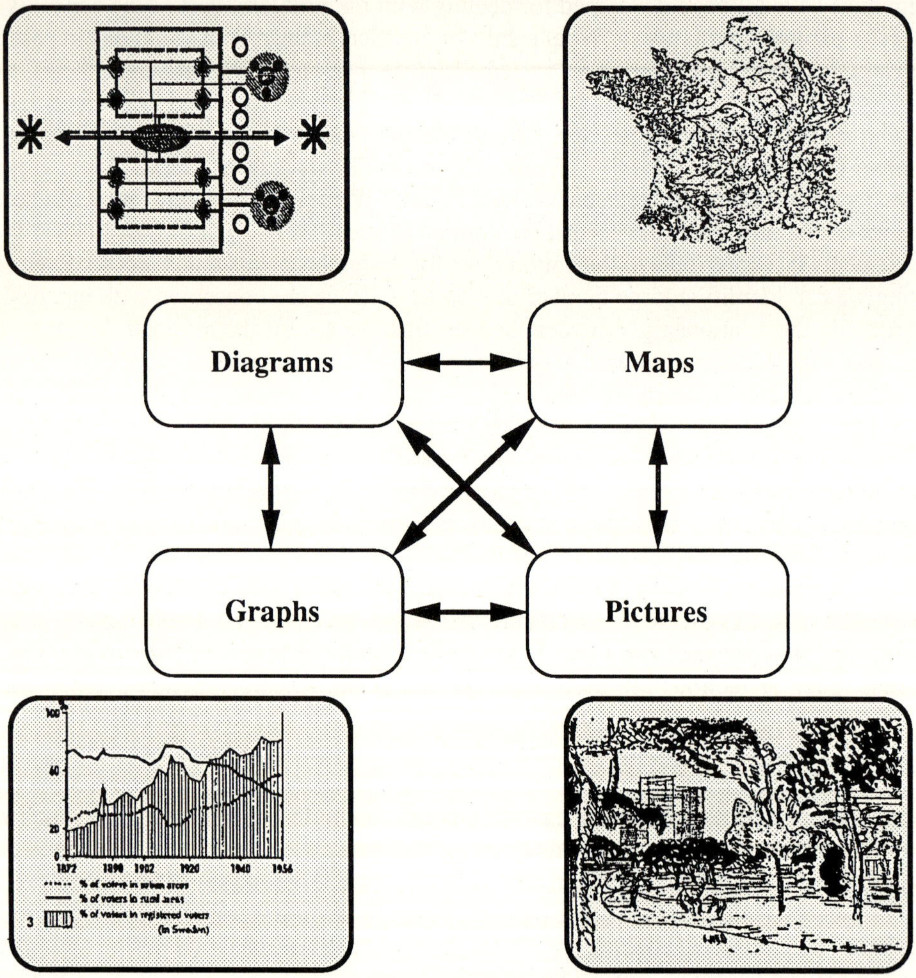

Figure 3. Inter-Media Linkages.

Diagram <--> Map Linkages

The possible linkages between diagrams and maps are many. In urban design, we often start with a simple concept diagram, and seek to apply the concept to a particular site, with all its details of topography, hydrology, vegetation, etc., to produce a plan. Or, starting with a map, we may produce a diagram revealing the essential structure of some phenomena. The process of abstracting here separates form-concepts from particular topography and details of geography. Many urban design studies start with just such abstractions, simplifying the essence of a study area into a ring, or star, or grid, or 'spaghetti' structure, etc. As maps are already abstractions, it is largely a matter of degree when crossing the threshold. Many useful graphics are ambiguous in this regard - subways line maps are typically more diagrammatic than topographic maps, but more map-like than the most abstract diagrams.

Automating the extraction of a diagram from a map, or the elaboration of a diagram into a map, is a challenge to pattern recognition techniques and knowledge based approaches. Exploring the relationship between maps and diagrams in the broadest sense - as, for example, between a land-use diagram and an illustrative site plan - is in many ways the essence of the early stages of design. Moving easily between these media, reconciling inconsistencies and letting insights from one medium constrain developments in the other, is a quintessential design process. It is likely that a computing environment which supports both representations from the outset, and therefore contains diagrammatic constraints on maps, will be a useful one for comprehensive design exploration.

Diagram <--> Graph Linkages

The most obvious connection between diagrammatic representations and graphs and charts is to identify some aspects of essential form in a chart - for example, rising, falling, erratic, stable - and to represent these diagrammatically, as an abstraction of the graph analogous to the abstraction of a map discussed above. The diagram may, in a sense, be considered a first derivative of the chart.

The mechanics of using diagrams as input, and getting graphs as dependent output are less obvious. One possibility is to understand that certain diagrammatic decisions have quantitative implications - increased circulation conflict or reduced access to open space, for example - and that graphs of these implications can be produced as output from diagrams.

Diagram <--> Picture Linkages

The automated extraction of a diagram from a picture is another challenge to pattern recognition, though there may be some obvious examples in landscapes with strong horizontal components identifying a vanishing point, or clear skylines, for example.

To produce a picture from a diagram is a many-from-one proposition, that crosses the extreme from most propositional to most pictorial, and whose purpose or utility is therefore unclear. The query "What might this diagrammatic decision look like?" - i.e., what are the implications in another medium - is often asked, but usually answered by passing through an intermediate less abstract form; typically a plan or a map. This suggests that one path from diagram to picture is through an intermediate map.

Diagrams might serve as a powerful indexing and retrieval mechanism for stored images, using diagrammatic criteria to classify and characterize complex visual information. A retrieval system that produces images previously indexed by diagram is an easily conceived, but doubtless difficult to implement, image archiving device.

Map <--> Graph Linkages

The most obvious connection between map representations and graphs and charts is to use the map(s) as input, and derive and illustrate characteristics of the map(s); or to illustrate comparisons between two or more maps.

For example, in the visual analysis of a road, we might ask the question "What is the sequence or rhythm of wooded versus open spaces along the length of the roadway?" The answer to this query, which depends on map information (i.e. land cover, vegetation), is best represented as a linear graph, in which the x-axis is station (horizontal distance), and the y-axis some representation (bars, or connected lines, e.g.) of variation in land cover. Multiple such attributes (land cover, presence of water, residential density, etc.) can be conveniently graphed as multiple bars or lines in a graph. In another typical planning application, given a map of land uses, a simple procedure could extract Floor Area Ratios (F.A.R.'s), and produce a graph of these ratios.

The mechanics of using graphs as input, and getting maps as dependent output is essentially an exercise in knowledge based generation (Coyne, et al.1990). The questions "Where along a road is the residential density 1.0 units/acre?", or "What site plan arrangement would produce a specified F.A.R.?" are examples of one-to-many relationship - there are likely several places along the highway with the requested density, and there are indefinitely many possible maps of land use that could result in any specified F.A.R. Procedures to automate the production or generation of one specimen from a set of possible answers are not obvious, nor are they obviously useful. Seen as a simple search, a list of answers in the first case is perfectly acceptable; take them all, and subject them to further scrutiny. In the second example, the generation of a plan subject to constraints could be managed, with sufficient additional constraints and assumptions about the production of the plan - such an approach is one way of testing the validity of those constraints and assumptions.

Map <--> Picture Linkages

The linkage between map representations and pictures is an obvious one. Some examples (e.g.- Ervin, Gimblett & Itami 1989) have demonstrated the feasibility of linking stored video images to geographic coordinates so that map data may be 'illustrated' with images. More abstract pictorial renditions are possible as projected views from the cartographic data base; digital elevation models with roads and vegetation overlaid, for example. Given a method for projecting a view in the first place, changing a road alignment, or a configuration of land cover, could result in a corresponding change in the projected view.

Going the other way, from picture to map, is again complicated by the one-to-many problem. Inferring three dimensional coordinates in a two-dimensional projection is subject to ambiguity that can only be resolved by a set of external conventions, so automation is difficult. Reconstructing plan views from several perspective views of known orientation is possible, and has been used in archaeological and architectural investigations. Making a change in a picture, and having the change reflected in a map, is a prime example of a constrained interaction between media, requiring considerable research and development.

Graph <--> Picture Linkages

The above discussion of graphs<->maps linkages applies equally to linkages between graphs and pictures. With an appropriate algorithm for choosing or generating examples, an illustration of any quantitative criteria may either be retrieved from a stored data base; the example of residential densities is easy to imagine, for example. Graphical analyses of visual images are known - a histogram of frequencies in a satellite image analysis is just such a tool. Are there other analyses besides bandwidth that usefully summarize or capture information contained in a drawing or picture? If so, these might serve as the basis of other quantitative analyses of visual data.

Linkages - constraints - between media are critical in design reasoning. When a designer makes a diagram, she may or may not have an image of what the result should look like. Sometimes, when she does have such an image, it is incompatible with the diagram; a fact that remains to be discovered and reconciled in the process of changing the image, changing the diagram, until they are in agreement. Similarly, the traffic engineer may have a target graph of traffic frequency; the design problem is to find the map, or road alignment and intersection plan, that produces the desired graph. Or perhaps the target is a desired road alignment; the problem is to find a set of spot elevations that make it work. And at the same time, to have a particular view of the lake in the distance. And to be a grid, rather than a cul-de-sac system... Map, chart, picture, diagram; all must come together in a synthetic whole, but each has its own time, place and method for use. These media are distinct, but related.

Towards a Designers' Workstation

The previous sections have touched on some of the advantages of and possibilities for constrained linkages between representations (inter-media constraints). The remaining section of this paper is devoted to exploring some aspects of implementing this functionality in a "designers' workstation", for comprehensive multi-media computer aided design.

At designers' traditional drawing boards, media are mixed, explored and invented all the time. The choice of a representational medium for any particular design task is in part guided by convention, and in part by consideration of the inferential needs of the design task at hand. The level of abstraction, of detail, the appropriateness of such attributes as color, texture, etc. all enter into the decision. To support these needs computationally, we need in the first place a rich repertoire of representational devices and techniques, including multiple simultaneous graphic displays, animated and static, color and monochrome, large and small, etc. In addition, the requirements for exploring constrained interactions between media and representations include new forms of constraint management, as yet only anticipated.

A necessary first step is to begin to provide simple multi-media and 'hyper-media' technology at an integrated design workstation, and then to begin to provide constraints between representations. It is useful to imagine the kinds of uses to which such constrained linkages might be put in the service of environmental planning and design.

Each of the sections above identified some possibilities and problems with two-way linkages between media. In order to focus on the knowledge representation and manipulation, rather than the details of the technology (which are bound to change), the following scenario presumes an infinitely capable hardware manager, with all sorts of protocol interchange capabilities and arbitrarily large memory, large display(s), deep color, small resolution, etc. The following hypothetical scenarios reveal some of the breadth and complexity of design exploration offered by such a system:

"Imagine that all the red maples along the highway were to succumb to a virus. What would sides of the road in the western part of the state look like? Where might more views of water be revealed? " This requires a geographical analysis in the first place, to identify tree species and locations of water. Then an image processing component is required to 'brush out' areas of images and simulate views behind the brushed out areas.

"Make a graph of the visual quality (according to whatever metric) along this stretch of the road. Now insert the following design changes as maps in the database. Graph the new visual quality, and make a graph of the change." This requires a metric of visual quality, a mechanism for inserting changes in images, and procedures for automating the analysis of quality according to some derived parameters. The derivation may come either from recording the proposed changes, as processes, or the results, as state. The distinctions between these two approaches (essentially transaction processing) may be both efficiency and comprehensiveness, and deserve to be tested.

"Change this view as indicated by hand (edit by removing buildings and signs, changing vegetation, inserting new landscape features, etc.). Now please produce a plan view showing the altered condition." This most resembles the plan/section/perspective technology now well-understood in CAD systems, but may require some object-oriented implementation rather than projections from a single data base.

"Use this graph of daily traffic by type as a control so that as numeric values are changed, animated views of traffic at selected toll-booths are illustrated on the screen. Use a modal selection algorithm so that as density builds up, more travelers choose to use alternate routes." Here, the linkage between models and graphics is envisioned to support interactive dynamic modelling, examples of which are available in a variety of disciplines already.

Research Agenda - Computational Issues

A system of coordinated, constraint-based multi-media representations such as the one envisioned here, and the process or processes of constraint exploration, raise an immediate question about underlying database: is it one, or many? With one, data base consistency is possible; with many, almost impossible. With a single database, multiple representations are treated just as multiple projections, or views; with many databases, each may have several projections, and conversion between them becomes the operative question (McDonald, et al). As appealing as a single database seems from a management perspective, the reality of the multi-media environment is that it is, by definition, a multiple data base (Parsaye). Different media, or representations, are not just different projections from a single database; that's why they are used! Indeed, translations between them are not always possible - this is one of the key issues in the development of such a system.

In addition to the problems of projection and translation, there are the related questions of database consistency, indexing and retrieval. Consistency is much to be aspired for in many traditional database applications - 'truth maintenance' is a lofty and admirable goal - but in designing, inconsistency, ambiguity and creative conflict resolution are essential components. The database manager in such a system must be willing to 'suspend disbelief' at times, to carry inconsistencies and conflicts, and to put up with ambiguous and imprecise definitions. Designers, of course, work towards final states in which consistency is to be found, and ambiguity and conflict resolved, but the process maybe halting, circuitous, and almost certainly non-monotonic (Ginsberg 1987). Not only are the algorithmic aspects of this question complex, but the associated interface issues - how and when to signal conflicts to the user, whether the manager is conceived of as an 'error detecting daemon' or a specially invoked procedure, for example- are perplexing as well.

The essential characteristics of a designers' workstation as envisioned here is the organized management of complexity and multiplicity of representation. The computational techniques of *object-oriented design*, *message-passing* and *concurrent processing* have evolved in response to such complexity in other disciplines, and are likely candidates for the implementation of any designers' workstation or network of such stations, as they address most directly the problems of abstraction, information sharing and asynchronous operation.

Object-oriented design seems inevitable, because of the advantages of encapsulation, inheritance, generic functionality, and exception handling offered by the paradigm. Objects may be thought of as databases, in the multi-database approach, and representations may be part of the objects' interface. Modelling real-world systems as objects is a well-established technique for achieving modularity in software design, as well as forcing detailed exploration of the system at hand. Maintaining systematic databases of objects also raises questions of 'persistence' over time (Smithers1987), and offers possibilities for exploring design variants as variants of saved state. Object-oriented programming and data base development are surely tools that the programming designer will want to avail herself of in the process of articulating and exploring design knowledge.

Message passing is a technology related to (but not necessarily a part of) object oriented design. The notion that objects send and receive messages simply highlights the characteristic of encapsulation that the inner workings of objects are hidden from public view; the possibility that different objects respond differently to the same message captures an important part of the semantics of real world behavior. The possibility of building up a language of communication unique to a particular design problem or set of problems, by customizing objects and messages, seems to be an important part of communicating between multiple agents. The role of inter-agent communication, and variants such as 'blackboards', etc., has been the focus of a branch of AI research; the equivalent study of inter-agent communication in design processes is relatively new.

Finally, concurrent processes seem desirable, and inevitable, both on grounds of technological change and availability, and because, again, this approach models the real world so directly. A design project is as likely a collaboration between an architect, landscape designer, painter and civil engineer, whether these are in fact different people or just different points of view of a single designer. Each point of view has preferred media and representations, and may or not be willing to have his or her view translated to another's. This view of concurrent, communicating design systems closely resembles the computer science view of 'open systems' (Hewitt & De Jong 1981).

The integrated designer's workstation may also embody the principles of object-orientedness, message-passing and concurrent systems at a 'meta-' scale, that is, the design studio of the future (Mitchell 1990) may well be modelled as an interacting network of just such workstations. A major problem when multiple agents interact - designers, consultants, and so on - is the misunderstandings that arise when each use their own medium, embodying their own viewpoint. The solution, I suggest, is not to force all concurrently operating agents into a common representation, but rather to understand the problems related to constraints and conversion between representations.

Conclusions

Intra-medium constraint management systems for design - those that manage algebraic and logical relationships in relatively well-defined problem areas, are coming to be valuable partners in all kinds of design fields. The questions that remain, primarily involving languages for expressing and combining constraints, mechanisms for handling the inevitable conflicts between constraint systems - including questions of interface and human engineering factors - are non-trivial. This paper suggests that, in addition to pursuing that line of research, we must begin to understand the complexities of *inter-media* constraints, in which the underlying semantics, and not just the syntax or implementation, are still at issue. In addition to the computational approaches outlined above, more research on the cognitive role(s) of various forms of representation and on the forms of inference that accompany them, is required. We still know very little about the use of representations in design reasoning, the relationship(s) between maps, diagrams, graphs and pictures, or the essential nature of abstraction levels in environmental design.

The development of design tools and eventually CAD systems that integrate multi-media and constraint management is bound to both depend upon, and engender, experiments in representation. These experiments may very well result in new conventions, or new ways of seeing, explaining and understanding, that are alien to our present ways of graphic communications. Multi-media presentations should not become the equivalent of glossy renderings - reserved for final presentations - but should become useful working and exploratory devices for designers. Simulations of proposed environments need not be 'realistic' (the apparent goal of much computer graphics work and of the 'virtual reality' movement), but rather should be 'informative' - full of information both intentional and accidental. It is the intentional pursuit of accidental insights that characterizes synthetic design reasoning, and encouraging and enabling this kind of search is a major performance goal of the design of the designers' workstation.

Summary

Expression, propagation and satisfaction of constraints among diverse representations and multiple media are both necessary for comprehensive computational design support, and considerably more perplexing problems than the (relatively) well-understood numeric or logical constraint problems. A designer's workstation providing computational support for design will have to support at least four distinct representations : *diagrams*, simple line drawings representing propositional design knowledge; *maps*, whether raster or vector, representing attributes of the earth's surface; *graphs*, simple graphics displaying relations among tables of numeric data; and *pictures*, arbitrarily complex visual depictions. Translating from intentions expressed in one medium to implications in another requires considerable design knowledge, and more than a single database. Designers also require constraint systems that can support inconsistency, ambiguity and multiple meanings on the one hand, and that can help them explore implications in a variety of media on the other. It is likely that such a designer's workstation, to be effective, will have to implement such functionality and support dynamic interactions and simulations, using computational techniques including object-oriented database design, message passing and concurrent processing. Experiments, hypotheses, and solutions in this direction, however partial or tentative, will be central to any effort that seeks to explain, emulate or assist the integrative, synthetic reasoning that characterizes environmental design and planning.

References

Figures:
1.a) after Chermayeff and Tzonis - diagram of Columbia New Town.
1.b) after Alexander - diagram of Indian Village.
2.a) after Bertin p.153 - Map of France.
2.b) after Bertin p. 223 - Graph of registered voters.
2.c) after Fishman - Sketch of Green City by Le Corbusier.

Alexander, C. 1966. *Notes on the Synthesis of Form.* Cambridge: Harvard University Press.

Appleyard, D., K. Lynch, and J. Meyer. 1961. *The View from the Road.* Cambridge, MA: MIT Press.

Arnheim, R. 1969. *Visual Thinking.* Berkeley: University of California Press.

Bertin, J. 1983. *Semiology of Graphics: Diagrams Networks Maps.* Madison, WI: University of Wisconsin Press.

Borning, Alan, Robert Duisberg, Bjorn Freeman-Benson, Axel Kramer, and Michael Woolf. 1987. "Constraint Hierarchies." In *OOPSLA Proceedings 1987,* pp. 48-60. ACM SigPlan.

Brachman, R., and H.Levesque (eds.). 1985. *Readings in Knowledge Representation.* Los Altos, CA: Morgan Kaufman Publishers.

Chermayeff, S. and A. Tzonis. 1967. *Advanced Studies in Urban Environments: Toward an Urban Model.* Yale University, Institute for Applied Technology.

Coyne, R.D., M.A. Rosenman, A.D. Radford, M. Balachandra and J.S. Gero. 1990. *Knowledge-Based Design Systems.* Reading, MA: Addison-Wesley.

Date, C.J. 1981. *An Introduction to DataBase Systems.* New York, NY: Addison-Wesley.

Delisle, Norman, and Mayer Swartz. 1986. "Neptune: A Hypertext system for CAD Applications." In *Proceedings of ACM, SIGMOD, '86.* Washington, D.C.

Ervin, S. 1987. "Levels of Abstraction in Environmental Design: A Computational Approach." In *Proceedings, 1987 Conference on Planning and Design in Urban and Regional Planning* 91-96.

Ervin, Stephen. 1989. "Designing with Diagrams: A role for Computing in Design Education and Exploration." In McCullough, Mitchell & Purcell (eds.). *The Electronic Design Studio,* pp. 107-121. Cambridge, MA: MIT Press.

Fishman, Robert. 1989. *Urban Utopias in the Twentieth Century.* Cambridge, MA: MIT Press.

Fleisher, A., S. Ervin and M. Gross 1989. "CM2: A constraint-based environment for design exploration." *Final Report to NSF* #DMC86-11375, MIT DTM Group.

Freeman-Benson, Bjorn N.. 1990. "Kaleidoscope: Mixing Objects, Constraints and Imperative Programming." In *ECOOP/OOPSLA Proceedings 1990,* pp. 77-88. ACM Press/ Addison-Wesley.

Gimblett, R.H. and R. Itami. 1989. "Linking GIS with Video Technology to Simulate Environmental Change." *Proceedings, GIS/LIS 1989.* Falls Church, VA: ASPRS/ACSM.

Ginsberg, M.L. (Ed.) 1987. *Readings in Nonmonotonic Reasoning.* Los Altos, CA: Morgan Kaufman Publishers.

Gross, Mark. 1990. "Relational Modeling: A Basis for Computer Assisted Design." In McCullough, Mitchell & Purcell (eds.). *The Electronic Design Studio,* pp. 123-136. Cambridge, MA: MIT Press.

Gross, M., S. Ervin, J. Anderson, and A. Fleisher. 1988. "Constraints: Knowledge Representation in Design." In *Design Studies,* July 1988.

Hewitt, Carl & Peter De Jong. 1981. "Open Systems." *A.I. Memo* #691, Massachusetts Institute of Technology, Cambridge, MA.

Jonassen, David H., 1989. *Hypertext/hypermedia.* Englewood Cliffs, N.J. : Educational Technology Publications.

Katzen, May (ed.). 1981. *Multi-media communications.* Westport, CT : Greenwood Press.

Larkin, Jill and Herbert Simon. 1987. "Why a diagram is (sometimes) worth 10,000 words." *Cognitive Science,* vol. 11, pp. 65-99.

Liggett, Robin S., William Mitchell, and Milton Tan. 1990. "Multi-Level Analysis and Optimization of Designs."

McAleese, Ray (ed.). 1989. *Hypertext : theory into practice.* Norwood, NJ : Ablex Pub. Co.

McDonald, John Alan, Werner Stuetzle and Andreas Buja. 1990. "Painting Multiple Views of Complex Objects." In *ECOOP/OOPSLA Proceedings 1990,* pp. 245-255. ACM Press/ Addison-Wesley.

Milne, M. 1966. *Computer-Aided Design: An experiment with a method...* University of Oregon Department of Architecture, Eugene: University of Oregon Press.

Mitchell, William J. 1990. "The Design Studio of the Future." In McCullough, Mitchell & Purcell (eds.). *The Electronic Design Studio,* pp. 479-494. Cambridge, MA: MIT Press.

Nelson, Theodor H. 1984. "*Literary machines...* " (6th Ed.). Swarthmore, PA: Ted Nelson.

Nelson, G. 1985. "Juno - A Constraint Based Graphics System." *Computer Graphics (19) Siggraph Proceedings: 235-243.*

Newell, A., and H. Simon. 1972. *Human Problem Solving.* New Jersey: Prentice Hall.

Nielsen, Jakob. 1990. *Hypertext and hypermedia.* Boston: Academic Press.

Parsaye, Kamran et al. 1989. *Intelligent databases: object-oriented, deductive hypermedia technologies.* New York: Wiley.

Purcell, Patrick & Dan Applebaum. 1990. "Light Table: An Interface to Visual Information Systems." In McCullough, Mitchell & Purcell (eds.). *The Electronic Design Studio,* pp. 230 - 238. Cambridge, MA: MIT Press.

Robinson, P. 1989. "The Design Debate." *Computer Graphics World* (12) 4, pp. 101-106.

Smithers, Tim. 1987. "AI-Based Design and Persistent Object Systems." *DAI Research Paper* #329. University of Edinburgh, Edinburgh, Scotland.

Steinitz, Carl. 1990. "A Model of Visual Preference: Arcadia National Park." *Landscape Journal,* Fall 1990.

Tuftie, Edward. 1990. *Envisioning Information.* Cheshire, CT: Graphics Press.

van Bakergem, Dave. 1990. "Image Collections in the Design Studio." In McCullough, Mitchell & Purcell (eds.). *The Electronic Design Studio,* pp. 261 - 271. Cambridge, MA: MIT Press.

Vanier, Dana J. "HyperText: A Computer Tool to Assist Building Design." In McCullough, Mitchell & Purcell (eds.). *The Electronic Design Studio,* pp. 283-300. Cambridge, MA: MIT Press.

24 Recognizing Structures: Some Problems in Reasoning with Drawings

Richard White

EdCAAD
Department of Architecture
University of Edinburgh
Edinburgh, United Kingdom

This paper describes work on our current project aimed at developing a generalized system for performing automated reasoning tasks in various domains, using information extracted from drawings. It briefly describes the MOLE representation system, a frame-like formalism which can be used to build both description and inheritance hierarchies. The use of MOLE for representing graphical objects as well as the objects they represent is also described.The paper goes on to discuss some of the problems faced in the development of systems which can perform reasoning tasks on such representations. In particular, problems arising from the need to map the structures required by the application domain to the drawing description are outlined and a model which adapts existing Artificial Intelligence (AI) techniques to solve these problems is proposed.

Introduction

Our current project (SERC Research Project GR/F61868) is concerned with issues surrounding the extraction of knowledge from drawings, with the aim of allowing this knowledge to be used by applications to perform reasoning tasks. In particular we are considering how such knowledge can be used for assessing the fire safety of buildings, but our aim is that the system should be more general, and capable of supporting applications in any domain.

This paper describes our approach, using the MOLE formalism for representing objects and drawings (Tweed & Bijl 1988, White & Ramscar 1991). The basic knowledge representation scheme is described, along with a method of using it for describing drawings using logical relationships between segments. We propose a model which embodies a schema driven process of drawing analysis, with the schemata upon which a particular interpretation is based being chosen by their relevance to the current task as defined by the user. Mapping between the high level structures of the task domain and the users design description serve to prune the possible search space further.

Knowledge Representation in MOLE

The MOLE knowledge representation system has been more fully described elsewhere (Tweed & Bijl 1988), as has its relationship with a system following the classic frame convention (White 1990). This section will outline the basic knowledge representation system with a view to going on to discuss the description of drawings using this formalism.

Kinds, Slots and Fillers

The basic entities of representation are the *kind*, *slot* and *filler*. A kind (as in "any-kind-of-thing") is defined by a unique name, and a series of slots which make up its description. The description is completed by giving the slots values via their fillers. Thus the description of a cylinder head within a car engine might include:

```
cylinder-head:
   material <- alloy
   part-number <- 61842#45
```

where the kind *cylinder-head* has slots *material* and *part-number* which are filled by the values *alloy* and *61842#45* respectively the <- operator being the "assignment"operator for filling slots with values.

It is important to note that the slots represent decomposition of the *description* of an object rather than the object itself. Bearing this in mind, the relation between the kind and slot is "has-part". Thus the description of the kind *cylinder-head* has the parts *material* and *part-number*.

As well as atomic values, slots can be filled by other kinds, allowing hierarchical descriptions of complex objects to be built up. For example the description of a cylinder head may form part of a larger representation of an engine, which in turn may contribute to the description of a car:

```
car:
    body <-...
    engine <- #syskind001
    chassis <-...

syskind#001:
   bottom-end <-...
   cylinder-head <- #syskind002
   gearbox <-...

syskind#002:
   valves <-...
   piston <- #syskind003
   gasket <-...
```

```
syskind#003:
    material <- alloy
    part-number <- 61842#45
```

Elements of the resulting tree structure can be accessed by specifying the path that is traversed in reaching them:

```
car:engine:cylinder-head:piston:material <- alloy
car:engine:cylinder-head:piston:part-number <- 61842#45
```

These path specifications provide the means by which MOLE descriptions are defined and edited (White & Ramscar 1991).

It is therefore possible to build up structured descriptions of large and complex objects, expressing many levels of granularity within the hierarchy. MOLE does not impose any system of decomposition upon the user. They are free to describe an object to whatever level they require, using whatever method of breaking down the description they think appropriate. As we shall see this will lead to some profound difficulties when it comes to the development of systems for extracting meaning from drawings.

Instances

Another way of describing an object, or part of an object, is as a specific instance of some more general category of things. This is especially the case if we need to describe a number of things which can be described in a similar manner, with only minor differences in their representations.

MOLE allows the user to define one kind as an instance of another kind. The following structure might represent part of a description of a tenement block:

```
tenement:
    location <- guthrie-street
    walls <- stone
    roof <- slate
    number-of-flats <- 6
```

This is not a description of any particular tenement, but describes an imaginary "typical" block in Guthrie Street. If we want to describe a specific tenement then we can define it as an instance of this typical one:

```
number15 ^ tenement
```

where ^ is the *"instance-of"* operator.

Thus the structure describing *number15* inherits all the slots and values describing a typical Guthrie Street block, with the exception of *roof* which is over-ridden by the local value:

number15:
location <- guthrie-street
walls <- stone
roof <- slate
number-of-flats <- 6
roof <- felt

Note that the inherited slots, in italics, are not stored as part of the *number15* structure, but are available for evaluation in the same way as if they were. As with the decomposition of objects, MOLE places no restriction on the user as to how to organize inheritance with the exception that a kind cannot inherit from more than one other kind.

Counterparts

Finally, and recently, we have introduced the *counterpart* relation (Ramscar 1991). This enables structure sharing where two kinds share the same slots and fillers, and changes to one result in changes to the other. To use a simple example, if a rectangular room was specified, then the opposite sides would be defined as counterparts:

room: wall1:length <-10
wall2:length <- 5
wall3:length = wall1:length
wall4:length = wall2:length

where = is the counterpart operator.

Thus whenever *wall1:length* or *wall3:length* has their value changed the value of their counterpart will be changed also. This relation provides the means for users to include their own constraints on values within a design description.
With decomposition, inheritance and counterparts, MOLE provides a flexible means of representing any type of object. The following section describes how this formalism can be used for the representation of drawings.

Drawing in MOLE:

The Basic Ingredients

The current method of representing drawings in MOLE was developed several years ago in EdCAAD (Steel & Szalapaj 1983) and was based upon a desire to have a representation system which could combine graphic and abstract descriptions of objects within MOLE, and which would treat lines symbolically rather than mathematically according to a particular coordinate system. The method described here is based upon the metaphor of constructing drawings from pencil and ink lines as practiced by designers at a drawing board. However the achievement of the original aims is not inextricably linked to the use of this metaphor.

Part of the MOLE system (as distinct from the MOLE representation language) is a *drawing machine*, which takes graphical input from a designer and generates MOLE descriptions corresponding to the resulting graphical objects. The first step in the production of a drawing is for the designer to call up a top level kind, say *house-plan* by which the resulting descriptions can be accessed.

In line with the pencil and ink metaphor, the designer first lays down some "pencil-lines". These will later be "inked in" to produce the actual drawing. The pencil lines, or *construction lines*, act as carriers for the final ink lines, or *segments*, and have no physical dimensions other than an angle, relative to some pre-defined origin. The intersection of two construction lines defines a *construction point*, and two construction points, in turn, define the endpoints of a segment. Figure 1 shows a simple example of this process.

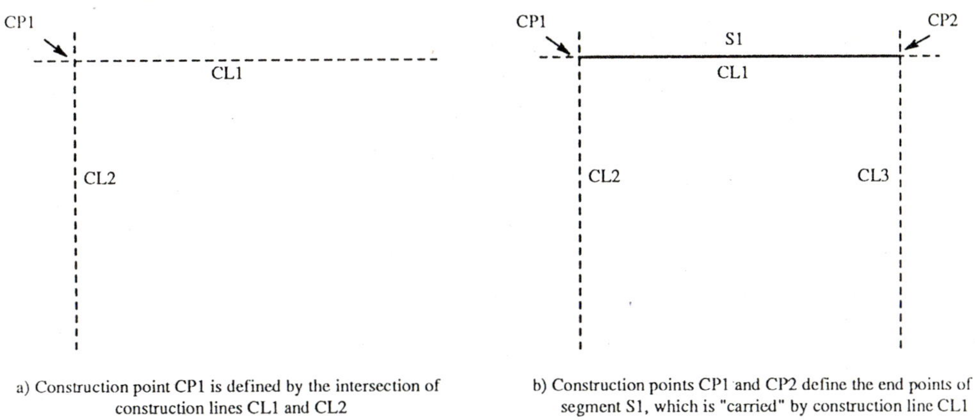

Figure 1. Drawing using construction lines.

As well as containing information about the construction lines which define them, construction point structures contain attachment information which defines how segment intersections will react as the drawing is manipulated graphically (see Steel & Szalapaj 1983 for a description of some of the problems of attachment). The segment structure contains slots for defining its endpoints, length and bearer, the latter pointing to a construction line which defines the angle of the segment. Further information referring to the style properties of the segment is also included. Figure 2 provides an example of segment and construction line descriptions for a rectangle.

While this description may appear over-complex for the description of a simple rectangle, the construction points and lines will be used as part of the definition of other shapes without the need for repetition. A single construction line can form the basis for more than one geometric form, even if they are non-congruent, and this feature allows separate objects within a drawing to be easily orientated with respect to one another. In effect, the user is defining their own grid to be used for the positioning and orientation of objects within the drawing. An advantage of this system is that lines on this grid need only be defined when needed (i.e. will not cover the entire drawing space) and are not limited to orthogonal orientations.

As the graphical elements are represented as MOLE expressions, it is possible for the designer to edit these expressions directly, and the drawing machine will reflect these changes in the drawing. Additionally, and more importantly, it allows for the addition of higher level structures to the drawing representation.

```
mole:[richard:[
    conline1:[angle<- 0],
    conline2:[angle<- 90],
    conline3:[angle<- 90],
    conline4:[angle<- 0],

    conpt1:[first_conline<- conline2,
        second_conline<- conline4],
    conpt2:[first_conline<- conline3,
        second_conline<- conline4],
    conpt3:[first_conline<- conline1,
        second_conline<- conline3],
    conpt4:[first_conline <- conline1,
        second_conline<- conline2],

    seg1:[      first_conpt<- conpt1,
        second_conpt<- conpt2,
        bearer<- conline4,
        length<- 3060,
        style<- "solid"],
    seg2:[      first_conpt<- conpt2,
        second_conpt<- conpt3,
        bearer<- conline3,
        length<- 2640,
        style<- "solid"],
    seg3:[      first_conpt<- conpt3,
        second_conpt<- conpt4,
        ...
        style<- "solid"],
    seg4:[      first_conpt<- conpt4,
        second_conpt<- conpt1,
        ...
        style<- "solid"]].
```

Figure 2. A rectangle defined in MOLE.

Building Larger Things

If we take the description of a simplified house plan that might be produced by the drawing machine (figure 3), it will consist of a large number of segment definitions, along with the construction line and point definitions supporting them. MOLE enables these bottom level descriptions to be linked together into higher level structure, for example into squares or rectangles, perhaps using the inheritance mechanism to produce generalized template descriptions.

The top level plan could then be described in terms of these higher level structures rather than the lowest level segment descriptions. This would convert a single one-layer description (figure 4a) into a two-layer description (figure 4b), and other layers could be added equally easily if required. The process of producing extra layers of description can be seen as *compositional* if carried out in a bottom-up manner as described here, with simple elements being combined to form more complex ones. Similar effects can be obtained using a *decompositional* or top-down manner, where description starts at the highest level and each level is split into lower level constituent parts until the basic level of representation is reached. MOLE supports both methods of structuring complex object and the criteria used for combining or decomposing elements to form new ones are solely the responsibility of the designer. Similarly the system does not limit the description hierarchy to binary trees, but allows any type of graph structures, including cyclic, to be built.

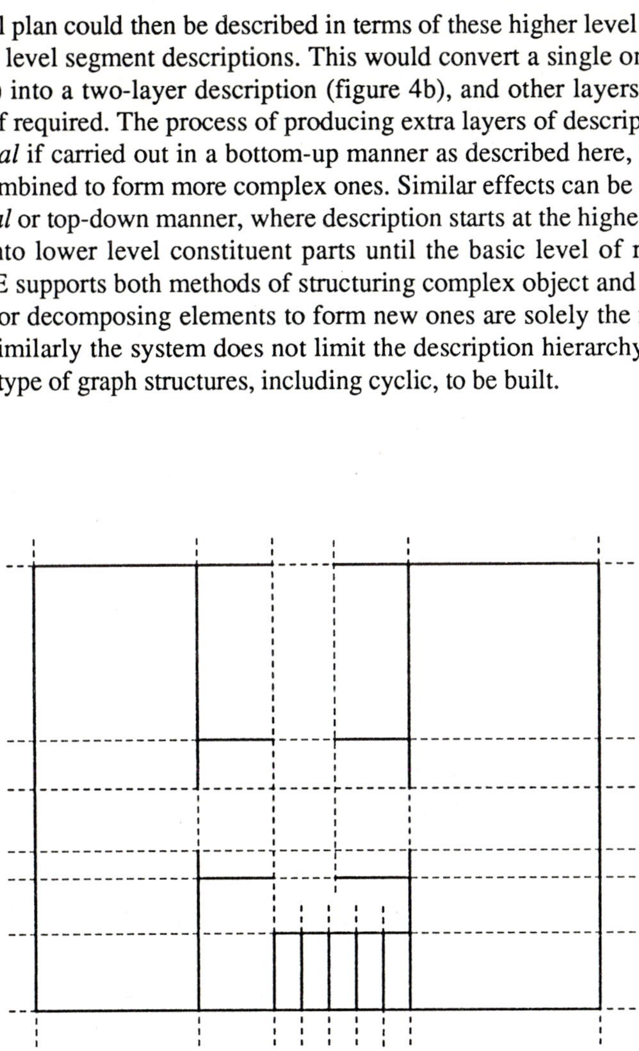

Figure 3. Simple plan of a house - ground floor.

What is to be Gained from Adding Extra Layers of Description

From the designers' point of view, drawings can be manipulated at levels higher than the basic segment descriptions, say at the level of the square. A designer can group a series of lines into a square, either graphically or by the direct editing of MOLE expressions, and then move the lines together as a square, rather than individually. This will be quicker, more efficient and lead to fewer errors.

Additionally it will be possible for the designer to view the design description at any one of a number of different granularities. The granularity of a description is an expression of how much detail is present. At high levels of description, there is less detail than at low levels. The granularity required of a particular view of a description will depend on the use to which that view is to be put. For example if the description of a building is to be used for town-planning, then nothing more might be required than a very high level description giving information about such things as its overall shape, size, and elevation. If the building was to be marketed to clients then they would want a lower level view of the description, with details of the number of rooms, their sizes etc. Finally, if the design description was to be used as a basis for the building process itself, then a still lower level view giving details of materials and quantities would be required. The careful structuring of the design representation could allow all these viewpoints to be accessed from one description.

Structuring the design description also leads to advantages from the point of view of building systems to manipulate this description automatically. Any such system will, at some stage, have to perform search operations on the plan description, to access certain drawing elements. In a flat, single layer, representation this effectively becomes a sequential search through all the elements of the drawing. This can be likened to searching for the definition of a single word in a random list of definitions - a long and tedious process. If intermediate levels of description are introduced, producing a tree structure, then the search is made easier and more efficient.

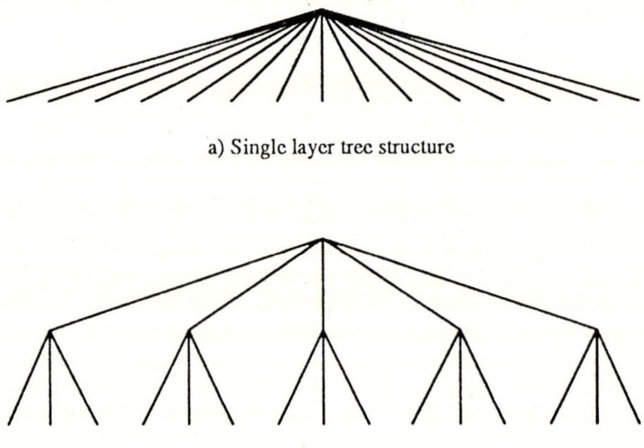

Figure 4. Tree diagrams showing addition of intermediate structures.

If we apply this to our previous problem of searching for word definitions, we might choose to put our definitions in alphabetical order of the first letter of each word. This can be imagined as a tree structure with a row of nodes representing each letter of the alphabet with a corresponding list of words under each. Thus if we know that the first letter of the word we are looking for is 'f' then we only have to search the sub-tree under the 'f' node. Further levels of organization can be introduced by ordering words within each sub-tree according to their subsequent letters until we have a dictionary! A more complete discussion of the problems of searching trees can be found in Korf (1987).

What Does the Designer Mean?

We have considered how large structures can be built, adding extra layers of description to a design. At this point it is useful to distinguish between *graphical* and *non-graphical* information. Graphical structures will primarily be created by the MOLE drawing machine and will consist of construction line, construction point and segment information.

Non-graphical information will consist of any structures representing facts about the object depicted by the drawing, rather than the drawing itself. These structures may be linked to elements of graphical information. Thus a designer may build a description of a house, consisting of a number of rooms, which in turn consist of a number of walls. As well as information about materials and dimensions, the structure may also point to the elements in the drawing which correspond to each of the walls, thus linking non-graphical and graphical information.

MOLE gives the designer the absolute freedom to link these two types of information in any way they wish, including the choice of adding no extra information to the drawing at all. If the designer were the only person to use the resulting knowledge structures then this would be no problem. However, certain complications arise when we try to perform some automated reasoning task upon the design description produced by the designer. The nature of such tasks will be varied, as it is one aim of our current research to show how a common formalism can be used as the basis of many applications. There may be different goals, one application may be giving feedback to the designer concerning how well their design conforms to certain regulations, another may be to assist the designer in complex calculations regarding the energy efficiency of a particular design.

Whatever the application, each will need to map different non-graphical concepts to the basic graphical objects in the drawing description. For example, our current project includes development of an application to judge how well a design conforms to fire safety regulations, and such an application will need to deal in terms of internal spaces, fire barriers and escape routes etc. It is unlikely that the non-graphical structures used by a designer will bear much relation to these. Even if the designer did have details of the structures used by a particular application, and structured her design description accordingly, problems would arise if the same design were to be used, perhaps at a later date, as data for a different one.

The precise nature of our problem, that of mapping structures from one domain to another will depend, to a large extent, on how much non-graphical information is supplied by the designer.

The Designer Doesn't Say - Analysis of Graphical Information

In some cases the designer may not have provided any information in addition to that produced by the graphics machine. Thus any description that exists refers purely to the drawing, and not to the object which the drawing is intended to depict. In some respect this problem is relatively simple and consists of imposing structure onto a structureless description. Thus the application might search through the drawing description searching for patterns which would fit the particular higher level descriptions it required.

This problem is similar to the high level pattern matching required of vision systems, and the models used to either explain human vision, or the implementation of computer vision systems may be of some help to us. In vision systems a mapping is sought between the representation of external stimuli produced by the low level vision system and a representation of the corresponding object in memory. In our domain, the graphical information, defined in terms of segments, can be likened to representations of the external stimulus and the high level, non-graphical structures the object representation in memory.

Amongst the many methods used for such processing (see Spoehr & Lehmkuhle (1982) - chapter 3 - for an overview) the *template* or *schema* based approach seems particularly suitable for our purposes. In this, memory contains a series of schemata representing prototypical examples of the objects which might be represented. A particular schema would contain information about those features shared by each member of the class. The external stimulus will be an instance of one of these schemata, and is matched by abstracting its representation until its class type is found.

A particularly pertinent example of schema driven image analysis is the ANON system (Pridmore & Joseph 1990). Designed for analyzing drawings of mechanical engineering drawings, it uses high level schemata to control all aspects of the interpretation process. A high level schema, describes general classes of objects within the drawing such as solid lines, junctions or outlines, and guides the interpretation process by specifying a set of rules for recognizing and combining lower level graphical entities. It is designed to deal with information at the pixel level, but the same approach is equally valid when dealing with analysis of MOLE descriptions.

In some respects our problem is easier than that faced by ANON's designers in that we do not have to try and decide which schema is the most appropriate to use. Our analysis will be goal driven, with the schema or schemata to be used in the interpretation of the graphical information depending on the task which the user has requested of the particular application. Associated with each task will be set of schemata, in the form of MOLE kinds, which describe the concepts which form the basis of that application along with some information about the geometry of these structures. For example, if one of the basic concept is a room, and associated with this is the information that rooms are rectangular, then when a user invokes an application task which refers to rooms, the analysis process will use the schema for rectangles in interpreting the graphical information in the design.

The use of such goal driven techniques will help to cut down the search space of the analysis process, ruling out a great many possible interpretations of the drawing that are irrelevant to the current task. However the process may still be slow, and subject to the ambiguities of interpretation that arise in all such systems. The process can be made more efficient, and less error prone, by using any non-graphical information that the user has supplied in the design description.

The Designer Does Say - Mapping of Non-graphical Structures

There is no reason why the approach described above should not be used even if the designer has specified some non-graphical information, with the application simply ignoring it, solely using the drawing machine information and its own schemata. However the efficiency and accuracy of the interpretation process as a whole will be improved if the explicit links between graphical and non-graphical information that the designer has provided can be used. This shifts the problem of determining mappings between graphical elements in the users design description and non-graphical structures in the application domain to that of determining mappings between two sets of non-graphical structures.

Such problems have been studied extensively in the field of analogical reasoning (Gentner 1988, Keane 1988, Holyoak & Thagard 1989). In this type of reasoning, a particular domain, known as the *base* is understood, and acts as a source of information which can be used to help understand a second, poorly understood domain, known as the *target*. A classic example is that of the use of the solar system to explain the Rutherford model of sub-atomic structure, where the sun corresponds to the nucleus of the atom and the planets, in orbit around the sun, correspond to the electrons in orbit around the nucleus.

Despite many different approaches, all models include some way of specifying the semantic similarity between elements of the two domains. There may be differences in the level at which this applies. For example in Gentner's 'Structure Mapping' model (Gentner 1983, Gentner 1988) any similarities between elements at the lowest level are ignored, with only functions or predicates playing an active part in the mapping process. In contrast Holyoak and Thagard (Holyoak & Thagard, 1989) propose a model based on parallel constraint satisfaction which allows semantic information between any level of element to be taken into account.

The problem with this, as far as we are concerned, is that it assumes at least a partial knowledge of the target domain, and the relationship between its elements and those in the base. What we need to do is to determine whether we have this type of information available to us when mapping MOLE structures, and at what level this information might exist.

Unfortunately we can trust very little of what the designer tells us. Even if they build a structure that has the same name as one used by the application, there is no reason to suppose that they refer to the same thing. For example a structure that the designer considers to be two spaces divided by a wall might be considered a single space by a fire safety application if the dividing wall offers no resistance to the progress of a fire.

So our problem, when attempting to map non-graphical structures, is determining at what level can we ground two structures, and say that they represent the same thing. As a MOLE kind is defined by its constituent slots and fillers, we are going to have to start at this level. A starting point might be to say that two structures can be considered equal if they share a number of slots with common fillers. This general principle will need to be adapted to deal with task definitions, and further information will be needed to allow it to work efficiently. For example, some slots are more important than others in defining the characteristics of an object. In a kind describing a cat, the slots specifying dentition and skeletal structure would be more characteristic and therefore more important than those specifying the animal's color and fur length. Any mechanism for matching kinds by their constituent slots will need some way of weighting the slots so that matches between important slots are more highly regarded than matches between less important ones.

Pragmatic factors are also commonly considered in analogical mapping processes (e.g Holyoak & Thagard 1989). Thus features of a domain that are considered central to the behavior of that domain are more likely to be mapped than those which are not. It is likely that similar factors will be useful in guiding our mapping process. In the domain of fire safety rules, for example, escape routes, such as staircases of fire escapes, are particularly important structures and will be mapped preferentially to other less important ones.

It is important to point out that our concept of importance, both at the slot and structure level, only extend to the application domain. We have no idea of the relative contributions of the various parts of the user's design descriptions. Nevertheless, these principles, form the field of analogical reasoning will prove to be important and useful in our task of determining potential mappings between designer and task non-graphical information.

What Do We Do if it All Goes Wrong?

Associated with attempts to map application structures to the drawing description produced by the designer is the problem of knowing what to do if the process fails. The application may be unable to find, or impose, any organization on the description to match the structures it uses. In this case it is likely that the application will simply fail.

Alternatively, matching structures may be found, but in a way that does not correspond to the organization of the drawing originally envisaged by the designer. This is more likely to be the case if no high level structures have been defined, but may occur even if they have. The misinterpretation of drawings is likely to lead to the designer becoming confused, and frustrated with the system.

A simple method of solving these problems would be to force the designer to organize her drawings using the structures required by the application, thus removing the need for the application to perform any mapping at all. This however implies a level of prescription which is completely at odds with the philosophy behind the development of MOLE (Tweed & Bijl 1988). It also implies that a different structuring would need to be imposed on a drawing for each application was to be used for. Whilst MOLE could support such a structure it would lead to an over-complex representation. Further problems would also arise if a description was to be used for applications other than those intended by the designer.

Many of these problems will be alleviated, by introducing some degree of dialogue between the designer and the application. The use of dialogue in explanation is a topic that is currently attracting much attention, (e.g. Cawsey 1989) and it is likely that a similar approach will be useful in the process of determining the structure of a designer's drawing. Whilst the precise approach will depend on how we eventually decide to structure the designer/application interface, dialogue will help us to get extra information if the search for napkins cannot proceed; to provide the designer with feedback as to what interpretations are being applied; and to give the designer the final choice in ambiguity resolution. Some consideration of the nature of the dialogue will be essential. For example, getting a balance between too much interruption in the design process and getting too little information for the mapping to be found will be particularly difficult. However, despite this, and other problems, a dialogue based approach will help considerably in the process of developing systems for automated reasoning with drawings.

Conclusion

It is important that the provision of design support tools within the MOLE environment does not impinge upon the flexibility of representation provided by that environment, despite the problems that this creates. We propose a system, based upon appropriate AI techniques, which will interpret design descriptions in any number of contexts, with the minimum of guidance from the designer themselves.

We suggest that the principles and problems at the heart of this system go beyond the interpretation of drawings by a single application and may be applicable to the wider problem of multi-user design systems. In any situation where more than one person is working on a design the problem of communication between them arises. In the case of pure pencil and paper designers, then there are conventions and symbols for specifying what different parts of a drawing mean. To an extent the problem is solved outside the design system itself. In developing MOLE for such situations we could take the same approach, insisting that designers communicate about their meanings outside the MOLE environment itself. However we can apply the principles used in mapping between designer and application structures to the case where we want to determine mappings between structures developed by two designers. The problem will be a lot less constrained, in that we have little knowledge about what either of the designers mean, and thus more complicated. However it would make an interesting and worthwhile extension to our current work.

Acknowledgments

The author is supported by SERC research grant GR/F61868.

References

Cawsey, A. J. 1989. "Explanatory Dialogues." *Interacting with Computers*, no. 1: 69-92.

Gentner, D. 1983. "Structure-mapping: a theoretical framework for analogy." *Cognitive Science, no.* 7: 155-170.

Gentner, D. 1988. "Analogical Inference and Analogical Access." In A. Prieditis (ed.). *Analogica*. London: Pitman.

Holyoak, K. J., and P. R. Thagard. 1989. "Analogical Mapping by Constraint Satisfaction." *Cognitive Science*, no. 13: 295-355.

Keane, M. 1988. "Analogical Mechanisms." *Artificial Intelligence Review*, no. 2: 229-250.

Korf, R. 1988. "Search: a survey of recent results." In H. Shrobe (ed). *Exploring Artificial Intelligence: survey talks from the national conferences on artificial intelligence*. Morgan Kaufmann.

Pridmore, T. P., and S. H. Joseph. 1990. "Integrating Visual Search with Visual Memory in a Knowledge Directed Image Interpretation System." In *Proceedings of the British Machine Vision Conference 1990*.

Ramscar, M. J. A. 1991. *Counterpart relationships in MOLE*. Technical Report, EdCAAD, Dept. of Architecture, University of Edinburgh.

Spoehr, K. T., and S. W. Lehmkuhle. 1982. *Visual Information Processing*. San Fransisco: W. H. Freeman & Co.

Steel S. W. D., and P. J. Szalapaj. 1983. *Pictures without numbers: graphical realization of logical models.* Technical Report, EdCAAD, Dept. of Architecture, University of Edinburgh.

Tweed, C., and A. Bijl. 1988. "MOLE: a reasonable logic for design." In P. J. W. ten Hagen, T. Tomiyama and V. Akman (eds). *Intelligent CAD Systems 2*. Berlin: Springer-Verlag.

White, R. H. 1990. *MOLE or ART - which way forward?* Technical Report, EdCAAD, Dept. of Architecture, University of Edinburgh.

White, R. H., and M. J. A. Ramscar. 1990. *A Quick Guide to Mole2*. Technical Report, EdCAAD, Dept. of Architecture, University of Edinburgh.

25 What Could Artificial Intelligence Know about the Knowledge Involved in the Design Process?

Khaldoun Zreik

CIMA
9, rue Barbanègre
75019 Paris, France

The nature of the knowledge involved in the design process is very specific and it is incompletely known. Its control becomes very complicated owing to the large number of dynamic parameters and functions which define the relationships between one another. So we consider two relevant facts:

1. all knowledge involved in the design process could not have been foreseen;
2. the help of computer technology in this domain is badly oriented.
Two major questions will be posed here:
a. what kind of design knowledge do designers explicitly master?
b. and which parts of it can computer technology represent today?

This paper aims to build a simple panorama of the knowledge involved in the architectural design process. Actors, resources and corresponding classifications of this knowledge and also its dynamic distribution will be presented. This paper also throws light upon how important are artificial intelligence sciences and tools for the improvement of the design process computability.

Introduction

One can figure out that the knowledge involved in the design process is divided into three domains: the explicit-known domain, the implicit-known domain, and the domain of the unknown.

The explicitly known domain consists of a set of conventional modelled knowledge and heuristics which is rapidly expressed, easily represented, and currently used or transferred to others. This domain of knowledge includes some part of intuitive knowledge and a large part of standard knowledge (technique, economics, regulation, etc.).

The implicitly known domain of knowledge includes all knowledge which can be felt but cannot be expressed or formulated properly from the beginning. In fact this domain concerns the greater part of knowledge involved in the design process.

According to Zeisel (Zeisel 1981), design consists of three elementary activities which are imagining, presenting and testing. On the other hand, Heath (Heath 1989) considers that innovative or original thinking and decision are possible at every stage of the design process. Thus the nature of imagining or innovative thinking is rather implicit.

Today most CAD systems deal only with the explicitly known domain of knowledge so they don't take into consideration all knowledge involved in the design process.

Does One Really Need to Model the Implicitly Known Domain?

In order to answer this question, many people are certainly endeavoring directly or indirectly to find out what the design process is about exactly or at least what is to be seen or understood in this domain? Furthermore what part of known knowledge will one be able to express clearly?
Some research works have tried to bring some positive answers which in practice have never been very convincing.
On the other hand it has been proved that integrating all the knowledge which could be involved in the design process is not always interesting. Thus a distinction must be made between uninteresting knowledge and knowledge which can not be formulated or represented properly.
Otherwise one must identify this problem and prevent CAD systems from taking this relevant fact into account by introducing at least a high level of interactivity which enables users to choose and integrate the different types of knowledge they manipulate. Finally the question remains the same: what kind of knowledge could and must be integrated in a CAD or Intelligent CAD system?
For these reasons we distinguish three kind of taxonomies to represent the knowledge involved in the design process: classical, professional and practical (see figure 1).

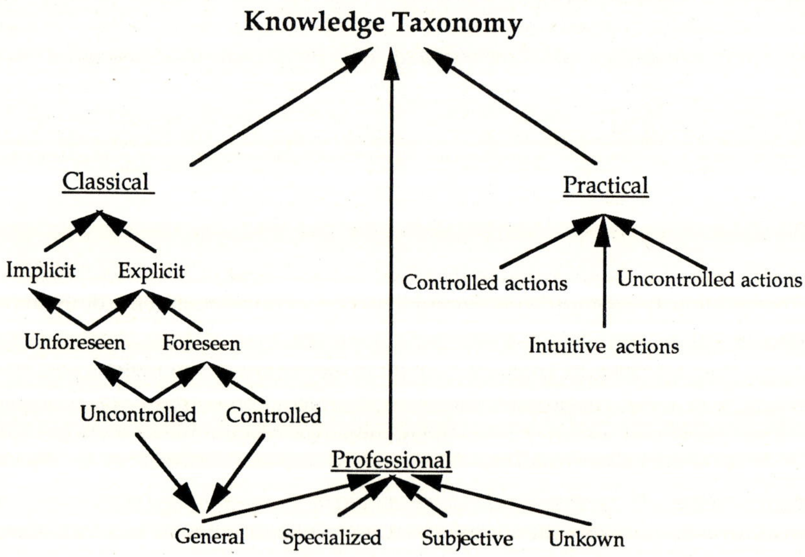

Figure 1. A knowledge taxonomy representation.

A Classical Taxonomy of Knowledge in Design: A Naïve Point of View

In this paragraph we suggest a general and naïve definition of the explicit and the implicit parts of knowledge which may be manipulated by the designer.

Explicit Knowledge

This is the type of knowledge which the designer claims as to be able to express clearly. Two classes can be distinguished:

The Foreseen Knowledge: it is the set of facts considered necessary in order to carry out an action or a task. It can be controlled or uncontrolled. The knowledge is controlled when one knows explicitly *when, where and how* to use it in a design process. Otherwise it is uncontrolled.

Today most CAD systems use only controlled knowledge by means of the AI techniques (Brown et al. 88) some of them can even integrate a set of unstructured complete knowledge which could be considered as uncontrolled.

The Unforeseen Knowledge: it is absolutely impossible to foresee all details about knowledge and particularly when one deals with the uncontrolled part of knowledge.

In fact all uncontrolled knowledge (UK) can eventually become controlled knowledge (CK) in an advanced stage of the design process, due to a transformation function T:

T(UKm) ---------> {CKn, X}

Up to now T can be presented as an interactive function between the system and the designer.

X can be the unforeseen or the implicit knowledge or set of facts required to integrate UKm or required when UKm is being integrated. If in certain situations X is empty {Ø}, then the UKm is a kind of unstructured complete knowledge which becomes certainty a controlled knowledge by using AI techniques (Miniton et al. 89).

Very few CAD systems can actually manipulate part of the unforeseen knowledge. This can be related on the one hand to the paucity of the knowledge acquisition tools used in CAD systems and on the other hand to the problem of managing a dynamic interactive man-machine system.

Implicit Knowledge

What is implicit knowledge? It is the knowledge which is felt though it seems impossible to express it in a given context. This is the very situation in which one misses the suitable tools (models or examples) to explain and to formulate an action or an object.

Implicit knowledge is the knowledge that one claims to understand, see and even use, but of which it is unfortunately impossible to tell anything (describe or explain) at a given time or in a given situation. Otherwise in certain situations or circumstances the implicit knowledge (IK) can become explicit knowledge (EK) as follows:

FT(IKm,S,T, X) ------> (EKn)

with:

FT: transformation function depending on:

S : given situation;

T : given time;

X : set of other parameters (sociology, psychology, information level, etc.).

Up to now the main operator of this function is the knowledge engineer whose elementary operations could be presented as follows (see figure 2):

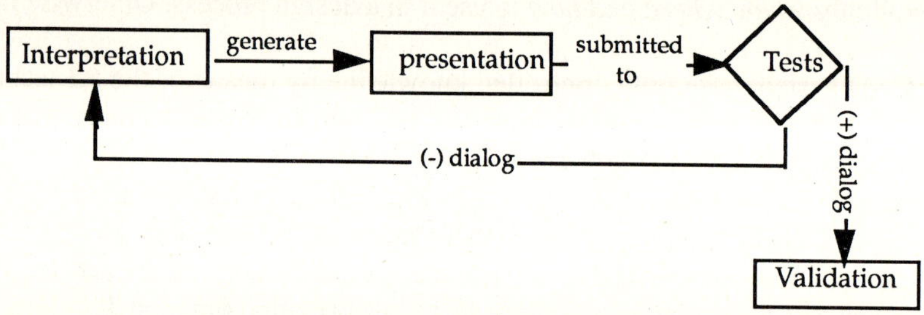

Figure 2. Knowledge engineer's elementary operations.

The system, the operator and even the knowledge engineer must be aware of this kind of knowledge. They should wait and be ready to seize on the proper moment and in the right situation to find it out. It is nearly impossible to decide when and where the opportunity will arise. This is why an intelligent computer memory can be a good assistant.
N.B.: If we accept this analysis we must admit that the certainty of both explicit and implicit knowledge is always suspect.

A Professional Taxonomy of Knowledge in Design: A Knowledge Engineer's Point of View

At a different level the knowledge engineer uses other parameters to classify the knowledge involved in the design process. These parameters are more specialized than those described previously. He tries indeed to acquire as much information as possible by using several techniques (Hart 86) (dialogue with experts, documentation, experimentation, etc.) and at the same time he matches this information according to the state of the art in the CAD systems technology.
The main objective of the knowledge engineer is to improve the reliability of a CAD system in the design domain. He often begins by selecting parts of the knowledge which can be modelled and he cuts off the rest. Then he chooses the system which seems the most adapted to the resulting knowledge base (KB) then he starts again to adapt the knowledge base to the chosen system and so on (see figure 3).

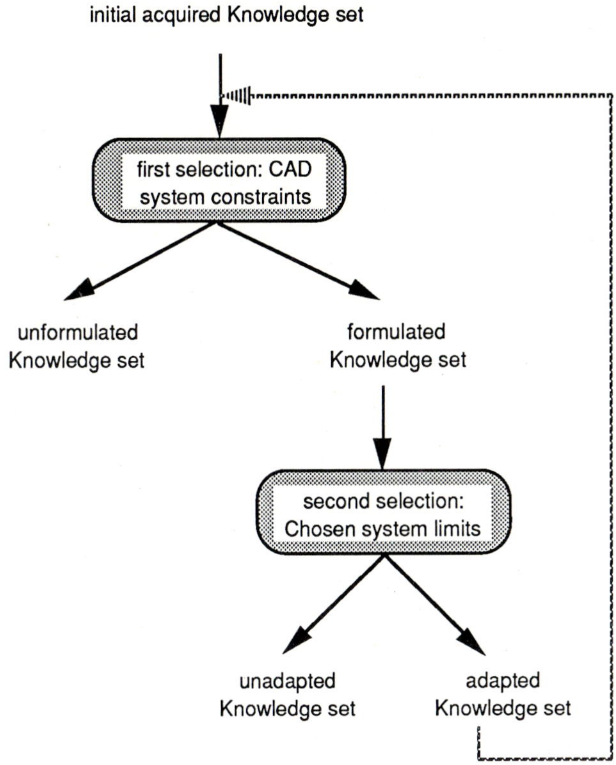

Figure 3. The knowledge selection process.

To throw light upon this idea, let us consider the problem of the architectural design where the knowledge engineer distinguishes and faces: the controlled general knowledge, the uncontrolled general knowledge, the specialized knowledge, the subjective knowledge and the unknown knowledge.

The Controlled General Knowledge (CGK)

The general knowledge in our example is the set of geometrical, technical and economical calculations, urban regulations, planning programs, etc. The controlled general knowledge is the explicit part of the general knowledge which is clearly represented and located. It consists of the formulated, published and taught knowledge. It can be manipulated by non-specialists. Generally most of this knowledge is nearly certain.

According to the artificial intelligence vocabulary, the controlled general knowledge can be defined as the part of knowledge for which the meta-knowledge is well known (i.e. when, where and how this knowledge must be used).

Let us consider the instance T and the situation S in which {G} is the set of general knowledge and {M} is the set of corresponding meta-knowledge. We can therefore define the set of controlled general knowledge {C} as follows:

it is an application Δ (T,S) of {M} on {G}:

$\forall T$ and $\forall S$, $\Delta(T,S)$: {M, G} ----> {C}, where $\{C\} \supset \{G\}$, that is

[$\forall$ c $\in$ {C}, $\exists$ m $\in$ {M} by which $\Delta(T,S)$:{M, G} ---> c]

The Uncontrolled General Knowledge (UGK)

This is the set of general knowledge which does not always have enough corresponding meta-knowledge for every situation. In other words it is the set of elements which belongs to the set of general knowledge and does not belong to the set of controlled general knowledge.

Let us consider {U} as the set of uncontrolled general knowledge, so we can represent it as follows: for the instance T0 in the situation S0

[$\forall$ u $\in$ {U}, $\neg\exists$ m Œ {M} by which Δ(T0,S0):{M, G} ---> u],

or

u $\in$ {U} if u $\in$ {G} and u $\notin$ {C}

{U} = {G} - {C}.

The Specialized Knowledge (SPK)

This is the set of the knowledge acquired by practice. The designer often faces in his practice different situations containing new constraints never manipulated before. In this case the designer generally solves his problem by analogy with other similar situations. So the specialized knowledge is a kind of experience consisting of the set of knowledge which allows one to deal with different situations.

In fact each designer stresses differently this part of knowledge according to his personal history, his degree of competence and his cultural background.

The specialized knowledge can be a simple knowledge, a set of knowledge or meta-knowledge.

At a given moment T0 and in a given situation S0 a specialized knowledge can become a controlled general knowledge at T1 or in S1 (with T1>T0 or S1 # S0). In fact it is perfectly natural that past and solid experiences should be transformed into general knowledge.

N.B.: experience proves that the specialized knowledge is not to be totally and automatically integrated into the controlled general knowledge; only the part of knowledge frequently used in design practice is interesting to be taken into account.

The Subjective Knowledge (SUK)

This is the set of knowledge that the designer may use to face a new situation or constraints never met before. In another way it could be the set of knowledge related to creative or innovative activities. A general characteristic of the subjective knowledge is that it is too difficult to explain. It nearly has never been told, written down or formulated. A new situation means that constraints and parameters have undergone some changes which do not allow us to adopt traditional solutions. According to the importance of these changes, designers face the following situations:

– The case of a known new situation:

1. The designer can recognize the type of the situation by analogy with previous situations and he tries to adapt a new solution for it. Here he uses much subjective knowledge.
2. The designer cannot recognize the situation via a similar one. This means that the most thought of relevant parameters and characteristics used to recognize the situation have been changed or annulled. The problem in this case is to find, introduce, redefine or rather to create some new concepts which can be useful in order to recognize the situation. In this case the designer begins by using his subjective knowledge as a key to the other kinds of knowledge which could be relevant in this situation.

– The case of an unknown new situation:

1. The designer knows only about some constraints and some parameters concerning the situation. In order to give a solution the designer uses, in addition to his general knowledge, parts of his subjective and specialized knowledge. Therefore he investigates the set of given parameters and constraints to verify the reliability of his solution-plan.
2. The designer has the full responsibility and liberty for a solution; it means that there is no given critical data to limit the number of possible solutions. Sometimes the designer suggests or more precisely tries to apply a new idea or an unexpected philosophy which can help him start a solution-plan. At the beginning the designer uses only some general knowledge or meta-knowledge. This allows him to acquire a new knowledge corresponding to his idea or philosophy. This new knowledge persists if it is successful; otherwise it will be annulled and the designer starts again. Therefore it can be supposed that in certain situations the designer uses meta-knowledge in order to generate a new knowledge; so we can consider the subjective knowledge in this case as a kind of meta-knowledge.

Thus several questions concerning subjective knowledge could be raised:

- Should meta-knowledge be defined before the concerned knowledge itself?
- Is there any rule or any parameter to control this process?
- Should meta-knowledge and knowledge be conceptually separated?
- When must these questions be taken into consideration?
- Etc.

The Unknown (U)

It could be an answer to many questions which have been asked for a long time. The unknown has never been told, explained, formulated, modelled nor even directly felt. Managing the unknown is an important criteria in expert competence.

N.B.: This paper does not give any direct solution to these problems. But it claims the importance of adapting a very high level of dynamic man/machine dialog controlled by knowledge acquisition and learning techniques to be associated to a CAD system.

A Practical Taxonomy of Knowledge in Design: The Designer's Point of View

In a pragmatic approach we consider that the knowledge engineer must develop and integrate the basic set of design knowledge. Then the dialog between the designer and the system must insure the evolvement of the domain knowledge. So in order to define an adapted man/machine dialog we must take into consideration the user's point of view which will be the principal future source of design knowledge.

In a design project the designer is somehow both the customer and the producer of knowledge. He manipulates several kinds of knowledge at different stages of his work; therefore he is the user of the known part of design knowledge.

Explicitly designer works by means of actions (declared goals) and not directly by means of knowledge. This means that the designer chooses an action then uses part of his knowledge to achieve it. But sometimes he chooses indirectly an action in order to investigate a knowledge later on. For example an architect chooses a type of facade in order to use a special form of window. In this case the set of knowledge concerning this window is the discrete goal and the type of facade is the declared one (see figure 4). So in this paragraph we are interested only in declared goals and we do not deal with discrete ones whose acquisition and manipulation cannot yet be controlled.

In this context the designer can have a very special point of view about the taxonomy of the set of knowledge he uses.

Maybe it can be represented in figure 5 in which we can recognize three kinds of trained actions: the controlled, the uncontrolled and the implicit actions.

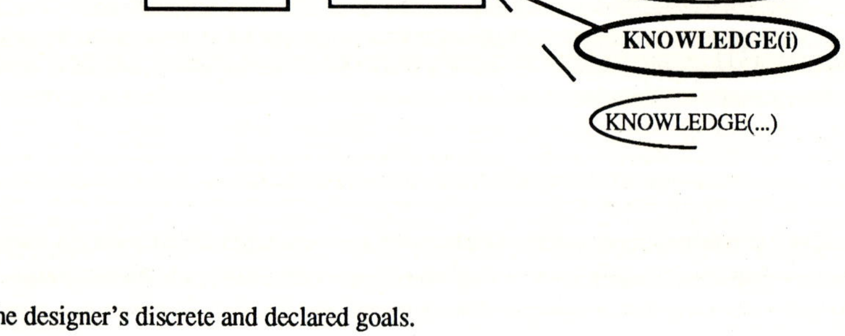

Figure 4. The designer's discrete and declared goals.

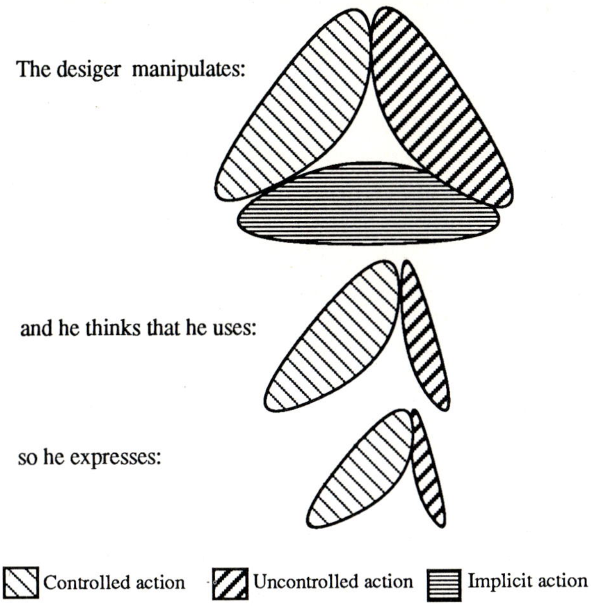

Figure 5. The designer's point of view.

The Controlled Actions

It is the part of actions that the designer knows very well how to use, why and when. Controlled actions usually use controlled general knowledge. For example the designer knows that facades, spaces and walls must all be defined before he locates the windows. Most traditional knowledge-based system techniques can manipulate this kind of action.

The Uncontrolled Actions

These actions are often made by the designer during the design process; yet he cannot specify precisely in advance why, when and how to use them. For example every designer knows that he sometimes has to define the location of the sanitary equipments. Knowledge engineers consider these actions as a set of uncontrolled general knowledge. Acquiring this kind of action must be dynamic and requires advanced knowledge acquisition tools based on machine learning techniques (Zreik 89).

The Intuitive (or Implicit) Actions

An intuitive action expresses in fact the cleverness and the competence of the designer. It is usually implicit and sometimes the designer can feel it only a long time after he has used it, generally when he faces a similar situation. To define the shape of a facade for a private house for example is often an implicit action. Architects usually explain their choice because of the need to please their customer.

Taking this fact into account can lead to the understanding of the role which should be played by the knowledge engineer or by the knowledge acquisition tools (KAT) to model in order to manipulate the design knowledge's world.

A Dynamic Distribution of the Knowledge Involved in the Design Process: A Knowledge Engineer's Point of View

Let us consider the design domain as it has been previously defined. To improve the performance of the design model we have tried to classify the different types of knowledge involved in the design process according to their importance in a given project.

The figure 6 shows some examples of knowledge distributions corresponding to certain projects at their first stage of design process. The following cases have been chosen to throw light upon these distributions and their variations:

Case 1 : designing a traditional project for a council house construction in a known regular urban area. In this case the controlled and uncontrolled general knowledge represent the most important parts of the knowledge involved in the design process.

Case 2 : designing a new civil monument in urban area. Here there is not any controlled or uncontrolled general knowledge at the first stage of the design process; only experience and subjective knowledge have to be relied on.

Case 3 : designing the shape and the location of a bay-window in a room. This action needs much subjective knowledge and some uncontrolled general knowledge in the advanced stages of design.

Case 4 : designing the installation of the heaters in a habitable space. The controlled general knowledge is the most important part of the knowledge used in this kind of application; some specialized knowledge could be useful in difficult situations.

Case 5 : designing a private habitation project. Here the part of uncontrolled general knowledge is as important as the part of specialized knowledge and it is thought that the part of unknown knowledge is very important.

Case 6 : designing an elevator in a existing council house. This well defined application uses much controlled general knowledge, some uncontrolled general knowledge and very little specialized knowledge. In this case the part of unknown knowledge is relatively less important than in the other cases (see cases 2, 3, 4, 5, 7, 8).

Case 7 : designing the shape of a building facade. Much controlled general knowledge is not needed when designing a facade. What is rather needed is much more specialized knowledge. The part of unknown knowledge is still very important.

Case 8 : designing a door. In this application the design knowledge is equally distributed between controlled general knowledge, uncontrolled general knowledge, subjective knowledge and unknown knowledge. In this situation the use of specialized knowledge is not as efficient as in the other cases (see cases 1, 2, 5, 6).

As he develops a knowledge-based system, the knowledge engineer always gives priority to the most available and common knowledge generally used in the domain.

In a design project it is not easy to determine which type of knowledge must be given the greater importance. This can be explained by the facts that on the one hand it is very rare to

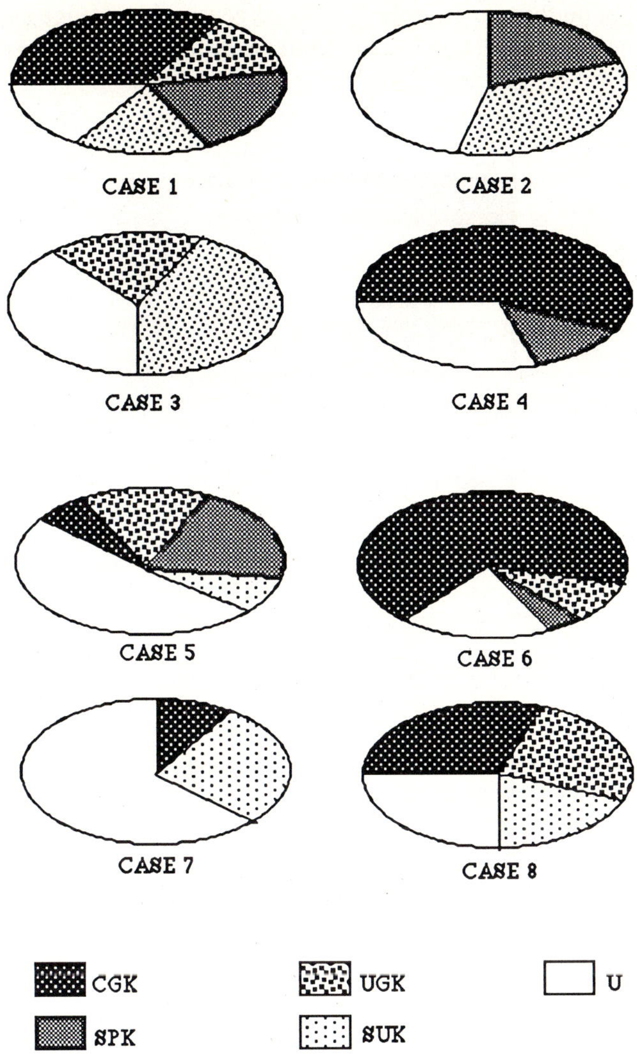

Figure 6. Design knowledge distribution considered by the knowledge engineer.

realize two similar design projects and on the other hand the distribution of the different types of knowledge involved in the design process is variable; there is no preliminary information about how it could or should be.

Figure 7 can help to explain this problem. We can immediately understand that the importance of each type of knowledge varies from one application to the other. It is fairly easy to prove that for the same type of application, the distribution could be changed in different circumstances.

Design knowledge distribution is somewhat dynamic. We can even consider our knowledge about "knowledge distribution" as being undefined and uncontrolled.

It is remarkable that on the one hand the controlled general knowledge and the subjective knowledge are omnipresent and on the other hand the differences between the uncontrolled general knowledge and the specialized knowledge are negligible.

n°case	CGK	UGK	SPK	SUK	U	total-H
case1	■	■	■	■	■	5
case2			■	■	■	3
case3		■		■	■	3
case4	■	■	■		■	4
case5	■		■	■	■	4
case6	■	■	■		■	4
case7	■			■	■	3
case8	■	■		■	■	4
total-V	6	5	5	6	8	30

Figure 7. A boolean representation of design knowledge distributions.

At any rate we cannot deny the importance of the general knowledge (both controlled and uncontrolled) in so many domains of design.
In fact those types of knowledge have been already integrated in many applications by the use of several programming techniques (Mitchell et al. 85, Mostow 89).
Most of the obtained results are not very satisfactory because cases similar to case numbers 2, 3, 5, 7 and even 8 are as often dealt with in architectural design as in other domains.
Therefore in certain situations (cf. cases 2, 3 and 5) it is not surprising that the general knowledge performances in the design process are not always sufficient to make CAD systems as useful as they should be.

Using Artificial Intelligence to Improve the Integration of the Knowledge Involved in the Design Process

Two different approaches are to be distinguished today when we speak about AI. First *the programming approach*: this refers to all available AI techniques and facilities used to help develop applications in varied domains. Then *the research approach*: it concerns the AI science which aims to improve the performance of computer reasoning.

AI Programming Techniques Approach in CAD Systems

AI tools have generally offered intelligent programming languages which have allowed non-programmers to prototype their own applications more rapidly.

AI programming techniques have brought a new dimension to the man/machine dialog in offering a simpler and unconventional language (nearer to the user's natural language).
It is considered that the user possesses already some knowledge to transfer; yet the available conventional language is not sufficiently adapted to help this user formulate all his known knowledge or his reasoning manner.

At the same time the use of AI techniques implies the help of knowledge engineers in critical cases. The knowledge engineer is very useful in such cases when the user finds it difficult to express and formulate directly his knowledge. Once knowledge is ready the knowledge engineer remains useful to model and transfer it precisely to programmers. Today in the development of particular cases the knowledge engineer encourages the user to give most of his knowledge.

Most of the time the greatest part of the knowledge acquired by knowledge engineers is controlled general knowledge; according to the chosen programming environment, one can wonder about acquiring other types of knowledge. As we have already mentioned it various AI tools can integrate some uncontrolled general knowledge.

Most AI project development actors mix specified knowledge with subjective knowledge which they often include in the uncontrolled general knowledge. It seems too early to evaluate the importance of AI programming techniques to be able to integrate all types of knowledge involved in the design process in CAD systems.

In a specific design domain using much general knowledge AI programming techniques have proved their utility; for example high-rise design (Maher 85), computer systems configuration (Dermott 82) and mechanical design (Brown et al. 88).

Finally using AI programming techniques has taught us that human intelligence is still to be investigated, particularly in regard to the building of intelligent systems.

AI Science Approach in CAD Systems

Let us consider now that AI techniques allow us to integrate satisfactorily only a great part of the controlled general knowledge and part of the uncontrolled general knowledge.
In this context the objective of AI science is therefore to enable computers to integrate the other kind of knowledge involved in the design process; it is also to increase and enhance continuously the quantity and the quality of integrated knowledge in CAD systems.

No doubt the integration of good knowledge acquisition paradigms using adapted learning apprentice systems (Mitchell et al. 85) in a CAD system environment will increase the quantity and enhance the quality of design knowledge-bases remarkably.

We have seen previously that uncontrolled general knowledge can become a controlled general knowledge by the addition of new meta-knowledge; this can be done through the learning of problem solving strategy heuristics (Mitchell et al. 84).
In a particular situation such as case n° 2 (see figure 6) for example, the designer uses only specialized knowledge and subjective knowledge. Then in order to make the CAD system useful it is necessary to endow it with the ability to learn. This could be achieved by the use of the techniques of explanation based learning (Miniton et al. 89), learning by analogy (Mostow 89) or learning from success and failure (Laird and Rosenbloom 86).

Is the use of these methods as easy as it seems? Naturally the answer is no. We cannot yet acquire or learn the different types of knowledge in using any of these methods. Consequently we must:
- determine the different types of knowledge involved in our problem in order to choose the most adapted learning concepts and tools. As design activity is not repetitive we can privilege a very interactive system associated with a learning apprentice system (Tecuci 88).
- use an incremental learning system based essentially on the principles of learning by analogy (Carbonell 86) and learning from examples (Dietterich et al. 84).
- admit that system users must be specialists in their domains.
- consider that a new knowledge is learnt when the following tasks have been achieved:
1. Acquiring a new knowledge = transfering it from the expert to the system;
2. Generalizing the acquired knowledge = transforming it into a general knowledge having semantic links with the other elements of the knowledge bases (Kodratoff et al. 86).
3. Validation of generalization = improving the new general knowledge by using the techniques of seeking similarity and an Intelligent Man/Machine Dialog (Guena et al. 1989).
So we can summarize the knowledge learning process as follows:
knowledge learning = knowledge acquiring + knowledge integrating (generalization + improvement).

Could AI Help to Select the Good Knowledge to be Learnt?

In fact this is the most important problem in design. In the first part of this paper we have suggested a classification of the knowledge involved in the design process. Then we have tried to locate the help of both AI techniques tools and theoretical methods in order to learn a new knowledge without any selection criteria concerning the nature and the importance of this knowledge.
The learning process is both dynamic and selective. In the design process a static hierarchy of knowledge, according to its qualitative or quantitative importance in the design project, does not exist.
Let us consider for example the plan 1 (see figure 8); it carries with it much information on architectural knowledge. It is not easy to recognize and select immediately the different types of manipulated knowledge, even the one that must be learnt.
But if we observe all the plans on figure 6 and if we try to find out where the differences lie or what the plans of this set have in common, we shall rapidly realize something about them: they are the plans of flats; their surfaces are the same, they have a living-room, a bathroom, etc.

So by introducing machine learning techniques such as learning from examples (Quinlan 89), learning by analogy (Mostow 89, Winston 80) or explanation based learning (Dejong 86, Schank et al. 89) AI could assist designers to find out some new concepts. But in order to obtain good results the knowledge engineer, the designer and the programmer must at once choose the most adapted methods to their applications and define an available model of knowledge representation corresponding to architectural design knowledge. Work carried on in this domain is very important (Akin 88, Flemming 88), (Radford et al. 85), etc.

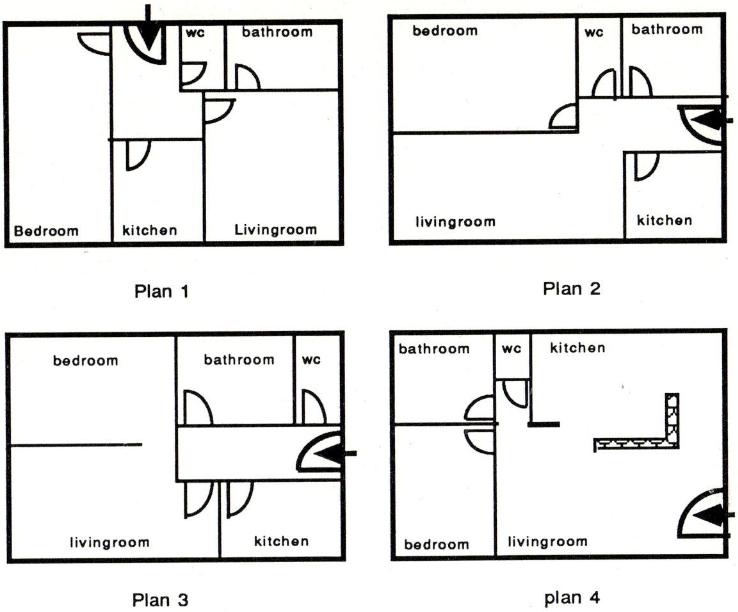

Figure 8. Set of architectural plans.

Conclusions

As a matter of fact what has been indirectly attempted in this paper is to grasp the nature of the knowledge involved in the design process. On the other hand we have tried to demonstrate that integrating all kinds of knowledge within a system is complex, not always necessary and it is not mastered yet.

We have suggested the use of AI tools such as machine learning techniques. This can be one element to model a really interactive design system in a set of limited possibilities.

Today AI techniques are very useful in several types of applications. If the performances of certain systems are sometimes not satisfactory, however the AI techniques alone must not be held as responsible. The complexity of the knowledge domain in design is not to be overlooked.

Today a large variety of available technologies must be used to enable us to improve the quality of design systems to insure a high level of interactivity.

References.

Akin, Ö. 1988. "Expertise of the Architect." In Michael D. Rychener (ed.). *Expert Systems for Engineering Design.* Pittsburgh, Pennsylvania: Academic Press edition, pp. 173-192.

Brown, D. C., and B. Chandrasekaran. 1988. "Expert System for a Class of Mechanical Design Activity." In D. T. Pham (ed.). *Expert Systems in Engineering*. IFS Publications/Springer-Verlag, pp. 334-360.

Carbonell, J.G. 1986. "Derivational Analogy: a Theory of Reconstructive Problem Solving and Expertise Acquisition." In R.S. Michalsky, J.G. Carbonell, T.M. Mitchell (eds.). *Machine Learning: An Artificial Intelligence Approach Vol 2*. Los Altos, CA: Morgan Kaufmann.

DeJong, G. F. 1986. "Some Thoughts on the Present and Future of Explanation-Based Learning." In R.S. Michalsky, J.G. Carbonell, T.M. Mitchell (eds.). *Machine Learning: An Artificial Intelligence Approach, Vol. 2*. Los Altos, CA: Morgan Kaufmann, pp. 571-590.

Dietterich, T.G., and R.S. Michalski. 1984. "A Comparative Review of Selected Methods for Learning from Examples." *Machine Learning an AI approach*, pp. 41-75. Springer-Verlag.

Flemming, U. 1988. "Rule-Based Systems in Computer Aided Architectural Design." In Michael D., Rychener (eds.). *Expert Systems for Engineering Design*, pp 93-110. Pittsburgh, Pennsylvania: Academic Press edition.

Guéna, F., and K. Zreik. 1989. "An Architect Assisted Architectural Design System." *AIENG 89*, Cambridge, UK.

Hart, A. 1986. *Knowledge Acquisition for Expert System*. Chapter 4, pp. 39-48. Kogan Page Ltd- U.K.

Heath, T. 1989. "Social Aspects of Creativity and their Impact on Creativity Modeling." Preprints of International Round-Table Conference, Modeling Creativity and Knowledge-Based. *Creative Design*, pp. 1-12. 11-14 December, Heron Island, 1989.

Kodratoff, Y., and J.G. Ganascia. 1986. "Improving the Generalization Step in Learning." In R.S. Michalsky, J.G. Carbonell, T.M. Mitchell (eds.). *Machine Learning: An artificial Intelligence Approach*, vol. 2. Los Altos, CA: Morgan Kaufmann.

Laird, J.E., P.S. Rosenbloom, and A. Newell. 1986. "Chunking in SOAR: The Anatomy of a General Learning Mechanism." *Machine Learning*, no. 1: 11-46.

Maher, M.L. 1985. "Hi-Rise and beyond: Directions for Expert Systems in Design." In *CAD* 17, no. 9: 420-427.

Mc Dermott, J. 1982. "R1: Rule-Based Configurer of Computer Systems." *Artificial Intelligence* 19, no. 1.

Miniton, S., J.G. Carbonell, C.A. Knoblock, D.R. Kuokka, O. Etzioni, and Y. Gil. 1989. "Explanation-Based Learning: a Problem Solving Perspective." *Artificial Intelligence* 40, no. 1-3: 63-118.

Mitchell, T.M., S. Mahadevan, and L.I. Steinberg. 1985. "Machine Learning, a Guide to Current Research." pp. 203-207. Kluwer Academic Publishers.

Mitchell, T. M., P.E. Utgoff, and R. Banerji. 1984. "Learning by Experimentation: Acquiring and Refining Problem Solving Heuristics." In *Machine Learning an AI Approach*, pp. 163-189. Springer-Verlag.

Mostow, J. 1989. "Design by Derivational Analogy: Issues in the Automated Replay of Design Plans." *Artificial Intelligence* 40, no. 1-3: 119-184.

Quinlan, J.R. 1989. "Induction from Structured Data." In *Australasian Conference on Expert Systems in Engineering, Architecture and Construction*, pp. 303-320.

Radford, A. D., and J.S. Gero. 1985. "Towards Generative Expert Systems for Architectural Detailing." *CAD* 17, no. 9: 428-434.

Schank, R.C., and D.B. Leak. 1989. "Creativity and Learning in a Case Based Explainer." *Artificial Intelligence* 40, no. 1-3: 353-386.

Tecuci, G. 1988. *DISCIPLE: A Theory, Methodology and System for Learning Expert Knowledge*. Thèse de doctorat, Université de Paris-Sud, Center d'Orsay.

Winston, P. 1980. "Learning and Reasoning by Analogy." In *Common ACM* 23 12, pp. 689-703.

Zeisel, J. 1981. "Inquiry by design: Tools for Environmental Behavior." Research, Brooks-Cole. Monterey, California.

Zreik, K. 1989. "Using Learning Apprentice System in Construction." In *Australasian Conference on Expert Systems in Engineering, Architecture and Construction*, pp. 339-358.

Application

26 The Impact of Computer Use on Design Practice

Richard Coyne

Department of Architectural and Design Science
University of Sydney NSW 2006 Australia

This paper presents a critical review of the impact of computing on design practice. It presents an overview of the impact as it relates to the intrusion of a highly technical resources into organizations. This involves a discussion of the changing nature of computing, the implications of training, management, and perceptions about the compatibility of computers and design. This leads to a consideration of less direct implications in terms of power structures, how computers influence the way we carry out intellectual tasks, the emphasis instilled by computers on form in design, and the influence of computers on attitudes of self worth.

Introduction

The influence of computers on design practice would appear to exceed that of other technologies. Computers become pervasive. They touch on almost every aspect of an organization: management, public relations, clerical tasks, and in the case of design practice, documentation and design. Some of the influences of computers arise out of the implications of managing a highly technical resource. But computers also change work practices. They affect the way people work together, they affect attitudes, and they impinge on power structures within organizations. There is nothing impartial about computers. By design or otherwise, they can serve as a mechanism for propagating certain value systems.

It can be argued that computing has only a relatively minor impact on the activity of design itself (or design decision making), other than in areas with a substantial engineering orientation. However, computers exhibit many indirect impacts on designers by changing the dynamics or organizations. Computers are commonly used in drawing documentation. Inevitably this brings with it the imposition of a new culture. Furthermore, it can be argued that the promises or threats of the possibilities represented by computers unsettles attitudes to design.

Although considerable attention has ben given to the impact of computer use on clerical workers (Otway and Peltu 1983, Turkle 1984, Wainwright and Francis 1984, Long 1987) there has been little in the way of formal studies of the impact of computers on the attitudes and work practices of designers. Some of the factors motivating computer use in architectural practice are discussed by Radford (1988), Radford and Stevens (1987), Stevens (1989) and Radford and Coyne (1989). Helpful summaries of the implications of computing in general form a social science perspective are provided by Kling and Iacono (1988), Danziger (1985) and a compilation of papers by Forester (1989). The discussion in this paper relates specifically to the impact of computing on the interests of designers. The views are derived from the author's own observations and interpretations of computer use in relation to academic institutions (Coyne 1989), corroborated by experiences in consulting and in discussions with other design practitioners.

The paper focuses primarily on computers as multipurpose devices and CAD workstations. A case could be presented that related communications technologies such as video, facsimile machines and electronic mail are exerting significant impacts on design practice, as they are on office practice in general (Marien 1989).

The argument presented in this paper is that certain implications of computing for design practice have gone largely unacknowledged. Computing has the potential as a focus for acrimony, and it can serve as a banner from behind which ideologies are espoused. Some of these issues will be confronted head on in this paper. The paper may assist in accounting for the difficulty organizations experience in making decisions about personnel, capital and training relating to computing. It also suggests some appropriate responses to these issues.

The Computer as a Technical Resource

The introductions of any new technology has ramifications. The nature of computing technology can be considered within four areas: making decisions about computers within a climate of change, changes to work practice the fact that computing requires intensive management, and the observation that work spaces occupied by computers appear to assume a certain ambience that influences the way people respond to them and work within them.

Making Decisions About Computers

The first concern relates to the rate at which computer technology is changing. In making decisions about computer resources it is helpful to be able to appeal to accepted practice. The difficulty here is that, whereas computer-aided drafting is obviously a current priority, there would appear to be no accepted norm of computer use in design practice. The scope of computer use is currently very wide, ranging across accounting, desktop publishing, drafting, three dimensional modelling, simulation, animation and image processing (photomontage).

The cost of commitment to any or all of these endeavors varies. Due to an increasing degree of standardization and the falling cost of equipment a commitment to some of these technologies can be tentative and incremental. Experimentation is affordable. This is less the case with elaborate CAD modelling and documentation tools. Apart from the relatively high cost of the facility the major burdens are the training overhead and the increasing value of the investment in computer drawings and models that accrues as the system is put into use. Once a commitment to a particular system has been made it becomes more difficult with time to shift allegiance from one CAD system to another. Of course, there are concerted efforts to standardize the way drawings are stored in CAD systems. The Initial Graphics Exchange Standard (IGES) format is an example.

Computer use has increased enormously over the past few years. Even during this short history there have been significant changes in the underlying technology. Coupled with this is a highly active market place where new products appear and disappear each week. There is every reason to expect that change will continue to be an influential feature of computing. The question arises as to what extent organizations should commit resources to an unsettled technology. Insufficient time has elapsed to monitor, evaluate and influence the course of events. So, added to the cost burden is the fact that patterns of computer use in practice are unstable.

As a consequence of the pattern of change, expertise in the area of system selection and management is in scarce supply. As the advice givers generally include vendors, junior staff members, experienced CAD operators and competitors anxious to justify their own decision making prowess, decision making in relation to computers can be expected to impose considerable stress on an organization. The lack of a clear source of advice sets up interesting dynamics within patterns of decision making in organizations, providing opportunities for enthusiasts at different levels and of different persuasions to exert influence. Computing is one area in which many less experienced workers can legitimately claim superior knowledge. Design schools are increasingly integrating computer use into the curriculum and the job of CAD operator would appear to be increasingly important as the first point of entry to the design professions for new graduates. Of course, these enthusiasts generally have less stake in the outcome of their advice.

Changing Work Practices and Attitudes

There is little doubt that the introduction of computers increases the repertoire of skills to be found within an organization. The need to acquire 'conventional' skills that a new employee is likely to encounter, such as understanding the nuances of office practice, can be met by training carried out on the job. However, the acquisition of computer skills generally requires considerable training. (Some CAD systems involve six weeks of full-time training.) There are several problems in relation to training. One is the cost of terms of fees (if the courses are external to the organization) and productivity losses. If the training is in-house then this means a commitment to an activity that is far removed from the normal concerns of practice. Another commonly reported problem with training is that the firm is effectively enhancing the prospects of its employees to bargain for more lucrative employment elsewhere. Some of the positive side effects that accompany the acquisition of new skills are the extra dimension of interest added to the work task, and the enhanced sense of self worth engendered by the opportunity for advancement.

Computing can also change the distribution of traditional work skills. For example, computers as word processors tend to change patterns of clerical support. It is the experience within many organizations, such as academic institutions, that some non-clerical or managerial staff are happy to take a greater role in the production of text documents. The development of the content of reports and other documents becomes more closely integrated with their production. This has implications in terms of autonomy, control and patterns of dependence. A redistribution of tasks that is more problematic can occur as skill as an operator becomes the major criterion by which workers are selected for particular projects. In the case of CAD systems this may mean those with the least design ability but the greatest enthusiasm and technical skill are carrying out the important design tasks.

A further negative effect of computers on work practice is that they can tend to over-formalize work tasks (Cozier 1983). This is manifested in the organization of drawings relating to a design project. The apparently disordered arrangement of material on and around a drawing board can be seen as a highly complex access system. Information is sorted and categorized according to some dynamic logic and changing system of priority. In spite of all the appeals to desktop analogues, the ordering of computer files is essentially two dimensional and tree-like. We can extrapolate this example to other aspect of office automation. Computers impose static ordering systems. Customizing computer systems to particular needs can induce workers to externalize their work practices, but in doing so ignore the subtle ad hoc operations that actually facilitate the task.

These are changes that computerization can make to work practices that are more difficult to pin down. There are ways in which the technology can take over as the central interest of the worker. These effects are less likely to be observed in the case of clerical tasks. Partly because of their design and their novelty computers tend to be used very consciously and deliberately in design and drawing. By contrast, conventional tools such as the T-square, set square and drawing board go largely unnoticed by their users. According to Winograd and Flores (1986) one of the goals of computer systems design is to instil the computer with a similar immediacy that a hammer has when wielded by a competent carpenter. Until this goal is achieved the design and documentation process often takes on the form of a challenge: how to do the task well with a computer. A special culture has arisen as support for the particular nature of working with computers. This culture provides special terminology, user groups, journals and societies. For many the hobby-like nature of the enterprise can provide the impetus for the development and promotion of expertise. The negative side is a distraction from the primary concerns of the design enterprise. Of course, some individuals and design organizations become specialists in CAD. CAD specialization also provides an opportunity for diversification during periods of economic stringency.

Of even greater significance on work practices are the likely long term effects of information technology. Computerization, tied in with telecommunications, may have the effect of breaking up locational dependence on the work place, though it is thought that the popularity of working at home will be suppressed by certain social needs (Forester 1989). Perhaps more likely is a general trend towards the decentralization of organizations away from the areas determined by clientele and support services to locations that are more convenient to employees.

Many of the changes that have occurred in the last number of years were unpredictable. The lesson is that there must be a preparedness to expect and challenge change within organizations. The distribution of work tasks and systems of reward and advancement should reflect the new distribution of expertise rather than reflect assumed but often outdated work practices.

The Critical Relationship Between Computers and Management

There are management implications in using computers, both personal and corporate. Computing tends to heighten the need for personal organization. The exercise of poor skills in managing files, disks and backups can be catastrophic. Time management is also critical. Whereas a last minute effort before a client meeting (involving manual drawing) produces a partial result at lease, a last minute effort in front of a computer can produce nothing. It is difficult to allow for contingencies in the event of file loss and system crashes.

As computers are a limited resource there is also the burden on the organization of managing the access of people to computers, and organizing schedules to optimize use. Other management issues involve the purchase and staging of acquisitions (both equipment and software); training; and maintaining databases, software and manuals. Many of these activities are essentially foreign to the traditional concerns of design practices. As computers become more pervasive the effective management of computer resources will become critical to the entire organization.

As computers are a failure prone and highly technical resource they also need managing. The technology currently seems to require individuals who are specialists or system managers. Modern computer installations are generally networked to facilitate the sharing of disk space, plotters, printers and digitizers, and to facilitate communications. Computing can be a distributed resource. This means that computers can be positioned around an entire building. The flexibility and power that accompanies this distribution also brings with it a certain dependence on centralized expertise. Due to the pervasive nature of computing, the role of the systems manager or specialist becomes far more critical than that of other technical and support staff within an organization.

Centralization and the intensity of management issues may render the workings of the entire organization prone to 'bottleneck effects'. The breakdown of the plotter means that there are no drawings; a break in the network disables half of the workstations; uncooperative technical support can bring a project to a halt. This becomes an even greater problem due to the inaccessibility of drawings and other documents to untrained project managers and supervisors—the bewildered project supervisor standing in a room full of blank computer screens.

An appropriate response to these issues is firstly to acknowledge the management implications of computerization in making resource decisions and selecting staff. A further response is to promote systems of management that reduce the bottleneck effect. This may mean: having backup personnel; ensuring that the technical skills are distributed wider than a single expert; partitioning networks and clusters of equipment so that failure in part of the system does not mean failure in the entire system; establishing fast maintenance and repair procedures; and establishing cooperation with other organizations for equipment exchange during a crisis.

There is an increasing need for design practitioners who are also systems manager. This suggests the need for specialist courses in computing and management within design schools that go beyond the general design curriculum. It also points to the need for continuing education of designers and managers.

Computer-Based Design Environments

Most computer use by designers is generally in the areas of documentation and 3D visualization. Due to advances in systems design and improved computer graphics the computer is proving more attractive as a medium for design expression generally (Radford and Coyne 1989). However, the idea of the computer as a tool for decision support or an 'intelligent assistant' is currently very limited, and advances in this area are the subject of considerable research effort both within and outside practice. These researches are generally accompanied by considerable questioning of the overall role of computers in the design process (Bijl 1989).

Apart from issues of software design, one of the major barriers to the use of computers in the design process lies in the nature of the spaces they occupy. Spaces occupied by computers have their own distinctive character. Computers are still expensive. For various reasons it makes sense to link computers together into networks. This sometimes means keeping them close together. So the first characteristic of spaces occupied by computers is that they tend to be gathered in coteries.

The second characteristic of these spaces is that they resist attempts at being personalized. Computers often have to be shared. A third characteristic of computer spaces is that they support a much narrower range of activities than many other spaces. There are restrictions to muscular activity imposed by the immediate task environment of keyboard, mouse and screen. Apart from the occupational health implications the restrictions create an environment in which people appear passive, and possibly introspective and uncommunicative (Bjørn-Andersen 1983). A fourth characteristic of computer spaces is that they hum, rattle and beep when in use. They also glow. Of course, when the computers are turned off they assume a different character again: cold and silent. The upshot of this is that to enter the presence of computers is to enter a special place.

Conventional drawing offices and design studios are also special places, although with a more sociable aspect. There may be a general ambience of disorder. Designers generally surround themselves with drawings, material from which inspiration may be drawn. Designer's workstations are very readily and rapidly personalized. There is generally a range of activities taking place: talking in groups, moving around the room, sharpening pencils, and drawing. To the extent that design is able to flourish in such an environment we may question the suitability of computer spaces as effective environments for design.

We can make further observations about computer spaces and the people in them. To work in front of a computer is to focus attention on a very small area (part of a computer screen). The nature of the task, which in its detailed execution often takes on the characteristic of an intense kind of game (matching wits with the computer by persuading it to scale a rectangle by one more pixel), seems to combine with the intense spatial focus to produce a mesmerizing effect. One's own experience is corroborated in observations of novices unused to working with computers. They are frequently surprised at the way their perception of time changes in front of a computer. They are surprised at the extent to which their obsession with detail is heightened.

The case against computer workstations as design environments can be supported further. Several people can gather around a drawing board. Drawing boards are large. They invite participations. Computer monitors are very much the domain of the user. Watching a computer operator at work is akin to reading a book over someone's shoulder. Participation in the task is about as welcome. The distorted and shadowy world reflected in a computer screen engenders a peculiar awareness of people and spaces. It is difficult to look over somebody's shoulder without arousing suspicion. Computer operators work as if they have eyes in the back of their heads.

None of this need matter. If design can flourish in a railway carriage, in the bath and while perched on a wooden stool then it can happen in front of a computer. The main lesson is that we need to be aware of the characteristics of the physical and social environment that generally attends computers. This may be a first step in overcoming the distaste of some designers towards 'computer culture'. We should not be averse to challenging the norms set by the designers and manufacturers of computers, computer networking systems, computer furniture and security systems. There is enormous scope for experimentation.

There are several approaches to handling computers in the workplace — from relegating computers to a back room to distributing and integrating the computer resource throughout the organization. The latter approach may serve not only to facilitate effective movement patterns, but also to offset any tendency to see the technology as precious and possibly menacing. The computer facility is sometimes employed as a selling point to promote a certain high tech ambience within the organization. The objective might be to enhance the sense of excitement, the sense that technology is at hand to solve our problems. As with a great deal of design there is scope for an appeal to myth and theater as much as ergonomics, efficient circulation and effective environmental control. Experiments in the design of architectural offices attest to this.

Computers and Ideology

Apart from the technological impacts of computing there are less direct sources of impact. There is something about certain technologies (such as television) that have far reaching effects. Computers and the attendant culture are incredibly influential. Computers change the way we think about ourselves. The issues in the following summary are not necessarily inherent in computing. They relate to the marketing and promotion of computers, our perceptions of ourselves and how we view machines. For good or ill people are not the same after working with computers.

Computing and Power

Mastery of any skills instils a sense of power and control. This applies to learning a musical instrument, throwing clay and operating or programming a computer. This manifestation of power serves an an enabling. There is also a sense of power that comes from belonging to a group — a trade, a profession, the cognoscenti — that has its own language and its own boasts. This phenomenon is certainly evident in the acquisition of computing skills (particularly programming), where entry is perceived to be difficult.

Some tasks assume connotations of power by virtue of their influence over a large number of people. So there is a sense of power in the practice of architecture or writing or the design of artefacts for mass production. Computing is the archetypal cottage industry. In computing, a finite amount of effort with modest resources can produce an infinity of outcomes. Even if the potential for mass production is not fully realized, the trappings are there: files can be copies and disseminated, building models can be viewed from an infinite number of angles, and generative algorithms can produce an infinity of patterns.

A further dimension to the power of computing is that it is possible to create something that resembles a world and then exercise mastery over it. This world may be some esoteric mathematical world, or the representation of a building or a city. You can fly over buildings, walk through walls and commit heinous acts of desecration in computer worlds, without reprisals. Computing to some becomes as engrossing as a game of chess or Dungeons and Dragons.

To what extent do these connotations of power make any impact on the actual relationships between individuals? The power would appear to be largely illusory. This illusion itself may also serve as a means of manipulation. Computer operators are content to dominate their own small worlds while others dominate them.

The distribution of real power, in a democratizing and egalitarian sense, would be expected to lie in the potential of computers as a medium of the dissemination of information and knowledge (for example, through the electronic mail system, databases and expert systems). There is evidence to suggest that there are subtle shifts of power to those with technical expertise, but some commentators, such as Gotlieb and Borodin (1973) and Danziger (1985), suggest that computing tends to reinforce existing power structures.

Subtle power plays are evident in organizations that use computing. The ability to orchestrate expensive capital acquisitions can serve as spectacular demonstrations of power by individuals and groups, especially where this is seen as a competitive enterprise. Within the organization, if the resources and expertise are centralized there is the necessity to grant permissions, and offer instructions and assistance when things go wrong. Again, this relates to the 'all or nothing' nature of the computing enterprise. A partially working computer is one that is not working at all, and partial knowledge is ignorance. So the co-operation of experts has to be thorough. There is enormous scope for condescension and the subtle misuse of power by the experts, where patterns of accountability are unclear. This problem is not new, but because of the pervasive nature of computing the effect of these power games can be all the more debilitating.

A further power dimension is the common perception that computing is on the ascendancy. It is a growing field. Practitioners with a foothold in the technology are in demand. A strong case could be presented that the aspirations of young designers or students relating to computing ar closely linked to perceptions of power in the employment market and in the world place. In academic institutions computer-related research finds favour with funding bodies. Computing has a high profile and impresses certain client groups. Even modest initiatives with computer are sometimes seen as innovative and advanced. Tied to this are Utopian expectations of computing ushering in a better world, better pedagogy, perhaps even better design. Some of the mythologies and ideologies behind computer advocacy are addressed in detail by Kling and Iacono (1988). Of course, the advocates and perpetrators of computing have a vested interest in its ascendancy.

There is no simple response to the power issue as it is an integral part of any enterprise involving people. The exercise of power in the market place that enhances the competitive enterprise can be debilitating when manifested within the organization itself. What would help the most is a general recognition of the potential of computing to amplify power problems, and a preparedness to set up mechanisms for accountability.

Computers and the Exercise of the Intellect

A further impact arises from am emphasis on method, order and organization instilled in computer users, and that pervades the way they tend to approach problem solving, even when computers are not being used. This is attested to by Kling and Iacono (1988) and Danziger (1985). We may suppose that there are two ways in which this influence is perpetrated. First, you have to be well organized to get what you want from computers. So computing instils good organizational habits. The second source is the views embodied within the culture that attends computers—the ideological trappings of the general discourse relating to computing. The discourse of the design theory and methods movement is one such source.

The advocacy of method is something of a tight rope act. There are aspects of the emphasis on method that are undesirable. These are summarized by Danziger (1985). First, there appears to be a tendency to undervalue, or fail to recognized knowledge that cannot be made explicit, and thereby potentially represented and manipulated in a computer. If it can't be put on a computer and made to work then it isn't worth knowing: "real life is life on line" (Kling and Iacono 1988). Second, there is a tendency to increase the importance of quantitative and technical criteria in making decisions. Third, there are tendencies to overestimate the reliability and significance of quantifiable information. This summary is supported by Weizenbaum's (1976) pejorative characterization of "instrumental reason".

The most extreme manifestation of these excesses in organizations is demonstrated by the 'scientific management' of Frederick Taylor at the end of the last century (Mumford 1983). According to this view individuals in an organization need a relatively narrow range of skills and the worker has little if any discretion. A corollary to this is that the worker only needs to be presented with information that is relevant to the task at hand. Computers tend to raise the specter of a resurgence of technical rationalism if not by the actual work practice changes imposed by computers then by the philosophical baggage that often accompanies the enterprise.

Although most computer advocates would decry any links with Taylorism, computing has developed and been promoted within theoretical frameworks that carry with them a strong bias towards 'rationalism'. This carries with it notions of objectivity gleaned from particular views of science and extended to other areas of human endeavor. This kind of thinking is under constant challenge (Coyne 1991a). An interesting illustration of the diversity of thinking in this area is the recent work of Winograd and Flores (1986) who present a critique of computing and artificial intelligence in the light of the 'post rationalism' of Husserl and Heidegger (Heidegger 1962). This theme is taken up in relation to design generally in Snodgrass and Coyne (1990, 1991) and Coyne and Snodgrass (1991a, 1991b).

Computers and the Emphasis on Form

The influence of computers in promoting the idea of 'design methods' is well known. There is also a readily observable phenomenon engendered by computer use that is less subtle and impinges heavily on the issue of design. This is a tendency of computing to focus on form—the shape of things and their configuration. There is no question that computing provides enormous scope for the exploration of matters relating to form in design. An interesting and recent example is provided by Oxman, Radford and Oxman (1988). This kind of activity is supported by the underlying capabilities of computing to configure symbols and the irresistible lure of computer graphics. The emphasis on form also spills over into theories of design as exemplified by Stiny's shape grammars (1980).

Of course, this tendency also reflects preoccupations within the architecture community generally. Leaving aside arguments about the importance of formal considerations in design, computing can tend to amplify and distort this preoccupation. Computers are generally employed for three dimensional modelling and visualizing. The time required for this activity alone has a distorting effect on the designer's perception of what is important. Furthermore, computing does not appear to support other considerations with the same opportunity for panache.

Of course computers can support other activities and there is enormous scope for experimentation. Computers have a role to play in participatory design. The computer can serve as a medium for bringing people together and facilitating the sharing of information. A simple example is the use of a wordprocessor or database file as a medium for storing, collating and analyzing information. This becomes particularly powerful when combined with networking that allows 'distributed input'. One interesting development is that simple tools are becoming available for tailor-making applications. So practices can embark on their own relatively inexpensive research and development. Media such a s Hypercard open up possibilities by providing simple yet novel ways of storing, manipulating and displaying design oriented information.

Computers and Models of the Mind

The final issue to be raised here is that computers influence the way we think about ourselves. The impact of computers on the attitudes of individuals to their self worth has been raised by Weizenbaum (1976) and Turkle (1984). The impact of computing on work has been one of the major causes of discontent with computing (Cooley 1980, Jones 1980). One of the manifestations of this influence also comes through contemporary models of human cognition.

Computing has been a major influence in contemporary models of cognition. Most notable has been the 'information theoretic' view of cognition presented by Newell and Simon (1972). At the very earliest stages in their development computers were seen as potential thinking machines. The corollary is that the brain is a machine with the mind as its program (Hofstadter and Dennett 1981). Critics of this approach include Searle (1987) and Dreyfus (1987). Rival positions within cognitive science gather around those who emphasize symbolic processing as a basis of cognition and those who support models based on low level 'connectionism' (Coyne 1991b). An appeal to computing features prominently in various dialogues within cognitive science and psychology.

At the lowest level, computing serves as a useful source of analogies. The most positive aspect of computing in this context is that computers have served to sharpen debate and stimulate the generation of important cognitive models. Similar claims could be made for the role of computing in helping to understand design and designers. Some recent accounts include those by Coyne (1988), Mitchell (1989), and an account with a different emphasis by Winograd and Flores (1986).

A negative effect is that computing can engender simplistic interpretations of human behavior, and thus design. The general mood of enthusiasm, the 'bandwagon effect', the lack of intellectual consolidation and the disproportionate recognition of modest achievements that often attends computer-based research can instil a sense of false security.

Conclusion

There is a certain inevitability about computing. There is also considerable resistance. Resistance from practitioners is based as much on the time and competence problems raised earlier in this paper as it is on ideology. Whatever the source, both of these factors (inevitability and resistance), lead to extremes of enthusiasm on the part of individuals. The supporters of computers tend to be enthusiastic. They are caught up with Utopian myths about computers, and they marshal their enthusiasm to overcome resistance amongst colleagues. There is an extent to which computing is oversold. However, the sober reflections of this paper should be modified by an appreciation of the motivating power of myths.

In the face of the daunting prospects and awesome responsibilities presented in this paper, what are the options? The precise response will depend on the management structure and the mechanisms for decision making in the organization. In loosely structured organizations, such as many architectural offices, the fall back position is to leave it to the enthusiasts to present their case for decisions in relation to computing.

In the short term, where there is a commitment to computerization, practices require competence in the management of technical resources, enthusiasm for the idea of computing, effective computer systems and able technical knowledge. The long term view should be to decentralize expertise within the organization. The computer enthusiasts should also be facilitators. As long as the concern of computers in design resides with the few there is the potential for some of the excesses described in this paper.

Acknowledgements

This work is supported by an ARC Grant, a Special Project Grant from the University of Sydney and a project grant from the Key Center of Design Quality, University of Sydney. Comments from Fay Sudweeks, Sid Newton, Adrian Snodgrass and Simon Hayman on drafts of this paper were much appreciated.

References

Bijl, A. 1989. *Computer Discipline and Design Practice: Shaping Our Future*. Edinburgh: Edinburgh University Press.

Bjørn-Andersen, N. 1983. "The changing roles of secretaries and clerks." In H.J. Otway and M. Peltu (eds.). *New Office Technology: Human and Organizational Aspects*, pp. 120-137. London: Frances Pinter.

Cooley, M. 1980. *Architect or Bee? the Human/Technology Relationship*. Sydney: Transnational Co-operative Limited.

Coyne, R.D. 1988. *Logic Models of Design*. London: Pitman.

Coyne, R.D. 1989. "The implications of computer use in architecture Schools." *ADTRA: Journal of the Architectural Design Teaching and Research Association* 1, no. 2: 5-12.

Coyne, R.D. 1991a. "Design reasoning without explanations." *AI Magazine* 11, no. 4: 72-80.

Coyne, R.D. 1991b. "Objectivity and the design process." *Environment and Planning B*, (to appear).

Coyne, R.D., and A.B. Snodgrass. 1991a. "Is designing mysterious? challenging the dual knowledge thesis." *Design Studies*. (to appear).

Coyne, R.D., and A.B. Snodgrass. 1991b. *Where do do design ideas come from? a case study of metaphor use.* Working Paper, Faculty of Architecture, University of Sydney, Sydney.

Crozier, M. 1983. "Implications for the organization." In H.J. Otway and M. Peltu (eds.). *New Office Technology: Human and Organizational Aspects*, pp. 86-101. London: Frances Pinter.

Danziger, J.N. 1985. "Social science and the social impacts of computer technology." *Social Science Quarterly* no. 66: 3-21.

Dreyfus, H.L. 1987. "Misrepresenting Human Intelligence." In R. Born (ed.). *Artificial Intelligence: the Case Against*, pp. 41-54. Beckenham, Kent: Croom Helm.

Forester, T. (ed.). 1989. *Computers in the Human Context: Information, Technology, Productivity and People.* Oxford: Blackwell.

Gotlieb, C.C., and A. Borodin. 1973. *Social Issues in Computing*. London: Academic Press.

Heidegger, M. 1962. *Being and Time*. New York: Harper and Row.

Hofstadter, D.R., and D.C. Dennett. 1981. *The Mind's I: Fantasies and Reflections on Self and Soul.* Harmondsworth, Middlesex: Penguin.

Jones, T. 1980. "A new society? The social impact of microprocessor technology." In T. Jones (ed.). *Microelectronics and Society*. Milton Keynes: Open University Press.

Kling, R., and S. Iacono. 1988. "The mobilization of support for computerization: the role of computerization movements." *Social Problems* 35, no. 3.

Long, R.J. 1987. *New Office Automation Technology: Human and Managerial Implications*. London: Croom Helm.

Marien, M. 1989. "IT: you ain't seen nothing yet." In T. Forester (ed.). *Computers in the Human Context: Information, Technology, Productivity and People*, pp. 41-47. Oxford: Blackwell.

Mitchell, W.J. 1989. *The Logic of Architecture*. Cambridge, Massachusetts: MIT Press.

Mumford, E. 1983. "Successful systems design." In H.J. Otway and M. Peltu (eds.). *New Office Technology: Human and Organizational Aspects*, pp. 68-85. London: Frances Pinter.

Newell, A., and H.A. Simon. 1972. *Human Problem Solving*. Englewood Cliffs, New Jersey: Prentice-Hall.

Otway, H.J., and M. Peltu (eds.). 1983. *New Office Technology: Human and Organizational Aspect*. London: Frances Pinter.

Oxman R., A.D. Radford, and R. Oxman. 1987. *The Language of Architectural Plans*. Royal Australian Institute of Architects Education Division, Red Hill, ACT.

Radford, A.D., and R. Coyne. 1989. "Architectural Computing: CAD versus 2B pencil for sketch design." *Architecture Australia*, May: 28-29.

Radford, A.D., and G. Stevens. 1987. *CADD Made Easy*. New York: McGraw Hill.

Searle, J.R. 1987. "Minds, brains and programs." In R. Born (ed.). *Artificial Intelligence: the Case Against*, pp. 18-40. Beckenham, Kent: Croom Helm.

Snodgrass, A.B., and R.D. Coyne. 1990. *Is designing hermeneutical?*. Working Paper. Faculty of Architecture, University of Sydney, Sydney.

Snodgrass, A.B., and R.D. Coyne. 1991. *Models, metaphors and the hermeneutics of designing*. Working Paper. Faculty of Architecture, University of Sydney, Sydney.

Stevens, G. 1989. "The social construction of computer-aided architectural design." *ADTRA: Journal of the Architectural Design Teaching and Research Association* 1, no. 2, pp. 51-56.

Stiny, G. 1980. "Introduction to Shape and Shape Grammars." *Environment and Planning B* no. 7: 409-462.

Turkle, S. 1984. *The Second Self: Computers and the Human Spirit*. London: Granada.

Wainright, J., and A. Francis, 1984. *Office Automation, Organization and the Nature of Work*. Aldershot, Hampshire: Gower.

Weizenbaum, J. 1976. *Computer Power and Human Reason*. Harmondsworth, Middlesex: Penguin.

Winograd, T., and F. Flores. 1986. *Understanding Computers and Cognition: a New Foundation for Design.* Reading, MA: Addison Wesley.

27 ESP — An Expert System for Property Revitalization

Robert E. Johnson

College of Architecture and Urban Planning
The University of Michigan
Ann Arbor, MI 48109, U.S.A.

This paper reports on the development of a knowledge based system that can help to assess the reuse potential of idle industrial property. It does not take the place of the architect or engineer, but allows for strategic design factors to be considered in very early and important property redesign and revitalization decisions. The idea is predicated on the judgment that there is a relatively systematic approach to evaluating the reuse potential of vacant property. A frame based approach together with a series of "if-then" rules are used to represent the knowledge domain and procedures required to perform a feasibility analysis. Rules for assessing the impact of the regional economy, industrial market trends, building configuration, building design strategies and the impact of building codes are included in this manner. A prototype of this system system has been implemented on both an Apple Macintosh computer using AAIS Prolog and an IBM AT compatible using Arity/Prolog.

Introduction

Between 1982 and 1987 over 350 factories closed in the State of Michigan (Molnar and Kahana 1989). An earlier study found that manufacturing plants in the nation's older industrial areas closed at the rate of over 3,000 per year during the 1970s. Vacant, obsolete industrial buildings are a significant problem for local communities that result in a loss of jobs, a decrease in the tax base, and cause significant urban decay of the surrounding neighborhood. Communities in the United States often do not have the resources or expertise to develop appropriate alternative strategies for the redesign and revitalization of these facilities. As a consequence, vacant industrial property sometimes sits idle for excessive periods of time or is disposed of in such a way that the potential value of the property is not realized.

Plant closing and abandonment are often the final result of a systematic process of disinvestment. Disinvestment (sometimes referred to as deferred investment) is the prolonged postponement of investment in plant and equipment. Strategies of deferred investment are typical when firms face a shortage of operating capital. Deferred investment in buildings has become, until recently, a standard way that universities in the United States have used to cope with budget shortages (Johnson et al 1987). However, while disinvestment may be a viable strategy for the private sector, it is often a disaster and very uneconomic when viewed from the perspective of the public sector. The subject of how to most effectively revitalize abandoned industrial facilities has been the subject of multi-disciplinary research at the University of Michigan for over a decade. This research "...shows clearly that annual community economic losses exceed comparable benefits to the abandoning firm. Thus, if the community costs of abandonment were a consideration of the firm, the economics of the move decision might be altered" (Industrial Development Division 1981).

The research reported here is set in this context, but has as its specific focus the role of the physical environment in this disinvestment process and subsequent revitalization efforts. The perspective in this paper advocates an integrative approach to this issue, where design decisions can only be evaluated sensibly within the larger socioeconomic and political context.

The overall goal of this research is to promote a more reasonable approach to decisions concerning the reuse of existing building infrastructure in order to help reverse the process of urban decay and shorten the time necessary to readjust buildings to changes in the market. In particular, the first objective of this research is to develop a systematic decision-making approach to assist in the redesign and economic revitalization of abandoned property. The second objective is to introduce a prototype expert system that implements this decision-making approach and that can be used by the non-expert to assist in making crucial early strategic decisions about what can be done to improve the economic viability of underutilized property. The initial data for this expert system was obtained from a study to revitalize a large number of obsolete industrial facilities in South Bend, Indiana, that were originally the central manufacturing facilities for Studebaker automobiles (Johnson et al 1987).

A Conceptual Approach to Economic Revitalization

There are many potential reasons why disinvestment occurs and plants close. These reasons include obsolete production technology, lack of sales, price competition from other companies, high labor rates, and inadequate facilities. The revitalization process is characterized by a complex range of problems requiring a range of solution approaches and strategies. An assessment of the issues associated with revitalization is a first step necessary to form a basis for an evaluation of the decision process.

Conceptually, the redesign and revitalization of an obsolete building can be considered a type of search problem (for a discussion of finding alternatives, see Simon 1981). In contrast to a more typical design problem, an existing state is already clearly identified. That state consists of the obsolete building and the social, economic and political context within which it exists. The goal is to change the existing state so as to reach a more satisfactory benefit/cost situation. Because the social, economic and political context are not generally open to manipulation by the decision maker these factors become constraints to the search process. The goal, therefore, may be defined more precisely as searching for a building reuse alternative that will represent a better "fit" within the existing socioeconomic context. Figure 1 illustrates the range of use alternatives that define the search space. It is, of course, always a possibility that the best alternative is the current state, i.e., do nothing.

Another way to conceptualize this problem is to think of it as a type of capital planning and budgeting decision process (Johnson 1990). As is the case with design, capital budgeting is an ill-structured problem that combines characteristics of both problem solving and strategic planning. Capital budgeting provides for the systematic review of a large number of possible alternatives. The output of this process is the determination of a cost-benefit ratio that results from each capital investment proposal. Within the context of building revitalization, the cost-benefit ratio provides one of the key factors that influences the final decision.

However, political and social factors are also important in finalizing decisions. Therefore, the result of a systematic analysis of alternatives can only be advisory. In the public sector, revitalization decisions are strongly influenced by perceptions of community priorities.

Problem Characteristics

As indicated previously, this research assumes that design decisions can only be made adequately by considering the larger, socioeconomic context within with the design exists. The acceptance of this view considerably increases the complexity of the decision making process. This complexity is characterized by five issues:

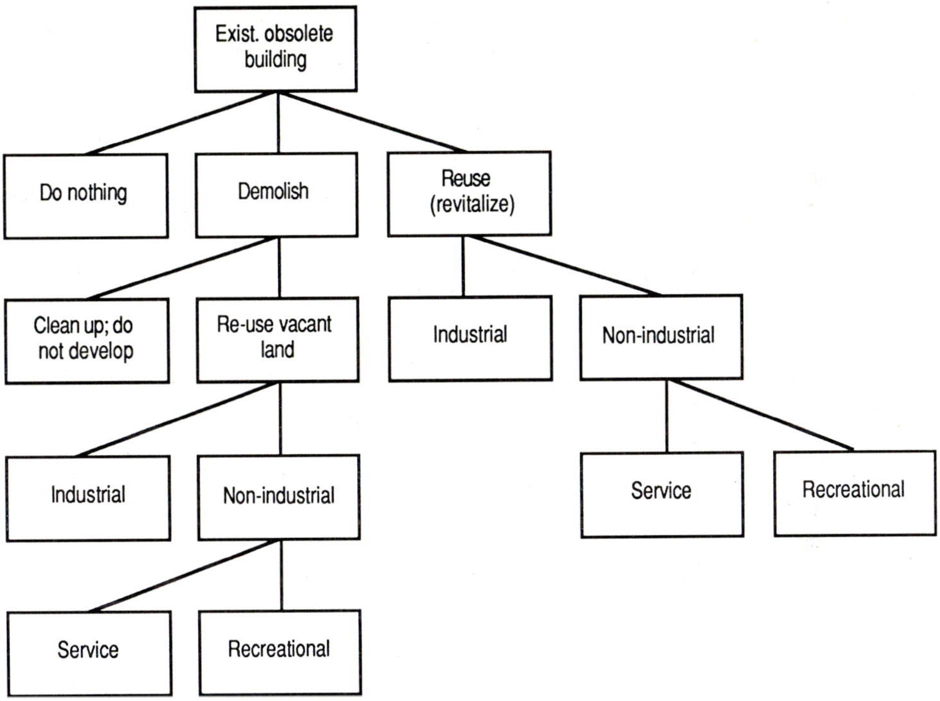

Figure 1. A Search Tree of Potential Reuse Categories for an Obsolete Building.

1) Political. The revitalization of vacant industrial buildings can often be very political and highly charged with emotions of special interest groups with opposing viewpoints about the problem. Historic preservationists are concerned about maintaining the integrity of the unique, historic nature of the building. Labor groups sometimes view these buildings as symbolic of past "sweat shops." The business community generally perceives these buildings through the singular lens of economic development. Finally, there is often a group representing the interests of new development who frequently see the problem solution as a simple case of demolition and reconstruction.

2) Multi-disciplinary. The comprehensive nature of the problem requires the development of knowledge from a variety of perspectives, including historical preservation, building

design (including all disciplines), site planning, city planning, economics (city and regional), and real estate. Developing a viable revitalization strategy generally requires the participation of many different disciplines, including economists, developers, engineers, architects, and land use planners. Because of this one can expect the utilization of a variety of different types of reasoning.

3) Complexity. Complexity is related partly to the multi-disciplinary nature of revitalization problems. A variety of different perspectives must be used to evaluate the feasibility of a large number of possible reuse alternatives.

4) Cost. Regardless of the outcome, revitalization decisions typically involve millions of dollars. If the decision is to do nothing, there will be a continuing negative impact because of lost property taxes. If the decision is to renovate, taxes or other funding sources must be obtained to reinvest in the facility. Even demolition can cost millions of dollars. Therefore, it is critical to articulate a clearly thought-out plan for any final decision that is proposed.

5) Uncertainty. Although many of the issues have an "objective" basis to them (e.g., structural evaluation) others are clouded in the uncertainty that usually surrounds planning for the future. There needs to be some method for adequately assessing this uncertainty.

Research Questions

The characteristics of the problem suggest some of the questions that have been explored during the course of this research. These issues include:

1) Given complexity of choices that are available, can the design decision maker be provided reasonably robust, "expert" guidance for improving the economic performance of an obsolete building?

2) While some building problems are unique and require creative, inventive solutions, there are also many problems where proven, reliable, cost-effective solutions exist. Can knowledge-based technologies be developed that apply these well-known solutions to complex revitalization situations.

3) Can an expert system, driven by both systematic and heuristic search procedures aimed at improving economic performance, be developed and implemented within the existing framework of current cost modeling system PC-based technologies?

4) Can knowledge-based technologies help deal with the ambiguity and incompleteness of information needed to make decisions about revitalization projects?

The Revitalization Decision Process

The overall organizational approach utilized in the development and analysis of the revitalization decision may be most effectively characterized as one of conjecture and refutation (Popper 1934) or generate and test (Simon 1981). Redesign of the obsolete facility to improve its economic viability is conceptualized as similar to developing a testable knowledge base about the facility. Part of that knowledge base is developed in conjunction with experts, if they are available. Another part of the knowledge base is developed by obtaining information about the context; and a third is developed by asking for subjective assessments about the building.

A general approach to the revitalization of vacant industrial buildings is outlined in figure 2. A use is proposed (conjectured) and efforts are made to test its viability. A failure to satisfy any of the major issues will result in a failure of the proposed use. Assuming that all of the rules are satisfactorily concluded, the financial feasibility of the proposed use is determined and compared with the prevailing market rate of return as well as with the rates of return for other proposed uses.

Problem Classification

The characteristics of the problem also suggest that a variety of reasoning approaches will be necessary to evaluate effectively the reuse potential of a vacant facility. Table 1 is a classification of the alternative reasoning types that are necessary for each major decision in the redesign of an obsolete facility.

Table 1. Problem Reasoning Classification.

Problem	Discipline	Reasoning type	Uncertainty
1) Is proposed use legal (zoning)?	Land use planning	rule-based	No
2) Is a zoning variance possible?	Political, legal	case-based	Yes
3) Is proposed use acceptable to historic preservationists?	Architecture, History	rule-based	Yes
4) Is the proposed use in demand in this economic context?	Real estate economics	rule-based or model-based	Yes
5) Is the building supply enough to meet market demand?	Real estate economics	model-based	Yes
6) Is the building condition acceptable?	Architecture, Engineering	rule-based	Yes
7) Is the building configuration acceptable?	Architecture, Industrial engineering	rule-based	Yes
8) Is proposed occupancy financially feasible?	Real estate economics	model-based	Yes

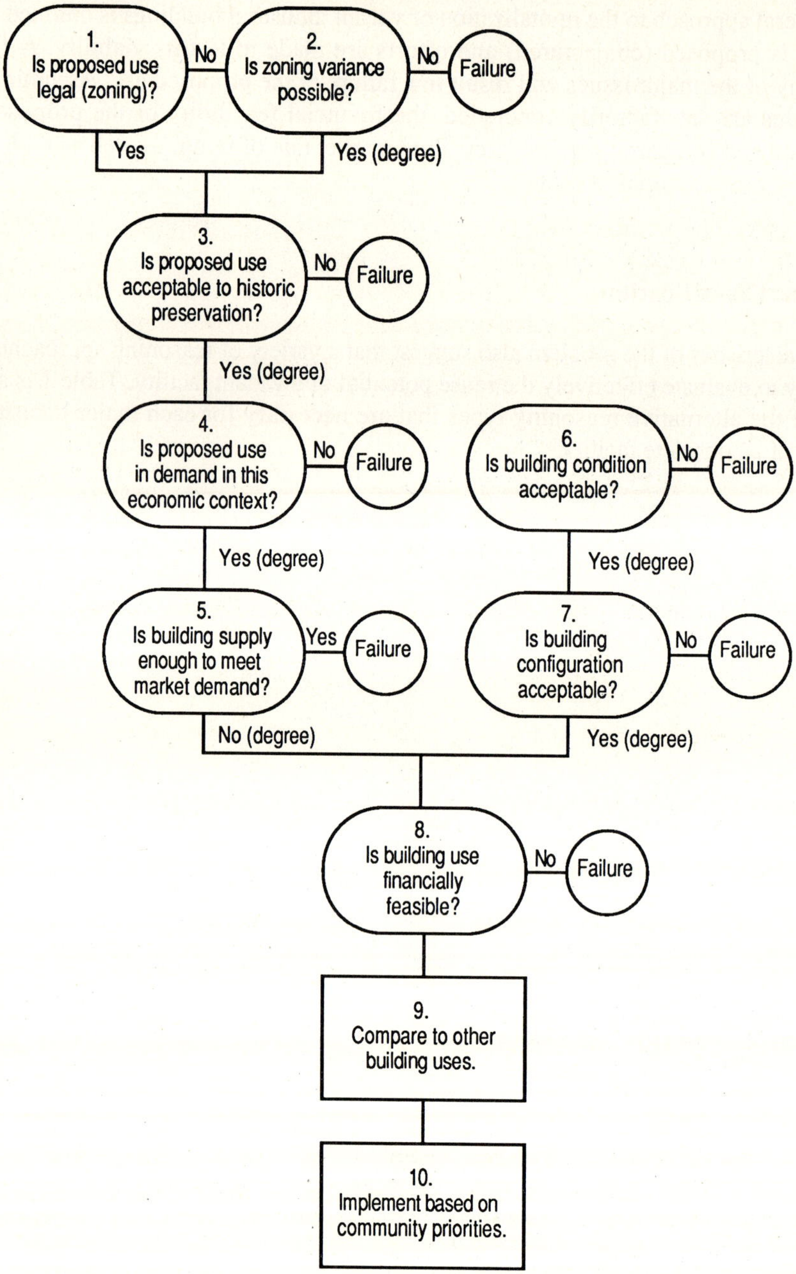

Figure 2. Decision Flow Chart.

Design and Implementation of the Expert System

The evaluation of underutilized industrial facilities can be a complicated, time consuming process. However, experience gained from research on this issue suggested that even though the process was complex, a relatively systematic approach to evaluating the reuse potential of surplus property could be identified. This previous research developed an understanding of the relative importance of major project variables and the degree to which these variables can be modified. As can be see in figure 3, there is a similarity between the thinking that is involved with reuse evaluation and that of expert systems. The rules and facts associated with the general procedures of feasibility analysis are combined with the specific facts relating to a building and its context in order to assess the feasibility of reusing that building.

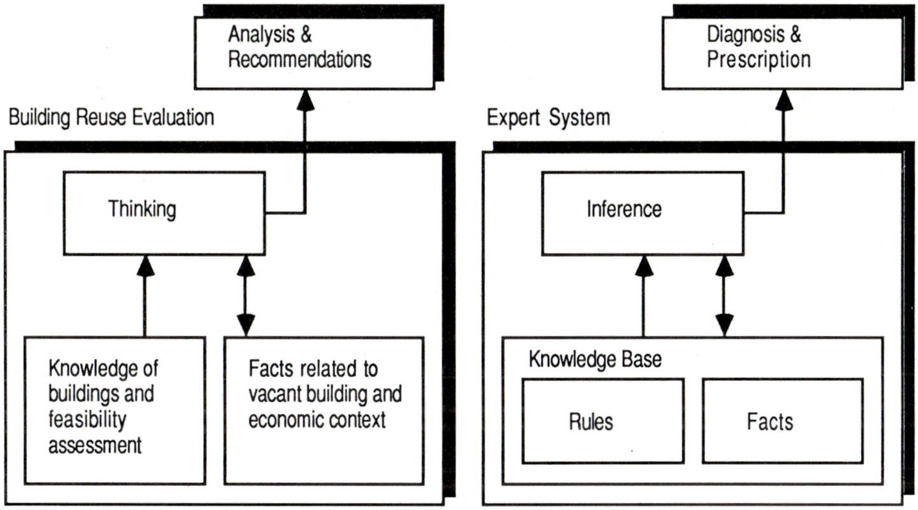

Figure 3. Comparing the Building Reuse Evaluation Process and Expert Systems.

Knowledge Representation: Hierarchical Decomposition

Figure 4 illustrates how building and community factors are arranged as objects (O), an attribute of the object (A) or a value of the attribute (V). Every object has at least one attribute and every attribute has one value. The objects are organized in a hierarchical fashion (e.g., the building object is a part of the project object). There may be more than one attribute associated with each object. For example, demand for a particular building use may be determined by either the absorption rate for that use or the employment rate associated with that use. Finally, values may either be numbers (e.g., the percent absorption rate) or one of a list of possible values (e.g., type of zoning use that is permitted). Both this basic structure and the rules that define the feasibility process are used to help organize the building reuse evaluation process.

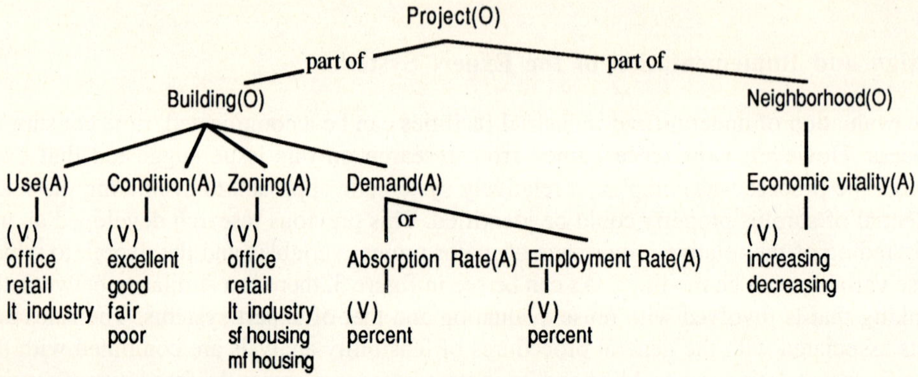

Figure 4. Hierarchical Organization of Rules and Facts.

Frame-Based Knowledge Representation

Knowledge is represented as frames (Winston 1984) within the hierarchical organization previously described. Frames are used in two ways. First, frames are used to represent information concerning the hierarchy of objects that combine to make up the building. An instance of this use of a frame is indicated in table 2.

Table 2. Frames Used to Represent Building Objects.

```
1) AN ABSTRACT REPRESENTATION OF THE ELEVATED-FLOOR FRAME
<Frame name>: elevated-floor
    <Slot-name>:            part-of
        <Facet-name>:       value   super-structure
    <Slot-name>:            load-capacity
        <Facet-name>:       value   *undefined*
        <Facet-name>:       if-needed               ask_integer
    <Slot-name>:            type
        <Facet-name>:       value   *undefined*
        <Facet-name>:       if-needed               ask_ako

2) A PSEUDO-REPRESENTATION OF AN INSTANCE
    elevated-floor
        part-of
                value       super-structure
        load-capacity
                value       200
        type
                value       wood floor

3) THE PROLOG REPRESENTATION OF AN INSTANCE
    oav(elevated-floor,part-of,super-structure).
    oav(elevated-floor,load-capacity,value,200).
    oav(elevated-floor,type,value,'wood floor').
```

The second use of the frame structure is to compare prototypes of prior situations (cases) that may assist in understanding the viability of reusing the vacant building (table 3). This type of representation is particularly useful in helping to determine if a zoning variance is possible for the proposed building use. The example below illustrates how the knowledge about cases can be packaged for use within the inference mechanism. This part of the knowledge base will be augmented as we increase our knowledge about situations in which zoning variances have been successful.

Table 3. Frames Used to Represent Cases.

```
1) AN ABSTRACT REPRESENTATION OF THE ZONING-VARIANCE FRAME
<Frame name>: similar-use-case
    <Slot-name>:            ako
        <Facet-name>:       value  zoning-variance-case
    <Slot-name>:            surrounding-land-use
        <Facet-name>:       value  *undefined*
        <Facet-name>:       if-needed              ask_ako
    <Slot-name>:            economic-impact
        <Facet-name>:       value  *undefined*
        <Facet-name>:       if-needed              ask_ako
    <Slot-name>:            economic-impact
        <Facet-name>:       value  *undefined*
        <Facet-name>:       if-needed              frame-get
    <Slot-name>:            case-law-reference
        <Facet-name>:       value  *undefined*
        <Facet-name>:       if-needed              frame-get

2) A PSEUDO-REPRESENTATION OF AN INSTANCE
    similar-use-case
        ako
                value      zoning-variance-case
        surrounding-land-use
                value      similar
        economic-impact
                value      moderate
        probability-of-variance
                value      likely
        case-law-reference
                value      'MICH PA 125.1045'

3) THE PROLOG REPRESENTATION OF AN INSTANCE
    oav(similar-use-case,ako,value,zoning-variance-case).
    oav(similar-use-case,surrounding-land-use,value,similar).
    oav(similar-use-case,economic-impact,value,low).
    oav(similar-use-case,probability-of-variance,value,likely).
    oav(similar-use-case,case-law-reference,value,'MICH 12.45').
```

Inference Mechanism

The inference mechanism is designed as a general purpose inference engine (see figure 5). The `generate_test` predicate conjectures a building use and tests that use against the knowledge base. `Show_rule` and `show_object` enable the user to query the status of the knowledge base. `How` and `Why` are standard queries to help the user assess the reasoning behind the outcome of the consultation. At present only the how predicate is implemented. The knowledge base also consists of predicates that manipulate frames and attached procedures. Predicates in working storage maintain the status of the knowledge base.

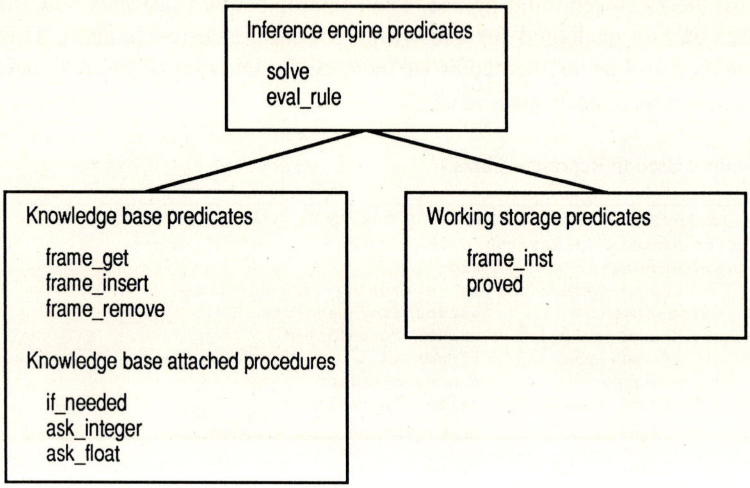

Figure 5. Architecture and Major Predicates of ESP.

Inexact Reasoning

The knowledge base of this system is a collection of human knowledge. Because much human knowledge is imprecise, uncertainty is frequently associated with both rules and facts. For example, although the number of floors in a building may be known for certain, it usually will not be possible to know with absolute certainty whether or not it will be possible to obtain a desirable zoning variance. This expert system accounts for such inexact reasoning by the inclusion of certainty factors (similar to the approach outlined by Lecont and Parker 1986). Numbers are used to express the degree to which the human expert believes the rules and facts are valid. Inexact reasoning then combines these different types of uncertainty into a global uncertainty measure associated with the final conclusion. The certainty factor, or level of confidence, that is associated with each rule ranges from 1.0 (completely known) to -1.0 (completely unknown). These certainty factors will need to be modified as experience is gained with the set of rules and as new rules are added. The certainty factor phrases associated with this version of the system are defined as indicated in table 4.

Table 4. Certainty Factors.

	Representative Cert. Fact	Low Cert. Fact	High Cert. Fact
definite	cf(1.00)	cf(1.00)	cf(1.00)
probable	cf(0.95)	cf(0.90)	cf(0.99)
likely	cf(0.75)	cf(0.60)	cf(0.89)
possible	cf(0.45)	cf(0.30)	cf(0.59)
do not know	cf(0.00)	cf(-0.29)	cf(0.29)
questionable	cf(-0.45)	cf(-0.59)	cf(-0.30)
unlikely	cf(-0.75)	cf(-0.89)	cf(-0.60)
not probable	cf(-0.95)	cf(-0.99)	cf(-0.90)
definitely not	cf(-1.00)	cf(-1.00)	cf(-1.00)

Prolog User Interface

The user interface has been developed to meet two objectives: 1) to facilitate ease of use and 2) to insure that the system is transportable among the widest number of computer systems (hardware and software). An example of the user interface is indicated in table 6. Although these goals are somewhat incompatible, a number of mechanisms have been adapted to enhance the ease of use. For example, in order to minimize the need for typing users select from a list of choices by entering the number of the item in the list. In addition, certainty factors are represented by more easily interpreted English text and are converted into numbers internally. The version of ESP that uses the Prolog user interface has been tested on both Macintosh (AAIS Prolog) and IBM compatible workstations (Arity/Prolog).

Table 6. Example of Prolog User Interface.

```
What is the exterior construction condition
   1. very good
   2. good
   3. fair
   4. poor
>> 2.

What is the certainty factor
   1. definite
   2. probable
   3. likely
   4. possible
   5. do not know
   6. questionable
   7. unlikely
   8. not probable
   9. definitely not
>> 1.
```

HyperCard Front-End

The weaknesses of a text-oriented, sequential question and answer interface become apparent when compared to generally available commercial software. A substantial amount of data entry is involved which can become tedious to enter. In addition, with the Prolog interface is not possible to correct easily items that were entered erroneously. Finally, the entry of information is easier to understand if the items are clustered together on a single screen.

The cost of developing a custom user-friendly interface can be considerable. Therefore, it was decided to experiment with HyperCard as a front-end to the ESP system. The HyperCard interface handles all data entry in a manner consistent with generally recognized user interface guidelines for Macintosh computers. Selections are provided through pop-up menus (figure 6), explanatory information is readily available (figure 7), and all parameters that are similar can be grouped within the contents of a single card to provide a better overview of the status of the object or attribute being addressed. Information collected through this manner is reformatted by a HyperCard script into Prolog predicates which are then written to a file. The ESP Prolog inference engine is automatically executed directly from a button located on a card.

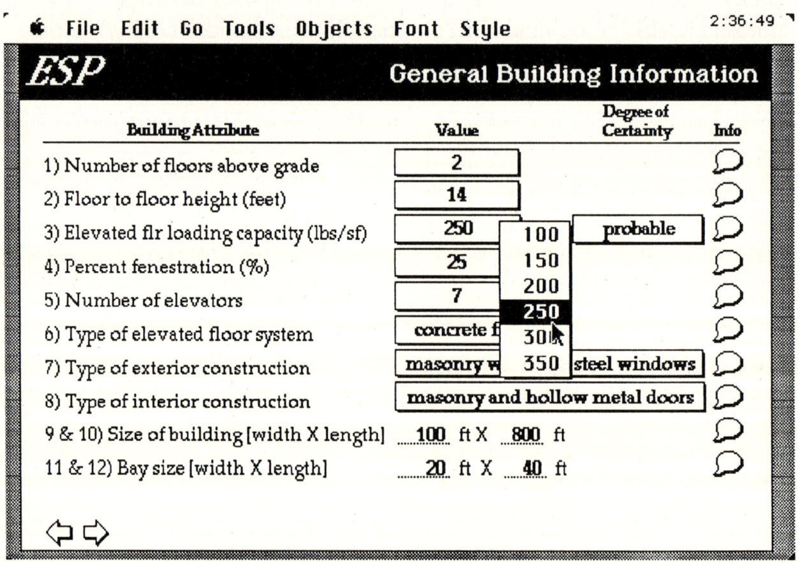

Figure 6. Example of HyperCard Pop-up Menus.

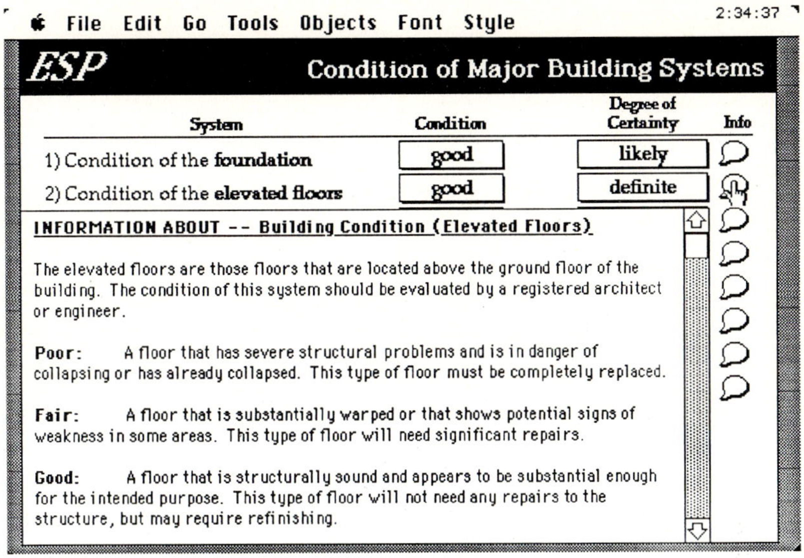

Figure 7. Example of Help Using "Tell About" Buttons.

Introduction to the Knowledge Base Rules and Facts

The knowledge base of the system contains the rules listed below. Internally, these rules are represented as Prolog predicates. In order to obtain an English-like listing it is necessary to use the predicate `show_all_rules` to display all the rules or `show_rule` to display only one of the rules. The sections below explain each the rules that exist in the knowledge base. The certainty factor, or level of confidence, that is associated with each rule ranges from 1.0 (completely known) to -1.0 (completely unknown). These certainty factors will need to be modified as experience is gained with the set of rules and as new rules are added.

In some cases these rules appear to be overly simplistic. There is a trade-off between developing an overly complex, but accurate set of rules and making a system that may be less accurate, but easier and quicker to use and to understand. The intent at this point in time is to develop a reasonable, comprehensive but still easy to understand set of rules for feasibility analysis.

Rule Set 1. Determine the Feasibility of the Proposed Building

```
RULE: feasibility of proposed building :
      if   building condition is acceptable
      and   building zoning is legal
      and   building market is exists
      and   building financing is feasible
      then it is likely (0.950000) that building proposal is possible
```

Expresses the fact that the building use that is proposed is possible if the building condition is acceptable; building zoning is legal; a market for the building exists, and that the results of a financial feasibility analysis are positive.

Rule Set 2. Assess the Overall Condition of the Building

```
RULE: building condition :
      if   foundation condition is very good, good, fair, or poor
      and   elevated floor condition is very good, good, fair, or poor
      and   roof condition is very good, good, fair, or poor
      and   exterior construction condition is very good, good, fair, or poor
      and   interior construction condition is very good, good, fair, or poor
      and   elevator condition is very good, good, fair, or poor
      and   mechanical system condition is very good, good, fair, or poor
      and   electrical system condition is very good, good, fair, or poor
      and   building structure is acceptable
      then it is likely (0.950000) that building condition is acceptable
```

The building condition is a function of all the condition of all of the major systems in the building as well as the basic configuration of the building. This rule indicates that the building system may be acceptable even when one or more building systems is determined to be in "poor" condition. This reflects that fact that the decision to reuse a building is primarily an economic decision, not a technical decision. This rule also indicates that rules may be interrelated with other rules. In this example, the building configuration is determined from a subsequent series of four rules (see Rule Set 3).

Within the system, the definition of "very good, good, fair, or poor" is mapped directly to the maintenance or renovation task ("min maint cost, avg maint cost, avg repair cost, max repair cost") needed to bring that building system up to its proper condition. A different maintenance or renovation cost is associated with each of these tasks. The items below are presented in order to facilitate the understanding of these judgments.

Rule Set 3. Evaluate Elevated Floor Load Capacity

```
RULE: office floor load capacity-wood floor :
      if   building use is office
      and   elevated floor type is wood floor
      and   elevated floor load capacity is greater than or equal to 150
      then it is definite (1.0) that building structure is acceptable

RULE: office floor load capacity-concrete floor :
      if   building use is office
      and   elevated floor type is concrete floor
      and   elevated floor load capacity is greater than or equal to 250
      then it is definite (1.0) that building structure is acceptable


RULE: retail floor load capacity-wood floor :
      if   building use is retail
      and   elevated floor type is wood floor
      and   elevated floor load capacity is greater than or equal to 200
      then it is definite (1.0) that building structure is acceptable


RULE: retail floor load capacity-concrete floor :
      if   building use is retail
      and   elevated floor type is concrete floor
      and   elevated floor load capacity is greater than or equal to 300
      then it is definite (1.0) that building structure is acceptable
```

This series of rules indicates the acceptability of the estimated floor loading capacity of the building. The required floor loading varies, depending on the live load (occupancy of the building) and the dead load (type of elevated floor system).

Rule Set 4. Compliance with Existing Zoning of the Property

```
RULE: compliance with current zoning-office use :
      if   building use is office compatible uses
      then it is definite (1.0) that building zoning is legal
RULE: compliance with current zoning -retail use:
      if   building use is retail compatible uses
      then it is definite (1.0) that building zoning is legal
RULE: possibility for obtaining a zoning variance :
      if   zoning variance is probable
      then it is likely (0.950000) that building zoning is legal
```

These rules govern whether or not the property meets existing zoning requirements. If the building use is compatible with current allowed uses, then there is a high degree of certainty that the zoning requirements have been met. However, if the proposed building use is not in compliance with zoning requirements, then a zoning variance must be obtained. The list of compatible uses will change, depending on the proposed use of the building.

Rule Set 5. Possibility for Obtaining a Zoning Variance

```
RULE: compatibility of proposed zoning with adjacent zoning :
      if   adjacent building use is building use
      then it is likely (0.95000) that zoning variance is probable

RULE: compatibility of planned use with surrounding use :
      if   adjacent building planned use is building use
      then it is possible (0.85000) that zoning variance is probable

RULE: impact on economic vitality of neighborhood :
      if   neighborhood vitality impact is positive
      then it is possible (0.85000) that zoning variance is probable
```

The probability that a zoning variance can be obtained is defined in these three rules. These rules indicate that a zoning variance is likely (but not definite) if the use of the surrounding buildings is the same as that of the building being analyzed. The probability of a zoning change is less (possible) if the planned, future use of surrounding buildings is the same as that of the building being analyzed and if it can be argued that the proposed building would have a positive impact on the economic vitality of the neighborhood.

Rule Set 6. Assessment of the Building Market

```
RULE: building marketability factors :
      if   building demand is positive
      and  building supply is positive
      and  building demand estimate is greater than building supply estimate
      then it is definite (1.0) that building market is exists
```

The assessment of the building market is operationalized by this rule, which simply compares the demand and supply of space associated with the proposed building use. If there is no demand for a given use, or if the supply exceeds the demand, then further consideration is unwarranted for that proposed occupancy.

Rule Set 7. Assessment of Building Supply and Demand Factors

```
RULE: demand for space using absorption rate :
      if   building absorption rate is greater than 0
      then it is definite (1.0) that building demand is positive

RULE: demand for space using employment rate :
      if   building employment rate is greater than 0
      then it is likely (0.950000) that building demand is positive
```

The demand for space is estimated in two ways. The first (and preferred) method is to evaluate the prevailing demand conditions by means of a market survey. Given the total building stock that is available for the proposed use, the market survey will define an absorption rate which can be used to estimate the space that can be absorbed each year.

Employment data is the second method used for estimating demand. This calculates space needs by multiplying the total employment for a given standard industrial classification (SIC) code by the current rate at which employment is increasing (or decreasing) times an estimate of the gross square foot of space per employee that is required for the proposed use. If employment is increasing, this should translate into a greater demand for space. It has a lower level of certainty but is generally easier to obtain from state employment security records.

```
RULE: supply of space using estimate of vacant space :
      if   building avg vacant sf (market) is greater than 0
      then it is likely (0.950000) that building supply is positive

RULE: supply of space using new building permits :
      if   building avg new sf (permits) is greater than 0
      then it is likely (0.950000) that building supply is positive
```

The supply of available space is obtained either through a market survey or through a evaluation of new building permits.

Rule Set 8. Assessment of Building Financial Feasibility

```
RULE: financial feasibility :
      if   building pre-tax equity rate of return is greater than or equal to
           building pre-tax market rate of return
      then it is definite (1.0) that building financing is feasible
```

The financial feasibility of the building is calculated using a standard pre-tax cash-on-cash rate of return analysis. The calculation proceeds in four stages: 1) estimation of the cost of renovation and land, 2) calculation of the mortgage debt service, 3) estimation of Net Operating Income (Potential Gross Income minus Operating Expenses), and 4) the calculation of the rate of return.

An Example of Results

After an evaluation of the building, the user may request an explanation of the solution by asking "how." Because the explanations can be quite detailed, they typically will be written into a text file that can then be read into a word processor, formatted as desired, and printed.

```
>> how.
The hypothesis is that: ("building proposal is possible")
The following has been established:
   building proposal [possible] is possible (with certainty of 0.726750)
   BECAUSE

   building condition [acceptable] is acceptable (with certainty of 0.902500)
   BECAUSE

   foundation condition [good] is very good, good, fair, or poor (with certainty of 1.0)
   and    elevated floor condition [good] is very good, good, fair, or poor (with certainty of
          0.950000)
   and    roof condition [good] is very good, good, fair, or poor (with certainty of 0.950000)
   and    exterior construction condition [good] is very good, good, fair, or poor (with certainty
          of 1.0)
   and    interior construction condition [good] is very good, good, fair, or poor (with certainty
          of 1.0)
   and    elevator condition [good] is very good, good, fair, or poor (with certainty of 0.950000)
   and    mechanical system condition [fair] is very good, good, fair, or poor (with certainty of
          1.0)
   and    electrical system condition [poor] is very good, good, fair, or poor (with certainty of
          1.0)

   building structure [acceptable] is acceptable (with certainty of 1.0)
   BECAUSE

   building use [office] is office (with certainty of 1.0)
   and    elevated floor type [wood floor] is wood floor (with certainty of 1.0)
   and    elevated floor load capacity [300] is greater than or equal to 150 (with certainty of
          1.0)
   and    elevated floor type [concrete floor] is wood floor <RULE FAILED>

   building use [retail] is office <RULE FAILED>

   building use [retail] is office <RULE FAILED>

   building zoning [legal] is legal (with certainty of 0.807500)
   BECAUSE

   building use [office] is office compatible uses [office,retail,light industry,multi-family]
      (with certainty of 1.0)

   building use [office] is office compatible uses [office,retail,light industry,multi-family] (
      with certainty of 1.0)

   zoning variance [probable] is probable (with certainty of 0.850000)
```

Conclusions and Acknowledgements

This paper has provided an interim report on the status of the ESP project. More development work needs to be conducted prior to a more comprehensive testing of the approach and additional rules need to be formulated for other building types. Rules also have to be developed for issues that have been identified but have not yet been factored into the rule base. Historic preservation is an example of one issue that still needs to be formalized in this decision process.

The primary purpose of this first phase of the project has been to demonstrate the viability of the concept and to identify areas for future research. It does appear possible to develop a systematic, knowledge-based approach to help evaluate the major options that face decision makers in the revitalization decision process. Further case studies need to be conducted in order to better understand the relative strengths and weaknesses of this approach. If this approach does turn out to be effective, then it may be possible to utilize a more generalized technique to evaluate alternative uses for a wider range of building types. The results of future research in this area may also have more direct applicability to the design of new buildings. Approaches used to improve the economic performance of an existing, underutilized building may have a direct applicability to approaches that can be used to improve the economic performance of an evolving building design.

The research reported in this paper was developed in part through funding by the Homer Hoyt Institute, a non-profit foundation which supports research in real estate and land economics. The extremely able assistance of Eduardo Sobrino, currently an Assistant Professor of Architecture at the University of Puerto Rico, in the initial design and implementation of the system is gratefully acknowledged as is the assistance of Wassim Jabi in the initial development of the certainty factors module of the system.

References

Johnson, Robert E. 1990. *The Economics of Building*. New York, NY: Wiley.

Johnson, Robert E., Yavuz Bozer, and Partricia Mondul. 1987. *Revitalization Strategies for the Studebaker Corridor*. Architecture and Planning Research Laboratory: Ann Arbor.

Johnson, Robert E., Ahmed Sherif and Franklin Becker. 1987. "Economics of University Research Laboratories: Policy Considerations." In *Construction Management and Economics*, vol. 5: 31-42. London: E & F.N. Spon Ltd.

Lecont, K., and D. Parker. 1986. "Control Over Inexact Reasoning." *AI Expert*. Premier issue, pp. 32-43.

Maher, Mary Lou. 1990. "Process Models for Design Synthesis." *AI Magazine*, no. 11 (Winter, 1990): 49-58.

Maloney, William D., Editor in Chief. 1990. *Means Assemblies Cost Data 1990* (15th ed.). Kingston, MA: Means.

Molnar, Lawrence, and Pinchas Kahana. 1989. *Geographical, Physical and Economic Analysis of Closed Industrial Plants in Michigan, 1982-1987*. Ann Arbor, MI: Office for Research on Industrial Facilities.

Parsaye, Kamran, and Mark Chignell. 1988. *Expert Systems for Experts*. New York, NY: Wiley.

Popper, Karl. 1934. *The Logic of Scientific Discovery*. New York, NY: Harper and Row.

"Revitalization of Industrial Buildings: An Investigation of Economic Impact Resulting From the Closing of Aged Multilevel Industrial Plants." 1981. *Part One: Analysis and Findings*. Industrial Development Division, Institute of Science and Technology, The University of Michigan.

Seldin, Maury, and Richard H. Swesnik. 1985. *Real Estate Investment Strategy*. New York, NY: Wiley.

Simon, Herbert. 1981. *The Sciences of the Artificial*. Cambridge, MA: MIT Press.

Winston, Patrick. 1984. *Artificial Intelligence*. Reading, MA: Addison-Wesley.

28 XNET2 - Methodical Design of Local Area Networks in Buildings

AN APPLICATION OF THE A4 INTELLIGENT DESIGN TOOL

Hartmut Ayrle

Institut für Industrielle Bauproduktion
Universität Karlsruhe
7500 Karlsruhe, Germany

XNET2 is a prototype program, that helps network planners to design Ethernet-conform data-networks for sites and buildings. It is implemented as an example application of the ARMILLA4 Intelligent Design Tool under Knowledge Craft. It is based on a knowledge acquisition phase with experts from DECsite, the network-branch of DEC. The ARMILLA Design Tool is developed on the basis of Fritz Haller's ARMILLA, a set of geometrical and operational rules for the integration of technical ductwork into a building's construction.

Our Perception of the Design Process

A discussion of intelligent software tools to support design processes must start with the formulation of underlying assumptions of the design process. During the development of A4 we picked up the following ideas:

Limited Competence

In a "problem-space" of limited complexity we can have unlimited competence in solving the problem - whereas in a "problem-space" of unlimited complexity, we can always only have limited competence in problem solving.

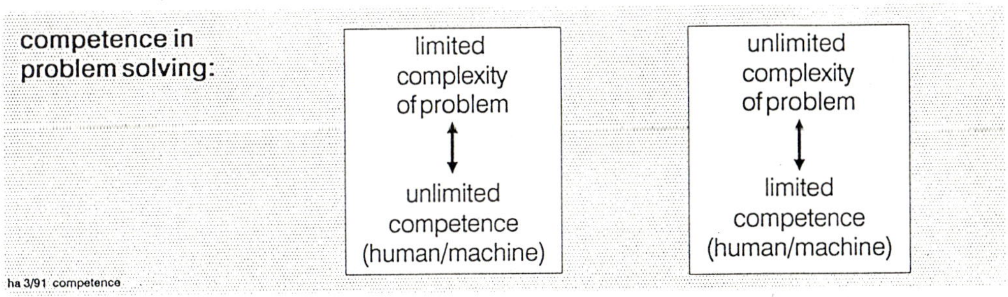

The complexity of a "problem-space" rises with the number of objects and the number of relations between the objects in it. We think that real-world design problems have the tendency to contain an unforeseeable number of objects with unforeseeable relations between them. Thus we do not claim either for a human or for an automatic planner anything like total competence in solving design problems.
In more detail, we state that the design of a building is normally incomplete in three aspects:

- time
- representation
- functions and related design knowledge

Temporal Incompleteness

If we regard a building as a system during its total lifetime and wish to support conscious design of its construction and all the following changes, then the design process is not completed until the final dismantling of the building. The initial design is only a special case of the permanent redesign. To limit design to the initial construction means to deny the consequences initial design have for the operation and quality of a building during its lifetime.

Representational Incompleteness

As every discipline in the design process looks at, designs, and operates a building from a different point of view, several worlds of symbolic descriptions of a building exist simultaneously. This statement is just another perception of the architect's coordination task and in our case of the design tool's coordination task its different models. In fact we are trying to establish a program that supports the handling and interaction of different descriptions for one identical building from different users.

In addition, the representation of a building in analogous or digital data is in principle incomplete. The representations we use are always only symbols for the real-world objects, only the building itself may be regarded as an analogous representation of a certain state in the design process. This leads to a new assessment of the contents of design documents. The statements they convey are always symbolic and thus may undergo more detailed consideration at some unforeseeable moment in the design process. A natural limitation of symbolic representation appears when the need for analogous physical distinction by using built models arises. CAD in this context is nothing more than an editor for the graphic parts of the symbolic representations of building models.

Incompleteness of Design Knowledge - Functional Incompleteness

Symbolic building models do not only contain descriptions of real-world objects but also knowledge about the appropriate way of designing and operating these objects. As there exist many differing descriptions of a building, the knowledge for design and operation is primarily distributed within the multiple descriptions and initially cannot be seen by every participating discipline. This is one source of design conflicts.

Furthermore, in building practice it is normal for planning agents a) to change their view of their design task during work, b) not to be integrated in the design team appropriately, or c) not to be integrated at all. This means that the multiple symbolic models of the building and the contained knowledge are changing due to functional redefinitions during the design process with unforeseeable effects. Again the design process is potentially incomplete, as regards the design and operational knowledge, about it.

In summary, we see the design process as an effort to handle design conflicts that inevitably appear in a human, real-world context. A software tool to support design tasks must treat design conflicts as constituent parts of the design process. The main service it may offer is to unravel and handle design conflicts and only at a second stage to possibly resolve them. Thus, intelligent design tools, which may contain expert systems as automatic planners, have to be designed and used as assistants to the human planner. The final responsibility for design decisions will stay with the human planner as long as the encoded competence of intelligent design tools can only be limited.

The Intelligent Design Tool A4

How do we handle these uncertainties in our "intelligent" design tool A4 ?

As it seems to be impossible to formulate a complete description of the manifold knowledge to be taken into account during the design process, we hand the formulation of semantic knowledge back to the different users, and focus on the possibility of coordinating them through a common syntax for the design and operating process. Only on such a platform can semantic knowledge be usefully formulated.

Design Methodology

We propose a common design methodology for all involved disciplines, that initially contains no knowledge about objects or procedures of the design task but is itself an aid to dynamically establish and handle symbolic representations of objects and procedures in multiple planning modules. It transfers the principles known from Methodical Construction in Mechanical Engineering to the field of Architecture and accomplishes the well-known incremental functional decomposition with the possibility of formulating constraints and constructive knowledge for every decomposition phase/module.

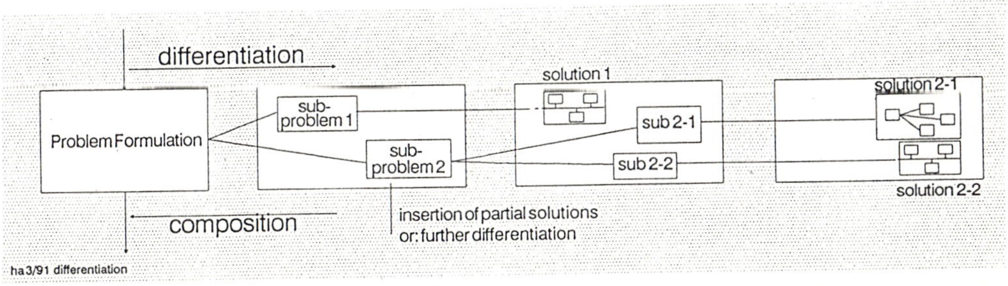

A planning agent starts to build a planning module with a graphic sketch of what he wants to plan that is what he wants to define more precisely - on an arbitrary scale of detail. He gives name, space and time to the problem he formulates, be it an object or process to be designed or operated. Then he starts filling in details of the problem. Every detail he gives can again be another problem to be solved later, or it can be a partial solution, that he creates himself or that is introduced from a prototype solution catalogue by him or by a planning automaton. The problem he started with is solved, when all details are decomposed so far that a solution for them can be found. Having solved a problem he can incorporate it into a larger problem formulation module, where it in turn may serve as a partial solution.

Dynamic Planning Model

During an initial decomposition process, the planning agent builds a series of program modules which represent his way of solving/decomposing the specific design task. Each module comprises the objects and knowledge for one decomposition step. One agent's modules form together his planning world and exist in parallel to another agent's modules.

As different planning agents build up their symbolic representations in a series of planning modules, we allow them to "publish" those parts, that may be relevant for other planners. Each agent can decide to declare "interests" that he has on other agent's objects or that other agents should have on some of his objects. That way a common planning world is gradually established alongside the multiple specialized planning worlds. The different planning agents will then use objects and procedures of multiple interest from the common planning world in their own process of detailing. Thus a network emerges, that reveals the dependencies of the different disciplines through the multiple use of objects or processes in the differing planning worlds. If one planning agent A changes the internal structure of an object or process, this change is passed on by a data-exchange-system (rather than an inflexible database-system) directly to all the planners B, C etc. who use this element in their decompositions.

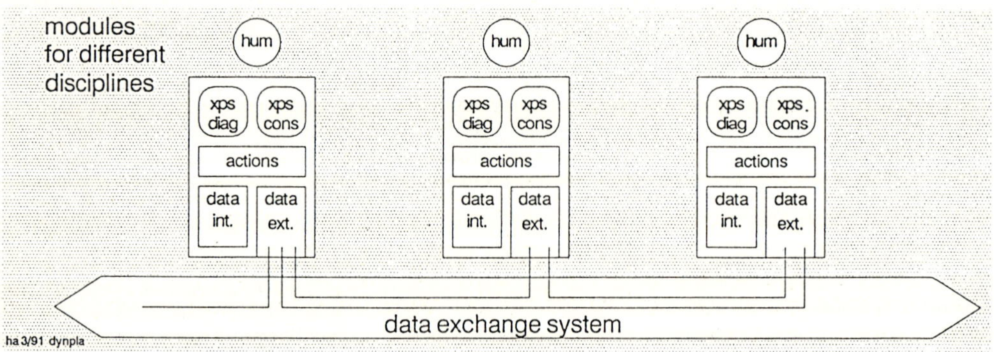

Conflicts may then be resolved in one of the following ways:

- The program notifies other users of the changed element, that a change occurred which might possibly cause a conflict; some notified users state no conflict with their current design and accept the change; some other users do state a conflict and try to resolve it by redesigning their internal plannings; if this is not possible, the originator is notified and the conflict has to be resolved either on the level of analogous face-to-face discussion or by means of a decision hierarchy.

This means that our program initially fulfills the task of coordinating different disciplines by bringing conflicts to the surface rather than trying to resolve them with design knowledge, which is in principle incomplete.

Design Constraints and Automatons

As we have seen, our program A4 initially only offers two automatisms: a) the operational support for the decomposition of a problem which keeps track of multiple uses of its elements and b) the notification of planners when conflicting designs become possible. So far, our system does not deserve the name of "intelligent" tool yet. How do we incorporate the human planner's knowledge into our system?

Our A4 system thus offers possibilities: a) to define constraints on the modification of object attributes that have to be fulfilled within a specific design subtask/module b) to define typical (partial) solutions for design subtasks in the form of prototype objects that represent elements which need no further detailing/decomposition c) to define knowledge for constructing solutions by finding and inserting partial solutions.

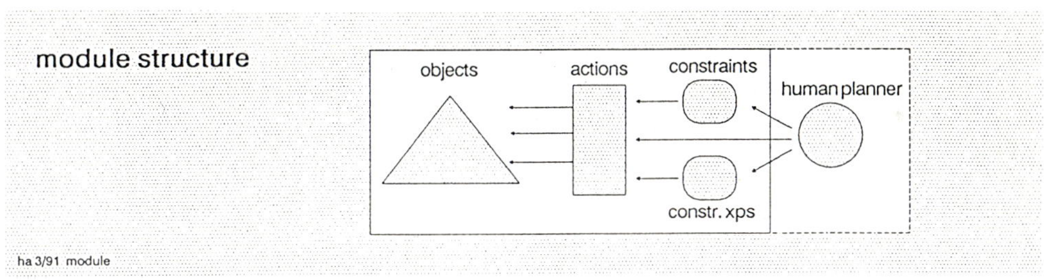

In our system, design knowledge is always appended to a certain design phase/module. In every design phase a planner works on, he can use the constraints, strategies or partial solutions that are formulated as relevant for it. He may examine this knowledge, lock its usage or add new knowledge through different appropriate editors, textual or graphical. Thus he has the choice between three work-modes with our design tool: a) pure manual design of building elements, with conflicts being shown for all elements, that he publishes to other planners; b) manual design controlled by the encoded constraints for the current design phase; c) automatic design driven by encoded strategic knowledge and prototype solutions.

Distinct series of design phases, that predefine appropriate levels of detailing/decomposition for a certain design task, are defined by a user's initial formulation of a design subtask. They also represent some knowledge of the design task, especially on a promising decomposition strategy. Nevertheless, the modules representing such a predefined process can be altered at any time for specific projects.

The representation of such knowledge in a software system has to be considered under software engineering aspects and I cannot discuss this subject here. It may be said however, that our experience in implementation points towards complex multilanguage software development-tools. They make it possible to represent different types of knowledge in different, appropriate languages - using only one language (LISP, Prologue, OPS etc.) brings too many problems in adopting the manifold ways of real-world reasoning to one single method of evaluation. We use the KnowledgeCraft development shell with an X-Windows based graphic interface builder.

The Role of the Graphic Interface

The graphic interface of our program is of special interest for us, firstly because we concentrate on a methodology for design, which produces questions on the realization of the methods. Secondly because we believe, that expert systems are only usable to the degree in which they are controllable. To give control over the software's influences on the design process, it is necessary to "show" what exists and what happens. As "a picture says more than a thousand words", we suggest that every object or operation to be planned, every design-process to be represented and every kind of knowledge to be incorporated in the program is best described and can best be investigated in graphic form. Of course there are things that are most efficiently described in words or formulas, but our preference lies towards graphic expressions.

Subsequently our program offers graphic and textual editors for several uses:

a) a CAD-like editor for graphic input and for the detailing of objects and graphic representations of processes;
b) a graphic editor for the relation network between the elements in the planning world;
c) an alphanumeric editor for textual definition of planning world elements or design knowledge;
d) a graphic editor for design knowledge which is under development.

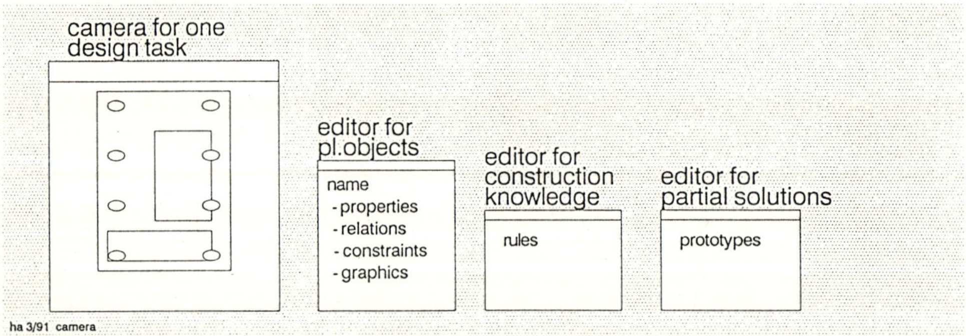

An Application Example: LAN-Design with XNET2

To give a more concrete picture of our program, I want to finish by giving you an impression of an expert system we are about to implement. In cooperation with Digital Equipment Germany we are building a design tool to support planning of Local Area Networks (LAN) for buildings under the name of XNET2.

The software is based on a thorough knowledge acquisition phase (about 1.5 many ears) which revealed important parts of the design knowledge of DECsite network planners. It uses the concepts of the A4 kernel explained earlier. The system predefines 4 design phases and 4 detailing levels for the LAN-planning process.

The phases of the LAN design process are:

a) an initial assessment of the site, its buildings and duct-possibilities and the existing and intended computer hardware installations to be connected;

b) the production of configuration alternatives that work on rough spatial and technical connection possibilities;

c) the accurate layout planning, that takes into account the exact measurements of existing rooms, possible ducts and permissible cable-lengths;

d) the definition of details for duct installation and the production of ordering lists.

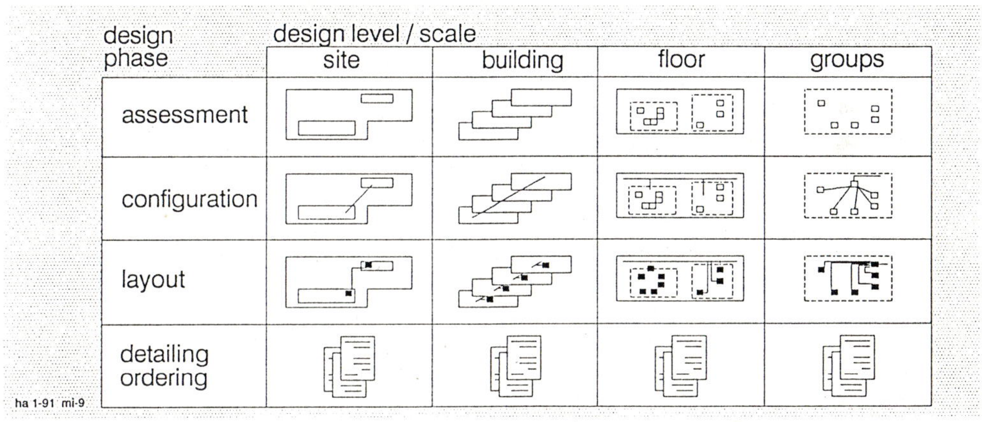

In each of these phases decision have to be taken on four levels of detailing: i) considering the whole site; ii) considering each building as a whole; iii) considering each floor in a building; and iv) considering groups of computers within one floor.

Our program offers 16 cameras on the planning world that represent those differentiation tasks. Appended to every camera is the constraint and strategic knowledge that we - in this case as A4 users - extracted from the DECsite experts and encoded into the program.

The user may start to build up the project-specific planning world at any phase and any level, by giving graphic descriptions of the buildings or computers or duct solutions or by giving textual descriptions of the hardware to be connected or new constraints to be considered. He is offered catalogues of typical hardware and cables from which he derives individual objects for the planning world. Thus he can manually produce a network concept for his project. At all planning levels, the user can call up a control routine, that checks his decisions against the available constraints and marks obviously wrong situations.

We also offer a planning automaton, that is based on the same incremental decomposition concept the whole system is designed for: The user may mark a region for which the program is to produce solution proposals. The software then starts to decompose: a) It tries to define groups of computers within the given region, that are obviously easy to connect. In order to do so it checks the technical connectability (port and cable types) and the proximity relations (all within one room, closer than n meters, depending on the cable type, etc.) and formulates a hierarchy of possible groupings. b) Then it starts to evaluate the existing prototype solutions for the current design phase and level and gives either possible alternative solutions or hands back the problem to the user as currently unsolvable.

The last statement must be understood correctly: the problem is currently unsolvable to the software, given the present state of the planning world and design knowledge. As soon as the user gives new informations or changes the planning world in some way, the same automatic process may be used again and may find a solution.

It is important to note, that we use collections of prototype solutions to select from rather than instructions for the generation of solutions. This takes more effort in evaluation but is necessary as we have encoded pure experience knowledge that up to now seems not to be expressible in generative form.

A generative method can be used when, during the layout planning phase, the system automatically tries to assign the roughly configurated cable-lines to existing or possible duct spaces. Here we use a modified Lee-algorithm to find possible cable and duct paths.

As XNET2 is completely based on the A4 system, it can be incorporated into a larger design tool, that holds modules for other design disciplines.

At our institute we run for example another expert system that supports planning and detailing of waste water duct systems in a building and shares parts of the symbolic building description with XNET2.

It is easy to think of a use for XNET2 in the maintenance of installed local area networks. As initial design is only a special case of redesign, most relevant data and knowledge for maintenance exists already and only few additional functions would have to be added, as for example timestamps for inspection intervals and test messages for hardware function checks.

Outlook

As we have seen, the A4 intelligent design tool models the design process as a decomposition process and supports the designer with a graphical interface and with means for constraints and constructive knowledge.

The critical point with the decomposition paradigm is, however, the process of decomposing a problem in exactly such a way, that partial solutions for sub-problems will be found. Expert excellence is the art of decomposing "correctly" and not towards a situation, where no solutions can be introduced. As pointed out in the XNET2 example, we are about to do more investigations in this field with the aim of producing an "automatic decomposition" support for A4 users.

References

Drach, A., L. Hovestadt. 1989. "Intelligente CAD-Systeme - Instrumente für die Planung und Verwaltung komplexer Gebäude." In *Proc. of the Intelligent Building Symposium*, Institut f. Industrielle Bauproduktion, Uni Karlsruhe.

Raetz Peter. 1989. "XNET: ein intelligentes CAD-System für die Planung von Lokalen Netzwerken in Gebäuden." Fortschrittsberichte 20/19. VDI Verlag.

VDI-Richtlinien zur Konstruktionsmethodik, Nr.2210-2217.

Ross, D.T. 1977. "Structured analysis - a language for communicating ideas." *IEEE Software Engineering* 1/77.

Minsky, Marvin. 1985. *The Society of Mind*. New York, NY: Simon & Schuster.

29 Architecture of a Knowledge-Based-System for the Detailing of Reinforced Concrete Columns

Christoph Meinecke, Raimar J. Scherer

Institut für Massivbau und Baustofftechnologie
Universität Karlsruhe
7500 Karlsruhe 1, Germany

This paper presents the hypothesis part of an expert-system for detailing reinforced concrete structures. The structural members on which the work is focused are columns. To generate a hypothesis - that means to configurate the reinforcement for a given structural member with an almost fixed geometry - needs different kinds of information, i.e. knowledge and a strategy to apply this knowledge. Therefore a hybrid system is chosen which combines object oriented organization to represent the fixed knowledge and a rule base to model the strategy and the dynamic knowledge.

Introduction

It is the aim to use CAD-systems for the construction of reinforced concrete structures and not only for the purpose of the graphical drawing. To achieve this aim a CAD-system is connected with an expert-system creating an intelligent construction system. An exclusively rule-based attempt seems to be not adequate since the description of a reinforced concrete structure is too extensive. A rule-based system combined with an object oriented data base is a tool to solve such a distinct problem.

Unit Construction System

A reinforced concrete unit is not only substructured in building components (e.g. continuous beams or frames) but on a second level these building components themselves are substructured in fundamental components (e.g. columns, frame corners or corbels) (Scherer 1990 a). This classification is made

- to generate an easier solution for the reinforcement layout (hypothesis)
- to simplify users control of this 'machine-made' solution
- to reduce the time for the verification made by the expert-system
- to increase the grade of repetition of the fundamental components for reducing
- the quantity of components.

The basic idea of these fundamental components are the D- (disturbance) and B- (bending) areas corresponding to the framework analogy (Schlaich 1987). Each fundamental component has typical reinforcement layouts. It is possible to describe in a parametric form its geometry and function by a rule base.

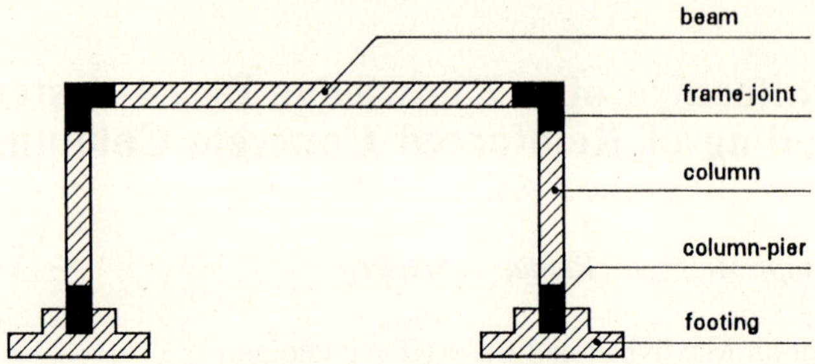

Figure 1. The building component 'frame' with its fundamental components.

The geometric description in parameters enables to model the whole range of variation for a fundamental component in one element. The primitive of the geometric description in parameters is the prisma. This description is comparable to the representation of the building components used in (Zlajpah 1990).

The functional description in parameters enables to model in one set of rules, all possible reinforcement layouts as a function of the requirements of the building component. The rules are substructured in accordance to the function of the reinforcement (compression, tension, shear, construction).

The advantage of this procedure is a finite number of fundamental components. Out of these components all possible building components and units can be assembled (see figure 2). The amount of these units however is infinite.

To use this unit construction system, the solution finding mechanism is subdivided in three steps. In the first step the unit is disassembled in building components and in fundamental components. In a second step the reinforcement of the fundamental component is generated and in the third step these fundamental components are reassembled into the building component and at last into the unit.

A full construction expert-system should include two different parts (Scherer 1990 b, Garret 1989): a hypothesis generating and a verification system. A hypothesis generating system constructs a solution - a verification system proves a solution. In this paper a hypothesis generating system for the detailing process of reinforced columns is presented. It is described how mechanisms which are specific for expert-systems are used to solve the detailing problem.

Requirements for the AI Tool

The AI (artificial intelligence) tool which is going to be used for such an attempt should provide the following features (Meinecke 1990):

- based on a symbol oriented programming language
- object oriented database
- rulebased knowledge representation
- allocation of expert-system typical mechanisms like rule matching algorithm
- possible connection of foreign programs with the shell to use existing numerical programs.

The tool that seems to be satisfactory for these requirements is Knowledge-Craft (KC) (Carnegie 1989). It provides the following components: an object oriented data base CRL (Carnegie Representation Language), a forward-chaining rule based knowledge representation CRL-OPS (an implementation of OPS-5) (Krickhahn 1987), a backward-chaining rule based knowledge representation CRL-PROLOG. KC is embedded in the LISP (Steele 1984).

KC could be characterized as an open expert-system-shell. That means the user has all the opportunities which are typical for expert-systems. He also has the possibility to introduce his own ideas into the system. This aspect was very important while choosing the shell. For example in KC there are following opportunities:

For the conflict resolution strategy there are two OPS-specific alternatives (LEX and MEA), but there is still the possibility to integrate a self defined solution strategy in the system. The CRL data base offers the opportunity to define relations between the classes in addition to the CRL-given relations. By this a special inheritance mechanism is created.

It is important to distinguish the knowledge which is required for the design problem in fixed knowledge, dynamic knowledge and in strategy knowledge. The fixed knowledge is represented in the CRL data base. Dynamic and strategy knowledge are modelled in CRL-OPS rules.

Object Oriented Data Base

The object oriented data base - further on called the taxonomy - is subclassified in three subtaxonomies:

- geometry
- material
- load.

Each of them stores facts to describe reinforced concrete columns. This classification is carried out for the sake of distinctness. Information about the geometry of the building components is stored in the geometry taxonomy. Information about the material is accumulated in the material taxonomy. The load taxonomy serves for the storage of facts to describe the load of columns.

The three fundamental ideas of object oriented knowledge representation are (Puppe 1988): inheritance hierarchy, attributive procedures and default values. The realization of these ideas is shown in the following chapters:

Inheritance Hierarchy

An object oriented database - with implicit inheritance hierarchies - is due to an economic data structure (Puppe 1988). Only individual properties of a class are stored at the class itself (Caspar 1990). Properties and occasionally their values with common character are stored in superordinated superclasses. Properties and their values are left from superordinated to subordinated classes. The same properties and values for different classes are stored in the data base only once, at a superordinated class.

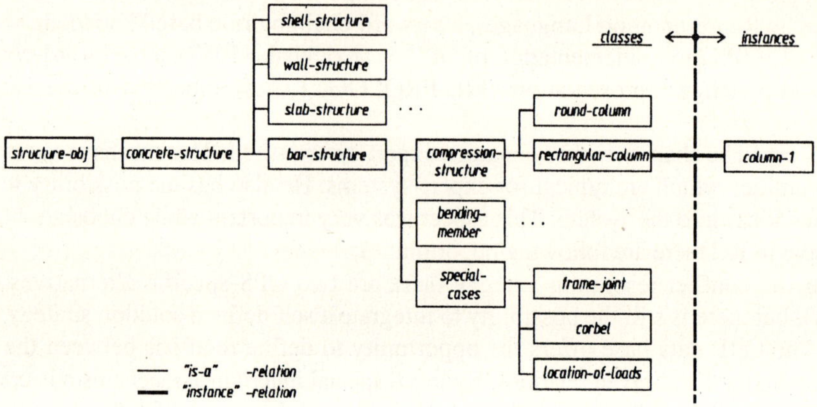

Figure 2. Extract of the geometry taxonomy.

```
(defschema concrete-structure
        (is-a structure-obj)
        (material-concrete )
        (material-steel )
        (environment-class-1 closed-rooms permanent-dry)
        ...
        (environment-class-4 susceptible-to-corrosion strong-chemical-attack)
        (environment-class )
        (ch-ds )                                        ; chosen-diameter long.rein.
        (c)                                             ; concrete-cover
        ...)
```

Figure 3. The class "concrete-structure".

Doing this there is no redundancy in a well shaped taxonomy. The use of this mechanism is shown in the figures 2 and 3. Globale properties like "material-concrete" and "material-steel" or "environment-class-_" are stored at the class "concrete-structure". The information is left to all subclasses of "concrete-structure" that are all concrete structures but they are stored only once in the taxonomy.

Attributive Procedures

This mechanism - or in other words: demons - serves also for an economic data structure. A demon is a program which is allocated to a certain property of a class. It determines the value of its property based on existing values of other properties. The demon is connected to the data base by special CRL commands.

The class "steel-bar" (see figure 4) contains the knowledge how the area of a single bar is calculated. It leaves this ability to its subclasses and their instances, e.g. to "diameter-20". The class "concrete-structure" (see figures 2 and 3) contains the information about the concrete cover for the reinforcement is provided. By German standards this concrete cover is dependent on the diameter of the chosen longitudinal reinforcement bars and the existing environment condition (see figure 5).

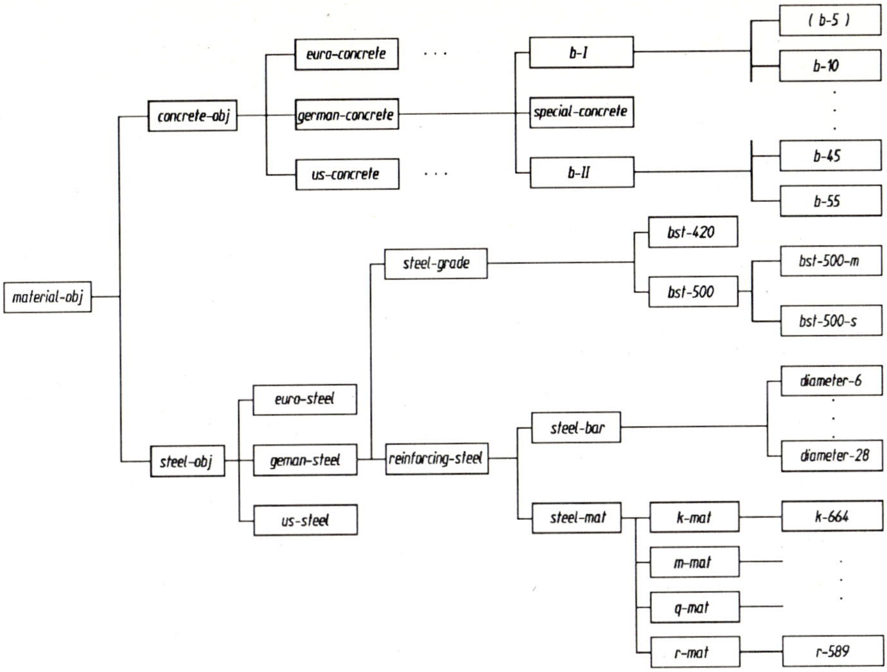

Figure 4. The material taxonomy.

The table shown in figure 5 is programmed as a demon which is guarding the property "c" (concrete-cover) of all concrete structures. This property and its demon are arranged at the class "concrete-structure". The demon is getting active each time the CRL-command "get-value...." is attaching the value of the property "c". If the diameter and/or the environment-conditions are not yet known the demon gives an answer with secure assumptions for the unknown details. Naturally this ability is left to all subclasses and their instances, that means to all concrete structures.

	1	2	3	4
	environmental conditions	diameter of the reinforcement d_s [mm]	minimum value for ≥ B25 min c [cm]	characteristic value for ≥ B25 nom c [cm]
1	structures in closed rooms e.g. in flats (incl. kitchen, bath room and laundry) offices, schools, hospitals commercial stores. - unless otherwise specified structures that are permanent dry	to 12 14, 16 20 25 28	1.0 1.5 2.0 2.5 3.0	2.0 2.5 3.0 3.5 4.0
..	....	....	....	....
4	structures susceptible to corrosion. E.g. frequent exposure of aggressive gases, deising salts or strong chemical attack	to 28	4.0	5.0

Figure 5. Extract of table 10 of the DIN 1045 (DIN1045 1988).

Default Values

Often it seems to be useful to have default values of certain properties in specific classes. During a session the user can accept these default values but naturally he can also change them. The default value for the arrangement of the reinforcement in rectangular columns with biaxial-load is the concentration at the corners (see figure 5). This design always has the larger lever arm towards the neutral axis.

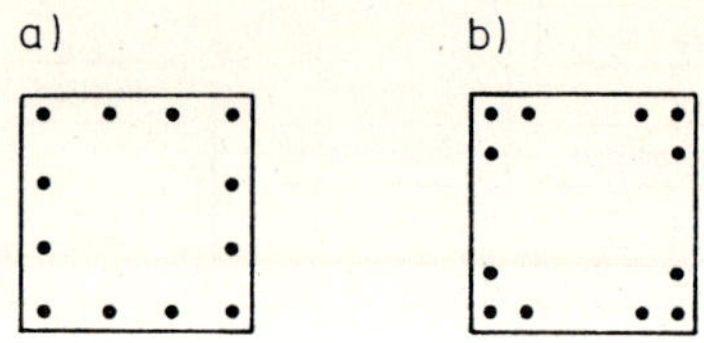

Figure 6. Longitudinal reinforcement distributed along the sides (a) and concentrated at the corners of a column (b) (DAfStb 1979).

Relations

For the design problem there is the necessity to leave knowledge under classes which do not have an original inheritance relationship. The classes representing the different forms of concrete (B-5 to B-55), the kinds of reinforcement steel or the reinforcement itself do not have such an original relation to all subclasses of "concrete-structure". A relation mechanism provides the chance to leave knowledge outside the classes. In the class "concrete-structure" (see figure 3) the properties "material-concrete" and "material-steel" and their inverse relation "is-used-in" utilized in the classes "b-5" to "b-55" and "bst-500-s" are not only properties, but also self defined relations.

Having chosen the materials the instance "column-1" e.g. has the value "b-35" for the property "material-concrete" and the value "bst-500-s" for the property "material-steel". All information stored in the classes "b-35" and "bst-500-s" is available for the instance "column-1". Relations are - like demons - connected to the data base by CRL mechanisms. The relations are properties in the classes. The values of these properties are the classes to which the relation is connected to.

```
{{ COLUMN-1                                   {{ B-35
        INSTANCE: RECTANGULAR-COLUMN                 IS-A: B-II
        MATERIAL-CONCRETE: B-35                      IS-USED-IN: COLUMN-1
        MATERIAL-STEEL: BST-500-S                    ...
...}}                                         }}
```

Figure 7. Extract of the instance "column-1" and the class "b-35".

Example for Encoding the German Standard DIN 1045

In standards knowledge is often represented in tables. In the following chapter it will be shown how this is reproduced. Generally only such knowledge is stored in the taxonomy which is due to one class (fixed knowledge). Knowledge concerning more than one class is represented as a rule. Figure 8 shows table 1 of the German standard DIN 1045 (DIN1045-1988). It is evident that the CRL-code of the class "b-35" shown in figure 9 is very close to the language of the standard.

	1	2	3	4	5	6
	concrete group	strength class of the concrete	characteristic strength β_{WN} (minimum value for the compression strength β_{W28}) [N/mm²]	mean strength β_{WS} (minimum value for the average compression strength β_{Wm}) [N/mm²]	mix	use
1	concrete B I	B 5	5	8	paragraph 6.5.5	unreinforced concrete
2		B 10	10	15		
3		B 15	15	20		un- reinforced and reinforced concrete
4		B 25	25	30		
5	concrete B II	B 35	35	40	paragraph 6.5.6	
6		B 45	45	50		
7		B 55	55	60		

Figure 8. Table 1 of the DIN 1045.

```
(defschema b-35
        (is-a b-II)
        (Is-used-In )
        (characteristic-strength-n/mm**2 35)
        (mean-strength-n/mm**2 40)
        (mix din-1045-6.5.6)
        (use unreinforced-concrete reinforced-concrete ))
```

Figure 9. The class "b-35".

Rule Base

There are two kinds of rules in the rule base. One kind of rule describes the construction knowledge that is necessary for the solution of the design problem. The other kind of rule represents strategy knowledge. They are used to describe the way how the solution of the design problem can be achieved.

Strategy Knowledge

The solution finding mechanism (recognize-act cycle) in a rulebased system is only controlled by the data status of the active classes and their instances. It uses the inference engine (Winston 1984)

- to select the rules, which match the instances (matching phase)
- to choose one of those rules (conflict resolution phase)
- to execute the actions specified in the selected rule (execution phase).

So it is not required to subdivide the rule base. But it became obvious that a lot of the data requests in the rules condition part only have control character. A large part of the aspired clarity would be lost. To model the strategy knowledge, the first phase of the recognize-act cycle is interfered by introducing a "context-object" into the data base (see figure 10) (Krickhahn 1987).

```
(defschema context-obj
        (is-a obj )
        (stack geometry forces long-rein tie-rein)
        (context ))
```

Figure 10. The "context-object".

The property "stack" contains all necessary contexts to become active during the session. Each of them must become active to generate a satisfactory result. The rule "control-ini" puts the first value of the property "stack" into the property "context", and deletes this special value in the "stack" property. The essential condition for this action is: the property "context" must not have any value.

```
(p control-ini
(context-obj
        ^schema-name <name>
        ^context ())
-(context-obj
        ^schema-name <name>
        ^stack ())
-->
(new-value <name> 'context (get-value <name> 'stack))
(delete-value <name> 'stack (get-value <name> 'context)))
```

Figure 11. The rule "control-ini".

All the other rules - those rules which represent the construction knowledge - have a context-object request in their condition part to prove the rule against the active context. To leave an actual context, there must be a precisely defined instance data status. If this data status is reached the value of the context-object's property "context" must be deleted to bring up the next context in the "stack". In each context there is a rule to manage this changeover. For the context "long-rein" this rule is shown in figure 12.

```
(p end-context-long-rein
(context-obj
        ^context 'long-rein)
-(rectangular-column
        ^instance 'rectangular-column
        ^long-bars ())
```

```
->
(delete-any-values 'context-obj 'context) )
```

Figure 12. The rule "end-context-long-rein".

Construction Knowledge

The basic knowledge to describe the construction of reinforced columns is formulated in standards, recommendations and textbooks (DIN1045 1988, DAfStb 1979). How this kind of knowledge is transferred into a shape the computer is able to understand is the purpose of this chapter.

In standards knowledge is often represented as a table. Above it is shown how such a table is represented in the taxonomy. If a table concerns more than one class it should be represented in rules. Such a table does not contain fixed knowledge, but rather a kind of dynamic knowledge. The data status of one class not only alters its own properties and their values but also properties and values of different classes (dynamic or interactive knowledge). Knowledge - not only stored in tables -but also structured knowledge as just described, is represented in the rule base.

Table 32 (DIN1045 1988) presents the permissible diameters for the longitudinal reinforcement bars in columns (see figure 13). How the second line of this table is performed is shown in figure 14.

	1	2
	smallest dimension of the cross section of the compressive member [cm]	smallest diameter d_{sl} [mm]
1	< 10	8
2	≥ 10 to < 20	10
3	≥20	12

Figure 13. Table 32 of the DIN 1045.

The condition part for the LHS (Left-Hand-Side) of the rule (shown in figure 14) checks first whether the active context is "long-rein" (longitudinal reinforcement). If the rule should fire the instance of the class "rectangular column" must have the minimum of width and depth ("min-d") between 10 and 20 cm. The class' property "has-diameter" may not have any values. Beyond this on the variable <name> the name of the instance is stored locally (e.g. "column-1").

```
(p 1045.tab.32-2
(context-obj
        ^context 'long-rein)
(rectangular-column
        ^instance 'rectangular-column
        ^schema-name <name>
        ^min-d { >= 10 < 20 }
        ^has-diameter ())
```

```
->
(new-values <name> 'has-diameter (get-values-if 'steel-bar 'diameter #'(lambda (x) (>= x 10))))
)
```

Figure 14. The rule "1045.tab.32-2".

In the conclusion part or the RHS (Right-Hand-Side) of the rule the value of the property "has-diameter" is determined. In the class "steel-bar" all available diameters are stored in its property "diameter". For the value of the column's property "has-diameter" only those diameters which are greater or equal than 10 mm will be taken. Afterwards the diameter for the longitudinal reinforcement will be chosen out of the values for this property.

To secure the stability of the reinforcement cage and to prevent wide cracks, the maximal distance of the reinforcement bars is set at 30 cm (DIN1045-1988). This is only effective for columns with larger dimensions than 40 cm. If the longitudinal reinforcement - which is necessary to ensure the structural analysis - is laid out in larger distances than 30 cm, constructive reinforcement must be build in with regard to the maximal distances between the reinforcement bars. Each bar has got the information about the distance to its next bar to the right ("delta-r") and about the name of this right neighbor ("bar-r").

```
(p constructive-reinforcement-b
(context-obj
        ^context 'long-rein)
(bar
        ^instance 'bar
        ^schema-name <name>
        ^is-used-in <structure>
        ^delta-r > 30)
(rectangular-column
        ^instance 'rectangular-column
        ^schema-name <structure>
        ^b > 40 )
-->
(const-rein <name>) )
```

Figure 15. The rule "constructive-reinforcement-b".

The rule "constructive-reinforcement-b" fires each time a bar has a larger distance to its right neighbor than 30 cm. Precondition is that the column's dimension "b" is greater than 40 cm. The layout of the new constructive bar or eventually bars (that depends on the distance "delta-r") is managed by the LISP-function "const-rein". This function creates the new bar or bars, calculates and determines the appropriate coordinates and values of the other necessary properties.

At last the function enters the new instance (s) into the data base. Of course the values of the properties "delta-r" and "bar-r" of the original longitudinal reinforcement bar are updated too. - Often it is very helpful to use such functions in the RHS to achieve a better performance.

Representation of the Results

There are at least two different ways to describe the results of the expert-system session: All information about the column, the longitudinal reinforcement bars and the ties is stored in one instance. The other possibility is that all information is stored in different instances: one for the concrete body of the column and one for each reinforcement bar and tie.

Representation as a Single Instance

This first proposal would have the advantage that all information about the column is stored at one place and the system has to handle only one result-instance. The shortcoming of this suggestion is that all information due to a single bar or a single tie has to be stored as one property of the result-instance. But such a property with a list value is not easy to handle. CRL and CRL-OPS do not have the possibility of working with a distinct element of a list value. CRL only has the possibility of working with the first element of a list value (get-value...) or of working with all of them (get-values...). So for each kind of data request it is necessary to produce a selfdefined request function. This does not seem to be very useful.

A way out could be to create a certain property for each important feature of a reinforcement bar or a tie at the result-instance. Using this solution all CRL mechanisms can be used. But the clarity of the result-instance is going to be lost because of the huge number of properties.

Representation in Several Instances

We chose the solution to create an instance of an adequate class not only for the concrete body of the column but also for each bar and tie. This solution has the decisive advantage that all CRL and OPS commands can be used on this data structure. Each bar or tie (represented as an instance) can be matched by CRL-OPS rules and can be manipulated by CRL-commands.

```
{{ COLUMN-1
        INSTANCE: RECTANGULAR-COLUMN
        MATERIAL-CONCRETE: B-35                ; material-concrete
        MATERIAL-STEEL: BST-500-S              ; material-steel
        LAYOUT: CORNER                         ; layout corner-concentrated
        H: 420                                 ; hight [cm]
        D: 40                                  ; width [cm]
        B: 40                                  ; depth [cm]
        MIN-D: 40                              ; minimum of depth and width [cm]
        HAS-DIAMETER: 12 14 16 20 25 28        ; has diameters (long. rein.) [mm]
        CH-DS: 20                              ; chosen diameter (long.rein.) [mm]
        CH-DTIE: 8                             ; chosen diameter (tie) [mm]
        AS: 35.8                               ; necess. area long. rein. [cm**2]
        CH-AS: 37.7                            ; chosen area long. rein. [cm**2]
        ENVIROMENT-CLAS: 2                     ; actual environment
        C: 3                                   ; concrete cover [m]
        ....
        TIE: 22                                ; quantity of ties
        LONG-BARS: 12}}                        ; quantity of long. bars
```

Figure 16. The instance "column-1".

```
{{ TIE-12
        INSTANCE: RECTANGULAR-TIE              ; rectangular tie
        IS-USED-IN: COLUMN1                    ; belongs to "stuetze-1"
        DTIE-U: 20                             ; distance to the next tie up [cm]
        NTIE-U: 13                             ; name of the next tie up
        STIE: 8                                ; diameter of the tie [mm]
        HOOK: 10                               ; end hook [cm]
```

```
DBR: 5                  ; bend radius[cm]
X: 180                  ; coordinates of the tie (x,y,z) [cm]
Y1: 16.6
Z1: 16.6
....
Y4: -16.6
Z4: 16.6
N: 12}}                 ; tie's number
```

Figure 17. The instance "tie-12".

Interface between the Expert-System and a CAD-System

The representation of the solution found by the expert-system takes place on a CAD-system. To increase the acceptance of this solution the user must always have the full control of the construction process. To realize this the system must work interactively. In other words the progress of a partial solution of the whole construction problem must be open for the ideas of the user. Not giving preference to a single CAD-system it is necessary to work out an interface which is able to connect the system with different CAD-systems. So the interface must have two parts: one part which is expert-system specific and the other one that is CAD-system specific.

The first part of the interface converts the information stored in the instances, which is described above into a datafile. This is realized as a LISP program. It is started as soon as a partial solution that should be proved by the user is worked out. The second part of the interface must transfer the datafile made by the first part in a form that the CAD-system will understand. For example at the UNICAD system (Hochtief 1989) these are extensions at the CAD-system's interface encoded in FORTRAN.

The aim is to implement the interface on a standardized exchange format. The most promising one seems to be STEP, because it has an object oriented concept. Currently the 2D draw exchange format is validated and will be a standard in Germany in the near future (DIN-NAM 1989). To use such a standardized drawing exchange format will have the great advantage that an interface made for one CAD-system can more easily be made suitable to other CAD-systems.

The Interactive Interface

In the system there are two kinds of interactive processes. The first one is used if the system needs information which is obtainable neither in the taxonomy nor in the rule base. Then the system will ask the user to supply it with that information. The other kind of interactivity is used to increase the acceptance of the system's solution: The entire process of constructing the reinforcement must be subdivided in partial solutions which the user can test more easily. This process must be managed by the interface, its function is a hypothesis/verification mechanism, what is described in the next paragraphs.

The system constructs a partial solution which is in conformity with the standards (hypothesis) and offers it on the CAD platform to the user. The user can accept this solution or change it. If he changes the solution, the system will test this user-made proposal and vrify if it conforms to the standards (verification).

If the system proves the user made solution was not acceptable the hypothesis/verification mechanism starts again. The system will work out a new solution which conforms to the standards. To generate this solution the system will change the user's nonconform proposal until it comes up to the standards. This new proposal is offered again and the user can accept it or naturally he can change it once again.

If the user's proposal conforms to the standards or the user does not want to change it the system will adapt it and will go on with the next step in generating a solution to the entire problem.

Future Developments

In the future our work will have the following focal points: It is very important to integrate the verification part into the system (Scherer 1990 b). This will achieve the full possibility for interactive work.The realization of the interface between CAD and expert-system based on a standardized data format is our second emphasis. A third one will be to integrate knowledge into the taxonomy and the rule base that represents different schools of construction to concrete structures (Franz 1988) (Leonhard 1977). Then the user will have the opportunity to decide which school is relevant for his construction.

Conclusions

The hybrid realization of a hypothesis generating system for the detailing of reinforced concrete columns by an object oriented and a rule based representation of the design knowledge and the design strategy is an encouraging attempt for the implementation of one part of a general expert-system which is undergoing development.

The hypothesis generating system is outlined as a production system not considering nonmonotonic reasoning and contradictive solutions. It generates a unique solution based on a strategy selected by the user. The structural member described in this paper covers only a specific and not very complex design region.

This allows us to concentrate on the object oriented presentation of the fixed knowledge and the rule based representation of the dynamic knowledge. In other design regions it may well be impossible to generate one unique and satisfactory solution. For example the connection process in which two separately designed fundamental components (e.g. column and frame-joint) are assembled into a building component (frame) can force the system to take back its solutions made for the reinforcement layout of one of the fundamental components (backtracking). Some ideas about how to manage these problems are given in (Mehrafza 1991). A redesign of one single fundamental component is necessary. Nonmonotonic reasoning technics have to be applied to make the process efficient.

Nevertheless our simple structural member proved the applicability of the combined object oriented and rule based implementation of the problem. Especially the object oriented representation of the fixed knowledge and the fixed strategy in a taxonomic form have proved their advantages compared with to a pure rule based representation. This result encourages us to use the hybrid object oriented and rule based implementation as an outline for the whole expert-system.

References

Carnegie Group Inc. 1989. "Manual of Knowledge Craft 3.2." Pittsburgh, PA.

Caspar, E. 1990. "Ingenieurgerechte Wissensrepräsentation am Beispiel eines objekt-orientierten Expertensystems für Stahlbau-Nachweise." (knowledge representation for engineers at the example of an object oriented expert-system for the prove of steel constructions). In J. Gauchel (ed.). *KI-Forschung im Baubereich.* Berlin: Verlag Ernst & Sohn.

Deutscher Ausschuß für Stahlbeton (DAfStb). 1979. *Heft 220.* (Heft 220: guideline for the construction of reinforced concrete members). Berlin: Verlag Ernst & Sohn.

Deutsches Institut für Normung e.V. 1988. *DIN 1045.* (DIN 1045: German standard for reinforced concrete structures). Berlin: Beuth.

Franz, G., and K. Schäfer. 1988. *Konstruktionslehre des Stahlbetons.* (construction of the reinforced concrete). Berlin: Springer.

Garret, J. H., and S. J. Fenves. 1989. "Knowledge-based standard-independent member design." *Journal of Structural Engineering* 115, no. 6: 1396-1411.

DIN-NAM 96.4.2. 1989. *STEP-2DBS.* (STEP-2D Building Subset, version 1.0, standardized exchange format - going to be standard in Germany). RIB e.V. Stuttgart.

Hochtief AG. 1989. *UNICAD-B Programmierhandbuch.* (UNICAD-B programers handbook). Frankfurt/Main, Essen.

Krickhahn, R., and B. Radig. 1987. *Die Wissensrepräsentationssprache OPS 5.* (the knowledge representation language OPS-5). Braunschweig: Vieweg.

Leonhardt, F. 1977. *Vorlesungen über Massivbau.* (lectures on reinforced concrete). Berlin: Springer.

Mehrafza, M. J., and R. J. Scherer. 1991. "Regelbasierte Formulierung von Varianten-Elementen in der Stahlbetondetaillierung." (rule based formulation of parameterized elements in detailing reinforced concrete buildings). In *Tagungsberichte der Dortmunder Expertensystemtage.* Dortmund.

Meinecke, Ch., and R. J. Scherer. 1990. "Expertensystem-Techniken im Vergleich zum normalen Programm am Beispiel der Stahlbetondetaillierung." (expert-system technics compared to the normal program at the example of detailing reinforced concrete structures). In *DAfStb-Forschungskolloquium.* Karlsruhe.

Puppe, F. 1988. *Einführung in Expertensysteme.* (introduction to expert-systems). Heidelberg: Springer.

Scherer, R. J. 1990-a. "Formen der Wissensrepräsentation in einem Expertensystem für die Stahlbetondetaillierung." (different kinds of knowledge representation in an expert-system for detailing reinforced concrete structures). In J. Gauchel (ed.). *KI-Forschung im Baubereich.* Berlin: Verlag Ernst & Sohn.

Scherer, R. J. 1990-b. "Expertensystem für die Planung und Bemessung der Bewehrung von Stahlbetonbauteilen." (expert-systems for the design of reinforced concrete structures). In R. Anderl (ed.). *CAD/CAM-Technologie.* Berlin: Springer.

Schlaich, J., K. Schäfer, and M. Jennewein. 1987. "Toward a Consistent Design of Structural Concrete." *PCI Journal,* May-June 1987.

Steele, G. L. 1984. *COMMON-LISP the language.* Digital Press.

Winston, P. H. 1984. *Artifical Intelligence.* Addison-Wesley.

Zlajpah, D., and J. Duhovnik. 1990. "AR_CAD: Regelbasiertes System für die Bewehrungsführung im Stahlbetonbau." (AR_CAD: a rule based system to model the reinforcement for concrete structures). In J. Gauchel (ed.). *KI-Forschung im Baubereich.* Berlin: Verlag Ernst & Sohn.

30 An Integrated KB-CAAD System for the Design of Solar and Low Energy Buildings

Edna Shaviv

Faculty of Architecture and Town Planning
Technion - Israel Institute of Technology
Haifa, Israel

Uriel J. Peleg

ACA-Architecture and Computer
Aids Ltd.
Ramat Gan, Israel

A knowledge-based computer-aided architectural design system (KB-CAAD) for the design and evaluation of solar and low energy buildings is presented. The KB-CAAD system is based on the integration of knowledge-based and procedural simulation methods with any available CAAD system for building representation. The knowledge base contains the heuristic rules for the design of passive solar buildings. Whenever possible, the knowledge base guides the designer through the decision making process. Yet, if the rules of thumb are not acceptable for the particular design problem, the KB-CAAD system guides the architect by using a procedural simulation model. We demonstrate by means of a case study, that not only does the KB-CAAD system lead to the design of better solar buildings, but that this process requires less time and labor than the process of building presentations by means of standard available CAAD systems.

Introduction

Different design tools for solar and low energy buildings were developed mainly since 1976 (SERI report 1980). These tools addressed different design stages. The first CAD tools to be developed were the comprehensive procedural simulations (deep knowledge). These tools were aimed for use on mainframes only and especially by researchers. Among the large simulations to be run on mainframes, we would like to mention the PASOLE simulation for passive solar design, developed by McFarland and used in Los Alamos National Laboratory (McFarland 1978) and TRNSYS for simulating the dynamic thermal behavior of active solar systems (Klein, et al. 1976). Other early examples of procedural simulation tools (that were aimed to be applied by researchers and designers) are BLAST (U.S Army 1977), ENERGY (Shaviv and Shaviv 1977), DEROB (Arumi 1979), ESP (Clark 1982), DOE-2 (LBL and LASL 1982), and SERIRES (Palmiter et al. 1982).

The cumbersome application of such heavy tools that run on mainframes led to the development of simplified procedural methods. These simplified methods were based on approximations, like steady-state assumption (ASHRAE 1972) and the correlations obtained from different detailed computer simulations. Typical examples are the "f-charts" method that was developed from the TRNSYS computer code (Beckman et al. 1977), and the SLR and LCR methods that are based on the PASOLE simulation tool (Balcomb et al. 1984).

Thus, the second approach to the design of solar and low energy buildings was based on simplified procedural methods and was not derived from first principles. It provides designers with an estimate of the expected thermal performance of different design alternatives. Shaviv (1989) claimed that the simple expressions that were developed to be manually solved are in most cases too cumbersome for this purpose (particularly for architects). As a consequence special computer programs were developed to solve the so called manual analysis methods. These approximate CAAD tools require detailed data of the building's design parameters, in the same way that the precise simulation tools do. The approximations differ from the precise tools in that they calculate energy consumption on an annual, monthly, or daily basis rather than hourly. The required climatological data for long time averages are naturally simpler than the hour by hour data. This advantage disappears when computers are used to perform the simulation. The storage requirements of hourly climatological data for each region seldom pose a problem even to small present day computers. We find that small computers can provide accurate efficient simulations at modest cost.

Looking back at the years 1976 to 1984, the rational behind the above mentioned approach is well understood. It was imaginary to predict that a time will come when architects will use the computer like a 6B pencil. Few architects and researchers, that entered the field of CAAD at the early 70's, believed in the use of computers as tools for energy conscious designs at that time. Such ideas were presented in CAD conferences by Clark, Greenberg and Shaviv (Pikes 1978). In 1977, Shaviv and Shaviv (1977, 1978 a,b) suggested a simulation model called ENERGY, which runs on a personal computer and could be used easily by architects. This model was based on interactive handling of the building data, using essentially a questionnaire expressed in daily architectural terminology. This approach can be contrasted with the non friendly thermal network physical presentation models, like the PASOLE code. The ENERGY model presented by Shaviv and Shaviv was planned for simple and easy use during the early schematic design stage. But as personal computers were rare at that time, the suggested approach seemed remote from reality.

The use of accurate CAD design tools seems more realistic to many people today. The above philosophy was advocated by Klein in the address he delivered when he was honored with the Abbot award for 'significant contribution to the field of solar energy' (Ases annual meeting, Denver, CO., 1988). Klein got the award for the development and implementation of the "f-chart" design method for sizing solar heating systems and his contribution in the development of TRNSYS computer code. In his speech he mentioned the fact that the "f-chart" was an important design tool when it was developed, as designers did not have at that time access to personal computers of todays power. Yet, he would probably not have suggested this method today.

The third approach, first suggested by Balcomb et al. (1984), is based on rules of thumb and acquired experience (wide knowledge). This approach was the latest to be developed, as it required the accumulation of knowledge and expertise. The heuristic rules provide designers with generalized appraisal of their choice of building orientation, geometry (massing), and choice of site treatments. The input required by this model is approximate and coarse compared to the input required by the procedural model. The knowledge-based evaluation model can therefore be applied at the early formative stages of the design process, where the impact of design choices on the energy performance of the building is more significant than choices made in later design phases (Shaviv 1977, Maher and Fenves 1985, Kalay et al. 1987, Schmitt 1987, Shaviv and Kalay 1990). Examples of early CAD tools based on this approach include an expert system developed by Gero and Coyne (1984), a design tool developed at CMU (Schmitt 1987), ARCADE (Antony 1987), and an expert system developed by Bharati (1990).

The early knowledge-based design tools for gross evaluation of thermal properties of design alternatives have the advantage that they do not require a full description of the building, and avoid the complication of preparing such detailed data. Yet, they suffer from the inherent over-simplicity of rules of thumb, which do not provide deep knowledge and are based on previously examined standard cases. Recently, we have seen new attempts to develop advanced knowledge-based energy conscious design tools based on integration with deep knowledge. Some of these works were presented in the ASHRAE symposium 'Artificial Intelligence in Building Design: Progress and Promise' (Pohl et al. 1990, Shaviv and Peleg 1990, Brown 1990, Tham et al. 1990, Papamichael and Selkowitz 1990).

Evaluation and Prediction at the Schematic-Conceptual Design Stage

The solar characteristics of passive solar and low energy buildings are determined at the schematic design stage. Therefore, the need for a good design tool during the conception stages is evident.

The procedural simulation CAAD tools provide an accurate evaluation of the predicted energy consumption and performance of a building. These tools require a detailed description of the building, which are not always known at the schematic stage. As a result, the usual practice is to use simple rules of thumb and approximate methods at this stage and leave the accurate evaluation, using more complex simulation tools, to the final design stage.

A few problems arise: First, rules of thumb do not always lead to a correct solution because they are based on, and relate to standard cases that were examined previously. Therefore, they may give incorrect recommendations for new innovative designs, which deviate substantially from the standard and frequently used cases. Second, major drawbacks may be discovered when accurate simulations of the building are carried out at the final design stage. Usually it is practically too late to draw new conclusions and introduce drastic changes.

In the same way that it is laborious to use simulation models at the early design stages, it is complicated to represent visually the building by applying any presently available 2D or 3D CAAD system. The reason being the cumbersome and tedious process of the introduction of the building's geometrical data. As a result most architects tend not to use these systems during the conceptual design stage but merely during the documentation of the final project.

The above difficulties call for a different and new computer-aided architectural design approach to handle the schematic sketch and evaluation process. The KB-CAAD tool, presented in this paper, combines geometric design with solar considerations. It is based on integrating a knowledge base with a procedural simulation model and any available graphic system for building representation. The knowledge base contains the heuristic rules for the design of passive solar buildings and is stored in the computer. Whenever it is possible to apply rules of thumb, it guides the designer through the decision-making process. However, when rules of thumb are not adequate for the particular design, the KB-CAAD system guides the designer by using the procedural simulation model.

The new design tool uses heuristic rules to automatically assign values to particular design parameters, such as wall thickness and composition, that are required input to the simulation model and to the graphic system for building representation. As a result, fewer data must be specified by the designer. By not having to insert detailed data describing the building, we benefit both in the schematic phase of design of energy-conscious buildings and in developing the two-dimensional and three-dimensional representations. Moreover, as some detailed data is assigned automatically by the system, the use of accurate simulations in the early design phases is possible. This method overcomes the possibility that the rules of thumb, which were developed for standard cases, may not apply to our innovative design.

The Complexity in Predicting the Thermal Performance of Buildings

The number of various energy-related design parameters needed for simulating the thermal performance of buildings is very large. The building data include the floor area and its volume, the area and heat capacity of the isothermal mass, the initial wall temperature conditions, and the internal heat gain according to a given schedule. This data includes also the information about the mode of operation, size of mechanical equipment (thermostat settings and hours during which the heater or cooler operate) and the number of air changes during day and night (due to infiltration and natural or forced ventilation). Information about the number of walls, including all opaque elements in the external envelope (such as roofs and floors) should be given. For each external element, the heat capacity, heat conductivity and thickness of each layer must be specified, as well as the albedo and emissivity of the element and its shading factors. The external element data also comprise of geometrical design parameters such as the azimuth, inclination and area of the element. The data incorporate the type, azimuth, inclination, shading coefficients, and area of each window located on this element as well.

Figure 1 shows part of the many energy-related design parameters that must be specified before a simulation can be run. The simulation used in the present case is the ENERGY code. This program solves simultaneously the heat transfer equation through all exterior walls, taking into account the thermal mass of each external wall and internal partitions. The simulation model calculates the energy consumption of the building during winter and summer (see Figure 2). In addition, it computes the maximum in-house summer temperature without air conditioning (Tmax-NV or Tmax-V) or with a fan only (Tmax-F). Most of these results, while of considerable importance to the user of the building, are not available in the approximate models. Special effort has been invested in the computer code ENERGY, to produce an algorithm that solves the implicit scheme of the time-dependent equation for the heat flow in an efficient way. Thus, to run an hour by hour simulation of a full-scale comprehensive building requires only 10 seconds on a Personal IRIS workstation.

An energy-conscious design process comprises the choice and assignment of appropriate values to the many design parameters presented in Figure 1. The process is complicated because many interdependent design parameters must be specified simultaneously.

To demonstrate this point, we have performed many simulation runs (Shaviv and Capeluto 1990), showing that the relationship between various design parameters is not universal and varies with the particular conditions existing in the building. This means that the same change in a given parameter may have different effects, all depending on the particular state the building is in(see Figure 2).

BUILDING'S GEOMETRY					
180.0					TOTAL FLOOR AREA
504.0					VOLUME OF BUILDING
6					NO. OF EXTERNAL WALLS
0.0					AZIMUTH OF REFERENCE WALL
INTERNAL PARTITIONS					
300.0					AREA OF INTERNAL MASS
8400.0					HEAT CAPACITY OF INTERNAL MASS
18.3					INITIAL TEMP. DISTRIBUTION
MECHANICAL SYSTEMS AND BUILDING USE POLICIES					
250					HEAT GAINS: CONSTANT
1000	18.0	22.0			HEAT GAINS: SCHEDULE
10000	07.0	22.0	18.0	19.0	HEATER: SCHEDULE; TEMP.SET
6000	07.0	22.0	24.0	28.0	COOLER: SCHEDULE; TEMP.SET
2	18.0	07.0	0.75	4.0	VENT: TYPE, SCHEDULE, ACH: DAY; NIGHT
ENVELOPE					
1					WALL NO 1
3					NUMBER OF LAYERS
500.0	1.40	0.02			(c,λ,d) 'OUTSIDE PLASTER'
75.0	0.23	0.20			(c,λ,d) 'YTUNG BLOCK 800'
450.0	0.87	0.01			(c,λ,d) 'INSIDE PLASTER'
180. 90.					WALL: AZIMUTH, INCLINATION
.65 .95					WALL: ALBEDO, EMISSIVITY
37.56					AREA OF WALL
90. 90. 90. 90.					SC-SUMMER: DIR,DIF; SC-WINTER: DIR DIF
1					NO OF WINDOWS AND SOLAR ELEMENTS
WINDOWS AND SOLAR ELEMENTS					(ON WALL NO 1)
1 18.00					WINDOW:TYPE;AREA
10. 50. 90. 90.					SC-SUMMER:DIR,DIF;SC-WINTER:DIR DIF
18. 07. 5. 3.5					U WINDOW:SCHEDULE;DAY;NIGHT

Figure 1. Part of the energy-related design parameters that should enter the simulation model ENERGY.

Figure 2 shows the thermal performance of a middle floor apartment with a large southern window in Jerusalem (a region of cold winters and mild summers) and in Tel Aviv (a region of mild winters and hot-humid summers). As an example, one can see that improving the walls' insulation, in the climate of Jerusalem, significantly reduces the energy consumption of the building (compare JE-SL with JE-IL). However, the same improvement in the climate of Tel Aviv will increase the total energy consumption of the building (compare T-SL with T-IL). Moreover, the improvement in the walls' insulation in a poorly ventilated building will deteriorate the summer thermal performance of the same apartment (see Tmax-NV and compared JE-SL to JE-IL). This is because the heat stored in the thermal mass is released to the unvented rooms, and the improved insulation prevents its loss through the building's envelope. Such conclusions could not be reached using approximate, steady-state calculations.

We see also that in Jerusalem the energy consumption for heating the building can be reduced by painting the walls dark (JE-SL compared with JE-SD). This factor is not significant in the well-insulated building (JE-IL, JE-IM, and JE-ID). On the other hand, light color is always preferable under summer conditions. Again, this factor is not significant if the building is ventilated well. These examples show that maximization or minimization of some design parameters will often lead to suboptimal solutions. Rather, trade-offs must be made to achieve a good balance. For instance, in Tel Aviv a light-colored, standard-insulated building behaves thermally as well as a dark-colored, better insulated building (T-SL compare with T-ID). Obviously it would be cheaper to paint the building white than to improve its insulation.

To overcome the difficulties of predicting the thermal performance of buildings, Shaviv and Kalay (1990) presented a process for designing energy-conscious buildings as a sequence of decisions made at different levels of abstraction. In each successive level more detailed and specific design parameters are explored. Accordingly, various energy-related design parameters are likely to be considered at different design stages (see Figure 3).

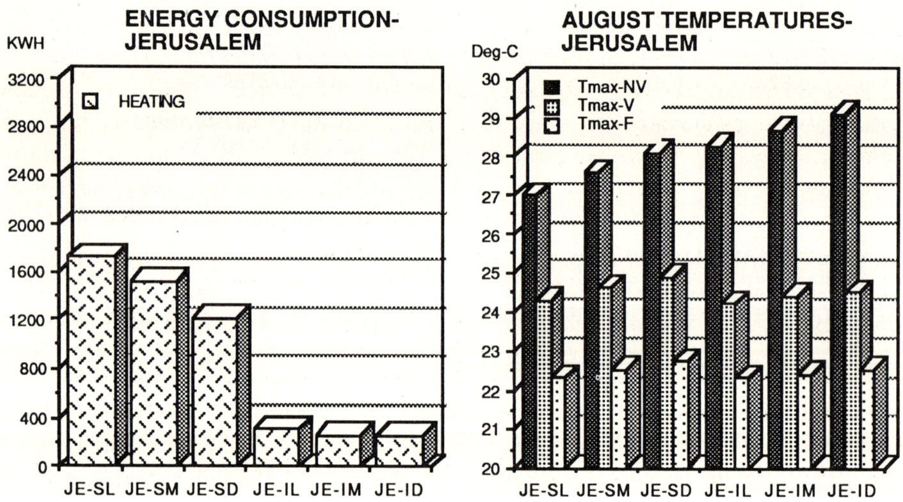

Figure 2. The energy consumption and thermal performance of a middle floor apartment with a large southern window in Jerusalem (above) and in Tel Aviv (next page). (JE:Jerusalem; T:Tel Aviv; S:standard insulation; I:Improved insulation; L:Light color; M:Medium color; D:Dark color; Tmax-NV:maximum in-house summer temperature with poor ventilation; Tmax-V: the same with good ventilation; Tmax-F:ventilation with fan.)

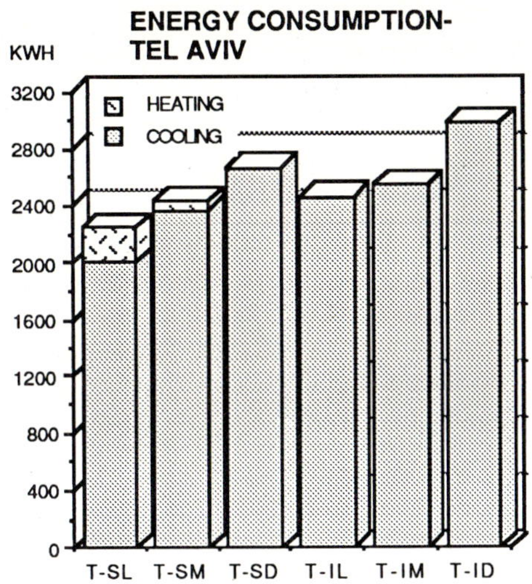

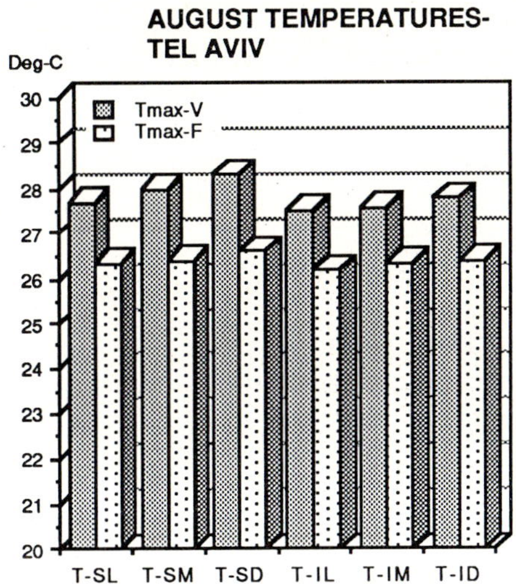

Most parameters are not assigned specific values early in the design process. Therefore, the designer is free to choose almost any value for the parameter of his current concern. As the design progresses, the previously assigned values may restrict the designer's freedom in choosing the values that are assignable to parameters considered later. For example, if the designer wishes to run an energy simulation at the schematic design phase in order to find the best proportion of the building in the Jerusalem climate, the designer must determine the materials from which the building will be constructed. If the walls were assigned a material composition of standard insulation, they must be painted with a dark color in order to reduce the energy consumption for winter heating. Once a dark color to the walls has been assigned, the designer must be careful to design the building with good ventilation for summer conditions, so as to avoid overheating. On the other hand, if the building is well insulated, colors have a negligible influence on its energy consumption, hence the designer is free to choose any color for the walls. To assist the designer at the early design process, the system could provide him or her with reasonable defaults for walls' insulation and color, based on the recommended R value for the climatic zone in which the building is located.

We presented the examples above to show that the complexity of evaluating the thermal performance of buildings warrants the use of accurate simulation models rather than approximated ones. But on the other hand, due to the strong interdependencies between different design variables, much expertise is required to reach good conclusions without actually running an excessive number of simulations. We believe, therefore, that integration of heuristic methods, in which such experience can be stored, and procedural simulation methods through which the former can be tested, will support all phases of energy conscious design and evaluation processes and will benefit from the advantages of both methods.

DESIGN PHASE	a.	b.	c.	d.	e.
TOTAL FLOOR AREA	•		+	+	
VOLUME OF BUILDING		•	+	+	
NO.OF EXTERNAL WALLS			•	+	
AZIMUTH OF REFERENCE WALL			•	+	
AREA OF INTERNAL MASS				•	+
HEAT CAPACITY OF INTERNAL MASS					•
INITIAL TEMP. DISTRIBUTION		•			
HEAT GAINS: CONSTANT	•				
HEAT GAINS: SCHEDULE	•				
HEATER: SCHEDULE; TEMP.SET		•			+
COOLER: SCHEDULE; TEMP.SET		•			+
VENT: TYPE, SCHEDULE, ACH: DAY; NIGHT		•			+
WALL NO 1					
NUMBER OF LAYERS				•	+
MATERIALS((c,λ,d)				•	+
" " "					
" " "					
WALL: AZIMUTH, INCLINATION			•	+	
AREA OF WALL			•	+	
WALL:ALBEDO,EMISSIVITY					•
WALL:SC-SUMMER,WINTER				•	+
NO OF WINDOWS AND SOLAR ELEMENTS			•	+	
WINDOW: AREA		•	+		
WINDOW: TYPE			•	+	
WINDOW: SC-SUMMER, WINTER		•			+
U WINDOW: DAY; NIGHT				•	+
U WINDOW: SCHEDULE		•			+

Figure 3. The design phase at which the various energy-related design parameters are first considered • and reconsidered +. The design phases are: a- Briefing, b- Pre-conceptual c- Conceptual, d- Preliminary, and e- Detailed design.

The Sensitivity Analysis of Various Design Parameters

The key questions that arise are:

- Is it necessary to design the building with all its details first, and only then run an energy simulation to obtain an accurate thermal evaluation?
- What inputs are important for running energy simulations during the early design stages?
- How rigorous must the data describing the building be at the early design stage?
- At the initial phases what values should be assigned to parameters, that are likely to be considered only at later design stages?
- How can values be assigned simultaneously to several parameters at the same design phase?

A large number of simulations were run and the results analyzed with the purpose to obtain answers to the above questions (Shaviv and Peleg 1989, Shaviv and Capeluto 1990, 1991). This study was carried for typical residential apartment buildings and for different climatic regions in Israel. The results were summarized and presented in an easy to comprehend graphical format (see for example Figure 4).

In Figure 4 we present some results that were obtained from the study that was carried out for residential buildings in Tel Aviv climate (Shaviv and Capeluto 1990, 1991). The design parameters in both cases are the geometrical ones (the building's proportions and its orientation). In the first case (Figure 4a) one can see that changing the building's proportion (the ratio of the length of southern and northern walls to the length of eastern and western walls, in a rectangle floor plan, is changed from 2:1 to 1:2) has a small effect on the energy consumption of the building. On the other hand, a change in the orientation of the building, so that the large window is not directed to the south, has a major effect on the energy consumption (Figure 4b). Other design parameters were examined in the same way.

The results obtained from the simulation model provide the knowledge base. This knowledge base contains case-specific rules that guide the system how to assign defaults to various design parameters. The knowledge base defines also the acceptable range of values for the design parameters that are considered at the different design phases. In addition, it includes the rules that guide the designer and the system as far as when to run a simulation, in order to provide rigor for the heuristics used by the early design phases. Lastly, the most important point to mention is the fact that the sensitivity analysis of the various design parameters shows that three different categories of parameters exist. They will be presented in the next chapter.

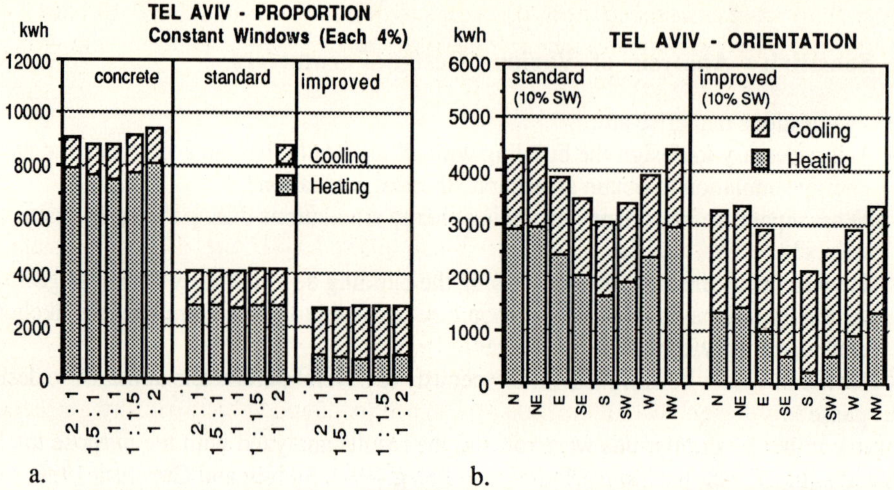

Figure 4. a. The influence of building's proportion on its energy consumption. **b.** The influence of building's orientation on its energy consumption. Both cases are for a standard and improved insulated building (Tel-Aviv climate).

Different Categories of Design Parameters

The three categories of design parameters that were found may be defined as follows:

a. A design parameter which has a strong influence on the energy performance and is insensitive to other design parameters. This kind of parameter should get its recommended value from the KB-CAAD systems as a default to ensure good energy performance. As it is not sensitive to other design parameters, its refinement can be carried out in the more advanced design phases.

b. A design parameter with a strong influence on the energy performance and that is sensitive to other design parameters. The KB-CAAD system has knowledge about type b parameters. Therefore, whenever needed, the system performs a series of simulation runs to guide the architect through the design of the particular building. This module of the KB-CAAD system provides deep knowledge and can overcome the problem that heuristic rules are valid for the average cases only.

c. A design parameter with a weak effect on the energy performance and that therefore is always insensitive to other design parameters. The value of this kind of parameter may be arbitrarily specified by the user or by the system as a default. A check in later design stages can be made to fix the exact value.

To summarize, the three categories of design parameters are: First, those for which default values can be specified by the knowledge base according to the specific climatic conditions and type of building. Only heuristic rules are used in this step (*case-specific defaults*). Second, those that have a significant influence on the energy consumption and are very sensitive to the other design parameters. These design parameters require a continuous guidance for their proper values. In this case heuristic rules are used with simulation analysis (*combined case-specific defaults tested by simulation evaluation*). And third, those that are free design parameters that can be arbitrarily specified, either by the system as defaults or by the designer (*arbitrary design parameters*).

The Building's Input

The knowledge-based system was first developed on a microcomputer as an open system that can be connected to a simulation design tool and to a commercial CAAD system. The connection between the different modules is carried out by files, which serve as an output for one module and as an input for the other one and vice-versa. This is not an ideal state, and we intend to run all modules in the future on the same workstation.

For the conceptual design phase, a 3D representation is important to allow visualization of the proposed design. The 3D representation can be obtained by using any available 3D software. In our case the input can be introduced by the commercial CAAD system ARC+ (ACA ltd. 1989). Yet, we found that this is not convenient, since each time one passes from the simulation run to the 3D commercial CAAD system, one must quit the CAAD software and re-enter it again. This will change when the KB-CAAD and the 3D commercial CAAD systems run on the same workstation under UNIX operating system that allows multi-processing. As simple 3D representation is sufficient at this stage, we developed a schematic 3D representation as a module of the KB-CAAD system. The use of the commercial 3D software is restricted to the documentation stage.

The building's input is given by defining the shape of each room as a polygon and by introducing the heights of the room at each corner (see Figure 5). The input file for the simulation evaluation (see Figure 6) is automatically created by the KB-CAAD system. It is implemented by interpreting the graphical input that was introduced by the designer and by assigning values, that are based on the heuristic rules, for the different design parameters. The values assigned by the KB-CAAD system guarantee to achieve good thermal performance of the building. The treatment of the different design parameters was carried out according to the three categories that were defined.

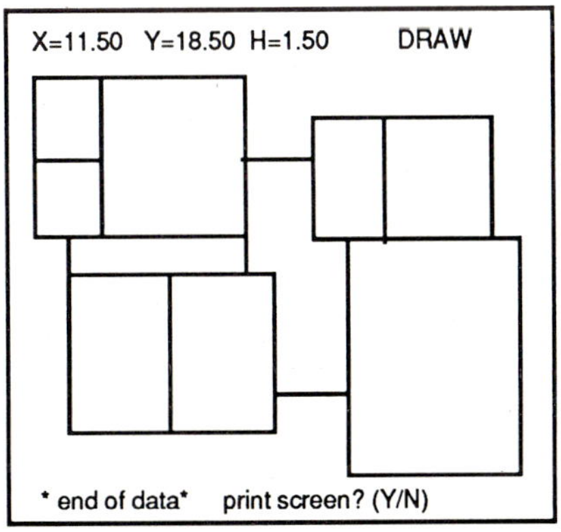

Figure 5. The introduction of the building geometry by a schematic plan (using the mouse) and heights at each corner (using the keyboard).

The different Treatment of Design Parameters

A. *Case-Specific Defaults*. The first category includes design parameters that according to some special conditions should be assigned default values from the knowledge base using heuristic rules. This category is classified into two sub-categories: design parameters that do not depend on the local climatic conditions but on the type of building (presented in Figure 6 by plain text) and those that depend on the local climatic conditions (presented in Figure 6 by bold text).

For example, in the first sub-category, one can find the internal heat gains and the schedule and temperature setting for operating the heater and cooler, while in the second subcategory one can find the recommended size of heater and cooler and the suggested walls' insulation. Based on the specific local climate and the designer's specification of the type of walls, the system suggests details for the walls, such as thickness, materials, etc. Detailed geometrical data for the design and representation of the building are introduced by the system automatically. This procedure saves labor and time, and the result is a better designed building.

ALT1-5					
BUILDING'S GEOMETRY					
146.3					TOTAL FLOOR AREA
351.2					VOLUME OF BUILDING
13					NO.OF EXTERNAL WALLS
5.0					AZIMUTH OF REFERENCE WALL
INTERNAL PARTITIONS					
203.2					AREA OF INTERNAL MASS
5690.					HEAT CAPACITY OF INTERNAL MASS
18.3					INITIAL TEMP. DISTRIBUTION
MECHANICAL SYSTEMS AND BUILDING USE POLICIES					
250.					HEAT GAINS:CONST.
1000	18.0	23.0			HEAT GAINS:SCHEDULE
5000	07.0	23.0	18.0	19.0	HEATER:SCHEDULE;TEMP.SET
5000	07.0	22.0	24.0	28.0	COOLER:SCHEDULE;TEMP.SET
18.0	07.0	0.75	4.0		VENT:SCHEDULE,ACH:DAY;NIGHT
18.0	07.0	**5.0**	**3.5**		U WINDOW:SCHEDULE;DAY;NIGHT
ENVELOPE					
1	WALL NO 1				
3	NUMBER OF LAYERS				
500.0	**1.40**	**0.02**			(c,λ,d) 'OUTSIDE PLASTER'
175.0	**0.23**	**0.20**			(c,λ,d) 'YTUNG BLOCK 800'
450.0	**0.87**	**0.01**			(c,λ,d) 'INSIDE PLASTER'
0. 90. *.65 .95*					WALL:AZ,INC,ALBEDO,EMISSIVITY
1		**45.60**			NO OF WINDOWS OR SOLAR ELEMENTS;AREA OF WALL
90. 90. 90. 90.					SC-SUMMER:DIR,DIF;SC-WINTER:DIR DIF
1		**5.28**			WINDOWS OR SOLAR ELEMENT:INDEX;AREA
10. 50. 90. 90.					SC-SUMMER:DIR,DIF;SC-WINTER:DIR DIF

....

....

1	WALL NO 3		
3	NUMBER OF LAYERS		
500.0	**1.40**	**0.02**	(c,λ,d) 'OUTSIDE PLASTER'
175.0	**0.23**	**0.20**	(c,λ,d) 'YTUNG BLOCK 800'
450.0	**0.87**	**0.01**	(c,λ,d) 'INSIDE PLASTER'
180. 90. *.65 .95*			WALL:AZ,INC,ALBEDO,EMISSIVITY
1		**43.60**	NO OF WINDOWS OR SOLAR ELEMENTS;AREA OF WALL
90. 90. 90. 90.			SC-SUMMER:DIR,DIF;SC-WINTER:DIR DIF
1		24.82	WINDOWS OR SOLAR ELEMENT:INDEX;AREA
10. 50. 90. 90.			SC-SUMMER:DIR,DIF;SC-WINTER:DIR DIF

Figure 6. Part of the building data file. Plain text is for building type defaults, Bold for local climatic conditions defaults, Italic for arbitrary non-geometrical parameters, Outline for arbitrary geometrical parameters that are introduced graphically, and Underline-outline is for the sensitive design parameters.

B. *Combined Case-Specific Defaults Tested by Simulation Evaluation.* The second category includes design parameters that have a great influence on the energy performance and are very sensitive to other design parameters. Therefore, continuous guidance for specific values should be provided by the KB-CAAD system, using the simulation model. In this category, one can find the recommended size of the southern glazing and the orientation of the building (presented in Figure 6 by underline and outline text).

The system treats the sensitive design parameters in two ways: First, the system presents a default solution that is based on the statistical cases. Second, it suggests a series of simulation runs for the specific case. Also, if for some reason, the user is unwilling to accept the recommended solution and suggests a different one, the system offers to perform simulation runs. Thus, continuous guidance is provided by the system.

For example, the suggested area of windows for specific climatic conditions and wall orientation is decided based on recommendations stored in the knowledge base as heuristic design rules. The recommended windows are introduced by the system automatically and presented in axonometric views (See Figure 7). The system locates each window in the middle of the specific wall. The designer is allowed, at this stage, to shift the windows anywhere on the given elevation, so that the best design is achieved according to his taste (see Figure 8). While shifting a window around a specific elevation, the designer can keep the area and size of the window fixed or can divide the proposed window into several smaller windows, while keeping the total window area equal to the area suggested by the system. Also the designer can change the recommended area or add more windows on other elevations (see Figure 9). At this point, the system offers to evaluate the thermal performance of the building for the new proposed design alternatives. The thermal performance of the building, as seen in Figure 10, will be presented graphically on another window of the powerful workstation. Since the system runs on a microcomputer, the evaluation starts only by clicking an item on a menu. This clicking initiates the creation of the building data file and the re-evaluation of the design by the simulation model. This continuous evaluation can be carried out because the knowledge base includes the information that windows belong to the category of sensitive design parameters for which continuous guidance by the system is critical.

The recommended orientation of the building for specific climatic conditions is also a sensitive design parameter and depends on the size of the windows located on each wall. The recommended orientation of the building in alternative 1 was 5° west of south. When the designer adds a window on the western and eastern walls (alternative 3), the system re-evaluates the best orientation for the specific case and suggests that the best orientation for that particular case is due south (see Figure 11). This module of the KB-CAAD system overcomes the difficulty that the heuristic rules, known to the system, are appropriate for average cases only by coupling the rules to a simulation model.

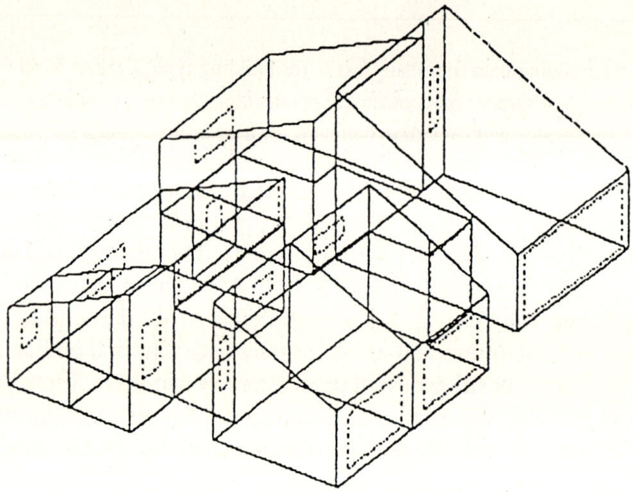

Figure 7. An axonometric view of the proposed building with the recommended area for each window (alternative # 1). The system locates the windows in the middle of each wall.

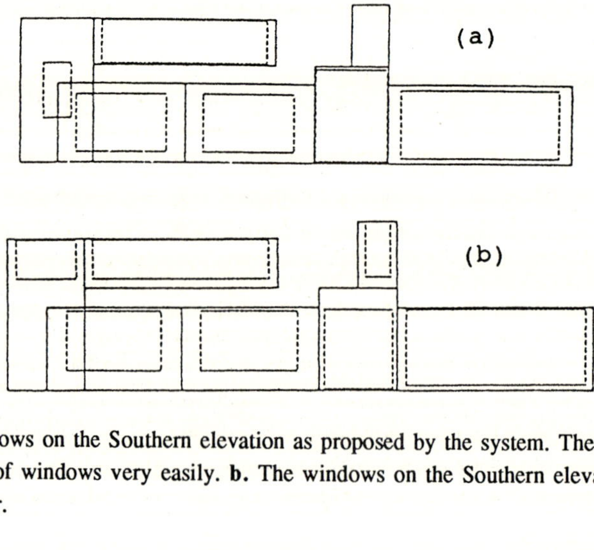

Figure 8 a. The windows on the Southern elevation as proposed by the system. The designer can now change the locations of windows very easily. **b.** The windows on the Southern elevation as they were changed by the designer.

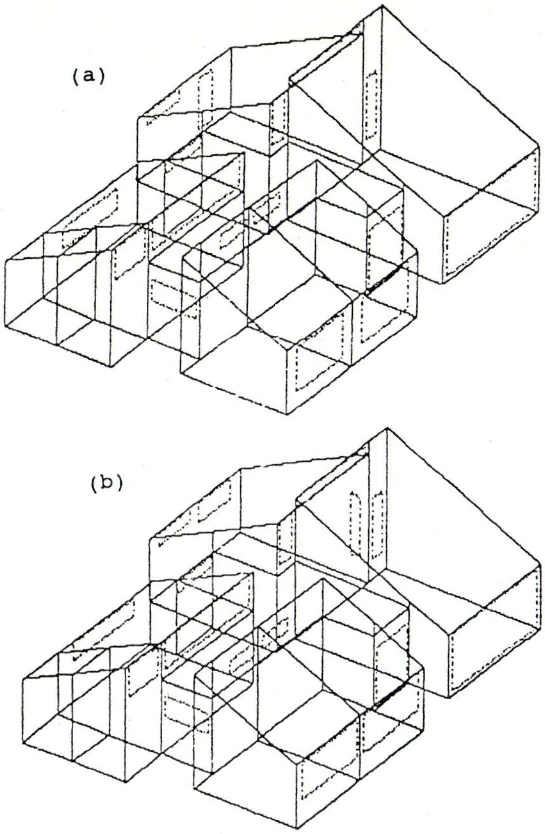

Figure 9 a. An axonometric view of alternative # 2. A new window is added to the Western elevation. **b.** An axonometric view of alternative # 3. A new window is added to the Eastern elevation.

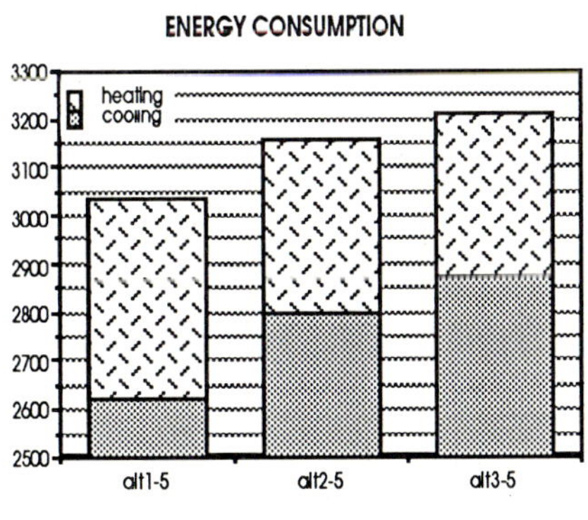

Figure 10. A comparison between the thermal performance of the three proposed building alternatives.

C. *Arbitrary Design Parameters*. The third category comprises design parameters that do not have a great influence on the energy performance of the building. They, therefore, can be treated as free parameters and may be determined arbitrarily, either by the system as defaults or by the designer. We classify this category of design parameters into two subcategories: design parameters that do not determine the form of the building and those that dictate the shape of it. In the first case, initial values will be given by the system as defaults, while in the second, we prefer to leave the decision to the designer. In both cases, these design parameters can be specified more explicitly in the advanced design stages.

The color of the building's envelope belongs to the first subcategory. It was found in the preliminary study that the color of the wall has a negligible effect on the thermal performance of a well insulated wall and vice versa. So a medium color is assigned first to the well-insulated walls by default (presented in Figure 6 by italic text). Once the design reaches advanced stages, we may decide to change the recommendation for the insulation of walls (which was given as a default). Therefore, at the advanced stages, the best color should be re-examined.

The building's proportions belong to the other subcategory. Here again, it was found that this design parameter has little influence on the thermal performance of the well-insulated, medium color building as long as the area of windows on each orientation is kept fixed and the suggested area of windows on the southern elevation can be achieved. In such a case, the authors suggest leaving these design parameters as free parameters. The designer can specify the form of the building according to personal taste and other functional considerations provided the recommended area of windows on the southern elevation is satisfied. The introduction of the free geometrical design parameters is carried out by the three-dimensional module of the KB-CAAD system. The KB-CAAD system interprets this graphical input and creates the numerical data file in the required format for the simulation run. These free geometrical design parameters are presented in Figure 6 by outlined text. If the orientation of the building changes, the recommended window area is recalculated, and the proportions of the building are re-checked. The system gives a warning if the southern walls do not comply with the suggested southern windows area.

CLIMATIC REPORT - ALT3-5 TEL AVIV

ANNUAL CONSUMPTION (KWH):

Total=3211 Cooling=2875 Heating=336

Inside Temperatures - January (with heater):

ave=19.5 max=22.2 min=17.4

Inside Temperatures - August (with cooler):

ave=25.2 max=27.0 min=24.0

PREDICTING INSIDE TEMPERATURES-AUGUST (Deg-C)

without cooler: **BUILDING IS TOO HOT**

ave=26.9 max=28.0 min=25.5

with fan: **BUILDING IS TOO HOT**

ave=25.9 max=27.4 min=24.1

BEST ORIENTATION IS DUE SOUTH (+-10 Deg)

Figure 11. A short report of the energy performance of the design alternative ALT3-5 (5° west of south).

Summary and Conclusions

We present in this work a new KB-CAAD tool for the schematic design and evaluation of passive solar buildings. The KB-CAAD system is based on an integration of knowledge-based and procedural simulation methods and any available commercial CAAD system for building documentations. The KB-CAAD tool combines the geometric design with solar considerations. This is done by applying a knowledge base that contains the heuristic rules for the design of passive solar buildings. The knowledge base is stored in the computer and provides the basis for guiding the designer through the decision-making process, whenever it is possible to use rules of thumb. Thus, the knowledge base controls some design parameters that should enter the simulation model. Yet, rules of thumb are not adequate to deal with particular projects, which involve deviations from standard designs. Should that be the case, the KB-CAAD system guides the architect by using the procedural simulation model.

The knowledge base was developed from recommendations obtained in a preliminary study performed by running many simulations. This knowledge base has two merits:

a. It saves the results of many simulation runs as rules for standard design cases and completes automatically the missing design information required to evaluate the thermal performance of the building.

b. It saves labor and time during building design and documentation by introducing automatically the geometrical and technical data required to present the building in two or three dimensions, based on the heuristic rules and the recommendations from the simulation study.

The case study presented here demonstrates the advantages of a knowledge-based design system. It shows that by using the knowledge-based CAAD system, not only can a better solar building be designed, but it takes (based on the case study shown in Figure 12) only about one-tenth of the time to introduce the geometrical data that would be required if only three-dimensional representation and documentation were desired. We believe that future CAAD systems should follow this suggested approach and should include a knowledge base to guide the designer during the different design stages.

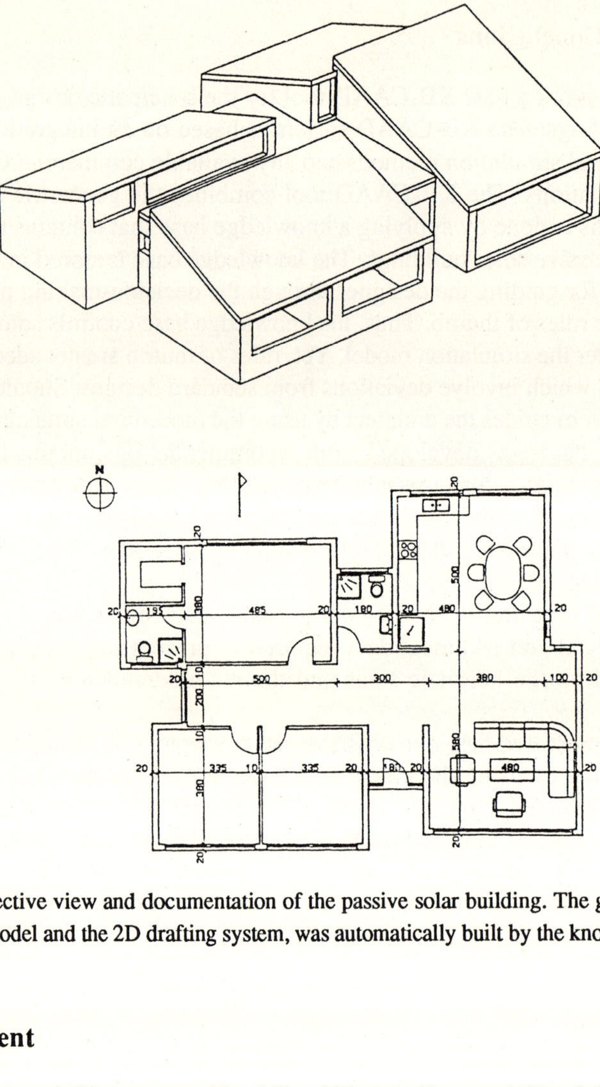

Figure 12. A perspective view and documentation of the passive solar building. The geometrical data base, needed for the 3D model and the 2D drafting system, was automatically built by the knowledge-based system.

Acknowledgment

The research was partially supported by Miami Energy Research Fund Grant number 022-470.

References

Antony, S. 1987. *ARCADE: Architectural Computer Aided Design Amender*. M. Arch. Thesis, School of Architecture and Planning, State University of New York at Buffalo.

ACA ltd. 1989. *ARC+ 3-D Architectural software - User's guide*. Israel.

ASHRAE. 1972. *Handbook of Fundamentals*. Atlanta, GA.

Arumi, F. N. 1979. *DEROB: Dynamic Energy of Building*. Numerical Simulation Lab., School of Architecture, University of Texas, Austin, Texas.

Balcomb, J. D., R. W. Jones, R. D. McFarland, and W. O.Wray. 1984. *Passive Solar Heating Analysis - A Design Manual*. LANL, ASHRAE ISBN 0-910110-38-7, Atlanta, GA.

Beckman, W. A., S. A. Klein, and J. A. Duffie. 1977. *Solar Heating Design by the F-Chart Method*. NY: Wiley-Interscience.

Bharati, J. 1990. "Evaluation of Designs for Energy Performance Using an Expert System." In Y.E. Kalay (ed). *Evaluating and Predicting Design Performance*. New York,NY: John Wiley & Sons, Inc.

Brown, G. Z. 1990. *Desirable Interface Characteristics of Knowledge-Based Energy Software Used by Architects*. ASHRAE Transactions, V. ST-96-2. Atlanta, GA.

Clark, J. A. 1982. *ESP: System Documentation Set*. University of Strathclyde, UK: ABACUS Publication.

Gero, J. S., and R. Coyne. 1984. "The Place of Expert Systems in Architecture." *CAD84*, pp. 529-546. Butterworth, Guilford, UK.

Kalay, Y. E., L. M. Swerdloff, and A. C. Harfmann. 1987. "A Knowledge-Based Computable Model of Design." In (J. Gero, ed.). *Expert Systems in Computer-Aided Design*. North Holland Publishing Co.

Klein, S. A., W. A. Beckman, and J. A. Duffie. 1976. "TRNSYS, A Transient Simulation Program." *ASHRAE Transactions* 82, Part 1. Atlanta, GA.

LBL and LASL DOE-2 reference manual. 1982. Version 2.1. Lawrence Berkeley Lab. and Los Alamos Scientific Lab.

McFarland, R. D. 1978. *PASOLE: A General Simulation Program for Passive Solar Energy*. Informal Report, LA-7433-MS. USA.

Maher, M. L., and S. J. Fenves. 1985. *HI-RISE: A Knowledge-Based Expert System for the Preliminary Structural Design of High Rise Buildings*. Report No. R-85-146, Department of Civil Engineering, Carnegie Mellon University, Pittsburgh, PA 15213.

Palmiter, L., T. Wheeling, and R. Judkoff. 1982. *SERIRES: Solar Energy Research Institute- Residential Energy Simulator*. SERI Report.

Papamichael, K. M., S. E. Selkowitz. 1990. "Modeling the Building Design Process and Expertise." *ASHRAE Transactions*, V. ST-96-2. Atlanta, GA.

Pikes, A. (ed.). 1978. *Proceedings of the 3rd Int. Conf. and Exhibition on Computers in Engineering and Building Design, Brighton*. England: IPC Science & Techn. Press.

Pohl, J., L. Myers, and A. Chapman. 1990. "A knowledge Based System for the Design of Passive Solar Buildings." *ASHRAE Transactions*, V. ST-96-2. Atlanta, GA.

Schmitt, G. 1987. "Expert Systems in Design Abstraction and Evaluation." In Y.E. Kalay (ed.). *Computability of Design*. New York, NY: John Wiley & Sons.

SERI report. 1980. "Analysis Methods for Solar Heating and Cooling Applications - Passive and Active Systems." SERI/SP-35-232R.

Shaviv, E. 1977. "A Model for Predicting Thermal Performance of Buildings and its Use in the Design for Minimal Energy Consumption." *The Building Center of Israel Quarterly* (in Hebrew), no. 4: 26-33.

Shaviv, E. 1979. "Building Design for Passive Energy Conservation." *PARC 79*, pp. 135-144. Berlin, Germany.

Shaviv, E. 1989. "The use of simulation models in the schematic design stage for the design of energy conscious buildings." In T.C. Steemers and W.Palz (eds.). Proceedings of the 2nd European Conf. on Architecture: *Science & Technology at the Service of Architecture*. Paris: Kluwer Academic Publishers.

Shaviv, E., and I. G. Capeluto. 1990. "The Influence of Geometrical Design Parameters on the Energy Consumption and Thermal Performance of Apartments Buildings-Part 1." *Research report* no. 0220474. Technion Research & Development Foundation Ltd. Haifa (In Hebrew).

Shaviv, E., and I. G. Capeluto. 1991. "The Influence of the Geometrical Design Parameters on the Passive Cooling and Heating of Buildings." *Proceedings of ISES 1991 SOLAR WORLD CONGRESS*. Denver, CO.

Shaviv, E., and Y. E. Kalay. 1990. "Combined Procedural & Heuristic Method to Energy Conscious Building Design & Evaluation." In Y.E. Kalay (ed). *Evaluating and Predicting Design Performance*. New York, NY: John Wiley & Sons, Inc.

Shaviv, E., and U. J. Peleg. 1989. "The Influence of Geometrical Design Parameters on the Energy Consumption and Thermal Performance of Buildings." *Research report* no. 0220474. Technion Research & Development Foundation Ltd. Haifa (In Hebrew).

Shaviv, E., and U. J. Peleg. 1990. "A knowledge Based System for the Design of Passive Solar Buildings." *ASHRAE Transactions*, V. ST-96-2. Atlanta, GA.

Shaviv, E., and G. Shaviv. 1977. "A Model for Predicting Thermal Performance of Buildings." *WP ASDM-8 report*. Faculty of Architecture & Town Planning, Technion, Haifa.

Shaviv, E., and G. Shaviv. 1978a. "Modelling the Thermal Performance of Buildings." *Building & Environment*, no. 13: 95-108. England: Pergamon Press Ltd.

Shaviv, E., and G. Shaviv. 1978b. "Designing of Buildings for Minimal Energy Consumption." *CAD* 10, no. 4: 239-247. England: IPC Business Press.

Tham, K. W., H. S. Lee, and J. S. Gero. 1990. "ICAD: An Intelligent Computer-Aided Design Environment." *ASHRAE Transactions*, V. ST-96-2. Atlanta, GA.

U.S. Army Construction Engineering Research Lab. 1977. *BLAST: Building Loads Analysis and System Thermodynamic Program*. AD-A048982/3ST, AD-A048734/8ST. USA.

31 Design Tools: Future Design Environments for Visualizing Building Performance

Murray Milne

Graduate School of Architecture and Urban Planning
University of California
Los Angeles, CA 90024-1467, U.S.A.

In the future of Computer Aided Architectural Design (CAAD), architects clearly need more than just computer aided design and drafting systems (CAD). Unquestionably CAD systems continue to become increasingly powerful, but there is more to designing a good building than its three-dimensional existence, especially in the eyes of all the non-architects of the world: users, owners, contractors, regulators, environmentalists...

The ultimate measure of a building's quality has something to do with how well it behaves over time. Predictions about its performance have many different dimensions; how much it costs to build, to operate, and to demolish; how comfortable it is; how effectively people can perform their functions in it; how much energy it uses or wastes. Every year dozens of building performance simulation programs are being written that can predict performance over time along any of these dimensions. That is why the need for both CAD systems and performance predictors can be taken for granted, and why instead it may be more interesting to speculate about the need for 'design tools'. A design tool can be defined as a piece of software that is easy and natural for architects to use, that easily accommodates three-dimensional representations of the building, and that predicts something useful about a building's performance.

There are at least five different components of design tools that will be needed for the design environment of the future.

Introduction

It is easy to say that computers will profoundly change the way architects design buildings. The tough question is to figure out exactly what that future design environment be like. These environments will be powered, at least in part, by a never-ending series of CAD system updates and new releases, each one more wonderful than the last at describing buildings in three-space. All of these computerized drafting systems are the direct linear descendents of the tradition of representing buildings that began in ancient times with papyrus, then in modern times with linen and India ink.

Computers make it possible, however, to do something that is profoundly different from what architects could do before. Like having a Magic Lamp with a Genie inside, we have the ability to bring a design to life, run it forward in time, and watch how it behaves - not just what it looks like, but how warm or cold it feels, how bright or dark it looks, what it sounds like, and how well it accommodates human activities. This opens a new world of opportunities that for future design environments that we are just beginning to explore.

However, there is a cost to be paid from letting that Genie escape from the lamp. Architects in the future will undoubtedly face a perpetual series of increasingly stringent performance criteria, in large part because computers make it possible to predict performance with increasing precision. A useful analogy might be the continually increasing sophistication of medical diagnosis and treatment. Once the resource is available, patients insist on nothing less, as will our clients for design services in the future. The only difference is that the building sciences lag far behind most other areas of technological development.

Another example might be the ever tightening standards imposed on the automobile manufacturers for fuel efficiency and emissions reduction. Here legislation drives technology. The same is already true in architecture where new building codes, especially in the areas of life safety, energy, and the environment have "made a market" for all sorts of technological innovations that otherwise would languish because they were judged non-economic. Certainly in the future this trend will only continue, given the ever-expanding aspirations for public safety, and concern for the environment, global warming, and the consumption of energy. The fact that software is already available which can predict how our buildings will perform, makes it inevitable that those criteria will be imposed sooner or later. In short, it will happen because we can do it.

Many architects will see all this as a threat to their design freedom, but others will see it as an opportunity to increase our profession's relevance and value to society, and to expand our own intellectual horizons.

CAD systems, like AutoCad for example, are becoming increasingly sophisticated at manipulating shapes, forms, colors, and textures in three-space. While they can represent reflected ceiling plans and wall details, they have no direct way to manipulate the luminous, thermal, or auditory environment, or even structural performance or life safety today. We need completely separate simulation models to do that. Unfortunately we have no obvious way to link all of them together or to the CAD system. The interface of each piece of software is so idiosyncratic that no one (not even an architect) can master them all.

It can be argued that the process of designing a building involves the simultaneous manipulation of two distinctly different models; the geometric representation of the building in three-space, and a time-line representation of each of the different measures of its performance, such as its energy consumption, visual comfort, operating cost, etc. In the olden days before computers, the architect's task was to externalize the former by hand, and to create fantasies about the latter.

Design Tools

What exactly is a design tool? It can be defined as a piece of computer software that has an easy-to-use interface, that allows the manipulation of the building's three-dimensional representation, and that shows the architect something useful about the performance of the building.

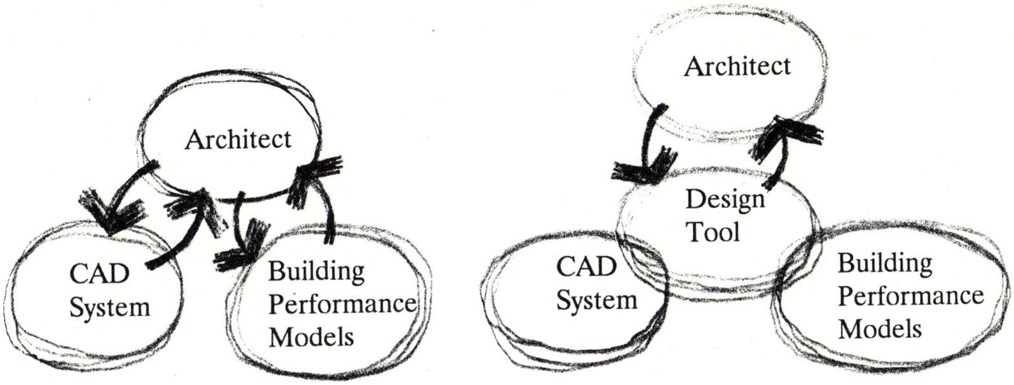

Figure 1. Future design environments will consist of at least four components, an architect plus three pieces of software: a CAD system, a Building Performance Model, and at the center a Design Tool that allows them to communicate with each other.

Today, architects can use many different kinds of CAD systems (AutoCad, ComputerVision, etc.), and many different kinds of performance models (BLAST, DOE-2, SUPERLITE, etc), but each has their own unique interface, and they do not talk to each other very well or share the same data. A design tool could sit between all three, acting as the interface for the architect to describe the building, then translating the building description to the performance model, and finally showing the architect how the building performs. A design tool may incorporate a complex building performance model, or may simply act as an interface to it. Similarly it may incorporate its own building description database or else access the CAD system's database.

Architects of course might still try to communicate directly with their building simulation routines, but the availability of an easy-to-use design tool that is more efficient and friendly is a much more attractive option, and in fact today very few architects have ever touched an energy simulation, daylighting model, or cost analysis routine. In the future, the same might even be true of CAD systems, because although some architects today have learned how to operate them, to be honest they require a great deal of training in arcane manipulation and otherwise unproductive effort. The amount of practice time required to maintain competency or to reach high proficiency is beyond the resources of the most influential and highest paid architects in the firm. That is why the CAD system sits on the desks of the lowest paid entry-level drafters. Senior people will never embrace it until it is easier to use, has greater power, and is more portable then a felt-tip pen and a napkin.

Imagine as an alternative, a thin notebook-size tablet with a flat full-color display plus some kind of sonic pen that allows the architect to draw in a building directly in three-space, then with the touch of a "virtual button" rotate it, cast shadows throughout the day, and look at its passive solar performance throughout the year, then plug into a network and share it with everyone else (1). When this 'fantasy' comes to pass, is there any doubt that sooner or later every chief designer will insist on using one?

Specifications of a Design Tool for a Future Design Environment

There will always be something unique about how an architect designs a building, whether a computer helps out or not. The dialogue between a human and a CAD system engages the human in imagining a three-space model of the building, manipulating it cognitively, then describing pieces of it to the computer. Next, another rather different process takes place in which the architect looks at the computer's representation of the building and tries to evaluate it against various mentally stored criteria. Compared to computers, architects are incredibly sophisticated at the cognitive manipulation of building form, but are virtually incompetent at making precise calculations on complex models to predict building performance. Manipulating the data-rich world of building performance is an ideal task for computers.
A fully integrated design environment of the future is probably a long way off, but at UCLA over the past few years my graduate students and I have developed and tested many different components for such a system; some parts were carried only through a proof of concept, while others are fully developed and are in wide use. The following five general categories describe most of the components that will be required in a Future Design Environment:

1. Establishment of initial design conditions;
2. Simplified three-dimensional data input;
3. Building performance predictions models;
4. Techniques for communicating complex data;
5. Automatic data conversion routines.

1. *Getting Off on the Right Foot: Initial Design Guidelines*
At the very beginning of the design process, the first few assumptions that the architect makes have a profound impact of the final design. These initial design decisions have far more influence than any other equal number of decisions made later in the process.
Consider for example, that at each different spot on planet Earth some ways of building will be more successful than others. Given the latitude and the hour-by-hour weather data, it is possible to say a great deal about the most appropriate design strategy. We have developed a program that reads the weather data for the site, then lists a set of design guidelines, rank ordered according to their relative importance (2). There is nothing very complicated about this, in fact there is general agreement about what the guidelines are and when they apply. The big problem is how to translate them into architectural form. Here is an application that is begging for an expert system.
In another program we have built an expert system that needs to be told only four things about the project (location, building type, floor area, number of stories), then it will 'design' a simple energy conserving building (3). It is not a very interesting building to look at, but when students use it as a basecase against which to test their own design, they find it is very hard to beat.
Dozens of other potential applications come to mind; topographic analysis, bubble diagrams, floor plan layout, code checks, perhaps automatically selected slide shows of comparable projects, or ultimately even a smart search through a CD-ROM of all the latest magazines.

2. *The Napkin: Quick Sketch as a Form of Non-verbal Inputs*

I wonder how many buildings have begun with a sketch on a paper napkin or the back of an envelope. The architect's earliest synthesis of relational and spatial issues needs to get instantly recorded and considered whole. Later versions become more literal and comprehensible, but the first sketch is just some squiggles and scratches that are incomprehensible to anyone who was not present at the conception. At this point the "building" is contradictory, ambiguous, and incomplete, certainly not something you would yet want to have to input into a solids modeler.

Imagine two or three architects around a drafting table, trying to solve a problem. The only thing an outsider would see is a series of incomprehensible sketches accompanied by grunting and head nodding, then suddenly one of them triumphantly draws another equally incomprehensible squiggle to which the others respond with relief, louder grunts, affirmative head nods, and now even spoken words will be heard like "yes...right...that's it."

Here is classic right brain activity, where information is being generated and shared without requiring intervening verbalization. Architects are especially skilled at this kind of non-verbal communication, especially as it relates to building form. It is one of our unique skills and one of the things that makes our profession so much fun. The kind of resonance and synchrony architects can feel with their co-designers, in the future must be part of their interactions with computers.

Something quite wonderful happens when the architect becomes completely immersed in the right-brain non-verbal world; there is magic in the speed and efficiency with which spatial concepts are generated and manipulated. Being forced to return to the verbal left-brain world is a jarring and disconcerting experience.

There is information in the act of drawing that computers could grasp; the weight of a line, the speed with which it is drawn, the sequence in which things are assembled. Imagine a computer program that knew if an X through a line meant to cut it in half here, or delete the whole line, or rotate everything about this point. Instead of a static drawing on a piece of paper, imagine a dynamic electronic image that could be stretched, rotated, flipped over, selectively erased, or de-constructed and re-formed in new ways. The real test of such a system would be if two architects who did not speak the same language, could work together on the same design. In fact, at UCLA we developed the prototype for such a system that can understand the architects gestures and modify the drawing accordingly (and it is now being marketed in Japan (4).

Another problem is how to assign non-spatial attributes without stopping to use words and numbers. For every piece of the building the computer needs to know its R-value, reflectivity, thermal mass, weight, cost, presence of a vapor barrier, order of assembly, etc. Imagine a set of paint-pots that the architect could dip into and flood different surfaces with something like off-white stucco, standing seam copper roof, or terra-cotta Mexican floor tiles (5). Imagine a box full of windows and doors that could be spotted onto the facade with a touch of the pen. The computer could of course render all of this in a spectacularly photo-realistic way, but more important is that now secretly attached to every surface is all the rest of the data needed to describe the building.

Most of the current CAD systems, although quite powerful, still do not have these capabilities. People who want to use them require a great deal of training (which is totally non-productive activity). Almost every action requires at least one translation between spatial and

verbal thinking which imposes an unnecessary cognitive load with its attendant inefficiencies and risks of error. Today's CAD systems virtually ignore non-spatial data, and in the end still only produce a frozen snapshot, having no way to bring the building to life and watch it run forward in time.
Thus the Design Environment of the Future needs some type of intuitively obvious way for an architect to communicate with a computer about how to describe three-dimensional building forms and see how they perform.

3. *Running the Clock Ahead: Building Performance Models*

Predicting the way a building might perform in the future is a fine art. Clearly there are many different ways to evaluate the success of a design; cost, energy, fame, number of design awards, etc. Obviously the degree of confidence of each of these different measures also varies widely.
Separate disciplines have sprung up around each of these building performance modeling areas. The oldest group is interested in simulating the structural behavior of buildings. But the fastest growing group is energy modelers; today there are dozens of different theoretical approaches and hundreds of different programs, all of which predict some aspect of how energy is used to heat and cool the building.
Three distinctions are worth pointing out: phase, focus, and speed. In each phase of the design process some kinds of energy models are appropriate while others are not. For instance, at the very beginning of the design process a model like BLAST or DOE-2 is useless; it requires the detailed input of every single building element, it takes a long time to execute, and produces stacks of tabular data. Instead what is needed is a model that works with a minimal "fuzzy" description of the building, executes in less time then it takes the architect's mind to wonder (probably about 15 seconds), and presents results in a way that can be instantly grasped by right-brain thinkers (6). As the architect's design becomes more focused, the model must also incorporate the more detailed representation and produce increasingly precise results. At every phase in this process, the design tool must show the architect if the latest decisions are moving the project in the right direction.
Large detailed energy models come into their own toward the end of the design development phase, when the building description is essentially complete, and when there is sufficient time to run a series of parametric studies to 'fine-tune' details of the design.
Daylight modeling of buildings has recently become a topic of considerable interest, but here too the issues of phase, focus, and speed apply. At the phase of the process when the design of the facade is being articulated, a daylighting design tool can help answer questions about how such things as the size and placement of windows, and the dimensions of fins, overhangs, sills, and interior lightshelves on light distribution throughout interior spaces. When the details of the electric lighting are being integrated, more highly focused parametric performance studies can be run (7). Computational techniques are known which will make it possible in the future to evaluate glare and visual comfort.
The final task for these models is code compliance (8). But because building laws and energy codes test against minimum standards, therefore it is reasonable to expect that a building designed with good design tools should easily exceed these minimum standards.

4. *Data-land: Envisioning Building Performance*

Sitting face to face at every terminal are two powerful information processors, a computer and an architect. Yet everything exchanged between them must pass through slow, low resolution devices that choke off precise complex communication (9).

The computer may 'know' how the building will perform, but the most challenging task is to devise effective ways to share the computer's knowledge with the human. At UCLA we have been working on ways to display building performance over time. We have developed a 3-D plot that shows the state of the variable for every hour of the day for every month of the year (10). The resulting shapes are easy to grasp at the highest level, and at the same time are rich with information at the most detailed level. The beauty and power of this approach is that it communicates in a direct right-brain mode, allowing the architect to pick up incredibly subtle distinctions that would otherwise be lost in a page full of numbers. Tufte defines information as the recognition of differences that make a difference. We have used this technique to display all kinds of different things about the building's performance; heat flow, illumination levels, cost of energy, ventilation rates, etc.

There are of course other ways to represent the performance of a building over time. For example, one could compute a kind of movie or video, and watch the way natural light moves through the room (11). But Architects might also like to know if there is adequate light to perform a specific task, are there brightness ratios that would cause direct or reflected glare for any user, and what is the probability that users will find the space visually comfortable (12). Imagine that the movie now shows a false-color representations of where and when any of these problems occur in the occupant's visual field; a checkerboard pattern shows where brightness ratios are too high, a splotch of purple shows the source of reflected glare.

5. *Transformers: Data Conversion*

We all know myths about how wonderful the world becomes when we simply transform our problems into another domain. A popular Christmas gift recently was a stuffed frog. When you reached inside his mouth and pulled him inside-out he became (you guessed it) THE HANDSOME PRINCE. Here a simple and elegant translation from one data structure to another is a solution to the problem - unless you happened to be a lady frog. In the real world of CAD however, it is hard to find very many successful examples. We have a few examples of going from frogs to toads (DXF to TIF for instance), but getting all the way to a prince is another matter. Imagine how delighted energy consultants would be if buildings could be instantly translated from AutoCad to DOE-2 (DXF to BDL) (13). Then again maybe they wouldn't be delighted, because the possession of this little bit of secret knowledge is one of the reasons architects need energy consultants, but the lack of it is also one of the reasons why so few architects ever do an energy analysis in the first place. Would buildings be better if architects could immediately flip from one domain into the other instantly seeing an energy analysis, a cost comparison, an illumination level plot?

Thus another thing that a design tool must be able to do is not only to let the architect talk to the CAD system about the building, but also to let the performance model query the CAD system about the building. The CAD system knows a lot of the information that the performance model needs, but unfortunately not in the format that it needs. It is safe to assume that every CAD system and every performance model has its own different way to store data, and it is not realistic to assume that any of them will be restructured simply to accommodate the needs of the other.

Epilogue

All this has been only speculation what lies in the future for CAAD. But we all must admit that no matter how certain we are, we really never can be sure exactly how the future will turn out:

> *The beautiful princess leaned down, and as her lips touched his green flesh there was a blinding flash .....*

Acknowledgements

All of the graduate students mentioned in this paper worked as Research Assistants with financial support from the UCLA Academic Senate, The University Energy Research Group, and the U.S. Department of Energy. In many cases they also wrote their Masters Thesis on this work. SOLAR-2 was developed in cooperation with Robin Liggett at UCLA, and DAYLIT and the SUPERLITE input interface were developed in cooperation with Marc Schiler of USC. The authors appreciation to all is gratefully acknowledged.

References

1. The earliest and most fascinating speculations about future design environments came from Nicholas Negroponte. His books The Architecture Machine and The Soft Architecture Machine are still the richest and most stimulating collection of ideas about the future. Currently as head of MIT's Media Lab he is working with a world class team of software and hardware people to bring it all off. Negroponte's original specification for a sketch-book size workstation also included the requirement that it be waterproof so he could use it in the shower, and flexible so he could roll it up. Except for these last two (slightly dubious) requirements, all of the rest of his predictions have come to pass and are commercially available today. All that remains now is to reduce their size, weight, and cost (which inevitably happens to all computer hardware in any case).

2. Our climate analysis design tool has been through a long process of evolution at UCLA. A little bit of its history might give a sense of how long this kind of software development takes and how everyone builds on the work of those who have gone before. Our first computer graphic representation of NOAA Monthly Average climate data was by Bruce (Ted) Anderson in 1979. A few years later, Yun Kim carried this work a step further, developing an interactive program that students first used in the Building Climatology class. Next Wade Hokoda wrote a program to read weather tapes then to plot hourly values and monthly averages on the psychrometric chart that Baruch Givoni had developed in his book Man Climate and Architecture (Van Nostrand Reinhold), on which was also laid out the comfort zone and the zones showing the most appropriate passive solar building design strategies. His program kept track of the hourly values in each zone of the psychrometric chart and generated a list of passive design strategies rank-ordered according to the percentage of hours each was effective.

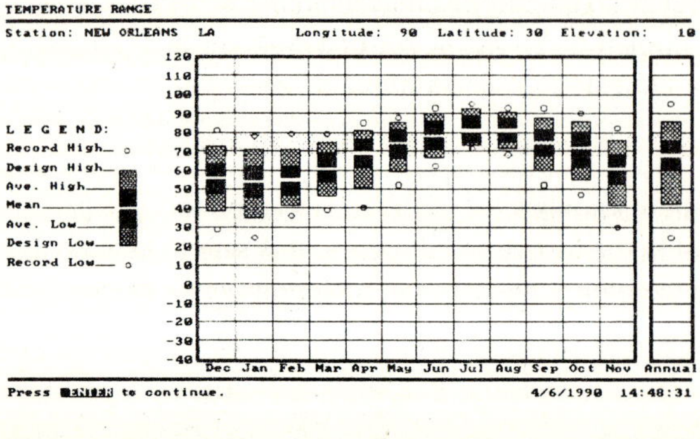

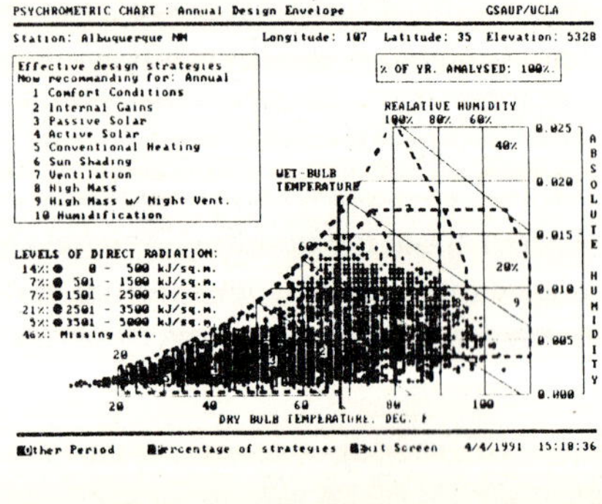

In his book Energy Conservation Through Building Design (McGraw-Hill), Don Watson included a chapter by Givoni and Milne that expanded on the technique of using the psychrometric chart as a design tool. When Watson and Ken Labs wrote their book Climatic Design (McGraw-Hill), they used this approach to identify the most appropriate passive design strategies for forty different cities, using a program written at Yale.

A micro-computer version of this design tool, called Climate Consultant was written at UCLA by Alex Acenas and Mark Clayton incorporating the list of fifty design guidelines that Watson and Labs developed in their book, it allows the architect to custom modify the climate "window" within which each guideline applies, in order to fine-tune the overall design strategy. Their program was not only friendly and colorful, but added new features like a Timetable of Bioclimatic Needs as developed by the Olgyay brothers in the 1940's. Currently this work is being pushed rapidly forward by Yung-Hsin Li who has added the capability of displaying wind data in a 3-D plot. He also automatically plots sun charts of the type Edward Mazria used in his book The Passive Solar Energy Book, except that he can overlay on these charts the Bioclimatic Timetable that showed the times when windows need to be shaded or to be exposed for direct gain. He is currently working on an expanded list of design guidelines and an expert system to aggregate them in more relevant ways.

3. Expert systems sometimes can be simple yet powerful, a very early example of which was written by Joel Loveland for SOLAR-5, to work at the very first moment of the design process. The architect only needs define four things; the building type, floor area, number of stories, and location of the nearest weather station. The program then creates a "building" complete with windows, sunshades, occupants, and lights.

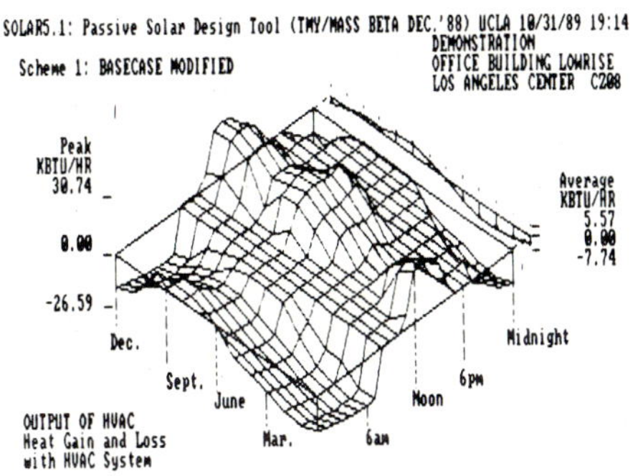

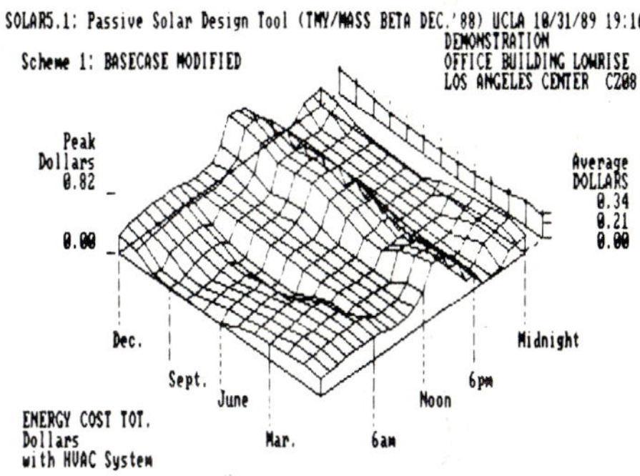

SOLAR-5 has a long history of development, beginning with the first version that we used in the Building Climatology class written by Shin Yoshikawa in 1978. Since then almost two dozen different Graduate Research Assistants have contributed to the project. The current version has all the attributes of a design tool as defined in this paper: the interface is friendly enough that beginning students are usually into their second of third design iteration within an hour after they first try it; the building can be described in a few minutes, it takes only a few minutes more for the energy model to calculate the buildings performance for all 24 hours and all 12 months; and finally the results are displayed graphically in a mode that portrays large quantities of complex data in a form easily grasped by architects or others trained in right-brain thinking.

4. The challenge of whether we could develop a completely non-verbal interface for architectural design problems was accepted by Yas Endo in his thesis of 1984. His CAD system watches the context, the sequence of prior events, to decide if the architect intends to enclose a form, erase a line, rotate a segment of the drawing, flip it over, etc. It can understand certain graphic input conventions like arrow heads and centerlines. At Takanaka Architects he has carried this work forward to the point where over a hundred systems have been marketed in Japan under the name of 'T-Board'.

5. At the University of Oregon, Charlie Brown suggested the paintpot metaphor as part of a Macintosh-based energy modeling system he was developing called Energy Scheming.

6. SOLAR-5 is being developed at UCLA to address these exact specifications of phase, focus, and speed.

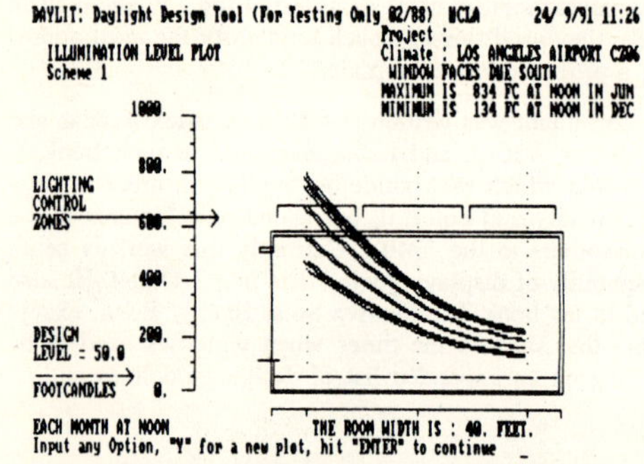

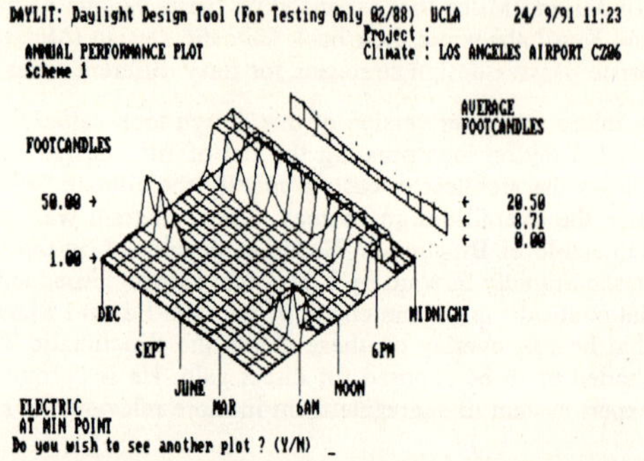

7. A design tool called DAYLIT was developed at UCLA to help architects develop building facades by showing them the distribution of light through their space from any combination of windows, skylights, or clerestories. It has the added power that it can show how the building performs for all 24 hours of the day and all 12 months of the year. In addition, automatic or manually controlled lights can be added in three different zones of the room, and the resulting savings in building electric energy consumption can be shown graphically in the same way. This work was supported by a grant from Southern California Edison.

8. The California Energy Commission performs a valuable service for architects in the state by making available at almost no cost, microcomputer programs for evaluating whether a building complies with the energy code: MICRO-CHECK, CAL-RES, SCM, etc. The first versions of these programs required a huge amount of input data but gave back only one piece of output data: "complies" or "fails". More recent versions, however, are more like design tools, identifying parts of the building that are most problematic, allowing multiple alternatives to be evaluated, simplifying the input process, and producing graphic output.

9. Edward Tufte has just published an exquisite book entitled, Envisioning Information (Graphics Press), which he designed as a "celebration of the escape from flatland". He presents wonderful examples of techniques for representing complex data in elegant and easy-to-grasp ways, all of which will particularly appeal to right-brain thinkers. He describes a multitude of techniques that he loosely collects under headings like Micro/Macro Readings, Layering and Separation, Small Multiples (in which he discusses the attributes of three-dimensional plots like those produced by SOLAR-5 and DAYLIT), Color and Information, and Narratives of Space and Time. He is correct when he suggests that his book could serve as a catalog for the collection in the (hypothetical) Museum of Cognitive Art, it is an intellectual and aesthetic delight.

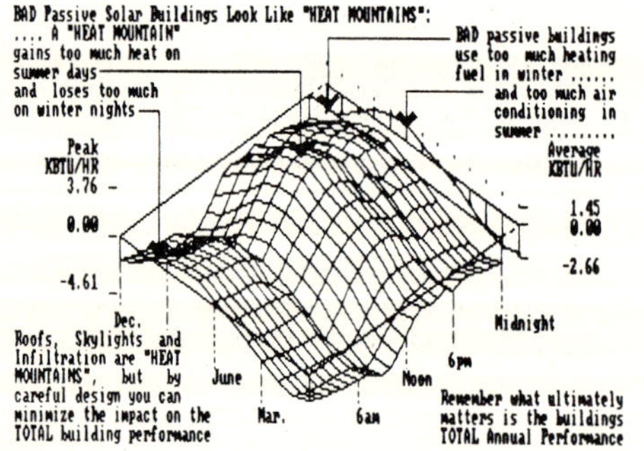

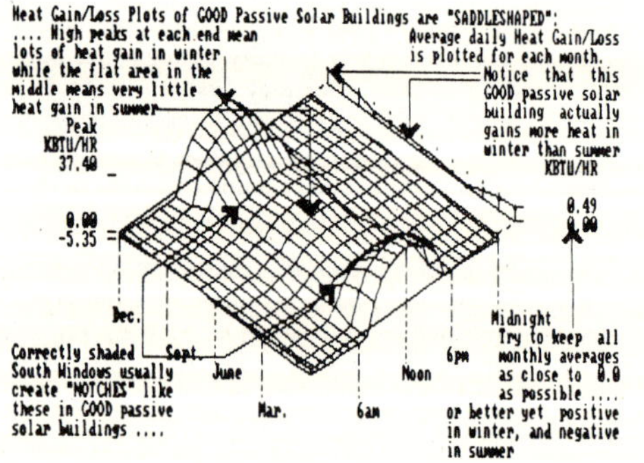

10. The three-dimensional plots produced by SOLAR-5 have proven to be exceptionally powerful in communicating complex data. A simple metaphor is helpful. Once students understand that the plot of a good passive solar building is saddle-shaped (maximum heat gain at mid-day in winter), and bad passive buildings are heat mountains

(peak gain at mid-day in summer). When students see their first SOLAR-5 plot, you sometimes see them visibly stiffen and recoil, but within minutes they have grasped the concept and have become intellectually intrigued. Then you see them leaning closer to the terminal, gesturing knowingly, and speculating if design changes like rotating the building a few degrees will reduce a bump here and fill in a valley there. Finally when you see the CRT screen covered with fingerprints you can be sure that they fully internalized the concept.

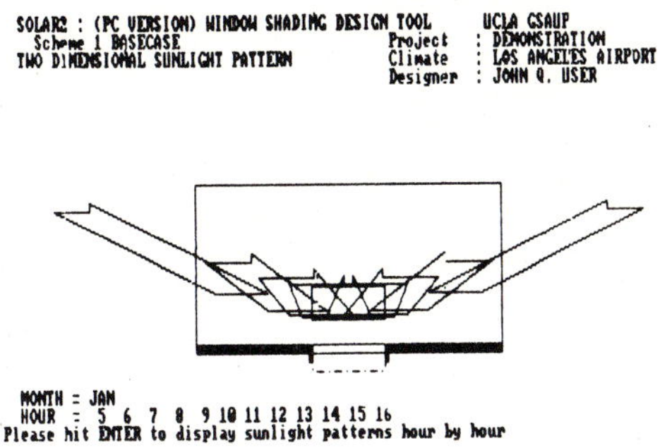

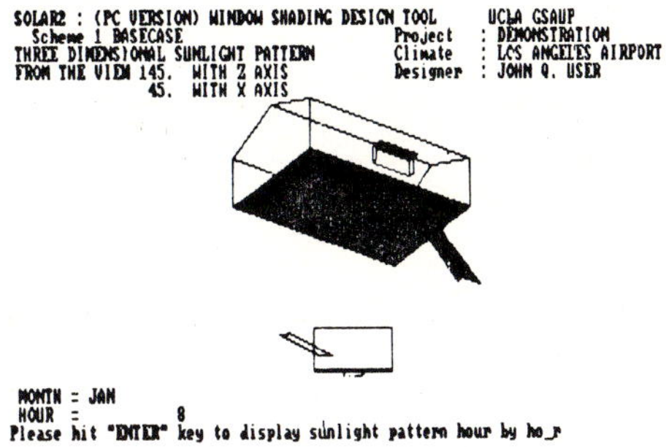

11. The first design tool we developed at UCLA was SOLAR-2. It shows a kind of time lapse plot of the sequence of sunlight penetration patterns as they move through the room for any month of the year. The designer can then change the window shape, fins, overhang, etc., and immediately see the new set of annual patterns. At the same time in the background it is calculating things like radiation through the glazing, percentage of window exposed to full sun, etc. Another interesting graphic that this program can generate is an axonometric view of the room, which when taken from the point of view of the sun is particularly useful to the designer because, for example, if full shading is needed it shows exactly which piece of glass is exposed, or if maximum solar gain is required it shows if any part of a fin or overhang is obstructing the window. The current micro-computer version of SOLAR-2 was written by Rong Sheu, and is described in his thesis of 1986.

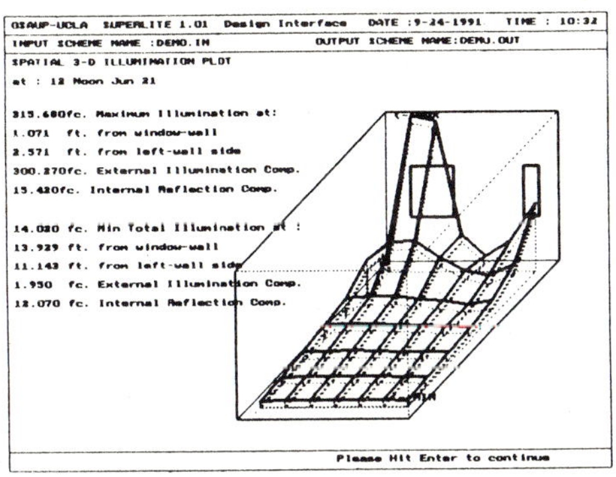

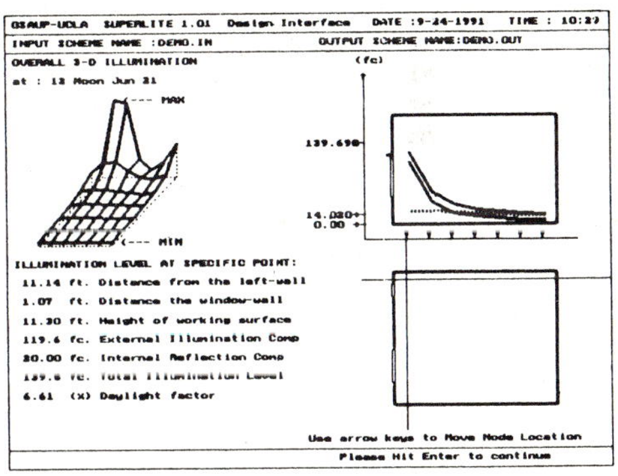

12. Currently there is a good deal of interest in programs that generate photo-realistic images, calculating and displaying the brightness of every surface in the room. The more complex programs like RADIANCE developed by Lawrence Berkeley Laboratory, require something like a weekend on a computer to generate an image. The SUPERLITE program, also by L.B.L. uses a more pragmatic approach of dividing all surfaces up into a relatively large grid, then calculating the radiant exchanges only at the centroid of each grid point. At UCLA we are currently in the midst of a joint research project with USC to develop a "user friendly" front end for SUPERLITE.

13. In fact at UCLA we have a number of systems that can make some impressive transformations between very different data structures. In 1986 Den Won Lin built an Auto-Lisp extension on AutoCad that would automatically generate a scheme description for SOLAR-5. If the Designer follows certain conventions like using reserved layers,

points defined counter-clockwise, and figures that must be enclosed, then by simply hitting "energy analysis" on the pull-down menu a complete SOLAR-5 run would be executed and the results instantly displayed.

Another thesis just completed by Joy Chen makes the conversion from AutoCad to SUPERLITE. It requires only that the perimeter of the desired space be identified by a special command, then all the three-space data would be written in the current format for SUPERLITE's .IN file. Upadi Yuliatmo is currently working under the joint USC/UCLA project to develop a translator between a generalized 3-D CAD system and the SUPERLITE .IN file.

32 The First CAAD Package (sketch based cad)

Mark de Vries, Harry Wagter

Section Calibre
Department of Architecture
Eindhoven University of Technology
Netherlands

In this paper a theory will be presented that can be used to develop a new type of CAD program. It supports architectural design and can be applied to the earliest stages of the design process. The theory is based on architectural knowledge and describes how sketched input can be used for CAAD programs. The theoretical backgrounds will be explained briefly.

Introduction

For the last 30 years much research has been made into computer aided design. The optimism of the early years disappeared when the tremendous complexity of the subject became clear. The idea of computer support for architectural design is still tempting. When research started about CAD at Calibre it was decided to work from the designers point of view. Clearly we are a very long way from the 'design assistant' (Negroponte 70) but less ambitious goals can be stated.

When a designer starts to work on a new design he must develop a basic idea about how to meet the requirements of the brief, and his own ideas of design. At this stage he could use computer assistance to help find out if his ideas are likely to be successful. The decisions at that early stage are very difficult to change in a later phase of the design process. Not only because the entire design depends on them and they therefore gain too much momentum, but also because it is simply too expensive to start all over again. If we want to work on a theory for CAAD it has to be one that is usable at the early stages of the design process.

A second consideration made while formulating the research goals, was that a majority of the architects are probably not going to accept a computer in their design process unless it does not force them to change their design techniques. This implies a serious restriction to the research. To a designer the most natural way of interaction with a CAAD program is through sketches. He makes these anyway and they provide a description of the design that may be usable in a computer program. Furthermore this eliminates the need to make a separate cad drawing of a design.

At Calibre research is carried out relating to the theoretical background that is needed for these kinds of CAAD programs. Up to now the design process has been studied and especially the design information that is generated during this process. At the moment only preliminary results can be presented.

The Design Process

Over the last three decades a great number of descriptions of the design process have been made. A significant number of them do not actually explain the process but give an overview of the various stages of the (building) process. When one takes a closer look at these theories that seek to explain the design process it is clear that almost every theory regard design basically as a 'generate and test' activity. There is no doubt that this is true, but when applied to the earliest stages of the design process these theories somehow fail to explain all that is going on.

One of the flaws is that they are unable to explain how the first ideas originate. Only after the designer has a clear view of what must be designed, and this is certainly not the case at the beginning of the process, can these theories be used to explain the rest of the process. The all important start of the process remains vague. A second flaw is that a false impression is given that the design process is well ordered. Again this may be true later in the process but it is not at the beginning. It can hardly be expected that an unstructured problem like design can be solved by well ordered techniques.

Thus it is clear that existing theories cannot be applied to the early design phase without modification. Study of design drawings and design processes has convinced us that there is a limit to the complexity of a design. This is true not only for the entire design but also for the intermediate stages. For instance only few designs consist of more than four recognizable parts. Parts, on their turn, are seldom composed of more than about 8 to 10 subassemblies. If during the design process the design exceeds these limits of complexity (i.e. too many parts) some elements must be combined into a new meaningful entity (de Vries & Wagter 1989). This process of combining, leads to a hierarchical description of the design and also to a rather fragmented design process since the parts are constantly changed during the design process.

When the basic subdivision of the design is completed, the first design stages are completed. The rest of the design process is concerned mainly with implementing the design brief in this basic design and with attaining the architectural quality of the design. In this respect the early design phase can be regarded as a process of creating a basic 'organization' (lay out) and 'hierarchy of building parts and functional entities'. In Dutch architecture these two aspects together are often called 'structure' or 'concept'. Students learn that without a good concept, no quality in design can be achieved and must learn for themselves to see when a concept fits the problem and when it does not. CAAD programs must concentrate on helping in the appraisal of a conceptual design as this forms the root of the entire design. When the starting point is good, quality in architecture can more easily be achieved. For our theory of the design process we have returned to the most basic description of design (Maver 68). We are only interested in the design information and this can be described by the simplest 'generate and test' loop. We are aware that this leads to a simplistic view of the design process, but for our research goals we do not yet need to know how the design process is structured. It is sufficient to regard the design process as the generation and appraisal of design information.

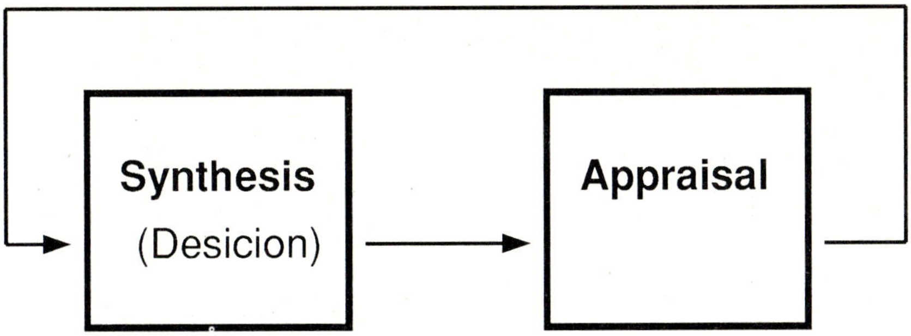

Figure 1. Primitive model of the design process.

This model describes the lowest level of design at which some information is generated and successively checked in an endless repetition. At every cycle some extra information about a design is added either by deciding about a new feature or by changing an existing feature.

Design Decisions

The 'synthesis' activity that was introduced in the previous paragraph can be regarded as a 'decision about a feature of the design'. In every cycle the designer makes a decision to change a feature. This is a primitive in the design process. It does not mean however that the feature that is decided about, is simple or singular or a detail. Decisions are made about arbitrary complex and global entities in the design. The model of the process does not invoke any restriction to the decisions. We will extend this very broad description to make it more useful.

The main question that arises now is: how can a decision about an entire building be the same as a decision about e.g. a doorknob? To architectural designers there is just a decision about one element. To them it makes no difference whether it is complex or not. The solution to this situation can be found in the important notion of 'hierarchical subdivision'. Each entity is part of a assembly and is not connected with other entities outside that assembly. This means that the number of interactions of an element is the same, no matter what hierarchical level the entity is on and this effectively conceals the complexity of design. At any point you can either see broad or deep but never both. The following schema may clarify this. In it each box is connected with 5 other boxes and with its parent. The level of complexity (or interactions) is constant at every level in the hierarchy.

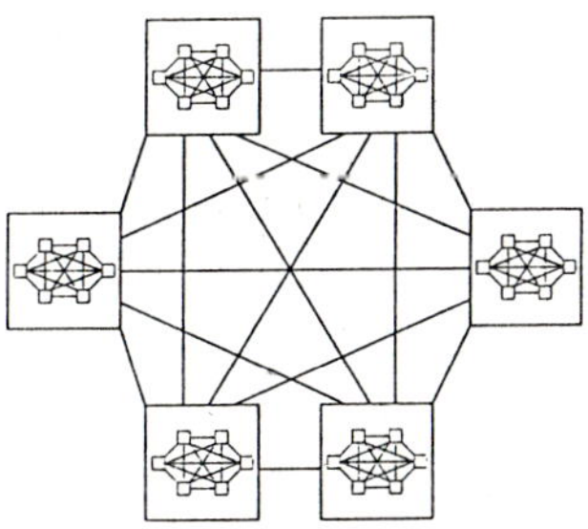

Figure 2. Hiding away complexity.

To describe this kind of information a concept of Marvin Minsky is adopted: 'Frames' (Minsky 85). Frames are a useful way to represent information and knowledge, especially if organized hierarchically. The use of frames makes it easy to construct 'is-a' and 'has-a' hierarchies with are important for representing architectural knowledge (Carrara 85). If frames are used as values to fill a slot of a certain frame this type of organization is easily achieved. Every decision in the 'synthesis' activity of the design process concerns a single frame or a single frame slot. Thus it is clear that architects need see no difference between the high level and low level decisions. The kind of information they are dealing with is the same: a single frame and its slots. A design can be regarded as a web of frames that are all linked through slot-filling relations. Every decision in the design process alters this frame hierarchy but can not invalidate it entirely, only parts of it may require modification after a change.

Minsky pointed out that frames, in fact are a means to represent knowledge. They are used to link properties to things. This enables humans to derive meaning from observations. They notice properties and their 'knowledge' frames are activated if these properties fill its terminals. Activated frames quickly suppress other possible interpretations thus leaving only one single interpretation active. This active interpretation fills in the default values for all slots that do not yet have a meaning and also pre-activates words and memories which are represented by other frame like structures in the brain.

It is not a single frame that forms the knowledge but the frame and its connection with other frames. For this reason the construction of new frames is very difficult. It is likely that most frames used in architectural design are based on other frames that were constructed earlier in life. Most likely new slots are appended to existing frames to add knowledge about the design process. This close connection with earlier knowledge has an advantage too, since it makes it easy for the designer to 'understand' how his design will be experienced by its users.

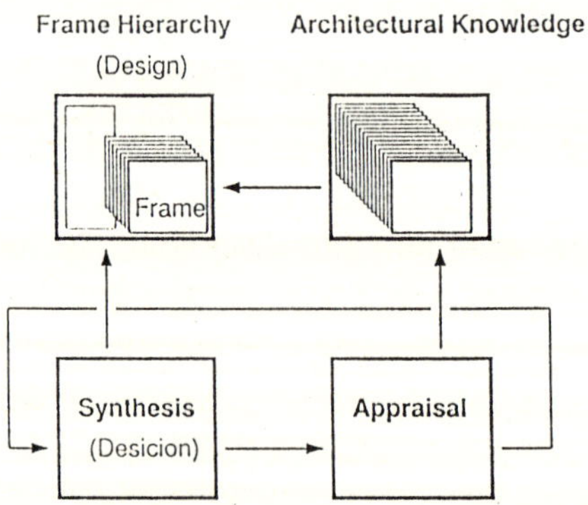

Figure 3. Design knowledge in the design process.

The important frame for 'design rooms' is most likely based on the frame that allows people to interact with rooms in daily life. The principles of enclosure, entrance, walking through, usage and so on are necessary for any human being. In the same way the knowledge of building types and styles is based on the common knowledge frames that allow people to see the difference between offices and domestic buildings. Not all design knowledge can be based on existing frames however. There is no direct equivalent to 'constructional organization or 'functional hierarchy'. These kind of frames must be developed by experience and the thorough understanding of the knowledge that is required, to do this is one of the most difficult parts of learning to design.

Design Frames

In the previous paragraph design information and knowledge was described as a hierarchy of frames. Our attempts to represent all this knowledge in this structure led to unexpected problems and proved to be very difficult. In fact we were unable to find a satisfying description. The reason we found for this is that some subframes need to refer to each other. This implies that the network of relations can not be shaped as a tree but must be a network with circular references. The following is one of our attempts to define a hierarchy of design information for a simple 'room' frame.

'Design Room' frame
-> Space
  -> shape
  -> edges
  -> spatial relations *
-> Position
-> Orientation
-> Size *
-> Height
-> Atmosphere
-> Relations
  -> functional *
  -> technical
  -> routes
-> Function
  -> activity
  -> furniture
  -> sizc *
  -> orientation *
  -> Space *

The subframes that are marked with an asterix are in some respect frame crossing. Some of their information will be used by other frames or subframes as well. Although this may be feasible from a neurological point of view, it leads to difficulties when one attempts to reason on these structures.

Different frame structures lead to similar self referential structures. We therefore adopted a different organization for part of the design knowledge, partially giving up the hierarchical structure. The design information was split in two parts, one describing the actual organization of the design, the other describing the components used in the design. The first part of the design information still can, and should, be described as a hierarchy in order to

overcome the problems of design complexity. This tree is stored mainly in short and long term memory. The second, more static, part of the design information can be described by a three dimensional frame array (Minsky 85, p293).
Frames of similar subjects are stored in levelbands, each band is used to represent a certain amount of abstraction. Frames are also grouped in different domains. A number of domains may share a single meta-frame representing a similar operation on all corresponding frames in the various domains.

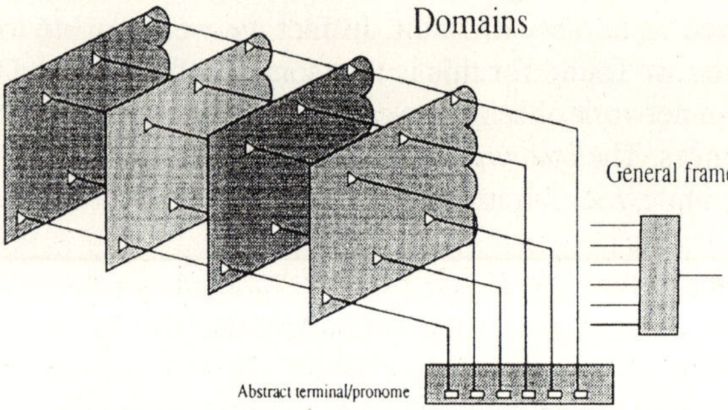

Figure 4. Related knowledge organized in a frame array.

So far we have not developed a 'final' description of design frames according to this domain based scheme but the preliminary results are promising. The following is our latest attempt, but it is likely to be changed considerably.

Domains:
- Functional
- Morphological
- Social
- Technical / Physical

Meta frame (abstraction)
- Boundaries
- Type
- Application
- Relations

Each of the terminals of the metaframe will be connected at the same time with frames in all corresponding frames in the different domains. When the abstraction gets activated all frames that are linked with it will be activated at the same time. Similarly if one of the domain dependent frames gets involved in some reasoning process all connected frames in other domains will be forced to undergo the same process, although this may have entirely different meanings in the other domains.

This description not only explains how certain design information can be shared by different frames, it also helps explain why design sketches can contain so little information.

Since all the information is connected in the frame array activating one part of the information will immediately also activate the corresponding information in the other domains. That information therefore does not need to be coded in the symbolic representation of the design decision as this is automatically derived.

Design Sketches

One aspect of the design process that is often somewhat neglected in theories about design is the design sketch. Yet it is virtually impossible to design without making sketches. They are usually considered as a side product of the design process but their role is more important than that. There are two major reasons for making sketches in the design process.

The first reason is that in buildings there are many spatial relations and constraints. It is very difficult to imagine these and it is much more efficient to sketch them and *see* if everything is correct. The second reason is similar to the frequently used explanation that sketches are a means of communicating the design. This can not be the real reason because most designers work alone and therefore do not need to communicate about the design. The fact is however that the design process takes considerable time and that it is frequently interrupted, either a scheduled interruption (e.g. at the end of each working day) or an unscheduled one because of the telephone, colleagues and so on. All these force the designer to concentrate on other things than the design. It would be very inefficient if he had to start all over again after being disturbed. Every designer must therefore take brief notes of the design process and this is exactly what the sketches are. After being interrupted the designer can look at his sketches and see what he had been working on and in effect this restores his state of mind and allows him to continue at the point where he was disturbed.

One can state that until recently most buildings, even buildings like the cathedrals, were designed without the use of sketches and sometimes even without plans. This criticism does not hold good however as these buildings were not designed in the same way as buildings are designed today. The building process for them depended on the knowledge of master craftsmen. These had learned how to lay out and construct buildings and taught this knowledge to their pupils. The main thing they did was to adapt a scheme to the given environment or to enlarge it if a larger building was required. If this failed measures to adjust the construction were taken and this knowledge was then passed on. In fact many cathedrals have collapsed at least once during construction and the same goes for some of the more ambitious Greek temples. This is in strong contrast with the current situation that requires that buildings have a different lay out and are built as fast as possible. It would be unacceptable today if a building collapsed during construction and had to be reconstructed using thicker walls and additional columns and supports. It is also difficult to rely on old designs that have proven to be useful. This has its influence on the way buildings are designed and with present day methods design sketches are inevitable.

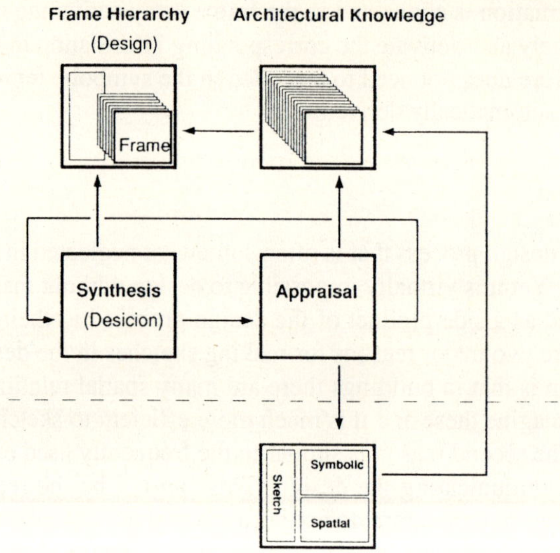

Figure 5. Sketches in the design process.

The use of sketches to remember the design process is not infallible though. One of the things that cannot be expressed in symbols is the strategy of the design process. This governs which actions will be performed but is not a part of the decision cycle and will therefore not be included in the sketches. In fact it can be observed that designers tend to finish their current design strategy before allowing themselves to be disturbed. If this is not possible because of the nature of the disturbance the design process is often changed abruptly. The designer can remember what he was doing but has forgotten why and what his plans were. He has no other option than to think of new goals and new plans for the design.

Theory

Theory in order to develop must make a connection between the design process and computers. As already pointed out in the previous paragraphs it must be based on the methods used by architects and be applicable at the early design phases. It is not the task of cad research to define new methods of design and it can certainly not be the intention of a tool to force a designer to adapt to an unnatural method.

The first research goal is to define a system that can interpret design sketches. This allows the designer to work in his normal fashion but at the same time enables the computer program to construct a more formal description of the design in a database. This database can be interrogated by various programs that the designer uses to assist in his appraisal of the design. This process should preferably require no extra attention from the designer other than a request for some information. If the designer must constantly turn to the computer to give some instruction the design process is interrupted too often to be performed properly. In the next figure the theory of how such system could be operating is given schematically. The various parts of this theory have been introduced in the previous paragraph.

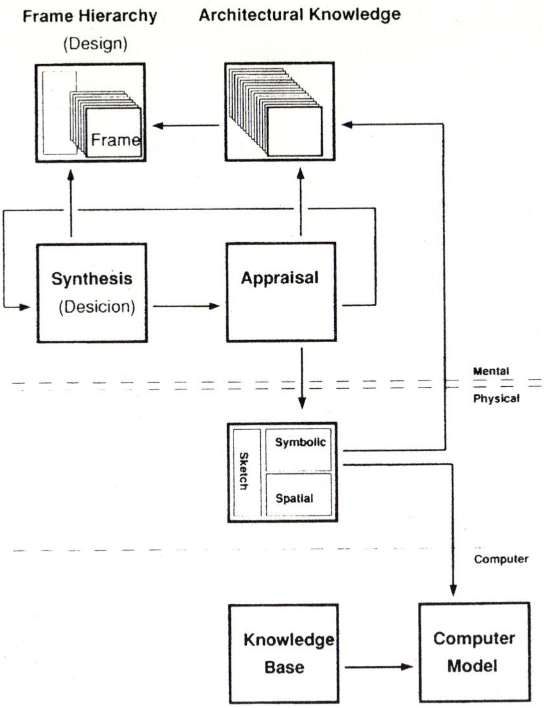

Figure 6. Principle of automated design interpretation.

At the center of the design process is the synthesis-appraisal cycle with its connected sketch activity. At the synthesis activity a frame in a frame hierarchy is modified. This frame hierarchy is in effect the design. After a decision has been made the results are checked using architectural knowledge. This is a large body of frames including relations and default slot values that forms the designers knowledge about architecture. Part of this knowledge is closely related to common knowledge about buildings yet another part has to do only with architecture or with the activities of design.

The principle of appraisal might be to try to match the design frame hierarchy with this general knowledge to *see* if some conflict arises. This is closely related to the way human beings normally reason and can be performed quite quickly. Most of the process can be performed simultaneously by different 'agents' in the brain. A conflict may then activate some frames that describe how a particular problem could be solved, or what strategy must be adopted to solve it. Strictly spoken these strategic decisions should be a separate part in the theory but they are left out so far, to keep things simple and because for CAAD purposes there is no particular interest in the way the design process is planned.

The general idea is that since every sketch activity is in fact a symbolic representation of a design frame, the interpretation of these symbols can be used to form a copy of the frame hierarchy in a computer database. The information that is available to do this interpretation is: the design made so far and a knowledge base of architectural knowledge. The usage of the design is crucial for the success of the interpretation. A program that scans a design sketch and tries to interpret it, cannot gather enough information to be successful.

Most frames / decisions are changed a number of times during the design process. Normally a changed decision is symbolized on top of the previous symbol. This makes sketches cluttered with lines and hatches. Without chronological information this is can not be interpreted. Another reason why chronological information is essential is that only few different symbols exist and many more possible meanings for them. Almost every design sketch can be described by closed polygons, bubbloids, lines (usually straight), arrows and few highly specialized symbols without dividing a single symbol into different primitives. It is not only the shape of the symbol but also its location and time (in the design process) that defines the frame it is representing. This information can not be derived exclusively from a final sketch. In a sense sketches can be regarded as a language. Only when the entire 'sentence' is heard can the meaning of it be understood.

Design sketches are used by designers to help regain track of thought after a disturbance. This implies that not all design information can be derived from the sketches. This is not a major problem for the interpretation of sketches, since they must contain enough information for the designer to identify the various frames of a design. Given a sufficiently large knowledge base this is all that an sketch interpreter must do to be able to construct a computer model of the design.

Product Models

Frames are a possibility for representing knowledge on an artifact derived from a psychological angle of incidence. This can be the basis of a design theory and it offers a structure for formalizing. A product model is a similar method for structuring applied to computers. It is inspired and based on the product life cycle approach. A product model offers a structure that probably will be of great use to formalize theories. The basic is a hierarchical decomposition of an artifact, or product, (e.g. a building) in sub-assemblies and parts (Turner 88). Every part is regarded as functional requirements (FU) that require a technical solution (TS). This method however lacks an approach to problems related to the design process itself. When it is formulated as functional requirements and technical solutions the design process seems to be omitted. The result of the proposed research should clarify and contribute to the description of what happens inside the so called 'hamburger structures'.

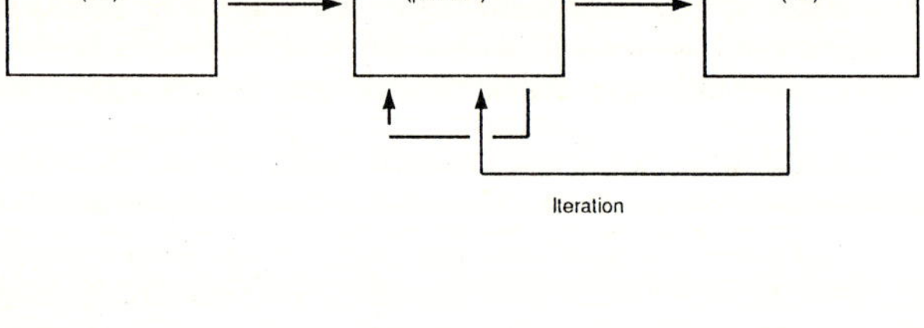

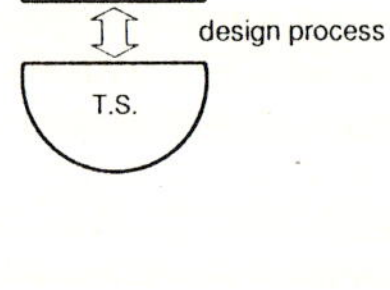

Figure 7. Product modelling.

Design Interpretation

The following example of an automated sketch interpretation is based on a prototype program that has been developed at Calibre. The program can interpret a certain class of simplified designs. The entire interpretation is performed automatically and requires no user supervision whatsoever. The prototype works by keeping track of every sketch action from the beginning of the design process onwards. From each sketch action, certain features are recognized and used in the interpretation.
The program is based on the assumption that every step in the design process can be monitored and is sufficiently small to be unambiguous (that is if enough context variables have been identified). In this prototype program 3 major variables were sufficient but for a more realistic program many more would be needed. The prototype recognizes the 'Shape', the 'Context' and the 'Phase'. The second feature describes the element that entirely or partially encloses the new shape. The third feature describes the probable phase the design process is in. This gives the program a hint of the most likely interpretation of the symbol.

Figure 8. left: Current sketch. right: current environment as seen by the computer Interpretation: 'Lot'.

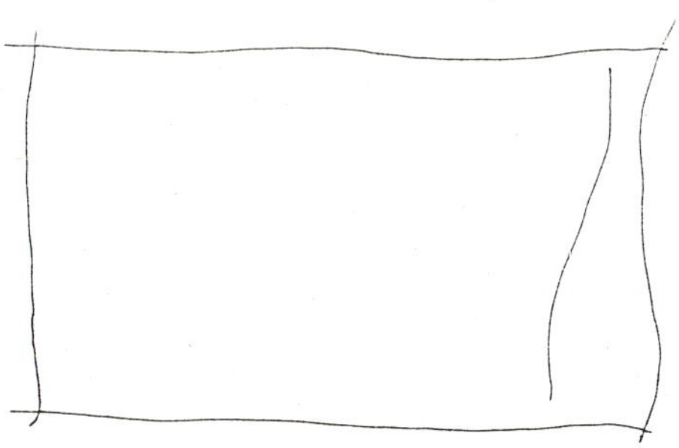

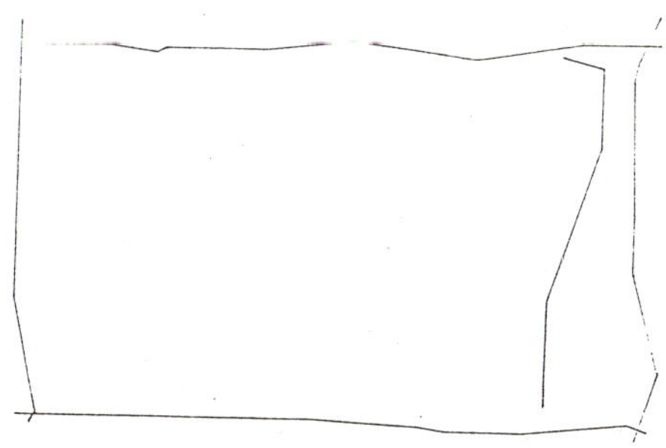

Figure 9. left: New symbol sketched. right: New symbol as seen by the computer.

This new symbol is recognized by the three sensors as follows:
'Shape' => Straight_Line; Vertical
'Context' => In_Lot; In_Buildable
'Phase' => Site_Layout
In the next illustration is shown how these features fill terminals of the frames that represent the different possible elements of the design.

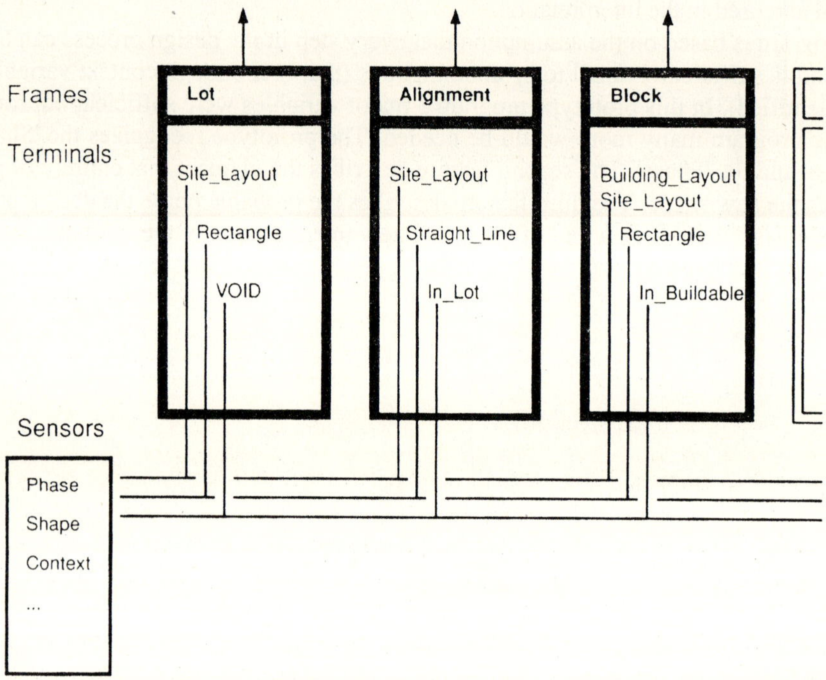

Figure 10. Recognizing frames from sketches.

The symbol will clearly activate the 'Alignment' frame. This frame will be connected to the sketch information in a hierarchical tree that forms the description of the design. The sketch will be straightened since the prototype can only handle orthogonal information. The information of the design is stored separately from the information about the elements. The first is modifiable whereas the latter is fixed. The information that is derived from the sketches can at any time be used to reactivate the proper frames.
In the prototype program the 'Alignment' frame is connected not only to the three sensors but also to some other frames. These describe some design information that is generally not sketched but derived from the information. For instance the 'Buildable Area' frame has four terminals that can be activated by 'Alignment' frames.

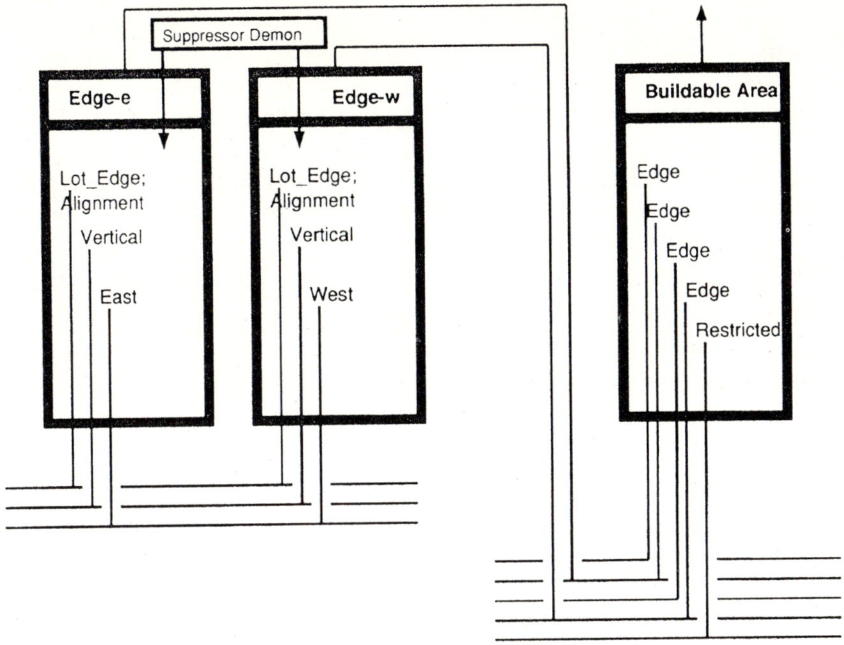

Figure 11. Deriving additional information from linked frames.

In this case two frames, 'Edge-w' and 'Edge_e' will get activated and the 'sensor demon' will get active because only one interpretation can be allowed. In this example there is not sufficient information and the demon will suppress the 'East' interpretation in favour of the west interpretation because of its relative position to the center of the 'Lot' symbol. Another 'Alignment' frame may later of course overrule this interpretation.
The activated 'Edge_w' frame will fill the appropriate 'Edge' terminal of the 'Buildable Area' frame. This has the effect of replacing the previous edge of the buildable area.

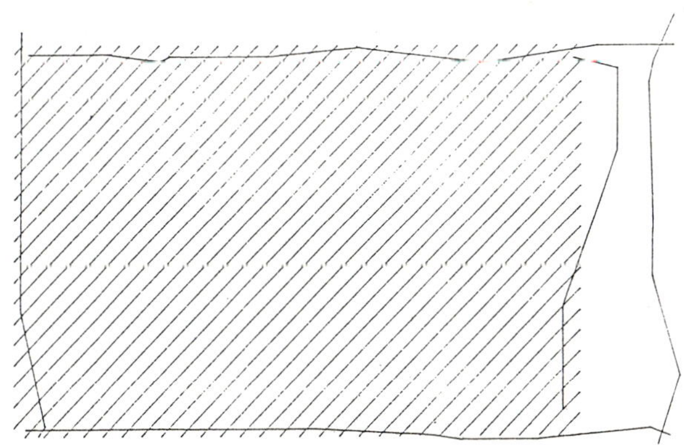

Figure 12. New sketch environment as seen by the computer.

Conclusions

So far we have tried to develop a theory of design that can be applied to the earliest stages of design and does explain how design information originates. Next we plan to address the definition of the architectural knowledge that is needed to do the actual interpretation of design sketches. Most of this research will be performed through prototype programs. These will be programmed to perform one specific task of the interpretation process and will be compared with human experts performing the same task. The final results of this research project are expected in approximately three years time.

References

Alexander, C. 1964. *Notes on the synthesis of form.* Harvard University Press.

Carrara, G., and Novembri, G. 1985. "Constraint bounded design search." In A. Pipes (ed.). *Computer Aided Architectural Design Futures.* London: Butterworths.

Maver, T. 1968. *The Strathclyde model of design process.*

Minsky, M. 1985. *The society of mind.* New York, NY: Simon & Schuster Inc.

Negroponte, N. 1970. *The Architecture Machine.* Cambridge, MA: MIT Press.

Turner, J. 1988. "AEC Building Systems Model, ISO TC 184/SC4/WG1 doc 3.2.2.4."

de Vries, M., and H. Wagter. 1989. "A CAAD model for use in the early design." In M. McCullough (ed.). *The electronic design studio.* Cambridge, MA: MIT Press.

33 Interactive Scene Walkthrough Using a Physically-Based Virtual Camera

Russell Turner, Francis Balaguer, Enrico Gobbetti, Daniel Thalmann

Laboratoire d'Infographie
EPF Lausanne
Swiss Federal Institute of Technology
CH 1015 Lausanne, Switzerland

One of the most powerful results of recent advances in graphics hardware is the ability of a computer user to interactively explore a virtual building or landscape. The newest three-dimensional input devices, together with high speed 3D graphics workstations, make it possible to view and move through a 3D scene by interactively controlling the motion of a virtual camera. In this paper, we describe how natural and intuitive control of building walkthrough can be achieved by using a physically-based model of the virtual camera's behavior. Using the laws of classical mechanics to create an abstract physical model of the camera, we then simulate the virtual camera motion in real time in response to force data from the various 3D input devices (e.g. the Spaceball and Polhemus 3Space Digitizer). The resulting interactive behavior of the model is determined by several physical parameters such as mass, moment of inertia, and various friction coefficients which can all be varied interactively, and by constraints on the camera's degrees of freedom. This allows us to explore a continuous range of physically-based metaphors for controlling the camera motion. We present the results of experiments using several of these metaphors for virtual camera motion and describe the effects of the various physical parameters.

Introduction

With the existence of graphics workstations able to display complex scenes containing several thousands of polygons at interactive speed, and with the advent of such new multiple degree-of-freedom interactive devices as the Spaceball, Polhemus 3Space, and DataGlove, it is now possible to create graphics applications based on a full 3D interaction metaphor in which the specification of the camera motion is given in real-time.

Interactive virtual camera motion is an important technique in a number of different computer graphics areas: animation, scientific visualization, CAD and virtual environment applications, all make considerable use of interactive virtual camera control in a three-dimensional environment to give the user the possibility of moving inside computer-generated virtual scenes (Baum et al. 1990, Magnenat-Thalmann and Thalmann 1986, Shinagawa et al. 1990). In architectural CAD applications, this gives both the architect and the client the ability to walk through virtual buildings and inspect them from any angle, allowing the architect to explore complex spaces and the client to provide feedback early in the design process (Brooks et al. 1986, Greenberg 1974).

In such systems, camera control using various input devices must be as natural and intuitive as possible so that the user is no longer conscious of it and can concentrate on the application task. However, the relationship between device input and virtual camera motion is not straightforward. Usually, a mathematical function or *filter* must be placed between the raw input device data and the virtual camera viewing parameters. This filter is usually associated with some sort of real-world metaphor such as *flying vehicle* metaphor, or *eyeball-in-hand* metaphor. Several recent papers have proposed and compared different metaphors for virtual camera motion control in virtual environments using input devices with six degrees of freedom (Ware and Osborne 1990, Mackinlay et al 1990). These are usually based on a kinematic model of control, where the virtual camera position, orientation, or velocity is set as a direct function of an input device coordinate.

One way to obtain more intuitive interactive camera control is to shift from a kinematic to a dynamic model, and to use some sort of physical laws to interpret the device input data. One such physical model that we propose is an interactive camera control metaphor based on physical modelling of the virtual camera, using forward dynamics for motion specification. This model is motivated by the following hypotheses:
- the interaction is natural because humans are used to physical "Newtonian" behavior
- it is a general parametric model with continuously variable behavior
- the parameters have physical meaning and are easy to understand

In this paper we present a physical description and mathematical derivation of the physical camera model. We then give our subjective impressions of the interactive "look and feel" of the model with different parameter settings using the Spaceball as an input device. We then present some examples of how this model could be used to aid interactive camera motion in a specific domain. Finally, a description of the implementation on a Silicon Graphics Iris workstation is given.

The Physical Camera Model

Like all physically-based modelling in computer graphics, the physical camera model is motivated by the assumption that human beings are best-equipped to deal with environments that resemble the natural world. Since the virtual camera is not normally seen, we are concerned with modelling not its physical appearance but rather its interactive response to the user. A natural virtual camera model is therefore most appropriately some kind of rigid body with mass that can be pushed or driven in various directions such as a moving vehicle or a real movie camera.

There exist a variety of real-world vehicles and camera mounts capable of moving in three dimensions from which to obtain an intuitive interaction metaphor. Although it would obviously be possible to physically model all of these, we have chosen to model an idealized real-world camera which is manipulated by a human being who exerts forces and torques on it. In this case, the behavior of the camera--the *virtual camera metaphor*--is determined by the mechanical properties of the camera. These properties can then be considered the parameters for our parametric virtual camera model.

Although real cameras and moving vehicles are complicated mechanical devices, their motions are determined for the most part by a few simple basic physical properties. Therefore, we have constructed an idealized physical model consisting of a single rigid body attached to a massless camera mount. The camera mount consists of three gimbals and three rails, one in each of the x, y, and z local coordinates, resulting in three Cartesian and three rotational degrees of freedom. Each of the gimbals and rails exerts friction and elastic forces on the camera.

The important mechanical properties of this model which affect its motion are its mass, its moments of inertia, and the coefficients of frictional and elastic forces imposed by the camera mount. The mass parameter specifies the amount by which the various forces will change the camera's linear velocity over time. The moment of inertia parameters affect, in an analogous way, the camera's response to the various torques. Usually a real camera's degrees of freedom are constrained in some geometrical way. For example, it may be placed on a dolly or a railway or tripod, constraining its linear motion to two, one and zero dimensions respectively. Likewise, the angular degrees of freedom may be restricted in one, two, or three axes by locking the gimbal bearings on the camera mount. Friction forces tend to reduce the linear and angular velocity of the camera over time and to oppose the applied forces and torques. There are several types of phenomenological friction forces used by physicists to model the dissipation of kinetic energy. We have found two, viscous friction and static friction, to be useful in our model. Viscous friction is proportional and opposite to the direction of motion, bringing the camera eventually to rest. Static friction is a constant force opposing the applied force, active only when the camera is at rest or below a threshold velocity. We have also found it useful to add an elastic parameter, in the form of a Hookian spring, to each degree of freedom. This elasticity is only important when the camera is at rest (i.e. static friction is active) and results in a more naturalistic transition from the static state to the dynamic state and back.

Motion Under External Driving Forces and Torques

Fortunately, the simplified camera model is quite easy to analyze physically and, from the point of view of classical mechanics, is a well understood problem (Feynman et al 1963). The general motion of a rigid body such as a camera can be decomposed into a linear motion of its center of mass under the control of an external net force and a rotational motion about the center of mass under the control of an external net torque.

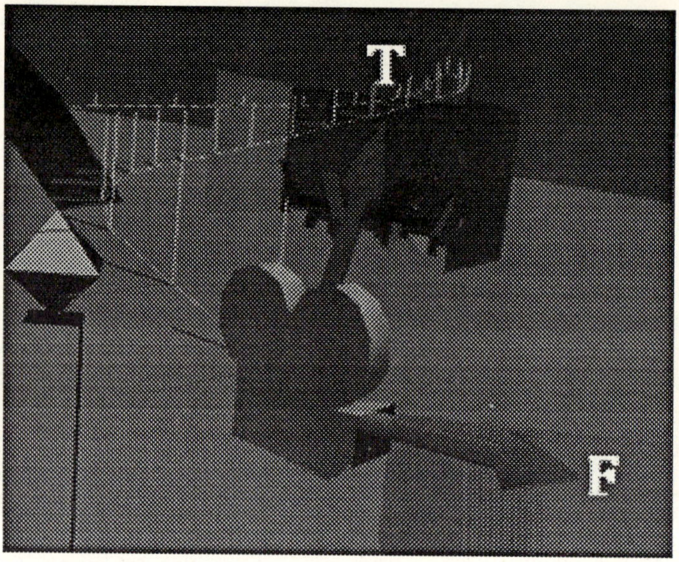

Figure 1. The virtual camera driven by a force and a torque.

Linear Motion

The linear motion under a total net force **F** can be computed by solving the differential equation

$$\ddot{\mathbf{X}} = \frac{\mathbf{F}}{m} \tag{1}$$

where m is the mass of the camera and **X** the position vector of its center of mass.

To compute the total net force **F** we have to take into account the driving force $\mathbf{F_d}$ and the forces that are generated by all the various frictions $\mathbf{F_f}$.

When the camera is moving at a speed below a given threshold velocity $\mathbf{v_s}$ and the driving force is smaller than a specified limit $\mathbf{F_s}$, we consider that the camera is in a static situation and that the frictions are caused by the springs that are present in the camera mount. Therefore we have

$$\mathbf{F_f} = k_{vs}\dot{\mathbf{X}} + k_{ss}(\mathbf{X} - \mathbf{X}_0) \tag{2}$$

where $\mathbf{X_0}$ is the position where the camera first entered the static situation, k_{vs} is the damping factor of the springs and k_{ss} the spring constant.

When we are at speeds higher than $\mathbf{v_s}$ or the driving force is bigger than $\mathbf{F_s}$, we consider the dynamic situation, where the frictions are mainly viscous. In that case we have

$$\mathbf{F_f} = k_{vd}\dot{\mathbf{X}} \tag{3}$$

where k_{vd} is the viscous friction coefficient.

It is useful to control the behavior of the camera separately for each of its principal axes. For this reason, the equations will be solved by projecting them onto the body-fixed reference frame, and a different value of the friction parameters will be specified for each one of the local axes.

Angular Motion

The rotational dynamics is expressed in a body-fixed reference system by the equation

$$\mathbf{I}\ddot{\theta} + \dot{\theta} \times \left(\mathbf{I}\dot{\theta}\right) = \mathbf{T_d} \tag{4}$$

where θ is the orientation of the camera expressed using Euler angles, **I** is the moment of inertia tensor of the body and is constant in the body-fixed reference frame, and $\mathbf{T_d}$ is the total net torque applied to the camera.

The modeling of the friction is analogous to the translational case. We can define ω_s to represent the threshold angular velocity and $\mathbf{T_s}$ to represent the threshold torque. In a static situation the friction torque $\mathbf{T_f}$ is given by

$$\mathbf{T_f} = k_{vs\text{-}rot}\dot{\theta} + k_{ss\text{-}rot}\left(\theta - \theta_0\right) \tag{5}$$

where θ_0 is the orientation where the camera first entered the static situation, $k_{vs\text{-}rot}$ is the damping factor of the springs and $k_{ss\text{-}rot}$ the spring constant.

In the dynamic case we have

$$\mathbf{T_f} = k_{vd\text{-}rot}\dot{\theta} \tag{6}$$

where $k_{vd\text{-}rot}$ is the viscous friction coefficient.

As for the translational case, it is useful to control the behavior of the camera separately for each of its principal axes, and a different value of the friction parameters will be specified for each one of the local axes.

Specifying the Camera's Behavior

The behavior of the virtual camera in response to user actions is completely specified by the parameters of the physical model of the camera. A different value of the friction parameters can be specified for every dimension in the reference frame attached to the camera. By this means we provide an easy and intuitive way for controlling the behavior of the model separately for each of the six degrees of freedom of the camera and several interesting camera motions or "camera metaphors" can be specified.

Modifying Mass and Inertia Tensor

The camera mass parameter determines the degree of acceleration control by the user. If all other parameters are set to zero, the camera maintains a steady velocity and changes its velocity only in response to user input, resulting in a pure acceleration control metaphor. Higher mass results in a smoother, more continuous motion and a higher degree of acceleration control, although it also makes it more difficult to bring the camera to rest at a given location. A high mass parameter is useful in situations where a smooth camera motion is desired, or where continuous motion is wanted with minimal input from the user, for example, tasks such as moving outside a building or inside large interior spaces.

In an analogous way, the inertia tensor determines the degree of torque control by the user over the camera orientation. A large inertia tensor results in smooth panning and tilting motions. This is often desirable because jerky camera rotation can be disorienting. Without a correspondingly high rotational friction parameter, however, it can be difficult to stop the camera from rotating. This is usually much more disorienting than the analogous translational situation. High inertia tensors are useful for the same sorts of tasks that high mass parameters are useful for: slow steady examination of a large scene. For more precise control up close to objects, a lower inertia tensor is preferable.

Viscous Friction Coefficient

The viscous friction parameter specifies the degree of velocity control. If the other parameters are set to zero, the camera metaphor becomes a pure velocity control one. Velocity control is useful for tasks where quick stopping and changes of direction are necessary, such as avoiding obstacles or inspecting objects up close. A typical architectural walk-through situation where a high viscous friction coefficient would be useful is a small room with furniture. One problem with high viscous friction camera metaphors is that the camera motions are not usually very smooth and the user must give continuous input while the camera is moving. For many interactive tasks, this is not a problem. For other tasks, a suitable combination of velocity and acceleration metaphors can be formed by adjusting various amounts of the mass and viscous friction parameters.

The rotational analog to the viscous friction coefficient is the rotational viscous friction coefficient, which determines the amount of angular velocity control. Angular velocity control is particularly useful because of the need to stop camera rotation quickly. The balance between the moment of inertia and the rotational viscous friction coefficient determines the smoothness of camera panning motions, and many real-world camera mounts have adjustable angular viscous friction controls.

Threshold Force and Velocity

A small static friction parameter establishes a threshold force below which the camera will stay stationary. The threshold velocity determines the speed below which the static friction force comes into effect, bringing the camera to rest more rapidly than the viscous friction forces. Changing these parameters can be useful for tasks in which the user wants to alternate between motion along different degrees of freedom. For example, moving the camera along only one axis at a time is easy as long as the threshold force is not exceeded in the other axes. Likewise, a task that involves hopping to a fixed location, looking around in different directions without moving, then hopping to the next location, is much easier with a small amount of static friction.

By setting the static friction parameter extremely high, its possible to, in effect, lock a particular degree of freedom, resulting in a constrained motion. For example, by locking one of the rotational degrees of freedom, the camera is forced to always maintain the same "up" direction, and by locking one of the translational degrees of freedom, the camera is forced to move in a plane. This can be useful to simulate a walking person's point of view. Locking the vertical and horizontal translational degrees of freedom, so the camera can only move forward and turn, results in a flying-vehicle camera metaphor.

Static Behavior: Damping Factor and Spring Constant

The spring constant and damping factor parameters control the vibrational behavior of the camera mount when it is in the static state. A small amount of damped vibration smooths out the jerkiness in the transition between dynamic and static states. It also provides a small degree of position control feedback while the camera is in the static state. In this way, a small applied force will move the camera slightly, but it will pop back to its rest position. A larger force, above the static friction threshold, will set the camera in motion. This allows the user to get an idea of what direction an applied force will act in before actually moving the camera's position. If the static friction parameter is set extremely high, then the camera becomes locked in the static state and a position control camera metaphor results.

Continuous Variation Between Different Behaviors

It is generally accepted that no one particular type of camera motion or camera control is appropriate for all tasks (Ware and Osborne 1990). In virtual building walkthrough, the user might require acceleration control for moving smoothly as he surveys the overall spatial organization of the building, while the task of inspecting some detail, where the camera viewpoint is close to the point of interest, might require more precise velocity control.

Unfortunately, genuinely useful tasks often require a combination of metaphors or a sequence of alternating metaphors. A common way to deal with this is to allow the user to continually change camera control metaphors by swapping through the different interaction modes. Modes can be changed by selecting menus, striking keys or mouse buttons. There are two problems with this technique. First it is obviously inconvenient and unnatural to continually change modes. The user has to stop performing his task to swap computer and mental modes. After a while, this can be distracting and will often inhibit the user from changing metaphors until the current one becomes really impracticable. Secondly, it is not necessarily true that there are only a finite number of discrete useful metaphors. There are, in fact, a lot of in between situations where no pure metaphor suits the task best (Mackinlay et al 1990).

The parameterized physical camera model provides a solution to this problem by giving us a way to control the camera behavior through its parameter values. For a given task, the user can experiment with the camera metaphor and tune the parameters interactively, through valuators, until a subjectively "best" set of parameters is found. These parameters can then be saved and restored, either automatically or by the user, whenever that particular task is encountered. Alternately, the user can interactively control certain camera parameters while he is performing his task. For example, a mouse button or foot pedal can be set to momentarily increase the amount of viscous friction, acting as a kind of break.

Ideally, however, the user should only be required to use a minimum of input and should not have to be overly aware of the camera metaphor at all. This can be achieved by having the application adjust the camera control parameters algorithmically as a function of position or some aspect of the task at hand. This is potentially the most powerful use of the parametric camera model.

For example, we have created a scalar viscosity field within a scene such that the camera viscous friction parameter increases in the vicinity of objects. This results in a camera metaphor that continuously varies from mainly acceleration control when the camera is far away from objects, to mainly velocity control when the camera is close to an object. In this way, the camera's behavior varies as a function of its distance from objects.

Figure 2. Exploring a scene.

Figure 3. Inspecting an object.

Implementation

Our dynamic camera control system is implemented on a Silicon Graphics Iris workstation in C using an object-oriented style of programming, on top of the Fifth Dimension 3D interaction toolkit (Turner et al 1990). In addition to the typical sorts of 3D classes, such as lights, hierarchical models and cameras, the toolkit abstracts every input device as an instance of an input device class. These input device objects communicate their data through a uniform event message protocol.

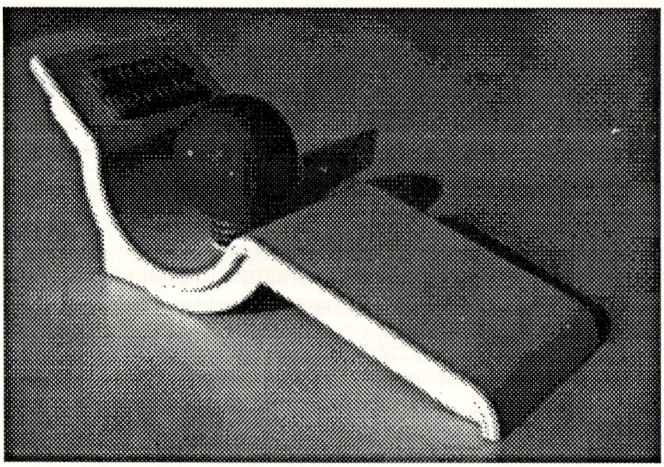

Figure 4. Spaceball six degree of freedom input device.

For interactive camera control, we have found the most natural input device to be the Spaceball, produced by Spatial Systems. It is composed of a rigid sphere containing strain gauges mounted on a plastic base in order to offer a comfortable rest position for the operator hand and arm. The position and orientation are specified by rotating or pushing the sphere in a certain direction. Although the sphere moves only slightly, the force and torque applied are measured and an incremental position and orientation is transmitted, at a configurable rate, to the host computer.

The interface between the input device objects and the camera object is implemented by a camera controller object. This object receives events from input devices, interprets the data according to a particular camera metaphor, and updates the camera object's position and orientation accordingly. Since our camera Controller involves a dynamic simulation, it also receives tick events from a clock object at regular time-step intervals.

At each time step, a numerical solution to the equations of motion (1) and (4) is calculated using a second-order approximation for the derivatives of **X** and **Θ**. This explicit procedure evolves the dynamic solution from given initial conditions. The current and the previous value of position and orientation are used to solve for the value at a small time Δt later. No oversampling is necessary, because the precision required is not high (the user interacts with the solver), and Δt represents the time increment between displayed frames. Our current implementation allows us to have an interactive display rate (more than 10 Hz) on a Silicon Graphics Iris 4D/80 with fully shaded scenes containing up to two-thousand polygons. The time spent for the dynamic computations is negligible with respect to the redraw time.

One of the advantages of this kind of software architecture is that various other devices, such as the Polhemus 3D, can be interchanged with the Spaceball as input to the Camera Controller. The use of this kind of devices is essential for providing an intuitive way of controlling the dynamic camera. Obviously, pressure-sensitive input devices are usually more appropriate because they provide a passive form of "force-feedback". In our case, the device that gave the best results is the Spaceball. Also, different types of Camera controllers with different behaviors can be swapped in and out, and the same controllers can be used to control Light objects or hierarchical models.

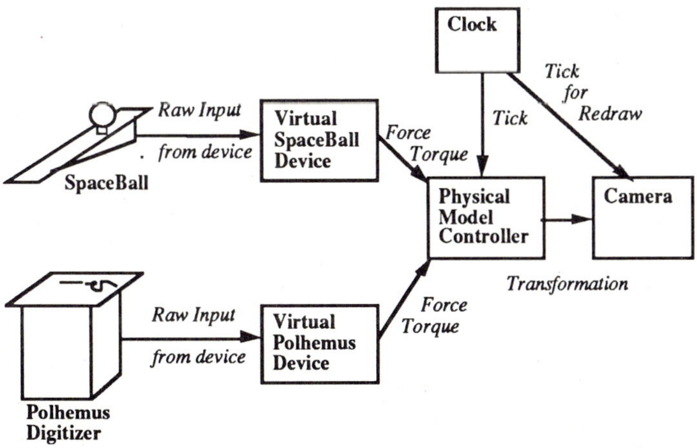

Figure 5. Event communication diagram for the camera controller.

Conclusions and Future Work

We believe that the physically-based camera control model provides a powerful, general-purpose metaphor for controlling virtual cameras in interactive 3D environments. Because it is based on a real camera model, it is natural for the user to control. Its parameters are physically-based and, therefore, easy to understand and intuitive for the user to manipulate. Its generality and control parameters make it configurable to emulate a continuum of camera behaviors ranging from pure position control to pure acceleration control. As it is fully described by its physical parameters, it is possible to construct more sophisticated virtual camera control metaphors by varying the parameters as a function of space, time, application data or other user input. Also, when used with force-calibrated input devices, the camera metaphor can be reproduced exactly on different hardware and software platforms, providing a predictable standard interactive "feel".

We are currently working on extending our model to specify camera paths for computer animation, and on exploring different kinds of algorithmic control of the camera parameters by creating various types of parameter fields within the scene space. We are also planning to use the dynamic model approach for other kinds of interactive tasks such as modelling, assembling, and specifying the animation of different kinds of objects.

Acknowledgements

The authors are grateful to Angelo Mangili for his technical help.The research was partly sponsored by *Le Fond National pour la Recherche Scientifique*.

References

Baum, R., and J.W Wingel. 1990. "Real Time Radiosity Through Parallel Processing and Hardware Acceleration." *Proceedings 1990 Workshop on Interactive 3D Graphics*. ACM: 67-75 .

Brooks, F.P. Jr. 1986. "Walkthrough - A Dynamic Graphics System for Simulating Virtual Buildings." *Proceedings 1986 Workshop on Interactive 3D Graphics*. ACM: 9-22.

Feynman, R.P., R.B. Leighton, M. Sands. 1963. *The Feynman Lectures on Physics*. Reading, MA: Addison-Wesley.

Greenberg, D.P. 1974. "Computer Graphics in Architecture." *Scientific American* 230, no. 5: 98-106.

Hahn, J.K. 1988. "Realistic Animation of Rigid Bodies." *Computer Graphics* 22, no. 4: 299-308.

Mackinlay, J.D., S.K. Card , and G. Robertson. 1990. "Rapid Controlled Movement Through a Virtual 3D Workspace." *Computer Graphics* 24, no. 4: 171-176.

Magnenat-Thalmann, N., and D. Thalmann. 1986. "Special Cinematographic Effects Using Multiple Virtual Movie Camera." *IEEE Computer Graphics & Applications* 6, no. 4: 43-50.

Shinogawa, Y., T.L. Kunii, Y. Nomura, T. Okuno, and Y. Young . 1990. "Automating View Function Generation for Walkthrough Animation Using a Reeb Graph." *Proceedings Computer Animation 90*, pp. 227-238. Tokyo: Springer.

Turner, R., E. Gobbetti, F. Balaguer, A. Mangili, D. Thalmann, and N. Magnenat-Thalmann. 1990. "An Object Oriented Methodology Using Dynamic Variables for Animation and Scientific Visualization." *Proceedings Computer Graphics International 90*, pp. 317-328. Springer-Verlag.

Ware, C., and S. Osborne. 1990. "Exploration and Virtual Camera Control in Virtual Three Dimensional Environments." *Proceedings 1990 Workshop on Interactive 3D Graph-ics*. ACM: 175-183.

Watson, V. 1989. "A Breakthrough for Experiencing and Understanding Simulated Physics." *ACM SIGGRAPH Course Notes on State of the Art in Data Visualization*, IV-26 - IV-32.

34 Leaving the Planar Universe

P. Durisch, E. Anderheggen

Professur für Informatik
ETH Zürich
CH 8093 Zürich, Switzerland

A computer program is presented which generates realistic images of planned buildings embedded in their future environment through photomontage. The planar universe of conventional photomontaging is extended to three dimensions. During an interactive pre-processing step, a three-dimensional model of the building's environment is created: Geometrical data is retrieved photogrammetrically from a number of site photographs. Atmospheric parameters and the relative weights of the components of natural daylight are also retrieved from the photographs. The final image, combining the artificial model of the building and the photographs of its surroundings, is rendered by an extended ray-tracing algorithm in three-dimensional object space.

Introduction

Among the traditional methods which support the delicate job of judging the visual impact of planned buildings on the landscape or cityscape are: images (plans, perspective drawings, photomontages) and three-dimensional hand-crafted models. There is a justification for all of these. Observation, however, reveals that they are either unable to show the subtle effects which make up the overall appearance of a building, inflexible for case studies, or expensive due to the invested 'artistic power'. Thus, finding cheap methods to provide accurate sources to judge the aesthetic properties of planned buildings seems to be a worthy goal.

A fundamental requirement is that a building must be integrated into its environment (landscape, cityscape). Photomontages try to combine some artificial objects and a particular existing environment which is represented by photographs. Both parts are essentially three-dimensional. Therefore, in the following brief review we discuss the technique of photomontage in a more general context: the combination of separately generated images of three-dimensional objects.

Early hidden-surface algorithms like the Newell, Newell & Sancha algorithm (Newell et al. 1972) or the z-buffer (Sutherland et al. 1974) use depth priority to render objects which do not interact, except that they may hide each other. The A-buffer (Carpenter 1984) is an extended z-buffer with increased resolution which handles transparent objects. Porter & Duff (Porter et al. 1984) use priority operators to combine fore- and background with image information available on a sub-pixel level (α-channel). z-buffer and α-channel have been combined by Duff (Duff 1985). Nakamae et al. (Nakamae et al. 1989) subdivide each image row into a number of virtual scanlines and store information for virtual scanline segments. Object depth information is required by all of these algorithms.

Photomontages with artificial computer-generated objects and backgrounds from digitized photographs are shown by (Uno et al. 1979), (Feibush et al. 1980) and (BD&C 1990). Maver et al. (Maver et al. 1985) construct a CAD model based on geometrical data retrieved from aerial photographs by photogrammetrical methods. Nakamae et al. (Nakamae et al. 1986) extract information about the current weather- and illumination conditions from the photographs. They also approximate parts of the environment by planar faces, mainly for adding and removing fog effects. They do not use photogrammetrical methods, just topographical maps. Kaneda et al. (Kaneda et al. 1989) map data of aerial photographs onto a terrain model based on cartographic data and integrate artificial objects into the three-dimensional terrain. This allows changing the observer position freely but is of limited use when details of the environment are required, especially those visible in horizontal views. Terzopoulos et al. (Terzopoulos et al. 1988) present an animation showing artificial objects copied into a real background scene which is approximated by planar surfaces.

If the full physical description of a scene is given and if it is known how light interacts with matter, then the spatial and spectral distribution of the light energy which reaches the image plane of an arbitrarily oriented camera (the eye of the observer) is completely defined. For the translation of the energy distribution into a color image, the physiological properties of the human visual system have to be considered. A color image of the scene can be computed algorithmically, which is 'correct' within the scope of the models which are used for the simplified simulation of the physical world we live in.

The new building is a three-dimensional object. Photomontages represent the existing environment by one or more photographs which are 'flat' projections of a three-dimensional scene. For a correct integration of an artificial object into its environment, a three-dimensional description of the environment is required. The environment generally consists of objects of arbitrary complexity with respect to size, shape, color, texture, shadow and reflection. Some information is lost due to the finite number of photographs; yet other information appears in more than one photograph and is therefore redundant.

Computer vision and photogrammetry deal with the problem of the (automatic) interpretation of images and the problem of measuring objects appearing in images. This paper does not present methods for automatic image interpretation or object measurement. Instead, during a preprocessing step, information is extracted interactively from the photographic images (program PREPARE). In a second step, the image which shows the planned building embedded in its environment is rendered by an extended ray-tracing algorithm (program RENDER). To the benefit of the non-technical reader, we concentrate on a descriptive overview of our work. Therefore, we do not use formulae. A detailed and more technical discussion of the models and methods can be found in (Durisch 1991).

Preprocessing

The interactive preprocessor PREPARE is designed for retrieving geometrical and non-geometrical information from a number of digital color images which represent the environment of the planned building (natural environment).

– Coordinate systems. 3D cartesian world-coordinates define locations in object space. The world-coordinate system may be selected arbitrarily. 2D cartesian image-coordinates define locations in the image plane of a central perspective projection. 2D cartesian bitmap-coordinates define locations in the pixel raster of a digital image.

– Image acquisition. A Rolleiflex 6006 camera with known interior orientation was used to take 60x60 mm color slides of the natural environment from several arbitrarily selected positions. The data of the interior camera orientation consists of the image-coordinates of eight hairline crosses (fiducial marks) visible on the slide, the center and amount of the radial image distortion due to the non-ideal optics of the camera (radial distortion), and the normal distance from the projection center to the image plane of the central perspective projection (calibrated focal length). The slides were digitized with 8 bits per RGB color channel and stored each in an image file.

– Image orientation. The linear mapping between image- and bitmap-coordinates is determined from the fiducial marks' image-coordinates (part of the interior orientation) and their bitmap-coordinates (identified manually on the workstation screen using a pointing device). The fiducial marks are not affected by the radial distortion. Therefore they define the image-coordinate system in the image plane. The image orientation is done separately for each image.

– Distortion correction. Each image with a significant radial distortion is geometrically corrected to eliminate the distortion effect. The corrected image is resampled to the same resolution. A 4x4 pixel wide piecewise cubic filter (Mitchell et al. 1988) is used for the reconstruction of continuous image data from discrete samples. Distortion correction results in a nonlinear image stretch and is computationally expensive.

– Resection in space. The exterior orientation of the camera (three world-coordinates of the camera position, three angles of the camera rotation) is determined from the known world-coordinates of at least three control points and their corresponding image-coordinates (identified manually). This is called resection in space. A system of six nonlinear equations has to be solved iteratively by a Newton-Raphson algorithm, starting from a user-specified estimation of the solution. At each iteration step, the increment is determined by solving the system of linearized equations at the location of the current solution. If there are more than three control points, the system of nonlinear equations is redundant and the increment is calculated by solving a system of Gaussian normal equations built from the linearized equations (Björck et al. 1979).

The result of the resection in space is converted to a 4x4 matrix which expresses the linear mapping from homogeneous world- to homogeneous image-coordinates. Since this mapping will be done very often during the rendering step, its linearity is essential for the speed of the calculation. The nonlinear component of the mapping is eliminated by the distortion correction if we assume that the radial distortion is the only error introduced by the non-ideal optics of the camera. The resection in space is done separately for each image.

– Intersection in space, planes and polygons. The world-coordinates of a point in object space can be determined from its image-coordinates which are identified manually in at least two images. This is called intersection in space. Three points in object space define an infinite plane. The image-coordinates of a pointing device can be mapped directly to a plane in object space. The plane is intersected with the ray from the projection center through the point in the image plane which is defined by the image-coordinates of the pointing device. Points retrieved by intersection in space or by mapping locator image-coordinates to a plane or a polygon in object space (see below) are stored in the point buffer. Planes are stored in the plane buffer.

The geometry of a polygon is defined by its co-planar vertices, specified in clockwise or counter-clockwise order. The world-coordinates of the vertices are retrieved from the point buffer. The non-geometrical properties of a polygon are defined by an *image tag* and a *material tag*. The image tag references one of the images, the material tag references a member of the material library. The referenced material description defines one part of the polygon's material properties, the other part is retrieved at rendering time from one of the images which represent the natural environment. Polygons are stored in the polygon buffer.

– Atmospheric Parameters. An object which moves away from the observer changes its color depending on the distance and the current weather conditions. What the observer perceives is the apparent color of the object. 'Far away' the apparent color cannot be distinguished from the horizon color. The light reflected from the object towards the observer defines the true color of the object. The *atmospheric model* describes this color shift. It is a nonlinear equation which yields the apparent color of an object, depending on its true color, the horizon color and the spectral transparency of the atmosphere. The spectral transparency describes the amount of light which is neither absorbed by the atmosphere nor scattered away from the normal direction of light propagation within a unit distance.

The attribute 'spectral' means that a physical quantity is wavelength dependent. The terms 'intensity' and 'color' are sometimes used interchangeably. Without giving precise definitions, it should be pointed out that intensity expresses the light energy while color is a quantity which results from the perception of light by the human visual system. The 1931 CIE XYZ color space (Judd et al. 1975) is based on the spectral energy distribution of the light and on the properties of the human visual system. For simplicity, we use the term 'color' in this discussion, though we implicitly refer to the corresponding spectral energy (or intensity) distribution of the light. RGB triplets are converted to CIE XYZ and expanded into a spectral distribution (or spectrum) before they are used by any of the models.

The *first inversion of the atmospheric model* involves solving the equation of the atmospheric model for the spectral transparency of the atmosphere: Given are the horizon color (identified manually) and the apparent colors of a number of objects of the same opaque ideally-diffuse reflecting material at various known distances from the observer (identified manually on previously determined planes or polygons in object space). Each color sample contributes one equation to a (redundant) system of nonlinear equations. For each wavelength in the visible spectrum, this is solved iteratively for the unknowns which are the true color of the object and the spectral transparency of the atmosphere. The former is of no interest and can be dismissed, since it expresses no general property of the scene. See (Nakamae et al. 1986) for a similar approach which does not consider wavelength dependency.

The *second inversion of the atmospheric model* involves solving the equation of the atmospheric model for the true color of an object: Given are the object's distance from the observer, the horizon color and the spectral transparency of the atmosphere (both by the first inversion of the atmospheric model) and the apparent color of the object.

– Illumination Parameters. Natural daylight is assumed to be composed of direct sun light, uniformly incident diffuse light from the hemisphere of the sky above the horizon (sky light) and uniformly incident diffuse ambient light. The relative weights of the illumination components are dependent on the actual weather conditions.

The direction to the sun is determined by a point on an object and its corresponding point on the object's shadow (by intersection in space). The direction to the zenith (the highest point of the sky hemisphere) is determined similarly, e.g. by two points on the same vertical edge of a house. Since the world-coordinate system may be selected arbitrarily, the zenith direction is not known a priori. The sky hemisphere is subdivided into a number of discrete facets. Each unobscured sky facet contributes to the illumination at a point on an object. The sun direction, the zenith direction and the granularity of the sky discretization define the illumination geometry. The ambient light represents a part of the global illumination.

The *illumination model* describes the behavior of light at an interface between two materials. It is an equation which yields the approximate spectral intensity distribution of the light which leaves the material interface in a given direction, depending on the illumination and the materials on both sides of the material interface.

The *first inversion of the illumination model* involves solving the equation of the illumination model for the relative weights of the illumination components which make up natural daylight: Given are the scene geometry and the illumination geometry, the relative (normalized) spectral intensity distributions of the illumination components and the true colors of a number of points located on objects of the same opaque ideally-diffuse reflecting material (identified manually on previously determined planes or polygons in object space). The true color of each sample is first determined from its apparent color by the second inversion of the atmospheric model. Each sample point may be located on a face which is oriented in a different direction or hidden from direct sunlight and/or part of the incident sky light. Each sample contributes one equation to a (redundant) system of linear equations. For each wavelength in the visible spectrum, this is solved (by the Gaussian least squares method) for the unknowns which are the relative weights of the illumination components. The weights are averaged within the visible spectrum. See (Nakamae et al. 1986) for an approach without sky light and without considering wavelength dependency.

The *second inversion of the illumination model* involves solving the equation of the illumination model for the spectral reflectance of an object. Given are the scene geometry and the illumination geometry, the spectral intensity distributions of the illumination components (by multiplying the relative intensities by the previously determined weights) and the true color of a point on an object of an opaque ideally-diffuse reflecting material. The true color of the sample is first determined from its apparent color by the second inversion of the atmospheric model.

– Environment Descriptions. The *natural environment description* contains geometrical data (polygon geometry, illumination geometry) and non-geometrical data (polygon attributes, light source attributes, atmospheric parameters) about the natural environment of the planned building. Most of the data is retrieved from the images which represent the scene. The interior and exterior camera orientation associated with each image and the names of the image files are also specified. The *artificial environment description* contains the description of the artificial world, including the planned building and additional light sources, if required. It can be generated by any CAD system but it has to be converted to the required data format. DXFCONV is a converter for the widely used DXF format (Autodesk

1988) for data interchange between CAD systems. DXFCONV has also been developed within this research project. The environment descriptions are both stored in an ASCII file.

Rendering

The ray-tracer RENDER generates one or several images, showing the planned building embedded in its future environment. It is (yet) another extension of conventional ray-tracing introduced by Whitted (Whitted 1980) in his classical paper.

– Input. RENDER reads the natural and the artificial environment description and accesses the files of the (distortion corrected) images used during the preprocessing step. If there is no artificial environment description present, RENDER works like a conventional ray-tracer. Hierarchically organized object bounding volumes allow to reduce the number of ray-object intersections. The bounding slab approach by Kay & Kajiya (Kay et al. 1986) was implemented. A set of rendering parameters allow to trade off speed versus image quality. There is a library which contains spectral and non-spectral material data and spectral light source data. Each member is a separate ASCII file which is referenced by its name. Therefore, extending the library is very simple. Material data (refraction indices, absorption coefficients of conductors, spectral reflectance values) and light source data (relative spectral energy distributions of standard illuminants) can be found in physical tables (CRC 1987, Ditchburn 1976, Jenkins et al 1976, Purdue 1970, Sala 1986, Judd et al 1975).

A spectral distribution at 1 nm increment is reconstructed from the tabulated spectral values and reduced to a number of spectral samples by low-pass filtering and sampling. The spectral samples represent the spectral distribution during the simulation (Hall 1989). Since RGB values are device-dependent, they are not used for the specification of material and light source properties.

Color data available as RGB triplets only, e.g. data from the image files, are converted to CIE XYZ in a first step. Then they are expanded into a spectrum. Since light with different spectral composition may map to the same XYZ triplet (metamers), there exist an infinite number of solutions to the expansion problem. We determine a spectrum as the linear combination of three non-overlapping box functions, with a constant value of 1 in the red, green and blue domain of the visible spectrum, respectively, and 0 otherwise. Glassner (Glassner 1989) uses linear combinations of other, i.e. trigonometric functions.

– Extended ray-tracing. Several approaches for photomontaging use three-dimensional data about the natural environment. In spite of this, most of them still work partly in object space (e.g. depth comparisons) and partly in image space (e.g. pixel by pixel combination of foreground and background). Our approach uses ray-tracing which works entirely in object space. To our knowledge, ray-tracing has not been used so far for rendering photomontages. There are a number of extensions of conventional ray-tracing which are described below:

Setup. One of the images which represent the natural environment (input images) is selected (current input image). The interior and exterior orientation of the camera which was used to take the current input image represents an observer in object space, which remains unchanged during the rendering of the current output image.

The current input image is a projection of the natural environment onto the image plane of the camera. The boundaries of the current output image are defined by a rectangular frame in the same image plane but they are completely independent from the boundaries of the current input image. The same is true for the number of pixels within the image boundaries.

Independent pixel processing (repeated for each sample within each pixel on each output image line). An initial ray is sent into the scene, originating at the center of projection. Several cases are identified:

Case A. The initial ray does not hit any artificial or natural object: the image-coordinates of the point where the ray penetrates the image plane are mapped to bitmap-coordinates of the current input image. The correspondence between image- and bitmap-coordinates has been established earlier. Image data is retrieved by accessing the current input image file at the calculated bitmap location. A 4x4 pixel wide piecewise cubic filter can be used optionally for the reconstruction of continuous image data from discrete samples. The (reconstructed) RGB triplet is expanded into a spectrum, reduced to a number of spectral samples and returned.

Case B. A non-initial ray does not hit any artificial or natural object: the horizon color is returned if the ray direction is above the horizon.

Case C. Any ray hits an artificial object: the illumination model is evaluated for the illuminating artificial and natural light sources and the result is returned. Depending on the material and the illumination model, a reflected and/or a refracted ray may be spawned.

Case D. Any ray hits a natural object: the intersection point is mapped from world- to bitmap-coordinates of one of the input images. This is the current input image, if the ray is the initial one, otherwise it is the input image referenced by the object's (polygon's) image tag. Image data is retrieved by accessing the input image file at the calculated bitmap location. The (reconstructed) RGB triplet is expanded into a spectrum and reduced to a number of spectral samples. These represent the apparent color of the intersected object. Its true color is determined by the second inversion of the atmospheric model. The spectral reflectance of the object material is determined from the true object color by the second inversion of the illumination model. All other material properties come from the material which is referenced by the object's material tag. The spectral reflectance is used by the illumination model. If the natural object does not have an image tag, all material properties come from the material which is referenced by the object's material tag. This allows one to change the appearance of natural objects by redefining their material properties. Several subcases are identified:

Case D-1. The natural object is illuminated by an artificial light source: the illumination model is evaluated, the result is added to the color retrieved from the input image and the sum is returned.

Case D-2. The natural object is illuminated by a natural light source: since the illumination effect is already visible in the input image, the unaltered color retrieved from the input image is returned.

Case D-3. The natural object is shaded from the illumination by a natural light source due to artificial objects only: the illumination model is evaluated with a *negative* contribution of the blocked natural light source (as if there were no artificial objects), the result is added to the color retrieved from the input image and the sum is returned.

Depending on the material and the illumination model, a reflected and/or a refracted ray may be spawned for each of the three subcases.

Selecting another current input image with the corresponding camera parameters during the setup step allows us to generate a different view of the same scene without any changes in the natural or artificial environment description.

– Output. After determining the spectral intensity distribution of the light incident on a location in the image plane, a continuous spectral distribution at 1 nm increment is again reconstructed from the spectral samples (Hall 1989). The spectral intensity distribution is multiplied by the CIE color-matching functions and integrated over the visible spectrum to get the CIE tristimulus values X, Y and Z (the coordinates of the 1931 CIE XYZ color space). Finally, these are converted to the RGB color space of a specific output device (Judd et al. 1975).

The program VIEW which was also developed within this research project, is able to show a complete image or the finished part of an image, the computation of which is still in progress. This allows us to interrupt the calculation of not very promising images. Practical experience shows that this can save much time. VIEW may run on a local workstation, while RENDER runs concurrently on a remote host. Data is transferred in ASCII format (e.g. through a UNIX pipe). Output is in ASCII or in binary format. ASCII format is required if the image is rendered on a remote machine, since binary files are usually incompatible across different computers.

Conventional ray-tracing is a strictly additive process, whereas our approach extends it to an additive *and* subtractive process. The extension does not require any changes in the illumination model which always adds illumination. The key is to pass a *negative* contribution to the illumination model in case D-3.

Example 0. Campus ETH-Hönggerberg

The example shows a scene on the campus of ETH-Hönggerberg, Zurich, which was used to test the program. It is a purely academic example, but it is well suited to illustrate the various effects which can be simulated. The natural environment was represented by 3 images.

Image 1 (figure 1, top left) shows the original natural environment on a sunny day in late fall. The gallery (supports, roof and floor), the horizontal lawn plane and the main background buildings were approximated by planar polygons during the preprocessing step. The material tags of the polygons reference the same opaque dielectric ideally-diffuse reflecting material with a flat reflectance characteristic within the visible spectrum. The image tags of the polygons reference the current input image (any image which is selected in the rendering process during the setup step). Samples on the lawn plane were used to determine the spectral transparency of the atmosphere (first inversion of the atmospheric model). Samples of various incident illumination were selected on the concrete wall of the background building on the left. They were used to determine the relative weights of the components of natural daylight (first inversion of the illumination model).

Image 2 (figure 1, top right) shows some primitive solids embedded in the natural environment: an aluminium torus around the center support, an iron-oxide cone and a floor consisting of brick and granite tiles. Note the shadow of the natural support cast onto the artificia torus, the geometrically correct interpenetration of the cone with the gallery and the shadow of the torus cast onto the ground.

Figure 1. Images 1 to 4. From left to right, top to bottom.

Image 3 (figure 1, bottom left) is similar to image 2. There is a marble torus and the cone has a bumpy surface which was simulated by a stochastic perturbation of the local normal vector. The image tag was removed from the polygon which represents one of the background walls. Its material tag references a textured stone material. Since this polygon extends to ground level, the foliage in front of the wall disappears. A solid white glass sphere is placed in the foreground where it acts like a lens (things visible through the sphere appear reversed and upside down). As a consequence of the principle of ray-tracing, only those natural objects which are part of the three-dimensional model of the natural environment are visible through the sphere (some of the background objects are missing). Note the two shadows of the sphere: one caused by the occlusion of direct sunlight, the other by the occlusion of light coming from the distributed light source which represents the sky hemisphere.

Image 4 (figure 1, bottom right) is a close-up of image 3. It was created by shrinking the rectangular image boundaries in the image plane.

All images were rendered with a resolution of 512x512 pixels and anti-aliasing. Image rendering time was between 3.4 and 7.6 CPU hours on a CONVEX-C2 computer for a single image. The geometrical model of the natural and artificial environment consisted of 18 light sources (16 of them due to the discretization of the sky hemisphere), (1 sphere) and a total of 719 convex polygons (38 of them from the natural environment description).

Example 1. Bridge at Büren an der Aare

The example shows the projected wooden bridge at Büren an der Aare, Canton Bern (project by Walder & Marchand AG, Gümligen, Moor & Hauser AG, Bern). The new bridge is intended to replace the historical wooden bridge of 1821 which was destroyed by a fire in 1989. The natural environment was represented by 8 images.

Image 5 (figure 2, top left) shows the original natural environment on a sunny summer morning. The house on the left (walls, balconies and roof) and the horizontal water plane were approximated by planar polygons during the preprocessing step. The material tags of the polygons of the house all reference the same opaque dielectric ideally-diffuse reflecting material with a flat reflectance characteristic within the visible spectrum. The image tags of all polygons reference the current input image. Samples on the water plane were used to determine the spectral transparency of the atmosphere (first inversion of the atmospheric model). Samples of various incident illumination were selected on the house and used to determine the relative weights of the components of natural daylight (first inversion of the illumination model). Note the remaining parts of the burned bridge. The supports will be used for the new bridge.

Image 6 (figure 2, top right) shows the new wooden bridge with a tiled roof embedded in the natural environment. Note the specular reflection on the water and the shadow of the artificial bridge cast onto the natural water. The regularity of the reflection is destroyed by a stochastic perturbation added to the local normal vector of the water surface. The new bridge hides the remaining parts of the old one.

Images 7 and 8 (figure 2, bottom left and bottom right, respectively) show an alternative view of the same scene. Except for the parameters which determine the macroscopic roughness of the water surface, the environment descriptions remained unchanged; only the current input image and the corresponding camera parameters were changed.

All images were rendered with a resolution of 512x512 pixels and with anti-aliasing. Image rendering time was between 3.7 and 4.9 CPU hours on a CONVEX-C2 computer for a single image. The geometrical model of the natural and artificial environment consisted of 18 light sources (16 of them due to the discretization of the sky hemisphere) and a total of 440 convex polygons (16 of them from the natural environment description).

Figure 2. Images 5 to 8. From left to right, top to bottom.

Example 2. Courtyard at Rütschistrasse, Zurich

The example shows a study for the redesign of a courtyard at Rütschistrasse, Zurich (project by Architekturwerkstatt Rütschistrasse, Dr. G. Scheibler, Zurich). The idea behind is to enlarge the apartments by expanding the buildings by a 2.5 m thick layer towards the courtyard. The natural environment was represented by 9 images.

Image 9 (figure 3, top left) shows the original natural environment on a winter day with overcast sky. The illumination is therefore completely diffuse and consists of sky light and ambient light only. Parts of the houses and the horizontal ground plane were approximated by planar polygons during the pre-processing step. The material tags of the polygons all reference the same opaque dielectric ideally-diffuse reflecting material with a flat reflectance characteristic within the visible spectrum. The image tags of the polygons reference different input images. The atmospheric effect has not been taken into account. Samples of various incident illumination were selected on the walls of the white house in the corner and used to determine the relative weights of the components of natural daylight (first inversion of the illumination model).

Images 10, 11 and 12 (figure 3, top right, bottom left and bottom right, respectively) show three variants of the projected buildings embedded in the natural environment. Note the specular reflections of natural and artificial objects in the windows. There is a diffuse shadow below the arcades. The somewhat noisy appearance is due to a coarse discretization of the sky hemisphere.

All images were rendered with a resolution of 512x512 pixels and anti-aliasing. Image rendering time was between 2.6 and 3.9 CPU hours on a CONVEX-C2 computer for a single image. The geometrical model of the natural and artificial environment consisted of 5 light sources (4 of them due to the discretization of the sky hemisphere) and a total of convex polygons between 2,695 and 3,349 (16 of them from the natural environment description).

All images in the examples section were rendered using an adaptive sampling strategy. Adaptive sampling involves devoting more time to interesting image regions. Based on the statistical variance of the returned color values, 4 to 16 rays per pixel were used, resulting in an average between 4.03 and 4.48 rays per pixel. Spectral distributions were reduced to a total of 9 spectral samples within the visible spectrum.

Conclusions

The generated images show some of the subtle effects which make up the overall appearance of a building: the three-dimensional shapes and their proportions, the surface textures and colors which are determined by the selected materials, the proportions between brightness and darkness, light and shadow, the integration of the object into its environment with respect to its scale and the materials used, and the effects which are determined by daytime, season, current weather conditions and by the selection of the observer position with respect to fore- and background (Leonhardt 1984).

Once the interactive preprocessing step is completed, case studies can be investigated flexibly by simply changing the artificial environment description and rendering a new image. The rendering parameters allow to trade off speed versus image quality. Therefore, at an early stage of the design process, 'quick looks' can be generated, e.g. at low resolution or by using simpler models. Tabulated physical data is used directly in an extendable library. This frees the user from 'inventing' some fundamental material and light source properties, though some of the coefficients still have to be selected empirically. The rendering algorithm works entirely in object space. It is a straightforward extension of conventional ray-tracing and does not require any changes in the illumination model. Consistency with the models is maintained during the preprocessing and the rendering step. Machines with large main memory allow to keep the whole input image(s) in memory. This speeds up the access of input image data.

Figure 3. Images 9 to 12. From left to right, top to bottom.

Drawbacks are the need for special equipment: a calibrated camera and a machine for fast floating-point calculations. Moreover, it would be highly desirable to replace the interactive pre-processing step by (semi)automatic methods.

Our thanks go to the Institute for Geodesy and Photogrammetry at the ETH Zurich for giving us the permission to use their photographic equipment, to Dr. U. Walder for providing us with the plans of the bridge in example 1 and to Dr. G. Scheibler, the architect of the study in example 2. Finally, we thank the reviewers for their helpful comments.

References

Autodesk. 1988. *AutoCAD 10 Reference Manual*. Appendix C: Drawing Interchange and File Formats.

BD&C. 1990. "Computer graphics facilitate approvals." *Building Design & Construction* 31, no. 7: 16.

Björck, A., and G. Dahlquist. 1979. *Numerische Methoden*. 2. Auflage. München: Oldenburg.

Carpenter, L. 1984. "The A-Buffer, an Antialiased Hidden Surface Method." Proceedings of SIGGRAPH '84: *Computer Graphics* 18, no. 3: 103-108.

CRC Handbook of Chemistry and Physics. 1987. 68th Edition 1987-1988. Florida: CRC-Press.

Ditchburn, R. W. 1976. *Light*. Third Edition. London: Academic Press.

Duff, T. "Compositing 3-D Rendered Images." Proceedings of SIGGRAPH '85: *Computer Graphics* 19, no. 3: 41-43.

Durisch, P. 1991. PhD Dissertation, ETH Zurich (to be published).

Feibush, E. A., M. Levoy, and R. L. Cook. 1980. "Synthetic Texturing Using Digital Filters." Proceedings of SIGGRAPH '80: *Computer Graphics* 14, no. 3: 294-301.

Glassner, A. S. 1989. "How to Derive a Spectrum from an RGB Triplet." *IEEE Computer Graphics & Applications* 9, no. 4: 95-99.

Hall, R. 1989. *Illumination and Color in Computer Generated Imagery*. New York: Springer Verlag.

Jenkins, F. A., and H. E. White. 1976. *Fundamentals of Optics*. Fourth Edition. New York, NY : McGraw-Hill.

Judd, D. B., and G. Wyszecki. 1975. *Color in Business, Science and Industry*. Third Edition. New York, NY: John Wiley & Sons.

Kaneda, K., F. Kato, E. Nakamae, T. Nishita, H. Tanaka, and T. Noguchi. 1989. "Three Dimensional Terrain Modeling and Display for Environmental Assessment." Proceedings of SIGGRAPH '89: *Computer Graphics* 23, no. 3: 207-214.

Kay, T. L., and J. T. Kajiya. 1986. "Ray Tracing Complex Scenes." Proceedings of SIGGRAPH '86: *Computer Graphics* 20, no. 4: 269-278.

Leonhardt, F. 1984. *Brücken, Ästhetik und Gestaltung*. 2. Auflage. Stuttgart: Deutsche Verlags-Anstalt.

Maver, T. W., C. Purdie, and D. Stearn. 1985. "Visual Impact Analysis - Modelling and Viewing the Natural and Built Environment." *Computers & Graphics* 9, no. 2: 117-124.

Mitchell, D. P., and A. N. Netravali. 1988. "Reconstruction Filters in Computer Graphics." Proceedings of SIGGRAPH '88: *Computer Graphics* 22, no. 4: 221-228.

Nakamae, E., K. Harada, and T. Ishizaki. 1986." A Montage Method: The Overlaying of the Computer Generated Images onto a Background Photograph." Proceedings of SIGGRAPH '86: *Computer Graphics* 20, no. 4: 207-214.

Nakamae, E., I. Takao, T. Nishita, and S. Takita. 1989. "Compositing 3D Images with Antialiasing and Various Shading Effects." *IEEE Computer Graphics & Applications* 9, no. 2: 21-29.

Newell, M. E., R. G. Newell, and T. L. Sancha. 1972. "A New Approach to the Shaded Picture Problem". *Proceedings ACM National Conference*, pp. 443-450.

Porter, T., and T. Duff. 1984. "Compositing Digital Images." Proceedings of SIGGRAPH '84: *Computer Graphics* 18, no. 3: 253-259.

Purdue University. 1970. *Thermophysical Properties of Matter*. Thermophysical Properties Research Center.

Sala, A. 1986. *Radiant Properties of Materials*. Physical Sciences Data 21. Warsaw: PWN.

Sutherland, I. E., R. F. Sproull, and R. A. Schumacker. 1974. "A Characterization of Ten Hidden-Surface Algorithms." *Computing Surveys* 6, no. 1: 1-55.

Terzopoulos, D., and A. Witkin. 1988. "Physically Based Models with Rigid and Deformable Components." *IEEE Computer Graphics & Applications* 8, no. 6: 41-51.

Uno, S., and H. Matsuka. 1979. "A General Purpose Graphic System for Computer Aided Design." Proceedings of SIGGRAPH '79: *Computer Graphics* 13, no. 2: 25-32.

Whitted, T. 1980. "An Improved Illumination Model for Shaded Display." *Communications of the ACM* 23, no. 6: 343-349.

35 Creating Architecture Models by Computer-Aided Prototyping

Bernd Streich

Lehr- und Forschungsgebiet
Computergestütztes Entwerfen und Konstruieren
in Raumplanung und Architektur
University of Kaiserslautern
D 6750 Kaiserslautern, Germany

In the future architects or urban planners will probably ask for architectural models based on CAD-generated model data, in addition to the usual graphical representation. A stereolithography process makes this possible. Currently, at the University of Kaiserslautern there is a research project investigating and evaluating possible applications for this technology in the fields of architecture and town planning. The first results of this research project are described in the following article.

Introduction

Since computer-aided design has been established as one of the standard methods in the architectural design process, graphical representations of architectural designs with the aid of computers became very significant. The advantage is quite obvious. Graphical computer output can be easily produced by graphical displays, plotters or printers. But at the same time, architects go on building architecture models by hand this being the standard method to represent their designs. In the past, computers were not used. This situation, however, may be changed as soon as architects have some new methods to complete this open field of computer-aided facilities. In the future many architects or urban planners will probably ask that architectural models be created in addition to the usual graphical representations.

In the early 1970's, we observed the first relevant development in creating physical models of objects constructed from computer data files (Newman/Sproull, p. 299). The use of numerically controlled milling machines was the basis of this technology. Mitchell wrote in 1977 that by "interfacing production machinery with computer graphics systems, a very sophisticated design/production facility can be developed" (Mitchell 1977, p. 372). But this way of building architecture models could not meet architectural requirements. Especially hollow spaces which are an important element of structure in generating architecture models of, for example, the interiors of buildings - can not be realized. As a result, this way of creating architecture models did not gain much in significance in architecture and town planning.

This situation could now change. In the middle of the 1980s, a new technical development was to get attention because architectural applications were made possible, and some important architectural requirements were met. The heart of this new technology is the automatic production of physical forms based on photopolymer plastic together with a laser and a scanner controlled by a computer. As users in the discipline of mechanical engineering are able to create complex form structures, they characterize this process as computer-aided prototyping. The producer of this new tool calls it stereolithography.

If this new technology for creating architecture models by stereolithography becomes more important in the architect's work, two questions are to be answered:

1. Which possibilities for architects will be offered by the stereolithography and which presuppositions in relation to available CAAD-systems have to be met ?
2. Which essential architectural design aspects have to be taken into account and have to be considered critically?

This article gives information about first results of a research work entitled "study of potentialities of the computer-aided prototyping in architecture and urban planning" at the University of Kaiserslautern.

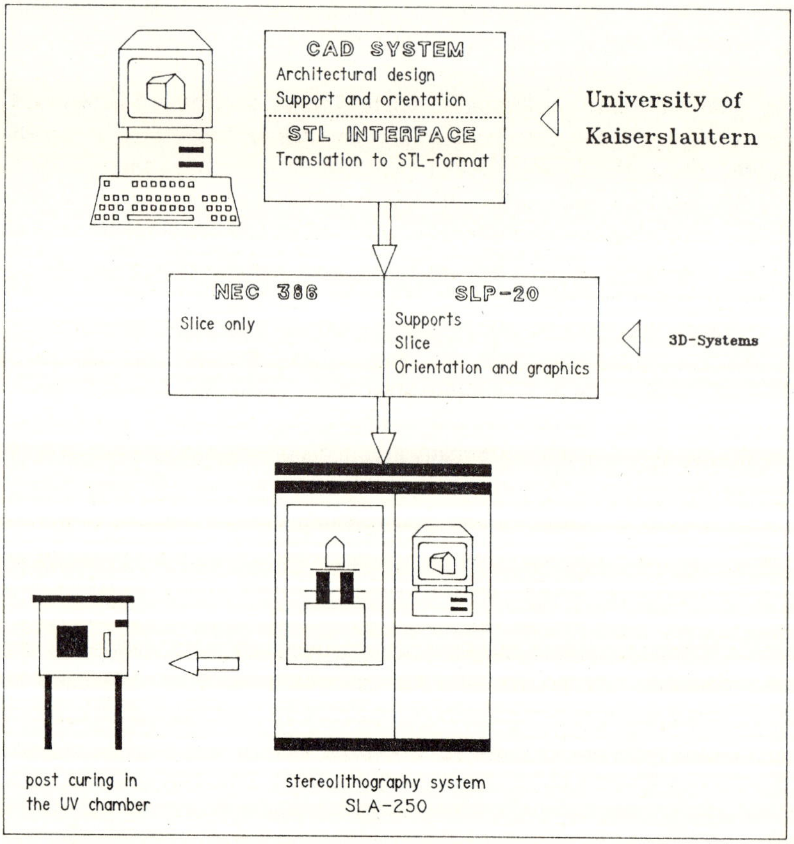

Figure 1. Main components of the stereolithography system and process of creating architecture models.

Technical Features of Computer-Aided Prototyping by Stereolithography

The stereolithography system combines three technologies: computer technology respectively computer-aided design, chemistry of photopolymer, and third, laser technology combined with scanner optics.

The system consists of the following main components (see figure 1):

- a slice-computer, which successively generates horizontal cross sections of the CAD-model layer by layer (slices) and builds a pattern of vectors controlling the x/y-scanner (the z-dimension is realized by a mechanical elevator);
- an ultraviolet helium-cadmium-laser, which is moved across the liquid surface with a mirror controlled x/y-scanner;
- a liquid photopolymer, which changes to solid when the laser with a high selective intensity hits the liquid material;
- a process box, in which the process of polymerization is being executed;
- a post-curing chamber to realize a higher solidity of the plastic material after this process.

The following steps are used to create a model:

First, the user generates an object by his CAD-system. After having generated CAD-data, the data file can be used to build a stereolithography model. Some interface conditions have to be met: first, the model data file has to represent only volumes; second, the surfaces of each volume have to be oriented topologically, so that it is possible to distinguish the volume outside from the volume inside; third, all volume surfaces have to be - under geometrical topic - plane and triangular. How to solve some problems by using exemplary CAAD-systems will be described in the next part of this article.

When the required model data file exists, the computer generates a new data file, a 'slice file', with the pattern of vectors which are representing cross sections of the model. The operator - using a CAD-modul of the stereolithography system - selects and attaches a post-support structure. This structure is built along with the part, holding it to the elevator, and supporting free-standing sections of the part (see figure 2). This completed CAD model, along with the support construction, is then passed over to the stereolithography unit, and the operator initiates the building program. Normally, after the stereolithography process the model is post-processed with brief exposure to ultraviolet light in the post-curing chamber. Then, the model can be removed from the support structure, ready for further steps of processing.

The exact building process works as follows: first, the support platform, i.e. the elevator, is positioned directly under the surface of the liquid plastic material. Then, the first slice will be hardened by the computer controlled scanner and laser. The laser beams the ultraviolet light in intervals of micro-seconds down to the liquid surface, where a great number of solid 'voxels', one per each laser impulse, develop. Between the light impulses, the laser is swept from one position to the other, so that all voxels form the desired slice at the end. In the next step, the elevator together with the first slice of the model sinks down into the liquid plastic material, so that the next slice can be formed. The measure of down sinking depends on the diameter of the slice, which is adjustable between 0.25 and 0.7 mm. After forming the second slice, the third slice will be generated and so on. So, the model will be built from bottom to top.

Due to the way the photopolymer model is built, sometimes it is necessary to construct a support design. Special model parts, which do not arise from bottom, i.e. from the elevator platform, to the top cannot be constructed without supports. For that reason a fully automatic process is not feasible. In architectural models, for example, support constructions have to be built in the case of hanging ceilings or roof overhangs.

In principle the model complexity only depends on the realizable diameter of the cross sections. The smallest realizable diameter is 0.5 mm, so that very complex model structures can be generated (the absolute minimum wall diameter is the width of the laser beam diameter, approximately 0.25 mm (6). Therefore, it is not only possible to create simple walls, roofs or window openings, but also fine structure elements upon these main objects of architectural design. On the other hand this theoretical possibility is unlikely to be realized because the production of fine structures as volume entities requires much effort.
Another limit of model configuration depends on the dimension of the stereolithography process box, in which the process of polymerization takes place. If the SLA-250 system is used, the size limit for the models will be 250 mm in a cube (a process box with 500 mm in a cube is available, too). Larger models can be produced in single parts or sections put together later.

Additionally, the joins can be filled with liquid photopolymer which solidifies in the post-processing chamber (or in sunlight; this method is useful in repairing model parts which have been broken off the model by carelessness). In architectural applications the joins can be left unfilled, in order to enable the viewer looking inside the buildings to see the order of all the rooms. For this purpose, model buildings will regularly be built storey by storey.

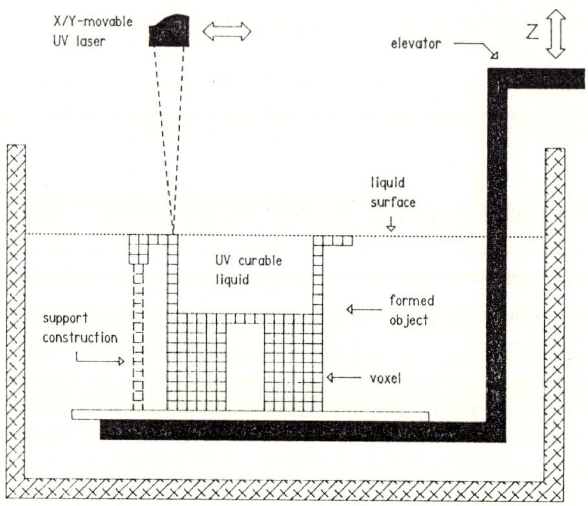

Figure 2. The stereolithography apparatus.

Available CAAD-Systems and Programming Software-Interfaces

The method of building models by computer-aided prototyping has found applications in mechanical engineering in building difficult prototype constructions. Architectural applications are still a great rarity. Up to now, there has not been any evaluation from the point of view of architectural design and questions of aesthetic nature have not been asked either. The reason for this is that the method of stereolithography is still new (first presented in 1987) and very expensive. Nevertheless stereolithography now seems to attract more attention as an important field for fundamental research in architecture.
Three kinds of graphical software systems with different types of model structures are used in the current research project. One is the geographical information system to represent terrain models based on raster data, the other ones are architecturally oriented design systems. If graphical software systems like these are to be applied in stereolithography, some interface conditions with a special data file structure, called STL-format, have to be considered:

- The data files have to represent volumes only; otherwise the computation of cross sections as a fundamental principle of the stereolithography method cannot be realized.
- All volumes must consist of plane surfaces (facets); other shapes are to be approximated to plane surfaces.
- All facets have to be oriented, so that it is possible to distinguish between volume inside and volume outside. The orientation will be realized by the point order of each facet polygon resp. by the direction of the normal vectors; in a right-handed coordinate system the outside surface is determined by a inverse clockwise order of each polygon.
- All these facets have to be exactly three-cornered in such a manner that between two end points of a polygon line a third point along this line must not exist; if necessary new three-cornered facets are to be added (see figure 3).
- All coordinate values have to be positive.

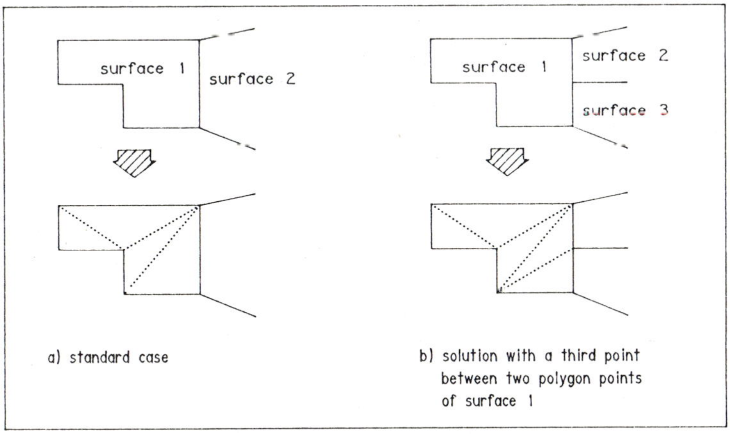

Figure 3. Generating a mesh of three-cornered facets for a polygonal surface.

Some new programs are to be written concerning the last two points especially.

The STL-file needs the following structure writing in C terminology:

```
char header [80];                /* 80 any given characters */
unsigned long NUMFACETS;         /* number of three-cornered facets */

/* next, storing 'NUMFACETS' three-cornered surfaces */

float i, j, k;                   /* components of the normal vector */
float x0, y0, z0;                /* coordinate triple of polygon point P0 */
float x1, y1, z1;                /* coordinate triple of polygon point P1 */
float x2, y2, z2;                /* coordinate triple of polygon point P2 */
unsigned short NUMATTR;          /* number of attribute bytes (not used;
                                 value is seeting to 0) */
```

The following problems in different kinds of graphical software systems have still to be solved:

a) Creating terrain models by using the geographic information system ERDAS

ERDAS belongs to the category of raster oriented geographic information systems. The transformation of raster data in a stereolithography data file is not difficult, so that this geographic information system is very suitable for testing purposes. But the suitability of the stereolithography for creating terrain models as a special field of application has to be verified, too.

The procedure for creating a terrain model from a ERDAS GIS-file and the stereolithography system is as follows:

The x/y-coordinates and the z size (representing the relief variations) of each pixel are known. As each pixel, geometrically, represents an area, and not exactly a point in mathematical mind, first all central points of each pixel will be set as vertices of a square gridded network. Subsequently the transformation in STL-file can start. Remembering the requirements of STL-files, the square grid is to be transformed in a mesh of triangles. For that reason the central point of each grid cell must be calculated, whereby the z value is derived by averaging the z values of the four neighboring grid points of the original network (see figure 4). After this procedure the triangular mesh of the surface relief is ready.

Additionally, a triangular mesh of the four side planes and of the base plane has to be computed. Now the whole terrain model is complete as a volume, ready to build the physical model by stereolithography (see figure 5).

Some further informations may be interesting:

- In a first test a terrain model was planned with a size of 100*100 pixels. Later, a reduction onto 25*25 pixels was done. The reduced model came up to testing purposes.

– The number of triangles was calculated with the following formula:

$$4mn + 2(n + m) - 10,$$

wherein n is the the number of pixels in x direction and m the number of pixels in y direction.

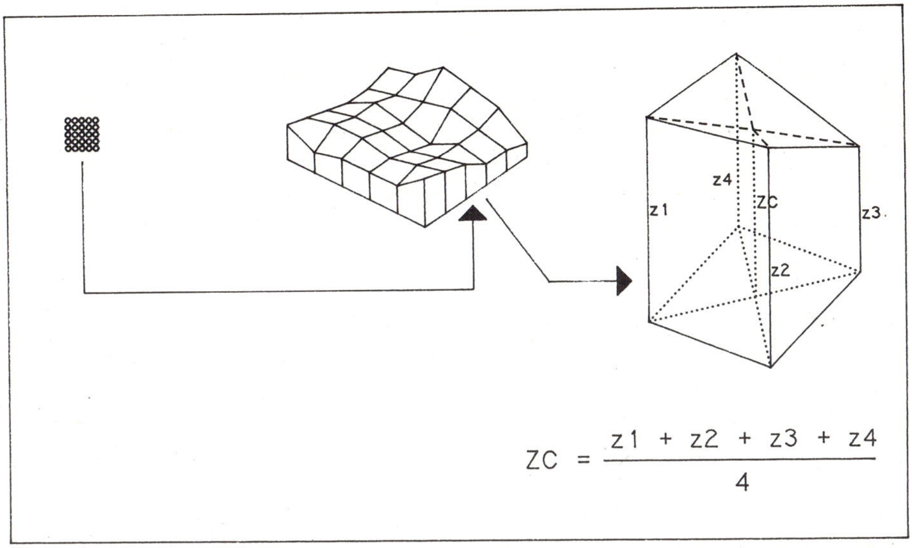

Figure 4. Generating a triangular mesh of a square gridded network based on a raster GIS.

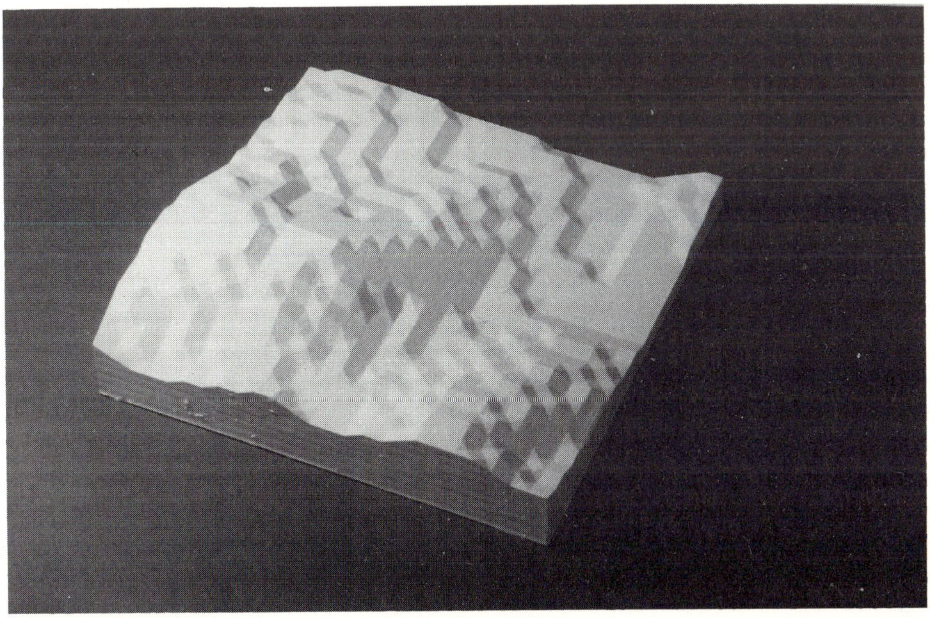

Figure 5. Terrain model generated by stereolithography.

Hence it follows that by using data files within 1000*600 pixels (this value corresponds with usual GIS-maps) nearly 2,400,000 triangles and, with 50 bytes per each triangle, about 120 MB storage capacity is needed. The terrain model in figure 5 only needs about 130 KB as binary file.
- The model size was chosen about 20*20 cm. Each pixel area represents 40 m in reality in scale of 1:5,000.

b) Creating an architecture model by using a quasi volumetric based CAAD-system
As to the structure of data files, the use of stereolithography to create architectural models requires higher qualities than is necessary in the described GIS-system. A minimal condition is the existence of a CAAD-system based on a surface-oriented model structure. But it is better to use a volumetrically based CAAD-system, because the principle of the stereolithography process is volume-oriented, too.

The CAAD-system, which was first used for testing purposes , can be classified as a quasi volumetrically based system. This means, that the most important architectural details like walls, floors and ceilings, generated by user interface, are to be handled as volumes (in the system used all these entities are called "wall elements"; openings are stored as negative wall elements), but in the data file there doesn't exist a corresponding full volumetric storage model. Some architectural entities or design macros (f. e. staircase symbols in a groundplane) are stored as faces. But additionally, in the data files all 'volumes' can be identified by their topological polygon order, which implies the differentiation in volume inside and outside. So, for stereolithography applications, only detached faces are to be deleted (f. e. 2D-symbols; see above). Lastly this has the advantage too, that in the data file all faces of each 'volume' are physically connected. The denotation of volumetric model could only be used if these faces were logically connected in a full volumetric model description, with corresponding file pointers from the data set containing the faces, to the data set containing the volumes.

Unlike the terrain model the technical interest in building architectural models aims at the effective use of the possibilities of hollow spaces as the most important form characteristic of computer-aided prototyping with stereolithography. Therefore, as a first test only a building with outer walls, roof, floor and some openings (windows, door) was constructed. In the next test, the inner walls, inner doors, staircases and some other building details were included, as well. In both cases, Le Corbusier's building in the Weissenhofsiedlung of Stuttgart was modelled.

To create both model versions, the following procedure was used:

After using the CAAD-system to create the data file containing the original quasi volumetric data, this file was transformed into a STL-file as described above. This has the advantage that similarities between the implemented "starbase"-interface of the CAAD-program and the needed STL-format of the stereolithography system can be used. Except for the polygon orientation (see above), the CAAD-system only knows triangles and four sided polygons. All volume surfaces, which have more than four polygon points, will automatically be divided into triangles by the program.

Therefore, the situation in transforming the original data file should not be difficult. But three essential problems have still to be solved by developing new software interfaces:

- It is not sufficient to generate a new diagonal line if a four sided polygon is to be trans formed into STL-format, because this polygon can be concave and the inconsistency of polygon orientations must be corrected (see figure 6).
- It is necessary to analyze all face polygons, if there are polygon points which belong to neighboring polygons. If such points are detected, they have to be included into the current face polygon, too.

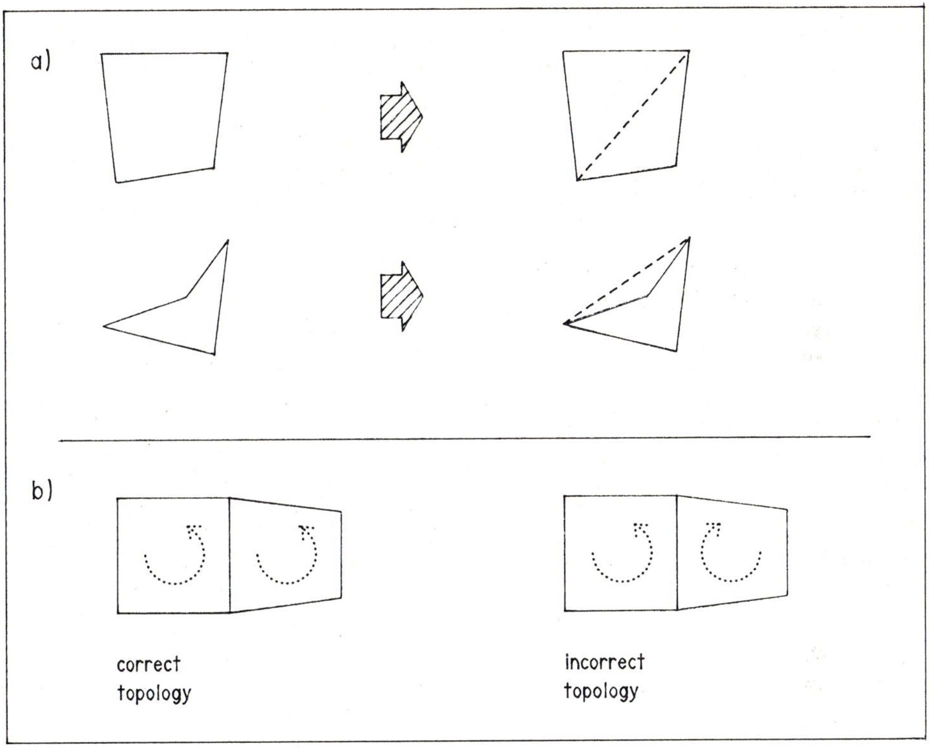

Figure 6. Polygonal conditions on transformation into STL-format: a) generating a diagonal line is not sufficient; b) polygon orientation must be corrected.

- As the polygon orientation of faces describing building openings is always turned contrary to the normal wall faces, the right orientation has to be computed.

If all these conditions comply with a program written in C (150 KB source program), the fully automatic conversion of the original data set in STL-format can start.

Some additional information may be of interest, too:

- The number of faces according the model shown in figure 7 is about 7000 (as mesh of triangles) with 320 KB storage capacity as binary STL-format. The data conversion from original CAD data to STL data format takes 180 minutes execution time using a 486 processor with mathematical co-processor and 25 MHz (a first, non-optimized program

version was executed). The stereolithography process itself takes two days execution time.
- The size of Le Corbusier's Weissenhof building was fixed at 14*9 cm (scale 1:100; maximum scale could be 1:30 using the stereolithography configuration with a process box of 50 cm in a cube).
- Costs range between 10,000 and 15,000 DM.

First the whole building was built in one process; storeys were not produced in single parts. The final model version with more details, inner walls and others can be seen in figure 7 and 8. A pure surface-based CAAD-system will be used, too, although for this much more programming work than for a volumetric model has to be done.

Figure 7. Model of Le Corbusier's building in the Weissenhofsiedlung generated by stereolithography.

Evaluation under Architectural Design Aspects and Possible Implications on Future CAAD Environments

After having discussed the technical features of stereolithography and the solution of problems in programming software-interfaces, now some questions concerning architectural design aspects must be answered. There are two arguments which make such reflections: necessary. Firstly, sometimes the image of stereolithography models has a technical character like a mechanical workpiece; some critical questions about aesthetics cannot be altogether settled. Secondly, in the future, reflections on all developments in CAAD will become more relevant to theoretical presuppositions about architecture (see Mitchell 1990, p. X). Both of these points are connected with the question of possible implications for future CAAD environments.

From the view of architectural design, there are three different aspects, viz. the new procedure for making architecture models, the combination of this technique with graphically oriented CAAD-systems and finally the evaluation from an aesthetic point of view. Other criteria for evaluation, like cost, or needed manpower to work with the system, will not be discussed here. And, of course, the important topic of ecological harmlessness of the photopolymer and the chemical process must be examined, too, but this cannot be cleared up in this paper.

Then follow viewpoints which show the new possibilities of this technique in building architecture models as examples:

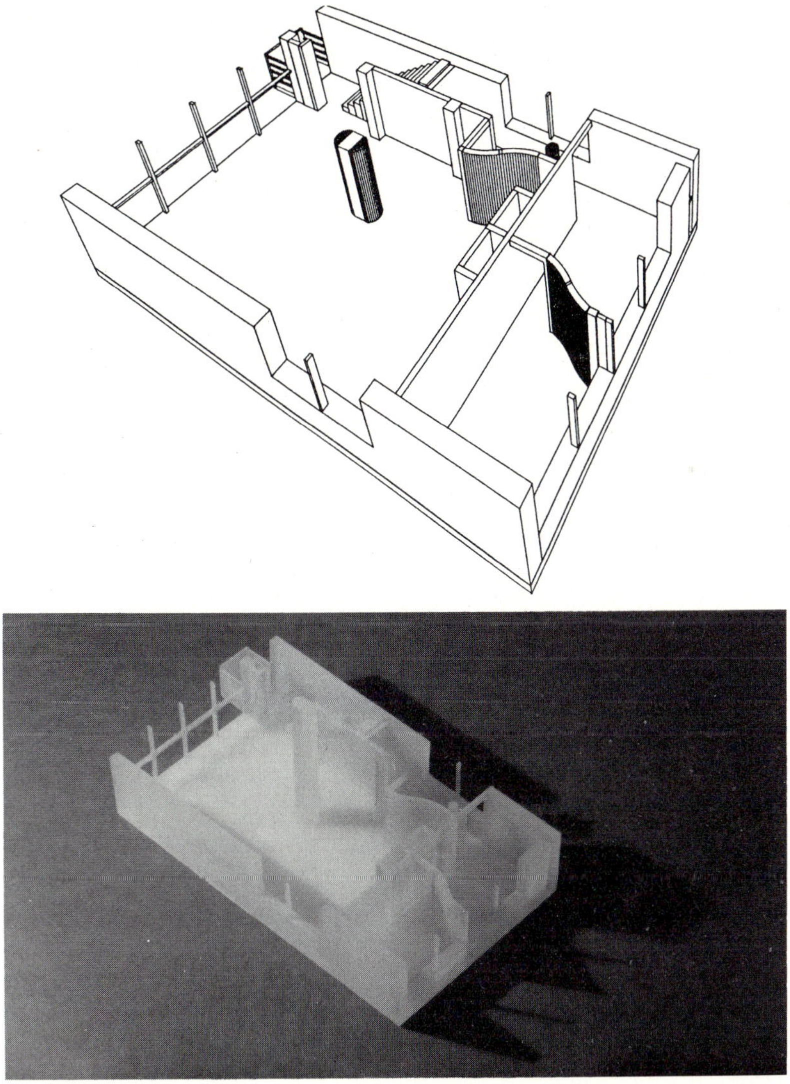

Figure 8. The first storey of the crated architecture model: plotter output and realized model.

- The spectrum of realizable shapes is nearly unlimited. In principle all thinkable shapes, which can be produced traditionally by hand, are feasible by stereolithography. The shapes can be plane, curved or free formed. Volumes can be hollow or not. Openings and holes can be placed at any position. In the inner spaces of hollow volumes further volumes can be constructed. Fine and filigran structures upon the surfaces are realizable. Compared to the stereolithography method, alternative methods, e.g. using milling machines controlled by computers, are significantly limited in form generating. Possible restrictions due to the stereolithographic building process (see above) can be avoided by creating single parts of the model (avoiding roof overhangs by the construction of roofs and assembling the walls separately).

- A combination of solid photopolymer parts together with traditional material, which is usually taken for architectural models is conceivable, too. The model part construction with complicated forms (f. e. architectural surface structures like used by Frei Otto) can quickly be generated by computer-aided design.

- In two ways, the model parts are always generated with precision using this method: first, the method itself has an inherent exactness, because the adjustable thickness of the cross sections which successively generate the model can be chosen at less than 1 mm (see above). The second aspect, however, is more important: the architectural design and its graphical representation together with exact dimensioning can be transformed to a stereolithography model. This procedure is extensively automated, and no manual step is included. Therefore, manipulations are reduced to a minimum.

The most interesting advantage of the stereolithography method for architectural applications is the possibility of combining computer-aided architectural design with the computer-aided construction of architecture models. Architects traditionally use two complementary kinds of design representation: drawings and architecture models. Up to now, only the graphical representation has been supported by computer technology, but not the building of architectural models. This gap has been filled, because now computers are able to generate both kinds of design representation in all the complexity which is needed by an architect:

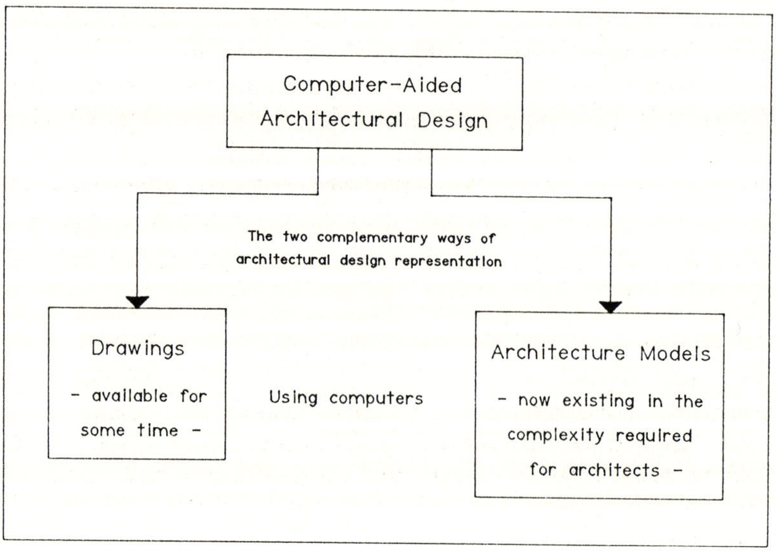

Architects can use design representation by computer generated architecture models in three important domains:
- in architecture design competitions when a quickly generated physical model identical with the CAD data-file and graphics is wanted or needed;
- to support real estate marketing, computer generated models could be a useful vehicle to persuade clients or art committees;
- as an alternative to graphical design representations whenever wanted.

One can imagine that future CAAD-systems may offer these new possibilities: architects will be able to create physical models directly from CAD-generated three-dimensional model data. It will be easy to implement a procedure into the CAD command environment, written in an easy to handle user programming language. User programming language means that the user can expand his CAD-system to any new purpose if desired, such as in building architecture models (well thought out CAAD-programs contain user programming languages; and, of course, there exist some good arguments that architects, who use CAD-systems extensively, should learn programming techniques, too). If no full automatical process is possible, because free-standing sections exist (see above), a few interactive work steps will help; perhaps the development of knowledge-based systems as an integrated component of all powerful CAAD systems may reduce or solve some of these problems in the future. The essential result of all these considerations is that now architects have got a new tool in computer-aided design, beside drawings,which corresponds, to the traditional methods of architectural design representation.

Some aesthetic considerations concerning the actual situation when applying this method are now given:

- The visual image of stereolithography models cannot satisfy all the specific requirements for the aesthetics of architecture models. The color of solid photopolymer varies from yellow to beige and light-brown. It is translucent, but not clear and transparent. If the diameter of volume is chosen near a minimum, the material appears white and more transparent. No other colors can be used. This means that the realizable colors are very restricted, and they have no equivalence to real architectural objects.

- As the photopolymer plastic consists of homogeneous material, no color differentiation for special details, is possible. Therefore, fine or filigran structures cannot be seen well sometimes.

- The surface of the model is rough due to the diameter-adjusted cross sections during the stereolithography process and uneven because there are photopolymer rests upon the model surface (see process of polymerization in figure 2). To remove this roughness, a manual treatment is necessary (normally this must be done every time).

The aesthetic deficiencies will continue to exist for a time. But the situation could change, if this - just four year old - technology develops further. An important topic for architects will be the possibility in choosing different colors which can be realized during (!) the building process. Theoretically in the future the polymer chemistry might help in the following way, the photopolymer molecules would have to have a specific structure which would vary by changing the wavelength of the laser beam. That would be a very promising breakthrough for applications in architecture. But it is also true that development in research for polymer chemistry and laser technology exclusively for architectural/aesthetic purposes is not a realistic proposition without public research funds (architectural applications are too small in commercialization).

Even without more technological progress, manual treatment can be done. In this way, varnishing or the use of illumination effects can improve the visual impression of these architectural models.

Finally, it can be remarked, that on the one hand the possibilities in design making and design representation will be expanded. Many design solutions generated by CAAD can not only be visualized and verified by graphical representation but also by physical models. On the other hand the construction of architectural models as a domain of handicraft might become computerized successively. An analogous development to what has happened in graphical architectural representation might occur. This would be regrettable. As long as this method is only regarded as one new tool beside others, however it is acceptable for architects and their aesthetic pretensions, too.

Conclusions

The present article is about the first results of a research work entitled: "study of potentialities of the computer-aided prototyping in architecture and urban planning". First are the technical features of the new technology, the main components and the process of the stereolithography method have been described. Then some conditions, restrictions and conclusions when using the stereolithography system were discussed. After this some information about available CAAD-systems and programmed software-interfaces were given. Two graphical software systems are used: a geographic information system to create terrain models for urban and regional planning purposes and, secondly a volumetrically based CAAD-system to create three-dimensional architecture models. Tests of interface together with a surface-based CAAD-system are in progress. The final part contains some remarks about aspects of architectural design using computer-aided prototyping and possible implications for future CAAD environments including some critical reflections on these subjects.

The general conclusion is that creating architecture models with computer-aided prototyping is an important field for fundamental research in architecture. Many software interfaces connecting this new technology with diverse other CAAD-systems can be programmed if necessary. Further research seems really promising because this technology is still developing. The next step concerning architectural research will be the evaluation during architectural design competitions. Furthermore its integration in suitable CAAD-systems will occur and some technical improvement in applications for architects and urban planners will probably be instigated.

References

Buchloh, C. 1990. *Steine räumlich denken.* Stereolithographie für den Prototypenbau. *iX* 6.

Dötsch, E. 1989. "Mit Stereo Lithographie Modelle und Teile ohne Form." *Kunststoff-berater* 10.

Mitchell, W. J. 1977. *Computer-Aided Architectural Design.* New York.

Mitchell, W. J. 1990. *The Logic of Architecture. Design, Computation and Cognition.* Cambridge, MA.

Newman, W. M., and R. F. Sproull. 1981. *Principles of Interactive Computer Graphics.* 2nd Edition.

The 3D Systems, Inc. 1989. *Stereo Lithography Interface Specification.* Valencia, CA.

36 The Reconstruction of the Past: the Application of New Techniques for Visualization and Research in Architectural History

Patricia Alkhoven

Department of Architectural History
University of Utrecht
3512 HD Utrecht, The Netherlands

This paper focuses on the visualization of historical architecture. The application of new Computer-Aided-Architectural-Design techniques for visualization on micro computers provides a technique for reconstructing and analyzing architectural objects from the past. The pilot project describes a case study in which the historical transformation of a town will be analyzed by using three-dimensional CAD models in combination with bitmap textures. The transformation of the historic town will be visualized in a space-time computer model in which bitmap textures enable us to display complex and relatively large architectural objects in detail. This three-dimensional descriptive model allows us to survey and analyze the history of architecture in its reconstructed context. It also provides a medium for researching the dynamics of urban management, since new combinations and arrangements with the individual architectural objects can be created. In this way, a new synthesis of the graphic material can reveal typologies and the architectural ordering systems of a town.

The Historical Project

Ever since Aldo Rossi's "The Architecture of the City", interest of architects and historians in the comprehensive analysis of the city has assumed enormous proportions (Rossi 1984). In search of design solutions, the history of the place (locus) and context is once more being taken into account. A successful urban development design presupposes a thorough knowledge of the city, its elements, its history and its dynamics. The city is to be conceived of as a collection of architectural 'facts' which can only be understood through an examination of the historical process.

The complex analysis of the dynamics of urban processes demands a careful examination of the elements which form the city and the forces that work upon it. The elements that constitute the city can be separated in permanent and semi-permanent phenomena. In general, public monuments (church, town hall, etc.) are more or less permanent structures while houses and shops are considered semi-permanent elements, since their appearance is highly dependent on *fashions* in design. In the same way we could view the houses as relatively permanent structures and their facades which are renovated every twenty or thirty years as semi-permanent. The facades and interiors of shops nowadays even change every three to five years.

The image of a city may change as a result of (government) planning and development plans but also through economic factors, restoration or through destruction in wartime. In any of these cases explicit decisions are made concerning the visual appearance. This is what Rossi calls "the problem of the politics of choice" (Rossi 1984).

Studying the history of architecture only makes sense when interpreted from the past to the present. Although we will always view the past with our knowledge of today, we could, to some extent, try to reconstruct past events based on contemporary literature, writings and visual material. The transformation of a city could only be viewed in relation to its past and future. It is not possible to understand the city in autonomous fragments of time, since there are no clean-cut boundaries between two different periods and styles. There will always be a period of transition in which contrasting ideas will overlap. And this is specifically what architectural historians try to examine: the tradition of ideas and their application.

An analysis of the transformation which Paris has undergone over time has recently been carried out by the French group headed by architect-historian Bruno Fortier. His investigation of the development of representational fragments of Paris shows how the city, independent of large-scale planning interventions, organizes itself. In every period the city of Paris would have had a *library of ideas* at its disposal from which design ideas could be chosen (Fortier 1989). Fortier's detailed graphical description, which revealed the different stages of Paris' urban development, was highly attractive and educational. With his research he demonstrated a method to *learn from the past in order to design for the future*. Following the research of Fortier the Italian architect Bernardo Secchi studies the structures, patterns and rules of the dynamics of urban processes in Sienna (Secchi 1989). Both Fortier and Secchi approach their subject much as an archaeologist would do, studying individual elements and rejecting rigid typological and morphological analyses. In order to demonstrate how the city evolved, not only do they use historical maps, but they also integrate information extracted from these maps in their own designs.

We think, following the historical research of Fortier and Secchi, that a detailed visual description of the architectural achievements of the past could, besides acquiring a better understanding of that past, possibly help us to draw conclusions from it for the future. The difference between their research and our project is, that we will use computer-aided-design techniques in order to decompose and analyze the *opaque presence* (Porphyrios 1980) of the city and to survey its *library of ideas* and the choices made in urban management.

The Application of CAAD to Historical Research

The few projects in which CAAD has been used to visualize or analyze historical architecture concentrate on the *ideal city*, its purpose being in most cases educational (Pelt and Seebohm 1990). There is nothing to be said against studying the conventional images of The Greek City, The Renaissance City or The Baroque City, but the fact remains that cities never exist in that ideal form. A city is always a synthesis of different architectural styles, a collage of different forms which have come down to us through the ages.

Architectural historians who study *real* architecture, work with imperfect, heterogeneous and often incomplete material when studying the transformation of a city. By studying very precisely the subtle transformation over time it is possible to trace the agents and forces that have produced the image of the city. In many cases we have a general knowledge of the choices made in urban management but the most difficult problem is to detect the real underlying *politics of choice*. For this, detailed examination is needed. This examination will not gain much by studying the major monuments of our cultural heritage, because the major monuments are permanent elements. They function as *landmarks* in the city and the city is often recognized solely on the basis of those monuments (Lynch 1960). The real organization of the city, however, has been performed by the more vernacular (semi-permanent) architecture from which we can *read* the subtle transition in styles and ideas.

The problem of the *computability of history* with respect to research into real cities has hardly been touched upon, with the possible exception of a study named "Messina 1908, The Invisible City" in which a library of three dimensional elements formed the basis for the reconstruction of a destroyed city (De Cola et al. 1990). The problems involved in the visualization of historical architecture and in using CAAD as an analyzing tool seem to be similar to those encountered in the field of design, namely the enormous amount of computer memory required to deal with large numbers of details.

Researching the Changing Image of the City: a Case Study

This case study describes the first stages of a research project concerning the urban development, the structure of the street pattern and the exterior of the building blocks of Heusden, a small fortified town in the Netherlands. The historical transformation of this town is studied by using three-dimensional computer models in combination with bitmap textures in which all aspects of restoration and renovation as well as urban management can be analyzed. The transformation of the architectural object within its urban context will be analyzed in a *space-time computer model*.

The town of Heusden was chosen for a case study because its architectural image has changed several times in the twentieth century. Heusden was fortified in the sixteenth and seventeenth centuries by a fortification system modern for its time, and during the Dutch Golden Age (17th century) it was a famous garrison town. Due to economic factors and the departure of the garrison, Heusden's prosperity came to an end in the nineteenth century. In 1904 the old town harbor was filled in and turned into public gardens. At the end of World War II a part of the town was destroyed, including the town hall and part of the church. During the Reconstruction period after the war (1945 - 1965), a new town hall was built and plans were made to dig out the fortifications and to build blocks of flats on the outskirts of the town. The plans were never realized. Instead of these plans a radical restoration plan was adopted involving repair of the fortifications, reconstruction of the historical street structure and restoration of the old style of building. The town harbor was re-excavated. During this restoration an old map by J. Blaeu (1649) had great influence on the realization of the reconstructed seventeenth century image of Heusden.

Although the initial idea of the project was to research only the urban development in the twentieth century, it soon became evident that the seventeenth-century map by Blaeu should serve as a reference in order to properly understand the transformation process of the urban morphology.

Methodology

We formulated some starting points for this project. We would use commercial CAD and rendering software for micro computers. As far as the computer models are concerned, the landscape would only be modelled at a very abstract level. Except the water level of the town harbor and the fortifications, the terrain would not be modelled and, as a consequence, all the houses would be modelled on the same level. Since the computer models are research models, photo realistic rendering was not an issue. Rendering would only be used to a limited extent to clarify some ambiguous elements or to make the image a little more realistic. Important factors for this project were the three-dimensional urban structure and information about the facades and the houses. Of less importance were the wall treatment (texture), pavement, vegetation and realistic coloring. Colors would be used either as symbols or to separate functions.

These starting points imply that it is not important HOW an architectural object is being visualized (realistically, idealistically or fictitious) but WHY it is being represented in the computer model. In fact, a well defined argument WHY we choose to pay attention to an object strictly determines HOW the object must be represented. Similarly, the level of detail is strongly dependent on what purpose the computer model will serve. The distance from which the model is to be viewed is a determinant of how detailed the model must be. When one is analyzing a three-dimensional structure of a complete town, details do not have to be displayed. When displaying a small block of houses, details do need to be visualized in the model. Decisions concerning data input are therefore very important and also strictly define the subject to be studied. Further, one has to keep in mind that the desired quality of the results must always justify the time spent obtaining them.

The interpretation of the visual sources is one of the main problems in architectural history. The most reliable information can be drawn from an existing building but in most cases historical buildings have been (partly) destroyed or lost and we then have to rely on drawings and pictures, etc. The problem with historic drawings is that they have not always been carefully carried out, they are often idealizations and differ from the reality as built because changes were made during the building process. Thus, the reliability of drawings and the conventions of depiction used in them have to be carefully analyzed.

Every drawing is an abstraction from reality. Through the ages different conventions of depiction and representation have evolved. A set of traditional visual codes made patterns or types of houses visible in drawings. In the course of time these codes were repeatedly replaced by other codes. In order to detect different patterns the sets of visual codes were all necessary extractions from the real objects (Mitchell 1990). An unavoidable consequence of this process of abstraction is the loss of information (Davis and Hersh 1986). To the architectural historian such loss of information seems to be inexcusable. We, on the contrary, think that the process of abstraction and decomposition can offer knowledge in return about the composition and synthesis of an object (Alkhoven 1989 a+b). Abstraction allows us to ignore unnecessary details so that the essential elements of an object become apparent.

The examination of an architectural object requires us to have knowledge about its structure, visual representation and abstraction before we can draw inferences. During the process of decomposition decisions can be made about which elements are important for the project and which elements can be left out.

Once a satisfying abstract visual description of every object has been obtained, the transformation over time can be analyzed. After the analysis, new syntheses or combinations with the individual architectural elements can reveal new patterns and types.

The three-dimensional model shows the architectural object in its context. For every time-phase one model will be made. The conventional but most instructive way to show the development over time is juxtaposition of the phases from the same viewpoint. The other possibility is animation by time-sequencing. For the time being we have chosen juxtaposition. The new synthesis shows different combinations of the facades in two-dimensional models.

In connection with this project, several questions can be formulated with respect to the application of CAAD and visualization techniques to architectural historical research. How useful is CAAD in this kind of research and what is the extra information we can extract from computer visualization? How can the method of analysis and new synthesis help us to understand the political choices made in the field of restoration? Could this project have been carried out in the conventional way?

Reconnaissance

Before defining the final planning of the project we decided to carry out experiments on some houses at the Fishmarket in Heusden to study the level of detail and abstraction needed for the project. At the same time we would test the development over time with *time-coordinates*. With time-coordinates it is possible to show the changing form of a building or town over a certain period of time. Every phase is stored with a time-code while the whole development is stored in a single file. Running the file from Time 1 to End shows an image by image animation of the development of the object. We used a simple surface modeler (Axis) that involved the use of time-coordinates. Cadastral maps 1:1000 were digitized, and the houses with the details (windows, doors) drawn on the planes were stored with the first phase time-code, i.e. the phase 1943. Based on pictures and drawings, etc., we entered the changes made in the following decades in the same file, defining the new time-code for every object. During the twentieth century four different phases of development emerged.

Juxtaposition of the four phases shows that the appearance of nineteenth century elevations had changed into a Dutch seventeenth century style of building with several mullions in the window-frames. In figure 1 it can be seen how the heterogeneous graphical sources can be normalized and integrated into a single computer model. Though only those elements that served the purposes of the project were represented, the model is sufficiently detailed to explain the transformation of the houses. Although we were fairly satisfied with the result, the drawing of all the details on the planes required much time and computer memory and, more importantly, changing the details for every period was not as easy as we thought it would be. Experiments with the latest rendering software in which scanned or painted facades (bitmap-textures) were projected onto the planes turned out to work much better. We therefore abandoned the technique of using time-coordinates and instead we organized the transformation process in *layers of time*.

Figure 1. Juxtaposition of the four phases of the Fishmarket development. 1943; 1968; 1976 and 1990. Perspective of the Fishmarket.

Now, the project could be carefully planned in distinct work phases:

1. Data acquisition (topological maps, military maps, postcards, drawings, designs, paintings, engravings, texts, etc.)
2. Analyzing the conventions and reliability of a certain number of old maps and making a three-dimensional reconstruction of the map by Blaeu (1649).
3. Replacing the abstract and idealized picture given by Blaeu by more realistic images.
4. Reconstructing the transformation of the town in layers of time: 1900, 1943, 1990 (three-dimensional descriptive model).

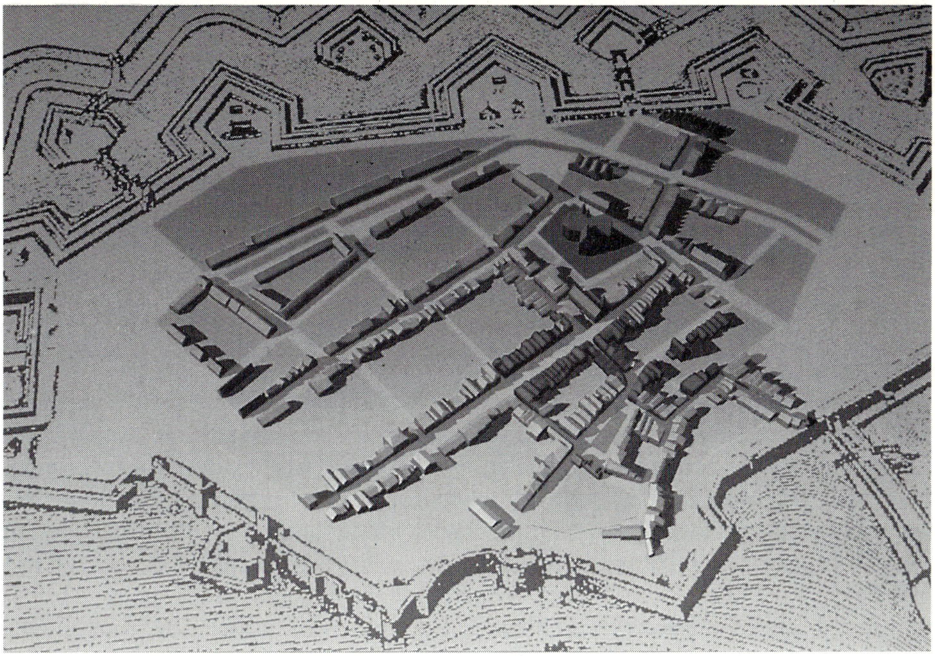

Figure 2. Scanned map (1649) combined with three-dimensional model (1965).

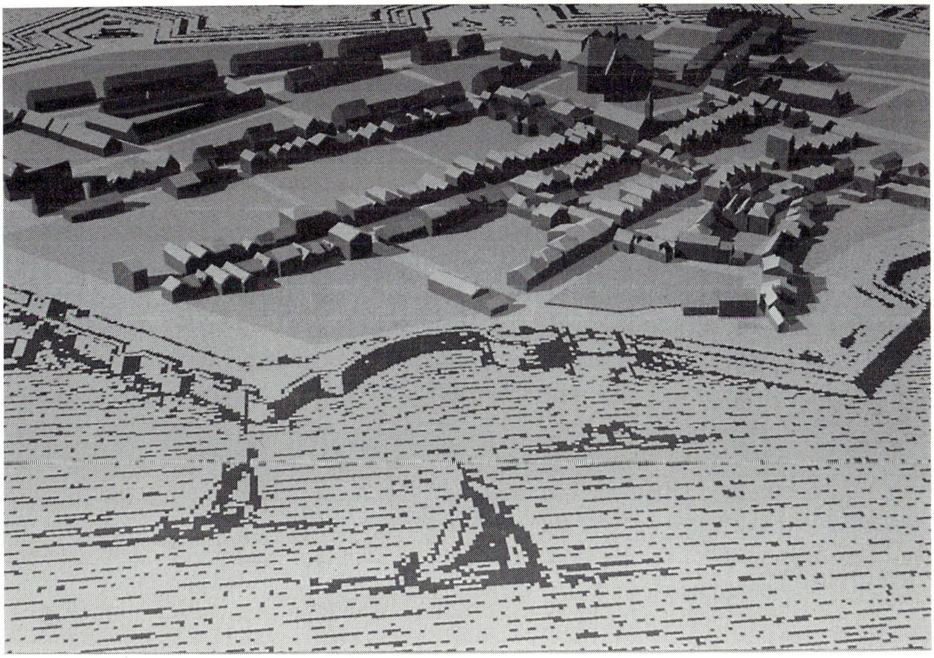

Figure 3. Scanned map (1649) combined with three-dimensional model (1965).

5. analyzing the choices made in urban management by ordering the visual material in new combinations (new synthesis).

The first step was to collect the visual material to build the computer models. We needed cadastral maps with accurate measurements and drawings from which we could derive the relative dimensions. Further, we needed aerial photographs for the roofs, and any material from which we could derive visual information about the facades and the other elevations. An extensive collection of postcards and photographs produced at the turn of the century provided the basis for that part of the development. In 1943 all the street walls in Heusden were carefully measured and recorded in a complete set of detailed designs which included almost every single house. These designs formed a good basis for tracing the history back to 1900 and plotting developments into the future. From the last thirty years an enormous amount of information was available.

Since the map depicted by Blaeu in the Townbook of the Netherlands (1649) had played an important role in the realization of the recent restoration, the next step was to analyze the map's conventions of depiction and abstraction. To find out to what extent reliable information could be drawn from this map, we made a two-dimensional computer projection of the outlines of the building blocks and the fortifications of both the map by Blaeu and a recent map. From this projection it became apparent that there was a discrepancy between the two maps which caused a difference of about 15 degrees in the direction of the streets. The old map was also elongated in a downward direction. The streets were depicted too wide and the perspective was probably chosen in order to show the town to its best advantage. By scanning a part of the old map and combining this bitmap image with a three-dimensional model of the town of 1965, it became even clearer how the town plan had been manipulated in the old map, although, in general, the old gates still connect to the modern street pattern (fig. 2 - 3). An explanation for this could be that Blaeu had a contemporary military map of the fortifications at his disposal in which the town plan was drawn in afterwards.

The Reconstruction of the Map by Blaeu (1649)

When the map by Blaeu was compared with contemporary and later images, the basic forms of the houses seemed to have been represented quite correctly. The facades and the arrangement of the windows and doors, however, were standardized. We investigated these abstract facades which resulted in a typology. It consisted of about 15 types, which had different heights and widths. Following contemporary drawings and prints, it was possible to trace the possible variety of the facades and analyze it in terms of the typology.

First, the computerized map was visualized exactly following the depiction by Blaeu. There were several considerations underlying the decision to visualize the map. Based on the new technology in rendering and the typology we believed it would be relatively easy to make a computer model. The visualization would represent the idealized appearance of Heusden's Golden Age and would be subjected to further analysis. The second step would be to rescale the computer model and to replace the idealized representation by Blaeu by a more realistic view based on visual and written information about the houses.

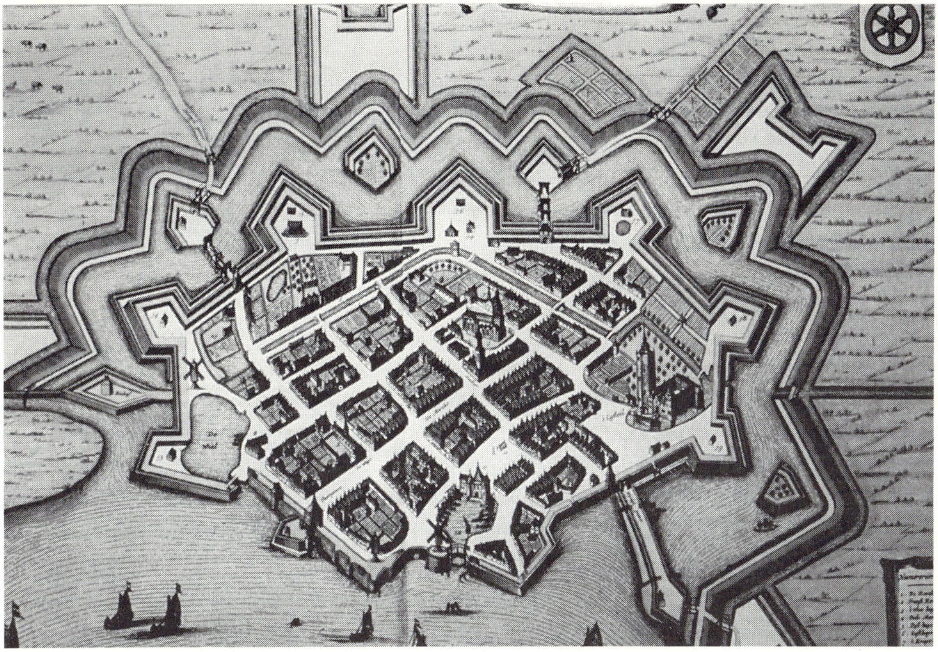

Figure 4. The Map by Blaeu from the Townbooks of the Netherlands (1649).

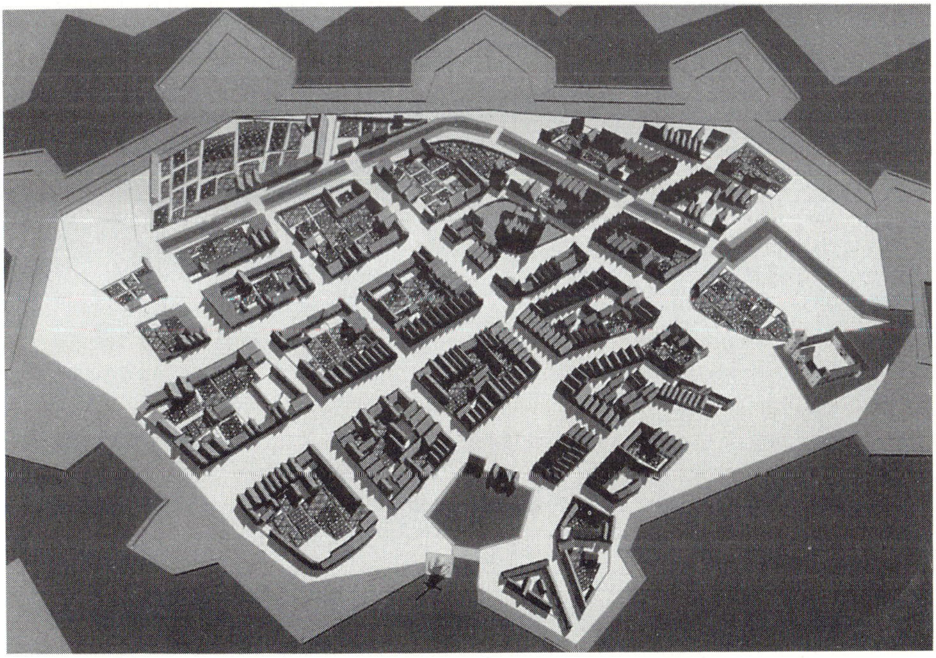

Figure 5. Three-dimensional computer visualization of the map by Blaeu.

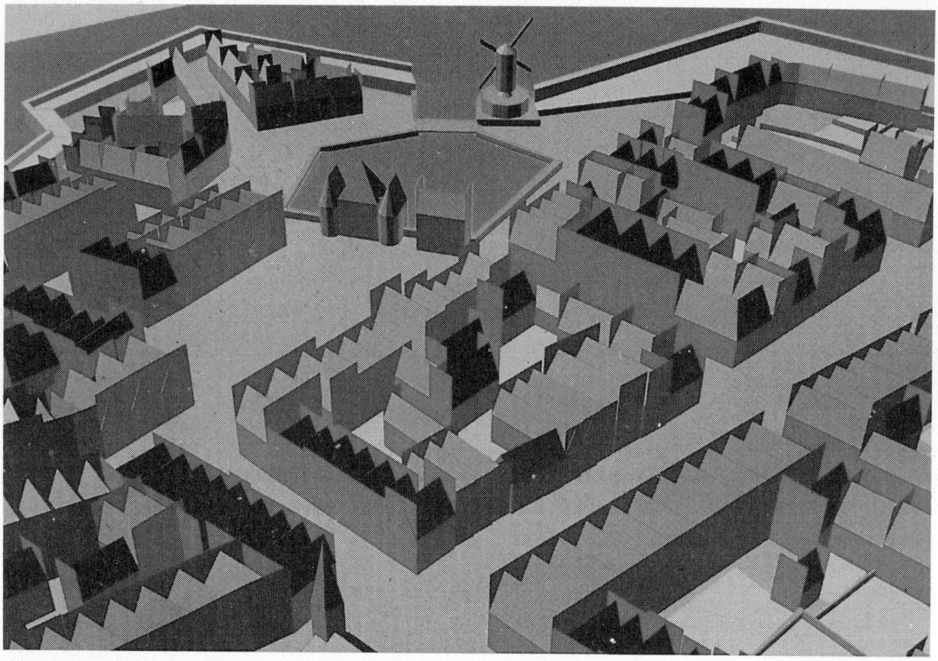

Figure 6. The basic model without effects and bitmap textures.

Figure 7. Perspective with effects and bitmap textures switched on.

The old map was digitized and scaled to 1:1000. Since there were almost no contemporary measurements of the houses available, we had to rely on the relative dimensions from the map. Every house in the model consisted of four sides and a roof and two vertical planes for the top-roofs. A bitmap texture of every facade type was painted in Autodesk Animator. By assigning a color number to a texture map a texture library for the project was set up. Every plane in the model was assigned a color number which corresponded to the color number of the texture. The ratio of the texture maps and the plane on which it was projected should match. The rendering software (RenderStar2) linked the textures to the planes in the model. The vertical planes on which the top-roofs were projected were not completely used by the textures of the stepped gables. The unused parts were rendered transparent so that the real stepped gables became visible, even from the other side. Thus, instead of building the facades in three dimensions, a screen of painted facades was put in front of the volumes of the houses. The advantage of this *scenographical architecture* is that the appearance of the facades can easily be changed by assigning new color numbers.

At that stage the reconstruction was actually finished. All the houses could be viewed from all sides but the real *landmarks* of the town (church, castle, townhall, fishmarket and mills) were missing. Without these elements the town seemed dead and for many people unrecognizable. So much so that when the real research-model was finished we decided to do some additional work to make the town look more realistic. Apart from the above mentioned landmarks, we designed the gardens and did some work on the fortifications. Because it was not our intention to create beautiful pictures we only refined the images to an acceptable extent (fig. 4 - 7).

The second step was to rescale part of this model following the cadastral map of 1832 (the first map with precise measurements) and to *repaint* the facades about which we could find visual information. As for the other houses, we continued our research in literature and we looked for paintings of seventeenth-century houses. Basing ourselves on this visual material, we *created* three different types of seventeenth-century houses from which bitmap textures were painted. Actually, here one could speak of the replacement of one abstract pattern by another abstract pattern. Then the planes in the model were assigned new color numbers and the image was rendered. Now the facades could be viewed from a closer point of view, since the repainted facades were much more detailed. The rigid severeness of Blaeu's map had been replaced by a more dynamic picture (fig. 8).

Three-dimensional Descriptive Computer Model

From both the map by Blaeu and the remodelled map we could derive the old structure of the town and houses. That information was useful for the time-model 1900 - 1990 which we were about to build. We decided not to visualize the period between 1650 and 1900, since the main lay-out of the town hardly changed until 1904 when the town-harbour was filled in. In general, the appearance of the houses had followed the standard Dutch architectural styles. Most of the stepped gables were replaced during the eighteenth century by cornice-facades and the windows were filled in with larger surfaces of glass.

We had to divide the town plan up into eight parts which we would study successively, since the hardware could only handle part of the data at a time. When all the parts will have been analyzed they will be merged into a single model. We will discuss here the first part that has been finished: the Fishmarket and the town harbor neighborhood.

The cadastral map of 1900, plans from 1943, 1965 and 1990 showing the outlines of the fortifications and the building blocks as well as the lots were digitized. We started by building the Fishmarket model of 1943, since we had a complete set of information at our disposal. With the data of the exact width and height of the facades and the depth of the lots we could easily build a correct three-dimensional model.

The transformation of every house was investigated and a scheme was designed displaying the image of every house in the researched periods, the dimensions of the facade and its color number. This scheme was used as a reference while building the model and connecting the textures. The method we used was the same as the visualization of the old map. Instead of using the typology, the more probable image of the facades of every single house on the Fishmarket (as recorded in the scheme) was painted in Autodesk Animator. These bitmap textures were connected to the planes in the model. After the 1943 phase the other *layers of time* were modelled in the same way. Viewing the phases one after the other, a kind of animation showed the whole transformation over time (fig. 9 - 11).

This descriptive model provides information about the plan, the three-dimensional structure of the houses and about the appearance of the facades in different periods. One can see how the Fishmarket area has developed over time by examining the models from the same viewpoint. However educational the models might be, the static viewpoint of a three-dimensional model does not allow us to get a clear picture of the development of every house at the same time. Further, the three-dimensional descriptive model does not explain how and why the houses were changed, which houses were reconstructed or what the dynamics of urban management had been.

New Syntheses

In order to solve this problem we needed to build new models in which the individual architectural elements were detached from their context. Using the bitmap textures, we were able to create several combinations with them: houses or facades of the 17th, 18th, 19th and 20th centuries; buildings of historical importance; the restored buildings in chronological order (1965 - 1990) and buildings restored by architects. We had chosen these combinations because we thought that each of these combinations would reveal to us aspects of the choices made by the local government or by architects involved about how the town should look like.

Although only a small part of the town had been involved so far, some conclusions could be drawn from these two-dimensional models. The period 1900 - 1943 shows mostly ad-hoc interventions. Some houses were built in contemporary style (Jugendstil) between 1905 - 1915. Many shops were renovated with display windows. After World War II the houses that were destroyed during the war were in most cases rebuilt the way they were.

Figure 8. Heusden's Fishmarket as it might have looked like in the seventeenth century.

Figure 9. Three-dimensional model showing the Fishmarket in 1900.

Figure 10. Three-dimensional model showing the Fishmarket in 1943.

Figure 11. Three-dimensional model showing the Fishmarket in 1990.

The real changes in the image of the town started with the 1965 Development Plan on the basis of which almost every single house in Heusden was renovated or reconstructed. The Development Plan itself was based on the spatial structure as can be seen on the map by Blaeu. In general, the spatial structure of the houses did not change much, since the old structure was still intact. The transformation of the image of the city can best be seen in the treatment of the facades.

Most attention seemed to be given to houses that originated in the seventeenth century and the houses that were assigned as public monuments. It is striking that almost without exception these houses were reconstructed in a Dutch seventeenth century style, though not all the stepped gables were rebuilt. Some seventeenth century houses that had had their facades renovated in the eighteenth or nineteenth centuries, were now reconstructed in a Dutch seventeenth-century style with mullions in the window frames. There is another example which confirms a preference for the image of seventeenth-century (or early eighteenth-century) architecture. In the windows of a mid-nineteenth century mansion mullions divided the window into thirty-five lights, as would have been done in the late seventeenth century or at the beginning of the eighteenth century. The building looks even older than it originally was (fig.12 - 13).

Buildings from the beginning of this century (Jugendstil) were in most cases demolished and replaced by types or abstractions of buildings that existed at the same place before. The houses that were not reconstructed in seventeenth-century style, were mostly restored following the image of the 1900 postcards. The new synthesis of the restored buildings in chronological order demonstrate that buildings were more radically reconstructed in the beginning of the restoration (probably because there was more money available for restoration work) than in the later period. The architects involved also had great influence on the transformation of the facades. Some architects had chosen to reconstruct the seventeenth-century (or early eighteenth-century) image or to use the 1900 postcards as their guides, others maintained the main appearance of the facades while using modern elements in addition.

The above described project has not yet been concluded. In the near future, the other parts of the town will be visualized in order to analyze their transformation over time. Some of the formulated questions can only be properly answered after the whole town has been visualized and analyzed.

Now that we are at the end of the description of this pilot project we must answer the question about whether or not this project could have been carried out in the conventional way. The models displaying the new synthesis are very simple and could have been drawn by hand, but it would have taken very long (we analyzed about twenty models!). In spite of the fact that it might indeed be possible to do this in the traditional way, we think that computer models are much more flexible and easy to manipulate. The data can easily be changed or reordered. In this way every possibility and combination can be explored. From the new synthesis direct visual proof can be derived about how the town has changed. From the educational point of view the models displaying the new synthesis do not look very attractive. We therefore think that there should be two different ways of using the computer models: one in which only the essential elements are displayed which serve the research-project (new synthesis) and one which is rendered more realistically for showing to the public (three-dimensional model).

Conclusions

The application of CAAD and visualization techniques in architectural historical research provides a method for analyzing the transformation of historical architecture and the dynamics of urban management. Although this project could have been carried out in the conventional way, i.e. with or without making drawings by hand, computer visualization seems very useful in normalizing heterogeneous graphic material. The process of extracting information from the opaque presence of the architectural sources produces detailed knowledge of the object under study. A computer visualization demonstrates direct visual feedback and proof of the analysis. Further, the reconstruction of the seventeenth-century map appeared very useful in analyzing some cartographic conventions and typologies which so far had been obscure. From the project described above one can conclude that the results are highly dependent on detailed delimitation of the boundaries of a project and on argumentation regarding the choices for every step taken. The combination of three-dimensional models and texture maps opens the possibility to manipulate relatively detailed architectural objects in a flexible way. They also enable us to apply two levels of abstraction. A three-dimensional model, which is visually very attractive and instructive, describes the architectural object in its context. The new synthesis, however, serves as a research model displaying the isolated architectural objects in different combinations. This makes the synthesis very flexible but less educational. Although the educational value of abstract hidden-line images might be sufficient to support the research project, more realistically rendered images seem to heighten the sense of *the town coming alive*.

Figure 12. Buildings of historical importance. 1900, 1943 and 1990.

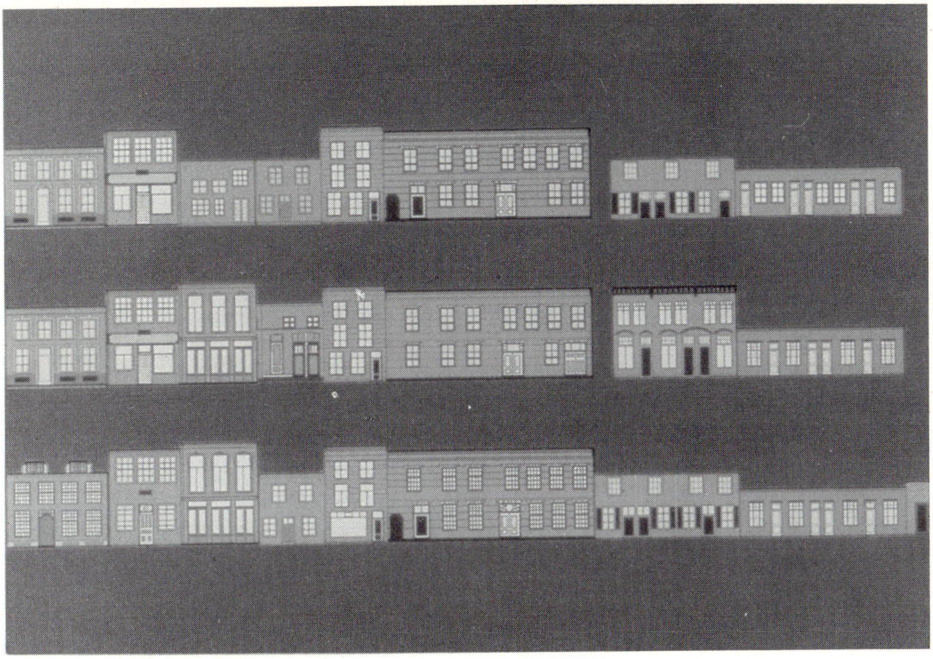

Figure 13. Some buildings restored by the architect Peetoom.

Technical Notes:
Hardware: 33 Mhz. 386/387, 10 MB., 1024x768 in 256 colors. Software: Axis, RenderStar2, AutoCad (release 10), Autodesk Animator. The final pictures were calculated at the resolution of 4096x2732 and processed by a digital slide recorder.

Acknowledgements

The author would like to acknowledge the technical assistance of the research and development department of Modern Medium, Amsterdam (NL). Most of the software used in this project (Axis, RenderStar2) has been developed by Modern Medium. The software was used whilst still in an experimental stage.

References

Alkhoven, P. 1989a. *Representatie en Abstractie in Architectuur, theorie en geschiedenis van visualisatiemethodes bij architectonische representaties.* (Representation and Abstraction in Architecture, Theory and History of Visualization Methods in Architecture). Masters thesis University of Leyden, the Netherlands.

Alkhoven, P. 1989b. "De Computer als Laboratorium van de Architectuurhistoricus." (The Computer as Laboratory of the Architectural Historian). In *Inleiding in de Beeldverwerking*. Computer & Humanities, University of Utrecht, the Netherlands.

Davis, P.J., and R. Hersh. 1986. *Descartes' Dream.* Harcourt Brace Jovanovich.

De Cola, S., B. De Cola, and F. Pentasuglia. 1990. "Messina 1908, The Invisible City." In M. McCullough, W.J. Mitchell, and P. Purcell (eds.). *The Electronic Design Studio*, Architectural Knowledge and Media in the Computer Age. Cambridge, MA: MIT Press.

Fortier, B. 1989. *La Metropole Imaginaire*. Liege-Bruxelles.

Lynch, K. 1960. *The Image of the City*. Cambridge, MA: MIT Press.

Mitchell, W.J. 1987. *The Art of Computer Graphics Programming*. Van Nostrand Reinhold Company.

Mitchell, W.J. 1990. *The Logic of Architecture*. Cambridge MA: MIT Press.

McCullough, M., W.J. Mitchell, and P. Purcell (eds.). 1990. *The Electronic Design Studio*, Architectural Knowledge and Media in the Computer Age. Cambridge, MA: MIT Press.

Pelt, R.J. van, and T. Seebohm. 1990. "Of Computer Memory and Human Remembrance: History of Urban Form Through Three-Dimensional Computer Modeling." In P. Jordan (ed.). *ACADIA 1990 Proceedings "From Research to Practice"*.

Porphyrios, D. 1981. "On the Methodology of Architectural History." *Architectural Design Profile*.

Rossi, A. 1984. 1966. *The Architecture of the City*. Cambridge, MA: MIT Press.

Secchi, B. 1989. *Un progetto per l'urbanistica*. Turin.

37 Free Hand Plotting Is It Live or Is It Digital?

W. Davis van Bakergem, Gen Obata

Urban Research and Design Center
Washington University
St. Louis, MO 63130, U.S.A.

Free hand plotting is a technique for creating the illusion of hand drawn sketches by means of a CAD system. Utilizing a single pen plotter and altering the holding device, squiggly line drawings can be produced which have a hand made quality and character. In addition, a software technique using postscript can be used to create images that appear to be hand drawn. This paper describes and illustrates both the pen and software techniques for creating these squiggly line drawings. It further proposes several explanations for the unusual viewer response and suggests potential applications.

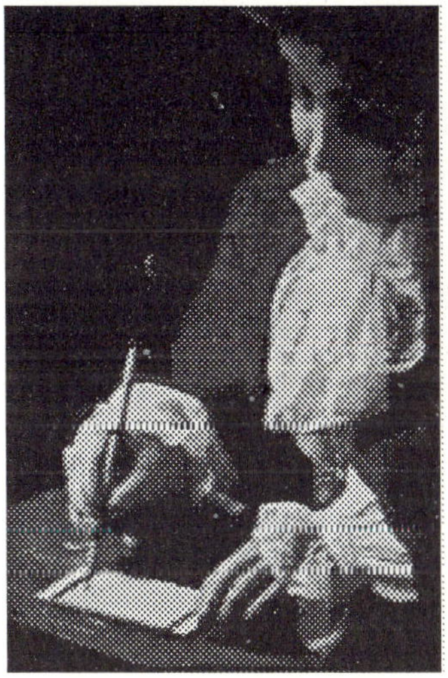

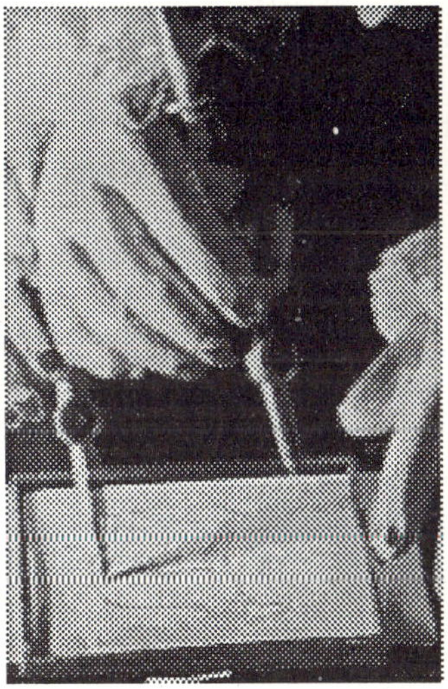

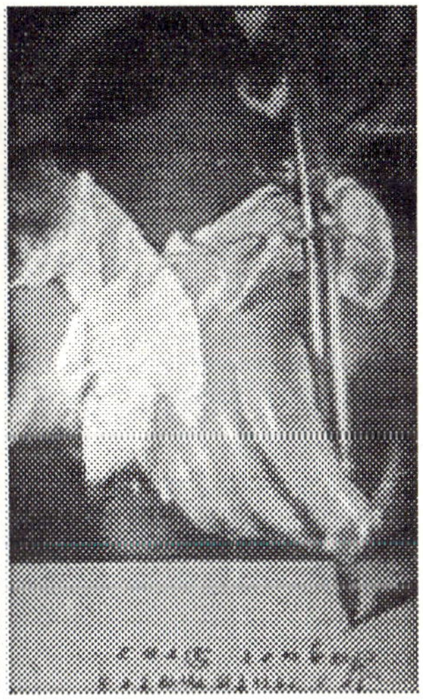

Figure 1. The Draughtsman. **Figure 2.** Draughtsman detail. **Figure 3.** The Writer.

Introduction

The idea of a machine producing a sketch seems like a contradiction. Making a machine behave like a human and produce human-like creations has been an elusive goal for many inventors. Golems, homunculi, androids, automatons, and robots have fascinated us for centuries. Some early efforts in the eighteenth century included a Swiss watchmaker Jaquet-Droz who built several of the first androids which were exhibited in Paris in 1775. The Writer, the Musician and the Draughtsman were three androids which he created that have appeared at various exhibitions throughout the years (see figures 1-3). These early efforts were primarily demonstrations of the capabilities of current technology and typically were displayed in a carnival sideshow-like setting. In many respects they were similar to the illusions created by magicians to thrill the members of royal courts.

More recently, with the development of digital computing, the search for artificial intelligence (arguably an oxymoron) has become a serious topic for research and has profound implications for our future. These high speed, powerful computers have stimulated a debate regarding the ability of computers to think and several have been labeled 'thinking machines'. Once again the capacity of a machine to 'perform' human functions astonishes and amazes the casual observer. The mathematician and logician Alan Turing devised a test to judge whether or not 'intelligence' has been achieved. For example, if a person is communicating through a teletype machine with a computer and through another teletype machine with a human and cannot tell which is which, then some form of artificial intelligence has been realized.

In the realm of computer-aided-design (CAD), the production of drawings was the initial mission of early commercial CAD software and hardware. The mechanical production of working drawings for architectural and engineering applications demanded precision and accuracy, and the 'toolkits' of these systems were analogous to the traditional drafting tools which have been in use for hundreds of years. Plotting hardware was developed with speed, precision and reliability as primary performance criteria and the capacity of these machines to outperform a human draftsman is impressive. It is amusing to see a group of people watching a high speed plotter in action for the first time; they will stare for a long time at the pen racing along the paper — almost as if a ghost were in the machine. Competition in the pen plotter market demanded faster, more precise machines capable of drawing with very fine lines and multiple colors. Engineers of plotters succeeded to the point of vastly surpassing the capabilities of a human draftsman. The drawing quality and character takes on the appearance of having been produced by a "perfect" draftsman. In the architectural profession there is a need for other types of drawings besides precise, dimensioned ones. Architectural drawing types include renderings and sketches which are usually created by a human renderer. More recently, the renderer has been aided by the use of a computer drawing that serves as an underlay which can then be re-sketched and enhanced by hand. In a sense, digital information is being translated into hand-drawn or analog information, receiving the nuances and subtle marks that only a human hand can add. Within this context of machine perfection, a technique was developed at Washington University's Urban Research and Design Center for making the machine produce "sketches" (see figure 4).

Figure 4. Squiggly pen plot.

Technique Described

This new technique was discovered with the help of an obsolete Ioline single pen plotter. The plotter is an Ioline model LP3700 that had been donated to the School by an alumnus; it is slow, noisy and requires operator attention when plotting with more than one pen width or color. One night, having used up all the pens designed for use by the plotter, a cheap drawing pen was jammed into the holder and because the pen was slightly loose, a squiggly line drawing resulted. By using a slow plotter and rigging it to draw imprecise, inaccurate, random lines, the illusion of a machine producing a hand drawn sketch was created. The detachment of the pen from the grip of the plotter introduced deliberate wobble into the pen motion. The pen wobbles, skips and randomly produces a hand-drawn effect (see figures 5-6). Three variables which affect the drawing's character were identified: pen looseness, pen type and pen speed.

Looseness variable. Some degree of wobble control was introduced by devising several types of simple holding devices to allow any pen, pencil, marker, or drawing instrument to be held at varying degrees of looseness. With the aid of three machine screws at the bottom of the holder and three near the top, the pen's looseness may be adjusted to fine tune the wobble in the pen. Further trials in wobble control led to the addition of a metal cylinder with a diameter greater than the pen's barrel diameter. With the cylinder holder, the looseness could be tightly controlled and as well was made relatively consistent. The pen is held in place by a binder clip (see figure 7) which permits the pen to move freely within the metal cylinder. When the plotter lifts the cylinder, the pen follows. The pen's weight is the only pressure on the paper. Several drawings illustrating a variety of pen looseness are displayed on the following pages.

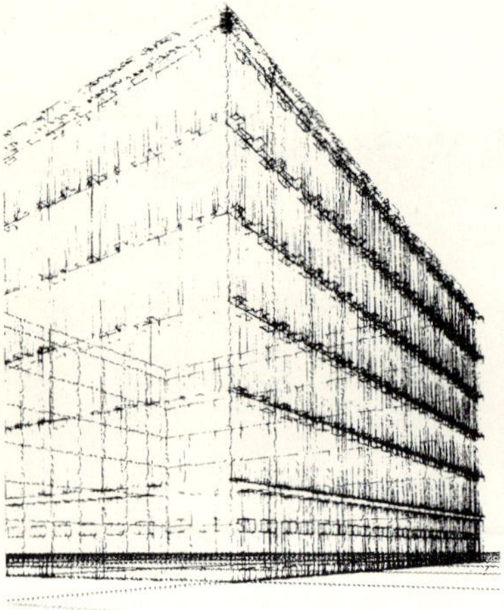

Figure 5. Early Squiggly Line Plot.

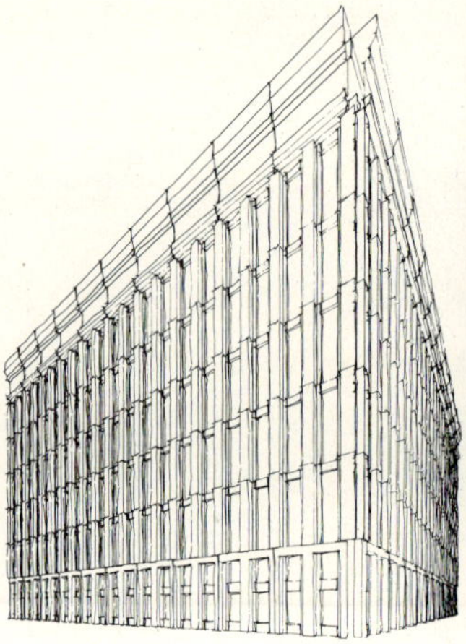

Figure 6. Squiggly Pen Plot.

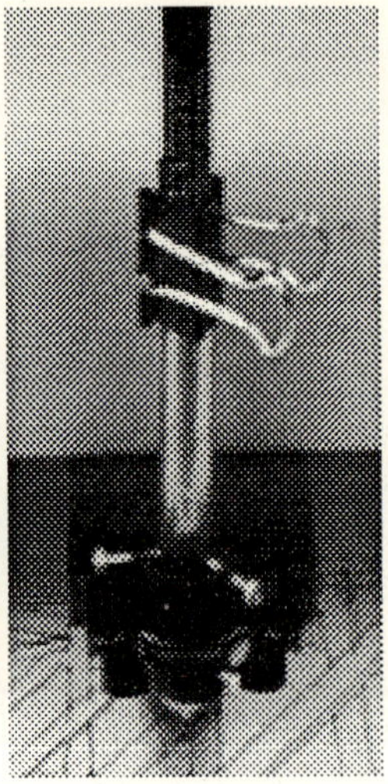

Figure 7. Pen Holder.

Media variable. Since the pen's weight is the only pressure, selecting media with free flowing inks or very soft lead is necessary to achieve sufficient drawing density for legibility. Felt tip markers, pencils, paint markers, charcoal pencils, crayons, and other implements can be used for different effects (see figure 8). Each "pen" and its degree of looseness result in slightly different drawing "styles". The best pen discovered was a PenStix which comes in three line widths and has a tough vinyl nib capable of withstanding the repeating impacts. Since the plotter takes cut sheets of paper, a wide variety of drawing paper, tracing paper, mylar, and even watercolor paper can be used as a drawing surface. One of the most convincing "hand drawn" effects is achieved by plotting on cheap, yellow tracing paper. Since the only pressure is the weight of the pen, the yellow trace does not tear.

Speed variable. The variable of speed of the pen also permits slight variation in the effects created (see figure 9). Control by pen speed is closely related to pen type and especially to the rate of ink flow. A speed of 12 inches per second seems to work for most of the media tested.

Figure 8. Charcoal Plot with hand smudge.

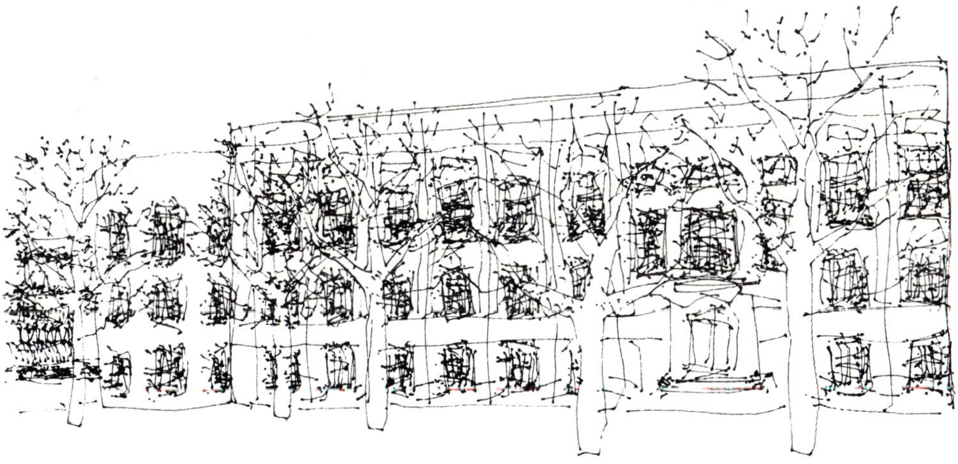

Figure 9. Severe wobble in pen plot.

The result of this trial and error approach to the media (various holding devices, marking pens, speeds and papers) was a surprisingly high level of control in affecting various drawing "styles".

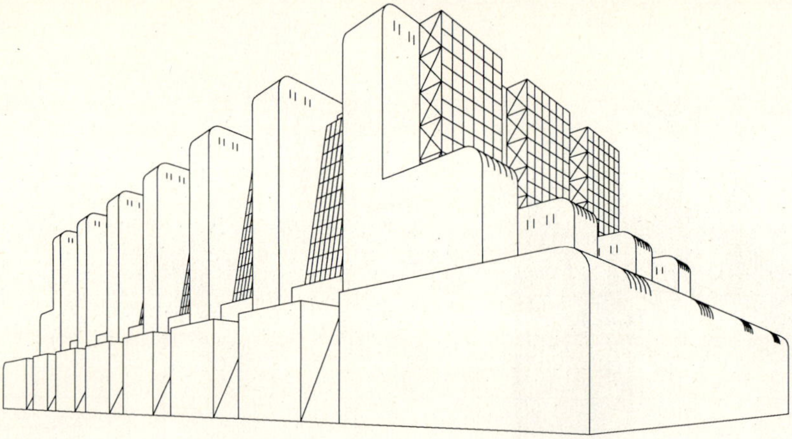

Figure 10. Mendhelson's Labor Hall: laser print.

Figure 11. Squiggly pen plot: mild wobble.

Figure 12. Squiggly pen plot: severe wobble.

Figure 13. Grove of trees: laser plotter.

Figure 14. Grove of trees: squiggly pen plot.

Figure 15. Palm trees: laser plot.

Figure 16. Palm trees: squiggly pen plot.

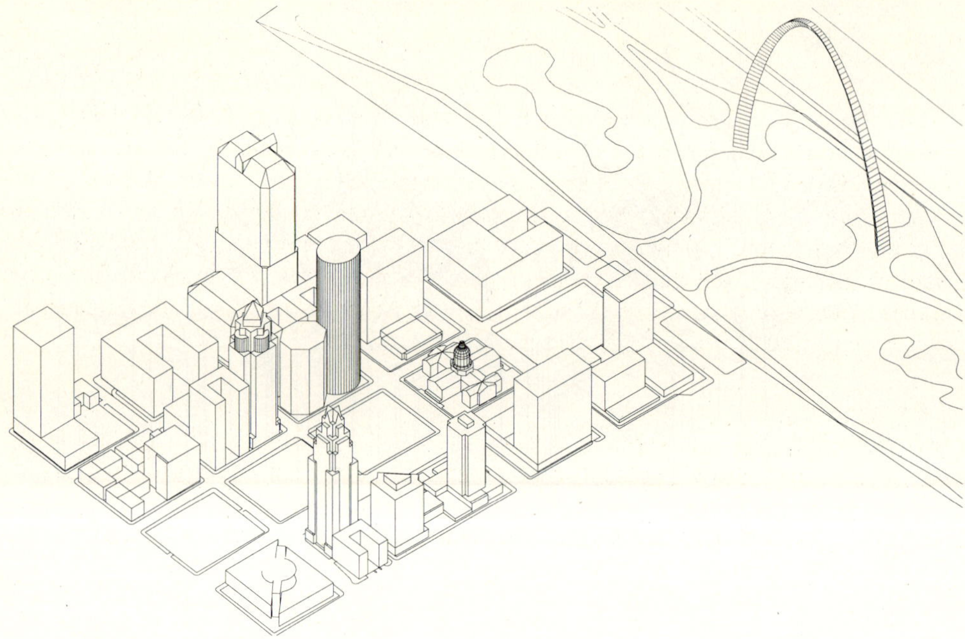

Figure 17. St. Louis laser plot.

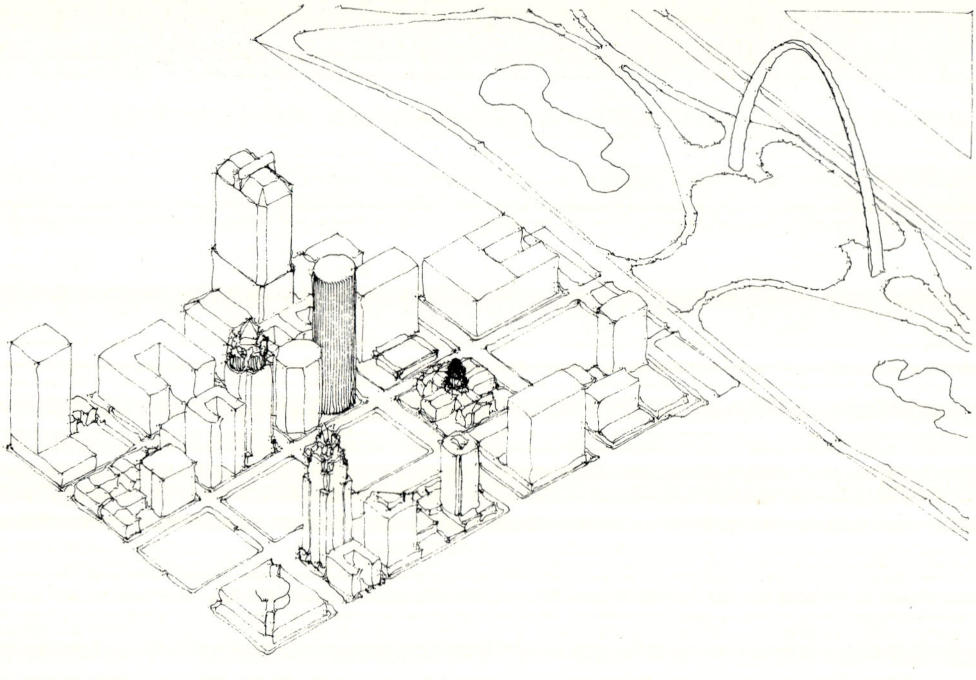

Figure 18. St. Louis squiggly pen plot.

Software Technique Explored

As a result of the interest generated by the squiggly line pen plots, Nathan Huebner, a director of software development at Hellmuth, Obata and Kassabaum, Inc. in St. Louis, developed a postscript version of a squiggly line plot generator. Several variables were found to be controllable which would produce the effect of a sketch. Prior to plotting the user would use the "set sketch" command to create to a postscript file based on the default sketch settings or values selected for a specific effect. The postscript freehand line program modifies each line according to three essential variables which can be adjusted in the program: line thickness, line end dots and line squiggle.

Line thickness:
Additional end thickness - The line ends are thickened. This gives the illusion that the person drawing the lines is pressing the pen harder at the beginning and end of each line (or moving the pen faster and slower).
Thickness drop-off - This allows for the thickness to change abruptly or gradually across the whole line.

Figure 19. Line thickness 1.

Figure 20. Line thickness 3.

Line end dots:
Dot percentage - Dots appear at the end of a certain percentage of the lines drawn.
Dot diameter - The diameter of the dots at line ends can be adjusted .
Dot length - The line end dots can be divided into short lines by changing the length of the dot.
Dot gap - The gap between the end of the line and the dot can be adjusted.

Line squiggle:

Average segment length - The length of the squiggles along the line can be made longer or shorter to give the effect of more or fewer squiggles.

Long frequency - This is the angular change per segment measured in degrees for the sine curve of the squiggle. The long adjustments affect the entire line. This sine curve is the first of two.

Long amplitude - This is the distance +/- from the original line that the sine wave can vary.

Short frequency - This is the angular change per segment measured in degrees for the sine curve of the squiggle. The short adjustments affect the entire line. This is the second sine curve of two.

Short amplitude - This is the distance +/- from the original line that the sine wave can vary.

This postscript version is as effective as the wobbling pen technique in creating the illusion of hand drawn sketches. Because the objective is to “mess up” the drawing a bit, the subtle differences in the effects is not significant. In fact, a thorough testing of the postscript variables by holding some constant and varying others resulted in slightly different “styles", but the net effect of creating the illusion of hand drawn sketches was achieved no matter which setting was used. Several examples of the postscript sketches are illustrated on the following page.

Figure 21. Short amplitude .3.

Figure 22. Long amplitude .9.

Figures 19-22 illustrate two of the "set sketch" variables which may be altered to achieve subtle differences in the plots. The differences in these drawings can be seen if examined closely, but it is apparent from the entire sequence of forty-eight drawings produced for this comparison that the subtleties are not significant. It's the fact that they are not hard line, straight edged drawings which makes them read as sketches.

Viewer Response

The most surprising result of this serendipitous discovery was the response of architects and students to these "hand-drawn" sketches. Astonishment and amazement that these drawings were machine made was the most common reaction and stimulated an exploration of more control of the technique. In all cases, viewers seemed more attracted to the "free hand" plots. In an effort to understand the attraction/ acceptance of these drawings, a simple survey was developed which requested a reaction to a comparison between conventional laser plot images and the squiggly line plots. Both the loose pen and postscript versions were included and shown adjacent to a hard edged plot of the same data. A free, open response using descriptive adjectives was requested of seventeen faculty members of the School of Architecture. Two sample survey forms with responses are shown on this page. The results were consistent in the choice and type of descriptors. Although one respondent thought it was "silly" to use a computer in such a manner - maintaining that computers produce a certain type of drawing and shouldn't be used otherwise.

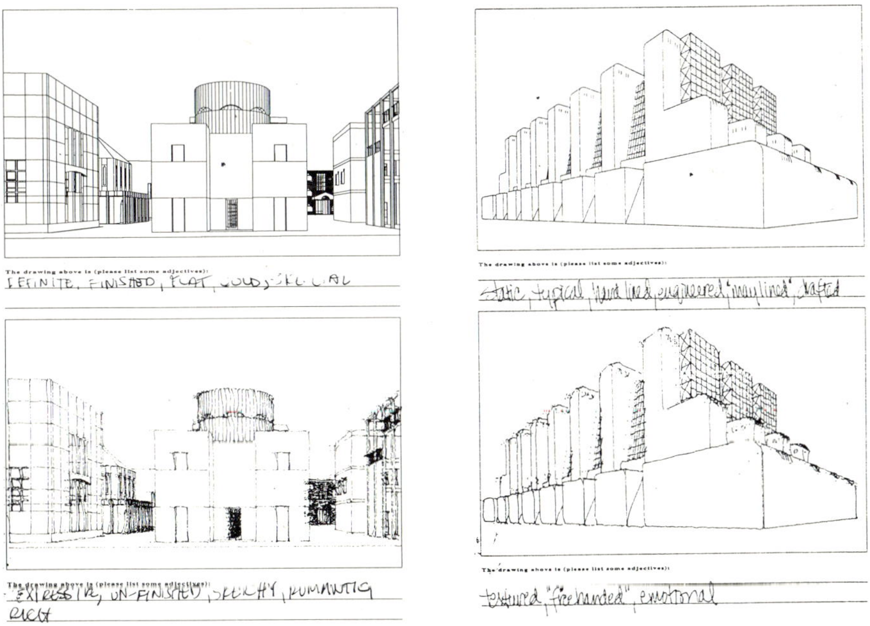

Figure 23. Sample survey forms.

Listed below are the adjectives used by the survey respondents to describe the plots.

Adjectives used to describe laser plots:

definite, finished, flat, cold, skeletal, clean, sharp, precise, neutral, stiff, distant, abstract, sharp, concise, authentic with respect to design, nice, absolute, angular, repetition, vertical, surface, rounded corners, good for this style of building, severe, hard, tight, impersonal, perfect, mechanical, deliberate, hardline, computer drafted, volumetric, quantitative, studied, unshaded, accurate, qualityless, fixed, static, typical, engineered, maylined, drafted.

Adjectives used to describe the squiggly plots:

expressive, unfinished, sketchy, romantic, rich, simplex, soft, free, suggestive, romantically, terrifying, disruptive, ambiguous, base, rhythmic, tumbling, interplay, movement, messy, undisciplined, lacks control, organic, tender, flexible, casual, relaxed, amusing, humane, informal, soft, focus, quick, imprecise, freehand trace overlay, loose, qualitative, wiggly, dotted, hairy, loose, thinking, working,in progress, open, developing, alterable, textured, freehanded, emotional.

There are several possible explanations for this apparent "attraction".

Man made vs. mass produced objects - The illusion that these images are hand drawn in part accentuates the level of astonishment because highly developed drawing skills are regarded as an enviable talent, and the time invested in a unique drawing assigns a high value to that effort. In addition, one of the characteristics of hand made objects is imperfection, or to put it in more positive terms, the human touch. For example, a ceramic pot may have marks and clues that it is man made and unique even if in some minute way. On the other hand machine made products are expected to be perfect and easily produced and therefore each one is devalued because it can be easily replaced by an identical copy. Moreover, computer plots have devalued drawings by storing the digital record of the drawing data; once described, many identical copies can be made. A complete, perfect and final drawing can be discarded with no second thought because it can be reproduced easily. Hand made objects and hand drawn sketches are usually valued because of their uniqueness. It is interesting to note here that the squiggly line pen plots produced for this paper were carefully stored and regarded as unique objects. While their data is in the records, the unique instance of the drawing is not.

Sketches permit interpretation - In addition to the issue of uniqueness, the incomplete quality of these drawings leads to a certain openness. Hard line drawings send the message of decisiveness and finality, while sketches encourage a more active engagement by the viewer in the interpretation of what the image is representing. A fuzzy sketch allows for filling in the gaps and reading it as representing emerging ideas. Several of the survey responses implied a reading of emerging ideas and work in progress.

Complexity is more engaging - The squiggly line drawings contain more complexity and therefore hold attention and interest more effectively than an image which is understood quickly. The idea of complexity could also apply to hard line drawings as well, but when the drawing is produced from the same data the squiggly line pen plots are more complex because of the addition of random movements of the pen.

Fuzzy image are closer to reality - The hard line computer plots appear much flatter than the squiggly line drawings. The evenness of the line weights of hard line drawings gives objects a cardboard cutout look while the fuzzy edges of the squiggly line drawings allows for the observer to interpret more rounded corners of objects and greater depth of field.

Potential Applications

A potential use for these free hand plots might be found in examining the distinction between presentation and design graphics. Sketches are utilized for both types but for different reasons. Presentation sketches are usually created to help visualize an unbuilt scene by means of experiential views and are produced when final decisions have been made. Even if the drawing is constructed by mechanical means, it is usually traced over by hand for the final rendering and detailing. These squiggly line plots offer the opportunity to create presentation images which render the natural landscape in a more believable and convincing style. Design graphics, on the other hand, are created while the design is emerging. Sketchy drawings of designs in progress have meant sketchy ideas and an interim working mode. Hand-drawn ink on mylar and other finished drawings are typically completed when final decisions have been reached and significant changes are unlikely if not impossible. One of the drawbacks of CAD drawings for early schematic design is the impression that the design has been worked out to a greater level of detail than it has. In fact, many designers have commented that working on a CAD system demands a higher level of detailed decisions at an earlier stage of the design. Each line entered into the computer has exact coordinates associated with it. While sketches are well suited for indecisiveness, most CAD systems cannot accept a fuzzy, approximate line. Most commercial CAD systems were not developed with assisting design thinking as the primary motivation but were meant to be precise drafting tools for production. Powerful capabilities are at hand once the drawing or model has been created including parametric variations, infinite viewing angles and many output media. These squiggly line plots are one potential type of output which create the illusion of a hand drawn sketch and they can be useful in the presentation of design ideas in progress. These drawings can be useful in communicating design ideas to clients and others where the data in fact represents intermediate design decisions and not final, precise conclusions. These plots may find applications in both presentation and design graphics. This usefulness legitimizes these fakes.

Figure 24. Laser plot.

Figure 25. Postscript squiggly plot.

Figure 26. Squiggly pen plot.

Concluding Observations

There is, of course, a fundamental contradiction in these drawings. The precise definitions of lines, polygons and other graphic elements which are stored in the computer are intentionally and randomly jumbled to affect an imprecise quality. They are a new means to an old end. One of the more surprising aspects of this development is that simply a loose pen can create such believably high quality drawings.

There is no intelligence in a loose pen and the operator still must resolve all the issues of graphic techniques in drawing just as with more conventional CAD drawings. Prior planning and thinking to produce a drawing (rather than view a model) are necessary for effective control and results. For example, to effect vignetting, or softening of the edges of a drawing, explicit alterations to the data must be made prior to sending the plot to the plotter. (Yanking the pen out in mid-plot works, but getting it back in is a feat of hand eye coordination). Certain data are more convincing as a squiggly line drawing than other data. For example, trees that look strange when plotted as hard-lined plots are believable as squiggly line drawings.

One might conclude that these free hand plots represent a reversal of the meaning of free hand sketches. When sketching by hand, emerging ideas are given some degree of manifested form in a process of visualizing the current state of the design, and, in fact, there are theories which propose direct connections between design thinking and hand motions in sketching. Here drawing firms up fuzzy thinking. The act of drawing and observing the drawn image becomes in integral part of the design process - an iterative loop between thinking, drawing and seeing. On the other hand, these free hand plots loosen up hard data to create the illusion of a sketch. They back away from representing the data as it exists in the machine and could be used to indicate that although the data is precise, the thinking about the design is still evolving.

References

The images of androids are from

Carrera, Roland, and Fryer, David. 1984. "Androids." *FMR*, no. 6: 65-92.

Johnson, George. 1986. *Machinery of the Mind*. New York, NY: Times Books.

The postscript code for the squiggly line laser plots was written by Nathan Huebner of HOK Inc. in St. Louis, Missouri.

38 Data Generation for CAAD with Digital Photogrammetry

Horst A. Beyer, André Streilein

Institute of Geodesy and Photogrammetry
ETH-Hönggerberg,
CH 8093 Zurich, Switzerland

The rapid advances in sensor technology and processing hardware make the development of a Digital Photogrammetric System for Architectural Photogrammetry possible. This system is able to acquire images with sufficient resolution for Architectural Photogrammetry. Geometric and topologic information for a CAAD-System can be derived with manual and/or semi-automated methods. This paper describes the current status of such a system which is under development at the Institute of Geodesy and Photogrammetry in cooperation with the Chair of Architecture and CAAD, both at the Swiss Federal Institute of Technology in Zurich.

Introduction

The basic hardware requirements and the data flow are given. Primary processing steps are outlined. An example project is discussed from data capture over photogrammetric calibration to the three-dimensional object description of an architectural object. The functionality of the software package DEDIP (Development Environment for Digital Photogrammetry) relevant to the data generation for CAAD is explained using the example project. Issues of image acquisition systems are explained and requirements shown. An outlook on software developments to increase the level of automation is given.

Data Flow in a Digital System for Architectural Photogrammetry

Figure 1 shows data flow and hardware components involved in the data generation for CAAD with Digital Photogrammetry. Images can be acquired with film cameras as well as with cameras using solid-state sensors. Conventional film cameras still provide for an unsurpassed resolution. Images with over 6000 by 6000 pixels would be required to match the resolution of a medium format film camera. The disadvantage of film cameras is that the film must be developed and digitized before the data is available for processing. Solid-state cameras have the advantage that their data is immediately accessible.

On the lower end of solid-state sensor based imaging systems are Still Video Cameras. They use analog recording on floppy disks and the image size is in the order of 512 x 512 pixels. On the upper end are cameras which use standard sensors with displacement methods and high resolution area sensors. Former create images with 2994 by 2330 (Kontron ProgRes

3000, *Kontron 1990)* to 5500 by 7050 (Rollei RSC, *Luhmann 1990)* pixels, but can only be used for stationary objects and under stable lighting conditions. Cameras with high resolution area sensors are available with up to 4048 x 4048 sensor elements *(Janesick et al., 1990)*. Prices for still video cameras range from several hundred to several thousand Swiss Francs. High-resolution cameras start at about sFr. 20000 and reach beyond sFr. 100000. The advent of imaging systems for High Definition Television (HDTV) will lead within the next years to a large decrease of prices for cameras with an image size of 1920 x 1035 pixels. The image quality of Still Video Cameras will be vastly improved by the incorporation of digital recording technologies.

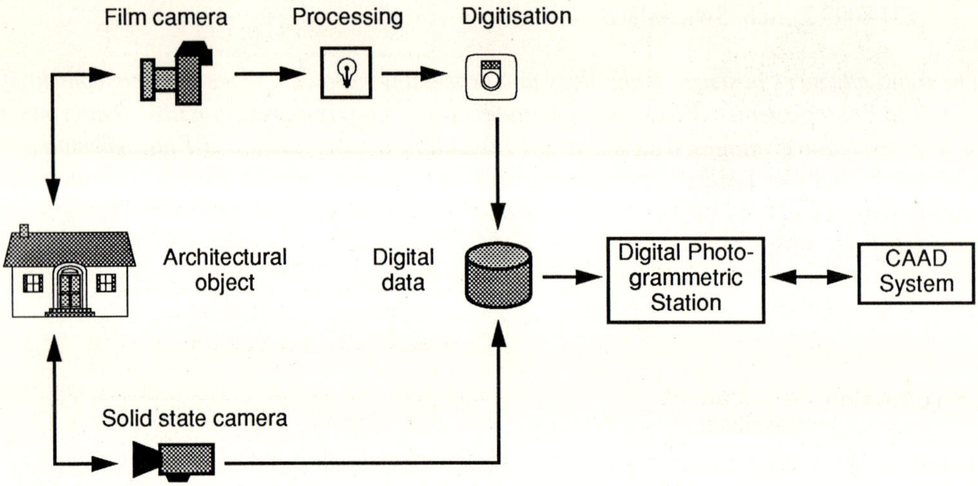

Figure 1. Data flow and hardware of a Digital System for Architectural Photogrammetry.

Data Processing is performed on a Digital Photogrammetric Station. Currently the Digital Photogrammetric Station and CAAD-System are different units, but could already be based on identical hardware platforms. An interaction between and/or integration of the CAAD-System and the photogrammetric processing system will be necessary in the future. The CAAD-System can support interactive measurements by an operator and will be required to provide a priori information for automatic measurement procedures.

Figure 2 depicts the processing steps of data generation for CAAD with Digital Photogrammetry. After the image acquisition an orientation and calibration must be performed. Some basic geometric information on the object and/or the camera-stations from which the images were taken must be provided by other means. Usually the three-dimensional object coordinates of well defined features (e.g. signalized points) are used, but the distance between two points is also sufficient under certain conditions. After the orientation and calibration the geometric relation among all images and between images and object are known. This is used for the measurement of the architectural features. The three-dimensional coordinates of a feature can be computed once it has been identified and measured in at least two images. The location of features in all other images can thereafter be predicted from their three-dimensional position. This enhances the measurement speed and improves the reliability of the measurement process. The semantic identification of features is currently performed interactively. This could be supported by information from the CAAD-System and/or an expert system.

All tasks, from image acquisition to the data transfer, are performed with the software package DEDIP (Development Environment for Digital Photogrammetry, *Beyer 1987; Grün and Beyer 1991*). It provides, among others, modules for image acquisition, interactive measurement of pixel coordinates, a bundle adjustment program, and measurement of architectural features. The current capabilities of the system will be shown in the following sections with a practical project.

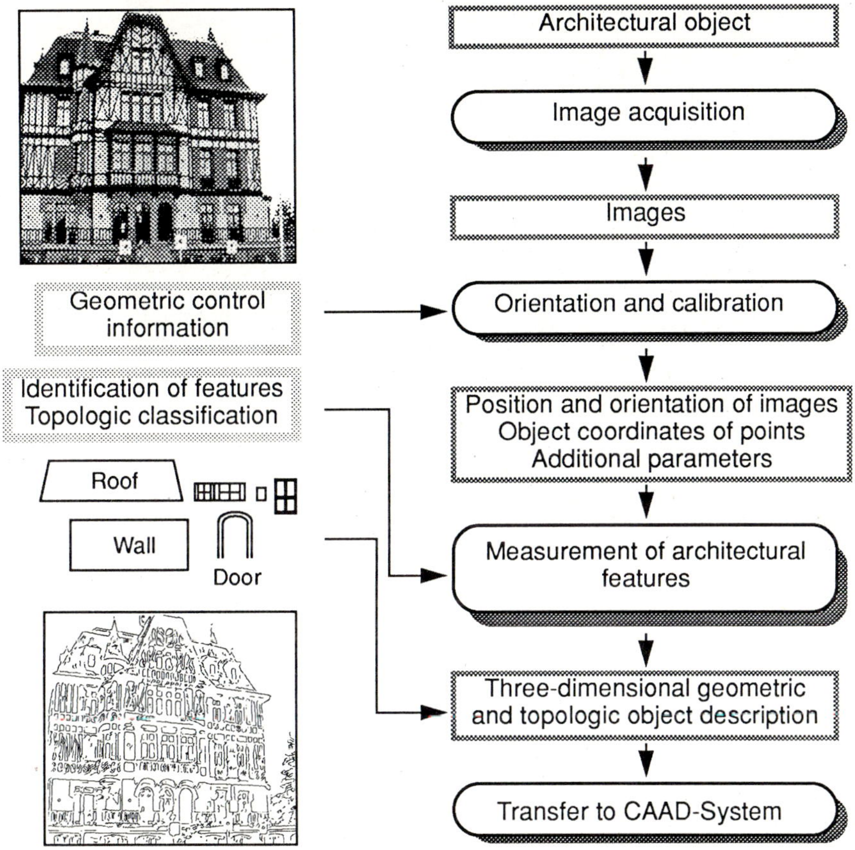

Figure 2. Processing steps in Digital Architectural Photogrammetry.

Project Villa Cassel: Architectural object

The timber frame house Villa Cassel is chosen to demonstrate the capabilities of the existing system. Villa Cassel was built for the English banker Sir Earnest Cassel at the turn of the century. It is located in a nature reserve of the Swiss Alps close to Riederalp (Wallis). Figure 3 shows the surroundings and the back facade of Villa Cassel. The front facade, which is 21 m wide and 17 m high, was used in this project.

Figure 3. Villa Cassel, Wallis, Switzerland.

Figure 4 gives a schematic representation of the house and the camera-stations. A Canon CI-10 color Still Video Camera was used to take two images at each of the four camera-stations. One image was acquired with the camera upright and the other with the camera rotated by ninety degrees around its optical axis. The sensor is 8.8 by 6.6 mm and the images have a size of 508 by 466 pixels.

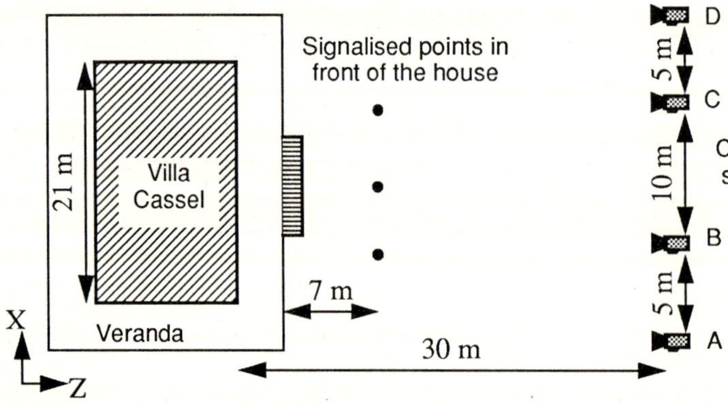

Figure 4. Object and camera configuration.

Orientation and Calibration

Before any measurement of architectural features can be done, the position and orientation of all images and camera-stations must be determined. This was performed using points signalized with targets consisting of black circles on a white background. The three-dimensional object coordinates of all signalized points were determined with theodolites to an accuracy better than 3 mm. Figure 5 shows an image taken at camera-station B (see Figure 4). The three signalized points in front of the house and the 19 targets on the facade are identifiable.

Figure 5. Image taken with a CI-10 from station B.

The pixel coordinates of the signalized targets were measured with Least Squares Template Matching. After a transformation from the pixel to the image coordinate system, the coordinates were introduced in a bundle adjustment program together with the three-dimensional object coordinates of 5 signalized points (control points). The position and orientation of all images, the object coordinates of all points, and the additional parameters were computed by a least squares adjustment with the bundle adjustment program of DEDIP *(Karara 1989; Beyer 1990)*. The additional parameters are used to compensate for the effects of systematic errors introduced by the non-ideal geometric characteristics of the imaging system. The reference coordinates of the other 17 signalized points were withheld from the bundle adjustment. The coordinates of these points were used to verify the accuracy by comparing the values obtained by the bundle adjustment with the reference theodolite values. Without calibration (no additional parameters are used) the accuracy of the 17 check points is in the order of 200 mm. With calibration the accuracy is in the order of 16 mm in object space, which corresponds in image space to 1/4 of the pixel spacing. This is quite good considering that the camera uses a color sensor and that the image quality was significantly degraded by the analog recording on the floppy disk of the still video recorder.

The importance of calibration can also be demonstrated with the influence of the systematic errors on the image coordinates as shown in Figure 6. The regular grid represents the position of points at a 5 mm spacing, if no systematic errors were present. The deformed grid shows the influence of the systematic errors. The vectors between the two grids indicate the correction of the image coordinates by the additional parameters. The vectors at the points are differences to the reference positions projected into the images. The effects of systematic errors are approximately 20 times larger than the attained accuracy. A good calibration is therefore a prerequisite for any precise extraction of geometric information.

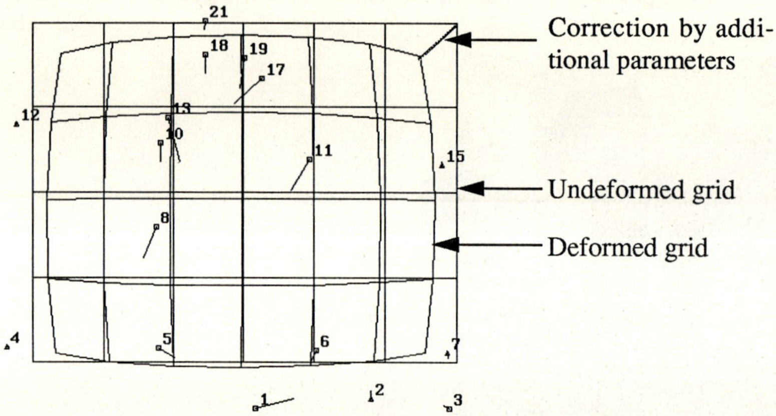

Figure 6. Influence of systematic errors showing the large deformations in relation to the achieved accuracy. Relation (point vector:grid) = 10:1.

Measurement of Architectural Features

After orientation and calibration the geometric relation of object and images is reconstructed. This can be relied on for the measurement of architectural features. The features must be detected and classified according to topologic classes. Geometric primitives describing each feature are measured. The features and their topologic classification depends on their use in the CAAD-System. In the following, the resolution requirements of imaging hardware with respect to architectural features are explained. Thereafter, measurement approaches for basic geometric primitives are addressed.

Camera Resolution

It was shown above that the geometric accuracy of standard CCD-cameras, and in particular of Still Video Cameras, would be sufficient to map an entire architectural object of this size with two images. The practical problem lies in the fact that the geometric accuracy is only achieved for large signalized points with good contrast. The characteristics of architectural features are very different. The resolution of the camera must be suited to imaging of the features to be mapped. Some of the problems and requirements are demonstrated in the following.

Figure 7 shows part of a window in two images acquired with the CI-10 camera. It is very difficult to decide which pixels represent the corresponding parts of the window corner in the left and right image. The pixels of images acquired with the Canon CI-10 correspond to an area of 38 mm by 33 mm on this object. A feature must span several pixels to be identifiable and measured with sufficient precision. Therefore features must span at least 120 mm on this object. On the contrary, when using the high-resolution ProgRes 3000 camera an area of 6.9 mm by 7.1 mm on the object would correspond to one pixel, under otherwise identical conditions. This camera could be used to extract features spanning only 20 mm on this object.

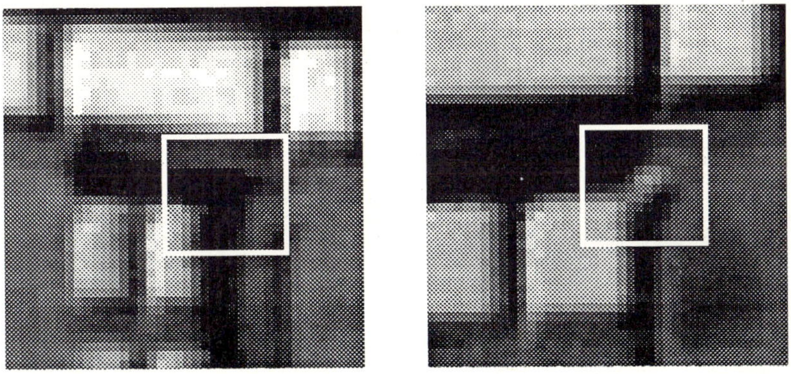

Figure 7. Window in two images demonstrating the difficulty to identify corresponding features due to insufficient camera resolution.

The difference in resolution is demonstrated in Figure 8. It shows zoomed portions of a close-range testfield. The images were taken with a standard solid-state camera (Figure 8 a) and the high-resolution camera ProgRes 3000 (Figure 8 b). The great difference in resolution of these two cameras is conspicuous. This demonstrates the need for high-resolution solid-state imaging systems.

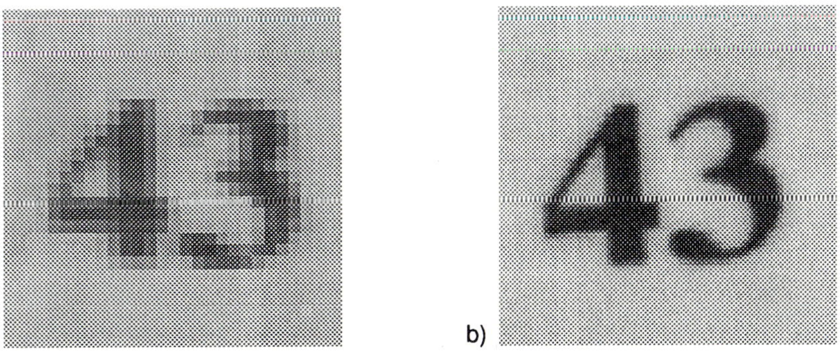

a) b)

Figure 8. Comparison of standard solid-state camera (a) and ProgRes 3000 (b) with images of a testfield.

Precise Feature Location

In this project Least Squares Template Matching (Gruen 1985J) was applied to measure the precise position of signalized points. It uses a template (artificial image of the feature) as reference and determines the position via an iterative procedure through the least squares fit of an affine transformation between template and patch (image region). Initially, the patch is taken at the approximate position from the image. This can for example be indicated by the operator in an interactive measurement mode. In subsequent iterations the patch is resampled using updated values for the affine transformation with a user defined interpolation algorithm from the data of the image. Figure 9 shows an enlargement of a part of the original image, the patch at the initial position, the patch after convergence of the algorithm, and the template.

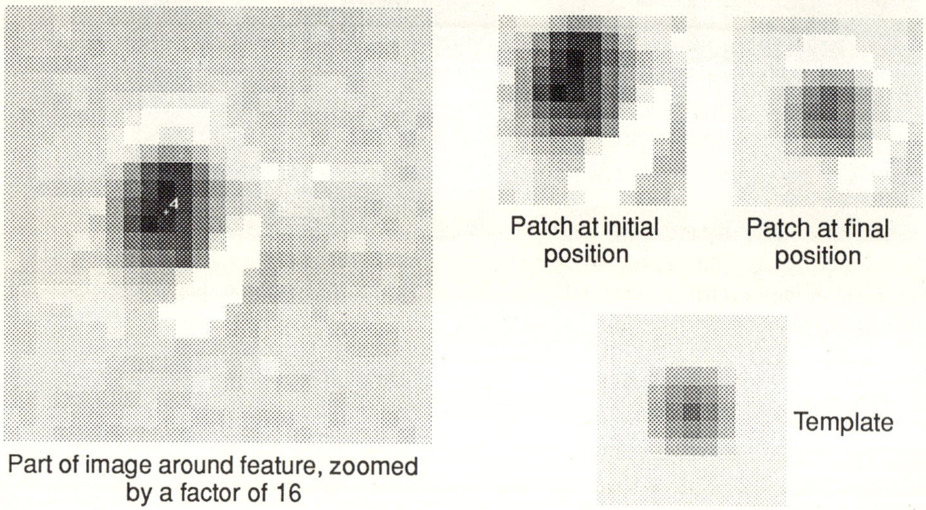

Figure 9. Image with point and number at final position, patches at initial and final position, and template of a target measured with least squares template matching.

Least Squares Template Matching provides a very high precision. In practical applications an accuracy corresponding to a tenth of the pixel spacing can be achieved for well defined features. Under laboratory conditions accuracies of a few hundreds of a pixel have been achieved. Least Squares Template Matching can be used to measure signalized points as well as architectural features, provided an artificial template can be generated for the feature. It is therefore a very precise and general measurement method.

Measurement of Points

The simplest method to determine the location of straight lines is to measure the coordinates of their end points. Potentially, the pixel coordinates of those points can be measured manu-

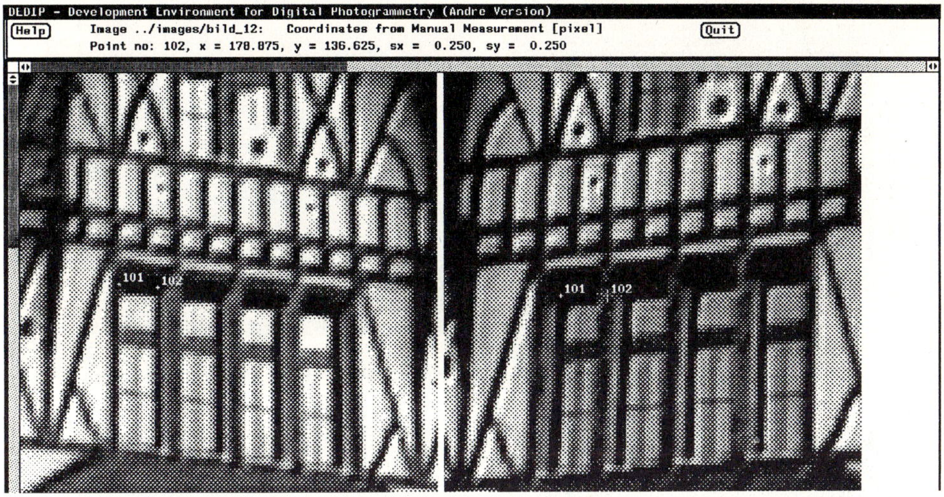

Figure 10. Layout of screen for measurement of points.

ally, semi-automatically and full automatically. Only the manual and semi-automatic measurement modes have been used in this project. Figure 10 shows a typical configuration of the workstation screen for the manual measurement of architectural points with DEDIP. The regions of the images, in which the coordinates of features are to be determined, were displayed on the screen and the operator measures the coordinates of corresponding points with the cursor. The images were zoomed to improve the precision of the manual measurements. Here only two images are displayed, but several regions of interest can be viewed simultaneously. A screen layout with four images was efficiently used in this test. The measured coordinates as indicated with marks and their respective numbers are shown in the figure.

Measurement of Points via Line Following

Figure 7 shows a related problem to the resolution requirements for the measurement of architectural features which have been explained above. The vertices describing the image feature are often not well defined for photogrammetric tasks. In these cases the linear boundaries of the object contain more information than the vertices. The measurement technique shown here takes advantage of this, by first locating the linear elements of the feature to be measured, and then deriving the vertices/corners as intersections of these lines. Figure 11 shows an example of this technique. The initial position of the linear element is indicated by the operator with the cursor (see Figure 11 a).

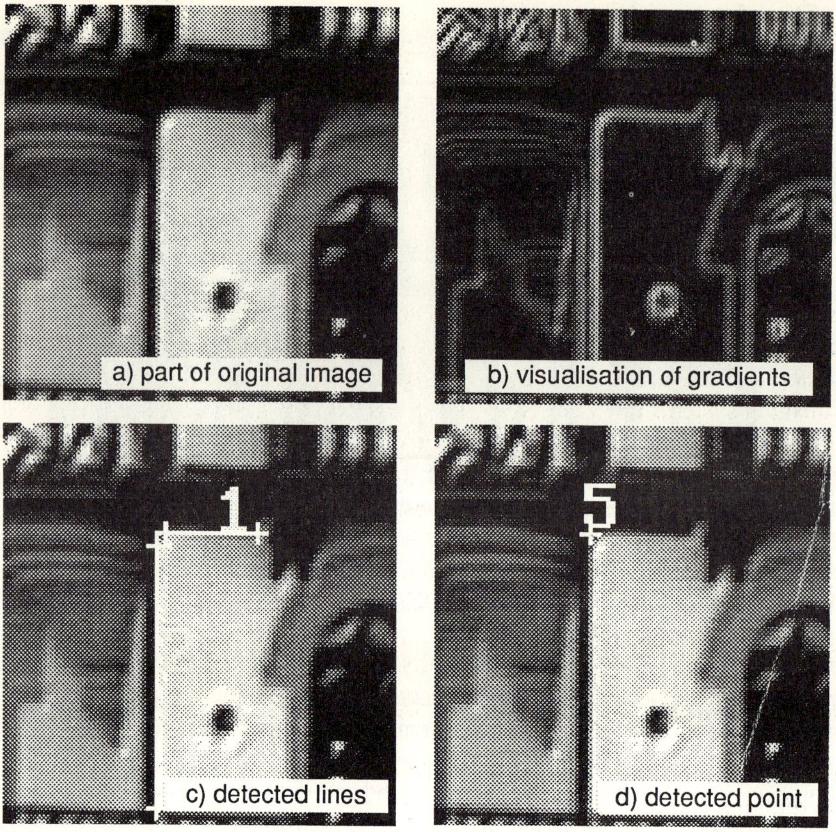

Figure 11. Example for measurement of points via line following. Line no. 1 and line no. 2 define point no. 5.

Starting from this, the line is tracked by the algorithm using the first partial derivatives of the image, which are visualized in Figure 11 b. Finally, a straight line is fitted to the results by following that line (see Figure 11 c). The points defining the architectural feature are computed as intersections of selected straight lines (see Figure 11 d). The first results of this measuring technique have been very encouraging.

Outlook

Some of the basic measurement methods to determine geometric primitives were described. These methods can be extended so that the operator can select feature classes to be measured. A priori information on each feature class can be used to support the operator. Such a system would provide a high level of automation as compared with existing measurement approaches. The system could furthermore be supported by information from a CAAD-System and/or an expert system. This includes knowledge of architectural styles, the

construction of features, and objects built out of several lower level features. Measurement routines adapted to special characteristics of features could be selected automatically.
The data representation would therefore ideally be performed in a format easily convertible to that of a CAAD-System. The features already measured could be used to reconstruct the object through CAAD and to support through visualization the interactive measurement and/or guide the automated recognition and measurement. Such a combined system would include algorithms of a Digital Photogrammetric Station and a CAAD-System.

Conclusions

The potential of Digital Photogrammetry as an important data source for CAAD has been demonstrated. The accuracy requirements can already be achieved with standard CCD-cameras for well defined and sufficiently large features. It has been shown that high-resolution digital imaging systems are required to image architectural features with sufficient detail to be identifiable and measurable with sufficient precision. Manual and semiautomatic measurements can already be performed with great ease. The improvement of the semiautomatic measurement procedures and the development of fully automatic measurement systems represents an interesting and challenging research and development topic. A major problem to be solved is the connection of semantic information to the three-dimensional data. To solve this problem an interaction between a Digital Photogrammetric System and a CAAD-System is conceivable and desirable.

Acknowledgments

The geodetic reference data and imagery of this project was acquired by W. Hardegen as part of a diploma thesis investigating the geometric characteristics of Still Video Cameras and the applicability to Architectural Photogrammetry. We would like to thank him for his fine work. The research project "Digital Architectural Photogrammetry and CAAD" is funded by ETH-Zurich.

References

Beyer, H.A. 1987. *Einige grundlegende Designfragen zu einer Entwicklungsumgebung für Digitale Photogrammetrie auf den SUN Workstations.* (DEDIP Development Environment for Digital Photogrammetry). Unpublished.

Beyer, H.A. 1990. "Calibration of CCD-Cameras for Machine Vision and Robotics." *SPIE,* vol. 1197, pp. 88-98. Automated Inspection and High Speed Architectures III.

Gruen, A. 1985. "Adaptive Least Squares Correlation: A Powerful Image Matching Technique." *South African Journal of Photogrammetry, Remote Sensing and Cartography* 14, no. 3: 175-187.

Grün, A., H. Beyer. 1991. "DIPS II - Turning a Standard Computer Workstation into a Digital Photogrammetric Station." *ZPF- Zeitschrift für Photogrammetrie und Fernerkundung,* no. 1: 2-10.

Hardegen, W. 1989. *Untersuchungen zum Einsatz von Still Videokameras in der Architekturphotogrammetrie.* Diplomarbeit, Institut fur Geodäsie und Photogrammetrie, ETH Zürich.

Janesick, J.R., T. Elliot, A. Dingizian, R. Bredthauer, C. Chandler, J. Westphal, and J. Gunn. 1990. "New advancements in charge-coupled device technology - sub-electron noise and 4096 x 4096 pixel CCD." *SPIE,* vol. 1242, pp. 223-237. Charge-Coupled Devices and Solid State Optical Sensors (1990).

Karara, H.M. 1989. *Non-Topographic Photogrammetry*. Second Edition. American Society of Photogrammetry and Remote Sensing.

Kontron, 1990. *ProgRes 3000*. Product Information, Munich (FRG).

Luhmann, T. 1990. "Image-recording systems for close-range photogrammetry." *International Archives of Photogrammetry and Remote Sensing*, vol. 28, part. 5/1: 86-95.